Best Practices in the Behavioral Management of Chronic Disease

Volume II
OTHER MEDICAL DISORDERS

Edited by Jodie A. Trafton, Ph.D. and William P. Gordon, Ph.D.
Institute for Disease Management

Published by Institute for Brain Potential

Best Practices in the Behavioral Management of Chronic Disease
Institute for Disease Management, Los Altos, CA

Acknowledgements:

We would like to acknowledge the research assistance of Tatiana Mejia, M.A., Marie Gordon and Brie Linkenhoker, Ph.D., the editorial assistance of Joan Zimmerman and Linda Williams, and the production assistance of Patricia Fullerton and Emmit Hancock.

Jodie A. Trafton, Ph.D. and William P. Gordon, Ph.D., Editors

All guidelines and discussions are presented as examples or generalized information only and should never be used as the basis for a legal document. They are intended as resources that can be selectively used and adapted with the advice of legal and medical resources to meet state, local and individual hospital, and specific departmental needs and requirements.

The editors have made every effort to ensure the accuracy of the information herein, particularly with regard to drug selection, dose and behavioral treatments. However, appropriate information sources should be consulted, especially for new or unfamiliar drugs or procedures. It is the responsibility of every practitioner to evaluate the appropriateness of a particular opinion in the context of actual clinical situations and with due consideration to new developments. Authors, editors and the publisher cannot be held responsible for typographical or content errors found in this publication.

Orders: 866-992-9399
Customer Service: 650-960-3536

Library of Congress Cataloging-in-Publication Data
Best Practices in the Behavioral Management of Chronic Disease
Volume I: Neuropsychiatric Disorders
ISBN 978-1-932745-15-3   Library of Congress Control Number: 2007932255

Best Practices in the Behavioral Management of Chronic Disease
Volume II: Other Medical Disorders
ISBN 978-1-932745-32-0   Library of Congress Control Number: 2007932255

Copyright © 2006-2007 by Institute for Disease Management, a division of Institute for Brain Potential (IBP).

IBP is a non-profit organization dedicated to providing advances in Behavioral Medicine through publications and conferences. IBP is a 501 (c) (3) organization (tax identification number 77-0026830) founded in 1984 as Institute for Cortext Research and Development. The Institute has trained over one million health professionals in the neurobehavioral sciences and has published books in the fields of Neuropsychology and Behavioral Medicine.

Printed in the United States of America

VOLUME II: OTHER MEDICAL DISORDERS

Contact Information and Additional Grant Support

Chapter 1: PRIMARY PREVENTION OF CANCER

Barbara K. Rimer, Dr.PH[1], Karen Glanz, Ph.D., M.P.H[2]
[1]Lineberger Cancer Center
University of North Carolina at Chapel Hill
Department of Health Behavior and Health Education
302 Rosenau Hall, Campus Box 7440
Chapel Hill, North Carolina   27599-7440
brimer@unc.edu

[2]Behavioral Sciences and Health Education
Rollins School of Public Health
Emory University
1518 Clifton Rd,, N.E.
Atlanta, GA 30322
kglanz@sph.emory.edu

Chapter 2: SCREENING FOR CANCER: THE DILEMMA OF EARLY DECTECTION FOR PROSTATE CANCER

Kathryn L. Taylor, Ph.D., Nicole L. Africano, M.Phil., Jennifer Cullen, Ph.D., Tara W. Lamond, L.G.S.W., Randi Williams, B.A., Kimberly Davis, Ph.D.
Cancer Control Program, Lombardi Comprehensive Cancer Center,
Georgetown University Medical Center
2233 Wisconsin Ave, Suite 317
Washington, DC 20007
taylorkl@georgetown.edu

Chapter 3: DOT AND BEYOND: COMPREHENSIVE MANAGEMENT OF TUBERCULOSIS

Sonya S. Shin, M.D., Jennifer Furin, M.D. and Jennifer Singler
Partners In Health/Program in Infectious Disease and Social Change
Department of Social Medicine
Harvard Medical School
641 Huntington Avenue
Boston, MA 02115
Sshin@pih.com

Chapter 4: ENHANCING ANTIRETROVIRAL ADHERENCE: A REVIEW OF PUBLISHED REPORTS OF RANDOMIZED CONTROLLED TRIALS AND ON-GOING NIH-FUNDED RESEARCH

Jane M Simoni, Ph.D.[1], David Pantalone, MS, Pamela Frick, PharmD, MPH[21], Barbara J Turner MD, MSEd[3]

[1]Department of Psychology
[2]Department of Pharmacy
University of Washington
Box 351525
Seattle, WA 98105-1525
[1]Jsimoni@u.washington.edu , dwpant@u.washington.edu
[2]pamfrick@u.washington.edu
[3]Division of General Internal Medicine
University of Pennsylvania School of Medicine
1122 Blockley Hall
423 Guardian Drive
Philadelphia, PA 19104-6021
Bturner@mail.med.upenn.edu

Chapter 5: PRIMARY PREVENTION OF CARDIOVASCULAR DISEASE

Lora E. Burke, Ph.D., MPH, RN
University of Pittsburgh
415 Victoria Building
Pittsburgh, PA 1526
lbu100@pitt.edu
This paper was supported in part by the National Institute of Diabetic, Digestive and Kidney Disorders (RO1 DK58631 and RO1 DK58387).

Chapter 6: BEHAVIOR CHANGE INTERVENTIONS IN CORONARY ARTERY DISEASE: REVERSING OR RETARDING ARTHERSCLEROTIC DISEASE

Jan Lisspers, Ph.D., D. Med.Sci.[1], Orjan Sundin, Ph.D.[2]
[1]Research Group for Behavioral Medicine and Health Psychology
Department of Social Sciences
Mid Sweden University Campus
Ostersund, Sweden
Jan.lisspers@miun.se
[2]Department of Clinical Neuroscience
Karolinska Institute
Stockholm, Sweden

Chapter 7: BEHAVIORAL AND LIFESTYLE INTEVENTIONS FOR THE
TREATMENT OF HYPERTENSION

Thomas Pickering, M.D., Ph.D., FRCP
Behavioral Cardiovascular Health and Hypertension Program
Columbia Presbyterian Medical Center
PH 9-946, 622 W 168th St
New York, NY 10032
Tp2114@columbia.edu

Chapter 8: BEHAVIORAL MANAGEMENT OF HEART FAILURE

Michael W. Rich, M.D., Valerie Emery, R.N.
Cardiovascular Division
Barnes-Jewish Hospital
Washington University Medical Center
660 S. Euclid Ave.,
Box 8086
St. Louis, MO 63110
1Mrich@im.wustl.edu
2Emeryv@msnotes.wustl.edu

Chapter 9: MEDICAL THERAPY FOR COPD

Bartolome Celli, M.D.[1], Claudia Cote, M.D.[2]
[1]Chief of Pulmonary and Critical Care
St. Elizabeth's Medical Center
Professor of Medicine
Tufts University School of Medicine
736 Cambridge Street
Boston, MA 02135-2997
Bartolome_Celli@cchcs.org

[2]University of South Florida
VA Medical Center Bay Pines (111A)
PO Box 5005
Bay Pines, FL 33744
Claudia.Cote@med.va.gov

Chapter 10: PREVENTION AND TREATMENT OF VIRAL HEPATITIS

Jane N. Zuckerman, M.D., FFPM, Arie J. Zuckerman, M.D., FRCP
WHO Collaborating Centre for Reference and Research on Viral Diseases
Royal Free and University College Medical School
University College London
Rowland Hill Street
London NW3 2PF, UK
a.zuckerman@rfc.ucl.ac.uk

Chapter 11: TYPE 1 DIABETES MELLITUS

Tim Wysocki, Ph.D., A.B.P.P
Division of Psychology and Psychiatry
Nemours Children'c Clinic
807 Children's Way
Jacksonville, FL 32207
Twysocki@nemours.org
Preparation of this chapter was supported in part by the following grants from the National Institutes of Health to the author: RO1-DK43802 "Behavior Therapy for Families of Diabetic Adolescents", RO1-DK50860 "Intensive Therapy for IDDM in Youth: Outcome Predictions", U10-HD41918 "Continuous Glucose Sensors in Youth: Biobehavioral Study"

Chapter 12: BEHAVIORAL SELF-MANAGEMENT OF TYPE 2 DIABETES: KEY ISSUES, EVIDENCE-BASED RECOMMENDATIONS AND FUTURE DIRECTIONS

Diane K. King, M.S., O.T.R., Russ Glasgow, Ph.D.
Clinical Research Unit
Kaiser Permanente Colorado
P.O. Box 378066
Denver, CO 80237-8066
diane.king@kp.org
russg@ris.net

Chapter 13: BEHAVIORAL MANAGEMENT OF CHRONIC DENTAL DISORDERS: METHODOLOGICAL AND RESEARCH ISSUES

Susan Reisine, Ph.D , Julie Wagner, Ph.D.
Department of Behavioral Sciences and Community Medicine
University of Connecticut School of Dental Medicine
263 Farmington Ave
Farmington, CT 06030-3910
Reisine@nso1.uchc.edu
Juwagner@uchc.edu
Acknowledgements: Preparation of this chapter was supported in part by the UCONN Center for Interdisciplinary Research in Women's Health, NIH Grant # 5K12 HD01409

Chapter 14: A REVIEW OF INTERVENTIONS FOR IMPROVING ADHERENCE WITH LONG-TERM PHARMACOLOGICAL THERAPY

Cynthia Willey, Ph.D., Brian J. Quilliam, Ph.D.
Department of Applied Pharmaceutical Sciences
College of Pharmacy
University of Rhode Island
41 Lower College Road
Kingston, RI 02881-0809
Cwilley@uri.edu

Chapter 15: IMPACT OF CULTURE ON TREATMENT ADHERENCE
Michael Lara, M.D.
Medical Director
Gardner Family Care Corporation
San Jose, CA
Mlaramd@sbcglobal.net

Chapter 16: INCREASING AND MAINTAINING PHYSICAL ACTIVITY IN CLINICAL POPULATIONS
Janet Buckworth, Ph.D., FACSM, Leigh Sears, M.S.
Sport and Exercise Sciences
349 Larkins Hall
337 West 17th Ave
Columbus, OH 43210-1284
Buckworth.1@osu.edu

Chapter 17: BEHAVIORAL MANAGEMENT OF OSTEOPOROSIS
Deborah T. Gold, Ph.D., Jane G. Hertel
Departments of Psychiatry and Behavioral Sciences, Sociology and Psychology: Social and Health Sciences
Box 3003, Duke University Medical Center
Durham, NC 277110
dtg@geri.duke.edu

Chapter 18: CHRONIC DISEASE MANAGEMENT AND TELEMEDICINE
Professor Richard Wootton
Centre for Online Health
Level 3, Foundation Building
Royal Children's Hospital
Herston 4029, AUSTRALIA
r.wootton@pobox.com

Chapter 19: TELEHEALTH: A PARADIGM FOR MANAGING CHRONIC AND PREVENTABLE DISEASES BY TARGETING BEHAVIORAL RISK FACTORS
William Gordon, Ph.D., Brie Linkenhoker, Ph.D.
Institute for Brain Potential
PO Box J
Los Altos, CA 94023
In4brain@mindspring.com

Preface to the 2006 Edition

The Centers for Disease Control estimate that chronic and preventable diseases kill over 1.7 million Americans annually, and almost half of the population has at least one chronic disease. The World Health Organization's 2005 report on chronic disease lays out a global objective of reducing chronic disease mortality by 2 percent annually over the next decade. If this goal were realized, 36 million lives would be saved. The report emphasizes that the scientific knowledge to achieve this goal already exists, however, with over 100,000 peer-reviewed articles concerning behavioral medicine, it is difficult to keep pace with advances.

Best Practices in the Behavioral Management of Chronic Disease is designed to be the most comprehensive review of evidence-based research of its kind. Written by national and international experts in the management of chronic diseases, *Best Practices* is divided into two volumes.

Volume I presents advances in preventing and managing Neuropsychiatric Disorders. The work includes three chapters on theoretical approaches, and new chapters for the 2006 edition focusing on Message Framing, Insomnia, and the Prevention of Suicide. Over half of the chapters were updated for 2006 edition including those concerning the management of stroke, as well as the management of chronic pain, cancer pain, and obesity.

Volume II presents advances in preventing and managing other medical disorders. The 2006 Edition contains new chapters on Cancer screening, secondary prevention of heart disease, prevention and management of osteoporosis, and management of hypertension. Revised chapters include those concerning adherence to anti-retroviral medication, managing type 2 diabetes, medication adherence, and physical activity.

The chapters are organized to review the best controlled clinical trials, focusing on long-term, randomized samples. The results are summarized in helpful tables. Authors present key insights, important advances, practice recommendations, and limitations of current knowledge.

The book identifies effective clinical, community and public health interventions for reducing chronic disease, and is a valuable resource for health professionals, decision-makers, researchers, and students. We hope you find this work helpful in your efforts to prevent and manage chronic disease.

PRIMARY PREVENTION OF CANCER

Barbara K. Rimer and Karen Glanz

THE RELATIONSHIP BETWEEN BEHAVIORS AND CANCER

For hundreds of years, it has been known that some cancers are preventable. In the 20th century, both cancer risks and knowledge about the preventability of some cancers grew, as exemplified by the rise and fall of the tobacco epidemic in the United States over the 20th century. Similarly, the availability of both healthy and unhealthy foods increased over the last century as did knowledge about the relationship of certain foods and nutrients to cancer. A landmark paper published by Doll and Peto in 1981 included the first comprehensive analysis of the proportions of cancer deaths attributable to different factors, including those that are modifiable. They concluded that 30% of cancer deaths were due to tobacco and 35% to diet (Doll and Peto, 1981). Except for infections, no other factor accounted for more than 7% of mortality. Byers et al. (1999) recently updated the prior work of Doll and Peto (1981) and McGinnis and Foege (1993). They estimated that, with redoubling of efforts to reduce the prevalence of known cancer risk factors, U.S. cancer incidence rates could be reduced by 19% and cancer mortality rates reduced by 29% by the year 2015 (Byers et al., 1999).

While the molecular revolution in biology made astonishing contributions to our understanding of cancer in the last quarter of the 20th century, the most dramatic reductions in cancer incidence and mortality in the developed world for the foreseeable future are likely to result from population shifts in unhealthy behaviors--e.g., decreases in the prevalence of smoking, intake of high-fat and high-calorie foods, physical inactivity, and unprotected exposure to the sun (McGinnis and Foege, 1993; Byers et al., 1999; Lippman and Hong, 2002; Greenwald, 2002; Glanz and Vogt, 1999). Even small decreases in unhealthy behaviors or small increases in healthy behaviors can have substantial impact when they occur on the population level.

In this chapter, we provide a brief overview of the key behaviors proven to reduce the development of cancer--primary prevention. We then provide brief summaries, based on published evidence reviews, of the interventions shown to be effective in reducing several cancer-related health behaviors--tobacco use, lack of exercise, not eating five or more fruits and vegetables per day, alcohol use, and inadequate sun protection. Because most of these topics are covered in other chapters, our review is brief.

For health-protective behaviors like avoiding smoking and other tobacco products, and maintaining a healthy diet, appropriate weight, and regular physical activity, the same behaviors that reduce the risk of cancer also reduce risks for several other serious, prevalent chronic diseases, e.g., heart disease, diabetes, and stroke. Thus, there are multiple benefits from changing these behaviors. This is important for clinical providers since there is synergy in the message across behaviors. In addition, since negative health behaviors tend to cluster, there is also efficiency in a combined approach to health behavior change (Colditz et al., 2000).

It is not hyperbole to conclude, as Peto (2001) did, that "The most important discovery in the history of cancer epidemiology is the carcinogenic effect of tobacco". In the U.S., use of tobacco remains the greatest cause of morbidity and mortality (Lippman and Hong, 2002).

The role of diet in cancer causation is both more complex and more controversial than that of tobacco. Doll and Peto concluded that about one-third of British deaths could be avoided by dietary change (Doll and Peto, 1981; Peto, 2001). Although most experts agree that adults should eat five or more servings of fruits and vegetables per day (and, increasingly, adults are being urged to eat nine or more servings a day), there is much more debate about the impact of specific micro and macro nutrients (Glanz and Vogt, 1999).

There also is growing recognition of the inter-relatedness of diet, weight, and physical activity, and of the relationship between post-menopausal weight gain in women and cancer initiation and progression (IARC, 2002; Peto, 2001; Colditz et al., 2000). There is general agreement that overweight is a risk factor for breast cancer and a host of other diseases (Peto, 2001). The evidence is sparser regarding obesity and other cancers, such as prostate cancer. The evidence is accumulating about the cancer preventive benefits of regular, aerobic exercise, especially for colon cancer (U.S. Department of Health and Human Services, 1996; Peto, 2001; Colditz et al., 2000).

Altering alcohol use may be important for certain subgroups, e.g., women who drink and are at higher risk for breast cancer, and smokers with high alcohol intake at higher risk for head and neck cancer. However, the message for the first group is a complicated one since modest alcohol intake may be protective for heart disease.

There is compelling evidence that the greatest risk factor for skin cancer is exposure to ultraviolet radiation, or UV radiation, which comes mainly from the sun (Gallagher, 1997; Green et al., 1999). It is believed that lifelong protection from the sun's rays would prevent most skin cancers.

The application of proven behavioral interventions could reduce population incidence and mortality from cancer and other diseases. Such interventions are needed, because the population prevalence of several key health-protective behaviors remains sub-optimal, as show in Table 1.

This chapter describes the state of current knowledge about efficacious preventive interventions for reducing tobacco use, improving diet, physical activity and appropriate weight-for-height, moderating alcohol intake, and avoiding sun exposure. The brief comments that follow provide a context for other issues that are less major emphases in cancer prevention today, and for which there are few data on behavioral interventions related to cancer prevention.

Other behavioral risk factors for cancer

There are several exposures and related behaviors that cannot be considered solely cancer-specific risk factors, or that may be more often thought of as risk factors for other diseases. Thus, behaviors that would be expected to reduce risk of cancer, such as avoidance of multiple sexual partners (related to AIDS), using alcohol in moderation, if at all (related to heart disease), and prevention of virus exposure have been encouraged primarily for prevention of these other diseases. For this reason, studies of interventions to improve these behaviors have focused on other disease related outcomes, rather than cancer outcomes. As noted by Doll and Peto (1981), virus exposure is a relatively minor cause of cancer in the developed world, although in the developing world, the story is quite different, as evidenced by the important roles of HPV, hepatitis-B virus, and Helicobacter Pylori (Peto, 2001) in cancer etiology. However, HPV testing is increasingly being considered as an important component of cervical cancer detection in the United States (Saslow et al., 2002), and it may become a cancer prevention focus in the next decade. Vaccines for this and other cancer precursors are in trials or on

Table 1. Population Prevalence of Selected Adult Health Behaviors

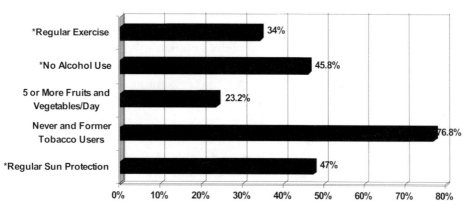

Exercise data: *Defined as moderate or vigorous physical activity for 20-30 minutes a day, 3 or more days per week. National Health Interview Survey 1998, National Center for Health Statistics, Centers for Disease Control and Prevention
Alcohol data: *Defined as not having a drink in past month. Behavioral Risk Factor Surveillance System 1999, National Center for Chronic Disease Prevention and Health Promotion, Centers for Disease Control and Prevention
Nutrition data: Behavioral Risk Factor Surveillance System 2000, National Center for Chronic Disease Prevention and Health Promotion, Centers for Disease Control and Prevention
Tobacco data: Behavioral Risk Factor Surveillance System 2000, National Center for Chronic Disease Prevention and Health Promotion, Centers for Disease Control and Prevention
Sun protection data: *Defined as very likely to practice at least one of three sun protection behaviors: sunscreen, protective clothing, seek shade. Behavioral Risk Factor Surveillance System 1998, National Center for Chronic Disease Prevention and Health Promotion, Centers for Disease Control and Prevention

the horizon and ultimately, could revolutionize cancer prevention. Genetic influences on cancer are important, but the proportion of cancers that result from mutations in cancer susceptibility genes is small--usually estimated to be 5 percent of cancers or less (Welcsh et al., 2002). However, because the risk is small in population size but large in individual risk, persons with high genetic risk, and especially those with known mutations, should be considered an important group to receive cancer prevention interventions. Unfortunately, we have little data to indicate the preventive benefit of any interventions in genetically at-risk populations, with the exception of surgical interventions to prevent breast cancer and data showing that tamoxifen use prevents breast cancer among women at high risk for the disease. Also, for now, the number of proven chemopreventive therapies is very small, e.g. Tamoxifen for breast cancer in

high risk women. However, over time, we expect that chemopreventives will be added to behavioral treatments for cancer prevention. Thus, treatments of the future may include behavioral interventions and chemoprevention therapies, much as the treatment for nicotine addiction often relies on behavioral treatment and a pharmacologic agent.

PREVENTIVE INTERVENTIONS TO REDUCE CANCER RISK

With this background, we turn to the behavioral interventions for which there is sufficient, high quality evidence of efficacy. There is a voluminous literature in some areas (e.g., tobacco use research, dietary change, exercise), although not all related to cancer, and a growing literature in other areas (e.g., sun exposure). Moreover, the cancer evidence overlaps with that reviewed in other chapters. We rely primarily on evidence reviews conducted by respected bodies using accepted methods (e.g., the U.S. Preventive Services Task Force, CDC's Guide to Community Preventive Services).

Behavioral interventions should build on the evidence base of epidemiologic research that demonstrates a connection between an exposure and disease outcomes. This is especially important, because few studies themselves provide the proof of principle one may find in basic science studies or clinical drug development research. *Thus, no single behavioral study demonstrates a causal relationship between smoking cessation and reductions in tobacco-related mortality.* Most likely, the lag-time between onset of smoking and cancer is too long to easily demonstrate such a link although recent state-wide intervention studies have sought to measure such linkages. In most cases, population level data obtained from the nation's cancer

surveillance system are used to make the case that large-scale behavior changes can shift cancer incidence and mortality. Before behavioral studies are undertaken, and especially before behavioral interventions are applied on a population basis, there should be excellent epidemiologic and basic science evidence about the phenomenon.

As an example, decreases in smoking among men in the 1960s, 1970s, and 1980s finally led to decreases in mortality from male lung cancer at the end of the 1990s (Annual Report to the Nation, 2001; 2002). These changes generally occur over decades or more. For this reason, the evidence base for cancer control research focuses on altering a behavior (e.g., smoking) that is linked clearly to a cancer outcome (e.g., lung cancer) as shown in Figure 1 below. (Anderson, 1999; Hiatt and Rimer, 1999; Rimer, 2000).

Figure 1.

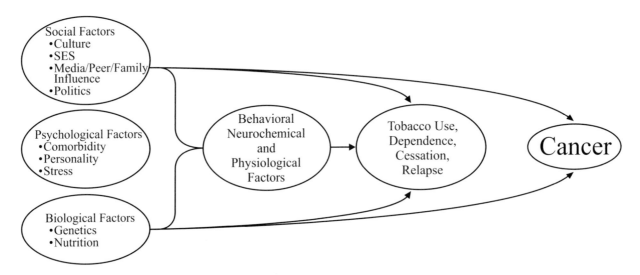

Adapted from Anderson, Office of Behavioral and Social Sciences Research, NIH, 1999.

Smoking Cessation

As noted earlier, there are now a number of excellent reviews of the smoking cessation literature. One of the most thorough and accessible reviews is the updated guideline, Treating Tobacco Use and Dependence (http://www.surgeongeneral.gov/tobacco/treat

ing_tobacco_use.pdf), Fiore et al., June 2000). This guideline was sponsored by a consortium of seven Federal Government agencies and nonprofit organizations. The review includes several recommendations with direct relevance for clinicians with patients who smoke. Most important, all patients who use tobacco should be offered at least one treatment, based on their willingness to quit tobacco use. The guideline concluded that brief treatments are effective, and every patient who uses tobacco should be offered at least one brief treatment. There is a strong dose-response relation between the intensity of tobacco dependence counseling and its effectiveness. Three types of counseling and behavioral therapies were found to be especially effective and should be used with all patients attempting tobacco cessation: provision of practical counseling, provision of social support as part of treatment, and help in securing support outside treatment. The guideline also recommends several first-line pharmacotherapies that increase long-term abstinence rates, including Buproprion SR, nicotine gum, nicotine inhaler, nicotine nasal spray and the nicotine patch.

The updated guideline strengthened the statements about the association between counseling intensity and successful treatment outcomes. In addition, the guideline noted the value of interventions like telephone counseling and counseling that helps smokers obtain support outside the treatment context. As described in the guideline and elsewhere, clinicians should routinely follow the 5 A's: Ask about smoking behavior, Advise smokers to quit, Assess aspects of the smoker's particular smoking typology, readiness to quit and facilitators and barriers to quitting, Assist the smoker to quit by providing help, using brief interventions where appropriate, and Arrange follow-up, especially by asking the smoker how he/she is doing on follow up visits. A Quick Reference Guide for Clinicians provides specific, useful information for clinicians about how to help patients stop smoking successfully (http://www.surgeongeneral.gov/tobaccotoba qrg.htm), Fiore et al., October 2000). Interested readers should consult Volume I Chapter 10 for more detail on effective smoking cessation interventions.

More recently, the Guide to Community Preventive Services (Hopkins et al., 2001) strongly recommended several community and health care system strategies as having a strong evidence base. These include increasing the unit price for tobacco products and mass media campaigns combined with other interventions. The Guide strongly recommended reminders from health care providers (clinicians) plus provider education with and without patient education, and also recommended provider reminders. Multicomponent patient telephone support interventions also were strongly recommended (Hopkins et al., 2001). The community approaches complement health care system strategies. Detailed information about each of the recommended strategies can be found in the published review and on the Guide website www.thecommunityguide.org.

Only a few states have conducted large-scale campaigns that have included mass media and other types of interventions, including increased taxes and other relevant policy changes. Data from Massachusetts and California are perhaps the best example of the potential impact of such combined, well-funded interventions. Data from the BRFSS were used to assess the impact of these statewide interventions by examining changes in cigarette prevalence. During 1990-1992, per-capita consumption of cigarettes declined by 6.4% in MA, 11% in CA and 5.8% in the remaining states (Harris et al. 1996).

Healthful Nutrition

There has been considerable research on behavioral interventions related to dietary change. A recent evidence review commissioned by the National Cancer Institute (NCI) through The Agency for Healthcare Research and Quality (AHRQ) examined the available literature for the two most-often studied dietary behavior outcomes which are thought to increase risk (high dietary fat intake) or reduce risk (high fruit and vegetable consumption) for some cancers (Ammerman et al., 2002; Agency for Healthcare Research and Quality [AHRQ], 2000). The main goal of the review was to examine the overall effectiveness of behavioral dietary interventions for promoting dietary change, and a secondary aim was to identify the types of interventions that are most effective and for whom.

The majority of the published studies reviewed reported significant dietary changes in terms of reducing intake of dietary fat and/or increasing fruit and vegetable intake. Average increases in fruit and vegetable consumption were 0.6 servings per day, and decreases in energy intake from fat averaged 7.3% across the studies reviewed. Two intervention components that seemed to be particularly promising for behavior change were goal setting and small groups. Also, interventions were generally more successful for people at increased-risk for disease than in general, healthy populations (Ammerman et al., 2002; AHRQ, 2000). It is likely that interventions for increased-risk persons were more intensive than were interventions aimed at the general population, but the review did not examine an indicator of intensity across studies. The evidence review conclusions were constrained by the lack of similarity across studies in terms of design, measures, intervention strategies, and analytical approaches. Nevertheless, the findings suggest future research directions and are informative for synthesizing the body of evidence to date.

Physical Activity

Attention to increasing physical activity has addressed both individually-oriented strategies and community-wide approaches, including information dissemination and environmental and policy changes. The Task Force on Community Preventive Services conducted systematic reviews of community interventions to increase physical activity and released its recommendations regarding interventions for which there is sufficient evidence to support their efficacy in 2001 (Task Force on Community Preventive Services, 2001). Because the evidence for physical activity in preventing cancer has emphasized lifelong physical activity – not only adult activity – their recommendations for both youth and adults are relevant to this chapter.

The Task Force recommends six types of interventions. Two are informational approaches: communitywide campaigns and point-of-decision prompts to encourage use of stairs. Three are behavioral and social approaches, i.e., school-based physical education and social support interventions in community settings, and individually adapted health behavior change programs. The remaining recommended intervention to increase physical activity involves environmental and policy approaches – enhanced access to places for physical activity, combined with informational outreach activities (Task Force, 2001).

The Task Force found insufficient evidence on which to base recommendations for classroom-based health education focused on information provision, behavioral skills training, and social support interventions in family settings because of inconsistent findings. There were an insufficient number of studies to make a recommendation regarding mass media campaigns, college-age physical education, and health education. They also did not recommend classroom-based health education focusing on reducing television viewing and video game playing, due to the lack of a demonstrated link between reduced TV or video game use and increased physical activity (Task Force, 2001). The conclusion of "insufficient evidence" does not mean that an evidence review found the intervention to be ineffective; rather, it means that the current scientific evidence from high quality intervention studies precludes inferring that the intervention is efficacious at the present time. This is an area in which more research clearly is needed.

Weight Control

The prevalence of overweight and obesity in adults and children has increased to epidemic proportions in recent years, especially in the United States and other developed countries. There is now sufficient evidence for a cancer-preventive effect of avoidance of weight gain for cancers of the colon, post-menopausal breast cancer, and cancers of the endometrium, kidney and esophagus (IARC, 2002). Therefore, weight gain prevention is likely to reduce the risk of these cancers; however, there currently is no direct evidence that weight reduction in overweight persons will reduce the risks of cancer (IARC, 2002) (See Volume 1, Chapters 14 and 15).

The study of weight gain prevention is in a very early stage, although a few principles are generally agreed upon. First, weight status is the result of a complex interplay of genetic, environmental, and behavioral factors; and second, a lifestyle marked by moderation in food intake and daily physical activity must be sustained to prevent weight gain and/or reduce excess weight (Cummings et al., 2002). The preceding discussions of interventions to promote healthy nutrition and physical activity are relevant to achieving these goals. However, a recent empirical analysis of the amount of physical activity required to prevent unhealthy weight gain or maintain weight loss showed that these goals require a much higher level of routine exercise than is recommended for prevention of cardiovascular disease (Erlichman et al., 2002). Thus, more intensive physical activity promotion is probably required for weight control, and food intake is likely to be a necessary central component of weight gain prevention.

Given the high and increasing prevalence of overweight, public health action is needed to achieve broad cancer-preventive potential (IARC, 2002). One recently completed trial, the Diabetes Prevention Program (DPP), demonstrated that an intensive lifestyle intervention could be effective in achieving significant weight loss/maintenance in a large group of ethnically diverse overweight persons with impaired glucose tolerance (IGT) (DPP Research Group, 2002). The intervention involved individual case management using "lifestyle coaches," frequent contact with participants, a 16-session behavioral self-management program, supervised physical activity, individualization, a flexible maintenance program, and an extensive network of training, feedback, and clinical support. Participants achieved a 58% reduction in their incidence rate of diabetes, maintained a minimum 7% weight loss, and averaged 30 minutes per day of moderate intensity physical activity (DPP Research Group, 2002). The DPP's findings are impressive, and raise the question of how public health and health care systems might adapt this type of intervention for integrated weight management systems (Pronk et al., 2002). Clearly, dissemination of this type of effective, yet highly intensive, strategy will require cooperation between government, the private sector, communities and individuals and would entail an unprecedented investment in reducing chronic disease risk (IARC, 2002).

Alcohol Use

It has been estimated that about 7% of cancers are due to alcohol use (Doll and Peto, 1981; Byers et al., 1999; Colditz et al., 2000). Alcohol use and smoking act synergistically to increase dramatically the risk for head and neck cancer (Lippman and Hong, 2002). Alcohol alone is a causative agent in cirrhosis-related hepatocellular cancer

(Colditz et al., 2000). For breast cancer, one to two drinks/day have been shown to increase risk, and there is a dose-response relationship. Turning this knowledge into a prevention message is complex, because not using alcohol may decrease risks for breast cancer while increasing risks for cardiovascular disease. For now, women should be informed about the breast cancer-alcohol use relationship. This may be especially relevant for women at high risk for breast cancer. Colditz et al. (2000) have recommended abstinence for women at high risk for breast cancer. However, we are aware of no data that prove that decreasing alcohol use also decreases cancer risk. Some studies of patients at high risk for developing breast cancer (e.g., Lerman et al., 1995) have educated women about the relationship between alcohol use and breast cancer but have not reported changes in alcohol use.

Approaches to counseling and education should vary according to the nature of the risk. For example, the message for women with high risk for breast cancer would be very different from that given to heavy alcohol and tobacco users at high risk for head and neck cancer. The message to the latter group should be unequivocal whereas the former would benefit from being given the available data, including the risks for breast cancer and heart disease, and advised to make informed personal decisions.

Reducing Sun Exposure

Skin cancers are among the most common cancers, yet they are also among the most preventable. Most skin cancers can be prevented by reducing sun exposure (i.e., ultraviolet radiation, or UVR exposure): seeking shade, using sunscreen properly, and wearing protective hats and clothing (US Department of Health and Human Services, 2000).

Although awareness about skin cancer is growing, the practice of preventive behaviors remains variable, and is relatively low in many populations. For example, fewer than one-third of U.S. adolescents engage in any form of sun protection, such as wearing a hat, using sunscreen, or staying in the shade on sunny days (Cokkinides et al., 2001). Thus, a variety of intervention strategies have been proposed for changing behaviors related to UVR exposure and their determinants, including media campaigns, educational programs, and changes in sun-protective environments and policies. Because UVR exposure during childhood is believed to account for a significant proportion of total lifetime exposure and thus to play a causative role in skin cancer, children and their caregivers are the main audiences for many of these interventions.

A comprehensive evidence review of the efficacy of health promotion intervention strategies for reducing UVR exposure in specific populations and settings is now in progress, under the sponsorship of the Task Force on Community Preventive Services. The key question addressed is: What interventions, or combination of interventions, are most effective for increasing sun protection behaviors (SPB's) [using sunscreen, hat use, shirt use, sunglasses, shade seeking, and sun avoidance]? A report is forthcoming in 2003, and preliminary conclusions are reported in a book chapter that is now in-press (Glanz et al., 2003). The chapter expands on the Task Force's review to include both controlled efficacy trials and effectiveness studies in real-world settings.

Key conclusions of the evidence review are as follows: Prevention programs in specific settings, such as recreation areas/programs and outdoor workplaces, can achieve significant improvements in sun protection behavior. Most school-based programs have led to changes in knowledge, but have not achieved recommended behavioral changes. Comprehensive, community-wide programs can increase solar protection behaviors and reduce UVR exposure; however, such programs have not been attempted in the United States so it is unclear whether they would be as effective as they have been in Australia, where skin cancer rates are the highest in the world. Media programs show promise for increasing awareness about skin cancer and UVR exposure (Glanz et al., 2003). There are several categories of interventions for sun protection for which there is insufficient evidence to recommend whether or not they should be adopted.

Skin cancer rates are increasing, and more attention should be devoted to designing and evaluating programs to effectively reduce exposure to ultraviolet radiation, especially in high risk populations. Intervention studies in the area of skin cancer prevention, as in all areas of cancer prevention, should attend to the issues of study design, measurement, and cost-effectiveness.

FUTURE DIRECTIONS AND UNANSWERED RESEARCH QUESTIONS

There are no simple solutions for achieving behavioral changes to prevent cancer. One source of optimism lies in the fact that key behavioral recommendations for cancer prevention are the same as those to help prevent other chronic diseases. This greatly increases the prominence and potential to direct resources toward encouraging people not to smoke, to eat a healthy diet, to get regular physical activity, to avoid overweight, and to consume alcohol moderately if at all. Sun protection behaviors, too, can have non-cancer-related benefits, in preventing photoaging of the skin.

Large scientific literatures have accumulated that deal with strategies for achieving health-enhancing changes in risk behaviors. The available evidence confirms the difficulty of maintaining behavior changes over long periods of time, and the importance of repeated efforts, health provider support, and supportive environments and policies. Brief advice from health professionals, as well as more intensive programs and counseling for smoking cessation, dietary change, and physical activity promotion, have all been shown to enhance or support people's efforts at self-change. Individualized communications that are directed to a person's specific barriers and facilitators to change also are effective. These can be of many kinds, including in person counseling as well as computerized communications.

The available evidence is limited with respect to identifying which types of people can benefit from less and more intensive interventions, and provides limited guidance about how to encourage unmotivated persons to participate in behavioral management opportunities. Future studies should explore who can benefit from low-intensity interventions and how to reach those who are least interested in change, but who may need it the most.

In the years ahead, new epidemiological research will help to fine-tune our focus on behavioral risk factors for cancer. For example, dietary constituents such as fish oils, tomatoes, and soy products might become the focus of interventions to reduce cancer risk among certain population groups. In addition, some emerging risk factors, such as HPV, may be shown to have greater population relevance and we will be challenged to build on existing behavioral research to tackle these issues.

As we mentioned earlier, no single behavioral study demonstrates a cause and effect relationship between changes in risk behavior and reductions in cancer incidence or mortality. Such experimental studies, if they were undertaken, would require incredibly large samples and long follow-up periods. Ultimately, population level data obtained from the nation's cancer surveillance system should help us to make the case that large-scale behavior changes can shift cancer incidence and mortality.

Acknowledgements

We thank Kelly Blake, MPH for her work on the table.

REFERENCES

Agency for Healthcare Research and Quality. (2000) Evidence Report Number 25. Efficacy of behavioral interventions to modify dietary behavior related to cancer risk. www.ahcpr.gov/clinic/epcsums/dietsumm. htm, accessed January 2003.

Ammerman AS, Lindquist CH, Lohr KN, Hersey J. (2002) The efficacy of behavioral interventions to modify dietary fat and fruit and vegetable intake: A review of the evidence. Prev Med 35:25-41.

Anderson NB. (1999) A Definition of Behavioral and Social Sciences Research for the National Institutes of Health. Bethesda, MD: National Institutes of Health, Office of Behavioral and Social Sciences Research.

Byers T, Mouchawar J, Marks J, Cady B, Lins N, Swanson GM, Bal DG, Eyre H. (1999) The American Cancer Society challenge goals. How far can cancer rates decline in the U.S. by the year 2015? Cancer 86:715-727.

Cokkinides V, Johnston-Davis K, Weinstock M, O'Connell M, Kalsbeek W, Thun M, Wingo PA. (2001) Sun exposure and sun-protection behaviors and attitudes among U.S. youth, 11 to 18 years of age. Preventive Medicine 33: 141-151.

Colditz GA, Atwood KA, Emmons K, Monson RR, Willett WC, Trichopoulos D, Hunter DJ. (2000) Harvard report on cancer prevention. Volume 4: Harvard Cancer Risk Index. Cancer Causes Control 11:477-488.

Cummings S, Parham ES, Strain GW. (2002) Position of the American Dietetic Association: Weight management. J Am Diet Assoc 102:1145-1155.

Diabetes Prevention Program (DPP) Research Group. (2002) The Diabetes Prevention Program (DPP): Description of lifestyle intervention. Diabetes Care 25:2165-2171.

Doll R, Peto R. (1981) The causes of cancer: quantitative estimates of avoidable risks of cancer in the United States today. J Nat'l Cancer Inst 66:1191-1308.

Edwards BK, Howe HL, Ries LAG, Thun MJ, Rosenberg HM, Yancik R, Wingo PA, Jemal A, Feigal EG. (2002) Annual report to the nation on the status of cancer, 1973-1999, featuring implications of age and aging on U.S. cancer burden. Cancer 94:2766-2792.

Ehrlichman J, Kerbey AL, James WP. (2002) Physical activity and its impact on health outcomes. Paper 2: Prevention of unhealthy weight gain and obesity by physical activity: An analysis of the evidence. Obes Rev 3:273-287.

Fiore MC, Bailey WC, Cohen SJ, Dorfman SF, Goldstein MG, Gritz ER, et al. (June 2000) Treating Tobacco Use and Dependence. U.S. Department of Health and Human Services. Public Health Service. (Available at http://www.surgeongeneral.gov/tobacco/tr eating_tobacco_use.pdf)

Fiore MC, Bailey WC, Cohen SJ, Dorfman SF, Goldstein MG, Gritz ER, et al. (October 2000) Treating Tobacco Use and Dependence. Quick Reference Guide for Clinicians. U.S. Department of Health and Human Services. Public Health Service. (Available at http://wwwsurgeongeneral.gov/tobacco/to baqrg.htm)

Gallagher RP. (1997) Sun exposure and non-melanocytic skin cancer. In: Grob JJ, Stern RS, McKie R. (Eds.) Epidemiology,

Causes and Prevention of Skin Diseases. New York: Blackwell Science, pp. 72-75.

Glanz K, Saraiya M, Briss P. (2003, in press) Impact of intervention strategies to reduce UVR exposure. In Hill D, Elwood M, English D (Eds.), Prevention of Skin Cancer. Amsterdam: Kluwer Academic Publishers.

Glanz K, Vogt TM. (1999) Cancer prevention for women. In Goldman M, Hatch M (Eds.), Women and Health. New York: Academic Press, pp. 977-985.

Green A, Whiteman D, Frost C, Battistutta D. (1999) Sun exposure, skin cancers and related conditions. J Epidemiol 9 (6 Suppl.):S7-S13.

Greenwald P. (2002) Cancer prevention clinical trials. J Clin Oncol 20:14s-22s.

Harris, JE, Connolly GN, Brooks, D et al. (1996) Cigarette Smoking Before and After an Excise Tax Increase and an Anti-Smoking Campaign—Mass, 1990-1996, MMWR, Nov 8, 1996:966-970.

Hiatt RA, Rimer BK. (1999) A new strategy for cancer control research. Cancer Epidemio Biomark and Prev 8:957-964.

Hopkins DP, Briss PA, Ricard CJ, Husten CG, Carande-kulis VG, Fielding JE Alao MO, KcKenna JW, Sharp DJ, Harris JR, Woollery TA, Harris KW, The Task Force on Community Preventive Services. (2001) Reviews of evidence regarding interventions to reduce tobacco use and exposure to environmental tobacco smoke. Am J Prev Med 20:10-15.

Howe HL, Wingo PA, Thun MJ, Ries LA, Rosenberg HM, Feigal EG, Edwards BK. (2001) Annual report to the nation on the status of cancer (1973 through 1998), featuring cancers with recent increasing trends. J Natl Canc Inst 93:824-842.

International Agency for Research on Cancer. (2002) IARC Handbooks of Cancer Prevention. Volume 6. Weight Control and Physical Activity. Vainio H, Bianchini F (eds). Lyon: IARC Press.

Lerman C, Lustbader E, Rimer BK, Daly M, Miller S, Sands C, Balsham A. (1995) Effects of Individualized Breast Cancer Risk Counseling: A Randomized Trial. J Natl Canc Inst 87: 286-292.

Lippman SM, Hong WK. (2002) Cancer prevention science and practice. Cancer Res 62:5119-5125.

McGinnis JM, Foege WH. (1993) Actual causes of death in the United States. JAMA 270:2207-2212.

Peto R. (2001) Cancer epidemiology in the last century and the next decade. Nature 411:390-395.

Pronk NP, Boucher JL, Gehling E, Boyle RG, Jeffery RW. (2002) A platform for population-based weight management: Description of a health plan-based integrated systems approach. Am J Manag Care 8:847-857.

Rimer BK. (2000) Cancer control research 2001. Cancer Causes Control 11:257-270.

Saslow D, Runowicz CD, Solomon D, Moscicki AB, Smith RA, Eyre HJ, Cohen C. (2002) American Cancer Society guideline for the early detection of cervical neoplasia and cancer. CA Cancer J Clin 52:342-362.

Task Force on Community Preventive Services. (2001) Increasing physical activity: A report on recommendations of the Task Force on Community Preventive Services. MMWR 50(RR18):1-16.

U. S. Department of Health and Human Services. (2000) Healthy People 2010, Objective 3.9. Washington, DC: US DHHS, January 2000.

U.S. Department of Health and Human services. (1996) Physical activity and health: A report of the Surgeon General. Atlanta: Centers for Disease Control.

Welcsh PL, Owens KN, King MC. (2002) Insights into the functions of BRCA1 and BRCA2. Trends Genet 16: 69-74.

SCREENING FOR CANCER: THE DILEMMA OF EARLY DETECTION FOR PROSTATE CANCER

Kathryn L. Taylor, Nicole L. Africano, Jennifer Cullen, Tara W. Lamond, Randi Williams, Kimberly Davis

When early detection or prevention efforts lead to unequivocal improvements in disease outcome, screening to detect early stage disease can be extremely beneficial. In this case, developing interventions to increase the number of people screened is key to improving public health. Often, however, our ability to detect those with asymptomatic disease precedes the development of empirically validated treatments to reduce the impact of the disease. When this occurs, appropriate behavioral interventions are more complex, and questions of when and whether people should be screened for a disease arise. In this chapter, we focus on prostate cancer screening, an example of a disease which can be detected early, although the benefits of early detection and treatment are unproven.

Definition of a Useful Screening Test

Prior to reviewing the literature on prostate cancer screening, we first provide an overview of how screening tests are evaluated for the general population. Screening is defined as the population-based assessment of asymptomatic individuals in an effort to detect disease. The definitive goal of any screening test is to reduce mortality and morbidity, not simply early detection. If a screening test does not accomplish a reduction in mortality and/or morbidity, it only serves to increase awareness of the cancer diagnosis for a longer period of time, but without any benefit (i.e., lead-time bias).

As outlined by Kramer and Brawley (2000), the criteria that define the usefulness of a screening test include the following: 1) the test and subsequent follow-up must be acceptable to those eligible for screening, as highly invasive tests won't decrease population-based cancer mortality because people won't adhere in large enough numbers; 2) disease burden must be substantial in the population, as screening for rare diseases won't impact mortality on a population basis; 3) the asymptomatic stage of disease must be detectable and prevalent; if a disease cannot be found prior to the onset of symptoms, early detection cannot occur; 4) the possibility of cure must be present primarily during early stages of disease. If a cancer can be cured at any stage that it is detected, screening asymptomatic individuals does not pay, as simply waiting for the symptoms to present and then treating them will yield the same outcome; and 5) treatment of early stage disease must reduce disease-specific mortality (although there is some debate about the reliance on disease-specific vs. all cause mortality; Black et al., 2002). In either case, screening and treatment must reduce mortality, and not just show an improvement in survival from the time of diagnosis. The first four criteria are necessary but not sufficient to demonstrate the benefit of a screening test (Kramer and Brawley, 2000). Although the last criterion is sufficient to demonstrate benefit, most cancer screening tests do not meet this criterion. Finally, as Kramer and Brawley (2000) argue, efficacy and morbidity of screening must be considered in light of the efficacy of available treatments. When considering whether a screening test is worthwhile, one must simultaneously consider whether the treatment is worthwhile. If there is not an effective treatment that has been shown to reduce disease-related mortality, then detection of the disease will not be fruitful and the implementation of screening must be questioned.

BACKGROUND INFORMATION
Introduction

In 2005, it is expected that prostate cancer will be diagnosed in 232,090 men and will be responsible for 30,350 deaths in the U.S. (Jemal et al., 2005). Prostate cancer is the leading cancer diagnosed in men, and the second leading cause of cancer death among men. The lifetime prevalence of prostate cancer is 1 in 6 men, which compares to a lifetime prevalence of breast cancer of 1 in 7 women (Jemal et al., 2005). The 1996 national expenditure for treating prostate cancer (excluding screening costs) was 4.5 billion (Brown et al., 2002). In spite of the significant disease burden presented by prostate cancer, the utility of screening asymptomatic men for prostate cancer remains controversial, as it has not yet been demonstrated by a randomized trial that early diagnosis and treatment of prostate cancer reduces disease-related mortality. Results from the National Cancer Institute's (NCI) Prostate, Lung, Colorectal, and Ovarian (PLCO) Cancer Screening trial (Prorok et al., 2000) will not be available for approximately ten years. Thus, men and their health care providers are compelled to sift through conflicting information and come to their own conclusions about the usefulness of screening.

There are racial disparities in the incidence, mortality, and five-year survival rates of prostate cancer. African American men are at increased risk for the disease: the incidence is 1.6 times greater among African American men compared to white men, and mortality is 2.4 times greater among African American men compared to Caucasians (Jemal et al., 2005). African American men are somewhat more likely to be diagnosed with poorly differentiated and unknown tumor grade, and less likely to be diagnosed with a well differentiated or moderately differentiated tumor grade, compared to white men (Stanford et al., 1999). Although the gap is lessening, the five-year survival rates (1995-2000) also demonstrated this racial disparity, as African Americans had a 96% five-year survival rate, compared to 100% among white men (Jemal et al., 2005).

While the professional community continues to debate the merits of screening, thousands of asymptomatic men in the U.S. are seeking and/ or receiving screening. In addition, some men are being screened by their physicians in the absence of a discussion of the pros and cons of screening. In spite of the widespread nature of screening, several studies have demonstrated a low level of knowledge and a lack of awareness of the limited evidence for the benefit of screening (e.g., Mercer et al., 1997; O'Dell et al., 1999; Taylor et al., 2002). Thus, most men being screened are under the impression that the medical community unequivocally accepts the benefits of screening. Similar situations have occurred in the past, when hotly debated cancer screening techniques were in widespread use prior to the completion of definitive studies, and the tests either did (cervical cancer screening; e.g., Laara et al., 1987) or did not (lung cancer screening; Collins and Barry, 1996) ultimately prove effective, as defined by a reduction in disease-related mortality. As the ultimate efficacy of prostate cancer screening is not yet known, it is imperative to educate men to promote informed screening decisions in a manner that does not encourage one decision over the other.

Overview of the Prostate Cancer Screening Controversy

The incidence of prostate cancer has increased dramatically within the past decade, primarily due to the use of prostate specific antigen (PSA) as a screening test (Potosky et al., 1995). Although data suggest that prostate cancer is being diagnosed at earlier stages, there is not yet evidence of a reduction in disease-specific mortality, which is the primary measure of screening effectiveness (Potosky et al., 1995; Lu-Yao et al., 2002). Some re-searchers argue that the shift to earlier-stage diagnosis is evidence that screening is effective, although others argue that diagnosing prostate cancer early may not necessarily lead to fewer deaths (i.e., a lead-time bias), that PSA may simply be detecting more indolent cancers (i.e., length bias; Mandelson et al., 1995), or that PSA testing may result in overdiagnosis (detection of disease that otherwise would not have caused a clinical problem; Etzioni et al., 2002; Yao and Lu-Yao, 2002). Overdiagnosis is a special case of length bias, and is thought to be a particular problem when diagnosis occurs at an older age, as death due to other causes is more likely.

The positive predictive value (PPV; true positives/all persons with a positive result) of both the digital rectal exam (DRE) and PSA can be quite low, even when the tests are combined (e.g., 32% to 71%; e.g., Mettlin et al., 1996), resulting in a false positive rate between 29% and 68%. Thus, in addition to their uncertain efficacy, these tests may lead a sizeable portion of men without cancer to undergo a biopsy. As a result, recommenda-tions for prostate cancer screening by professional and governmental organizations vary considerably. For example, the NCI does not recommend for or against prostate cancer screening, while the American Cancer Society (ACS) recommends annual screening beginning at age 50, and at age 45 for African American men. Importantly, the ACS empha-sizes that information should be provided to men about the benefits and limitations of testing (Smith et al., 2001). In addition to the shortcomings of the screening tests, the fundamental controversy concerns what is not yet known about treatment effectiveness and

the long-term side effects associated with treatment.

Overview of the Controversy Surrounding Treatment of Early Stage Prostate Cancer

Although several options are available for the management of localized prostate cancer, no option is clearly superior to others. After a structured review of the available literature, the American Urological Association concluded that there was insufficient evidence to clearly recommend radical prostatectomy, radiation therapy, or expectant management (Middleton et al., 1995). They recommended that factors such as life expectancy, current health, and patient preference for therapeutic options be considered in the treatment decision. Recently, Holmberg et al. (2002) reported that men who were randomly assigned to receive a radical prostatectomy were less likely to die of prostate cancer compared to those assigned to expectant management after six years of follow-up. There was no group difference in all cause mortality, which has been described as a more reliable outcome (Black et al., 2002). These are encouraging, although modest, results in an unscreened population. In an editorial accompanying this article, Walsh (2002) concluded that until additional trials have been completed, physicians are still compelled to educate patients about their options. Further, although it is unknown whether similar results would be obtained in a highly screened U.S. population, a recent observational report using SEER data (1987-1997) indicated that increased screening rates did not result in reduced prostate cancer mortality, regardless of the treatment modality (Lu-Yao et al., 2002).

Men deciding about options for manage-ment of their localized prostate cancer are faced with potential trade-offs between survival and quality of life. In exchange for a *potential* survival benefit from therapy with curative intent, men face significant and common treatment-related side effects, including treatment-related death, incontinence, erectile dysfunction, bowel dysfunction, bleeding, and urethral strictures (Madalinska et al., 2001; Middleton et al., 1995; Steineck et al., 2002). Adverse effects of therapy have an impact on patients' quality of life, and while adverse effects differ between treatments, general health-related quality of life is similar in men treated with either option (Potosky et al., 2000). Thus, since survival benefits of the different management strategies are as of yet uncertain, and men's preferences for outcomes of therapy may influence the decision regarding management choice, men should be informed of potential outcomes and should be encouraged to examine their own values in deciding upon treatment for their prostate cancer. Further, given these uncertainties surrounding treatment and the implications they have for early detection, we contend that men should also have an understanding of these treatment issues prior to a diagnosis, when making a decision about screening.

Overview of Prostate Cancer Risk Factors

The etiology of prostate cancer is not well understood. Established risk factors include older age, African-American race, and family history of prostate cancer in a primary male relative (Powell et al., 1999; Cotter et al., 2002; Hoffman et al., 2001). Age is among the strongest predictors of prostate cancer occurrence (Powell et al., 1999; Cotter et al., 2002).

African American men aged 50-69 years have higher PSA levels, less favorable Gleason scores, more advanced stages of disease, and a higher recurrence rate than white men (Powell et al., 1999; Hoffman et al., 2001). However, among men aged 70-79 years, differences within these parameters have not been found between African American and white men (Powell et al., 1999). It has been recommended that African

American men be tested for prostate cancer at an earlier age than white men, as they may experience a more rapid growth rate of prostate cancer (Powell et al., 2000).

Other factors (e.g., diet, lifestyle behaviors, hormones, sexual factors) have been identified as potential causal factors associated with prostate cancer. A family history of prostate cancer in a primary relative (i.e. father or brother) is another important risk factor for prostate cancer development (Cotter et al., 2002). Men with a family history of prostate cancer are diagnosed at an earlier age than those who lack a family history (Cotter et al., 2002). African American men report a family history of prostate cancer more often than white men and tend to be younger at diagnosis (Cotter et al., 2002).

Dietary factors have been linked to prostate cancer among African American men (Hayes et al., 1999; Kolonel et al., 2000; Vogt et al., 2002; Vogt et al., 2003; Giovannucci et al. 1993; Whittemore et al., 1995). Increased consumption of foods high in animal fat has been linked to prostate cancer among African American men (Hayes et al., 1999). Animal fat, but not vegetable fat, has been related to risk of prostate cancer (Giovannucci et al., 1993). Red meat represents the food group with the strongest association with prostate cancer (Giovannucci et al., 1993). Crude estimates suggest that differences in saturated fat intake account for about 10% of black-white differences in incidence of prostate cancer (Whittemore et al., 1995).

Intake of legumes has been found to be inversely related to prostate cancer (Kolonel et al., 2000). Intake of yellow-orange and cruciferous vegetables may also protect against the disease (Kolonel et al., 2000). Lycopene has been associated with decreased risk of prostate cancer (Vogt et al., 2002). Serum lycopene concentrations have been found to be lower in African American men than white men and this may contribute to a racial disparity in incidence (Vogt et al.,

2002). Intake of selenium is another element that may protect against prostate cancer (Vogt et al., 2003). Higher selenium intake may result in a reduced risk of disease (Li et al., 2004; Vogt et al., 2003).

Heavy alcohol consumption (>3 drinks per day) has been linked to elevated risk of prostate cancer and this finding is consistent in African American and white men (Hayes et al., 1996). Disease risk has not been attributed to tobacco use (Hayes et al., 1996).

A strong association has not been found with regard to the impact of testosterone on the development of prostate cancer (Platz et al., 2000; Kubricht et al., 1999). Although prostate growth is androgen dependent, no difference has been found in testosterone levels in men with and without prostate cancer (Kubricht et al., 1999). However, levels of insulin-like growth factors have been found to be significantly lower in African American men than in white men (Winter et al., 2001). It is interesting to note that these lower levels of growth hormones are found in a population of men at increased risk of developing prostate cancer.

There is some debate in the field of prostate cancer research as to the effect of sexual factors on the development of prostate cancer. Some studies have found no relation between lifetime frequency of sexual intercourse and risk of prostate cancer (Rosenblatt et al., 2001). However, a recent study has suggested that high ejaculation frequency is related to decreased risk of prostate cancer (Leitzmann et al., 2004). Finally, incidence of prostate cancer is not associated with history of vasectomy (John et al., 1995).

Finally, there are some ongoing prevention trials in the field of prostate cancer research. The Prostate Cancer Prevention Trial (PCPT) was designed to test whether the drug finasteride can prevent prostate cancer (Thompson et al., 2003). Men assigned to take finasteride were 25% less likely to develop prostate cancer and the trial was

stopped early because of the clear finding that finasteride reduced the risk of disease. However, men taking finasteride who were diagnosed with prostate cancer appeared to have a higher Gleason grade than those not taking finasteride (Thompson et al., 2003). The NCI's Selenium and Vitamin E Cancer Prevention Trial (SELECT) trial is currently enrolling participants to test whether selenium and Vitamin E may also prevent the development of prostate cancer (Klein et al., 2001).

Screening Parameters

While knowledge of the PSA protein and its primary expression in seminal fluid has been acknowledged since the early 1970's, its use as a serum marker for clinical detection of prostate cancer began in 1987 (Brosman, 2004; Stamey, 1987). Dissemination of this test occurred rapidly throughout the US and led to a dramatic rise in the incidence of early-stage prostate cancer (Potosky, 1995) by the early 1990's. According to established reference ranges, men with PSA values ≤ 4 ng/mL (PSA protein per 1 mL serum) are labeled as "normal" while those above 4 ng/mL are considered to have "elevated" PSA levels. The sensitivity of the PSA blood test ranges between 46% and 89% and the specificity of the PSA ranges from 59% to 91%, depending on the study (Catalona. 1994). It is important to note that factors other than prostate cancer, including inflammation of the prostate gland (prostatitis), benign prostatic hyperplasia (BPH), age and race can contribute to higher PSA serum levels (NCI-PDQ, 2004). Recently, PSA values of less than 4.0 have begun to be classified as abnormal, due to a recently published study from the PCPT that examined end-of-study biopsies among men assigned to the placebo arm of this trial (Thompson et al., 2004). This study found that prostate cancer was present in 15.2% (449/2950) of men whose PSA value fell within the established normal range (i.e., ≤ 4.0 ng/mL). However, men detected with high grade disease constituted only 14.9% (67/449) of the men detected with cancer, or 2% (67/2950) of the men with a PSA value of ≤ 4.0. These data suggest that lowering the PSA value considered to be abnormal may detect more cancers, but may also contribute to the problem of overdiagnosis due to prostate cancer screening.

Age- and race-specific ranges have also been proposed (Oesterling et al, 1993; Henderson et al., 1997; Cooney et al., 2001). While it is clear that a man's age plays an important role in interpreting PSA reference ranges, not all researchers agree as to the usefulness of race-specific ranges (Catalona et al., 2000). There is also evidence that use of free-to-total PSA ratios can be used to improve test specificity (Ozdal et al., 2004; Parsons et al., 2004a; Haese et al., 2004; Parsons et al., 2004b; Raaijmakers et al., 2004, Catalona, 1996). However, the benefit of using these combinations of tests may be modest when PSA >4 ng/mL (Etzioni et al., 2004). Moreover, some researchers have cautioned against use of such ratios in determining whether a cancer biopsy should occur (Ciatto et al., 2004). Other measurements such as PSA velocity (change in PSA over time), PSA doubling time, and PSA density (total serum PSA divided by tumor volume) might also serve as useful indicators of cancer presence (Benson et al., 1992; Carter et al., 1992).

An important consequence of improving PSA test accuracy could be a reduction in the number of unnecessary prostate biopsies. Although it has not yet been determined whether prostate cancer screening reduces disease-specific mortality, there is clear morbidity associated with undergoing testing, including physical discomfort during biopsy and anxiety associated with awaiting test results. Still awaited are results from the randomized clinical trials of PSA screening on prostate cancer-specific mortality, including the Prostate Lung, Colorectal and Ovarian (PLCO; Gohagan et al., 2000) trial being conducted through the NCI, and the European Randomized Study of Screening for Prostate Cancer (ERSPC; deKoning et al., 2002) trial. Both trials are anticipated to shed light on screening-related survival benefits.

Search Terms and Inclusion/Exclusion Criteria Used for This Review

We used the following terms in our Medline search for relevant articles: a) prostate cancer prevention, prostate cancer risk, prostate cancer screening and detection (DRE, PSA, prostate biopsy), prostate cancer symptoms, and pros-tate cancer statistics. b) prostate cancer screening AND 1) knowledge, 2) health beliefs/ attitudes; and c) prominent authors in this area (e.g., O. Brawley, I. Powell, M. Litwin. S. Woolf).

The inclusion criteria were articles published from 1995 to 2004, with the exception that we included seminal articles published in the early 1990's, particularly when there were few recent articles on a particular topic. Articles must have been published in refereed journals, and all study designs were included (cross-sectional and longitudinal surveys, focus groups, case-control studies, cohort studies, and randomized trials). We excluded studies which had a primary focus on: prostate cancer treatment outcome studies (including quality of life outcomes), the cost of treatment, and black/ white survival differences. We also excluded abstracts and conference presentations.

OVERVIEW OF INTERVENTIONS DESIGNED TO INCREASE UPTAKE OF CANCER SCREENING TESTS
Breast, Cervical, and Colorectal Cancer Screening

Unlike prostate cancer screening, the utility of breast, cervical, and colorectal cancer screening is widely accepted and recommended by virtually all scientific and professional groups. Screening for these cancers is encouraged as there have been a number of trials to demonstrate a reduction in disease-specific mortality (Gates, 2001). A 20% to 30% decrease in mortality has been shown as a result of mammography in a number of studies conducted with normal-risk women over the age of 50 who were screened every 1 to 2 years (Brawley and Kramer, 2005; Nystrom et al., 2002; Anderson et al., 1988, 1997). Despite these studies, there is still some controversy regarding the impact of mammography on mortality reduction (e.g., Olsen and Gotzsche, 2002; Green and Taplin, 2003). Regarding cervical cancer screening, there have been no randomized clinical trials to date to show that cervical cancer screening with the Pap test reduces mortality.However, a number of cohort and case-control studies have shown a 20% to 60% reduction in cervical cancer mortality (NCI, 2004; Laara, 1987; Sigurdsson, 1993; USPSTF, 2003) indicating the effectiveness of the Pap test. Randomized controlled trials using the fecal occult blood test (FOBT) show a 15-30% reduction in death from colorectal cancer (USPSTF, 2003; Pignone et al., 2002; McCleod 2001; Ault and Mandel, 2000). Although the ongoing PLCO trial is expected to provide the first U.S. randomized trial data on the utility of the flexible sigmoidoscopy, several case control studies have already established the benefit of this procedure, demonstrating a 60-80% reduction in disease-related mortality (Newcomb et al., 1992; Selby et al., 1992; Muller et al., 1995).

Adherence to these recommended screening tests has increased in recent years, particularly for mammography. In 1995, the median percentage of women who had a mammogram or breast exam was 56.3%, compared to 63.4% in 2002 (Behavioral Risk Factor Surveillance System [BRFSS], 2002). In 2002, 95.2% of women reported having had a pap smear in comparison to 94.1% in 1995 (BRFSS, 2002). Despite the more recent evidence demonstrating that there are several methods (including the fecal occult blood test (FOBT), flexible sigmoidoscopy, colonoscopy and barium enema) that all reduce the incidence of colorectal cancer, the percentage of individuals who are non-adherent to colorectal screening remains high: in 2002, only 48.1% of adults aged 50 and older had undergone sigmoidoscopy or colonoscopy in the past ten years (BRFSS, 2002). Even though there has been an overall increase in screening rates, there are several subgroups defined by sociodemographic and cultural differences whose rates remain lower than the national average (Hiatt et al., 2002).

We have provided a brief overview of some of the most widely studied methods of increasing the rates of these effective cancer screening tests (Pasick et al., 2004). These methods include: 1) patient based (i.e. personalized print communication and tailored telephone counseling), 2) physician based (i.e. medical record prompt for physicians), and 3) office based (i.e. cancer screening checklist for office employees to monitor when tests are due, ordered, and completed) interventions.

Roetzheim et al. (2004) conducted a cluster-randomized trial to assess effectiveness of the Cancer Screening Office Systems intervention. This program was designed to promote screening among disadvantaged populations in primary care settings. The intervention consisted of two components: 1) a cancer-screening check-list indicating whether specific cancer screening tests were due, ordered, or completed, and 2) identification and review by office staff of patients within the recommended screening age, for the provider to then determine which cancer-screening tests were required. Of the 1,237 subjects who completed a 12-month follow up, the intervention increased the odds of mammograms (OR=1.62, 95% CI, 1.07-9.78, P=.023), fecal occult blood tests

(OR=2.5, 95% CI, 1.65-4.0, P<.0001), and produced a trend toward greater use of Pap smears (OR=1.57, 95% CI, 0.92-2.64, P=.096). The Cancer Screening Office Systems intervention significantly increased the cancer screening rates, suggesting that this intervention might be effective in other primary care settings.

A three year randomized field trial was designed to evaluate the impact of tailored interventions on mammography in an HMO setting (Lipkus et al., 2000). Subjects (N = 1099) were randomized to one of three groups (telephone counseling, tailored print, or usual care) and followed for 36 months. Telephone counseling was more effective at promoting mammography than was tailored print or usual care (71%, 67%, 61%, respectively; p < .006). The findings suggest that telephone counseling is a more effective intervention than print when trying to improve women's adherence to breast cancer screening.

In a trial conducted to evaluate three interventions designed to increase pap smears among women at high risk for cervical cancer, Bowman et al. (1995) randomly assigned subjects to receive an educational pamphlet, letters inviting attendance at a woman's health clinic, or letters from physicians. Of the 659 women interviewed, 36.9% (95% CI: 29.8-44) of the women who received letters from the physicians, 25.9% (95% CI; 19.2-32.6) who receiv-ed the educational pamphlet, 22.6% (95% CI; 16.2-29) who received the invitation to the clinic, and 24.5% (95% CI; 17.7-33.3) of the control group reported screening at the six month follow up, respectively. These results suggest that physicians can have a significant effect on patients' attendance at future screenings.

Church et al. (2004) conducted a randomized trial that used direct mailing of an FOBT kit among residents of a community in which colorectal cancer screening had been promoted. The sample (N = 1451) was randomly assigned to one of three groups: 1) control group (no intervention), 2) FOBT kit with reminders to return it, and 3) FOBT kit without reminders. The responses from the one-year follow-up were used to estimate the one year change in self-reported screening rates. The one year rate change in absolute percentage for FOBT adher-ence was 1.5% (95%CI = -2.9% to 5.9%) for the control group, 16.9% (95% CI = 11.5% to 22.3%) for the direct mail with no reminders group, and 23.2% (95% CI = 17.2% to 29.3%) for the direct mail with reminders group. The one year rate changes for self-reported adherence to any colorectal screening test were 7.8% (95% CI=3.2% to 12%) for the control group, 13.2% (95% CI=8.4% to 18.2%) for direct mailing of FOBT with no reminders group, and 14.1% (95% CI=9.1% to 19.1%) for direct mailing of FOBT with reminders group. The direct mailing of the FOBT kits with follow-up reminders increased overall rate of adherence to colorectal cancer screening, suggesting that this method may be an effective way to promote more proactive colorectal screening behaviors.

In summary, these trials show that there are a number of different methods that can be used to improve the overall adherence to breast, cervical, and colorectal screening tests. A number of randomized trials are still underway and their findings may show further strategies in which interventions can be used to impact screening behaviors.

Prostate Cancer Screening

Although some researchers believe that the population-based shortcomings of screening also apply to men at high risk for the disease (e.g., Brawley, 2003), there is a dissenting argument, which states that in spite of the lack of firm evidence for the utility of screening, African American men and men with a strong family history should be screened due to their high risk status (e.g., Farkas, 1997; Powell, 1994; Mettlin et al., 1993; Gelfand et al., 1995). As African American men tend to present with advanced disease, have higher incidence and mortality rates (Kosary et al., 1995) and have significantly lower screening participation rates, most intervention studies designed to increase screening rates have targeted African Americans. There have been approximately 6 studies designed to increase the rates of screening among African American men (Weinrich et al., 1998; Myers et al., 1999; Powell et al ., 1997; Powell et al., 1997; Black et al., 1993; Freeman et al., 1995; Stone, 1998). We have described two of these studies below.

Weinrich et al. (1998) conducted a quasi-experimental study to measure the effect of four educational interventions on participation in a free prostate cancer screening program. The 4 educational interventions were randomly assigned to 222 community study sites. Interventions included: traditional education (controls), peer-education only, client-navigator only, or a combination intervention (peer education and client-navigator interventions). Of 1,717 men (71% African American), 1114 (65%) had a free prostate cancer screening test (DRE or PSA). African American men were significantly less likely to participate in screening than their Caucasian counterparts (61% vs. 75%). Significant interventions for African Americans were peer-education only (OR = 1.40, p = 0.04) and client-navigator only (OR = 1.91, p = 0.0001). Neither of these interventions was significant for Caucasian men. However, the client-navigator only intervention was a significant predictor of screening participation for the sample as a whole (OR = 1.77, p= 0.0001). These results highlight the positive impact of combining educational strategies delivered through community-based organizations for increasing prostate cancer screening among African American men as proposed by Powell (1994).

In another study, Myers et al. (1999) randomized 413 African American men to either "minimal" or "enhanced" intervention. Mini-mal intervention included a mailed letter inviting men to a no-cost clinic visit where information about prostate cancer and early detection and a free prostate cancer early detection exam would be made available. The enhanced intervention provided the minimal intervention plus a culturally sensitive and personalized educational booklet about prostate cancer, early detection and a tailored risk factors and symptoms form. Adherence was defined as men who made an office visit for education and an early detection screen within 1 year of completing a baseline telephone survey. Thirty-nine percent of the sample received a screening test. Adherence was significantly higher (OR = 2.6, CI: 1.7-3.9) in the enhanced intervention compared with the minimal intervention (51% vs. 29%) group. Age (OR = 1.7, CI: 1.1-2.8), marital status (OR = 1.8, CI: 1.2-2.9), belief that an early detection exam should be performed in the absence of symptoms (OR = 2.3, CI: 1.3-4.0), and self-reported intention to have a screening exam (OR = 1.9, CI: 1.2-2.9) were all predictors of adherence. The researchers concluded that a tailored "enhanced" intervention could influence adherence to prostate cancer early detection in African American men.

Results from both of these studies indicate the ability of educational interventions to increase rates of prostate cancer screening. Culturally sensitive information and/or use of a role model to educate men appear to be important by personalizing prostate cancer as a major health concern. Evidence from these and other studies demonstrate that African American men will participate in screening if it is accessible, particularly through community networks and if information is presented in an individualized manner. However, due to the controversies in prostate cancer screening, the current trend has shifted away from interventions designed to increase screening, in favor of interventions designed to increase men's knowledge and informed decision making. These interventions are reviewed following the subsequent section.

KNOWLEDGE, AWARENESS, AND BEHAVIOR ASSOCIATED WITH PROSTATE CANCER SCREENING

Increased publicity has magnified public concern about prostate cancer as a disease that causes death in a substantial number of men each year. As a result, the number of men seeking screening is on the rise (Breen et al., 2001). However, this increased awareness has not led to a corresponding increase in knowledge about prostate cancer (Diefenbach et al., 1996; Mercer et al., 1997; Myers et al., 1996; O'Dell et al., 1999, Taylor et al., 2002; Wilt et al., 2001). This situation is due in part to the uncertainty in the medical community about exactly what should be communicated to the public.

Some research has focused on the issue of informed consent and prostate cancer screening (Davison et al., 1999; O'Connor et al., 2001; Schapira et al., 2000). In the absence of a definitive medical recommendation for screening, patients' personal values and preferences become crucial to their screening decision. But in order to play a meaningful role in the screening decision, patients need to have the relevant information available to them. For example, important aspects of prostate cancer screening are its uncertain efficacy, and the disagreements among experts as to whether screening extends life. Thus, unlike other cancers (e.g., colon or cervical), it is not necessarily the case that a higher rate of prostate cancer screening will lead to a better outcome. On the other hand, we may eventually learn that early detection does lead to improved cure rates, making screening the best choice one could make. Thus, patients must learn to weigh the potential (but as yet unproven) benefits of screening with its potential limitations.

There is a large literature on the prediction of cancer screening behaviors, using several theoretical orientations, including the Transtheoretical Model (TTM; Prochaska, 1994) and the Health Belief Model (HBM; Aiken et al., 1994). Much of this research concerns mam-mography and breast self-examination, although increasingly, studies have focused on prostate cancer screening. We have provided a brief description of some of the studies conducted before 2000, and a more detailed description of more recent research.

One's history of prostate screening has been related to knowledge regarding prostate cancer, and both knowledge and screening history are positively related to intent to undergo screening in the future (O'Dell et al., 1999; Myers et al., 1996). Education, income, and urban residence have been positively associated with prior screening (Price et al., 1993) and willingness to undergo screening in the future (Robinson et al., 1996). Further, several studies demonstrated the low level of knowledge regarding prostate cancer, particularly among African American men (Price et al., 1993; Myers et al., 1994; Myers et al., 1996; Brown et al., 1990). Patient education studies designed to increase knowledge and increase rates of screening among African American men have reported that brief print-based interventions result in an increase in knowledge of symptoms and risk factors (Collins, 1997), as well as an increase in rates of screening (Myers et al., 1997).

Below we present more recent studies that have assessed prostate cancer-related knowledge, attitudes, beliefs, and behaviors. Studies are organized in the following order: 1) focus group studies and 2) observational survey studies (Randomized intervention studies are described in the following section and Table 1).

Focus group studies have addressed the barriers to screening (Meade et al., 2003; Nash and Hall, 2002), what men know and misconceptions about prostate cancer (Clarke-Tasker and Wade, 2002; McFall et al., 2004), and what men want to know and how they want to learn new information (Chan et al., 2003; Meade et al., 2003; Taylor et al., 2001). Several misconceptions about prostate cancer have been revealed, as well as a lack of knowledge about the screening controversy. In some cases, these studies have been useful in helping to design educational interventions that are targeted to African American men (McFall et al., 2004; Taylor et al., 2001).

Given the relatively recent beginning of behavioral and psychological survey research in prostate cancer, it is not surprising that in general, the literature is beset with methodological limitations. Chief among the limitations are cross-sectional designs and small, biased samples, which often occur due to the difficulty of accessing and accruing random samples of participants. As in the focus group studies, the outcomes of interest were typically knowledge (Agho and Lewis, 2001; Ashford et al., 2001; Chan et a., 2003; Steele et al., 2000; Taylor et al., 2002), barriers to screening (Gwede et al., 2002; Weinrich et al., 2003), perceived risk for the disease (Fearing et al., 2000; Honda et al., 2004; Taylor et al., 1999) and intention to follow-up on an abnormal screening exam (Myers et al., 2000). Three recent studies have used either a random digit dial sampling strategy (Ashford et al., 2001; Schwartz et al., 2004) or the National Health Interview Survey, a nationally representative sample (Honda et al., 2004). Recent studies have been more likely to include an assessment of men's understanding of the screening controversy (e.g., Schwartz et al., 2004; Chan et al., 2003; Taylor et al., 2002), suggesting that researchers are becoming more aware of and more interested in addressing the uncertainties associated with prostate cancer screening.

Behavioral and psychological research in prostate cancer must focus on developing effective methods of educating men about the current state of the science, and helping men to make the best screening decision for themselves. Until biomedical research has a definitive answer regarding the utility of screening, a major role for behavioral and psychological research is to develop and evaluate educational materials that accurately reflect what is known and not known about prostate cancer, and to help men understand these complicated issues so that they may determine the side of this debate with which they are most comfortable. Below we have reviewed the interventions that have been conducted to date.

REVIEW OF PROSTATE CANCER SCREENING EDUCATIONAL MATERIALS

Current educational materials for prostate cancer screening include printed pamphlets and brochures, Internet information, videos, and books. To a lesser degree, consumer magazine and news updates describe prostate cancer statistics and topics relevant to prostate cancer, but do not necessarily focus on screening. Further, most materials are designed for men in general, regardless of ethnic/racial background; thus, currently there is a lack of educational materials that are designed specifically for African American men. Three exceptions are the CDC's guide "Prostate Cancer Screening: A Decision Guide for African Americans" (October 2003), Taylor et al.'s (2001) guide "The Right Decision Is Yours: A Guide To Prostate Cancer Check-ups," and Hamm's (2000) guide, "What Black Men in their 40s [50s, 60s] want to know about Prostate Cancer." Papers have not yet been published on the evaluation of these three projects. This section provides a review of the randomized trials that have examined the use of various educational materials for screening, a sampling of Internet websites, and a summary of available videos and books.

Table 1: Randomized Trials of Educational Materials for Prostate Cancer Screening

Author(s)	Sample	Design	Outcome
Flood, AB, Wennberg, JE, et al. (1996)	Two studies reported. Total N = 568 men age 50 and older, All white Ave age range = 63.6 – 66.5 Some college = 53.6% - 78.4%	Two quasi-randomized trials. For study 1, men *seeking free prostate cancer screening* were preassigned to view an **educational videotape** (N=184) or **a control videotape** (N=188) (PCEC in conjunction w/ Schering Corp., pro-screening). For study 2, men *scheduled to visit* a general internal medicine clinic viewed either the **educational videotape** (N=103) **or no videotape** (N=93). Videotape: "The PSA Decision: What YOU Need To Know" (Foundation for Informed Medical Decision Making [FIMDM])	Men who viewed the educational videotape were better informed about PSA tests, prostate cancer and its treatment. If cancer were found, they preferred "watchful waiting" over surgery or radiation therapy. Most men in control groups of both studies preferred active treatment over watchful waiting (73% & 61%, respectively). Men in both control groups said chances were "high" to have PSA test in next 2 years; those who viewed the educational video were less inclined. Among scheduled clinic patients, men who viewed the educational video were less likely to have a PSA test.
Wolf, AM, Nasser, JF, Wolf, AM, Schorling, JB (1996)	N = 205 men aged 50 yrs or older with no prior PSA screening Ave age = 65 Intervent. = 62.1% white, 37.9% "nonwhite" 69.6% not HS grad Control = 63.7% white 36.3% "nonwhite" 67.6% not HS grad	Four university-affiliated primary care practices were used to accrue men; predominantly low SES status. RCT in which patients either received a **scripted (oral) informational intervention (read aloud by a trained research assistant)** or a single sentence about PSA test	Patients who received the informational intervention less interested in undergoing screening (similar impact w/ higher educated as well). Family history positively associated w/ interest. Age negatively associated w/ interest (with advancing age, less interest in screening).
Davison, BJ, Kirk, P., Degner, LF, Hassard, TH. (1999)	N=100 men aged 50-79 scheduled for a periodic health exam (PHE) All white Ave age = 62.1 High school or more = 56%	RCT in which men were assigned to receive **verbal and written screening information** (about controversy and pros/cons of PSA and/or DRE) either prior to PHE or after PHE Control: Investigator talked to men about general issues prior to exam.	Men who received screening information prior to PHE had a significantly more active role in making screening decision, and had significantly lower levels of decisional conflict. No significant differences in anxiety or actual screening behavior.

Table 1: Randomized Trials of Educational Materials for Prostate Cancer Screening

Author(s)	Sample	Design	Outcome
Volk, RJ, Cass, AR, Spann, SJ. (1999)	N=160 men aged 45-70 scheduled for office visit at family medicine clinic Intervention: Ave age = 58.5 Race = 48% White, 18% Black, 10% Mexican-Amer., 2% Other Education =49% some college or more Control: Ave age = 59.5 Race = 49% White, 12% Black, 15% Mexican-Amer., 4% Other Education = 42% some college	RCT in which men were assigned to receive a **videotape/brochure** & utility assessment, or videotape/brochure only, or a brochure at 2 week follow-up (control group). Videotape: "The PSA Decision: What YOU Need To Know"	Videotape intervention group led to increased knowledge of prostate cancer (75% improvement in knowledge questions answered correctly). At two-week follow-up, 62% of intervention patients vs. 80% of control patients planned PSA testing. The percentage of subjects wanting the PSA test in the intervention group decreased by 17%, where there was no significant difference in control group.
Volk, RJ, Spann, SJ, Cass, AR, Hawley, ST (2003)	N=160 men aged 45-70 scheduled for office visit at family medicine clinic (Same sample as above)	RCT described above. This paper provides the one-year follow-up findings.	At one-year, 34.3% of intervention subjects had PSA testing compared to 55.2% of controls; the groups did not differ in rate of DRE. The groups did not differ in their satisfaction with their screening decision over the past year. The intervention group had higher knowledge, but their mean score was lower than it was at baseline.
Schapira, MM, VanRuiswyk, J. (2000)	N=257 men aged 50-80 Intervention: Ave age – 69.4 Race – 95% White Control: Ave age – 70.4 Race – 90% White, 5% Black	Men were receiving primary care at a VA Hospital in Milwaukee RCT in which men either received an **8-pg illustrated pamphlet** ("Questions and Answers about tests for Prostate Cancer") or a comparison pamphlet containing basic prostate cancer information	The illustrated pamphlet was effective in improving knowledge of prostate cancer screening tests (e.g., 95% of intervention group were aware of the possibility of false-negative results compared with 85% of comparison group) and of the natural history of prostate cancer. No differences found in use of PSA tests.

Table 1: Randomized Trials of Educational Materials for Prostate Cancer Screening

Author(s)	Sample	Design	Outcome
Frosch, DL, Kaplan, RM, Felitti, V. (2001)	N=176 men among 4 studies Men were recruited through the Health Appraisal screening prog in the Dept. for Preventive Med, Kaiser Permanente, San Diego CA. Age range = 63.11 – 64.26 yrs Education: High school or less: 14 -28.8% College: 46.7-67.4% Grad degree: 17.4-26.2% Ethnicity: African American: 0 -11.1% Hispanic: 2.3 -13.3% Asian: 4.3 – 9.5% Native Amer: 0 – 4.7% Caucasian: 68.9 – 85.7%	Four-arm randomized trial in which participants were randomly assigned to 1 of 4 groups: 1) Usual Care (statement about PSA as screening test for PCa) 2) Discussion (25 minute talk on risks and benefits of screening, PCa, and risks/benefits of tx) 3) **Video** ("The PSA Decision: What YOU Need To Know") 4) Video and Discussion – Video followed by time to ask questions	The proportion of men selecting PSA testing was about 98% with usual care, 82% with discussion, 60% with videotape, and 50% with both the videotape and discussion. Participation in any intervention significantly increased knowledge compared to usual care. Participants in the intervention groups were more likely to choose watchful waiting over surgery or radiation, if they were diagnosed with prostate cancer (81.8%, 72.7%, 67.5%, 35.7% of participants in the discussion, video, video/discussion, and usual care, respectively)
Wilt, TJ, Paul, J., Murdoch, M., et al. (2001)	N=342 men aged 50 and over who had clinic appointments at VA medical center Ave age = 71; 90% White	RCT to determine whether a **mailed educational pamphlet** ("Early prostate cancer") affected men's knowledge about early detection of prostate cancer.	Men who received the pamphlet were better informed than men in usual care group (by higher proportion of correct answers to questions about natural history of prostate cancer, whether treatment lengthens lives of men w/ early prostate cancer and accuracy of PSA testing). The groups did not differ in testing for PSA in the year after the index clinic visits.

Table 1: Randomized Trials of Educational Materials for Prostate Cancer Screening

Author(s)	Sample	Design	Outcome
Frosch, DL, Kaplan, RM, Felitti, VJ. (2003)	N=226 men aged 50+ Internet group: Ave age– 62 Race – 94% White Education – 95% some college and beyond Video group: Ave age – 62 Race – 88.4% White, 5% Asian, 4% Hispanic Education – 90% at least college and beyond	Men were accrued from the Health Appraisal Clinic of the Dept. of Preventive Med. at Kaiser Permanente in San Diego RCT (pre and posttest) in which men scheduled for a physical exam were randomly assigned to access a **website (47 slides similar to video)** or view a **videotape** (FIMDM) in clinic prior to deciding about screening	Contrary to hypotheses, men assigned to video 1)were more likely to view the material than men assigned to internet; 2) had significantly greater increases in knowledge; 3) were more likely to decline PSA tests. However, men who reviewed the entire internet presentation showed similar increases in knowledge. There was a significant shift in treatment preferences post-test, where men assigned to video were more likely to endorse watchful waiting (76.8%) than those assigned to internet (53.2%).
Gattellari, M, & Ward, JE (2003) Note: Booklet available in article	N= 248 men aged 40-70 recruited from the practices of 13 local general practitioners in Sydney All white (Australian) Ave age – 54 Education: 20% before school cert. 16% school certificate 34% trade or univ qualified 30% university degree	RCT in which men received an **evidence-based (EB) booklet** ("Should I have a PSA test?") or government-published pamphlet	Men who received EB booklet had significantly improved knowledge and lower levels of decisional conflict. Both groups had lower levels of interest in PSA screening at post-test.
Gattellari, M, & Ward, JE (2004, in press)	N = 421 men from Australian community accrued from random selection of white page telephone directory Ave age – 58 Education: 15.4% before school cert. 47% school certificate 37.6% university degree	RCT in which men received an **evidence-based (EB) booklet**, leaflet (standard care), or video ("The choice is yours: testing for prostate cancer")	Men in all 3 groups had significantly improved knowledge at post-test. Men who received the EB booklet had lowest levels of decisional conflict. Men who received the EB booklet also were least likely to accept a scenario-based recommendation by a physician to undergo PSA screening.

Randomized Trials of Prostate Cancer Screening Educational Materials

As of 2005, there have been 11 published and 2 unpublished randomized trials that have examined three different types of educational materials for prostate cancer screening (pamphlet, video, Internet; See Table 1). Six trials have studied the impact of providing written and/or verbal information to men prior to the opportunity to be screened (Wolf et al., 1996; Davison et al., 1999; Schapira et al, 2000; Wilt et al., 2001; Gattellari et al., 2003; Gattellari et al., 2004). Wolf et al. found that patients who received the scripted (verbal) informational intervention were less interested in undergoing screening compared to a control condition. Davison et al. randomized men to either receive verbal and written information about screening or to listen to an investigator talk about general health issues for men prior to a health exam. They found that men who had received the screening information had a significantly more active role in making a screening decision and had significantly lower levels of decisional conflict. There were no significant differences in anxiety or actual screening behavior. Schapira and VanRuiswyk (2000) reported that men who had received an illustrated pamphlet decision aid containing quantitative information (vs. a comparison pamphlet containing basic prostate cancer information) had improved knowledge of screening tests. Similarly, Wilt et al. (2001) found that men who had received a pamphlet prior to a clinic appointment were better informed than the usual care group. However, similar to Schapira's findings, the groups did not differ in rates of PSA screening. Gattellari et al. (2003) showed similar findings, whereby men who received an evidence-based booklet vs. a government-published pamphlet had significantly improved knowledge and lower levels of decisional conflict. Regardless of the information received, men had lower interest in PSA screening at post-test. Finally,

Gattellari and Ward (2004) have recently compared their evidence-based booklet with a leaflet and video in a randomized trial of men recruited from the community. Their findings indicated that men in all 3 groups had significantly improved knowledge at post-test, with men who received the booklet indicating lowest decisional conflict. Men who received the booklet were also less likely to agree to a doctor's recommendation for PSA screening (presented as a scenario question at post-test), compared to men who received the leaflet or video. It is important to note that only the Gatellari studies had a separate "decision aid" to assist men in working through their values and thoughts about prostate cancer screening.

Five published trials have studied the use of an established 22-minute videotape ("The PSA Decision: What You Need to Know", Foundation for Informed Medical Decision Making (FIMDM), 1994) in providing information to men about prostate cancer screening (Flood et al., 1996; Volk et al., 1999; Frosch et al, 2001; Frosch et al., 2003; Partin et al., 2004). Flood et al. (1996) conducted two quasi-randomized trials with the videotape in two different settings: one setting involved men attending free screening at a clinic who either viewed the FIMDM videotape or a control videotape (a pro-screening tape produced by a pharmaceutical company), and one setting involved men scheduled for a routine medical visit who viewed either the FIMDM videotape or no videotape. Findings indicated that men who viewed the FIMDM videotape were better informed about PSA tests, prostate cancer, and its treatment. Men in the control groups were significantly more inclined to have a PSA test in the next 2 years compared to those in the intervention condition group. Most men in the control groups of both samples preferred active treatment over watchful waiting, whereas men who viewed the FIMDM intervention videotape preferred no active treatment if cancer were found.

Volk and colleagues (1999) randomly assigned men to one of three conditions: 1) FIMDM videotape and the accompanying brochure, 2) FIMDM videotape plus a utility assessment exercise, or 3) a brochure only. Similar to Flood et al.'s findings, men assigned to the FIMDM videotape had increased knowledge of prostate cancer. At the two-week follow-up, 62% of intervention patients vs. 80% of control patients planned to undergo PSA screening. These subjects were contacted again at the one-year follow-up (Volk et al., 2003) to assess whether they had undergone screening, their satisfaction with their decision, and knowledge retention. The researchers found that 34.3% of the intervention subjects had been screened, compared to 55.2% of the control subjects; the groups did not differ in the rates of receiving the digital rectal exam (DRE) or on satisfaction with their screening decision.

Frosch and colleagues (2001) conducted a four-arm randomized trial in which men were assigned to receive 1) usual care (a statement about PSA as screening test for prostate cancer), 2) a discussion (25 minute talk on benefits and risks of screening, prostate cancer, and risks/benefits of treatment), 3) the FIMDM videotape, or 4) a combination of the FIMDM videotape and discussion. The proportion of men selecting PSA screening was 98% with usual care, 82% with discussion, 60% with videotape, and 50% with both videotape and discussion. Participation in any intervention significantly increased knowledge compared to usual care. Further, similar to Flood et al.'s findings, participants in the intervention groups were more likely to choose watchful waiting over surgery or radiation, if they were diagnosed with prostate cancer.

More recently, Frosch and colleagues (2003) randomly assigned men to access an Internet website (which had 47 slides similar to the FIMDM videotape) or view the FIMDM video-tape in a clinic prior to making a decision about screening. Contrary to their hypotheses, men assigned to the videotape were more likely to view the material, had significantly greater increases in knowledge, and were more likely to decline PSA testing. However, men who reviewed the entire website had similar increases in knowledge.

In another recent randomized trial, Partin and colleagues (2004) randomly assigned primary care patients aged 50 and older to receive a mailed pamphlet, mailed video (FIMDM), or usual care. The primary objective of the study was to compare the impact of the pamphlet and the video on knowledge, decision-making participation, screening preferences, and testing rates. They found that knowledge scores for the intervention groups were moderately higher than the control group. Men who received the pamphlet (41%) were more likely to discuss screening with their doctor than those who received the video (35%) or those who received the usual care (32%). While the groups did not differ significantly in their PSA screening rates at the 2 week or 1 year follow-up, pamphlet and video groups were less likely to intend to have a PSA relative to the control group (65%, 63%, and 74%, respectively).

There have been two unpublished trials as well. One trial developed and examined the use of a brochure and videotape designed specifically for African-American men entitled "The Right Decision is Yours: A Guide to Prostate Cancer Check-ups" (Taylor et al., 2001; Taylor et al., in preparation). The other unpublished trial developed and examined the impact of "balance sheets" for influencing men's beliefs and attitudes regarding prostate cancer screening, their intention to get prostate cancer screening, and their prostate cancer screening behavior (Hamm, 2000). To date, 7 balance sheets have been created ("What Hispanic Men in their 50s [60s] want to know about Prostate Cancer," "What White Men in their 50s [60s] want to know about Prostate Cancer," "What

Black Men in their 40s [50s, 60s] want to know about Prostate Cancer"). Results from these two trials are forthcoming.

Each of the studies described in this section demonstrated an improvement in knowledge and seven reported a lower rate of screening (or intent to screen) as a result of the educational interventions. Although these studies have demonstrated the ability of various educational modalities to improve knowledge about screening, it is important to note that participants in 11 of these 13 trials were predominantly white men, indicating a need for future studies to include larger samples of African-American men.

Unevaluated Educational Materials

Internet-Based Information: There are a number of Internet websites that provide information about prostate cancer screening, diagnosis, and treatment. We have listed several of the more well-known websites in Table 2. To our knowledge, only the Virginia Commonwealth University website (www.acorn.fap.vcu.edu/ psa) has undergone an evaluation to examine its impact on knowledge acquisition and other outcomes (S.H. Woolf, personal communication, 1/15/05). The ACS, the Centers for Disease Control and Prevention (CDC), and the NCI all have comprehensive information online about prostate cancer, including online versions of hard-copy pamphlets (e.g., the NCI's "What You Need to Know About Prostate Cancer"). Of those organizations, only the CDC has a booklet (hard-copy and online) for African-American men, noted earlier.

Books: Numerous books are available about prostate cancer, screening, diagnosis, and treatment. For example, "Dr. Walsh's Guide to Surviving Prostate Cancer" (2001) includes chapters on the prostate, causes of prostate cancer, prevention, diagnosis and staging, treat-ment, and side effects of treatment. Similarly, Sheldon Marks' "Prostate and

Cancer: A Family Guide to Diagnosis, Treatment and Survival" (2003) is a comprehensive text with descriptions of anatomy, diet and nutrition, prostate cancer screening tests, diagnosis and treatment. Another popular book is Pamela Ellsworth et al.'s (2002) "100 Questions and Answers about Prostate Cancer," which covers basic questions about the disease such as risk factors and causes, methods of prevention, screening, and diagnosis, available treatments and how to choose among them, and ways of coping with common emotional and physical difficulties associated with the diagnosis and treatment. The authors are a prostate cancer survivor and two urologic surgeons who team up to provide both patient and physician perspectives in answering these questions.

Both Internet sites and books remain a popular means of educating men and their family members who are self-directed in their quest for knowledge about prostate cancer screening. However, to date, the impact of these sources on knowledge, satisfaction, and screening behavior has not been studied.

CHALLENGES AND POTENTIAL SOLUTIONS ASSOCIATED WITH PROSTATE CANCER SCREENING EDUCATION

Challenges

There are multiple challenges inherent to the education of patients about controversial medical procedures such as prostate cancer screening. For numerous reasons, it is increas- ingly difficult for the public and for health professionals to consider the full spectrum of facts about screening effectiveness. Further, for African American men, their increased risk serves to only further complicate these already difficult issues. Thus, for the next ten years, until the results from the PLCO Cancer Screening Trial are released, improved methods are needed to assist men in understanding these complex issues. If the PLCO results do not

Table 2: Websites for Prostate Cancer Screening

(Sites specific to African American men marked in bold)

Website (All sites last accessed February 16, 2005)	Title/Design	Literacy Level When Provided
American Cancer Society (ACS) http://www.cancer.org/docroot/CRI/CRI_2_3x.asp?dt=36	"Detailed Guide: Prostate Cancer" (Includes guideline statement for detection)	Flesch-Kincaid Grade Level: 12 (Standard writg approx. equates to 7th-8th gr level) Flesch Reading Ease: 32.6 (Scores from 0-100; standard writing averages 60-70)
American Cancer Society http://www.cancer.org/docroot/CRI/CRI_2_1x.asp?dt=36	"Overview: Prostate Cancer"	Flesch-Kincaid Grade Level: 9.5 Flesch Reading Ease: 55.3
American Cancer Society **http://www.cancer.org/docroot/NWS/content/NWS_2_1x_Prostate_Screening_Benefits_African-Americans.asp**	Studies mentioned on ACS site along w/ ACS recommendation for AA men	
American Cancer Society www.cancer.org/docroot/PED/content/PED_1_5X_Lets_Talk_About_It.asp	"Let's Talk About It" Information on a free community-based program developed by the ACS and 100 Black Men of America to increase awareness and knowledge of prostate cancer among African American men. Informational pamphlet available (not online).	
American Academy of Family Physicians (AAFP, 2001) www.aafp.org/x19519.xml www.aafp.org/PreBuilt/prostate_patient_tool.pdf (Contact: Dr. Ted Ganiats)	First website includes section about prostate cancer screening counseling tools Second website is a tool entitled "Should you get a PSA test? A Patient-Doctor Decision"	
Agency for Healthcare Research and Quality (AHRQ) www.ahrq.gov/clinic/3rduspstf/prostatescr/prostatwh.htm	Has links to studies and fact sheets on prostate cancer screening	
Cancer Education http://www.cancereducation.com	Has links to prostate cancer information from medical websites as well as webcast discussions (requires RealOne Player)	

Website (All sites last accessed February 16, 2005)	Title/Design	Literacy Level When Provided
Centers for Disease Control and Prevention (CDC) www.cdc.gov/cancer/prostate/decisionguide **http://www.cdc.gov/cancer/prostate/prospdf/aaprosguide.pdf** **http://www.cdc.gov/cancer/prostate/resourcematerials.htm**	"Prostate Cancer Screening: A Decision Guide [for African Americans]" The third website listed is for prostate cancer resources/publications.	Flesch-Kincaid Grade Level: 8.2 Flesch Reading Ease: 57.6
Dept. of Family Medicine, Virginia Commonwealth University (copyright Alex Krist, Robert Johnson, Steven Woolf) www.acorn.fap.vcu.edu/psa	"Should you get a PSA test? A Patient-Doctor Decision"	Flesch-Kincaid Grade Level: 9.6 Flesch Reading Ease: 53.8
www.Healthfinder.gov	Listed in CDC booklet Has 25 links to other websites for information (e.g., CDC's booklet, NCI's PDQ on screening, NCI's fact sheet on PSA, familydoctor.org on treatment, etc)	N/A (mainly links to other sites)
National Cancer Institute (NCI) http://cis.nci.nih.gov/fact/5_29.htm	"The Prostate-Specific Antigen (PSA) Test: Questions and Answers"	Flesch-Kincaid Grade Level: 10.4 Flesch Reading Ease: 54.8
NCI Prostate Cancer Outcomes Study http://www.cancer.gov/newscenter/pcos	Gives a description of the Prostate Cancer Outcomes Study	
NCI Prostate, Lung, Colorectal, & Ovarian (PLCO) Cancer Screening Trial www.cancer.gov/prevention/plco	Gives a description of the PLCO screening trial	
National Comprehensive Cancer Network (with ACS) www.nccn.org/patient_gls/_english/_prostate/index.htm	"Prostate Cancer: Treatment Guidelines for Patients" (Version IV/July 2004)	Flesch-Kincaid Grade Level: 10.4 Flesch Reading Ease: 56
National Prostate Cancer Coalition www.pcacoalition.org	General education on prostate cancer	
Prostate Cancer Education Council www.pcaw.com	General information on PCAW (Prostate Cancer Awareness Week)	
U.S. Preventive Services Task Force www.ahcpr.gov/clinic/uspstf/uspsprca.htm	Recommendations for screening	
US TOO www.ustoo.com	Prostate cancer education and support	

provide a definitive recommendation for or against screening, then these issues will need to be addressed continually. We have detailed several of the difficulties of educating the public and health professionals about prostate cancer screening.

First, because health professionals and the general public are urgently seeking to reduce the number of deaths due to cancer, new technologies for detection or prevention frequently make their way into clinical use prior to completion of the research needed to determine their effectiveness and potential detrimental effects (Curry et al., 2003). As a result, certain tests and procedures have become an accepted part of clinical care by many patients and physicians, making it difficult to effectively communicate opposing arguments. In the current environment, men often appear predisposed to screening and may see opposing information as irrelevant or incorrect (Taylor et al., 2001). As the majority of men are already aware of the potential benefits of screening (Taylor et al., 1999; Schwartz et al., 2004), the challenge is to present the limitations of screening in a way that is understandable and engaging to men who have already decided to be screened. A further challenge that may limit men's openness to learning the potential downsides of screening is that men do not want to regret not having been screened (Clark et al., 2001). The fear is that choosing not to be screened and then later learning that one has prostate cancer could result in a deep sense of regret that one did not take advantage of the possible benefits of screening.

Second, media reports have reinforced the beliefs regarding the effectiveness of prostate screening by presenting imbalanced information. The detrimental role that the media plays in public health education has received a lot of recent attention (Schwartz and Woloshin, 2004; Schwartz et al., 2002a, 2002b; Schwartz and Woloshin 2002). Due to the time pressure associated with media

publications, as well as the need to have an attention grabbing and easily understandable headline, media messages are often incomplete, one-sided, and misleading regarding generally accepted practices vs. con-troversial practices. Furthermore, it has been shown that the scientific community obtains a significant amount of information from the lay press, which only serves to further the spread of incomplete information (Phillips et al., 1991).

Third, there appears to be the need to 'do something,' even if doing something is not necessarily believed to result in a better outcome than doing nothing (Chapman and Elstein, 2000). Many people have become very focused on reducing the likelihood that they will be diagnosed with prostate cancer, such that taking a chance that screening *may* help them appears to be a better option than avoiding the potential harms of screening. Further, men want peace of mind about prostate cancer, and also to feel like they have control over their own health, i.e., that they are doing something active about their health (Taylor et al., 2002).

Fourth, the nature of the procedures used for prostate cancer screening has undoubtedly contributed to their widespread acceptance. In spite of the fact that colorectal cancer screening has been demonstrated to reduce disease-related mortality and is uniformly encouraged by virtually all physicians and medical organizations, a recent national survey revealed that men are significantly more likely to have been screened for prostate cancer than for colorectal cancer (Sirovich et al., 2003). This finding may be associated with the nature of the screening tests for these two cancers, i.e., that acceptance by the public has been so widespread because the prostate cancer screening tests are relatively quick and easy, compared to the invasiveness of most of the tests used for colorectal cancer screening. We speculate that the rates of screening for these two cancers would be reversed if the characteristics of the screening tests were different.

Fifth, until recently, cancer screening has been thought of as 'taking a risk,' as people were risking finding out something negative, i.e., that they had cancer. Currently, largely due to the role of the media promulgating the message that cancer screening is good and that detecting cancer early will save lives, *not* screening is now seen as taking a risk (Schwartz et al., 2004). Because people are known to be risk averse when it comes to outcomes that are positively framed (Kahneman and Tversky, 1979), which, in this case is the chance of living longer due to screening, getting screened is the least risky (i.e., the risk averse) course of action to take. In fact, screening is often marketed as the 'safest course of action' and screening has come to be viewed more as an obligation than a choice (Schwartz et al., 2004). This national enthusiasm for cancer screening increases the likelihood that new technologies will continue to be adopted prior to the completion of the necessary research, thereby increasing the likelihood of overdiagnosis and overtreatment in a variety of diseases (Schwartz et al., 2004).

In summary, educating the public about prostate cancer screening, or about similarly controversial health-related procedures, requires consideration of multiple issues, beyond the simple presentation of the facts in an understandable format. Because of the rapidity with which new technologies are accepted into clinical use by both physicians and patients, health educators are frequently put in the position of asking the public to rethink something they had already decided upon and now consider a non-issue. This problem is likely to become increasingly widespread. Therefore, innovative methods to help the public contend with making health-related decisions for which there is no accepted right or wrong answer are essential.

Potential Solutions

One of the proposed methods for assisting the public with making an informed screening decision is shared decision making (SDM; e.g., Woolf, 1997). SDM is the active collaboration between clinicians and patients that allows patients to participate fully in their own medical care, particularly when a decision regarding a controversial procedure or treat-ment must be made. There are many obvious advantages that SDM has for the prostate cancer screening decision, including a) the provision of up-to-date information by clinicians, b) clinician expertise that can help patients sort out the various trade-offs involved in the decision (Woolf, 2001), c) the patients' ability to have their questions answered, d) the ability of clinicians to take into account patients' preferences for various outcomes, and e) the involvement of the patient in the decision, which may have a positive impact on patients' overall satisfaction with their medical care (Jansen et al., 2004).

On the other hand, there are several limitations of SDM as a method to educate men and help them to make a decision about prostate cancer screening. First, not all pat-ients wish to be involved in their medical decisions, particularly older and sicker patients (Woolf, 2001). It may be difficult for clinicians to engage an older cohort of patients, and/or patients who have other competing health concerns. Second, it has been documented that SDM can be difficult for clinicians to carry out, due to competing demands for time during the office visit and due to physicians' lack of expertise and training in SDM (Barry, 1999; Braddock et al., 1999; Dunn et al., 2001; Woolf, 2001). A third limiting factor in the success of the doctor/patient discussion is that due to the controversial issues discussed previously: doctors are apt to have strong beliefs on one side or the other, thereby reducing the likelihood of a balanced presentation on the risks and benefits of screening (Woolf, 1995).

Thus, although it is possible that the traditional, individual, doctor/patient discussion will provide the needed education about the benefits and limitations of prostate cancer screening, there are several potential impediments to the success of this method. Additional methods of patient and physician education are needed for patients to be able to provide truly informed consent for difficult health decisions such as prostate cancer screening (Braddock et al., 1999; O'Connor et al., 1999). For example, educational materials that allow for varying degrees of involvement of men would provide the flexibility to address the needs of men who do/do not want to make the decision themselves. In addition, complimentary materials for clinicians are needed, to assist them in effectively explaining all sides of the issue to patients. Below we have described decision aids, which may offer one potential solution to the shortcomings inherent in SDM.

Decision aids are psychosocial interventions that are distinguished from traditional patient education tools by their explicit focus on helping individuals make consequential decisions (Llewellyn-Thomas, 1995). Decision aids have a greater level of detail about potential options and attempt to assist patients in making a choice between the options. Further, decision aids are intended to foster realistic expectations of the potential outcomes, help patients weigh their preferences for the advantages and disadvantages, and encourage patients to engage in shared decision making (O'Connor et al., 1999). Decision aids are typically based upon expectancy-value models of decision-making such as subjective expected utility (SEU) theory (O'Connor et al., 1998).

There have been three recent reviews of randomized trials using patient decision aids (AHRQ, 2002; O'Connor et al. 1999, 2001). These reviews reported that, relative to control conditions, decision aids resulted in improved knowledge, reduced decisional conflict, and inconsistent findings for the screening decision. Importantly, decision aids did not increase anxiety among participants, but they also did not impact satisfaction with the decision or the decision making process. There is evidence that decision aids resulted in patients becoming more active in decision making, compared to usual care (Davison and Degner, 1997; Davison et al., 1999), and that detailed information often results in more conservative health decisions (i.e., less likely to undergo a test or treatment; O'Connor et al., 2001). Finally, O'Connor et al. (1999) and Braddock et al. (1999) have concluded that usual care methods of educating patients about complex decisions are not adequate. O'Connor et al. (1999) noted several issues that require further work, including the impact of decision aids on persistence of a particular choice over time, and assessing whether certain types of decision aids work best for different types of people.

The availability of patient educational materials and interactive decision aids is becoming widespread, particularly as the number of controversial diagnostic and treatment procedures increases. Decision aids may be particularly useful for medical decisions in which information about outcomes is uncertain and for decisions that require subjective judgments about the benefits relative to the risks for various options. This describes the situation faced by all men who must decide whether to undergo prostate cancer screening, with limited outcome data available to guide their decision.

Because the potential benefits of prostate cancer screening have become so widely accepted among the public (Schwartz et al., 2004), conducting patient and physician education on an individual basis is unlikely to reach large enough numbers of men to counteract the largely one-sided media blitz and the public's eagerness for screening. For the public to appreciate the ongoing debate in prostate cancer screening, and for men to be able to make an informed decision for themselves, a concerted, widespread media and/or internet campaign will be needed, in which large groups of men are exposed to these ideas at one time. The idea that prostate cancer screening may not necessarily be a useful screening strategy is such a foreign idea to most people, in addition to containing many difficult concepts (e.g., overdiagnosis), that it will take repeated exposures in multiple formats for it to begin to take hold on a population basis. As a follow-up to a media/ internet campaign, more detailed materials (e.g., print, video, interactive computer-based formats) would need to be widely available, for both physicians and patients, as described above. Based on our experience in working to educate men about the prostate cancer screening dilemma over the past several years, it is our opinion that it will require the same intensive efforts that we are accustomed to utilizing when *promoting* a health behavior. Further, this message is particularly difficult to deliver given that it is not a message that says 'do something,' and instead says 'stop, learn about issues that are contrary to what you have learned previously, think about how the issues apply to you, and then decide what is best for you,' and thus may require particularly innovative methods of delivery.

In spite of the arguments above, given the relative closeness of the release of the PLCO results (approximately ten years), it is probably premature to launch a major campaign to educate men about the prostate screening controversy. Instead, we would recommend developing and disseminating health education materials (see section below) which provide balanced information on both sides of the controversy. In the hopes that the PLCO results will support the utility of screening for all men, then the job of health educators and clinicians will be relatively straightforward, as the pro-screening message is largely in place. However, if the results from the PLCO do not support screening or are not definitive in one direction or the other, then it would be appropriate and necessary to launch a major campaign to publicize these results, in an effort to reduce the continued occurrence of overdiagnosis of prostate cancer.

CRUCIAL ISSUES TO ADDRESS IN EDUCATIONAL MATERIALS FOR PROSTATE CANCER SCREENING

Throughout the paper we have detailed the issues that need to be addressed in prostate screening educational materials, and we will summarize them here. All of these issues listed below are considered essential and are not presented in any particular order.

1) A definition of the word 'screening,' a complete description of the tests used for screening (PSA and DRE), including the definition of a normal vs. an abnormal result, and the accuracy of the screening tests (i.e., specificity and sensitivity).

2) A description of the anatomy and function of the prostate and symptoms of prostate cancer.

3) Risk factors for prostate cancer, including the three widely accepted factors (older age, family history, and race), as well as a discussion of the possible role of dietary fat, selenium, and vitamin E. Although it may be premature to recommend that men change their diet to prevent prostate cancer, a recommendation for maintaining a diet that is low in fat and high in fruits and vegetables should be included to encourage men to make a positive step toward overall and cardiac health.

4) A decision tool or balance sheet to help men understand whether their own preferences lean more toward screening or toward not screening.

5) The incidence of prostate cancer in the population, and the differences in incidence as they vary by racial and age groups. Further, a description of the natural history of prostate

cancer should be included, i.e., that prostate cancer is often slow growing and may not cause clinical problems if not detected by screening. The comparison of the likelihood of death due to prostate cancer vs. due to other causes is instructive, as prostate cancer is the fifth leading cause of death among men over the age of 45, which is often surprising for men.

6) An explicit description of the advantages and potential disadvantages of prostate cancer screening. We have excerpted the tables below from our most recent booklet.

How Screening May Help	*How Screening May Cause Problems*
• **If your results are normal--** It can help you feel relieved and less worried to find that you do NOT have prostate cancer.	• **If your results are abnormal -** You may NOT have cancer. But you may have to go through an uncomfortable test (biopsy) to find that out.
• **If your results find early prostate cancer—** You may have more treatment options. Some of these options may have fewer side effects.	• **If your results find early prostate cancer** Treatment may cause you to have problems holding your urine and bowel movements (incontinence) and having sex (impotence).
• **If your results find early prostate cancer—** Treatment may help you to live longer.	• **If your results find early prostate cancer** Treatment may not help you to live longer. We really still do not know for sure.
• **If your results find early prostate cancer--** It may be a **fast-growing** (aggressive) cancer that needs to be treated right away.	• **If your results find early prostate cancer** You could end up getting treated for a **slow-growing** cancer that would have never caused you any problems and did not need to be treated.

7) The sequence of events that may occur when a screening result is abnormal, including a description of the usual diagnostic work-up procedures, a description of usual treatment options for early stage disease, and the potential side effects of these treatments. Men need to be encouraged to consider treatment issues when deciding about treatment, with a particular focus on the fact that it is not yet known whether the treatment of early stage disease will reduce prostate cancer related death.

In addition to these specific content areas, educational materials should encourage men to seek alternate sources of information and support in this decision, including information from national organizations, health professionals, and friends and family. In a single source of information, it is virtually impossible to present all of the issues that are pertinent to a screening decision. Finally, for printed materials, the importance of presenting the information in a readable format in as easy a reading level as possible cannot be over-emphasized.

CONCLUSIONS AND RECOMMENDATIONS

Much of the research to date has focused on the barriers to increasing screening, as opposed to exploring issues surrounding men's understanding of the controversy. It is our contention that, given the current controversy, the understanding of the barriers to screening and the methods of increasing screening are less important than developing methods of how to educate men about the advantages and disadvantages of screening. However, as noted in the review of the literature above, much of what is known about men's understanding of the controversy and effective methods to communicate that controversy was conducted in studies that largely included samples of Caucasian men. Thus, further studies of African American men need to focus on the development and evaluation of effective communication methods with regard to the screening controversy, particularly when strongly held beliefs in support of screening are already in place. Although all men need information and support in making the screening decision, it is particularly difficult for African American men, given their high risk status and the focus of media attention and much of the medical establishment on increasing screening. Although it seems as though the safest decision is to recommend that all men at high risk get screened, it must be remembered that the difficulties with screening (overdiagnosis being primary) are still present, regardless of the sample being screened. Providing screening to men without giving them every opportunity to understand the current state of the science is unethical. Until the results of the PLCO trial are available, the task at hand is to help men make the best decision for themselves, based on a clear understanding of the available data.

REFERENCES

Agency for Healthcare Research and Quality. Impact of cancer-related decision aids. Summary, Evidence Report/Technology Assessment: Number 46. AHRQ Publication No. 02-E033, July 2002. Agency for Healthcare Research and Quality, Rockville, MD. Available at: http://www.ahrq.gov/clinic/epcsums/caaidsum.htm. Accessed 1/2/05.

Agho AO, Lewis MA. (2001) Correlates of actual and perceived knowledge of prostate cancer among African Americans. Cancer Nurs 24(3): 165-171.

Aiken LS, West SG, Woodward CK, Reno RR. (1994) Health beliefs and compliance with mammography-screening recommendations in symptomatic women. Health Psychol 13: 122-129.

American Cancer Society. (2004) Can prostate cancer be found early? Available at: http://www.cancer.org/docroot/CRI/content/CRI_2_4_3X_Can_prostate_cancer_be_found_early_36.asp. Accessed 12/30/04.

American Foundation for Urologic Disease. (2004) Prostate Specific Antigen. Available at: http://www.afud.org/conditions/psa.asp. Accessed 12/30/04.

Anderson I, et al. (1988). Mammographic screening and mortality from breast cancer: malmo Mammographic Screening Trial. BMJ 297(6654):943-8.

Anderson I, et al. (1997). Reduced breast cancer mortality in women under age 50: updated results from the Malmo Mammographic Screening Program. Journal of the National Cancer Institute. Monographs, (22):63-7

Ashford AR, Albert SM, Hoke G, Cushman LF, Miller DS, Bassett M. (2001) Prostate carcinoma knowledge, attitudes, and screening behavior among African-American men in Central Harlem, New York City. Cancer 91(1): 164-172.

Ault MJ, Mandel SA. (2000). Screening for colorectal cancer. New Engl J Med 343: 1652-1654.

Barry MJ. (1999). Involving patients in medical decisions. How can physicians do better? JAMA 282(24):2356-2357.

Behavioral Risk Factor Surveillance System. BRFSS Prevalence Data, Nationwide – 2002, Women's Health. Have you ever had a mammogram? Retrieved 12/13/04 from http://apps.nccd.cdc.gov/brfss/display.asp?cat=WH&yr=2002&qkey=311&state=US.

Benson MC, Whang IS, Olsson CA, McMahon DJ, Cooner WH. (1992). The use of prostate specific antigen density to enhance the predictive value of intermediate levels of serum prostate specific antigen. J Urol 147(3 Pt 2):817-821.

Black BL, Schweitzer R, Dezelsky T. (1993) Report on the American Cancer Society Workshop on Community Cancer Detection, Education, and Prevention Demonstration Projects for Underserved Populations. CA Cancer J Clinicians 43(4):226-233.

Black WC, Haggstrom DA, Welch HG. (2002). All-cause mortality in randomized trials of cancer screening. J Natl Cancer Inst 94(3):167-173.

Bowman J, Sanson-Fisher R, Boyle C, Pope S, Redman S. (1995) A randomized controlled trial of strategies to prompt attendance for a Pap smear. J Med Screen 2(4):211-218.

Braddock CH 3rd, Edwards KA, Hasenberg NM, Laidley TL, Levinson W. (1999) Informed decision making in outpatient practice: time to get back to basics. JAMA 282(24): 2313-2320.

Brawley OW. (2003). Introduction: Cancer and health disparities. Cancer & Metastasis Rev 22 (1): 7-9.

Brawley OW, Kramer BS. (2005). Cancer screening in theory and in practice. J Clin Oncol 23(2): 293-300.

Breen N, Wagener DK, Brown ML, Davis WW, Ballard-Barbash R. (2001). Progress in cancer screening over a decade: Results of cancer screening from 1987, 1992, and 1998 National Health Interview Surveys. J Natl Cancer Inst 93(22):1704-1713.

Brosman SA. (2004). Prostate-specific antigen. Available at: http://www.emedicine.com/med/topic3465.htm Accessed 12/30/04.

Brown ML, Potosky AL, Thompson GB, Kessler LG. (1990). The knowledge and use of screening tests for colorectal and prostate cancer: data from the 1987 National Health Interview Survey. Preventive Medicine, 19(5): 562-574.

Brown ML, Riley GF, Schussler BS, Etzioni R (2002). Estimating health care costs related to cancer treatment from SEER-Medi-care Data. Med Care, 40 (8): IV-104-IV-117.

Carter HB, Pearson JD, Metter EJ, Brant LJ, Chan DW, Andres R, Fozard JL, Walsh PC. (1992). Longitudinal evaluation of prostate-specific antigen levels in men with and without prostate disease. JAMA 267(16):2215-2220.

Catalona WJ. (1996). Clinical utility of measurements of free and total prostate-specific antigen (PSA): a review. Prostate Suppl 7:64-69.

Catalona WJ, Partin AW, Slawin KM, Naughton CK, Brawer MK, Flanigan RC, Richie JP, Patel A, Walsh PC, Scardino PT, Lange PH, deKernion JB, Southwick PC, Loveland KG, Parson RE, Gasior GH. (2000) Percentage of free PSA in black versus white men for detection and staging of prostate cancer: a prospective multicenter clinical trial. Urology 55(3):372-376.

Catalona WJ, Richie JP, Ahmann FR, Hudson MA, Scardino PT, Flanigan RC, deKernion JB, Ratliff TL, Kavoussi LR, Dalkin BL, et al. (1994). Comparison of digital rectal examination and serum prostate specific antigen in the early detection of prostate cancer: results of a multicenter clinical trial of 6,630 men. J Urol 151(5):1283-1290.

Centers for Disease Control, U.S. Department of Health and Human Services. (2003) Prostate cancer screening: a decision guide for African Americans. CDC Pub #99-7692.

Chan EC, Vernon SW, O'Donnell FT, Ahn C, Greisinger A, Aga DW. (2003) Informed consent for cancer screening with prostate-specific antigen: how well are men getting the message? Am J Public Health 93(5):779-785.

Chapman GB, Elstein AS .(2000) Cognitive processes and biases in medical decision making. In Decision Making in Health Care, GB Chapman and FA Sonnenberg (Eds.), Cambridge University Press, New York.

Church TR, Yeazel MW, Jones RM, Kochevar LK, Watt GD, Mongin SJ, Cordes JE, Engelhard D. (2004) A randomized trial of direct mailing of fecal occult blood tests to increase colorectal cancer screening. J Nat Cancer Inst 96(10):770-780.

Ciatto S, Rubeca T, Confortini M, Pontenani G, Lombardi C, Zendron P, Di Lollo S, Crocetti E. (2004). Free to total PSA ratio is not a reliable predictor of prostate biopsy outcome. Tumori 90(3):324-327.

Clark JA, Wray NP, Ashton CM (2001) Living with treatment decisions: regrets and quality of life among men treated for metastatic prostate cancer. J Clin Oncol 19(1):72-80.

Clarke-Tasker VA, Wade R. (2002) What we thought we knew: African American males' perceptions of prostate cancer and screening methods. ABNF J 13(3):56-60.

Collins M. (1997). Increasing prostate cancer awareness in African American men. Oncology Nursing Forum 24(1):91-95.

Collins MM, Barry JJ. (1996). Controversies in prostate cancer screening: Analogies to the early lung cancer screening debate. JAMA, 276(24):1976-1979.

Cooney KA, Strawderman MS, Wojno KJ, Doerr KM, Taylor A, Alcser KH, Heeringa SG, Taylor JM, Wei JT, Montie JE, Schottenfeld D. (2001) Age-specific distribution of serum prostate-specific antigen in a community-based study of African-American men. Urology 57(1):91-96.

Cotter MP, Gern RW, Ho GY, Chang RY, Burk RD. (2002) Role of family history and ethnicity on the mode and age of prostate cancer presentation. Prostate 50(4):216-221.

Curry SJ, Byers T, Hewitt MA. (Eds.); National Cancer Policy Board, Institute of Medicine, National Research Council. (2003) Fulfilling the potential of cancer prevention and early detection. Washington, DC: National Academies Press.

Davison BJ, Degner LF. (1997). Empowerment of men newly diagnosed with prostate cancer. Cancer Nursing 20(3):187-196.

Davison BJ, Kirk P, Degner LF, Hassard TH. (1999) Information and patient participation in screening for prostate cancer. Patient Educ Couns 37(3): 255-263.

DeKoning HJ, Auvinen A, Berenguer Sanchez A, Calais da Silva F, Ciatto S, Denis L, Gohagan JK, Hakama M, et al. (2002). Large-scale randomized prostate cancer screening trials: program performances in the European Randomized Screening for Prostate Cancer trial and the Prostate, Lung, Colorectal, and Ovary cancer trial. International Journal of Cancer 97(2):237-244.

Diefenbach PN, Ganz PA, Pawlow AJ, Guthrie D. (1996) Screening by the prostate-specific antigen test: what do the patients know? J Cancer Educ 11(1):39-44.

Dunn AS, Shridharani KV, Lou W, Bernstein J, Horowitz CR. (2001) Physician-patient discussions of controversial cancer screening tests. Am J Prev Med 20(2):130-134.

Ellsworth P, Heaney JA, Gill O. (2002) 100 Questions & Answers About Prostate Cancer. Jones and Bartlett Publishers.

Etzioni R, Berry KM, Legler JM, Shaw P. (2002). Prostate-specific antigen testing in black and white men: an analysis of Medicare claims from 1991-1998. Urol 59(2):251-255.

Etzioni R, Falcon S, Gann PH, Kooperberg CL, Penson DF, Stampfer MJ. (2004). Prostate-specific antigen and free prostate-specific antigen in the early detection of prostate cancer: do combination tests improve detection? Cancer Epidemiol Biomarkers Prev 13(10):1640-1645.

Farkas A. (1997) The importance of screening African Americans for prostate cancer. J Natl Med Assoc 89(12):779-782.

Fearing A, Bell D, Newton M, Lambert S. (2000) Prostate screening health beliefs and practices of African American men. ABNF J 11(6):141-144.

Flood AB, Wennberg JE, Nease RF Jr., Fowler FJ Jr., Ding J, Hynes LM. (1996) The importance of patient preference in the decision to screen for prostate cancer. Prostate Patient Outcomes Research Team. J Gen Intern Med 11(6):342-349.

Foundation for Medical Decision Making. Dartmouth, Hanover, NH. (1994) The PSA decision: what you need to know, a shared decision-making program. [video]

Freeman HP, Muth BJ, Kerner JF. (1995)

Expanding access to cancer screening and clinical follow-up among the medically underserved. Cancer Pract 3(1):19-30.

Frosch DL, Kaplan RM, Felitti V. (2001) The evaluation of two methods to facilitate shared decision making for men considering the prostate-specific antigen test. J Gen Intern Med 16(6):391-398.

Frosch DL, Kaplan RM, Felitti VJ. (2003) A randomized controlled trial comparing internet and video to facilitate patient education for men considering the prostate specific antigen test. J Gen Intern Med 18(10):781-787.

Gates TJ. (2001) Screening for cancer: Evaluating the evidence. Am Fam Phys 63(3): 513-522.

Gattellari M, Ward JE. (2003) Does evidence-based information about screening for prostate cancer enhance consumer decision-making? A randomized controlled trial. J Med Screen 10(1):27-39.

Gattellari M, Ward JE. (2004) A community-based randomised controlled trial of three different educational resources for men about prostate cancer screening. Patient Education and Counseling (in press). Available online at: http://www.sciencedirect.com. Accessed 1/5/05.

Gelfand DE, Parzuchowski J, Cort M, Powell I. (1995). Digital rectal examinations and prostate cancer screening attitudes of African American men. Oncol Nurs Forum 22(8):1253-1255.

Giovannucci E, Rimm EB, Colditz GA, Stampfer MJ, Ascherio A, Chute CC, Willett WC. (1993) A prospective study of dietary fat and risk of prostate cancer. J Natl Cancer Inst 85(19): 1571-1579.

Gohagan JK, Prorok PC, Hayes RB, Kramer BS; Prostate, Lung, Colorectal and Ovarian Cancer Screening Trial Project Team. (2000) The Prostate, Lung, Colorectal and Ovarian (PLCO) Cancer Screening Trial of the National Cancer Institute: history, organization, and status. Control Clin Trials 21(6 Suppl): 251S-272S.

Gwede CK, Forthofer MS, McDermott RJ. (2002) Awareness of prostate cancer screening tests among African-American men in under-served neighborhoods: need for community outreach. J Oncol Manag 11(5):36-41.

Haese A, Graefen M, Huland H, Lilja H. (2004). Prostate-specific antigen and related isoforms in the diagnosis and management of prostate cancer. Curr Urol Rep (3):231-240.

Hamm RM. (2000) What Black men in their 40's [50's, 60's] want to know about prostate cancer. University of Oklahoma Health Sciences Center.

Hayes RB, Brown LM, Schoenberg JB, Greenberg RS, Silverman DT, Schwartz AG, Swanson GM, Benichou J, Liff JM, Hoover RN, Pottern LM. (1996). Alcohol use and prostate cancer risk in US blacks and whites. Am J Epidemiol 143(7):692-697.

Hayes RB, Ziegler RG, Gridley G, Swanson C, Greenberg RS, Swanson GM, Schoenberg JB, Silverman DT, Brown LM, Pottern LM, Liff J, Schwartz AG, Fraumeni JF Jr, Hoover RN. (1999). Dietary factors and risks for prostate cancer among blacks and whites in the United States. Cancer Epidemiol Biomarkers Prev 8(1):25-34.

Henderson RJ, Eastham JA, Culkin DJ, Kattan MW, Whatley T, Mata J, Venable D, Sartor O. (1997). Prostate-specific antigen (PSA) and PSA density: racial differences in men without prostate cancer. J Natl Cancer Inst 89(2):134-138.

Hiatt RA, Klabunde C, Breen N, Swan J, Ballard-Barbash R. (2002) Cancer Screening Practices from National Health Interview Surveys: past, present, and future. J Natl Cancer Inst 94(24):1837-1846.

Hoffman RM, Gilliland FD, Eley JW, Harlan LC, Stephenson RA, Stanford JL, Albertson PC, Hamilton AS, Hunt WC, Potosky AL. (2001). Racial and ethnic differences in advanced-stage prostate cancer: the

Prostate Cancer Outcomes Study. J Natl Cancer Inst 93(5):388-395.

Holmberg L, Bill-Axelson A, Helgesen F, Salo JO, Folmerz P, Haggman M, et al. (2002) A randomized trial comparing radical prostat-ectomy with watchful waiting in early prostate cancer. New Engl J Med 347(11):781-789.

Honda K, Neugut AI. (2004) Associations between perceived cancer risk and established risk factors in a national community sample. Cancer Detect Prev 28(1):1-7.

Jansen SJ, Otten W, van de Velde CJ, Nortier JW, Stiggelbout AM. (2004) The impact of the perception of treatment choice on satisfaction with treatment, experienced chemo-therapy burden and current quality of life. Br J Cancer 91(1):56-61.

Jemal A, Murray T, Ward E, Samuels A, Tiwari, RC, Ghafoor A, Feuer EJ, Thun MJ, American Cancer Society. (2005) Cancer statistics, 2005. CA Cancer J Clin 55(1):10-30.

Kahneman D, Tversky A. (1979) Prospect theory: an analysis of decision under risk. Econometrica 47(2): 263-291.

Klein EA, Thompson IM, Lippman SM, Goodman PJ, Albanes D, Taylor PR, Coltman C. (2001) SELECT: the next prostate cancer prevention trial. Selenum and Vitamin E Cancer Prevention Trial. J Urol 166(4):1311-1315.

Kolonel, LN, Hankin JH, Whittemore AS, Wu AH, Gallagher RP, Wilkens LR, John EM, Howe GR, Dreon DM, West, DW, Paffen-barger RS Jr. (2000)Vegetables, fruits, legumes and prostate cancer: a multiethnic case-control study. Cancer Epidemiol Biomarkers Prev 9(8):795-804.

Kosary C, Reis L, Miller B. (1995) SEER cancer statistics review, 1973-1992: Tables and graphs. (NIH Publication No. 96-2789). Bethesda, MD: National Cancer Institute.

Kramer BS, Brawley OW. (2000). Cancer screening. Hematol Oncol Clin North Am 14(4):831-848.

Kubricht WS 3rd, Williams BJ, Whatley T, Pinckard P, Eastham JA. (1999) Serum testosterone levels in African-American and white men undergoing prostate biopsy. Urology 54(6):1035-1038.

Laara E, Day NE, Hakama M. (1987). Trends in mortality from cervical cancer in the Nordic countries: association with organised screening programmes. Lancet 1(8544):1247-1249.

Leitzmann MF, Platz EA, Stampfer MJ, Willett WC, Giovannucci E. (2004) Ejaculation frequency and subsequent risk of prostate cancer. JAMA 291(13):1578-1586.

Li H, Stampfer MJ, Giovannucci EL, Morris JS, Willett WC, Gaziano JM, Ma J. (2004). A prospective study of plasma selen-ium levels and prostate cancer risk. J Natl Cancer Inst 96(9):696-703.

Lipkus IM, Rimer BK, Halabi S, Strigo TS. (2000) Can tailored interventions increase mammography use among HMO women? Am J Prev Med 18(1):1-10.

Llewellyn-Thomas HA. (1995) Patients' health-care decision making: A framework for descriptive and experimental investigations. Medical Decision Making 15(2):101-106.

Lu-Yao G, Albertsen PC, Stanford JL, Stukel TA, Walker-Corkery ES, Barry MJ. (2002) Natural experiment examining impact of aggressive screening and treatment on prostate cancer mortality in two fixed cohorts from Seattle area and Connecticut. BMJ 325(7367): 740.

Madalinska JB, Essink-Bot ML, de Koning HJ, Kirkels WJ, van der Maas PJ, Schroder FH. (2001) Health-related quality-of-life effects of radical prostatectomy and primary radiotherapy for screen-detected or clinically diagnosed localized prostate cancer. J Clinical Oncology 19(6):1619-1628.

Mandelson MT, Wagner EH, Thompson RS. (1995) PSA screening: a public health dilemma. Ann Rev Pub Health 16: 283-306.

Marks S. (2003) <u>Prostate and Cancer: A family guide to diagnosis, treatment and survival.</u> 3rd edition. Cambridge, MA: Perseus Publishing.

McCleod RS. (2001) Screening strategies for colorectal cancer: A systematic review of the evidence. Can J Gastroenterol 15:647-660.

McFall SL, Hamm RM, Volk RJ. (2004) Exploring beliefs about prostate cancer and early detection in men and women of three ethnic groups. Under review.

Meade CD, Calvo A, Rivera MA, Baer RD. (2003) Focus groups in the design of prostate cancer screening information for Hispanic farmworkers and African American men. Oncol Nurs Forum 30(6):967-975.

Mercer SL, Goel V, Levy IG, Ashbury FD, Iverson DC, Iscoe NA. (1997) Prostate cancer screening in the midst of controversy: Canadian men's knowledge, beliefs, utilization, and future intentions. Can J Pub Health 88(5):327-332.

Mettlin C, Jones G, Averette H, Gusberg SB, Murphy GP. (1993) Defining and updating the American Cancer Society guidelines for the cancer-related checkup: prostate and endo-metrial cancers. CA Cancer J Clin 43(1): 42-46.

Mettlin C, Murphy GP, Babaian RJ, Chesley A, Kane RA, Littrup PJ, et al. (1996) The results of a five-year early prostate cancer detection intervention. Investigators of the Am-erican Cancer Society National Prostate Cancer Detection Project. Cancer 77(1):150-159.

Middleton RG, Thompson IM, Austenfeld MS, Cooner WH, Correa RJ, Gibbons RP, et al.(1995). Prostate Cancer Clinical Guidelines Panel Summary report on the management of clinically localized prostate cancer. The American Urological Association. Journal of Urology 154(6):2144-2148.

Myers RE, Chodak, GW, Wolf TA, Burgh, DY et al. (1999) Adherence by African American men to prostate cancer education and early detection. Cancer 86(1): 88-104.

Myers RE, Hyslop T, Wolf TA, Burgh D, Kunkel EJ, Oyesanmi A, Chodak GJ. (2000) African-American men and intention to adhere to recommended follow-up for an abnormal prostate cancer early detection examination result. Urology 55(5):716-720.

Myers RE, Vernon SW, Carpenter AV, Balshem AM, Lewis PG, Wolf TA, Hilbert J, DeFonso LR, Ross EA. (1997) Employee response to a company-sponsored program of colorectal and prostate cancer screening. Cancer Detect Prev 21(4):380-389.

Myers RE, Wolf TA, Balshem AM, Ross EA, Chodak GW. (1994). Receptivity of African-American men to prostate cancer screening. Urology 43(4):480-487.

Myers RE, Wolf TA, McKee L, McGrory G, Burgh DY, Nelson G, Nelson GA. (1996) Factors associated with intention to undergo annual prostate cancer screening among African American men in Philadelphia. Cancer 78(3):471-479.

Nash C, Hall C. (2002). Prostate cancer in Akransas. J Ark Med Soc 98(10):331-338.

National Cancer Institute (2004). Cervical Cancer Screening: Evidence of Benefit. Retrieved February 15, 2005 from http://www.nci.nih.gov/cancertopics/pdq/scre ening/cervical/HealthProfessional/page3

O'Connor AM, Fiset V, DeGrasse C, Graham ID, Evans W, Stacey D, et al. (1999) Decision aids for patients considering options affecting cancer outcomes: Evidence of efficacy and policy implications. J Nat Cancer Inst Monograph (25):67-80.

Nystrom L, et al. (2002) Long-term effects of mammography screening: updated overview of the Swedish randomised trials. Lancet 359: 909-19.

O'Connor AM, Stacey D, Rovner D, Holmes-Rovner M, Tetroe J Llewellyn-Thomas H, et al. (2001). Decision aids for people facing health treatment or screening decisions. The Cochrane Database of Systematic Reviews (3):CD001431.

O'Connor AM, Tugwell P, Wells GA, Elmslie T, Jolly E, Hollingworth G, et al. (1998) A decision aid for women considering hormone therapy after menopause: decision support framework and evaluation. Patient Education and Counseling 33(3):267-279.

O'Dell KJ, Volk RJ, Cass AR, Spann AL. (1999) Screening for prostate cancer with the prostate-specific antigen test: are patients making informed decisions? J Fam Pract 48(9): 682-688.

Oesterling JE, Cooner WH, Jacobsen SJ, Guess HA, Lieber MM. (1993) Influence of patient age on the serum PSA concentration. An important clinical observation. Urol Clin North Am 20(4):671-680.

Ozdal OL, Aprikian AG, Begin LR, Behlouli H, Tanguay S. (2004) Comparative evaluation of various prostate specific antigen ratios for the early detection of prostate cancer.
BJU Int 93(7):970-974.

Parsons JK, Brawer MK, Cheli CD, Partin AW, Djavan R. (2004) Complexed prostate specific antigen (PSA) reduces unnecessary prostate biopsies in the 2.6-4.0 ng/mL range of total PSA. BJU Int 94(1):47-50.

Partin MR, Nelson D, Radosevich D, Nugent S, Flood AB, Dillon N, Holtzman J, Haas M, Wilt TJ. (2004) Randomized trial examining the effect of two prostate cancer screening educational interventions on patient knowledge, preferences, and behaviors. J Gen Intern Med19(8):835-842.

Pasick RJ, Hiatt RA, Paskett ED. (2004) Lessons learned from community-based cancer screening intervention research. Cancer 101(5 Suppl):1146-1164.

Pignone M, Rich M, Teutsch SM, et al. (2002) Screening for colorectal cancer in adults at average risk: A summary of the evidence for the U.S. Preventive Task Force. Ann Int Med 137:132-141.

Platz EA, Rimm EB, Willett WC, Kantoff PW, Giovannucci E. (2000) Racial variation in prostate cancer incidence and in hormonal system markers among male health profes-sionals. J Natl Cancer Inst 92(24):2009-2017.

Potosky AL, Legler J, Albertsen PC, Stanford JL, Gilliland FD, Hamilton AS, et al. (2000) Health outcomes after prostatectomy or radiotherapy for prostate cancer: Results from the Prostate Cancer Outcomes Study. J Natl Cancer Inst 92(19):1582-1592.

Potosky A, Miller BA, Albertsen PC, Kramer BS. (1995) The role of increasing detection in the rising incidence of prostate cancer. JAMA 273(7):548-552.

Powell IJ. (1994) Early detection issues of prostate cancer in African American men. In Vivo 8(3): 451-452.

Powell IJ. (1998) Keynote address: prostate cancer among African-American men—from the bench to the community. J Natl Med Assoc 90(11): S705-S709.

Powell IJ, Banerjee M, Sakr W, Grignon D, Wood DP Jr, Novallo M, Pontes E. (1999) Should African-American men be tested for prostate carcinoma at an earlier age than white men? Cancer 85(2):472-477.

Powell IJ, Banerjee M, Novallo M, Sakr W, Grignon D, Wood DP, Pontes JE. (2000) Should the age specific prostate specific antigen cutoff for prostate biopsy be higher for black than for white men older than 50 years? Urology 163(1):146-148.

Powell IJ, Heilbrum L, Littrup PL, Franklin A, Parzuchowski J, Gelfand D, Sakr W. (1997) Outcome of African American men screened for prostate cancer: the Detroit Education and Early Detection Study. J Urol 1581(1):146-149.

Price JH, Colvin TL, Smith D. (1993). Prostate cancer: Perceptions of African-Amer-ican males. J Natl Med Assoc 85(12):941-947.

Prochaska JO, Velicer WF, Rossi JS, Goldstein MG, Marcus BH, Rakowski W, Fiore C, Harlow LL, Redding CA, Rosenbloom D, et al. (1994) Stages of change and decisional balance for 12 problem behaviors. Health Psychol 13(1): 39-46.

Prorok PC, Andriole GL, Bresalier RS, Buys SS, Chia D, Crawford ED, Fogel R, Gelmann EP, Gilbert F, Hasson MA, Hayes RB, Johnson CC, Mandel JS, Oberman A, O'Brien B, Oken MM, Rafla S, Reding D, Rutt W, Weissfeld JL, Yokochi L, Gohagan JK; Prostate, Lung, Colorectal and Ovarian Cancer Screening Trial Project Team. (2000). Design of the Prostate, Lung, Colorectal and Ovarian (PLCO) Cancer Screening Trial. Control Clin Trials 21(6 Suppl):273S-309S.

Raaijmakers R, Blijenberg BG, Finlay JA, Rittenhouse HG, Wildhagen MF, Roobol MJ,

Schroder FH. (2004). Prostate cancer detection in the prostate specific antigen range of 2.0 to 3.9 ng/ml: value of percent free prostate specific antigen on tumor detection and tumor aggressiveness. J Urol 171(6 Pt 1):2245-2249.

Robinson SB, Ashley M, Haynes MA. (1996) Attitudes of African Americans regarding screening for prostate cancer. J Natl Medical Association 88(4):241-246.

Roetzheim RG, Christman LK, Jacobsen PB, Cantor AB, Schroeder J, Abdulla R, Hunter S, Chirikos TN, Krischer JP. (2004). A randomized controlled trial to increase cancer screening among attendees of community health centers. Ann Fam Med 2(4):294-300.

Rosenblatt KA, Wicklund KG, Stanford JL. (2001). Sexual factors and the risk of prostate cancer. Am J Epidemiol 153(12):1152-1158.

Schapira MM, VanRuiswyk J. (2000) The effect of an illustrated pamphlet decision-aid on the use of prostate cancer screening tests. J Fam Pract 49(5):418-424.

Schwartz LM, Woloshin S. (2002) Marketing medicine to the public: a reader's guide. JAMA 287(6):774-775.

Schwartz LM, Woloshin S. (2002). News media coverage of screening mammography for women in their 40s and tamoxifen for primary prevention of breast cancer. JAMA 287(23): 3136-3142.

Schwartz LM, Woloshin S. (2004) The media matter: a call for straightforward medical reporting. Ann Intern Med 140(3):226-228.

Schwartz LM, Woloshin S, Baczek L. (2002) Media coverage of scientific meetings: too much, too soon? JAMA 287(21):2859-2863.

Schwartz LM, Woloshin S, Fowler FJ Jr, Welch HG. (2004) Enthusiasm for cancer screening in the United States. JAMA 291(1):71-78.

Sigurdsson, K (1993) Effect of organized screening on the risk of cervical cancer. Evaluation of screening activity in Iceland, 1964-1991. Int J Cancer 54(4):563-70.

Sirovich BE, Schwartz LM, Woloshin S. (2003) Screening men for prostate and colorectal cancer in the United States: does practice reflect the evidence? JAMA 289(11): 1414-1420.

Smith RA, von Eschenbach AC, Wender R, Levin B, Byers T, et al. (2001) American Cancer Society guidelines for the early detection of cancer: Update of early detection guidelines for prostate, colorectal, and endometrial cancers. CA: A cancer journal for clinicians 51(1):38-75.

Stamey TA, Yang N, Hay AR, McNeal JE, Freiha FS, Redwine E. (1987) Prostate-specific antigen as a serum marker for adenocarcinoma of the prostate. N Engl J Med 317(15):909-916.

Stanford JL, Stephenson RA, Coyle LM, Cerhan J, Correa R, Eley JW, Gilliland F, Hankey B, Kolonel LN, Kosary C, Ross R, Severson R, West D. Prostate Cancer Trends 1973-1995, SEER Program, National Cancer Institute. NIH Pub. No. 99-4543. Bethesda, MD, 1999.

Steele CB, Miller DS, Maylahn C, Uhler RJ, Baker CT. (2000) Knowledge, attitudes, and screening practices among older men regarding prostate cancer. Am J Public Health 90(10):1595-600.

Steineck G, Helgesen F, Adolfsson J, Dickman PW, Johansson JE, Norlen BJ, et al. (2002). Quality of life after radical prostatectomy or watchful waiting. New Engl J Med 347(11):839-840.

Stone BA. (1998) Prostate cancer early detection in African-American men: a priority for the 21st century. J Natl Med Assoc 90(11 Suppl): S724-S727.

Taylor KL, Turner RO, Davis JL 3rd, Johnson L, Schwartz MD, Kerner J, Leak C. Improving African American Men's Knowledge of the Prostate Cancer Screening Dilemma: A Randomized Intervention. In preparation.

Taylor KL et al. (2000) The right decision

is yours : a guide to PCA check-ups. [brochure and video]

Taylor KL, DiPlacido J, Redd WH, Faccenda K, Greer L, Perlmutter A. (1999) Demographics, family histories, and psychological characteristics of prostate carcinoma screening participants. Cancer 85(6):1305-1312.

Taylor KL, Shelby R, Kerner J, Redd W, Lynch J. (2002) Impact of undergoing prostate carcinoma screening on prostate carcinoma-related knowledge and distress. Cancer 95(5): 1037-1044.

Taylor KL, Turner RO, Davis JL 3rd, Johnson L, Schwartz MD, Kerner J, Leak C. (2001) Improving knowledge of the prostate cancer screening dilemma among African American men: an academic-community partnership in Washington, DC. Public Health Rep 116(6):590-598.

Thompson IM, Goodman PJ, Tangen CM, Lucia MS, Miller GJ, Ford LG, Lieber MM, Cespedes RD, Atkins JN, Lippman SM, Carlin SM, Ryan A, Szczepanek CM, Crowley JJ, Coltman CA Jr. (2003) The influence of finasteride on the development of prostate cancer. N Engl J Med 349(3):215-224.

Thompson IM, Pauler DK, Goodman PJ, Tangen CM, Lucia MS, Parnes HL, Minasian LM, Ford LG, Lippman SM, Crawford ED, Crowley JJ, Coltman CA Jr. (2004) Prevalence of prostate cancer among men with a prostate-specific antigen level < or =4.0 ng per milliliter. N Engl J Med 350(22):2239-46. Erratum in: N Engl J Med 351(14):1470.

U.S. Preventive Services Task Force. Guide to Clinical Preventive Services. 3rd ed. Washington, DC: Office of Disease Prevention and Health Promotion; 2003. Retrieved February 15, 2005 from http://www.ahrq.gov/clinic/uspstf/uspscerv.htm

Vogt TM, Mayne ST, Graubard BI, Swanson CA, Sowell AL, Schoenberg JB, Swanson GM, Greenberg RS, Hoover RN, Hayes RB, Ziegler RG. (2002) Serum lycopene, other serum carotenoids, and risk of prostate cancer in US Blacks and Whites. Am J Epidemiol 155(11):1023-1032.

Vogt TM, Ziegler RG, Graubard BI, Swanson CA, Greenberg RS, Schoenberg JB, Swanson GM, Hayes RB, Mayne ST. (2003) Serum selenium and risk of prostate cancer in U.S. blacks and whites. Int J Cancer 103(5): 664-670.

Volk RJ, Cass AR, Spann SJ. (1999) A randomized controlled trial of shared decision making for prostate cancer screening. Arch Family Med 8(4):333-340.

Volk RJ, Spann SJ, Cass AR, Hawley ST. (2003). Patient education for informed decision making about prostate cancer screening: a randomized controlled trial with 1-year follow-up. Ann Fam Med 1(1):22-28.

Walsh PC. (2002) Surgery and the reduction of mortality from prostate cancer. New Engl J Med 347(11):839-840.

Walsh PC, Worthington JF. (2001). Dr. Patrick Walsh's guide to surviving prostate cancer. New York: Warner Books.

Weinrich SP, Boyd MD, Bradford D, Mossa MS, Weinrich M. (1998) Recruitment of African Americans into prostate cancer screening. Cancer Pract 6(1):23-30.

Weinrich SP, Boyd MD, Weinrich M, Greene F, Reynolds WA Jr, Metlin C. (1998) Increasing prostate cancer screening in African-American men with peer-educator and client-navigator interventions. J Cancer Educ 13(4):213-219.

Weinrich SP, Weinrich MC, Priest J, Fodi C. (2003) Self-reported reasons men decide not to participate in free prostate cancer screening. Oncol Nurs Forum 30(1):E12-E16.

Whittemore AS, Kolonel LN, Wu AH, John EM, Gallagher RP, Howe GR, Burch JD, Hankin J, Dreon DM, West DW, et al. (1995) Prostate cancer in relation to diet, physical activity, and body size in blacks, whites, and Asians in the United States and Canada. J Natl Cancer Inst 87(9):652-661.

Wilt TJ, Paul J, Murdoch M, Nelson D, Nugent S, Rubins HB. (2001) Educating men about prostate cancer screening. A randomized trial of a mailed pamphlet. Eff Clin Pract 4(3):112-120.

Winter DL, Hanlon AL, Raysor SL, Watkins-Bruner D, Pinover WH, Hanks GE, Tricoli JV. (2001) Plasma levels of IGF-1, IGF-2, and IGFBP-3 in white and African-American men at increased risk of prostate cancer. Urology 58(4):614-618.

Wolf AM, Nasser JF, Wolf AM, Schorling JB. (1996) The impact of informed consent on patient interest in prostate-specific antigen screening. Arch Intern Med 156 (12):1333-1336.

Woolf SH. (1995) Screening for prostate cancer with prostate-specific antigen. An examination of the evidence. N Engl J Med 333(21):1401-1405.

Woolf SH. (1997) Shared decision-making: the case for letting patients decide which choice is best. J Family Pract 45(3): 205-208.

Woolf SH. (2001) The logic and limits of shared decision making. J Urol 166(1):244-245.

Yao SL, Lu-Yao G. (2002) Understanding and appreciating overdiagnosis in the PSA era. J Natl Cancer Inst 94(13):958-960.

COMPREHENSIVE MANAGEMENT OF TUBERCULOSIS: DIRECTLY OBSERVED THERAPY AND BEYOND

Sonya S. Shin, Jennifer J. Furin, and Jennifer M. Singler

"You have to understand our situation in this country—we work hard, but sometimes we don't have enough to eat... If there were enough food, enough work in our country, then there wouldn't be so many sick people. This illness, tuberculosis, is increasing. It's attacking so many people. I'm worried that my children will get sick as well. I got sick because I was with my mother when she was sick, constantly taking care of her. And then my brother got sick. They both died of TB. Why do so many of us get sick? There are so many people who have gotten tuberculosis, and there will be many more. There are some people who don't want to get better; they become demoralized. Why should we take these medicines, complete the treatment that you give us, if the situation is the same —no work, no food?" Luz Ramirez, TB patient in Lima, Peru

In a dusty slum in Northern Lima, Peru, Ana Maria lies on a small cot in the corner of her family's one room shack. She is exhausted after having been awake all night, coughing. Thankfully, there was no blood this time. Ana Maria knows she is sick. Her weight has fallen dramatically, and she has daily fevers. She watched the same thing happen to her brother, who died just a year ago, leaving his wife and small children with no home, no income. His family now crowds in with Ana Maria and her two daughters in a one-room shanty whose roof is nothing more than tarp. Winter has settled in, and the air is damp and cold. Ana Maria earns what little money she can for her family selling chewing gum on a busy street, but it is never enough to keep them all fed. As she rises from bed, she wonders how they will survive. As she dresses for work, she is wracked with another coughing spell that shakes her thin frame to the core. She knows tuberculosis well and fears this is what she has. She has heard that there may be treatment for her at the health center, strong medicine that can kill the bacteria that are destroying her lungs. She is unsure, however, when she can get to the center, as missing even a small amount of time selling on the street may make the difference between eating little or going completely hungry that night.

Tuberculosis—long thought to be a disease of the past—is one of the leading infectious killers of adults in the world today. It is estimated that one third of the world's population, roughly 2 billion people, is infected with the bacteria that causes tuberculosis. Estimates of mortality range from two to three million deaths per year (WHO, 1997; WHO, 2002). Globally, a majority of the tuberculosis burden is felt in poor countries, with 54% of cases occurring in Africa and Asia (WHO, 1999). In rich countries, tuberculosis has been and remains a disease of the poor, striking in particular the homeless and institutionalized (Nardell, 1989), the foreign-born (CDC, 1998), and those living with HIV (Murray, 1991; Moore et al., 1999). In the United States, TB incidence is about 6.8 per 100,000 population with a death rate of around 4%, although these numbers are much higher among persons with HIV, poor people, and racial and ethnic minorities.

Tuberculosis is caused by *Mycobacterium tuberculosis*, one of a group of mycobacteria with a mycolic acid cell wall. Since the introduction of the first antituberculous drug, streptomycin, in the 1950s, physicians and patients have been challenged by the complexities of TB therapy. Early strategies of monotherapy with streptomycin soon proved inadequate due to the mycobacteria's capacity to mutate and produce drug-resistant strains. Other antituberculous agents soon followed, allowing for combination therapies, with improved clinical outcomes when administered for prolonged durations of 12 months or more. However, daily injectables and a high pill burden posed formidable difficulties for patients; not surprisingly, completion of a year of therapy was the exception rather than the rule. Side effects were common, including hearing loss, renal failure, gastrointestinal disturbances and hepatitis. Even worse, irregular therapy (such as monotherapy) allowed for selection of drug-resistant strains, further diminishing the chance of cure. Currently, drug-resistant strains of *M. tuberculosis* have been found in over one hundred countries, and in some "hot spots" prevalence exceeds 3% (WHO, 2002). A majority of drug-resistant cases occur in patients who have received prior treatment for TB, although spread of already resistant strains appears to be on the rise.

Fifty years after the initial discovery of antituberculous therapy, newer drugs permit shorter courses (of six to nine months) with fewer adverse effects. A typical treatment regimen consists of three to four medications taken once daily for two months followed by a two-drug regimen taken twice weekly for an additional four months. Indeed, patients with tuberculosis, when successfully treated for pan-susceptible disease (i.e. disease that is sensitive to all known antituberculous medications) will be cured more than 95% of the time. Yet, even as late as 1994, the worldwide average cure rate for tuberculosis was a dismal 43%, primarily due to lack of access to therapy (Raviglione et al., 1997).

What then are the barriers to favorable treatment outcomes, especially in resource-poor settings? As previously mentioned, the practical difficulties of successfully completing a prolonged multidrug regimen results in irregular treatment. Indeed, irregular therapy has been significantly associated with treatment failure (Fox, 1983). Even in the first decade of tuberculosis therapy, treatment non-compliance was identified as a major risk factor for poor treatment outcome (Fox, 1958). Fox describes his disheartening experience in Madras, where 20% of those TB patients treated at home had a negative urine test (detecting metabolites of an antituberculous drug) at least once each month during the first six months of treatment. Fox found it difficult to elucidate the reasons behind patient non-compliance, citing side effects, lack of food, religious motivations, as well as "forgetfulness" and "indolence," as contributing factors. He acknowledges that "very little is known of the motives which impel a patient to take medicine and the best way to get him to do so," and reiterates the WHO Study Group's recommendation to invest in "research employing the disciplines of both the medical sciences and the social sciences" to further understand and remediate the roots of noncompliance.

Research on nonadherence comprises one of the largest themes in both medical and social science literature on behavioral interventions in tuberculosis. Mainstream dogma has attributed noncompliance to "self-destructive" attitudes and beliefs on behalf of the patient (Addington, 1979). Most authors acknowledge that predictors of nonadherence are difficult to identify in any consistent manner (Addington, 1997; Sbarbaro, 1985; Vermiere, 2001). Nonetheless, three models of theory in social sciences guide the motivations behind the majority of strategies developed to improve adherence in TB patients.

The first model may be called the paternalistic model; this model places primary responsibility in the patient, who may "comply" and thus obey the physician's indications, or else, in an act of "self-destruction," ignore medical orders due to a variety of motivations (Addington, 1997). Here, patients are viewed as "passive, obedient and unquestioning recipients of medical instructions" (Vermiere et al., 2001). The motivations behind their actions are of secondary importance, because the final decision—to comply or to defy medical orders—is viewed as either right or wrong. The solution that logically stems from this model is directly observed therapy (DOT), wherein the capacity for noncompliance is essentially removed from the patient. Instead, the patient receives every dose of every TB medication under direct supervision of a health worker or layperson. Mandatory incarceration is another strategy that is based on this explanatory model of patient noncompliance.

A more recent model that arose out of the movement of patient autonomy views the patient as rational decision-maker, wherein patients make informed decisions based on their attitudes, knowledge, and cultural beliefs (Donovan and Blake, 1992; Vermiere et al., 2001). Here, even if the patient goes against the physician's advice, this decision is viewed as the correct decision, from the patient's point of view, which may weigh factors that the physician or caregiver is unable to take into account or comprehend. Therefore, the relation of the patient's actions to the physician's advice is one of "concordance" rather than compliance. Solutions to noncompliance based on this theory are centered around creating a cooperative alliance with the patient, based on a sound patient-doctor relationship, heightened physician communication skills, and detailed patient education about the nature of TB therapy and the disease itself. Additional incentives, reminders, positive feedback, and cultural considerations further reinforce the

overall goals for enhancing compliance: "improving patient comprehension, patient recall and patient motivation" (Vermiere et al., 2001). Cuneo and Snider reflect this theory in their nine action steps to improve compliance—patient education, incentives, reminders, tailored therapy, self-monitoring behavior, health contracts, supervised therapy, following-up on broken appointments, and training for health care personnel (Cuneo and Snider, 1989). They write: "We must educate ourselves to learn how to reach society's disenfranchised members to provide relevant educational interventions and other services" (Cuneo and Snider, 1989).

This model acknowledges that noncompliance is not simply a failing on the part of the patient, but rather a shared responsibility between patient and physician. Yet, like the paternalistic model, the concordance model is almost equally shortsighted in its failure to consider the impact of larger societal forces—such as poverty and political instability—which remove the individual agency from the patient, thus resulting in nonadherence due to neither indolence, forgetfulness, ignorance, nor cultural beliefs. Sumartojo points out that many of the commonly cited factors that predict nonadherence fail to consider the "environmental, structural, and operational factors that are beyond the patient's control. It is important that researchers challenge assumptions that attribute adherence problems exclusively to patient; such attributions may bias providers against certain kinds of patients and limit the providers' willingness to make needed changes in health care services" (Sumartojo, 1993).

A third model considers nonadherence within the context of programmatic failings, as well as socioeconomic stressors that not only contribute to patient nonadherence but are also the very factors which place these same individuals at risk of developing TB. Sumartojo writes: "Many patients with tuberculosis suffer from severe problems: homelessness, poverty, substance abuse. In successful comprehensive services, the wide diversity of difficulties faced by patients is recognized, and they are provided the additional assistance that makes the medical care and control of tuberculosis possible." Particularly in resource-poor settings, patient adherence must be contextualized within these larger factors which often overshadow individual cultural beliefs and health-related preferences of the individual.

Farmer and colleagues consistently argue for the need to consider these larger societal factors when discussing or remediating the causes of noncompliance. In summarizing common reasons for nonadherence, most of the factors he mentions are far beyond the sphere of patient autonomy: "economic barriers (including 'hidden costs' of transportation, etc.); drug stock-outs, inconvenient clinic hours or locations; errors in prescribing or dispensing medications; discontinuation of therapy due to perceived adverse effects; and patient misconceptions (Farmer et al., 2001)." He believes that the myopic perspective among many who study patient compliance is due to their disregard for "the relationship between the social reproduction of inequalities and the persistence of TB. Our failure to discern a political economy of risk for both the development of multi-drug resistant (MDR) TB and also for suboptimal treatment may be related to a desire to link our (perfectly legitimate) investigations of the shaping of personal experience by culture to (inaccurate) claims of causality (Farmer et al., 1999)."

Arising from this contextualized theory of noncompliance is a comprehensive strategy aimed at addressing not only the immediate medical issue of TB and its treatment, but also social and economic factors which place the patient at risk of nonadherence, often regardless of the patient's knowledge of the disease process and desire to complete treatment. For example, even if a patient knows that TB is fatal without treatment, if she must continue to work to feed her children and is unable to receive her medications outside of her work hours or unable to afford bus fare to the clinic, her poverty, not surprisingly, places her at risk not only for contracting TB but for a bad outcome due to nonadherence. As Johansson observes about noncompliant TB patients in Vietnam, "They did not seem to have a real choice, or it was too complicated to combine the two [options of work and TB treatment]" (Johansson et al., 1996).

Even in rich countries, TB is a disease of the poor and marginalized, and we argue that poverty and social instability are two of the strongest risk factors for acquiring the disease and for doing poorly once sick with TB. Analysis of behavioral factors related to tuberculosis and its management without contextualizing tuberculosis as a disease of poverty often results in misguided or myopic interventions that fail to improve the health of patients in a meaningful way. Unfortunately, the behavioral and social science literature regarding tuberculosis treatment is guilty of this shortcoming, assuming individual agency and thus focusing on individual factors that affect "compliance" with therapy rather than complex social forces that place people at risk.

As practitioners caring for patients with tuberculosis, how are we to best manage these complex health and social problems? What are the "best behavioral practices" we can put into place to ensure that patients with tuberculosis have excellent clinical outcomes? Because socioeconomic forces play such a dominant role in shaping the outcome of patients with TB, it is our belief that any behavioral intervention must be placed in the context of larger structural factors if it is to be successful. The remainder of this chapter will review the literature on behavioral interventions aimed at improving the efficacy of TB treatment. (Table 1.) In doing so, we will attempt to identify successful interventions that have had an impact on health outcomes of patients with tuberculosis. The studies chosen to review in the chapter came from a literature search on the topics of tuberculosis and adherence to therapy. Papers were found either in Medline or using the Cochrane Database of Systematic Reviews. Because the topic was broad, not every paper from each area could be reviewed. Rather, studies that were felt to be representative of the broader literature in the subsections discussed were selected. A variety of methodologic approaches were included in the review as it was felt each would yield different types of data that might be of use to the reader.

DIRECTLY OBSERVED THERAPY

As soon as it was apparent that self-administration of TB therapy was fraught with the risk of nonadherence, the concept of directly observed therapy for TB medications was introduced (Fox, 1958). As previously mentioned, DOT entails "supervised swallowing;" a health care worker or lay person observes the patient's ingestion of every dose of TB treatment (Garner, 1998). Having previously demonstrated success in

Table 1: Studies of behavioral interventions for TB treatment

Study and type	Population	Intervention	Outcome
Directly Observed Therapy			
Bayer et al., 1998 *Retrospective ecological study of TB control programs*	28 TB control programs with 100 or more incident cases of TB in any one year	DOT v. standard care. Also, assistance for substance abuse, mental illness, homelessness, training, federal funding	Treatment completion rates were 80% in 1990 when DOT rates were 16%; treatment completion rates were 87% in 1994 when DOT rates were 49.4%
Kamolratanakul et al., 1999 Prospective randomized trial	837 new smear-positive TB patients in Thailand, 1996-1997	DOT v. SST (self supervised therapy). choice of supervisor (staff, CHW, family), patient convenience	Cure: 76% DOT v. 67% SST (p=0.004) Treatment completion: 84% DOT v 76% SST (p=0.006) ; Default: 7% DOT v 13% SST (p=0.005)
Zwarenstein et al., 1998 Prospective randomized trial	216 TB patients in Cape Town, South Africa, 1994-1995.	DOT by nurses in clinic v. SST	60% among SST v. 54% DOT group achieved treatment completion (NS)
Zwarenstein et al., 2000 Prospective randomized trial	156 TB patients in Cape Town, South Africa, 1994-1995.	SST v. clinic DOT v. lay health worker DOT	59% among SST v. 57% among clinic DOT v. 74% among LHW-DOT achieved treatment success (NS)
Walley et al. 2001 Prospective randomized trial	497 TB patients in Pakistan 1996-1998.	DOT by facility of community health worker v. DOT by family v. SST	Cure: 64% health worker DOT v. 55% family DOT v. 62% SAT (NS)

Physician/Staff Motivation, Training and Supervision			
Jin et al., 1993 *Prospective randomized trial*	1300 TB patients in Korea; intervention at level of health center; 7 health centers included	Intensive supervision and staff motivation v. routine staff supervision at 7 health centers	513/651 (78.8%) v. 423/649 (65.2%) completed treatment in intervention v. control health centers. Cure rates also higher in intervention group (RR 1.7 [1.4-1.9])
Prompts, Reminders, Contracts, Defaulter Action			
Lange, 1986 *Prospective randomized study*	38 patients with latent tuberculosis infection in Los Angeles county	Medication calendars to track adherence with isoniazid prophlyaxis	No change in adherence. Of note, a high dropout rate was noted among both groups after 2 months of therapy.
Paramasivan et al., 1993 *Prospective randomized study*	200 TB patients in Madrid	Reminder letters to patients who did not collect drugs	88% (intervention) v 73% (control) completion, RR 1.2 [1.1 – 1.4]
Patient and Family Education			
Seetha et al., 1981 *Prospective randomized study*	235 patients with TB in India	Education, family involvement through home health visitor	60% intervention v. 28% control collected all antituberculous drugs over first 3 months (p< 0.05)
Sanmarti et al., 1993 *Prospective randomized study*	318 primary school children with latent tuberculosis infection in Barcelona	education given every three months 1: during home visit 2: by phone 3: by MD at clinic 4: leaflet (control);	75/79 (93.6%) (1); 75/80 (93.7%)(2); 64/82 (78%)(3); 55/77 (71.4%)(4) completed treatment. Tested for presence of drug, too – significantly higher in all intervention groups v. control
Wobeser et al., 1989 *Prospective randomized study & historical control*	82 patients with latent tuberculosis infection in 1986 and 1987 in Canada	Six weeks of DOT and education versus no DOT nor education; compared with historical cohort from 1986.	Medication adherence 81% (intervention) vs. 52% (control) vs. 25% (in 1986) (p < 0.001) Effect lost after intervention ended
Incentives and Enablers			
Morisky, 1990 *Prospective randomized study*	88 patients with active TB and 117 with latent tuberculosis infection each randomized into two groups	Behavioral counseling in patient's language and monetary incentive ($10 to cure TB, $5 for prophylaxis) v. usual care with tracing of defaulters	Adherence in terms of pill taking in prevention group: 68% intervention group v. 38% control (p< 0.001) Adherence in terms of pill taking in treatment group: 93% v. 90% (NS) Completion of treatment in prevention group: 64% in intervention v. 27% control (p=0.001) Completion of rx in TB group 97% in intervention v. 91% control (NS) Also higher rates of appointments kept and mean proportion of drugs taken in intervention group

Chaisson et al., 2001 *Prospective randomized trial*	Approx 300 drug users with latent tuberculosis infection in Baltimore	DOT v. SST with peer counseling v. routine care. Also, randomized within each group to receive either immediate or deferred monetary incentive ($10 monthly)	No difference between groups was noted
Pilote et al., 1996 *Prospective randomized study*	240 homeless patients with latent tuberculosis infection	Money ($5) for group 1, peer health adviser for group 2, usual care for group 3	69/82 (84%) group 1 v. 62/83 group 2 (75%) v. 42/79 (53%) group 3 completed treatment
Comprehensive, Community-Based Services			
Curry, 1968 *Historical control*	Three neighborhood clinics in San Francisco among the Chinese, African Americans, and the homeless	Creation of neighborhood TB clinics with improved clinic hours, shorter wait, social services, home visits for missed appts	94% v 66% adherence over time, defined as number of appointments kept
Werhane et al., 1989 *Case control*	164 TB patients in Chicago 1976-1987	Care provided in specialized TB clinic with reduced waiting time, transportation money, social /financial assistance, comprehensive medical care	85% v 12% treatment completion among patients receiving care at TB clinic versus general medical clinic (p < 0.0001)
Famer et al., 1991 *Case control*	86 TB patients in rural Haiti	DOT by CHW, financial/nutritional assistance, travel assistance, home visits	cure rates: 100% (intervention) v. 57% (control)
Chaulk et al., 1995 *Case control study*	466 TB patients in Baltimore v. other U.S. cities	DOT, outreach, transportation, housing, trackers	89.8% completed rx among DOT v. 53.4% among non-DOT
Tulsky et al., 2000 *Propsective randomized trial*	138 homeless adults with latent tuberculosis infection in San Francisco	Biweekly DOT plus a financial incentive v. biweekly DOT plus a peer health adviser v. usual care	Completion of 6 months therapy 44% among DOT plus financial incentive v. 19% among DOT plus PHA v. 26% usual care
Malotte et al., 2001 *Prospective randomized trial*	163 drug users with latent tuberculosis infection in California between 1994-1997.	Group 1: DOT by outreach worker + incentive, Group 2: active outreach, Group 3: DOT at study site and incentive ($5/visit)	Group 1 took 71% prescribed medications; group 2 13%; group 3 68% (p< .001); treatment completion 53% among group 1; 4% among group 2; and 60% among group 3 (p< .0001)

Mushtaque et al., 1997 *Retrospective study*	5238 TB patients in Bangladesh; no control group	DOT by CHW, contracts, monetary incentives for both patients and CHWs, immunizations, improvements in water and sanitation, family planning, treatment of infections, staff supervision	Cure rate achieved was 85%
Mangura et al., 2002 *Retrospective case control study*	343 TB patients in Newark, New Jersey	SST with selective DOT v. universal DOT v. universal DOT with nurse case management	Treatment completion was three to six times higher among patients who received DOT in addition to nurse case management compared with the selective DOT and with universal DOT

leprosy treatment, directly observed therapy was applied to TB therapy as early as the 1950s; it was ultimately revised and officially adopted on the global level in 1991 by the 44th World Health Assembly (WHO, 1991). In 1994 the World Health Organization christened the new strategy DOTS (directly observed therapy, short-course), and made it a cornerstone for the management of tuberculosis worldwide (WHO, 1994). The WHO defined DOTS as a comprehensive treatment package with five essential technical and managerial components, including political commitment, improved laboratory facilities for case detection via smear microscopy, a continuous drug supply, universal direct observation of medications which are provided for free, and a data tracking and recording system.

In the United States, universal DOT was implemented in 1993 (Bayer and Wilkinson, 1995). Prior to that time, DOT was applied selectively to "unreliable" patients, based on the assumption that DOT for "reliable" patients would incur excessive and unnecessary expenses. It was not until an outbreak of TB in New York City in the early 1990's that the Advisory Council for the Elimination of Tuberculosis voted to make universal DOT federal policy. Even so, many

in the United States still argue that universal DOT is unjustifiable both in terms of cost and infringement on patient autonomy (Annas, 1993).

DOT remains the most widespread behavioral intervention in TB treatment to date. Surprisingly, the effectiveness of DOT is still debated. While numerous studies describe DOT-based programs, at the time of this writing there are only four randomized controlled trials evaluating DOT in the treatment of patients with TB. It bears mentioning that while the focus of DOT has been on patients receiving treatment for active TB, this strategy has also been applied to prophylactic treatment for latent TB infection (LTI), which entails administration of a single drug, isoniazid, once daily for 6 to 9 months. One randomized controlled trial exists in this field, which is reviewed in Table 1.

Two of these trials were performed by Zwarenstein and colleagues in South Africa (Zwarenstein et al., 1998; Zwarenstein et al., 2000). The first trial was conducted in two regions with historically high default rates among persons being treated for tuberculosis (Zwarenstein et al., 1998). 1177 patients starting treatment for active pulmonary tuberculosis were recruited; exclusion criteria included patients with MDR-TB, severe illness, or intention to receive supervised therapy at their school or workplace. Patients meeting eligibility criteria were randomized to receive DOT versus self-supervised therapy (SST). DOT patients attended clinic during working hours and received medications under nurse supervision; adherence was recorded by the clinic nurse. SST patients collected medications from the clinic weekly and kept track of their own treatment adherence via a self-report card. Among the 294 patients who were randomized, only 216 were included in analysis because of the subsequent exclusion of drug-resistant cases, non-TB cases, and "community-supervised" cases (see discussion of Zwarenstein et al., 2000). The primary outcome was cure or treatment completion. There were no differences between the two groups of patients, with favorable outcomes seen in 60% of self-supervised patients versus 54% of patients receiving observed therapy, a difference that was not statistically significant. These data lead the authors to conclude that self-supervised therapy could result in improved rates of treatment success; they speculate that the infringement of patient autonomy and the interference with the authoritarian act of supervision with the patient-caregiver relationship may negate any positive impact of DOT in their treatment setting.

There have been several critiques of this trial. First, the number of patients participating in the study was low, in part due to the exclusion of a large number of eligible patients for multiple reasons, including the fact that they were seeking employment. Second, positive outcomes in both groups were low and well below the targeted WHO goal of 85% cure. Finally, the DOT system implemented in the study was rigidly designed, requiring attendance at a clinic during working hours and without any flexibility in the observation strategy. Finally, the time of follow-up was not specified, and

in particular, rates of relapse were not assessed (Hill et al., 2002).

The second study by Zwarenstein et al. (2000) was part of the previous randomized controlled trial. 174 patients from Elsies River, a Cape Town suburb, were recruited. Among these, 156 were randomized to receive either SST versus community DOT (by a lay health worker) versus clinic DOT. No significant difference in treatment outcomes was observed among the three interventions. On stratified analysis, community DOT was associated with improved treatment success among new patients and females. Potential weaknesses of the study include a high cross-over rate from SST and community DOT to clinic DOT, and failure to recruit a population sufficient to meet sample size calculations to detect a 20% difference in outcome. The authors speculate that due to a small sample size, their study may have failed to demonstrate a true benefit of lay health worker DOT on treatment outcome.

The third randomized controlled trial of DOT versus SST came from Thailand and yielded conflicting results to the South Africa study (Kamolratanakul et al., 1999). The study was a large randomized trial involving patients with pulmonary tuberculosis being treated at 8 district hospitals, 3 provincial hospitals, and 4 referral centers in Thailand. A total of 837 patients were eligible; 415 were randomized to DOT and 422 to SST. Patients randomized to the DOT group were permitted to choose among health center staff, community members, or family members as their DOT workers. Of note, 86% chose a family member as their supervisor. If community or family members were selected, home visits were made by health center staff twice per month to perform pill counts and check treatment adherence cards. In the SST group, patients received their medications for one month at a time. Outcomes examined included cure, treatment completion, and default rate. No patients were lost to follow-up. In this study, the authors found that 76% of patients with DOT were cured compared with 67% of patients who were self supervised, a statistically significant difference (p=0.004). Similarly, 84% versus 76% of patients in the DOT versus SST groups, respectively, completed therapy (p=0.006), while 7% versus 13%, respectively, defaulted from treatment (p=0.005). The authors contend that their results support the effectiveness of DOT, in particular when the DOT setting is flexible enough to accommodate patients' work and transportation limitations. The authors note that studies conducted in South Africa were less flexible, thus possibly explaining the studies' discrepant results. This study has also been criticized, however, for cure rates that fail to meet WHO standards and for potential limitations as a reproducible model given that health center staff were paid to perform DOT home visits; in addition, relapse rates are not reported. It bears mentioning, however, that few countries in the world (< 20%) actually meet WHO standards and the results from this study are fairly typical for those seen under program conditions globally.

The final randomized controlled trial comparing DOT with SST was undertaken in Pakistan, a country with no existing National Tuberculosis Program (Walley et al., 2001). The study was carried out in three sites in Pakistan in order to determine how best to implement a national strategy to combat tuberculosis. As a part of this study, tuberculosis services in the 3 sites were "strengthened" overall—that is, they were reformed to reach standards for "developing" countries as regards tuberculosis treatment. A total of 497 patients with newly diagnosed sputum-positive tuberculosis were enrolled in the study and assigned to 3 different intervention groups: the first consisted of DOT provided by health workers, either community or facility based (170 patients);

the second was DOT provided by family members (165 patients); and the third was self-administered therapy (162 patients). The main outcome of interest was cure. The study found no difference between the 3 groups, with cure being achieved in 64% of patients receiving DOT from health workers, 55% of patients receiving DOT from family members, and 62% of patients receiving self supervised therapy. Outcomes of all three strategies were improved when compared to an historical control, likely reflecting the overall investment in infrastructure that accompanied this study. The authors of this study thus conclude "there was no additional benefit from direct observation of treatment over and above service strengthening whether supervision was by health workers or family members." This study has also been criticized for low cure rates and for the fact that overall service improvement may have negated any benefit of DOT.

In a follow-up survey, the authors found that DOT patients reported the primary factors contributing to nonadherence to be "poor health, cost and time of travel, occupation, waiting time, for women no-one to accompany her, social events, and unfriendly staff" (Walley et al., 2000). While they suggest an "emphasis on patient-friendly services" as an area of improvement, they fail to mention the overriding impact of larger elements of poverty and societal restrictions and stigma on treatment outcome, or the need to address such elements to improve patient outcome.

The data from these randomized controlled trials of DOT are difficult to interpret. Nonetheless, Volmink and Garner found that in a meta-analysis of these four studies, there was no difference in outcomes (cure, and cure plus treatment completion) in those groups who received DOT verses self-administration (Volmink and Garner, 2002). In addition, the lack of impact was observed regardless of the DOT worker's identity (i.e. health professional, lay worker, or family/community member). The authors suggest that the significant effect of DOT on treatment outcomes in the Thailand study may have been due to two outstanding characteristics of the Thai study. First, theirs is a well-resourced TB program, unlike the programs in South Africa and Pakistan; second, the patient-oriented approach of assigning the supervisor of the patient's choice and conducting home visits with outreach workers may have additionally contributed to the impact of DOT.

What then of other studies of DOT? Although surprisingly few randomized controlled trials of DOT exist, numerous observational studies done of DOT have been published. Three recent reviews (Chaulk and Kazandjian, 1998; Volmink et al., 2000; Hill et al., 2002) have been conducted on the published body of DOT literature, and all arrive at similar conclusions: that a DOT program with integrated services addressing the diverse medical, financial, and psychosocial needs of the patient is more effective than DOT alone.

Whereas DOT alone may not be effective in improving the outcome of TB treatment, "multifaceted programme inputs" that often accompany DOT account in large part for the success (perhaps mistakenly) attributed to directly observed therapy (Garner, 1998). Volmink and Garner have repeatedly argued that these very "accoutrements" of DOT— including incentives, programmatic strengthening, patient reminders, and assistance with social and medical services— may be fundamentally more important than DOT itself. They caution the need to "disaggregate the effect of the specific strategy [of DOT] from the investment of time and money that usually accompanies it" (Volmink et al., 1997). In their critical review of DOT, Volmink et al. examine 32 studies on DOT (Volmink et al., 2000). They found that programs using DOT were heterogeneous in

nature and almost all employed other strategies in addition to the supervision of doses in order to improve patient outcomes. In fact, randomized trials demonstrated the effectiveness of reminder letters, patient assistance by community health workers, monetary incentives and increased staff supervision. (These studies will be reviewed later in this chapter.) The authors caution against the tendency of most studies to focus on DOT as the key factor in improving patient outcomes, suggesting that concomitant financial investment in programmatic infrastructure, training and supervision, and financial, social, and nutritional patient support should be explicitly enumerated in all DOT programs.

A second review of DOT literature examines 34 publications of DOT-based interventions (Hill et al., 2002). The authors note that multiple program elements likely contribute to favorable patient outcomes, including better case management, improved laboratory techniques, and improved program staffing. While they conclude that DOT alone likely has a beneficial impact on treatment outcome, they acknowledge that "it is artificial to evaluate DOT in the minimal sense of observed drug ingestion while ignoring other benefits that are integral to a patient-oriented holistic DOT program." In fact, they argue that patient-staff contact, education, psychosocial support, management of adverse effects and concurrent medical issues, as well as incentives and enablers should be considered integral to the DOT package. In addition, "referral to other medical and social services in the treatment center of community, nutritional support, counseling regarding HIV infection, and access to housing and health insurance" are equally important to DOT caseholding, particularly in working with indigent TB patients (Hill et al., 2002).

A third review of DOT performed by the Public Health Tuberculosis Guidelines Panel resulted in a consensus statement issued in 1998. The committee reviewed 497 articles related to TB treatment, among which 27 studies were eligible with treatment completion as an outcome (Chaulk and Kazandjian, 1998). The authors of this study conclude that patients receiving "enhanced" DOT programs (those with social, financial, nutritional incentives) are more likely to complete treatment successfully.

Proponents and opponents of DOT alone all seem to agree that incorporation of support services into DOT-based interventions not only offers a favorable option from the patient's point of view (Perlman and Salomon, 2000), but more importantly provides (albeit sometimes minimal) stabilization of the tenuous access to health services by many of society's most marginalized patients. In particular, insufficient and unreliable services greatly impact patient adherence and are most common in lower- and middle-income settings where TB prevails (Barker and Millard, 2000).

Yet, despite the widespread recognition that supplementary programmatic and patient support is necessary, such services are commonly considered "extra" or outside the realm of usual care. Studies rigorously examining the impact of these additional interventions are sparse. The following section reviews several studies that evaluate the effectiveness of a variety of interventions (and combinations thereof), including staff supervision, reminder letters, monetary incentives, nutritional and transportation reimbursements, patient and family education, and improvement of comprehensive medical and social services.

PHYSICIAN/STAFF MOTIVATION, TRAINING AND SUPERVISION

Motivation and education of TB health care providers has been proposed as one way to strengthen TB services and improve patient outcomes. One study examining this hypothesis was a randomized control trial investigating the impact of intense staff training (Jin et al., 1993). The study was carried out in seven health centers in Korea, and centers were randomized to either receive intensive education and "motivation" or not. Patient outcomes at the different health centers were then assessed. Rates of treatment completion among patients who received care at a health center receiving staff-level interventions were higher compared with patients who attended control clinics (79% versus 65% treatment completion). Sputum smear conversion was also higher within the intervention group. This study suggests that some intervention aimed at the level of health care providers may prove to be beneficial for TB patients.

PROMPTS, REMINDERS, CONTRACTS, DEFAULTER ACTION

A randomized controlled trial was conducted on patients with TB in Madras who defaulted on clinic attendance. Patients were randomized to receive up to two reminder letters versus no intervention (Paramasivan et al., 1993). Despite high rates of illiteracy, 17 of the 29 (59%) of those who received letters returned to clinic, compared with 4/31 (13%) of those in the control group. This intervention is focused on a short-lived impact (attendance of a single clinic appointment) and it is not clear whether reminders etc. would be able to sustain long-term adherence to TB treatment.

A small study was done by Lange and colleagues (1986) to assess the impact of a daily reminder—a treatment calendar—on treatment completion rates among individuals with latent tuberculosis infection in Los Angeles county. A total of 38 patients were randomized into an intervention group which received a calendar reminding them to take their daily medications which they would then mark with their initials, and a control group.

Although in the first month of the study more patients in the intervention group reported taking their medication, by the end of the second month almost all patients in both the control and intervention groups had dropped out of the study, rendering its results difficult to interpret. These studies, taken together, suggest that while reminders may be a useful initial intervention, they are unlikely to have a sustained benefit over time.

PATIENT AND FAMILY EDUCATION

Seetha and colleagues (1981) evaluated an interventional strategy that they term "motivational" among a group of patients with active TB in India. The intervention included a series of at-home patient and family education sessions conducted at regular intervals throughout the course of therapy. The outcome variable of interest was collection of antituberculous drugs from the health center. Among patients who received at-home "motivational" and education sessions, 60% collected antituberculous drugs over the 3 month period of the study, as compared with 28% in the control group, a difference which was statistically significant. One potential problem with this study is that collection of medications does not necessarily correlate with compliance or improved health outcomes for patients.

Sanmarti et al. (1993) conducted a randomized controlled trial in which parents of Barcelona schoolchildren with latent TB infection (LTI) were educated on the importance of adherence to prophylactic therapy (Sanmarti et al., 1993). Parents were randomized to receive educational sessions every three months in one of three settings: during a home visit conducted by a nurse, through a telephone call conducted by a nurse, or by a physician in clinic. The control group received an informational leaflet. Although 43 subjects (13.5%) were lost to follow-up, attendance at the last clinic visit was significantly higher among those receiving educational counseling from a nurse, regardless of the setting. Rates among those counseled by a physician were not significantly higher than the control group. The presence of drug metabolites in the urine was significantly more common in each intervention group when compared with the control. Other factors that may have affected attendance at clinic visits—including stuctural constraints on attendance—were not assessed.

Wobeser and colleagues performed a randomized trial looking at adherence with a six-month course of preventive therapy among a group of patients with latent tuberculosis infection. Patients were randomized into two groups: the first received DOT and an educational program, while the control group received neither. Among patients in the intervention group, adherence was 81% compared with 52% among the control group, a statistically significant difference (p<0.05). The two groups were also compared with an historical control group from the preceding year and both were found to have higher rates of treatment completion, although it is unclear as to why this might be the case.

These studies show that education of patients may have some effect on surrogate outcome markers for patients with latent tuberculosis infection and active TB. The outcome measures used, however, were not rigorous and it is unclear if the benefits of education can be sustained. Furthermore, there is little mention made on how educational interventions may be mitigated by socioeconimic circumstances, which are known to play a major role in TB outcomes.

INCENTIVES AND ENABLERS (MONETARY, FOOD)

Substantial literature exists to support the positive impact of incentives and enablers in improving patient compliance and treatment outcome. In one study, Bock and colleagues found they were able to improve completion rates among 55 patients with tuberculosis who were missing more than 25% of scheduled doses by providing them with five-dollar grocery coupons for each appointment kept compared with historical controls (Bock et al., 2001). In a study done using subway tokens at increasing intervals among tuberculosis patients in New York City, Davidson and colleagues found that increasing incentives was significantly associated with improved adherence in a multivariable analysis (Davidson et al., 2000).

Indeed, this strategy is felt to be cost-effective and is widely employed, although primarily in resource-endowed settings. In one survey of public health departments in the United States it was found that almost all states had programs for tuberculosis treatment which offered incentives for staying in therapy, including food, transportation, and ancillary services (Buchanan, 1997). In particular, several randomized controlled trials support the use of monetary and nonmonetary incentives to improve patient adherence in the treatment of active or latent TB.

In a study which compared counseling and monetary incentives to routine care, Morisky et al. randomized low-income Los Angeles patients with LTI or active TB to receive either counseling in the patient's native language plus a monetary incentive ($5-10) versus usual care (Morisky et al., 1990). Among those patients who received prophylactic therapy for LTI, rates of treatment completion were significantly higher in the intervention group. However, among those with active tuberculosis, there was no significant difference in completion rates among the intervention versus control group. A similar result was also found when the outcome variable of interest was appointment keeping, with those in the active TB group showing no difference between the intervention and control strategies but those with LTI showing a statistically significant

difference between the two groups, with intervention participants keeping 64% of appointments versus 47% among controls (p< 0.003). In terms of percentage of medication taken, both patients with active TB and LTI who received the intervention took a statistically significantly higher percentage of their medications (p < 0.001). One of the critiques of this study is the inability to identify which of the two interventions (counseling versus incentives) is actually associated with improved outcomes.

In response, Malotte and colleagues conducted a randomized controlled trial to determine the impact of monetary incentives as well as that of active outreach on adherence among patients receiving DOT for LTI (Malotte et al., 2001). All 202 patients recruited for the study were active drug users and had a positive tuberculin skin test; among these, 169 agreed to participate although six were subsequently dropped from the study due to discontinuation of prophylaxis because of prior isoniazid therapy, isoniazid-related toxicity, or development of active TB. Patients were assigned to one of three groups: 1) DOT by an outreach worker at a location chosen by the participant, plus $5 at each visit; 2) DOT by an outreach worker at a location chosen by the participant without monetary incentive; or 3) DOT at a community site plus monetary incentive. Among these groups, only 2/55 (4%) of participants in Group 2 completed treatment, while 28/53 (53%) in Group 1, and 33/55 (60%) in Group 3 completed therapy. While treatment completion rates in Group 2 were significantly lower compared with both other groups (p<0.0001), no significant difference in completion rates was noted between Groups 1 and 3. Similarly, the percentage of medications taken on time was significantly lower among patients in Group 2 (12% v. 72% in Group 1 and 69% in Group 3). Thus while monetary incentives clearly improved patient adherence, outreach-based DOT or the addition of outreach-based DOT to incentives did not significantly improve completion rates.

Pilote and colleagues conducted a randomized trial among homeless men known to have positive results on tuberculin skin testing to assess the impact of a monetary incentive ($5) to either the patients or peer advisors in attending an initial appointment for evaluation of tuberculosis (Pilote et al., 1996). Among those patients who received the incentive, 69/82 (84%) attended their appointment; among those whose peer advisors received the incentive, 62/83 (75%) attended, and among the control group, 42/79 (53%) made their appointment. Both intervention groups had significantly higher attendance rates compared with the control group; there was no significant difference in attendance between the two intervention groups.

In an effort to explore the optimal timing of monetary incentives (as well as the impact of DOT) on adherence to TB prophylaxis, Chaisson and colleagues conducted a randomized controlled factorial design trial in which 300 drug-using individuals in Baltimore with LTI were assigned to receive either: 1) DOT by an outreach nurse, 2) Self-administered therapy (SAT) with peer counseling (1 to 2 times a month), or 3) SAT without peer counseling (Chaisson et al., 2001). In addition, patients were also randomly assigned to receive either immediate (given after each month) or deferred (given at the end of treatment) incentive of $10 per month. None of the interventions resulted in a significant difference in treatment completion rates, although there was a trend toward higher rates of treatment completion among those receiving an immediate incentive (83%) compared with those who received a deferred incentive (75%) (p=0.09).

That monetary and non-monetary incentives should improve patient adherence

is not surprising, given the prevalence of poverty among patients with TB. Certainly, lack of transportation, unwillingness to take medications when hungry and with empty stomachs, and the necessity of work often pose insurmountable obstacles to TB treatment unless seemingly minor "incentives" are provided to allow patients to "choose" to adhere to therapy. Indeed, what some researchers refer to as incentives and enablers could just as easily be seen as integral health care for poor people.

While incentives alone have thus been shown to have a significant impact on treatment completion for LTI, whether they also have a positive effect on cure rates for patients with active TB or on mortality has yet to be determined. While the use of incentives acknowledges many barriers these patients face in receiving appropriate healthcare, such a strategy is short-sited in failing to produce a lasting effect on those barriers. Only through a truly integral approach to TB treatment services can lasting improvement in health outcomes be effected.

COMPREHENSIVE, COMMUNITY-BASED SERVICES

Comprehensive, community-based services include improvement of program infrastructure (including uninterrupted drug supplies; convenient clinic hours; accessible locations; reliable funding), access to services (including removal of economic barriers including transportation and clinic visit costs; outreach services for those who do not attend clinics; provision of services in the native language spoken by each patient), and comprehensive medical and socioeconomic support (including counseling and health services for concomitant illnesses; case management to provide advocacy; financial, nutritional and housing assistance; and job placement). Such approaches are commonly community-based, utilizing local resources that allow for increased flexibility and comprehensive support and outreach. When complemented with a stable health service program and adequate resources, a community-based approach is often more successful in solving many of the challenges associated with patient adherence (Squire and Wilkinson, 1997).

While such an intervention may seem excessive or costly as a TB-treatment strategy, we argue that only by addressing the root causes of diseases of poverty (including tuberculosis) can we provide patients with the true agency to choose good health for themselves and their families, although we emphasize that TB treatment cannot wait for poverty to be eliminated. Rather, TB care needs to be implemented in a way that is mindful of and aims to address socioeconomic factors linked with development of the disease and poor outcomes, including malnutrition, substandard living conditions, and inability to access medical care. Furthermore, several TB-based interventions have demonstrated that this approach is indeed feasible and successful. Unfortunately, given the implications of implementing such wide-based interventions, randomized controlled trials in this area do not exist. Nonetheless, several well-designed case control studies provide critical insight into the impact of such interventions.

In one of the earliest studies to look at comprehensive, community-based TB services, Curry describes a city-based effort to target TB services among groups most likely to miss appointments in San Francisco (Curry, 1968). Over a period of five years, neighborhood-based clinics for TB care were established for the homeless, the Chinese-American community, and the African-American community. In addition to providing flexible hours and relative geographical accessibility, the clinics also provided home visits, social services, and telephone reminders to patients. Compared with a historical control group, patients

receiving care at the neighborhood clinics missed significantly fewer appointments, a sign of their more active involvement in TB care, with subsequent improved outcomes.

Another study that evaluated the impact of a community clinic providing comprehensive health services for TB patients was done by Werhane and colleagues in the Chicago area (Werhane et al., 1989). The clinic of interest was staffed by a clinical nurse specialist and a nurse epidemiologist, both of whom were responsible for active patient outreach as well as provision of TB care and social services. Patients were also provided with money for transportation costs. Patients receiving comprehensive care at the TB clinic were compared with those patients receiving care at the general medical clinic, and it was found that treatment completion was significantly higher among the group receiving care at the comprehensive TB clinic compared with the general medical clinic (86% versus 12%, p< 0.0001). The authors of this study conclude that provision of comprehensive TB services through a specialized clinic that also addresses other financial and social needs of patients is a way to improve treatment completion—and thus cure—of TB patients.

Comprehensive case management when combined with DOT has been shown to be effective in case control trials. Another study that demonstrates the importance of a comprehensive package of services—and not merely direct observation of medications—was done by Mangura and colleagues (Mangura et al., 2002). The study took place with several cohorts of TB patients in a New Jersey clinic between 1994 and 1996. A total of 343 patients received one of the following strategies: 1) self administered therapy with occasional DOT; 2) universal DOT; or 3) DOT with case management from nursing staff. Treatment completion was three to six times higher among patients who received DOT in addition to nurse case management, suggesting this strategy was superior to DOT alone and self-administered therapy. This study seems to provide more evidence that DOT coupled with other comprehensive services—in this instance nurse case management—may be linked to improved outcomes for patients suffering from TB.

Mushtaque and colleagues (1997) examined a community-based comprehensive system of services for both detection and control of TB in one district in Bangladesh. The program was started by the Bangladesh Rural Advancement Committee (BRAC) a non-governmental organization in the region, and relied on community health workers to actively seek patients with TB and follow them through the course of their disease. In addition, the patients and community were provided with educational materials about TB and case management services as well as improved access to clean water, sanitation, and family planning. Patients paid a deposit upon entering therapy, with a proportion of that money returned upon completion of treatment. Treatment compliance and cure rates were compared over three phases of implementation of the study, and with each year, cure rates improved from 81% to 85.9%. The authors of the study conclude that "in countries such as Bangladesh where the government infrastructure is poorly developed, particularly in rural areas, non-governmental organizations have a major potential role. In this BRAC tuberculosis program, the community health workers were successful in identifying tuberculosis and encouraging treatment compliance in their own villages."

Perhaps one of the most important studies done looking at comprehensive services for TB patients is a 1991 landmark study by Farmer and colleagues done in rural Haiti (Farmer et al., 1991). Haiti, the poorest country in the Western hemisphere, is characterized by high prevalence of TB and death from the disease is also common. The study was done in a rural area in Haiti's central plateau with high mortality rates from TB. A community health worker program was started to improve TB outcomes in the region, but poor health outcomes were still observed. According to the authors of the study, health workers asked "How had they failed to prevent these deaths, all of which were registered among adults in their 40s? Some community health workers felt that TB patients with poor outcomes were the most economically impoverished and thus the sickest; others attributed poor compliance to widespread 'beliefs' about TB as a disorder inflicted through sorcery...". In order to test these hypotheses and improve TB care, Farmer and colleagues carried out a study comparing two groups of TB patients. The first received comprehensive services, including financial aid, nutritional support transportation costs and daily visits from health workers. The second group received standard care, including free medical services and antituberculous medications. The results showed that the patients receiving comprehensive care had higher rates of sputum conversion (100% compared with 86.6% in the standard care group), lower mortality (0% versus 10%) and gained 10.4 pounds versus 1.7 pounds. Overall cure rate was 100% in the intervention group versus 56.7% in the usual care group. Both groups of patients, however, believed that sorcery played a role in their illness (83.3% versus 86.7%) demonstrating no clear link between causal beliefs about disease and patient outcomes. The authors of the study conclude: "hunger and poverty are the prime culprits in treatment failure, just as they are so often responsible for the reactivation of endogenous infection. Countries held in under-development would do well to invest meager resources in programs that address patients' nutritional status while assuring easy access to multidrug regimens."

CONCLUSION

TB treatment, like many chronic diseases, is challenged by complicated and prolonged multidrug regimens; however, the most fundamental challenge of TB treatment is its characteristic as a disease of poverty. The very socioeconomic forces which place an individual at risk of developing TB make it even more difficult for the patient to complete treatment: hunger, unemployment, difficult access to drugs, homelessness, violence, concomitant illnesses such as substance abuse and HIV. While many behavioral interventions to improve adherence to TB treatment have been assessed, most such interventions are still founded in the notion that patients make a decision regarding adherence, one based on their health beliefs, cultural attitudes, lifestyle preferences, etc. Behavioral and biomedical research on compliance with TB therapy demonstrates an overwhelming myopia in its failure to contextualize the sphere of individual agency within the larger economic and societal constraints in which the patient lives.

In this chapter, we have sought to critically review the most rigorous and influential studies examining behavioral interventions related to TB treatment (Table 2). While the largest body of literature on TB-related behavioral interventions focuses on DOT, and family education, may have a short-term impact, but in resource-poor settings, we question whether adherence to prolonged TB therapy can be sustained by staff motivation, reminders and/or education. While incentives do provide crucial material resources often needed to overcome barriers to treatment (and indeed have demonstrated a more robust benefit than previously mentioned behavioral interventions), a truly comprehensive approach to healthcare for impoverished TB patients should address the structural barriers to agency and health.

Links between TB and poverty are perhaps best summarized by Farmer and colleagues, who note that "cultural, political and economic factors, although inevitably important, cannot be of equal significance in all settings. Whereas cultural considerations, such as the nearly universal stigma attached to TB, may very well be of overriding significance in settings in the developed world, we would argue that they are often less so in Haiti, where so many factors are determined by economic constraints. The hoary truth that poverty and TB are greater than the sum of their parts is once again supported by data" (Farmer et al., 1991). Thus, best behavioral practices regarding TB must take into account the socioeconomic situations in which sick and poor TB patients find themselves. Attempts to address TB that are divorced from such an understanding will only lead to misconceptions on the parts of researchers and care providers, and poor health outcomes for patients. It is only when truly comprehensive care is offered to TB patients—including nutritional support, access to other medical services, and financial assistance, as well as efforts to address behavioral issues—that there can be hope to relieve the tremendous burdens of the millions suffering from the disease. equivocal evidence at best supports its efficacy when applied alone. Other interventions, such as staff motivation and supervision, patient reminders, and patientand family education, may have a short-term impact, but in resource-poor settings, we question whether adherence to prolonged TB therapy can be sustained by staff motivation, reminders and/or education. While incentives do provide crucial material resources often needed to overcome barriers to treatment (and indeed have demonstrated a more robust benefit than previously mentioned behavioral interventions), a truly comprehensive approach to healthcare for impoverished TB patients should address the structural barriers to agency and health.

Table 2: Summary of behavioral interventions for TB treatment

Intervention strategy	Effectiveness on TB treatment outcome	Potential Advantages	Potential Disadvantages
Directly observed therapy	Neutral	• Assurance that medications are being taken	• Strictest definition may place undue burdens on patients • Sense of coercion on part of patient • Focus on single patient • Does not address other risks for poor outcomes (i.e. malnutrition)
Reminders, prompters, contracts, defaulter action	Neutral	• Relatively low cost • Relatively easy to implement	• Places all responsibility with patients • Does not address larger structural factors that may interfere with adherence
Physician/staff motivation, training, and supervision	Somewhat effective	• Potential to benefit multiple patients • Longevity of intervention	• Does not address larger structural factors that may interfere with compliance • Does not address patient factors
Patient/family education	Somewhat effective	• Improved understanding of disease process and need for therapy	• Education not enough to improve adherence
Incentives/enablers	Effective	• Can help address some structural factors that interfere with compliance	• Unclear which enablers are most effective
Program infrastructure	Most effective	• Longevity of intervention • Potential to benefit multiple patients	• Initial up-front costs may be relatively high
Comprehensive, community-based patient services	Most effective	• Multi-pronged and best addresses larger structural forces that interfere with adherence • Potential to benefit multiple patients	• Initial up-front costs may be relatively high

Links between TB and poverty are perhaps best summarized by Farmer and colleagues, who note that "cultural, political and economic factors, although inevitably important, cannot be of equal significance in all settings. Whereas cultural considerations, such as the nearly universal stigma attached to TB, may very well be of overriding significance in settings in the developed world, we would argue that they are often less so in Haiti, where so many factors are determined by economic constraints. The hoary truth that poverty and TB are greater than the sum of their parts is once again supported by data" (Farmer et al, 1991). Thus, best behavioral practices regarding TB must take into account the socioeconomic situations in which sick and poor TB patients find themselves. Attempts to address TB that are divorced from such an understanding will only lead to misconceptions on the parts of researchers and care providers, and poor health outcomes for patients. It is only when truly comprehensive care is offered to TB patients—including nutritional support, access to other medical services, and financial assistance, as well as efforts to address behavioral issues—that there can be hope to relieve the tremendous burdens of the millions suffering from the disease.

MOST IMPORTANT RESEARCH QUESTIONS IN THIS FIELD

- What are the best research methodologies that can be used to assess the impact of many of the behavioral interventions discussed in this chapter? How can such methodologies best be implemented?
- How can complicated variables—including those associated with TB outcomes on a structural level—best be operationalized and evaluated?
- How can broad definitions of improved clinical outcomes be incorporated when evaluating the impact of improved program infrastructure and comprehensive

patient services– for instance, overall mortality with long-term follow-up, possibility of socioeconomic stability of patient or patient-family units, cost-effectiveness analysis ?
- How can strategies incorporated in the field of TB be used to address overlapping health issues affecting the poor – e.g. HIV, substance abuse, TB, homelessness – in a comprehensive manner?

SELECTED REFERENCES

- Sumartojo, E. (1993) When tuberculosis treatment fails: a social behavioral account of patient adherence. Am Rev Resp Dis 147: 1311-20.

- Volmink, J., Matchaba, P., and Garner, P. (2000) Directly observed therapy and treatment adherence. Lancet 355: 1345-50.

- Volmink, J., Garner, P. (1997) Directly observed therapy. Lancet 349:1399-40.

- Farmer, P. Robin, S., Ramilus S., and Kim, J.(1991) Tuberculosis, poverty and "compliance:" lessons from rural Haiti. Semin Resp Infect 6: 254-260.

- Bayer, B., Stayton, C., Desvarieux, M., et al. (1998) Directly observed therapy and treatment completion for tuberculosis in the United States: is universal supervised therapy necessary? Am J Public Health 88: 1052-8.

- Farmer, P. (1997) Social Scientists and the New TB. Social Science and Medicine 44(3): 347-358

- Vermiere, E., Hearnshaw, H., Van Royen, et al. (2001) Patient adherence to treatment: three decades of research. A comprehensive review. J. Clin. Pharm Ther 26: 331-342.

REFERENCES

Addington W. (1997) Patient compliance: the most serious remaining problem in the control of tuberculosis in the United States. Chest 76:741-3.

Annas G. (1993) Control of tuberculosis: the law and the public health. N Engl J Med 328:585-8.

Barker J, Millard J. (2000) Directly observed therapy and treatment adherence [Letter]. Lancet 356:1030-1.

Bayer R, Wilkinson D. (1995) Directly observed therapy for tuberculosis: history of an idea. Lancet 345:1545-8.

Bock N, Sales R, Rogers T, et al. (2001) A spoonful of sugar…improving adherence to tuberculosis treatment using financial incentives. Int J Tuberc Lung Dis 5(1): 96-98.

Buchanan R. (1997) Compliance with tuberculosis drug regimens: incentives and enablers offered by public health departments. American Journal of Public Health 87(12):2014-17.

Centers for Disease Control and Prevention. (1998) Recommendations for prevention and control of tuberculosis among foreign-born persons: Report of the working group on tuberculosis among foreign-born persons. Morbid Mortal Wkly Rep 47 (No. RR-16):1-49.

Chaisson RE, Barnes GL, Hackman J, Watkinson J, Kimbrough L, Metha S, Cavalcante S, Moore RD. (2001) A randomized, controlled trial of interventions to improve adherence to isoniazid therapy to prevent tuberculosis in injection drug users. Am J Med 110:610-5.

Chaulk CP, Kazandjian VA. (1998) Directly observed therapy for treatment completion of pulmonary tuberculosis: consensus statement of the public health tuberculosis guidelines panel. JAMA 270:943-8.

Cuneo W, Snider D. (1989) Enhancing patient compliance with tuberculosis therapy. Clin Chest Med 10(3):375-80.

Curry FJ. (1968) Neighborhood clinics for more effective outpatient treatment of tuberculosis. N Engl J Med 279:1262-7.

Davidson H, Schluger N, Feldman PH, Valentine DP, Telzak EE, Laufer FN. (2000) The effects of increasing incentives on adherence to tuberculosis directly observed therapy. Int J Tuberc Lung Dis 4(9): 860-865.

Donovan K, Blake D. (1992) Patient non-compliance: deviance or reasoned decision-making? Soc Sci Med 45(5):507-513.

Farmer P. (1999) Infections and Inequalities: The Modern Plagues. Berkeley: University of California Press.

Farmer P, Robin S, Ramilus S, et al. (1991) Tuberculosis, poverty and "compliance:" lessons from rural Haiti. Seminars in Respiratory Infection 6(4):254-60.

Farmer P, Walton D, Becerra M. (2001) International tuberculosis control in the 21st century. In: Tuberculosis: Current Concepts and Treatment. 2nd ed (Friedman L, ed), pp. 475-96. Boca Raton, FL: CRC Press.

Fox W. (1958) The problem of self-administration of drugs; with particular reference to pulmonary tuberculosis. Tubercle 39:269-74.

Fox W. (1983) Compliance of patients and physicians: experience and lessons from tuberculosis – I. Brit Med J 287:33-35.

Garner P. (1998) What makes DOT work? Lancet 352:1326-7.

Hill AR, Manikal VM, Riska PF. (2002) Effectiveness of directly observed therapy (DOT) for tuberculosis: a review of multinational experience reported in 1990-2000. Medicine 81(3):179-93.

Jin BW, Kim SC, Shimao T. (1993) The impact of intensified supervisory activities on tuberculosis treatment. Tubercle Lung Dis 74:267-72.

Johansson E, Diwan V, Huong N, et al. (1996) Staff and patient attitudes to tuberculosis and compliance with treatment: an exploratory study in a district in Vietnam. Tuberc and Lung Dis 77:178-83.

Kamolratanakul P, Sawert H, Lertmaharit S, et al. (1999) Randomized controlled trial of directly observed treatment (DOT) for patients with pulmonary tuberculosis in Thailand. Transactions of the Royal Society of Tropical Medicine and Hygiene 93:552-57.

Lange RA, Ulmer RA, Weiss DJ. (1986) An intervention to improve compliance to year-long isoniazid (INH) therapy for tuberculosis. J Compliance in Health Care;1:47-54.

Malotte CK, Hollingshead JR, Larro M. (2001) Incentives vs outreach workers for latent tuberculosis treatment in drug users. Am J Prev Med 20(2):103-7.

Mangura B, Napolitano E, Passannante M, Sarrel M, McDonald R, Galanowsky K, Reichman L. (2002) Directly observed therapy (DOT) is not the entire answer: an operational cohort analysis. Int J Tuberc Lung Dis 6(8):654-61.

Moore M, McCray E, Onorato I. (1999) Cross matching TB and AIDS registries: TB patients with HIV coinfection, United States, 1993-1994. Publ Health Rep 114:269-77.

Morisky DE, Malotte CK, Choi P, Davidson P, Rigler S, Sugland B, Langer M. (1990) A patient education program to improve adherence rates with antituberculosis drug regimens. Health Educ Q 17:253-67.

Murray J. (1991) Tuberculosis and human immunodeficiency virus infections during the 1990s. Bull Int Union Tuberc Lung Dis 66:21-5.

Mushtaque A, Chowdhury R, Chowdhury S, et al. (1997) Control of tuberculosis by community health workers in Bangladesh. Lancet 350:169-72.

Nardell E. (1989) Tuberculosis in homeless, residential care facilities, prisons, nursing homes, and other close communities. Semin Respir Infect 4:206.

Perlman DC, Salomon N. (2000) Directly observed therapy and treatment adherence [Letter]. Lancet 356:1030.

Paramasivan R, Parthasarathy RT, Rajasekaran S. (1993) Short course chemotherapy: A controlled study of indirect defaulter retrieval method. Indian J Tuberc 40:185-90.

Pilote L, Tulsky JP, Zolopa AR, Hahn JA, Schecter GF, Moss AR. (1996) Tuberculosis prophylaxis in the homeless: a trial to improve adherence to referral. Arch Intern Med. 156:161-5.

Raviglione M, Dye C, Schmidt S, Kochi A. (1997) Assessment of worldwide tuberculosis control. WHO Global Surveillance and Monitoring Project. Lancet 350:624-9.

Raviglione MC, Pio A (2002) Evolution of WHO policies for tuberculosis control, 1948-2001. Lancet 359:775-80.

Sanmarti L, Megias JA, Gomez MN, Soler JC. Alcala EN, Puigbo MR, Majem LS. (1993) Evaluation of the efficacy of health education on the compliance with antituberculous chemoprophylaxis in school children. A randomized clinical trial. Tubercle Lung Dis 74:28-31.

Sbarbaro J. (1985) Strategies to improve compliance with therapy. Am J Med 97(Suppl 6A):34-7.

Seetha, M., Srikantaramu, N., Aneja, K., Singh (1981). Influence of motivation of patients and their family members on the drug collection by patients. Indian J Tuberc 28: 182-190.

Squire SB, Wilkinson D. (1997) Strengthening "DOTS" through community care for tuberculosis: observation alone isn't the key. BMJ 315(7120):1395-6.

Sumartojo E. (1993) When tuberculosis treatment fails: a social behavioral account of patient adherence. Am Rev Respir Dis 147:1311-20.

Vermiere E, Hearnshaw H, Van Royen P, Denekens J. (2001) Patient adherence to treatment: three decades of research. A comprehensive review. J Clin Pham Ther 26:331-42.

Volmink J, Garner P. (1997) Directly observed therapy. Lancet 349:1399-40.

Volmink J, Garner P. (2002) Directly observed therapy for treating tuberculosis (Cochraine Review). The Cochrane Library. Issue 4. Oxford: Update Software Ltd.

Volmink J, Matchaba P, Garner P. (2000) Directly observed therapy and treatment adherence. Lancet 355:1345-50.

Walley J, Newell J, Khan A. (2000) Directly observed therapy and treatment adherence [Letter]. Lancet 357:1031.

Walley J, Khan M, Newell J, et al. (2001) Effectiveness of the direct observation component of DOTS for tuberculosis: a randomised controlled trial in Pakistan. Lancet 357:664-669.

Werhane MJ, Snukst-Torbeck G, Schraufnagal DE. (1989) The tuberculosis clinic. Chest 96:815-8.

World Health Organization (1991) Forty-fourth World Health Assembly. Resolutions and Decisions. Resolution WHA 44.8. WHA44/1991/REC/1) Geneva: World Health Organization.

World Health Organization (1994) WHO TB Programme. Framework for Effective Tuberculosis Control. WHO/TB/94.179 Geneva: World Health Organization.

World Health Organization (1997) WHO Report on the Tuberculosis Epidemic. Geneva: World Health Organization.

World Health Organization (1999) Global Tuberculosis Control, WHO Report 1999. Geneva: World Health Organization.

World Health Organization (2002) STOP TB Annual Report 2001. Geneva: World Health Organization.

Zwarenstein M, Schoeman J, Vundule C, et al. (1998) Randomised controlled trial of self-supervised and directly observed treatment of tuberculosis. Lancet 352:1340-43.

Zwarenstein M, Schoeman JH, Vundule C, Lombard CJ, Tatley M. (2000) A random-ised controlled trial of lay health workers as direct observers for treatment of tuber-culosis. Int J Tub Lung Dis 4(6):550-4.

ENHANCING ANTIRETROVIRAL ADHERENCE:
A REVIEW OF PUBLISHED REPORTS OF RANDOMIZED CONTROLLED TRIALS AND ON-GOING NIH-FUNDED RESEARCH

Jane M. Simoni, David W. Pantalone, Pamela A. Frick and Barbara J. Turner

INTRODUCTION

In 1987, zidovudine, also known as AZT, became the first nucleoside reverse transcriptase inhibitor (NRTI) approved for use as monotherapy against HIV. However, monotherapy was soon found to be ineffective due to rapid development of resistance. Combination therapies known as Highly Active Antiretroviral Therapy (HAART) became the standard of care in 1995. By mid-2003, twenty antiretrovirals with five distinct mechanisms of action were available for treatment, often as part of complex, multi-drug antiretroviral regimens. A complex regimen may have consisted of 3 to 6 medications taken at 3 separate dosing times, each dose consisting of 1 to 20 pills, with 2 doses needing to be taken with a meal containing 30-40 grams of fat and 1 dose on an empty stomach. However, recent years have seen the introduction of simplified regimens with more drugs that can be administered on a once a day basis (Benson et al., 2004; Busti et al., 2004; Jayaweera et al., 2004). Research efforts persist in making regimens continually less burdensome and with less complex dosing instructions. These once daily regimens have the potential to contribute to increased adherence overall, for patients who have not developed resistance to the component drugs.

Numerous reports have documented that intensive combinations of antiretroviral medications can inhibit viral replication and reduce HIV-1 RNA to undetectable levels in the blood (Friedland and Williams, 1999). Improved virologic, immunologic, and clinical outcomes have followed the introduction of HAART (Hogg et al., 1998; Palella et al., 1998), with precipitous declines in HIV-

associated morbidity and mortality (Deeks et al., 1997; Palella et al., 1998).

However, the high degree of success with HAART in achieving undetectable HIV-1 RNA levels reported in clinical trials (i.e., 60-90%) has seldom been achieved in everyday practice (Carpenter et al., 1997). Indeed, studies in primary care settings suggest that, on average, 50% of patients achieve undetectable HIV-1 RNA (Casado et al., 1998; Nieuwkerk et al., 2001). A primary reason for the lack of success in clinical practice appears to be either intentional or non-intentional poor adherence to medication regimens (Liu et al., 2001; Rabkin and Chesney, 1999). For example, Singh et al. (1996) reported that only 63% of HIV-positive patients took more than 80% of their prescribed doses, and Murphy et al. (2003) reported that only 6% of patients reported full adherence, with a mean level of 56% adherence. Another study at an inner-city public hospital with high rates of infection through injection drug use also noted suboptimal adherence (Simoni et al., 2002). Few studies have been conducted comparing adherence of once-daily HAART to more complex dosing schedules. Initial evidence indicates that, while patients' report a preference for once-daily dosing, patients on once a day regimens do not report significantly higher rates of adherence than those on more complex regimens (Stone et al., 2004). Clearly, there are many variables that influence adherence, not just dosing schedule alone.

Several studies have demonstrated how successful outcomes on HAART depend greatly on patients' adherence to these medications (Bangsberg et al., 2000; Garcia de

Olalla et al., 2002). For example, in a study by Knobel et al., 43% of patients had an undetectable HIV-1 RNA level (<500 copies/mL) at 12 months after starting HAART and poor adherence was the only statistically significant variable associated with failure to achieve virologic goals.

Although it has been stated that an acceptable level of medication adherence usually ranges between 75-100% (Little et al., 1999), the level of adherence with HAART needed to obtain optimal long-term benefits appears to be over 90% (Bartlett, 2002; Paterson et al., 2000; Singh et al., 1999). Compared to adherence for most clinical conditions, HAART requires an unprecedentedly high level of adherence for an indefinite time period for optimal viral suppression.

Several other factors render combination therapies especially challenging for patients. These include the relative absence of significant symptoms related to HIV until later in the course of the disease; the recommended treatment may be considered as only prophylactic by some patients; long duration of treatment; questionable treatment efficacy; and frequent side effects.

In sum, adherence has proven to be the Achilles' heel of antiretroviral therapy. Providers, patients, and health care officials now recognize that adherence to HAART regimens requires substantial initial and ongoing support and monitoring. Effective approaches to promote and improve patient adherence to antiretroviral therapy are beginning to appear, as the literature evolves from early pilot trials to more methodologically rigorous randomized controlled trials (RCTs).

In this review of the research on interventions to improve adherence to HAART, we consider various definitions of adherence as well as its correlates. Because interventions to promote adherence in non-HIV-infected patients are covered in Chapter 13 of this volume, we focus our review on interventions to enhance antiretroviral adherence for HIV treatment (specifically HAART). We review published reports of RCTs as well as federally funded studies that are in progress. We conclude with recommendations for practice and directions for future research.

CONCEPTUALIZING ADHERENCE AND ITS CORRELATES

There is no universally accepted definition for medication adherence. Haynes originally defined "compliance" as "the extent to which a person's behavior (in terms of taking medication, following diets or executing lifestyle changes) coincides with medical or health advice" (pp. 2-3; Haynes, 1979). Later the term "adherence" was promoted because it was thought to connote a more collaborative and less authoritarian relationship with the medical provider. Stedman's Medical Dictionary defines "adherence" as "the extent to which the patient continues the agreed-upon mode of treatment under limited supervision" (Jani, 2002). More recently, the term "treatment maintenance" has been advanced as more indicative of the collaborative relationship between the patient as an active and involved participant and the provider as the professional guide toward establishing an individualized plan for successful treatment (Noring et al., 2001). With respect to HIV/AIDS care specifically, "medication adherence" has been defined as "the ability of the person living with HIV/AIDS to be involved in choosing, starting, managing and maintaining a given therapeutic combination medication regimen to control viral (HIV) replication and improve immune function" (Jani, 2002).

Few studies use similar measures of adherence. Two common approaches to defining a categorical outcome are to consider (a) whether the patient missed any pills over a specific interval or (b) whether the patient has exceeded a set percentage of doses taken. The latter threshold approach also may consider the timing of taking the medications (Fogarty et al., 2002). Less commonly, adherence is analyzed as a continuous variable, such as the proportion of prescribed doses taken as measured by an electronic drug monitoring (EDM) device, self-report, or pill count; the percentage of pills available for consumption by pharmacy refill records; or the number of missed doses over a specified time period, such as the last 3 days. For a systematic review of self-report measures of HAART adherence, see Simoni, Kurth, Pearson, Pantalone, Frick and Merrill (in press).

Many correlates of non-adherence have been identified from cross-sectional studies across various illnesses. Ickovics categorized these factors into four groups (Ickovics and Meisler, 1997).*Patient characteristics* include socio-demographic factors (which are generally not strongly related to non-adherence), active alcohol or other drug use, lack of social support, nondisclosure, poor general health, and psychological impairment and distress. *Aspects of the provider and the patient-provider relationship* include the provider's belief in the medication and how much the provider conveys this confidence to patients; the provider's ability, knowledge, and time to implement interventions to help his or her patients; and specific aspects of the provider's relationship with his or her patients, including its duration, consistency, openness, friendliness, genuine interest, empathy, mutual trust, and respect. *Variables related to the treatment regimen or illness* include the regimen's complexity (i.e., large number of medications, frequent doses, dietary restrictions, long-term duration, severe side effects, and various forms of administration) and the number of side effects. Patients are less likely to adhere when their illness is chronic and has asymptomatic periods, non-curative treatment, or no immediate effects of non-adherence. Also, *contextual factors* include macro-level issues such as whether the medical practice or clinic is far from the patient's home or has lengthy delays between clinic contact and appointments, inconvenient hours of operation, long waiting periods, lack of services such as child care, poor privacy, and inconsiderate staff. Other contextual factors include systemic issues such as poor access to drugs or inadequate health insurance, life situation issues such as homelessness and lack of steady income, and institutional systems such as prisons or hospitals that do not provide adequate access to medications.

With respect to correlates of non-adherence to HAART specifically, a number of empirical studies and reviews have found that several factors were often associated with non-adherence, including symptomatic disease and presence of adverse drug effects, neuropsychological dysfunction, psychological distress, lack of social or family support, increased complexity of the HAART regimen, low patient self-efficacy, and inconvenience of treatment (Ammassari et al., 2002; Deloria-Knoll et al., 2004; Hinkin et al., 2004; Kerr et al., 2004; Murphy et al., 2004; Reynolds, 2004).

One review summarized empirical support for correlates of adherence to antiretroviral therapy by dividing the correlates into factors related to treatment regimen, social and psychological factors, institutional resources, and personal attributes (Fogarty et al., 2002); statistically significant associations across more than one study corroborated most of these relationships.

PREVIOUS REVIEWS OF ANTIRETROVIRAL ADHERENCE INTERVENTIONS

The seriousness and urgency of problems related to non-adherence to antiretroviral medications have sparked increasing attention to this issue and reports of adherence interventions for HIV-infected persons are beginning to appear with increasing frequency in the literature. At least four prior reviews have attempted to summarize current knowledge.

Haddad et al. (2002) reviewed controlled research studies published from January 1996 to April 1999 on interventions offering patient support and education to promote HAART and identified only one intervention study (Knobel et al., 1999) that met their strict selection criteria. This study involved a pharmacist who offered a single one-on-one individualized educational session designed to provide detailed information about therapy and to help the participants fit the medication regimen into their lifestyle, followed by telephone support. At 24 weeks, participants in the intervention condition self-reported significantly improved adherence compared to those in the control condition, but they were no more likely to achieve an undetectable HIV-1 RNA level.

Fogarty et al. (2002) reviewed the field through April 1999 and identified 16 interventions designed to enhance HIV medication adherence of which 12 were in conference abstracts and 4 were in published articles The interventions incorporated strategies that were cognitive (i.e., designed to teach, clarify, or instruct); behavioral (i.e., designed to shape, reinforce, or influence behavior); or affective (i.e., designed to optimize social and emotional support). Of the 16 reports, only 11 included data on intervention efficacy, and the effects of these interventions were generally weak. Among these, only five were RCTs, with a mean sample size of 58. Four of these reported no treatment effect between the intervention and control groups, and the fifth - - a directly observed therapy study of AZT adherence (Wall et al., 1995) reported temporary effects that disappeared after the end of the intervention.

A third review focused on reports of RCTs of interventions to enhance adherence to HAART that were published or presented at the International AIDS Conference in Barcelona in July, 2002 (Ickovics and Meade, 2002). The authors cited three promising interventions among the published reports: the

Knobel et al. study as well as ones by Tuldra et al. (2000) and Rigsby et al. (2000).

The Tuldra et al. study (2000), based on Bandura's self-efficacy theory (Bandura, 1982) involved a psychologist who provided a single one-on-one educational session about the importance of adherence and managing adherence problems with the goal of increasing the patient's self-efficacy. In addition, a daily dosage schedule was developed. During follow-up visits at 4, 24, and 48 weeks, adherence was reinforced and any problems addressed. At 48 weeks, 94% of the participants in the intervention group, and (69% of the controls achieved a level of adherence of 95% or greater as measured by self-report (p=0.008). In addition, 89% of the intervention group and 66% of the control group had a viral load $\leq$ 400 copies/mL (p = 0.026). However, these effects were based on only 70 of the original 116 participants.

The Rigsby et al. 2000 study involved cue-dose training and monetary reinforcement (Rigsby et al., 2000). In four weekly sessions, counselors trained patients to time their doses based on personalized cues such as meal times or regular daily activities. They also used feedback from an Electronic Drug Monitoring system (EDM). For example, if a particular dose was missed repeatedly, the counselor would suggest an alternative cue. In a second arm, cue-dosing was paired with weekly cash incentives for correctly timed EDM bottle openings. Incentives began at $2 per correct dose (within 2 hours of dosing time) and increased with each consecutive correct dose to a maximum of $10 per day. If doses were missed or not taken within 2 hours of the specified dosing time, the reinforcement was reset to $2. During the intervention (weeks 0-4), participants who received both strategies (but not those receiving only cue-dosing) demonstrated enhanced adherence according to EDM relative to controls. However, the change was not sustained at follow-up (weeks 5 to 12).

From the AIDS Conference presentations, Ickovics and Meade (2002) cited two successful RCTs, one involving an internet-based paging system and the other using continuous and personalized counseling. However, two other RCTs that were presented, one assessing a problem-solving and enhanced support intervention and the other based on motivational interviewing, showed no intervention effects.

Finally, the current authors (Simoni et al., 2003a; Simoni et al., 2003b) conducted an earlier review that identified 21 published studies of HAART adherence interventions, most of which were pilot or feasibility studies. Ten studies included control or comparison groups, but only seven of these included the randomization to treatment or control conditions that define RCTs. Of these, only four incorporated a follow-up period of assessment (i.e., Knobel et al., 1999; Murphy et al., 2001; Tuldra et al., 2000; Rigsby et al., 2000). Three of the studies are described above. The Murphy et al. study (2001) involved five alternating individual and group sessions of behavioral strategies, patient information, social support, cognitive-behavioral therapy, and psychiatric nursing over 7 weeks. However, at the end of intervention and at 3-month follow-up, there were no significant treatment effects according to self-reported adherence. In addition to these published reported, the authors located and described 39 ongoing federally funded studies of HAART adherence interventions.

DATA SOURCES FOR THE CURRENT REVIEW

For the current review, we updated and expanded earlier work, examining both the published literature and ongoing federally funded research.

Published Articles

We searched PsycINFO and MEDLINE for articles published through January 2005

that contained various combinations of the terms *HIV/AIDS, adherence, compliance,* and *intervention* (also keywords for specific types of interventions, such as *education, telephone, pager, peer,* and *alarm*). We selected from this list all research articles describing primary reports of interventions to enhance antiretroviral adherence among adults that employed an RCT design of random assignment to treatment or control conditions.

Ongoing research funded by the National Institutes of Health (NIH)

Additionally, we searched CRISP (Computer Retrieval of Information on Scientific Projects, an on-line database of ongoing federally funded biomedical research projects), using the terms *HIV, medication, adherence, non-adherence, compliance, noncompliance, antiretroviral, ARV,* and *HAART.*

FINDINGS FROM CURRENT REVIEW
Published Articles

Our review of the published literature identified 15 RCTs, which are summarized in Table 1. For each, we attempted to provide information on the participants (i.e., *N*, basic demographic description, eligibility criteria, geographic location); the intervention strategies (i.e., duration, modality, intervener, and any theoretical framework); and main findings (i.e., method of adherence assessment and group differences). Few reports included all of this information, leading to many omissions in the table.

The studies are listed in the table by intervention strategy. The first category of *Cognitive-Behavioral and Individualized Counseling and Education Strategies* includes eleven studies with motivational interviewing, stress management, individualized assessment and education provision, problem-solving, and skills training strategies. A trained facilitator or adherence counselor was usually the intervener, but, when a provider was

Table: Published Randomized Controlled Trials of Interventions to Enhance Antiretroviral Therapy Adherence (15)

Authors	Participants	Intervention Strategy	Main Findings
Cognitive-Behavioral and Individualized Counseling and Education Strategies			
Di Iorio et al., 2003	Patients from an HIV clinic in the South-east U.S. with CD4 <200 (N=20)	Arm 1: Biweekly nurse-delivered 3-session motivational interviewing intervention (n=10) Arm 2: SOC (n=10)	At 2-week F/U: - No significant differences in self-report adherence - Arm 1 participants reported being more likely to follow the medication regimen as prescribed
Goujard et al., 2003	Men and women who were not pregnant, no partner in study, no active psychiatric diagnoses. Multiple sites in France University-based clinics (N=367)	Arm 1: Specially trained staff physicians and nurses develop a personalized educational plan based on the individual's problems with adherence, consisting of planning card with stickers, 3 one-hour educational sessions, and pill boxes Arm 2: Wait-list control	At 6-month F/U: - Intervention participants reported significantly increased adherence between baseline and 6 months, maintained at 12- and 18- month F/U - No direct impact on viral load or CD4 count
Jones et al., 2003	Multiethnic sample (54% Af Am, 18% Hisp) of women with AIDS in Florida, New York, New Jersey (N=174)	Arm 1: Therapists provide 10 sessions of group cognitive-behavioral stress management plus expressive support-ive therapy (n=92) Arm 2: Similar time (10 sessions) & content (stress management and coping with AIDS) in a weekly video format, consisting of a 45-minute education video and 75-minute entertainment video (n=82)	At 15-month F/U: -No significant adherence differences between arms - Those with very low adherence reported post-intervention adherence gains (0-40%) in both Arm 1 (p<.001) and Arm 2 (p<.01)

Knobel et al., 1999	Patients in Barcelona, Spain with VL > 5,000 and CD4 < 200 (N = 170)	Arm 1: A single one-on-one session with a pharmacist providing individualized assessment and adherence advice with F/U telephone support available as needed (n = 60). Arm 2: SOC (n = 110)	At 24-week F/U: -Adherence levels over 90% (by self-report or pill counts) were identified for 77% of Arm 1 and 53% of Arm 2 (p<.002) -No group difference in rate of undetectable VL
Murphy et al., 2002	HIV clinic patients referred by provider because of non-adherence who self-reported missing ≥ 1 dose per week (N = 79)	Arm 1: Five alternating individual and group sessions of behavioral strategies, patient information, social support, cognitive-behavioral therapy, and psychiatric nursing over 7 weeks (n=17) Arm 2: SOC (n=17)	At end of intervention and at 3-month post-intervention F/U, results for remaining pts (as treated, n=33): - No significant treatment effect by either self-report of dose adherence or of schedule adherence
Pradier et al., 2003	HAART patients who attended a medical follow-up consultation at Nice University Hospital, France (N=246)	Arm 1: Nurse-delivered 3-session individualized counseling and education intervention based on motivational psychology and client-centered empathic therapies to enhance self-efficacy and skills (n=124) Arm 2: SOC (n=122)	At 6-month F/U: - Arm 1 showed significantly higher proportion of adherent patients and a significant viral load decrease - Across arms, proportion with undetectable viral load was not different
Rawlings et al., 2003	HIV+ women with a detectable viral load, recruited from 25 sites (N=195)	Arm 1: Four modules of education and counseling with patients and their caregivers plus routine counseling on adherence, delivered by a health care provider (n=96) Arm 2: Routine adherence counseling alone (n=99)	At 20-week F/U: - No self-reported or EDM-measured difference between treatment arms at any point during the trial - No differences observed in virologic indicators

Study	Setting/Sample	Intervention	Results
Safren et al., 2001	Community health center (Boston, MA) clients considered at risk for non-adherence because they were starting or changing medications or who self-reported <100% adherence in the 2 weeks prior to enrollment ($\underline{N}$ = 56)	Arm 1: Single-session intervention presented by clinician or videotape utilizing cognitive-behavioral therapy, problem-solving, and motivational interviewing techniques + F/U telephone call at 1 week ($\underline{n}$=30) Arm 2: Two weeks of minimal contact and self-monitoring with pill diary ($\underline{n}$=26)	- Arm 1 self-reported % of pills taken in past two weeks increased significantly from baseline to week 2 (74% to 95%). - Minimal adherence increase in Arm 2 (84% to 90%). - At 12-week F/U, levels were maintained.
Smith et al., 2003	Participants initiating or switching to a new regimen at the Infectious Disease Clinic, University of North Carolina, Chapel Hill ($\underline{N}$=43)	Arm 1: Individualized patient education and skills training intervention, delivered by a nurse or pharmacist, including information exchange, skills development, self-monitoring, goal setting, and social support and self-incentives enlistment ($\underline{n}$=22) Arm 2: SOC ($\underline{n}$=21)	At 12-week F/U: - Intervention group had higher and increasing EDM-measured adherence compared to control group (p<.0017) - No significant differences observed in virologic indicators
Tuldra et al., 2000	Consecutive patients starting 1st or 2nd antiretroviral regimen in a university-affiliated HIV clinic ($\underline{N}$ = 116)	Arm 1: Psychologist provided a single one-on-one education session about the importance of adherence and how to manage adherence problems based on self-efficacy theory. At F/U visits (4, 24, and 48 weeks), adherence was reinforced and problems addressed ($\underline{n}$=55) Arm 2: SOC ($\underline{n}$=61)	At 48-week F/U in as treated analysis ($\underline{N}$ = 70): - 94% of Arm 1 vs. 69% of Arm 2 achieved $\geq$ 95% self-reported adherence in past month. - 89% of Arm 1 vs. 66% of Arm 2 had HIV-1 RNA levels $\leq$ 400 copies/mL.

Weber et al., 2004	Swiss HIV cohort study VL< 50 copies/ml within last 3 months and on stable antiretroviral therapy; no injection drug use (N=60)	Arm 1: Individual, 45-minute, cognitive-behavior therapy sessions delivered by doctoral-level, licensed psychologists or psychiatrists with the frequency of appointments determined by the provider and the client (mean=11 sessions, range 3-25, each session over 1 year) (n=31) Arm 2: SOC (n=27)	At 12-month F/U: - EDM-assessed adherence not significantly different between arms - Proportion of pts with adherence >=95% was significantly higher in Arm 1 compared to Arm 2 (p=.01) - Over the course of the study, significant decrease in adherence in Arm 2 (p=.006) but not Arm 1 - No significant differences on virologic outcomes or psychosocial measures

Reminder Aids or Behavioral Strategies Only

Haubrich et al., 2001	Predominantly low-income patients from 5 university-affiliated HIV clinics in CA (N = 206)	Arm 1: Bi-monthly feedback of HIV-1 RNA results for 12 months Arm 2: Semi-annual feedback of HIV-1 RNA results	- No significant differences in self-report adherence or CD4 count were observed - Arm 1 had a significantly greater reduction in viral load than Arm 2 (p=0.003)
Rigsby et al., 2000	Mainly male, African American, formerly drug-using clinic patients in West Haven and Hartford, CT (N = 55)	Four weekly sessions of: Arm 1: CD: Counselor led personalized cue-dose training (subjects identify daily cues for remembering dose times) + weekly feedback from EDM (n=22) Arm 2: CD + CR: CD and weekly cash reinforcement for correctly timed EDM bottle openings (n=15) Arm 3: Control group: Counselor-led inquiries and encouragement about adherence (n=18)	- During intervention (weeks 0-4), CD + CR group (but not CD group) relative to controls had enhanced EDM adherence - During F/U (weeks 5-12), CD + CR group (but not CD group) had a significant loss of EDM adherence gains relative to controls

Safren et al., 2003	Community health center (Boston, MA) clients less than 90% adherent according to initial 2-week EDM (N = 44)	Arm 1: Pager text messaging system for dose reminders, meal timing, and appointments + EDM monitoring (no feedback given to participants) (n=34) Arm 2: EDM monitoring alone (n=36)	At the end of the 12-week intervention: - Arm 1 showed significantly greater improvement in EDM adherence than Arm 2 (p<.004)
Affective Strategies			
Mann, 2001	Multi-ethnic women (40% Af Am, 35% Hisp) of low socioeconomic status (N = 44)	Arm 1: Write for at least 10 minutes, twice a week, about "a somewhat positive future in which they only had to take one pill each day for HIV" (n=21) Arm 2: No writing assigned (n=23)	Data stratified by self-reported level of optimism at baseline; at 4-week F/U: - Low optimism: No differences in adherence across Arms. - High optimism: Arm 1 reported significantly lower adherence than Arm 2 (p<.05)

Notes. All participants were HIV-positive adults on combination antiretroviral therapy unless otherwise noted. For comparative results, $p \leq 0.05$ was considered significant unless otherwise noted. SOC = Standard of care. F/U = follow-up.

involved, it was typically a nurse or pharmacist. These interventions were delivered in group settings, one-on-one, or via both modalities. The three studies in the second category of *Reminder Aids or Behavioral Strategies Only* considered more frequent HIV-1 RNA monitoring, personalized cue-dose training, monetary reinforcement, pager text messaging, and EDM monitoring and feedback. The third category of *Affective Strategies* referred to those designed to optimize social and emotional support, as Fogarty et al. (2002) defined the term. The only study in this category employed expressive writing about an optimistic future in which adherence regimens would be far less burdensome.

Findings from the 15 RCTs are mixed: 10 studies reported at least some significant differences in either adherence or clinical impact between the intervention and control arms, but in the remaining 5 studies there were no between-arm intervention effects. The findings are difficult to interpret because of the heterogeneity in the studies. The intervention duration varied from one session with follow-up to 10 sessions. While some studies reported results immediately post-intervention, others followed their participants for a year or more. Few analyses were strictly intent-to-treat and sample size ranged from 20 to 244 with likely impact on statistical power. The methods to assess adherence varied from various self-report formats to EDM; clinical impact in terms of viral load or CD4 was often not assessed. Moreover, among the 10 studies reporting some intervention effects, there were sometimes differences in self-reported adherence but not in the more direct measures of clinical impact. Post-intervention gains often were not sustained at follow-up. Indeed, in only two studies were interventions effects found for both adherence

behavior and clinical outcome at follow-up (Tuldra et al., 2000; Pradier et al., 2003).

The data provide no clear directives about intervention length or comprehensiveness. For example, some very brief interventions were successful at improving self-report adherence (e.g., Knobel et al., 1999; Tuldra et al., 2000), while other more intensive and comprehensive strategies were not (Murphy et al., 2002; Jones et al., 2003). Similarly, the data are inconsistent with regard to the most helpful content of a successful intervention. For example, in two studies, cognitive-behavioral treatment was part of an efficacious strategy (Safren et al., 2001; Weber et al., 2004); in two others it was not (Jones et al., 2003; Murphy et al., 2002). Equivocal data such as these make it difficult for researchers and providers alike to confidently move forward with any one particular intervention strategy.

Ongoing Research Funded by NIH

Our CRISP search identified 51 abstracts for on-going federally funded research involving interventions to enhance antiretroviral adherence. A summary appears in the Appendix. For each abstract we present information about study design, sample size, nature and length of intervention, measure of adherence and any other outcome measure, such as CD4 lymphocyte count and HIV-1 RNA levels. The studies in progress are divided into the same categories above with the addition of *Directly Observed Therapy (DOT) or Modified DOT Strategies*, which involve a provider, outreach worker, or peer who delivers every dose (or, in the case of modified DOT, almost every dose) of prescribed medication and watches the patient ingest the medication. The expense and complicated logistics of having a professional home-deliver every single dose renders strict DOT unfeasible, but researchers have designed creative alternatives. Some interventions take advantage of having a captive population (e.g., in prisons, hospitals, or methadone clinics) or deliver only the morning dose of a twice daily regimen or only the weekday doses, leaving other doses to be self-administered. The average duration of the interventions varies considerably, with some involving a gradual tapering of observed doses; however, there seems to be no consensus as to the optimal timeframe.

Novel strategies currently being tested include telephone or computer-delivered interventions; the involvement of a romantic partner or other family member; the targetting of providers; optimization of social and emotional support through peer support groups, a convenient mnemonic device, management of side effects, and the treatment of depression as well as a variety of modified DOT interventions.

GUIDELINES FOR BEST PRACTICE

Our review of the literature suggests we lack the empirical data necessary to make strong recommendations regarding the most efficacious way to improve HAART adherence. However, these early RCTs offer some encouragement regarding a range of strategies, including even brief individualized counseling and education, reminder aids in the form of pager text messages, and cue-dosing with monetary reinforcement (at least for the short-term).

Providers will need to make choices about adherence interventions based on factors specific to their clinic setting and patient population as well. For example, some of the interventions, such as motivational interviewing and cognitive-behavior therapy, require expertise beyond the skills of most staff. Also, different patient populations (e.g., women, active injection drug users) may find some strategies more appealing and thus

potentially more efficacious than others. The research to date gives us little guidance about how to customize interventions for specific settings or target populations, although this will likely be necessary given the lack of robust intervention effects thus far.

In the absence of conclusive empirical data, providers can turn to lists of strategies recommended by experts, which are based on methodologically limited data, research from adherence in other fields, empirically demonstrated correlates of adherence, and clinical experience. For example, the Best Practices Guide published on-line by the American Public Health Association (Jani, 2002) proposes a 4-step practical approach: (1) assess factors that may influence adherence and function as potential barriers; (2) develop and maintain a therapeutic alliance with the patient; (3) monitor the level of medication adherence with multiple measures; and (4) implement multiple targeted interventions to resolve barriers to adherence. Unfortunately, we still lack an accurate and well-accepted measure of adherence and a clear approach to defining and addressing potential barriers.

Chesney offered more specific advice, emphasizing the patient's role and conceptualizing adherence as a skill that can be learned when the patient masters specific tasks (Chesney, 1997; Chesney, 2003). She suggested that providers strive to: clarify the regimen; tailor it to the patient's lifestyle; teach the patient how to keep a medication diary, establish a time to set out pills, establish set places for pill taking, plan ahead for changes in routine, make special plans for weekends and holidays; have clinics lower barriers to care; invite patients to become active partners in care; refer patients to social services; and follow-up, monitor, and track adherence over time.

Turner offered similarly prescriptive guidelines: simplify and explain the regimen, provide reminder devices, discuss side effects, provide social support, and treat concomitant psychological disorders and substance abuse (Turner, 2002).

The American Psychological Association, in its congressional testimony, recommended the following: clarify the regimen; tailor it to individual lifestyles; facilitate interaction with clinic staff; identify and remove personal barriers to adherence; refer patients with special needs such as substance abuse to appropriate treatment; enhance self-efficacy (e.g., offer positive feedback for new skills, demonstrate problem-solving and ways to integrate the regimen into their lives); and create a social environment conducive to adherence (e.g., enlist support from patient's social network and maintain support of clinical team) (The American Psychological Association, 1997).

Finally, Stone offered strategies for optimizing adherence based on research and clinical practice for each of the four main groups of factors found to correlate with adherence – those focused on the patient, regimen, clinical care setting, or provider (Stone et al., 2001).

SUGGESTIONS FOR FUTURE RESEARCH

The body of research on improving adherence to HAART is growing rapidly. The gold standard study is the RCT, but RCTs need to have appropriate theoretical frameworks; adequate sample sizes, psychometrically sound and clinically useful outcome measures, clear and consistent operationalization of adherence and outcome, and better adherence assessment methods (Wendel et al., 2001). Additionaly, the authors should report the results according to the CONSORT statement's (http://www.consort-statement.org/) guidelines to facilitate the evaluation of studies and

comparisons among them. Effective interventions will likely need to combine strategies, given the relatively small effects observed from studies of single interventions, as well as expand the breath of adherence issues addressed by these interventions. Most of the intervention strategies have focused on patient characteristics; interventions are needed that focus on the provider and the patient-provider relationship, variables related to the treatment regimen or illness, and contextual factors. Better communication and collaboration among investigators may enhance the development of knowledge and reduce duplication of efforts; in the Appendix we provide a list of on-going studies to help in this dissemination process and there is currently an adherence list serve for researchers and clinicians (Note: to join, contact the first author). Most importantly, researchers need to submit and editors need to publish reports of interventions with nonsignificant treatment effects if the field is to avoid past mistakes and the needless evaluation of unpromising strategies.

Multi-factorial interventions leave a study vulnerable to the critique that it is impossible to distinguish which aspect of the intervention is the most effective. It is important to emphasize to reviewers and to researchers that adherence studies likely need to provide a combination of interventions to promote a long-term behavior such as adherence to medication. Since adherence behavior is dynamic, often decreasing initially in response to side effects or disease status (Ickovics et al., 2002), further research is needed about the timing of interventions. Front-loaded, prophylactic strategies are probably best, but when should they begin and how long should they last? What type and quantity of booster sessions are required? Studies need to demonstrate, if possible, how much time is required for complex behaviors like HAART adherence to become habitual and how quickly such behaviors extinguish.

As successfully tested interventions emerge, we also need to address the issue of efficacy vs. effectiveness – what works in RCTs might not work in clinics challenged by limited staff time and resources and diverse patient populations. What kinds of ancillary medical and mental health providers can assist the physician, nurse practitioner, or physician's assistant in the job of promoting and reviewing adherence? Can pharmacists take on the additional work of adherence counseling and how can they be compensated for their time? Is there a role for non-health care providers, such as peers or near peers, in on-going adherence work?

Given the complex array of factors associated with non-adherence, no one strategy is likely to be effective for every patient. Therefore, different sets of targeted interventions may be needed for special groups such as children, pregnant women, or active substance users. For example, all patients do not need DOT, but it may be that DOT and self-efficacy training in the context of a drug treatment program is necessary to help drug users adhere successfully to therapy. Unfortunately, the cost of such highly individualized interventions render them unfeasible to incorporate into most clinics. Such cost-effectiveness data are needed in the long term to assess the practical value of various types of interventions to promote adherence.

Finally, the international AIDS pandemic requires us to consider HAART access and adherence in resource-poor settings (Farmer et al., 2001). Initial studies are disproving fears about inadequate adherence levels in developing countries, but other issues remain unresolved. For example, will DOT or other strategies such as culturally relevant information, motivational, and skills-building strategies be most cost-effective? Given the possibility of transmission of resistant virus to drug-naïve individuals, it is important when initiating HAART in resource-poor countries to emphasize the importance of adherence and the risk of sharing medications (Lange et al., 2004).

CONCLUSIONS

Initial optimism regarding the efficacy of HAART has dissipated in the face of the onerous challenges of maintaining nearly perfect adherence indefinitely. Current research on correlates of adherence to HIV medications offers preliminary support for the efficacy of strategies such as assessing and addressing individual patient needs and barriers, nurturing the therapeutic alliance as well as other sources of social support, employing comprehensive and individualized cognitive and behavioral strategies, and continuously monitoring adherence with a variety of assessment methods. Empirical research focusing specifically on interventions to bolster HAART adherence is in an nascent but quickly burgeoning stage of development. Results of 15 RCTs lend some support to a range of strategies, including even brief individualized counseling and education, reminder aids in the form of pager text messages, and cue-dosing with monetary reinforcement (at least for the short-term). However, even these encouraging findings were marred by methodological limitations. Finally, a review of ongoing federally funded research revealed 51 adherence intervention projects evaluating a diversity of adherence strategies. Fortunately, intensive work is underway to address the seemingly intractable problem of HAART non-adherence.

ACKNOWLEDGEMENTS
We acknowledge Daniel Leatham for his assistance in tabulating the CRISP data.

APPENDIX:
ONGOING RESEARCH ON HAART ADHERENCE INTERVENTIONS FUNDED BY THE NATIONAL INSTITUTES OF HEALTH

Cognitive-Behavioral and Individualized Counseling and Education Strategies

ATKINSON, J. H. (DA012800). Better Antiretroviral Adherence: HIV+ Amphetamine Users. For HIV+ methamphetamine-dependent persons in early recovery, conduct a 3-arm, 24-week RCT (N=75 in each arm) comparing (1) SOC, (2) 2-months of Adherence Training alone, and (3) 2-months of Adherence Training with Stimulant Relapse Prevention. Outcome measures (at 6-month F/U) will include adherence (self-report, electronic monitoring, serum antiretroviral drug concentrations), HIV RNA, urine toxicology, substance use, quality of life, and neuropsychiatric status.

BLANK, M.B. (NR008851). Nursing Intervention for HIV Regimen Adherence among SMI. For HIV+ persons with serious mental illness (SMI), RCT (N=300) comparing (1) SOC to (2) an integrated intervention delivered by advance practice nurses and case managers. Intervention participants reporting <80% adherence will be triaged into a more intensive version of the intervention that gradually adds (a) involvement of family and significant others in prompting participants through use of beepers or mobile phones, and then (b) directly observed therapy. Outcomes at 24-months will include adherence, CD4, viral load, and high risk sex and substance use.

CAMP, C. J. (MH069199). HIV/AIDS and Aging: A Cognitive Clinical Intervention. For HIV+ older adults, RCT (N=60) comparing (1) a combination of external aids (pill boxes, checklists, calendars) to remind participants with a face-to-face spaced retrieval intervention (where patients are taught to retrieve information at increasingly long temporal intervals after initial presentation), with (2) a spaced retrieval intervention conducted over the phone. Primary outcomes include adherence, CD4 count, and viral load.

CATZ, S.L. (MH063644). Adherence Intervention for Incarcerated Persons with HIV. For incarcerated persons, RCT (N=112) comparing (1) a telephone-delivered intervention based on the transtheoretical model of behavior change and including motivational interviewing and behavioral skills training strategies, to (2) a telephone-delivered health education control intervention.

CATZ, S. L. (MH065858). Adherence Intervention–Late Middle-Aged/Older Adults. For HIV+ late middle-aged and older persons, development and pilot testing of individual-level and group-level adherence interventions based on motivational interviewing techniques and behavioral skills training.

CHAISSON, R. E. (RR000052). Improving Medication Adherence Among HIV Infected Patients. For clinic medical staff seeing HIV patients, RCT comparing (1) information-intensive interview to increase the practitioner awareness of patients' adherence to (2) SOC. Primary outcome is the patient's HAART adherence.

CUNNINGHAM, W. E. (HS010858). HIV intervention development study. For racial and ethnic minority individuals with HIV, RCT comparing (1) case management and adherence counseling intervention, to (2) SOC. Primary outcomes include treatment adherence, HAART adherence, and viral load suppression.

DIIORIO, C. K. (NR004857-04). An Adherence Intervention for Antiretroviral Regimens. RCT (N=240) of 12-week intervention comparing (1) SOC with (2) one in-person introductory session and four telephone-based motivational interviewing sessions, written self-help materials, and a self-help videotape.

DIXON, D. A. (MH064906). CBSM, Psychological & Physical Health in HIV+ Children. For school-aged children with HIV (N=50), RCT comparing (1) SOC+ an 8-week group cognitive behavioral stress management (CBSM) intervention on affective distress, physical health and adherence, to (2) a wait list control. Outcomes measures (baseline, post-treatment, 2 months F/U) include adherence, viral loads, disease progression, psychological distress, and coping.

ERLEN, J. A. (NR004749). Improving Adherence to Antiretroviral Therapy. RCT (N=300+51 for attrition) of (1) a 12-week structured telephone delivered intervention and a 3-month maintenance program, (2) a 12-week structured telephone delivered intervention and a 3-month maintenance program + 3 boosters over the next 6 months, and (3) SOC. Primary outcome measure will be electronic event monitors, with secondary measures of adherence diaries, 4-day recall, the self-reported medication-taking scale, and number of missed appointments.

FEASTER, D.J. (DA015004). Adherence in Recently Sober HIV+ Women: Ecosystemic Tx. In recently sober women, 4-month RCT (N=196) of (1) structural ecosystemic intervention (SETA) which targets the women, their families, and their social networks, and (2) an attention-matched HIV health group. Outcomes measures include adherence (self-report, EDM) and viral load.

FISHER, J. D. (MH066684). Changing ART Adherence Behavior. RCT of (1) intervention using Motivational Interviewing techniques to deliver individually-tailored ART adherence-related information, motivation, and behavioral skills (IMB), and (2) SOC.

GOLIN, C. E. (MH001862). Adherence to Antiretroviral Therapy: A Controlled Trial. RCT of an (1) intervention that trains patients with HIV to participate in decision-making and provides feedback, and (2) SOC. Primary outcomes are patient participation, patient and physician satisfaction with the medical visit, and the impact of patient participation on adherence.

GRINSTEAD, O.A. (MH067495). Eco-systems Therapy: Men Reintegrating with Their Family. For HIV+ men leaving prison, RCT (N=186) of (1) a family therapy intervention, Structural Ecosystems Therapy (SET), for the men and their families, and (2) an individually focused HIV transmission risk reduction comparison intervention. Outcomes include sexual and drug-related HIV transmission risk and increasing HIV-related medical adherence.

GROSS, R. (MH001584). Adherence to Protease Inhibitors in HIV. Planned RCT will evaluate (1) SOC, (2) a EDM-based beeper as a "mnemonic aide," (3) a case management intervention based on the social problem solving model, or (4) both a beeper and a program of case management.

HECKMAN, T. G. (MH067566). A Coping Intervention for HIV-Infected Older Adults. For persons 50 years of age and older living with HIV disease (N=300), 3-arm RCT comparing (1) a face-to-face coping improvement group intervention based on Lazarus and Folkman's (1984) Transactional Model of Stress and Coping, (2) a face-to-face information-support group intervention; or (3) SOC. Outcomes (collected up to 8-months F/U) include comorbid health conditions, cognitive functioning, sources of life stress, ways of coping, psychological distress, social support, health services utilization, treatment adherence, and quality of life.

HOLZEMER, W. L. (NR004846). Outpatient Nurse Managed HIV Adherence Trial. RCT (N=222) testing (1) SOC and (2) Client Adherence Profiling-Intervention Tailoring (CAP-IT), implemented by nurse case managers during regularly scheduled home care visits. Investigators will measure adherence as well as CD4 lymphocyte count, HIV-1 RNA level, and antiretroviral therapy resistance.

HOSEK, S. G. (MH064348). A Pilot Adherence Intervention for HIV-Infected Youth. For HIV+ adolescents and young adults, pilot RCT comparing (1) a cognitive-behavioral depression and coping skills intervention to (2) SOC.

INGERSOLL, K.S. (DA016554). Development of CART for HIV adherence and cocaine abuse. RCT (N=50) of (1) a 4 session, dual-focused motivational interviewing intervention for HIV+ cocaine abusers that both increases medication adherence and reduces cocaine use, and (2) SOC.

JOHNSON, M.O. (MH068208). RCT of an HIV treatment side effects coping intervention. RCT (N=278) of (1) a piloted, theory-based, one-on-one, five-session side effects management intervention administered by trained HIV clinical staff, and (2) a wait list control condition receiving SOC.

KANOUSE, D. E. (MH061695). A Training Intervention to Enhance Adherence to HAART. For patients either initiating or restarting (after a hiatus of at least 6 months) a HAART regimen (N=270), a 3-arm, 5-site RCT of (1) an adherence training intervention with psycho-educational components alone, (2) the same psycho-educational intervention + a brief practice trial of an inert medication regimen that mimics HAART, and (3) SOC. The primary outcome (12-month F/U) will be adherence (self report, electronic monitoring), viral load, CD4 count, and genotypic resistance.

KONKLE-PARKER, D. J. (NR009186) Multidimensional HIV Adherence Intervention. For a low-income minority population of HIV+ adults, pilot RCT comparing (1) an Information-Motivation-Behavioral Skills (IMB) intervention + communication skills training, operationalized by two individual face-to-face sessions and five telephone calls tapering over a 6-month period, to (2) SOC.

KURTH, A. E. (PS000066). Computer Assisted Rx Education for HIV-Positives: Care+. For HIV+ adults, 3-arm RCT (N=210) of (1) Computer-Assisted Rx Education for Positives (CARE+) including an HIV risk assessment, medication monitoring, tailored feedback, stage-based skills-building videos, motivational interviewing counseling, an integrated health promotion plan, and printout with referrals, (2) a computer risk assessment (to control for intervention effect of assessment), and (3) SOC. Primary outcomes (9 months F/U) are adherence by plasma HIV viral load and HIV transmission risk behaviors.

LEVENSKY, E. R. (MH069178). Intervention for Increasing Adherence to HIV Medications. For HIV patients with identified poor HAART adherence, RCT (N=90) comparing (1) an individualized assessment-based intervention, to (2) SOC. Outcomes include (20 weeks F/U) adherence to (self-report, pill counts, pharmacy refill records), viral load, CD4 count, psychosocial variables.

LEWIS, S. J. (DA016133). Antiretroviral-TIP for Substance Users. For HIV+ drug-involved individuals who are HAART-naïve or who have been on an extended break from treatment (> 3 months), conduct a pilot RCT comparing (1) a four-session, theory-based intervention that focuses on preparation for adherence before treatment is initiated, emphasizes commitment to adherence through increased knowledge, physician-patient collaboration, and negotiation strategies for removal of barriers to adherence, to (2) SOC.

MALOW, R. M. (DA013802). Cognitive Behavioral Treatment (CBT) of HIV + Drug

Abusers. For recovering drug abusers, RCT (N=320) of (1) SOC and (2) Cognitive Behavioral Stress Management intervention specifically for recovering drug abusers. Endpoints include distress and quality of life, drug abuse relapse, unsafe sex, antiretroviral therapy adherence, and health status.

MCDONNELL, M. K. (NR008094). Motivating HIV+ Women: Risk Reduction and ART Adherence. RCT of (1) SOC of an eight session attention equivalent control condition of a health promotion program led by a nurse health educator, and (2) a group intervention based on motivational interviewing consisting of eight nurse-led 90-minute sessions over 4-months. Adherence will be measured by self-report via audio computer assisted self-interviewing (ACASI), EDM, and a Multi-Component Adherence Index, HIV-1 RNA levels and CD4 lymphocyte counts will be obtained by chart review.

MITRANI, V. B. (DA016543). Family Therapy Mechanisms in HIV+ Women in Drug Recovery. For HIV+ women (N=172) in drug recovery, 4-month RCT comparing (1) Structural Ecosystems Therapy (SET) for the women and their families, to (2) an HIV health group. Outcome measures (12-months F/U) include functioning (self-report, observational methods) as well as individual measures for the female participants, includeing drug use, HIV medication adherence, and HIV risk behaviors. individual functioning of her family members (psychological distress, drug use and parent report of problem behaviors in children).

NAAR-KING, S. (DA014710). Motivational Therapy/Reduce Risk Behaviors/ HIV/ Youth. For HIV+ youth (ages 16-24), pilot study of 3-month RCT (N=60) comparing (1) wait-list control to (2) Motivational Enhancement Therapy, an empirically supported risk reduction intervention targeting the triad of risk behaviors (drug use, sexual behaviors,

and health behaviors). Outcome measures will be collected a 6 and 12 months post-intervention.

PARSONS, J. T. (AA013556). Adherence Intervention for HIV + Alcohol Users. RCT of 8-session intervention comparing (1) an attention control condition of standard education to (2) motivational interviewing and behavioral skills training based on the Information-Motivation-Behavioral Skills model. Primary outcome measures will be the biological markers for HIV-1 RNA level, CD4 lymphocyte count, and tests for alcohol use. Other outcome measures will include self-reported adherence, prescription refill data (via pharmacy records), adherence to medical appointments (via chart review), and self-reported alcohol use and alcohol related problems.

REMIEN, R. H. (MH061173). Serodiscordant Couples, Medical Adherence and HIV Risk. For serodiscordant couples, RCT of (1) SOC and (2) a brief, structured, theory-based intervention with the couples. Investigators will measure adherence to HIV medications, clinic appointment attendance, and prescription refills. Secondary aims of the study are to examine the relationship between attitudes and beliefs about effective medical treatments and sexual risk and participants' behaviors.

REYNOLDS, N. R. (NR005108). Improving ARV Adherence: Effects of Telephone Follow-Up. RCT (N=200) of a 36-week RCT based on self-regulation theory comparing (1) weekly scheduled telephone sessions with registered nurses specializing in HIV care with 16 hour/day pager access to (2) SOC. Outcome measures (3 years F/U) include adherence, quality of life, clinical events, and virologic and immunologic indicators.

ROSS, D. (AI045403). Promoting Adherence to Antiretroviral Regimens. For HIV+

outpatients initiating a new antiretroviral regimen, testing a 6-month RCT (N=216) comparing (1) SOC to (2) an Enhanced Adherence Promotion condition that systematically addresses specific psychosocial issues associated with medication adherence. Outcome measures (through 24 weeks F/U) include adherence (pill counts, self-report), viral load, CD4 count, and genotypic viral resistance.

SAFREN, S. A. (DA018603). CBT for Depression & Adherence in HIV Methadone Patients. For HIV+ individuals receiving methadone maintenance for opioid dependence, RCT (with 12-months F/U) comparing (1) CBT targeting both depression and HIV medication adherence, and (2) a single session HIV medication adherence intervention in conjunction with physician feedback regarding baseline study assessments.

SAFREN, S. A. (MH066660). CBT for HIV Medication Adherence and Depression. For patients with major depression and a detectable HIV-1 RNA level, RCT of 4-month intervention comparing (1) a single-session adherence intervention with (2) CBT for both major depression and antiretroviral therapy adherence. Control Group participants will be re-assigned to CBT after the initial phase of the study if they have not improved on key outcome variables

SIMONI, J. M. (MH058986). Peer versus Pager Support to Enhance Antiretroviral Adherence. RCT (N=240) of 3-month intervention comparing (1) SOC, (2) carrying an alphanumeric programmable pager, (3) having an HIV+ buddy to give peer support, and (4) having both a pager and buddy. Adherence will be assessed with self-reports, pharmacy refills, 3-day recall telephone interviews, and EDM. HIV-1 RNA level and CD4 lymphocyte count will be assessed as clinical outcomes.

WEISS, S. M. (MH055463) and TOBIN, J. N. (5R01MH061208). Behavioral Interventions for Women with HIV/AIDS. Two linked interactive research project grant applications for a multi-site clinical trial focused on poor women of color living with HIV/AIDS. Phase I: RCT (N=450) of (1) individual psycho-educational comparison condition and (2) cognitive-behavioral stress management training combined with expressive-supportive therapy. Phase II: RCT comparing (1) individual health educational control with (2) a group skills training program. Outcome measures will include medication adherence, nutritional intake and physical activity, sexual risk taking and substance use behaviors.

Reminder Aids or Behavioral Strategies Only

PAUL, R. H. (MH065857). Improving adherence to HAART in HIV. RCT (N=125) comparing (1) SOC + a pre-programmed wristwatch that will deliver a mnemonic aid (MA) to facilitate HAART dosing, to (2) SOC alone. Outcomes include adherence (electronic monitoring, pill count), CD4/CD8 cell count, plasma viral load, psychosocial variables, and cognitive functioning.

ROSEN, M. I. (DA015215). Contingent Reinforcement of Compliance in Drug Users. For patients with recent substance abuse, RCT of (1) intervention: supportive advice around self-reported compliance and advice around the use of cues, and (2) Incentives combined with EDM-Feedback Therapy. The primary outcome measure will be adherence as measured by EDM.

WILSON, I. B. (DA015679). Understanding and Improving Adherence in HIV Disease. Multiple baseline RCT (N=150) comparing (1) SOC to (2) EDM data being fed back to physicians in the form of a report, prior to outpatient medical visits. Detailed patient interviews will collect adherence data in addition to the EDM. Primary outcome measures for the intervention study will be changes in adherence as assessed by EDM and changes in HIV-1 RNA levels.

Affective Strategies

BANGSBERG, D. R. (MH063011). Depression Treatment to Improve ARV Therapy Adherence. For HIV+ homeless and marginally housed persons with depression, RCT testing the efficacy of (1) SOC and (2) antidepressant therapy. Investigators will examine five primary aims, including depression treatment, antiretroviral therapy adherence, duration of sustained antiretroviral therapy treatment, initiation of treatment, and viral suppression.

IRONSON, G.H. (AT002035). Efficacy of an Emotional Disclosure Intervention in HIV. RCT (N=200) comparing (1) a 4-session emotional disclosure writing intervention to (2) a 4-session control intervention. Primary outcomes are: HIV disease progression (HIV RNA viral load, HIV and non-HIV somatic symptoms, urinary and salivary cortisol, CD4 T-lymphocytes), health status, psychosocial variables, and health behavior.

SIKKEMA, K. J. (MH062965). Intervention for Coping with HIV and Trauma. For individuals who are HIV+ and experiencing trauma-related stress and psychiatric distress, RCT (N=240) comparing (1) SOC support group and (2) an HIV and trauma coping group. Outcomes include measurements of psychiatric distress, quality of life, rates of adherence to medical treatment, levels of substance use and sexual risk behaviors, and health status as indicated by HIV symptomatology and CD4 lymphocyte count and HIV-1 RNA level.

DOT or Modified DOT Strategies

ALTICE, F. L. (DA017059). Direct Observed Therapy/ Community-Released

HIV+ Prisoners. For HIV+ individuals recently released from prison, RCT of (1) an established DAART+ intervention to (2) SOC. Primary outcomes will be biological markers (HIV-1 RNA levels, CD4+ count, genotype), clinical (retention in clinical care, HIV quality of life), and behavioral (adherence to ART, relapse to active drug use.)

ALTICE, F. L. (DA013805). Directly Observed Therapy Among Active Drug Users. For HIV+ individuals not in drug treatment but attending needle exchange programs, RCT of (1) modified DOT dispensed HAART (one dose DOT and, for a twice a day regimen, a programmed reminder to take their next dose on their own) to (2) SOC. Primary outcomes will be adherence, reduction in HIV-1 RNA levels, and time to development of a primary HIV-1 resistance mutation. Secondary outcomes include quality of life measures, health care utilization and entry into drug treatment.

ARNSTEN, J. H. (DA015302). Efficacy and cost of HAART DOT in methadone clinics. In methadone maintenance clinics, 24-week RCT of (1) HAART DOT in methadone maintenance clinics at which HIV primary care is provided versus (2) self-administered HAART. Outcome measures will include both biological markers (viral load, CD4 count) and adherence (self-report, electronic monitoring).

BANGSBERG, D. R. (MH064388). A RCT of HIV Adherence Case Management and Modified DOT. For a sample of homeless and marginally housed HIV individuals (N=336), a 3-arm, 6-month RCT comparing (1) Adherence Case Management (ACM), (2) Modified Directly Observed Therapy (MDOT), and (3) SOC. Outcomes include adherence (self-report ACASI, unannounced pill count), changes in HIV-1 viral load, development of viral resistance, and cost effectiveness of the intervention.

CHAISSON, R. E. (AI055359). <u>DOT-HAART for HIV-Infected South African Adults</u>. RCT (N=200) comparing (1) Peer-DOT-HAART using patient-nominated peer supervisors/advocates, and (2) or self-administration of a once-daily HAART-regimen, each for 24-months. Outcomes include treatment adherence, CD4 count, viral load, genotypic resistance, incidence of opportunistic infections.

FLANIGAN, T. P. (DA013767). <u>Directly Observed Antiretroviral Therapy for Active Substance Abusers</u>. For active substance users on a one-a-day antiretroviral therapy regimen, RCT (<u>N</u>=120) of 18-month intervention comparing (1) SOC with self-administration of medications to (2) 12-months of daily directly observed therapy (DOT) followed by a 6-month gradual tapering phase. Adherence will be assessed by patient self-report in an ACASI questionnaire. HIV-1 RNA quantification, drug resistance testing by genotype, and CD4 lymphocyte count determinations will be used to assess the effect of DOT on virologic suppression and development of resistance.

GOGGIN, K. J. (MH068197). <u>ART Adherence: Observed Therapy and Enhanced Counseling</u>. For patients starting a new HAART regimen, 3-arm RCT comparing (1) observed therapy + enhanced counseling (a motivational interviewing approach), (2) enhanced counseling alone, and (3) SOC. Outcomes include adherence and viral load.

MITTY, J. A. (DA017622). <u>DOT and Prevention for HIV(+) Persons Leaving Prison</u>. For HIV+ individuals transitioning to the community after release from the Adult Correctional Institution in Rhode Island, pilot testing (N=50) of an RCT comparing (1) a combined modified directly observed therapy and secondary prevention intervention, to (20 SOC. Outcome measures (during first 6-months post-release) will include viral load suppression and self-reported HIV-risk behaviors.

REFERENCES

American Psychological Association. (1997) APA Testimony on the Adherence to HIV/AIDS Drug Therapy. Retrieved July 29, 1998, from the World Wide Web: http://www.apa.org/ppo/aids.html.

Ammassari A, Trotta MP, Murri R, Castelli F, Narciso P, Noto P, Vecchiet J, D'Arminio MA, Wu AW, Antinori A. (2002) Correlates and predictors of adherence to highly active antiretroviral therapy: overview of published literature. J Acquir Immune Defic Syndr 31:S123-S127.

Babudieri S, Aceti A, D'Offizi GP, Carbonara S, Starnini G. (2000) Directly observed therapy to treat HIV infection in prisoners. JAMA 284:712-715.

Bamberger JD, Unick J, Klein P, Fraser M, Chesney M , Katz MH. (2000) Helping the urban poor stay with antiretroviral HIV drug therapy. Am J Public Health 90:699-701.

Bandura A. (1982) Self-efficacy mechanisms in human agency. Am Psychol 37:122-147.

Bangsberg DR, Hecht FM, Charlebois ED, Zolopa AR, Holodniy M, Sheiner L, Bamberger JD, Chesney MA, Moss A. (2000) Adherence to protease inhibitors, HIV-1 viral load and development of drug resistance in an indigent population. AIDS 14:357-366.

Bartlett JA. (2002) Addressing the challenges of adherence. J Acquir Immune Defic Syndr 29:S2-S10.

Benson CA, van der Horst C, Lamarca A, Haas DW, McDonald CK, Steinhart CR, Rublein J, Quinn JB, Mondou E, Rousseau F; FTC-303/350 Writing Group. (2004). A randomized study of emtricitabine and lamivudine in stably suppressed patients with HIV. AIDS 18(17):2269-76.

Broadhead RS, Heckathorn DD, Altice FL, van Hulst Y, Carbone M, Friedland GH, O'Connor PG, Selwyn PA. (2002) Increasing drug users' adherence to HIV treatment: results of a peer-driven intervention feasibility study. Soc Sci Med 55:235-246.

Busti AJ, Hall RG, Margolis DM. (2004). Atazanavir for the treatment of human immunodeficiency virus infection. Pharmacotherapy 24(12):1732-47.

Carpenter CC, Fischl MA, Hammer SM, Hirsch MS, Jacobsen DM, Katzenstein DA, Montaner JS, Richman DD, Saag MS, Schooley RT, Thompson MA, Vella S, Yeni PG, Volberding PA. (1997) Antiretroviral therapy for HIV infection in 1997. Updated recommendations of the International AIDS Society-USA panel. JAMA 277:1962-1969.

Casado JL, Perez-Elias MJ, Antela A, Sabido R, Marti-Belda P, Dronda F, Blazquez J, Quereda C. (1998) Predictors of long-term response to protease inhibitor therapy in a cohort of HIV-infected patients. AIDS 12:F131-F135.

Chesney M. (2003). Adherence to HAART regimens. AIDS Patient Care & STDS. 17(4):169-77.

Chesney MA. (1997) Compliance: How you can help. Retrieved December 12, 2002, from the World Wide Web: http://www.hivnewsline.com/issues/Vol3I ssue3/comply.html

Deeks SG, Smith M, Holodnly M, Kahn JO. (1997) HIV-1 protease inhibitors: A review for clinicians. JAMA 277:145-153.

Deloria-Knoll M, Chmiel JS, Moorman AC, Wood KC, Holmberg SD, Palella FJ; HIV Outpatient Study (HOPS) Investigators. (2004). Factors related to and consequences of adherence to

antiretroviral therapy in an ambulatory HIV-infected patient cohort. AIDS Patient Care STDS 18(12):721-7.

Dunbar PJ, Madigan D, Grohskopf LA, Revere D, Woodward J, Minstrell J, Frick PA, Simoni JM, Hooton TM. (2003) A two-way messaging system to enhance antiretroviral adherence. J Am Med Inform Assoc 10:11-15.

Farmer P, Leandre F, Mukherjee JS, Claude MS, Nevil P, Smith-Fawzi MC, Koenig SP, Castro A, Becerra MC, Sachs J, Attaran A, Kim JY. (2001) Community-based approaches to HIV treatment in resource-poor settings. Lancet 358:404-409.

Fogarty L, Roter D, Larson S, Burke J, Gillespie J, Levy R. (2002) Patient adherence to HIV medication regimens: a review of published and abstract reports. Patient Education and Counseling 46:93-108.

Friedland GH, Williams A. (1999) Attaining higher goals in HIV treatment: the central importance of adherence. AIDS 13:S61-S72.

Garcia de Olalla P, Knobel H, Carmona A, Guelar A, Lopez-Colomes JL, Cayla J A. (2002) Impact of adherence and highly active antiretroviral therapy on survival in HIV-infected patients. J Acquir Immune Defic Syndr 30:105-110.

Haddad M, Inch C, Glazier RH, Wilkins AL, Urbshott GB, Bayoumi A, Rourke S. (2002) Patient support and education for promoting adherence to highly active antiretroviral therapy for HIV/AIDS (Cochrane Review). Cochrane Database System Review:CD001442.

Haubrich RH, Little SJ, Currier JS, Forthal DN, Kemper CA, Beall GN, Johnson D, Dube MP, Hwang JY, McCutchan JA, the California Collaborative Treatment Group. (1999) The value of patient-reported adherence to antiretroviral therapy in predicting virologic and immunologic response. AIDS 13:1099-1107.

Haynes RB. (1979) Introduction. In D. W. T. R. B. Haynes, D. L. Sackett (Ed.), Compliance in Health Care (pp. 1-10). Baltimore, MD: Johns Hopkins University.

Hinkin CH, Hardy DJ, Mason KI, Castellon SA, Durvasula RS, Lam MN, Stefaniak M. (2004) Medication adherence in HIV-infected adults: effect of patient age, cognitive status, and substance abuse. AIDS 18:S19-25.

Hogg, R. S., Heath, K. V., Yip, B., Craib, K. J. P., O'Shaughnessy, M. V., Schechter, M. T., Mantaner, J. S. G. (1998). Improved survival among HIV-infected individuals following initiation of antiretroviral therapy. JAMA 279:450-454.

Holzemer WL, Henry SB, Portillo CJ, Miramontes H. (2000) The client adherence profiling-intervention tailoring (CAP-IT) intervention for enhancing adherence to HIV/AIDS medications: a pilot study. J Assoc Nurses AIDS Care 11:36-44.

Ickovics JR, Meade CS. (2002) Adherence to antiretroviral therapy among patients with HIV: a critical link between behavioral and biomedical sciences. J Acquir Immune Defic Syndr 31:S98-S102.

Ickovics JR, Meisler AW. (1997) Adherence in AIDS clinical trials: a framework for clinical research and clinical care. J Clin Epidemiol 50:385-391.

Jani AA. (2002, June) Adherence to HIV treatment regimens: Recommendations for best practices. Retrieved December 12, 2002, from the World Wide Web: http://www.apha.org/ppp/hiv/Best_Practices.pdf.

Jayaweera DT, Kolber MA, Brill M, Tanner T, Campo R, Rodriguez A, Chu HM, Garg V. (2004) Effectiveness and tolerability of a once-daily amprenavir/ritonavir-containing highly active antiretroviral therapy regimen in antiretroviral-naive patients at risk for non-adherence: 48-week results after 24 weeks of directly observed therapy. HIV Med 5(5):364-70.

Kerr T, Palepu A, Barness G, Walsh J, Hogg R, Montaner J, Tyndall M, Wood E. (2004). Psychosocial determinants of adherence to highly active antiretroviral therapy among injection drug users in Vancouver. Antivir Ther 9(3):407-14.

Kirkland LR, Fischl MA, Tashima KT, Paar D, Gensler T, Graham NM, Gao H, Rosenzweig JRC, McClernon DR, Pittman G, Hessenthaler SM, Hernandez JE, the NZTA4007 Study Team. (2002) Response to lamivudine-zidovudine plus abacavir twice daily in antiretroviral-naive, incarcerated patients with HIV infection taking directly observed treatment. Clin Infect Dis 34:511-518.

Knobel H, Carmona A, Lopez JL, Gimeno JL, Saballs P, Gonzalez A, Guelar A, Diez A. (1999) Adherence to very active antiretroviral treatment: impact of individualized assessment. Enferm Infecc Microbiol Clin 17:78-81.

Knobel H, Guelar A, Carmona A, Espona M, Gonzalez A, Lopez-Colomes JL, Saballs P, Gimeno JL, Diez A. (2001) Virologic outcome and predictors of virologic failure of highly active antiretroviral therapy containing protease inhibitors. AIDS Patient Care and STDs 15:193-199.

Lange, JM, Perriens, J, Kuritzkes, D, Zewdie, D. (2004) What policymakers should know about drug resistance and adherence in the context of scaling-up treatment of HIV infection. AIDS :S69-74.

Lanzafame M, Trevenzoli M, Cattelan AM,

Rovere P, Parrinello A. (2000) Directly observed therapy in HIV therapy: a realistic perspective? J Acquir Immune Defic Syndr 25:200-201.

Little SJ, Daar ES, D'Aquila RT, Keiser PH, Connick E. (1999) Reduced antiretroviral drug susceptibility among patients with primary HIV infection. JAMA 282:1142-1149.

Liu H, Golin CE, Miller LG, Hays RD, Beck CK, Sanandaji S, Christian J, Maldonado T, Duran D, Kaplan AH, Wenger NS. (2001) A comparison study of multiple measures of adherence to HIV protease inhibitors. Ann Intern Med 134:968-977.

Malow RM, McPherson S, Klimas N, Antoni MH, Schneiderman N, Penedo FJ, Ziskind D, Page B, McMahon R. (1998) Alcohol & drug abuse: adherence to complex combination antiretroviral therapies by HIV-positive drug abusers. Psychiatr Serv 49.

Mann T. (2001) Effects of future writing and optimism on health behaviors in HIV-infected women. Ann Behav Med 23:26-33.

Martin J, Sabugal GM, Rubio R, Sainz-Maza M, Blanco JM, Alonso JL, Dominguez J. (2001) Outcomes of a health education intervention in a sample of patients infected by HIV, most of them injection drug users: possibilities and limitations. AIDS Care 13:467-473.

McCance-Katz EF, Gourevitch MN, Arnsten JH, Sarlo J, Rainey P, Jatlow P. (2002) Modified directly observed therapy (MDOT) for injection drug users with HIV disease. Am J Addict 11:271-278.

McPherson-Baker S, Malow RM, Penedo F, Jones DL, Schneiderman N, Klimas NG. (2000) Enhancing adherence to combination antiretroviral therapy in non-adherent HIV-positive men. AIDS Care 12:399-404.

Mitty JA, Stone VE, Sands M, Macalino G, Flanigan T. (2002) Directly observed therapy for the treatment of people with HIV infection: a work in progress. Clin Infect Dis 34:984-990.

Murphy DA, Lu MC, Martin D, Hoffman D, Marelich WD. (2002) Results of a Pilot Intervention Trial to Improve Antiretroviral Adherence Among HIV-Positive Patients. J Assoc Nurses AIDS Care 13:57-69.

Murphy DA, Marelich WD, Hoffman D, Steers WN. (2004) Predictors of anti-retroviral adherence. AIDS Care 16(4):471-84.

Murphy DA, Roberts KJ, Hoffman D, Molina A, Lu MC. (2003) Barriers and successful strategies to antiretroviral adherence among HIV-infected monolingual Spanish-speaking patients. AIDS Care 15(2):217-30.

Nieuwkerk PT, Sprangers MA, Burger DM, Hoetelmans RM, Hugen PW, Danner SA, Ende MEVD, Schneider MM, Schrey G, Meenhorst P L, Sprenger HG, Kauffmann RH, Jambroes M, Chesney MA, Wolf FD, Lange JM, Athena Project. (2001) Limited patient adherence to highly active antiretroviral therapy for HIV-1 infection in an observational cohort study. Arch Intern Med 161:1962-1968.

Noring S, Dubler NN, Birkhead G, Agins B. (2001) A new paradigm for HIV care: ethical and clinical considerations. Am J Public Health 91:690-694.

Palella FJ, Delaney KM, Moorman AC, Loveless MO, Fuhrer J, Satten GA, Aschman DJ, Holmberg SD, The HIV Outpatient Study Investigators. (1998) Declining morbidity and mortality among patients with advanced human immunodeficiency virus infection. N Engl J Med 338:853-860.

Paterson DL, Swindells S, Mohr J, Brester M,

Vergis EN, Squier C, Wagener MM, Singh N. (2000) Adherence to protease inhibitor therapy and outcomes in patients with HIV infection. Ann Intern Med 133:21-30.

Rabkin JG, Chesney MA. (1999) Treatment adherence to HIV medications. In D. G. O. S. C. Kalichman (Ed.), Psychosocial and Public Health Impact of New HIV Therapies (pp. 61-82). New York: Kluwer Academic/Plenum Publishers.

Reynolds NR. (2004) Adherence to antiretroviral therapies: state of the science. Current HIV Research 2(3):207-14.

Rigsby MO, Rosen MI, Beauvais JE, Cramer JA, Rainey PM, O'Malley SS, Dieckhaus KD, Rounsaville BJ. (2000) Cue-dose training with monetary reinforcement: pilot study of an antiretroviral adherence intervention. J Gen Intern Med 15:841-847.

Rogers AS, Miller S, Murphy DA, Tanney M, Fortune T. (2001) The TREAT (therapeutic regimens enhancing adherence in teens) program: theory and preliminary results. J Adolesc Health 29:30-38.

Safren SA, Otto MW, Worth JL. (1999) Life-Steps: applying cognitive behavioral therapy to HIV medication adherence. Cognitive and Behavioral Practice 6:332-341.

Safren SA, Otto MW, Worth JL, Salomon E, Johnson W, Mayer K, Boswell S. (2001) Two strategies to increase adherence to HIV antiretroviral medication: life-steps and medication monitoring. Behav Res Ther 39:1151-1162.

Simoni JM, Frick PA, Lockhart D, Liebovitz D. (2002) Mediators of social support and antiretroviral adherence. AIDS Patient Care and STDs 16:431-439.

Simoni JM, Frick PA, Pantalone DW, Turner, BJ. (2003) Antiretroviral adherence interventions: A review of current literature and ongoing studies. Topics in HIV Medicine 11(6):185-198.

Simoni JM, Frick PA, Pantalone DW, Turner, BJ. (2003). Enhancing antiretroviral adherence: Review of an emerging field. In J. A. Trafton & W. Gordon (Eds.), Best practices in the behavioral management of chronic disease. Los Altos, CA: Institute for Disease Management.

Singh N, Berman SM, Swindells S, Justis JC, Mohr JA, Squier C, Wagener M. (1999) Adherence of human immunodeficiency virus-infected patients to antiretroviral therapy. Clin Infect Dis 29:824-830.

Singh, N., Squier, C., Sivek, C., Wagener, M., Nguyen, M. H., Yu, V. L. (1996). Determinants of compliance with antiretroviral therapy in patients with human immunodeficiency virus: prospective assessment with implications for enhancing compliance. AIDS Care 8:261-269.

Stenzel MS, McKenzie M, Mitty JA, Flanigan TP. (2001) Enhancing adherence to HAART: a pilot program of modified directly observed therapy. The AIDS Reader 11:317-328.

Stone VE, Hogan JW, Schuman P, Rompalo AM, Howard AA, Korkontzelou C, Smith DK, HERS Study. (2001) Antiretroviral regimen complexity, self-reported adherence, and HIV patients' understanding of their regimens: survey of women in the HERS study. J Acquir Immune Defic Syndr 28:124-131.

Stone VE, Jordan J, Tolson J, Miller R, Pilon T. (2004) Perspectives on Adherence and Simplicity for HIV-Infected Patients on Antiretroviral Therapy: Self-Report of the Relative Importance of Multiple Attributes of Highly Active Antiretroviral Therapy (HAART) Regimens in Predicting Adherence. J Acquir Immune

Defic Syndr 36(3):808-816.

Tuldra A, Fumaz CR, Ferrer MJ, Bayes R, Arno A, Balague M, Bonjoch A, Jou A, Negredo E, Paredes R, Ruiz L, Romeu J, Sirera G, Tural C, Burger D, Clotet B. (2000) Prospective randomized two-arm controlled study to determine the efficacy of a specific intervention to improve long-term adherence to highly active antiretroviral therapy. J Acquir Immune Defic Syndr 25:221-228.

Turner BJ. (2002) Adherence to antiretroviral therapy by human immunodeficiency virus-infected patients. J Infect Dis 185:S143-S151.

Wall TL, Sorensen JL, Batki SL, Delucchi KL, London JA, Chesney MA. (1995) Adherence to zidovudine (AZT) among HIV-infected methadone patients: a pilot study of supervised therapy and dispensing compared to usual care. Drug Alcohol Dependence 37:261-269.

Wendel CS, Mohler MJ, Kroesen K, Ampel NM, Gifford AL, Coons SJ. (2001) Barriers to use of electronic adherence monitoring in an HIV clinic. Ann Pharmacother 35:1010-1015.

PRIMARY PREVENTION OF CARDIOVASCULAR DISEASE

Lora E. Burke

INTRODUCTION

Coronary heart disease (CHD), the most common manifestation of heart disease, remains the number one cause of death and disability in the U.S. In 1968, following three decades of rising CHD mortality rates, (Daviglus and Stamler, 2001), the U. S. began to experience a downward trend in deaths due to CHD. However, during the 1990s the rate of that decline slowed. Several factors have been invoked to explain these trends. The decline in mortality rate is due to prevention counseling and lifestyle interventions that target individuals at increased risk, which have been shown to reduce morbidity and mortality (Ketola et al., 2000), as well as the prevention efforts of the national government and volunteer and private organizations (Daviglus and Stamler, 2001). Population surveys show that two-thirds of the people reported making several changes in their eating habits, including changes related to dietary fats, calories, blood cholesterol, and blood pressure; and that these changes were made because of advice from health professionals or information received from mass media. Concordant with these changes, the average serum cholesterol in the population declined from approximately 235 mg/dl in the 1960s to 205 mg/dl in the late 1980s and early 1990s (Cooper et al., 2000). Moreover, mean blood pressure levels are lower and the national statistics for smoking are lower (Burt et al, 1995; Garfinkel, 1997). The slowing of the mortality decline in the 1990s may be due to several factors, such as increased prevalence in the US population of overweight and obesity and type 2 diabetes, lack of physical activity, and a lack of interventions addressing these factors.

Among the array of factors related to the development of CHD, lifestyle factors play an important role. Included in lifestyle are consuming calorie-dense, high fat diets, smoking cigarettes, and leading a sedentary life. Documented evidence exists that reduction in CHD risk factors have lead to reductions in CHD incidence and mortality (Goldman et al, 2001). Widespread population-based educational programs, in addition to individual interventions, are responsible for widespread changes in risk factors such as consuming a high fat diet, leading a sedentary life, and having an elevated blood pressure or cholesterol level (Goldman et al., 2001; Daviglus and Stamler, 2001). The purpose of this chapter is to review tested behavioral interventions for the prevention of heart disease. Because several CHD risk factors, such as cigarette smoking, diabetes, and obesity are addressed in other chapters in this text, the focus of this chapter is primary prevention strategies for changing eating behaviors and physical activity patterns among children and adults.

REVIEW METHOD

The ensuing review addresses CHD primary prevention strategies with a focus on lifestyle changes. In conducting the search for randomized clinical trials (RCT) with at least one year of post-randomization follow-up, several electronic databases were searched, e.g., Medline, PsychInfo. The search strategy included several key terms, such as primary prevention of CHD, lifestyle, diet, exercise/physical activity, behavioral management and behavioral modification. In addition, relevant papers were hand-searched for additional citations. The review includes papers published since 1990. Despite the efforts employed in this search, it is possible that reports of RCT meeting the criteria were inadvertently missed. However, the 13 studies reviewed here are representative of primary prevention studies focused on changing eating or exercise behaviors to prevent the development of heart disease.

Table 1 outlines the sample, intervention and results of the 13 studies. Each study was given an effectiveness rating for the intervention strategy that was based on the clinical outcome and the retention of participants. The ratings are on a 4-point scale: 0 (neutral, no difference), 1 (mildly effective), 2 (moderately effective), and 3 (most effective). All studies were at least mildly effective in changing the targeted behaviors.

RESULTS OF REVIEW

The 13 studies reviewed are categorized as (1) interventions for children, (2) workplace interventions, and (3) community/clinical interventions. Two studies focused on school age children, while the other 11 studies addressed primary prevention in adults, two took place at worksites, four trials recruited participants from the general population, and four took place in primary care or general practice settings.

The Dietary Intervention Study in Children (DISC) reported sustained reduction in dietary fat intake at 7 years post enrollment, and most importantly, no difference in physical growth or maturation in those on the restricted diet compared to those in the usual care group (Obarzanek et al., 2001). The Child and Adolescent Trial for Cardiovascular Health (CATCH) enrolled students in the 3rd grade and reported sustained changes at the 8th grade level in reduced fat intake and regular, vigorous physical activity, although the number of minutes of activity was reduced by nearly 50% compared to the 5th grade level (Luepker et al., 1996; Nader et al., 1999).

The reduced physical activity observed among 8th graders in this study likely reflects the societal changes reported to occur at the time of adolescence, a problem that is especially prevalent among females (Kimm et al., 2002).

Studies conducted at worksites involved minimal intervention strategies and addressed multiple risk factors. Strategies included little or no one-on-one contact, but instead used individualized, computer-tailored health messages and involvement of workers to facilitate behavior change, e.g., workers actively participated in the planning and implementation of the program at one site (Emmons et al., 1999) while Campbell and colleagues (2002) used natural helpers or peer supports at their site. The Working Healthy Project reported significant changes at 2.5 years in participation in regular exercise and consumption of fruits and vegetables and fiber (Emmons et al., 1999). The Health Works for Women study reported similar changes at 18 months (Campbell et al., 2002). However, both of these studies suffered from attrition over time. In the Working Healthy Project, 63% of the sample completed the midpoint survey (Emmons et al., 1999) and 63% completed all three surveys in the Health Works for Women study (Campbell et al., 2002).

Of the five studies that recruited participants from the community, one targeted healthy lifestyle in pre-menopausal women (Kuller et al., 2001), one focused on dietary change in men at a specific industry (Knopp et al., 1997), and the remainder addressed exercise (Dunn et al., 1999; Castro et al., 2001; Bock et al., 2001). Kuller and colleagues (2001) reported 5-year results of the Women's Healthy Lifestyle Project, a cognitive-behavioral program targeting the prevention of weight gain and LDL-C rise in a group of pre-menopausal women. Results showed a 3.5 mg/dL increase in LDL-C, however, this was significantly less than the

8.9 mg/dL increase in the control group. Although the intervention was intensive (e.g., weekly group sessions) during the first six months, the improvements in risk factors and the 95% retention rate are impressive. The Dietary Alternative Study (DAS) recruited males with hyperlidemia and tested four fat-reduced diets, which resulted in significant reductions in dietary fat and calorie intake as well as reduced serum cholesterol levels (Knopp et al., 1997). It should be noted that individuals with combined hyperlipidemia (elevated cholesterol and triglycerides) experienced an increase in serum triglycerides and a reduction in HDL-C while on the 18%- and 22%-fat diets. However, similar to the previous study, the DAS intervention resulted in significant improvements in dietary intake and body weight. Follow-up in these studies was too short to draw any conclusions about decreased incidence of CVD, or about reduced mortality due to CVD.

Among the exercise studies, Dunn (1999) compared a 24-month lifestyle physical activity program with a structured exercise program. Over the course of the intervention, especially during the intensive first 6-month phase, the patterns of exercise between the two groups varied but the physical activity and structured exercise groups were comparable at 24-months in exercise as well as other risk factor improvement. Two studies focused on maintenance of physical activity. Castro and colleagues (2001) reported that the group receiving mail contact adhered better than the group receiving phone calls and mail reminders. Bock (2001) compared individual, motivationally-tailored materials to self-help exercise materials and showed significantly greater exercise time in the tailored material group. Across all the exercise studies, there was reduced adherence to the exercise protocol after the initial six months. The reader is referred to the chapter on exercise for additional information on this topic (See chapter 16).

Practice setting interventions involved either the physician or a nurse. The two physician interventions were limited to activities that could be performed within the context of a standard visit (Beresford et al., 1990; Ockene et al., 1999), while the nursing intervention added two to three counseling sessions to usual care (Steptoe et al, 1999). It is difficult to compare across these studies since each reported the observed changes in eating behavior differently. However, all three studies showed significant differences between the usual care and the intervention groups in fat intake. In addition to fat intake, two of the studies addressed other risk factors (e.g., cigarette smoking, blood pressure, and weight) and showed significant improvement in these outcomes (Ockene et al, 1999; Steptoe et al, 1999). In another trial, the intervention did not result in significant group differences (The ACT Writing Group, 2002). The Activity Counseling Trial (ACT) examined the effectiveness of two counseling interventions delivered by patient educators compared to advice given by the primary care physician (The ACT Writing Group, 2002). At 24 months post randomization, cardio respiratory fitness for women was equally improved across the two interventions and in men neither intervention was more effective than the recommended advice.

DISCUSSION

The 13 studies reviewed in this paper represent a group of participants that are diverse by age only. Progress in inclusion of both genders in study samples is evident in that few studies limited the sample to one gender (Knopp et al., 1997; Kuller et al., 2001) and those that did not had close to equal representation across genders. However, only the ACT Writing Group (2002) designed the study to examine gender differences. A lack of progress in inclusion of minority groups in clinical trials is noted since a previous review by this author (Burke et al.,

Study	Participants in Study (N); Per Group (n)	Intervention (Tx)	Outcome
		Interventions for Children	
Long-term safety and efficacy of a cholesterol-lowering diet in children with elevated low-density lipoprotein cholesterol: Seven-year results of the Dietary Intervention Study in Children (DISC). *Obarzanek E et al. Pediatrics, 2001:256-264.*	N = 663 children 8-10 years of age with elevated LDL-C at enrollment. Tx Group: 179 boys, 155 girls; UC Group: 183 boys, 146 girls Average length of follow-up at last visit was 7.4 years with 87.7 % of participants in attendance	Aim: test efficacy and safety of dietary intervention among children with elevated LDL-C. Intervention based on social learning and social action theories. Tx: individual and group counseling by nutritionist and behaviorists, monthly telephone contacts during first 3 years. In 4th year used motivational interviewing and stages of change in 2 group events and 2 individual visits with phone contacts as appropriate. Usual care: group was informed of cholesterol level, had annual measurements, and received educational publications on heart-healthy eating available to the public. **Effectiveness score:** 3.0 for sustained reduction in fat intake over 7 years.	**7-year Δ in fat intake, diet chol, and LDL-C** **Δ in % energy from total fat:** Tx Grp: -4.9 UC Grp: -3.1 P <.001 **Δ in % energy from sat fat:** Tx Grp: -2.3 UC Grp: -1.4 P <.001 **Δ in dietary chol:** Tx Grp: -19.0 UC Grp: -11.0 NS difference at 7 yrs. **Δ in serum LDL-C:** Tx Grp: -16.5 UC Grp: -14.7 NS difference at 7 yrs. No differences between groups in physical growth and maturation or in the proportion who met recommended nutrient intake.
Outcomes of a field trial to improve children's dietary patterns and physical activity. The Child and Adolescent Trial for Cardiovascular Health (CATCH). *Luepker RV et al. Journal of the American Medical Association 1996: 768-776.*	N = 5106 3rd grade students at time of enrollment in study. Con schools = 40; Tx schools = 56; 63% completed 3-year follow-up in 5th grade, Con Group (n = 473) and Tx Group (n = 709)	Aim: assess outcome of health behavior intervention focused on elementary school environment and curricula, home program for primary prevention of CVD. Tx Group: school based diet (30% fat, 10% sat fat, 600-1000 mg sodium; moderate to strenuous physical activity in Phys. Ed. class, classroom curricula on health; Con Group: usual health curricula, Phys. Ed. and food service program. **Effectiveness score:** 3.0 for long-term changes in dietary fat.	**3 year Δ in total fat intake, sat fat intake, and diet chol.** **Δ in % energy from total fat:** Tx Grp: -2.4 UC Grp: -0.4 P <.005 **Δ in % energy from sat fat:** Tx Grp: -1.2 UC Grp: -0.3 P <.005 **Δ in dietary chol:** Tx Grp: -16.9 UC Grp: +7.0 P <.10

Three-year maintenance of improved diet and physical activity: The CATCH cohort.
 	
Nader PR et al. Archives Pediatrics and Adolescent Medicine 1999: 695-704.
	N = 3714 (73%) of the initial CATCH cohort (5106 students), follow-up of the group at grades 6, 7, and 8.	No further intervention beyond 5th grade. Aim: assess at end of 8th grade the maintenance of intervention effects achieved at the 5th end of grade.	**At 3 years post intervention total fat intake, sat fat intake, and diet chol.**
			% energy from total fat:
			          Grade 3: Grade 5: Grade 8:
			Tx Grp: 32.6 30.3 30.6
			UC Grp: 32.7 32.2 31.6 P = .002
			% energy from sat fat:
			          Grade 3: Grade 5: Grade 8:
			Tx Grp: 12.7 11.5 11.3

Study	Participants in Study (N); Per Group (n)	Intervention (Tx)	Outcome

Nader et al, 1999 (cont.)		**Effectiveness score:** 3.0, sustained change in diet.	UC Grp: 12.7 12.1 11.8 P = .008
			Dietary chol:
			    Grade 3: Grade 5: Grade 8:
			Tx Grp: 223.3 205.4 207.3
			UC Grp: 215.7 226.8 216.4 P =.15
			Time (min.) spent vigorous physical activity:
			    Grade 5: Grade 8:
			Tx Grp: 59.2 30.2
			UC Grp 45.6 22.1 P = .001

Workplace Interventions

Study	Participants in Study (N); Per Group (n)	Intervention (Tx)	Outcome
The Working Healthy Project: A worksite health-promotion trial targeting physical activity, diet, and smoking. *Emmons KM et al. The Journal of Occupational and Environmental Medicine, 1999:545-555.*	26 worksites in RI and MA, ~ 337 employees per site participated in baseline assessment (63% of eligible employees): 51% (n=2761) completed intervention midpoint survey, and 83% of those (n=2055) completed the final survey at 2.5 years.	Aim: to improve physical activity, reduce dietary fat and increase fiber, fruit and vegetable intake, reduce cigarette smoking. Intervention based on a participatory strategies model with workers active participants in the planning and implementation of program. Intervention included several individually focused activities, as well as strategies targeting social norms and health-related worksite policies . Control sites had minimal standard of care intervention programs (self-help programs). **Effectiveness score: 2.0,** low retention.	**Outcomes at 2.5 years in the Tx worksite Ss, compared to Ss at the Con worksite:** **Physical activity:** Tx worksites Ss (51.2% vs 41.1%) more likely to report engaging in regular exercise (P <0.03). **Nutrition outcomes:** Tx worksites Ss had marginal increase (3.0 vs 2.6) in fruit and vegetable consumption (P<0.06); significant increase in fiber intake (9.2 vs 8.7 grams/day, P<001); % of calories from fat (33.0% vs 33.4%) was unrelated to Tx condition. **Smoking cessation:** No significant differences in quit rate.
Effects of a tailored health promotion program for female blue-collar workers: Health Works for Women *Campbell MK et al. Preventive Medicine, 2002:313-323*	Women >18 yrs. of age employed at one of 9 rural, blue-collar worksites. Of the 859 Ss at baseline, 63% (N = 538) completed surveys at baseline, 6 and 18 mos.	Aim: test the effect of a 2-component intervention on Ss' diet, physical activity, smoking cessation and cancer screening. Tx (4 worksites) included 2 individualized computer-tailored health messages and a natural helpers program at the workplace. Comparison groups (5 worksites) received a delayed, more minimal intervention (one computer tailored health message at 6 mos.) **Effectiveness score:** 2.0, minimal intervention led to changes in diet, exercise, and smoking.	**At 18 months, Ss at the Tx worksites compared to Ss at the Con worksites:** Increased fruit and vegetable intake 0.7 servings/day, no △ in Con Ss (P = 0.01) Tx Ss reduced fat intake more than Con Ss (NS) Tx site Ss increased aerobic, strengthening, and flexibility exercises; Con Ss decreased their exercise; at 18 months difference in flexibility significant (P < 0.004) Both groups reduced smoking rate by ~3% No differences in rate of screening (Pap test and mammogram) between groups

UC Group = Usual care group or control group; Tx Group = Intervention Group; Tx = intervention; △ = delta or change in score or value; chol = cholesterol; LDL-C = low density lipoprotein-cholesterol; sat fat = saturated fat; Ss = subjects or study participants

Community/Clinical Setting Interventions

Study	Sample	Intervention	Results
Dietary Intervention in Primary Care Practice: The Eating Pattern Study. *Beresford S et al., Am J of Public Health 1990:610-616*	N = 2121 (completed baseline interview) Tx Group: n = 1010 Con Group: n = 1111 Patients seen for routine appt. by primary care MD. N = 1818 completed 12-month interview: Tx Group: 859 (85%) Con Group: 959 (86%) Setting: 28 physician practices/6 clinics	Aim: reduce dietary fat intake, increase fiber intake. Tx had 2 components: 1. self-help booklet 2. MD endorsement MD introduced booklet at visit, follow-up letter 2 weeks post visit. Con group received usual care. **Effectiveness score:** 2.5, minimal intervention, moderate effect at 12 months.	**Fat, % Energy** 12-month mean Δ (95% CI) Tx: -1.54 (-1.88, -1.19) Con: -0.34 (0.66, -0.01) Mean Tx effect: -1.20 (-1.68, -0.73) P <.01 **Fiber, g/1000 kcal** Mean Δ (95% CI) Tx: 0.55 (0.27, 0.83) Con: 0.22 (-0.03, 0.49) Mean Tx effect: 0.32 (-0.06, 0.70) P >.05 **Total serum cholesterol** Both groups reduced chol level ~ 3.5 mg/dL
Effect of Physician-Delivered Nutrition Counseling Training and an Office-Support Program on Saturated Fat Intake, Weight, and Serum Lipid Measurements in a Hyperlipidemic Population: Worcester Area Trial for Counseling in Hylerlipidemia (WATCH). *Ockene I et al., Archives of Int Med. 1999:725-731*	N = 45 physicians in a HMO randomized to 1 of 3 groups (patients randomized to same 3 groups): 1.Usual care 2.MD nutrition counseling training 3.MD nutrition counseling training + office support. Patients had chol level in upper 25th percentile (N = 1162); 12-month data available on 927 Ss; 78.8%, 82.6%, and 82.7% in groups 1 to 3, respectively.	Aim: to evaluate effectiveness of a training program for MD-delivered nutrition counseling, alone and in combination with office-support program, on dietary fat intake, wt., blood LDL-C levels. MD training: 2 sessions: one 2.5 hrs. (didactic, videotape observation, role-playing), and one 30-min. individual tutorial. Patient intervention based on patient-centered counseling model (advise nutrition change, assess strengths and barriers, review patient's food frequency questionnaire, develop plan for change, and arrange follow-up); takes 8-10 minutes of clinic visit time. **Effectiveness score:** 3.0 for significant reduction in saturated fat intake and body wt.	**12-mos. Δ in fat intake, serum LDL-C, and body wt.** **Δ in % energy from sat fat:** Grp 1: 0.0 Grp 2: -0.1 Grp 3: -1.1 , P = .01 **Δ serum LDL-C:** Grp 1: -0.01 Grp 2: 0.02 Grp 3: -0.11, P = .10 **Δ body wt.:** Grp 1: 0.0 Grp 2: -1.0 Grp 3: -2.3 , P <.001
Behavioral counseling in general practice for the promotion of healthy behavior among adults at increased risk of coronary heart disease: Randomized trial. *Steptoe, A et al. British Medical*	20 general practices allocated to Tx and Con conditions in Great Britain. Patients recruited with ≥1 risk factors for CVD. N = 883 Tx: n = 316 Con: n = 567 58.9% (n = 520) completed 12-month assessment	Aim: to measure effect of behaviorally oriented counseling in general practice on healthy behavior and biological risk factors in patients at increased risk of CHD. General practice nurses trained in assessment of readiness for behavioral change and how to deliver behavioral counseling. Patients invited to 2 counseling sessions if had 1 risk factor, 3 sessions if 2 risk factors. Sessions last ≤ 20 min.; also had 1 to 2 phone	**12-mos. Δ from baseline in fat score, # exercise sessions, cigarettes/day** **Δ in fat score: (95% CI)** — % Δ Tx Grp: 7.1 (4.7-9.4) 23% Con Grp: 4.3 (2.5-6.0) 15% **Δ in # ex. sessions : (95% CI)** — % Δ Tx Grp: 8.2 (6.7-9.6) 146 Con Grp: 4.3 (1.5-7.1) 88.8 **Δ in cig./day (95% CI)** — % Δ Tx Grp: 8.0 (3.7-12.1) 38.5

Reference	Sample	Methods / Effectiveness	Results
Journal, 1999: 943-947 Steptoe et al, 1999 (cont.)		contacts between sessions. Fat score derived from dietary instrument, higher score better. **Effectiveness score:** 2.0; changes observed were very good but only 59% completed 12 months follow-up.	Con Grp: 2.7 (1.4-4.1) **Δ in systolic BP : (95% CI)** % Δ Tx Grp: 4.3 (2.3-7.0) 17.6 2.4 Con Grp: 1.8 (-0.05-4.1) 0.7
Long-term cholesterol-lowering effects of 4 fat-restricted diets in hypercholesterolemic and combined hyperlipidmic men: The Dietary Alternatives Study. Knopp R et al. JAMA, 1997:1509-1515.	N = 444 male employees of large industry who had LDL-C levels at 75th age-specific percentile (HC) and men who had elevated LDL-C and triglyceride levels at the 75th age-specific percentile (combined hyperlipidmic[CHL])	HC Ss randomized to diet 1, 2, 3, or 4 with 30%, 26%, 22%, or 18% fat, respectively. All CHL Ss randomized only to diet 1, 2, or 3. All Ss and spouse/partner were taught the diet and behavioral techniques to make dietary changes in 8 weekly 2-hour classes (attendance was 68%); 4-day food records were collected and reviewed with S at 1, 3, 6, 9, and 12 mos. **Effectiveness score:** 2.5 for changes in diet, weight, and serum lipids.	From baseline to 12 mos., significant reductions in total fat and calorie intake, and body wt. (2-3 kg loss) in all groups (P < .01). Plasma cholesterol levels were reduced. Tx Group: HC CHL Diet 1: 3.3% 5.2% Diet 2: 10.2% 4.0% Diet 3: 6.5% 4.4% Diet 4: 8.3% NA P <.01 **LDL-C levels decreased** Tx Group: HC CHL Diet 1: 5.3% 7.0% Diet 2: 13.4% 2.8% Diet 3: 8.4% 4.6% Diet 4: 13.0% NA P <.01 Unwanted effects observed in the HC Ss on diets 3 and 4 (HDL-C ↓, triglyceride levels ↑ sig.).
Women's healthy lifestyle project: A randomized clinical trial – results at 54 months. Kuller LH et al. Circulation, 2001:32-37.	N = 275 pre-menopausal women randomized to Assessment Only (Con) Group (n = 275) and Lifestyle Intervention (Tx) Group (n = 260); 95% of sample completed 54-month assessment.	5-year cognitive-behavioral program aimed at preventing increase in LDL-C, preventing wt. gain, and increasing leisure-time activity. Diet 25% fat, 7% sat. fat, 100 mg/day cholesterol; wt. loss goal of 5-15#; 1000-1500 kcal/week. Activity. Intensive group program 1st 6 mos. (dietary and behavioral change meetings weekly x 10, bi-weekly x 10); maintenance (mail/phone contact) to 54 mos. Assessments at 6, 18, 30, 42, and 54 mos. **Effectiveness score:** 3.0 for high retention over 5 yrs. and prevention of greater ↑ in serum lipids and weight, significant ↓ in dietary fat/cholesterol; however, intervention was intensive.	**Baseline to 54 mos.. Δ in risk factors:** Risk factor Δ Tx Con: LDL-C 3.5* 8.9 HDL-C 2.3 3.1 Triglycerides 18.2* 29.9 Systolic BP -0.12 0.20 Diastolic BP 1.5 2.2 Wt. in lbs. -.18* 5.2 Waist in cm -2.9* -0.46 **Δ in dietary components:** Sat fat, % -2.8** 0.6 Total fat, % -7.0** -2.1 Chol, mg -43** 16.0 *P<0.01, ** P<0.000 At 54 mos., 35% of the Ss in both groups had become post-menopausal.

Reference	Sample	Aim / Methods	Results
Comparison of lifestyle and structured interventions to increase physical activity and cardio-respiratory fitness: A randomized trial. *Dunn AL et al.* *JAMA, 1999:327-334.*	N = 237 sedentary 30-60 yr. old men (n = 116) and women (n = 119) with self-reported physical activity of <36 and <34 kcal/kg per day, respectively. Randomized to lifestyle physical activity program (n=122) or structured exercise program (n=115); 82% in lifestyle, 78% in structured exercise (ex.) completed 24 mos. assessment.	**Aim:** to compare 24-month intervention effects of lifestyle physical activity with traditional structured exercise on improving physical activity, cardiorespiratory fitness, and CVD risk factors. Intervention intensive for first 6 mos. Structured ex. group offered individual supervised sessions 3-5xs/wk. At state-of-the-art fitness center; lifestyle group met weekly in small groups for 16 wks., then bi-weekly until week 24. During 18-mos. follow-up period, groups met quarterly for group activities; also received monthly calendars, quarterly newsletters. **Effectiveness score:** 2.25 intensive intervention with limited sustained change at 24 months.	**Baseline to 24 mos. Δ in physical activity, cardio-respiratory fitness, and CVD risk factors (RF):** Both lifestyle and structured ex. groups significantly increased total energy expenditure and cardiorespiratory fitness from baseline to 24 mos.. P<.001 and P<.002, respectively. Both groups had similar increases in activity at 6 months and similar decreases from 6 to 24 mos. The structured ex. group had greater increases in fitness the first 6 mos. and greater decreases afterward; both groups were comparable at 24 months. Blood pressure, total chol:HDL-C ratio, and % body fat improved in both groups; the structured ex. group also showed reduced serum cholesterol.
Telephone versus mail interventions for maintenance of physical activity in older adults. *Castro C, King AC, and Brassington GS* *Health Psychology, 2001:438-444.*	Ss 50-65 years (N = 179) participated in either a high intensity or low intensity home exercise program for 1 year. At year 2, 140 (80 men, 60 women) agreed to be re-randomized. Equal proportions of Ss in each exercise intensity group were randomized to 1 of 2 maintenance programs.	**Aim:** to evaluate telephone and mail-mediated interventions on physical activity maintenance. Exercise was either high intensity (three 60-min. sessions/wk) or low intensity (five 30-min. sessions/wk) and year 2 maintenance was either phone and mail contact or predominantly mail contact. **Effectiveness score:** 2.5, good retention and low intensity Tx but effect decreased overtime.	**Adherence rates in year 1 and year 2:** During year 1, adherence rate in high intensity group was 88%, in low intensity group 81%; in year 2 adherence was significantly below year 1, high intensity group adherence was 73%, low intensity group adherence was 57%, (P <.0001). Ss in the predominantly mail-mediated program had sig (P <.05) better adherence rates than Ss in the phone/mail group throughout year 2.
Maintenance of physical activity following an individualized motivationally tailored intervention. *Bock BC et al.* *Annals of Behavioral Medicine, 2001:79-87.*	N = 194 healthy sedentary male and female adults recruited from the community; 80% completed 12-month assessment.	**Aim:** examine the maintenance of physical activity during the 6 mos. following a 6-mos. active intervention. Intervention compared 2 print-based formats: use of individualized, motivationally-tailored materials + motivation-matched self-help manual to enhance physical activity (IT), and standard high-quality self-help exercise materials (ST). **Effectiveness score:** 2.25, adequate retention but Ss showed backsliding at 12 months.	**At 12 months, Ss in the IT Group compared to Ss in the ST Group (based on self-report data):** Exercised 187.6 ±216.1 min/wk. Compared to 133±216.8 min/wk ST (P=.10) indicating both groups on average had reduced their exercise; 42% of IT Group were meeting or exceeding CDC/ACSM physical activity criteria compared to 25% of ST Group (P<.05).

UC Group = Usual care group or control group; Tx Group = Intervention Group; Δ = delta or change in score or value

			Baseline to 24-month Δ in VO₂ max:	

Effects of physical activity counseling in primary care: The Activity Counseling Trial: A randomized controlled trial.

The Writing Group for the ACT Research Group, JAMA 2002;677-687.

Inactive adults w/out hx of CHD being seen in primary care clinics.
Females: n = 395
Males: n = 479
~30% minority in sample

At 24-mos, 91.4% completed physical activity interview, 77.6% completed VO₂max.

Aim: determine the effects of 2 patient education and counseling interventions compared with current recommended care, and with each other, on cardioespiratory fitness and physical activity. Current recommended care (advice to exercise) delivered by MD, other intervention components delivered by patient educator.

Effectiveness score: 2.25, limited effect but relatively good retention for 2 years.

Baseline to 24-month Δ in VO₂ max:

	Males	Females
Advice:	-19.4	-16.2
Assistance:	39.4	58.5
Counseling:	-5.4	62.9

In females, VO₂max significantly higher in the assistance and counseling groups compared to advice only group; in males no significant between group differences.
For males and females, no significant differences in self-reported total physical activity at 24 months.

UC Group = Usual care group or control group; Tx Group = Intervention Group; Tx = intervention; △ = delta or change in score or value; chol = cholesterol; LDL-C = low density lipoprotein-cholesterol; sat fat = saturated fat; Ss = subjects or study participants

1997). Only two studies (ACT and CATCH) reported a minority representation that exceeded 14% while the majority of the studies reported that over 90% of the sample was comprised of whites. This leaves us with still unanswered questions about difference in response to behavioral interventions for primary prevention across gender and across ethnic groups. Moreover, it limits the generalizability of the reviewed studies.

Progress has been made in incorporation of primary prevention and brief behavioral counseling strategies by physicians and other health care professionals into routine patient visits in primary care settings. Studies reported by Beresford and by Ockene showed reductions in dietary fat intake that have important public health implications. For example, it has been suggested that a 1% lowering of calories consumed from fats applied on a population wide basis could result in a savings of 10,000 lives (Prentice and Sheppard, 1990). Because of the conditions associated with a high dietary fat intake (e.g., heart disease and cancer), shifting the entire population's fat intake downward can lead to a reduction in mortality rates. Both Beresford and Ockene's studies reported $\geq 1\%$ lowering in energy from fat calories, and most importantly, required less than 10 minutes to deliver. Ockene also demonstrated that involving the organization or system of health care delivery to support these interventions was helpful. These results support a combined approach of population-wide and individual interventions to reduce CHD incidence and mortality (Rose, 1990).

As can be seen in Table 1, the array of interventions varied widely, as did their intensity and duration. Each intervention incorporated behavioral rather than just educational strategies and showed improved behavior. However, there was decay over time in the improved behaviors, as noted in the studies with longer follow-up periods. While interventions have become increasingly successful in achieving behavior change the challenge of how to sustain those changes remains. The fundamental questions we are left with include what strategies work best for the long-term and when is a "booster" dose necessary? Do males and females respond differently to behavioral interventions? The Activity Counseling Trial results would suggest they do. What strategies are most effective in promoting good health and adherence to cardiovascular risk reduction strategies among minority or lower socioeconomic groups? These are questions that need to be answered in order to reverse the slowing of the trend in reduced CHD mortality and to achieve improved cardiovascular health across all strata of the population. The duration of most of the studies reviewed was two years or less, which is an insufficient period to demonstrate reduced mortality related to the intervention. However, these studies were based on the abundant evidence that behavioral change leads to reduced CVD mortality (Daviglus and Stamler, 2001; Goldman et al., 2001; Ketola, 2000).

The target population of the reviewed studies has implications for how and when we implement prevention strategies. The studies focused on children provided the longest follow-up period, ranging from five to seven years (Obarzanek et al., 2001; Luepker et al, 1996; Nader et al., 1999). In both studies there were sustained changes in dietary habits related to fat and cholesterol consumption. Identification and treatment of elevated lipids at an early age, as well as prevention of a rise in cholesterol, are relatively low cost strategies in the prevention of CHD compared to treating the elevation in adults and attempting to reverse well-established lifestyle habits that led to adverse risk factors (Daviglus and Stamler, 2001; Krauss et al., 2000). Knowing that atherosclerosis begins in childhood and leads to the death of a significant proportion of adults dictates that primary prevention begin in childhood, when it is possible to reverse the trend of increased risk factors and the development of coronary atherosclerosis (Tsimikas and Witztum, 2002).

In addition to age of the target population, the setting in which the study is conducted and the intensity of the intervention have implications for cost, duration, and long-term outcomes. Low-intensity interventions, such as use of peer groups in the work setting or provision of self-help materials can be as effective as more intensive, individually-delivered interventions. However, the potential of low-intensity interventions lies in their ability to reach large numbers of people. For example, the Working Healthy Project included 26 worksites with approximately 337 employees per site (Emmons et al., 1999). The strength of the study was its large sample and low intensity intervention that resulted in significant between-group differences in reported exercise and fiber intake. However, the effects were diminished by the fact that less than 50% of the sample completed the final survey at 2.5 years.

Studies conducted in clinical settings are beginning to adopt the model of low-cost, low-intensity interventions that can target large numbers of patients. Two examples of successful outcomes are the studies conducted by Beresford in a primary care setting that at 12 months had approximately 85% retention of over 2000 participants, and the study conducted by Ockene and colleagues (1999) based on physician training in patient-centered counseling. The latter study had 927 patients (80%) complete the study at 12 months and showed significant between-group differences in percent of energy consumed from fat, serum LDL-C level and body weight. The investigators reported that the overall cost of the intervention was $1.86 per patient per year, and that most of this cost was offset by reduced use of lipid-lowering drugs when the physician-training and office

support group was compared with the usual care or control group. These studies suggest that an intervention that is lower in intensity and cost can target a larger number of people, potentially be continued for an extended period of time, and thus have a significant impact on prevention of CHD through risk factor reduction.

All studies reported less than 100% retention and decay over time in the behavioral changes achieved. There are ample data from an array of settings, population groups, and types of interventions to demonstrate that, as the intervention is withdrawn or contact decreased, adherence declines. Maintaining behavior change remains the greatest challenge in risk factor reduction. Thus, we need to identify strategies to sustain the behavior changes we have been so successful in achieving for the short-term.

For additional reading in primary prevention of CHD, the reader is referred to a host of excellent papers, e.g. a review of primary care behavioral counseling interventions using an evidence-based approach (Whitlock et al., 2002), a summary of the evidence on counseling to promote a healthy diet in adults (Pignone et al., 2003), recommendations and rationale for behavioral counseling in primary care to promote a healthy diet (USPSTF, 2003), the Report from the Bethesda Consensus Conference on Prevention of CHD (Consensus Group, 2002), as well as review papers on behavioral interventions to modify diets (Ammerman et al., 2002) and lifestyle physical activity (Dunn et al., 1998). Additional resources for both the health care professional and patient are available at the American Heart Association web site (americanheart.org), in particular a program entitled, *The Heart Profiler,* which has assessment tools and extensive educational materials for the patient and evidence based literature for the professional. Dietary and exercise guidelines are available from several professional organizations (e.g., American Dietetic Association, American Diabetes Association, and the American College of Sports Medicine).

REFERENCES

Ammerman A, Lindquist C, Lohr K and Hersey J. (2002) The efficacy of behavioral interventions to modify dietary fat and fruit and vegetable intake: a review of the evidence. Prev Med 35: 25-41.

Beresford S, Curry S, Kristal A, Lazovich D, Feng Z, and Wagner E. (1997) A dietary intervention in primary care practice: the eating patterns study. Am Public Health Association 87 (4): 610-616.

Bethesda Consensus Conference on Prevention of Cardiovascular Disease (2002). Report of the 33rd Consensus Conference. Preventive cardiology: How can we do better? J American Coll Cardiol 40(4):580-651.

Bock BC, Marcus BH, Pinto BM, and Forsyth LAH (2001) Maintenance of physical activity following an individualized motivationally tailored intervention. Ann Behav Med 23(2):79-87.

Burke L, Dunbar-Jacob J, and Hill M. (1997) Compliance with cardiovascular disease prevention strategies: a review of the research. Ann Behav Med 19 (3): 239-263.

Burt VL, Cutler JA, Higgins M, et al. (1995) Trends in the prevalence, awareness, treatment, and control of hypertension in the adult US population: data from the Health Examination Surveys, 1960 to 1991. Hypertension 26:60-69.

Cooper R, Cutler J, Desvignc-Nickens P, et al. (2000) Trends and disparities in coronary heart disease, stroke, and other cardiovascular diseases in the United States: findings of the National Conference on Cardiovascular Disease Prevention. Circulation 103:3137-3147.

Campbell M, Tessaro I, DeVellis B, Benedict S, Kelsey K, Belton L and Sanhueza. (2002) Effects of a tailored health promotion program for female blue-collar workers: health works for women. American Health Foundation and Elsecier Science 34: 313-323.

Castro C, King A, Brassington G. (2001) Telephone versus mail interventions for maintenance of physical activity in older adults. American Psychological Association 20 (6): 438-444.

Daviglius ML and Stamler J. (2001) Major risk factors and coronary heart disease: Much has been achieved but crucial challenges remain. J Am Coll Cardiology 30(4): 1018-1022.

Dunn A, Marcu B, Kampert J, Garcia M, Kohl H and Blair S. (1999) Comparison of lifestyle and structured interventions to increase physical activity and cardiorespiratory fitness: a randomized trial. JAMA 281 (4): 327-334.

Dunn AL, Anderson RE, and Jakicic JM (1998) Lifestyle physical activity interventions: History, short- and long-term effects, and recommendations. Am J Prev Med 15(4): 398-412.

Emmons K, Linnan L, Shadel W, Marcus B and Adams D. (1999) The working healthy project: a worksite health - promotion trial targeting physical activity, diet, and smoking. J Occup Environ Med 41 (7): 545-555.

Garfinkel L. (1997) Trends in cigarette smoking in the United States. Prev Med 26:447-450.

Goldman L, Phillips KA, Coxson P, et al. (2001) The effect of risk factor reductions between 1981 and 1990 on coronary heart disease incidence, prevalence, mortality and cost. J Am Coll Cardiol 38:1012-1017.

Jones JL. (1977) Are health concerns changing the American diet? National Food Situation, NFS-159. Washington, DC: US Department of Agriculture 27-8.

Ketola E, Sipila R, Makela M. (2000) Effectiveness of individual lifestyle interventions in reducing cardiovascular disease and risk factors. Ann Med 32(4):239-251.

Kimm SYS, Glynn NW, Kriska AM, Barton BA, Kronsberg SS, Daniels SR, Crawford PB, Sabry ZI, and Kie,K. (2002) Decline in physical activity in black girls and white girls during adolescence. N Engl J Med 347(10):709-715.

Knopp R, Walden C, Retzlaff B, McCann B Dowdy A, Albers J, Gey G and Cooper M. (1997) Long-term cholesterol-lowering effects of 4 fat-restricted diets in hypercholesterolemia and combined hyperlipidemia men: the dietary alternatives study. JAMA 278 (18): 1509-1515.

Krauss, RM Eckel RH, Howard B, et al. (2000) Dietary Guidelines: Revision 2000: a statement for healthcare professionals from the Nutrition Committee of the American Heart Association. Circulation 102:2284-2299.

Kuller L, Simkin-Silverman L, Wing R, Meilahn E and Ives D. (2001) Women's healthy lifestyle project: a randomized clinical trial results at 54 months. Circulation 103: 32-37.

Luepker RV, Perry CL, McKinlay SM, et al. (1996) Outcomes of a field trial to improve children's dietary patterns and physical activity. The Child and Adolescent Trial for Cardiovascular Health (CATCH. JAMA 275(10)768-776.

Nader P, Stone E, Lytle L, Perry C, Osganian S, Kelder S, Webber L, Elder J, Montgomery D, Feldman H, Wu M, Johnson C, Parcel G and Lueker R. (1999) Three-year maintenance of improved diet and physical activity: the CATCH cohort. Arch Pediatr Adolesc Med 153 (7): 695-704.

Obarzanek E, Kimm S, Barton B, Van horn L, Kwiterovich P, Simons-Morton D, Hunsberger S, Lasser N, Robson A, Franklin F, Lauer R, Stevens V, Friedman L, Dorgan J and Greenlick M. (2001) Long-term safety and efficacy of a cholesterol-lowering diet in children with elevated low-density lipoprotein cholesterol: seven-year results of the dietary intervention study in children (DISC). Pediatrics 107 (2): 256-264.

Ockene I, Hebert J, Ockene J, Saperia G, Stanek E, Nicolosi R, Merriam P, and Hurley T. (1999) Effect of physician-delivered nutrition counseling training and an office-support program on saturated fat intake, weight, and serum lipid measurements in a hyperlipidemic population: Worcester area trial for counseling in hyperlipidemia (WATCH). Arch Intern Med 159 (7): 725-731.

Pignone MP, Ammerman A, Fernandex L et al. (2003) Counseling to promote a healthy diet in adults. A summary of the evidence for the U.S. Preventive Services Task Force. Am J Prev Med 24(1):75-92.

Prentice RL , Sheppard L. (1990). Dietary fat and cancer: Consistency of the epidemiological data, and disease prevention that may follow from a practical reduction in fat consumption. Cancer Causes Control 1:81-97.

Rose G. (1990) Future of disease prevention: British perspective on the US preventive services task force guidelines. J Gen Intern Med Suppl 5:S128-S132.

Steptoe A, Doherty S, Rink E, Kerry S, Kendrick T, and Hilton S. (1999) Behavioral counseling in general practice for the promotion of healthy behavior among adults at increased risk of coronary heart disease: randomized trial. BMJ 319: 943-947.

Tsimikas S, Witztum JL. (2002) Shifting the diagnosis and treatment of atherosclerosis to children and young adults: a new paradigm for the 21st century. J Am Coll Cardiol 40(12):2122-2124.

U.S. Preventive Services Task Force (2003) Behavioral counseling in primary care to promote a healthy diet. Recommendations and rationale. Am J Prev Med 24(1):93-100.

Whitlock E, Orleans T, Pender N and Allan J. (2002) Evaluating primary care behavioral counseling interventions an evidenced-based approach. Am J Prev Med 22(4):267-284.

BEHAVIOR CHANGE INTERVENTIONS IN CORONARY ARTERY DISEASE: REVERSING OR RETARDING ARTHEROSCLEROTIC DISEASE

Jan Lisspers and Orjan Sundin

INTRODUCTION

An overall decline of coronary artery disease (CAD) incidence and mortality rates began in the 1960s, and since then there has been substantial reductions in the Western world. The age-adjusted mortality associated with CAD has decreased by 20% during the last 10-year period, a development ascribed to therapeutic advances and primary and secondary prevention (Hunink et al., 1997). Despite declines in age-adjusted mortality, the aging of the population will cause CAD to remain a predominant cause of morbidity and mortality. By 2020, CAD is expected to account for at least one third of all deaths and become the major cause of death worldwide (Gaziano, 2001). Furthermore, although CAD incidence and mortality rates have decreased, absolute prevalence has increased, which implies a future increase in the financial burden associated with CAD (Hunink et al., 1997).

The lifetime risk of developing coronary heart disease after age 40 has been estimated to be 49% in men and 32% in women, respectively. Including other diseases secondary to atherosclerosis makes the likelihood of developing cardiovascular disease even greater. According to the American Heart Association coronary heart disease caused 494,382 deaths in 2002 and is the single leading cause of death in America today. Thirteen million people alive today, 7,100,000 males and 5,900,000 females, have a history of heart attack, angina pectoris or both. This year an estimated 1.2 million Americans will have a new or recurrent coronary attack. The overall mortality of patients with documented coronary artery disease (CAD) is 3% to 4% per year, but rises up to 10% after a myocardial infarction or unstable angina (Cheitlin, 1988), high-lighting the great need for rehabilitation and secondary prevention interventions. The direct and indirect costs of coronary heart disease in the US have been estimated to be $142.1 billion in 2005.

In this chapter we will describe how CAD progresses and the impact of lifestyle decisions on this physiological process. We then discuss key findings from health psychology that guide the development of interventions to improve lifestyle to reduce CAD. Finally, we review findings from randomized controlled trials of lifestyle interventions to reduce progression of CAD.

Pathophysiology of CAD

Coronary artery disease is an illness primarily caused by atheromatous plaque, principally developed in the innermost layer of the wall of coronary arteries. Regardless of whether a person is destined to develop CAD or not, the formation of these plaques begins as early as in the first or second decade of life for most people (Stary, 1983). The initiation and acceleration of coronary plaque development are hypothesized to be promoted by factors that damage the arterial endothelium cell lining. The mechanism by which this damage leads to CAD is complex; Repetitive injury to the artery wall promotes the replication of endothelial cells with increased cell membrane permeability to blood borne lipoproteins. Endothelial injury, as well as atherosclerotic development, is most commonly found at points in the arterial tree that are exposed to rapid alterations in the directions and strength of pulsatile flow (i.e. the carotid bifurcations and the curvature of the coronary arteries). Both injury of the inner membrane of the blood vessel wall and rapid flow alteration have been shown to be sensitive to factors such as transient blood pressure elevations, blood turbulence, and carbon monoxide (see

Bondjers et al., 1990 for a review). It is possible that this is one path through which behavioral and emotional factors influence the progression of CAD.

Typically by the age of thirty, the extent of fatty streaking in coronary arteries decreases and fibrous plaques predominate. While direct observation of the events necessary for progression from the initiation stage to actual formation of coronary plaques in humans is not entirely possible, the following factors undoubtedly play a significant role in the atherosclerotic process. Platelets adhere and aggregate into a fibrin clot consisting of connective tissue matrix proteins (synthesized by smooth muscle cells within the inner membrane of the blood vessel wall) and plasma derived lipid (predominantly cholesterol and its ester). This raised plaque evolves over a period of time, adopts a crescent shape (either eccentric or concentric) and bulges out into the media of the vessel wall, which then undergoes thinning and atrophy. The thickening of the inner membrane of the arterial wall, if allowed to grow, can eventually lead to arterial stenosis, a narrowing of the lumen, occlusion, and the clinical manifestations of CAD.

Alternative to this comparably slow, time-dependent plaque progression, plaques may develop by a more rapid process. That is, a slow plaque progression may be accentuated by expeditious rupture of the plaque surface. This surface rupture may be accompanied by hemorrhage into the plaque and/or luminal thrombosis, causing rapid plaque progression. The thrombosis eventually convalesces and becomes incorporated in the wall and the process of atherosclerosis perpetuates in this spurious manner. Rupture occurs most commonly at sites of high circumferential stress. The point of rupture is a function of the impact from various sources, such as the bending and twisting during heart contraction, variations in blood pressure, pulsatile flow, high wall shear stress, wall vibration, flutter, and the resistance of the fibrous cap (Richardson et al., 1989).

Any factor or mechanism that can influence these enlargement processes will contribute to the development and pathogenesis of the disease. Thus, it is no overstatement to say that CAD is multifactorially determined. When, and if, these plaques grow and impede the blood supply to tissues of the heart, myocardial ischemia may occur. And, if the metabolic demands of the heart tissue, at any time, greatly exceed what the coronary arteries can supply, or if the plaque ruptures, causing a thrombus, and further restricts the flow, the stage is set for a myocardial infarction.

IMPACT OF LIFESTYLE ON CAD PROGRESSION

It has long been known that elevated blood pressure (Berglund et al., 1978), smoking (Castelli, 1984) and high levels of serum cholesterol (i.e. low density lipoproteins) (Kannel, 1987), predict development of coronary artery disease. Furthermore, epidemiological research has demonstrated that the coexistence of two or more moderately elevated risk factors increases the risk beyond what would be expected from simple summing of single factors (Wilhelmsen, 1990). From these types of calculations three risk factors (the so called traditional risk factors) could be used to identify individuals at high risk of CAD. However, the traditional risk factor panorama does not explain more than 50% of the variance in the prediction of new cases of CHD. The need to search for auxiliary factors remains.

Among lifestyle factors providing additional contributions to the prediction of CHD are obesity (Hubert et al., 1983), dietary habits (Shekelle et al., 1981), alcohol consumption (Hennekens, 1986), exercise habits (Paffenberger, 1985), occupational stress (Karasek, 1982), social support (Berkman, 1984), type A behavior (Haynes and Matthews, 1989), type D behavior (Denollet, 1996), and vital exhaustion (Apples and Mulder, 1989).

Pathophysiologic mechanisms are believed to mediate the association between lifestyle and CAD progression. Alterations in lipid metabolism (Brindley et al., 1993), HPA-axis activity (Chrousos, 1995), physiological reactivity (Sundin et al., 1995), and inflammatory processes (Appels et al., 2000) may be mechanisms bridging the gap between behavioral factors and CAD incidence and progression. Most, if not all, of the known risk factors mentioned above modify these physiological processes and are closely related to behavior in everyday life.

Diet

Diet has been linked to progression of atherosclerosis for several decades (Paul, 1989). Saturated fat ingestion increases levels of total cholesterol and low-density lipoprotein (LDL) cholesterol (Paul, 1989), and decreases levels of high-density lipoprotein (HDL) cholesterol. This is usually accompanied by increased levels of triglycerides or very low-density lipoprotein (VLDL). Thus saturated fat consumption elevates traditional risk factors and contributes to the development of atherosclerosis (Breslow, 1991). Unsaturated fat ingestion, on the other hand, leads to a decrease in total cholesterol levels and to an increase in HDL cholesterol level which is detrimental to atherosclerotic development (Liebson and Amsterdam, 1999). Lipid and lipoprotein levels are not only influenced by dietary factors but also by genetic factors (Breslow, 1991). However, diet habits, in contrast to heredity, can be modified. High cholesterol concentration has been regarded as the main cause of coronary atherosclerosis, leading to recommendations of dietary changes from expert panels (Expert panel, 1988). However, interventions to accomplish these changes are more seldom addressed.

Lipid lowering therapy has improved survival rates and reduced CAD mortality (Scandinavian Simvastatin Survival Study Group, 1994; LIPID Study Group, 1998). Comprehensive diets, characterized by a low intake of total and saturated fats, and/or increased intake of marine or plant ω-3 fatty acids, also appear to be successful in reducing recurrent coronary events. De Lorgeril and co-workers (1999) demonstrated that the protective effect of such a Mediterranean diet is maintained up to 4 years after the first infarction. Several studies have shown that comprehensive dietary changes can result in both reduced levels of serum cholesterol and reduced cardiovascular complications and mortality (Ornish et al., 1990, 1998; Watts et al., 1992; Singh et al., 1992).

Smoking

Smoking is one of the most powerful risk factors for the development of CAD, and also one of the most effective and least expensive targets for preventing disease progression (Gersh et al., 2001). Several explanations have been suggested for the association between smoking and CAD. Smoking influences changes in blood lipid and lipoprotein concentrations (Craig et al., 1989). In an overview, Craig and colleagues found that smokers had significantly higher concentrations of total cholesterol, LDL, VLDL and triglycerides, and lower concentrations of HDL cholesterol. Smoking also stimulates increases in heart rate and blood pressure (Benowitz et al., 1984; Robertson et al., 1988), reduces oxygen delivery, impairs dilation of the coronary vessels and enhances platelet aggregation (Rigotti and Pasternak, 1996) possibly accelerating coronary plaque development (Grundy et al., 1998) and predisposing individuals to acute thrombosis (Burke et al., 1997).

Smoking cessation is highly beneficial in reducing mortality after myocardial infarction (Wilhelmsen, 1998). After smoking cessation, CAD risk rapidly decreases, probably due to the effect on thrombogenesis; By 3 to 4 years after cessation, the risk is equivalent to that of patients who never smoked (Rosenberg et al., 1990). On the other hand, patients who continue to smoke after acute myocardial infarction (AMI) have twice the risk of death from recurrent myocardial infarction than those who stop (Cavender et al., 1992). Patients undergoing coronary artery bypass graft

(CABG) who continue smoking one year after CABG more than double their risk for AMI and re-operation. The risk increases even more over time (Voors et al., 1996). Despite the well known risk of smoking, more than half of CAD patients resume or are still smoking six month to five years after the incident (Sebregts et al., 2000).

Exercise

When habitual physical activity levels are increased, subsequent cardiac mortality is decreased (Paffenbarger et al., 1993). Possible mechanisms for the beneficial effects of overall physical activity are the impact on total cholesterol and HDL cholesterol concentrations (Shepherd and Balady, 1999) independent of diet (Thompson et al., 1988), and the impact on triglycerides and VLDL. Furthermore, physical activity increases coronary blood flow, reduces blood pressure, promotes a more efficient cardiac use of oxygen, and increases vagal tone. Physical activity may also modify the harmful effects of other risk factors (Berlin and Colditz, 1990). Both Oldridge et al. (1988) and O'Connor (1989) reported that physical training reduces mortality in CAD patients. However, a major problem with exercise is the high drop out rate and low long-term compliance (Oldridge, 1988). Nevertheless, Taylor et al. (2004), in a recent meta-analysis, showed that all cause mortality was reduced (odds ratio = .80) among those who continued to exercise.

Stress

Both acute and chronic stress have long been considered as risk factors for CAD (Krantz et al., 1996). Acute stress promotes CAD in a number of ways. Stress activates the sympathoadrenal and pituitary-adrenocortical systems, which increase circulating catecholamines and cortisol plus heart rate and blood pressure. Acute mental stress results in increased platelet activation that may lead to plaque rupture and thrombosis (Krantz et al., 1996) perpetuating the atherosclerotic process. In the presence of atherosclerosis, increases in blood pressure, heart rate, and catecholamines lead to increases in myocardial oxygen demands that may result in acute myocardial ischemia (Krantz et al.. 1996). Stress also leads to increased LDL and decreased HDL cholesterol concentrations (McCann et al., 1990).

In a case control design involving about 25,000 participants from 52 different countries, Rosengren et al. (2004) reported that stress was more frequent a problem among CHD patients during a time period preceding their myocardial infarction. Chronic stress ultimately leads to physical or psychological impairment, unless the individual can control the demands in a satisfactory way. Appels and co-workers have shown that the end result of this adaptive break down (vital exhaustion) is associated with CAD development, subsequent AMI, and also to revascularization following percutaneous coronary intervention (PCI) (Appels and Mulder, 1989; Kop et al., 1994; see also Koertge et al., 2002) Stressors also influence lifestyle habits, typically increasing smoking, (Epstein and Perkins, 1988) and worsening dietary behaviors.

Management of CAD

Although still controversial (Jones and West, 1996; Campbell et al., 1998; Jolly et al., 1999), meta-analyses indicate that the addition of lifestyle interventions to standard rehabilitation regimens for CAD patients reduces recurrences and mortality as well as psychological distress (Nunes et al.. 1987; Linden et al., 1996). However, community-based risk-reduction trials have been less successful. In particular, short term psychological and lifestyle interventions have had limited or no success (Jones and West, 1996; Jolly et al., 1998), nor have larger scale clinical trials with long term clinical endpoints evaluating uni-factorial interventions (Berkman et al., 2003). This may be due to the fact that the consequences of CAD (i.e. myocardial infarction and angina pectoris) are typically unexpected and psychologically traumatic events. As such they involve demands that can tax or exceed the individual patient's adaptive resources. Successful coping with the illness demands personal adjustments, and the required lifestyle changes may be hard to accomplish (and perhaps become an additional hardship affecting the course of the disease [see Sundin, 1993]). Thus, depression, anxiety, exhaustion, and hostility (Öhman and Sundin, 1995; Lane et al., 1999) as well as lifestyle behavioral correlates to coronary risk factors, such as tobacco usage, exercise and diet habits, have been associated with disease progression and outcome. Since roughly 90% of CAD patients have more than one lifestyle related cardiovascular risk factor (Campbell et al., 1998) multi-factorial lifestyle intervention approaches, with emphasis on a broad spectrum of coronary risk factor reduction have attracted considerable interest and the need for more comprehensive and individually tailored rehabilitative efforts has been emphasized (Thompson et al., 1996; Franklin et al., 1997). Questions regarding the organization, duration, and delivery of such comprehensive approaches have therefore been asked (Thompson and de Bono, 1999) but not yet fully answered.

THE PSYCHOLOGY OF LIFESTYLE BEHAVIOR CHANGE

During the last 10-15 years, there has been a dramatic increase in the development of theoretical analyses, research and treatment methods of a cognitive nature. Focusing on this mental, internal, and private part of human behavior has led to the neglect of fundamental behavioral and learning principles (see, for example, "Why I am not a cognitive psychologist" by B.F. Skinner, 1977; or Skinner, 1985, 1988, 1989). Since these principles seem particularly important regarding habitual, everyday lifestyle behaviors, we analyze what can be learned from them in the development of interventions to improve lifestyle to reduce CAD.

Back to basics: Contingencies of reinforcement

From a strict behavioral perspective, the problems of changing lifestyle and health behavior, as well as the problem of long-term maintenance of early behavior changes, are fairly easily understood. The most important factors controlling future behavior, the immediate ("contingent") consequences of the behavior, generally have a much more profound influence on behavior than knowledge and anticipation of distant, long-term consequences, even if these are much more important or serious. The immediate positive and reinforcing effects help explain why people behave in health hazardous ways (e.g. smoking) even though they are aware of the negative and/or health detrimental long-term consequences

Behavior control through natural contingencies, whether extrinsic or in some way internalized as intrinsic motivators (Bellg, 2003; Sansone and Harackiewicz, 2000), also explains the difficulties experienced in changing lifestyle behavior, and in maintaining early changes: the new habitual lifestyle behavior patterns we are trying to help people acquire seldom have any obvious, naturally occurring immediate positive effects, and hence few naturally occurring contingent reinforcements. In fact, there are often short-term negative consequences of behavior change, including negative bodily, emotional, practical and social effects. Feasible positive effects are achieved later in a distant future, and are often much more uncertain, diffuse and unspecific (e.g. "perhaps staying healthy if I don't get ill for some other reason") and thus have very little contingent association with the behavior.

Other obstacles to lifestyle change are that the undesired lifestyle behaviors are extremely well established and habitual. They are "automatic" (they can be performed with very little conscious planning), and are closely integrated with many other habitual, everyday behaviors. Thus, changing one behavior will directly influence other high-frequency behaviors. Well-established life-style behaviors are connected to many discriminative stimuli (i.e. cues to action) and they can be maintained on "thin" schedules of reinforcement. Thus, although behaviors are performed frequently, positive reinforcement for them occurs infrequently; the behaviors, for this reason alone, become very resistant to extinction. Since undesired behaviors are frequently "normal", social lifestyle behavior patterns, discriminative stimuli, modeling opportunities, as well as instances of natural social reinforcement for the undesired behavior are numerous, and thus difficult to overcome.

A model for lifestyle behavior change

The above principles can be viewed as the basic behavioral and learning factors influencing behavior change, and any further theoretical analyses based on these are, consequently, refinements of these basic premises. Below, some general factors important to a model for lifestyle behavior change will be put forward, and some theoretical conceptualizations of interest will be presented. Of course, behavior change is an ever-continuing process - we are always learning and changing - and lifestyle behavior change is best analyzed as a sequential series of stages (Prochaska and DiClemente, 1983; Prochaska et al., 2002). Here the discussion will be focused on three chronological phases: (1) the decision to change lifestyle, (2) early behavior change and habit acquisition, and (3) adherence to and long-term maintenance of lifelong behavior change.

Deciding on a lifestyle change

It is unlikely that attempts to coerce or frighten someone into a new habitual way of life will be successful. The individual has to be persuaded (or given the opportunity) to take responsibility for his/ her own life and lifestyle. To be able to take conscious responsibility, and be motivated to take it, the individual needs information, knowledge and a change in attitudes – in other words, a change in cognitive behavior – favoring the new lifestyle behavior. On a general level, the most important knowledge is perhaps that every individual can, and does,

influence his own future health and that our everyday habitual lifestyle may be of the most vital importance to health.

What other kinds of information, knowledge and attitudes are important for motivating a decision to make a health-related lifestyle change? One of the most widely accepted theoretical models dealing with these problems is the Health Belief Model (HBM) (Rosenstock, 1974, Janz et al., 2002). Studies of the HBM have demonstrated that modeled factors are retrospectively associated with concurrent health behaviors, and can predict future health behavior (see for example Janz and Becker, 1984; Janz et al., 2002). The HBM model postulates that the likelihood of taking a specific health-related preventive action (e.g. to start a change of lifestyle) is mainly dependent on two different cognitive factors, namely (1) the perceived threat to ones health, and (2) the perceived "cost-effectiveness" of the recommended action. The perceived threat is dependent on the perceived vulnerability to the illness in question and to the perceived seriousness of contracting the illness. The cost-effectiveness estimate is based on the believed efficiency of the recommended actions in reducing the risk of contracting the illness weighted against the potential negative aspects or "costliness" of the behavior (i.e. being expensive, dangerous, unpleasant, inconvenient, time-consuming, and so forth).

To the formula for "cost-benefit" estimates which influence the probability of the desirable behavior change (Rosenstock et al., 1988) was added the individual's perceived self-efficacy (Bandura 1977; 1997), i.e. the confidence that one can effectively enough perform the particular behavior in question. This factor is a function of both past learning and present perceptions of the actual behavior required, and is, in practice, closely coupled with the process of acquisition and shaping of the new behavior pattern.

The acquisition of new skills and habitual behaviors

New knowledge and changing attitudes are seldom sufficient conditions for actual change of overt behavior: Many smokers know the detrimental effects of smoking and honestly think that they ought to quit smoking! To learn that your stress behaviors might increase your risk of suffering a myocardial infarction in the future, and that you ought to stay calmer, might at the very best give you a hint of what you should avoid doing. It does not however tell you how to accomplish this! The new "insights" must be accompanied by the shaping of a new, and sometimes rather complex behavior repertoire (for example stress management and non-Type A behavior). This learning process is for many different reasons (some of which will be evident from the following discussion) best accomplished through actual enacting and rehearsal of the desired behavior. Regarding cognitive concept of self-efficacy (Bandura 1977, 1997), note that even early writers proposed that "...there are both behavioral and cognitive influences upon perceived self-efficacy. Enactive attainments are the best source of self-efficacy, whereas vicarious experiences and verbal persuasions may be less effective in producing these changes" (Kaplan and Atkins, 1984). Thus, such cognitive factors of motivation are not primarily influenced by cognitive focused interventions but through procedures focused on changes and practicing of overt behavior.

Many of the factors important to successful lifestyle behavior change are dependent on the actual target behavior chosen. Other things being equal, the more culturally normal, close to the individual's previous everyday lifestyle, simple, socially valued, as well as the less time consuming, expensive, and so on the behavior is to the person, the easier the behavior change.

From a learning perspective, discussed earlier, there are two main areas of importance to understanding lifestyle behavior change, and the problems of achieving it: (a) the discriminative stimuli setting the occasion for, and (2) the consequences reinforcing or punishing the desired and undesired behavior respectively. Some examples of interventions influencing both the cues for the desired behavior, as well as the potential positive and negative consequences for them, might be: choice of as simple and "normal" target behavior as possible, making them easy to integrate into a normal every-day life; a gradual and thorough training (i.e. "shaping") of the desired lifestyle behavior to the point where it becomes habitual; usage of appropriate programmed and/or natural social reinforcement; individual goal setting/self-observation/feedback; "setting the stage for the new lifestyle" by rearranging the home/work situation or attaining material/resources for the behavior in question; involvement of peers or family members, and so on.

Maintenance of behavior change

Since the important positive effects of many changes in lifestyle behavior are encountered in the relatively distant future, the problem of behavior change maintenance is, generally speaking, to bridge this time gap between the behavior and long-term positive consequences. Basically this means finding short-term positively reinforcing consequences for the behavior. This might be accomplished through many different means, some of which were mentioned above regarding early behavior acquisition. At the same time a major objective during this phase must be to gradually fade out programmed interventions (both cues and reinforcements), and make sure that the desired lifestyle behavior comes under the control of naturally occurring consequences.

In an early publication, Lees and Dygdon (1988) put forward an intriguing learning conceptualization of the initiation and maintenance of exercise behavior which is of particular interest here. The hypothesis put forward is that one important factor explaining why some individuals continue exercising is that earlier unnoticed, neutral and/or even mildly aversive bodily sensations (such as muscle fatigue) become "conditioned positive reinforcers" for exercising. In other words, the continuers learned to appreciate and value the feelings of mild muscle fatigue, and understood its association to the long-term goals of their exercising. At least two factors are pre-requisites for this to take place, first the connection between mild muscle fatigue and, for example, the reduced risk of CAD has to be learned and understood (perhaps through education), and secondly, exercise must be increased gradually to avoid more adverse soreness (which instead might turn the early mild proprioceptive feedback into conditioned punishing stimuli). These principles are valid for other lifestyle behaviors as well, that is for stress management, diet and smoking, in the sense that there are also subtle proprioceptive signals which could become positive reinforcers if appropriately attended to.

RESEARCH ON THE EFFECTS OF LIFESTYLE BEHAVIOR CHANGE ON THE PROGRESSION OF CAD

Above, we have argued that the development of coronary artery disease and the subsequent risk for serious - sometimes life threatening - cardiac illness is a consequence of everyday behavior. Well known biological risk factors and precursors of cardiac events such as hypertension, hyper-lipidemia, abdominal overweight, diabetes and the like, are in themselves largely influenced by lifestyle behaviors such as stress management, tobacco usage, or diet- and exercise habits. Therefore any attempts to help people avoid future cardiac events, whether in primary or in secondary prevention ought to be focused on helping the individual change everyday lifestyle behaviors. Interventions and preventive attempts should be able to influence the basic coronary disease itself in terms of the formation and development of coronary artery atherosclerosis, as well as subsequent clinical coronary events.

On the other hand, we have proposed that changing habitual everyday behavior is not an easy task, even if these lifestyle habits are related to future health risks. Thus, there is a need for the development of intervention methods that are efficiently optimized for supporting long term, lifelong behavior change. In this endeavor we probably need to utilize basic psychologic-ally, and especially behaviorally based theoretical and empirical knowledge – knowledge which we argue has not yet been fully exploited in practical applications.

Below, we review all identified published controlled studies that have explicitly evaluated the effects of interventions focused on lifestyle behavior change on the progression of coronary artery disease (through the use of quantified computer assisted coronary angiography, QCA). For each study we will briefly summarize (a) the design of the intervention program, (b) the effects achieved on coronary atherosclerosis, and (c) the effects on clinical coronary/cardiac events.

In a series of inspiring publications Ornish and co-workers (Ornish et al., 1990; Gould et al., 1992; Gould et al., 1995; Ornish et al., 1998) studied the effects of comprehensive lifestyle changes on athero-sclerotic plaque progression in coronary arteries ("The Life Style Heart Trial"). Coronary artery lesions were assessed through quantitative coronary angiography and patients were randomly assigned to either a usual-care control group (n=19), or a treatment group (n=22). The treatment group participated in a 12 month intensive program for comprehensive lifestyle changes, consisting of a week-long retreat to teach the lifestyle intervention and regular group support meetings over one year.

The goals of the lifestyle change program included stress management (relaxation/meditation/yoga, 1 hour/day), healthy vege-tarian diet (10% fat with a restriction of caffeine and alcohol usage), regular moderate aerobic exercise (at least 3 hours per week, at least 30 minutes per session, mostly walking), as well as smoking cessa-tion. The group support meetings (4 hours, twice a week) were aimed at providing social support to help participants achieve and maintain the lifestyle changes, as well as promote communication skills and the expression of emotions in relationships at home and work.

When quantitative coronary angiography (QCA) tests were re-administered after 12 months, the average percentage diameter stenosis of the coronary arteries had decreased from 40.0 to 37.8 percent in the treatment group. In the control group there was a continuing progression of stenosis from 42.7 to 46.1 percent. In 82% of the intervention subjects the change was in the direction of regression, while 53% of the control subjects experienced progression of the lesions.

A 5-year follow up indicated that a modest further regression of coronary atherosclerosis had occurred in the intervention participants, while there was a substantial continued progression in the control subjects, reaching an average of 52 percent diameter stenosis (Ornish et al., 1998). Also, the follow-up study confirmed that these differences in the development of the coronary artery stenosis were associated with corresponding differences in severity of myocardial perfusion abnormalities; The modest regression of stenosis seen in the lifestyle intervention subjects was associated with a decrease in size and severity of perfusion abnormalities compared to an increase and worsening for the control subjects.

There was also a clear effect on the risk of cardiac events during the 5-year follow-up period. Twenty-five events occurred in the intervention group (which included 28 subjects, Mean=0.89 events per subject), while there were 45 events in the control group (20 subjects, Mean=2.25). This resulted in a significantly elevated risk for any event in the control group compared to the intervention group (Relative Risk=2.47).

One of the first published controlled studies to, at least partly, confirm the initially sensational results from the Lifestyle Heart Trial was the "STARS-study" ("St Thomas' Atheroma Regression Study", London; Watts et al., 1992). This study demonstrated that changes in diet alone, especially if these changes coincided with a decrease in serum cholesterol, led to positive effect on the development of atherosclerotic plaque, and a decrease in cardiac events.

Ninety male coronary patients referred for coronary angiography but without an imminent need for a revascularization procedure were randomized to either a dietary intervention or to a control group. Intervention group patients were instructed individually by a dietician, and prescribed a "heart-healthy" diet characterized by a reduction in total fat to 27% of total calories, saturated fatty acids to 8-10%, and polysaturated fatty acids increased to 8%. Overweight subjects received special counseling to encourage weight loss. At follow-up visits every third month, assessments were made, dietary compliance was discussed and support was given by the clinician. All participants also received standard individualized, cardiological follow-up and treatment which, if indicated, included antihypertensive treatment, counseling against smoking, and general advice about weight loss and exercise.

At a 3-year follow-up (average 39 months), coronary angiograms (QCA) showed significant changes in the development of coronary atherosclerosis in favor of the intervention group compared to the control group. In 15% of the diet intervention subjects an overall progression occurred, compared to 46% of the control subjects. Regression of atherosclerosis was observed in 38% of the intervention group while in only 1 subject (4%) in the control group. Thus the average severity of the stenosis (percentage diameter stenosis) increased significantly in the control group (+5.6) compared to the intervention group (-0.5).

As in the Ornish study, there was a significant effect of the intervention on the risk for cardiovascular events. While 36% in the control group experienced any clinical cardiac event during the follow-up, only 11% of the diet intervention subjects did, which constitutes a 69% relative risk reduction in the intervention group compared to the control group.

Another early and ambitious study in this area was done by Schuler, Hambrecht, Niebauer and co-workers in Heidelberg, Germany (see Schuler et al., 1992; Hambrecht et al., 1993; Niebauer et al., 1995; Niebauer et al., 1997). In this study 113 males with CAD (stable angina pectoris and documented coronary artery stenosis) were randomized either to an intervention group (n=56) or a control group (n=57) receiving "usual care" and then followed for up to 6 years (when 80% of the subjects were available).

The intervention program targeted diet and physical activity. In the diet change intervention participants "stayed on a metabolic ward during the initial 3 weeks, where they were instructed how to lower the fat and cholesterol content of their regular diet on the basis of the American heart Association recommendations, phase III (protein 15%, carbohydrates 65%, fat <20% of calories, total cholesterol <200mg, poly-unsaturated/saturated fatty acids ratio >1" (Niebauer et al., 1997, p.2535). They were furthermore instructed to participate in regular group exercise sessions (at least 2 of 4 times per week) and exercise on their own at home on a cycle ergometer for at least 30 minutes each day. Compliance with the program was followed based on individual log books, and the effects of the diet and exercise changes were evaluated for each subject at regular check-ups (assessing body weight, metabolic and hemodynamic variables) every third month during the first year and once each year thereafter. Five times a year, sessions for both patients and their spouses were conducted for discussions about problems related to the diet and exercise habits, and psychosocial topics. The control group subjects receiving usual care stayed only one week on the ward "where they received identical recommendations on physical exercise and on how to lower their dietary fat intake. Adherence to these guidelines was left to their own initiative, and 'usual care' was rendered by their private physicians" (Niebauer et al., 1997).

After the first year of more intensive intervention (Schuler et al., 1992), there was evidence of a clear overall retardation of CAD progression in the subjects in the intervention group. In the intervention group 30% showed an overall regression of stenosis compared to only 4% of the controls, and 42% of the control group had a progression compared to half as many among the intervention subjects (20%). At the 6-year follow-up these differential effects were again confirmed. The average stenosis diameter had changed only marginally in the intervention group (from 58.9% to 62%, not significant) while there was a significant worsening for the control group subjects (from 54.7% to 66.6%). Overall, no control subject showed regression of the coronary lesions while 19% of the intervention subjects did. Furthermore, in 74% of the controls there was evidence of progression of the stenosis compared to 59% of the intervention subjects.

In this study, contrary to the other studies reviewed here, there was no evidence of a positive effect of the intervention on the risk or frequency of clinical coronary events.

The SCRIP-program ("The Stanford Coronary Risk Intervention Project"; Haskell et al., 1994; Quinn et al., 1994; Gordon and Haskell, 1997) was developed based on the general premise that programs for cardiovascular disease risk reduction and secondary prevention should include basic components such as: "...(1) initial evaluation and risk assessment; (2) identification of specific goals for each CAD risk factor; (3) formulation and implementation of an individualized treatment plan including lifestyle modification and pharmacologic interventions for accomplishing specific risk reduction goals; (4) effective long-term follow-up to enhance compliance and revise the treatment plan as indicated; and (5) a mechanism for outcomes-based, long-term assessment of each patient" (Gordon and Haskell, 1997). Hence the program was focused on aggressive modification of multiple CAD risk factors via comprehensive, individualized modification of lifestyle behavior. Lifestyle areas included a low-fat and low-cholesterol "heart-healthy" diet, physical exercise, weight loss, smoking cessation, as well as appropriate secondary preventive medication, and employed a physician-supervised, nurse case-manager team model with consultation from other health professionals, such as a dietitian and psychologist in specific focus areas (Gordon and Haskell, 1997).

All program activities were conducted on an individual basis, and participants initially met with a nurse case manager to design an individualized program and goal planning based on the subject's initial risk profile and lifestyle habits, as well as on resources and motivation for making lifestyle changes. The subjects were also instructed in more detail in the different lifestyle change areas by other health professionals in the team. Patients were also prescribed appropriate drug therapy (primarily cholesterol-lowering drugs) as indicated and when lifestyle changes in themselves did not meet the cholesterol reduction goals. During the four years of the study, intervention subjects returned to the clinic every 2 or 3 months to have their progress assessed (e.g. lipid levels, body weight, and blood-pressure). Further assistance in their lifestyle change efforts were provided individually. Between these regular visits contact was maintained using telephone and mail.

In the study, 300 male (n=259) and female (n=41) patients, with arteriographically documented CAD, were randomly assigned to the above described program (n=145) or to usual care provided by their own physician (n=155), and followed for a period of 4 years. Both groups demonstrated a progression of coronary atherosclerosis. The rate of progression was however significantly less (47% less decrease in minimum lumen diameter) in the intervention group compared to the usual care control group. There were about twice as many subjects demonstrating a regression in the intervention group (20%) as compared to the control group (10%), whereas there

was no difference in the proportion with disease progression (50% in both groups).

Over the 4-year follow-up period, 20 subjects (14%) of the intervention group subjects experienced a total of 25 clinical coronary events, while 34 control group subjects (22%) experienced 44 events among them. These differences between groups were significant, and constitute a 36% relative risk reduction for any coronary event in the intervention group compared to the control group.

At the start of our own intervention project (Lisspers et al., 1999a; Lisspers et al., 1999b; Hofman-Bang et al., 1999a; Hofman-Bang et al., 1999b; Sundin et al., 2002; Lisspers et al., 2005) we had the opportunity to take an active part in the development of an intervention program in a newly started cardiac rehabilitation and secondary prevention unit. The explicit goal was to apply behaviorally oriented intervention methods (see "A model for lifestyle behavior change" above) in order to promote long-term lifestyle behavior changes important in the CAD pathology process. Lifestyle areas covered in the program included stress management (with a strong emphasis on Type A-behavior and training in applied relaxation), diet (a low-fat, low-cholesterol diet was served and instructed following Swedish official guidelines, total fat: <35%, saturated fat: <10%, protein: 15%, carbohydrates: 60%), smoking (and other tobacco usage) cessation and exercise habits (at least 30 minutes at least three times per week, at least low-moderate intensity such as brisk walking).

The program had a total duration of 12 months, starting with a 4-week residential stay at the intervention unit located in a rural area in northern Sweden. This very intensive initial phase contained a combination of group oriented (5-8 participants in closed groups) and individual intervention components. The group sessions consisted of a structured series of lectures, discussion seminars and practical skills training sessions in each of the different lifestyle areas, conducted by appropriate health professionals such as psychologist, dietician, physical exercise therapist, physician, and so on. There was also an explicit emphasis on the participants' own, self-initiated and self-controlled activities: they were assigned daily homework and skill training in all lifestyle areas, to be performed individually between the group sessions. Spouses were invited to participate in the program during the third week.

Each participant was furthermore assigned a personal "case manager" (specially trained nurses) together with whom he/she had a series of individual, structured interview sessions during the residential phase. The aim of these sessions was to analyze each participant's individual situation, lifestyle behavior pattern and resources for behavior change. The sessions were also used to achieve an individualization of all material covered elsewhere, and hence, to promote motivation and preparedness for behavior change. Furthermore, this contact between the case-manager and the participant also aimed at providing individualized feedback and reinforcement, as well as emotional and motivational support during the initial behavior change efforts during the residential stay and the reminder of the 12-month intervention period. The main practical outcome of these initial individual face-to-face sessions was the participant's very concrete planning of how to carry out the actual lifestyle changes, both on a short- and long-term basis. Priorities and personal goals were explicitly specified in a written plan.

After the residential phase, the intervention continued with an 11-month home-based maintenance phase. This phase included regular follow-up contacts by mail and telephone between the participant and his/her case manager. During the first three months after departure, participants kept a daily self-monitoring diary regarding their diet, exercise, stress management/relaxation, and smoking habits. These diaries were mailed to the case manager every fortnight. Feedback was sent back to the participants in the form of graphs showing the progress

of behavior change, as well as personal feedback comments from the case-manager. The frequency of the support was gradually faded out, and from the fourth month onwards the diaries were sent in and feedback returned on a monthly basis. All this material also formed the basis for telephone contacts between the case manager and the participant for verbal feedback, emotional/motivational support, problem-solving and re-planning on at least three pre-planned occasions, after three, eight and 11 months of the maintenance phase.

This program was evaluated in a randomized, long-term study (Lisspers et al., 1999b; Hofman-Bang et al., 1999a; Hofman-Bang et al., 1999b; Lisspers et al., 2005), where patients recently successfully treated with percutaneous coronary intervention (PCI) were randomized either to an intervention (n=46) or a standard care control group (n=42). Coronary angiography was performed at inclusion and at the 24 months' follow-up. Non-treated lesions were analyzed with the quantitative computer-assisted technique (QCA). Coronary events (AMI, CABG, PCI, cardiovascular mortality) were recorded from hospital records for up to a minimum of 60 months (M=6.5 years).

At the 24 months' QCA assessments, the control group showed significantly more pronounced progression of the atherosclerotic lesions (a decrease of 0.09mm minimum lumen diameter) than the treated group (0.03mm; Hofman-Bang et al., 1999b).

Across the entire follow-up period, the intervention group had a significantly lower rate of all coronary events (30% vs. 51%; relative risk reduction: 43%), as well as of cardiovascular mortality (2% vs. 15%; relative risk reduction: 87%) compared to the control group. In this study we found no difference between the groups during the first 12 months, i.e. the intervention phase, as regards to the number of subjects experiencing coronary events. Consequently, the difference between the two groups was more pronounced after the end of the 1-year intervention phase, with an event rate of 42% among control subjects, and 17% among the intervention group subjects, constituting a relative risk reduction of 58% for the intervention group compared to the usual care control group (Lisspers et al., 2005).

In a recent 1-year study conducted in New Delhi, India by Manchanda et al. (2000), 42 male patients with chronic stable angina and angiographically proven CAD were randomized to either a usual care control group (including pharmacological risk factor control, advice on AHA step 1 diet and moderate aerobic exercise) or a "Yoga lifestyle intervention program (YLI)". The YLI program started with a four day stay at a yoga residential center with introduction to and training in the various yogic lifestyle components, including different techniques for stretching, breathing, relaxation, meditation, as well as diet change and moderate aerobic exercise. Spouses were invited to accompany the patients. The yogic exercises were to be carried out for about 90 minutes daily. Compliance was followed-up and motivated during visits to the yoga center every other week, and once a month during evaluation visits to the cardiac clinic.

At the 12-month follow-up repeated coronary angiography was used to analyze the development of CAD. There was no significant progression of coronary stenosis in the intervention group, while there was a definite worsening (a significant mean increase from 60 to 68% diameter stenosis) in the control group. The difference between the groups was highly significant. In the intervention group 20% of the lesions showed regression, while only one (2%) was found among the control subjects. Three lesions (5%) in the intervention subjects had progressed compared to 37% in the control group.

Clinical coronary events (in this case only PCI - or CABG interventions) during the study period differed between the groups. Only one (2%) yoga lifestyle intervention subject needed such treatment while 8 (14%) control subjects were treated, which constitutes a relative risk ratio of 5.45 for the control group compared to the intervention group.

CONCLUSIONS

The modification of lifestyle based risk factors can have profound effects on CAD, even on variables like recurrence rate, mortality, and the actual progression/ regression of coronary atherosclerosis. However, the results from many different intervention trials published throughout the years vary, and the main reason for this appears to be that the achieved rates of actual changes in lifestyle behavior are often low and/or variable, especially with regard to the long-term maintenance of behavior changes. The problem is consequently not, as has been discussed, if it is worthwhile or cost effective to change lifestyle. The problem is to develop rehabilitation interventions that reliably lead to meaningful changes in lifestyle behavior. That is, the compliance and adherence with the program goals are the main problems, as is the long-term maintenance of achieved behavior changes.

The six studies reviewed here all show that interventions focusing on change of lifestyle behavior, such as diet, exercise, smoking and stress management, have clear and beneficial effects on cardiovascular disease processes, even when compared to the relatively efficient standard care of today. Interestingly, the studies come from different parts of the world; There are three studies conducted in Europe (in Great Britain, Germany and Sweden, respectively), two in the US and one in India. The findings are remarkable since they all, from a methodologically sound perspective, demonstrate that an aggressive focus on behavioral modification of risk factor related lifestyle habits can help coronary patients achieve long-lasting changes in biological parameters, of such magnitude that the underlying coronary disease progression can be reversed, halted or slowed down. An even more dramatic consequence of this comprehensive behavioral approach is the decrease in the long-term coronary recurrence risk. Thus, these behaviorally based lifestyle interventions not only alleviate unnecessary suffering in an already burdened patient group, but also save lives.

Although it is problematic to delineate more explicitly the specific components of the individual programs essential for the effects, a common denominator among them is the explicit and aggressive focus on actual behavior change as well as prolonged contact for maintenance and compliance support, often extended for a full year or even up to several years. Even though the results are dramatic and convincing, most of reviewed studies are rather small and often based on selected samples of participants which of course pose restrictions of the conclusions that can be drawn. Taken as a whole though, this body of evidence does clearly indicate, that further development, deployment and, most importantly, large-scale evaluation of such interventions are warranted. Two other areas now also seem important to address. First, in order to achieve the greatest effects on long-term lifestyle behavior changes, and to optimize cost-effective intervention formats usable in a more general practice, specific components of the intervention need to be examined. Secondly, it is time to focus on more mechanistic questions: Is there a direct relation between the degree of behavior change and the progress of CAD? Perhaps, the overall adherence to the lifestyle changes was related to the degree of changes in the coronary lesions. For example, subjects in 'The Life Style Heart Trial' (Ornish et al., 1990; 1998) adhering the most to the program had the greatest regression of atherosclerosis, while those who did not change their lifestyle experienced a further worsening of the condition. This finding is of importance since such "dose-response" associations indicate a casual relationship.

On the other hand, much uncertainty still remains concerning the degree of change that is needed in each lifestyle behavior area, and if changes in all areas are equally important to influence disease progression. It is possible that smaller changes in a broad range of different lifestyle areas is as, or even more, important than larger changes in a single or a few areas.

Coronary artery disease is subject to a multitude of etiologic and influencing factors, factors closely connected to different lifestyle behavior areas. Hence, it seems reasonable that an optimal intervention program should be directed towards changing multiple factors involved. The most important lifestyle factors appear to be physical activity/exercise, stress management, diet, and smoking. Behavioral psychology methodologies and approaches have an obvious importance in promoting this endeavor.

REFERENCES

Appels A, Bar FW, Bar J, Bruggeman C, de Baets M (2000) Inflammation, depressive symptomtology, and coronary artery disease. Psychosomatic Med 62(5): 601-5.

Apples A, Mulder P, (1989) Fatigue and heart diseases. The association between vital exhaustion and past, present and future coronary heart disease. J Psychosomatic Res 33: 727-738.

Bandura A. (1977) Self-Efficacy: Toward a unifying theory of behavioral change. Psychological Rev 84(2): 191-215.

Bandura A. (1997) Self-Efficacy: The exercise of control. New York: Freeman & Co.

Bellg AJ. (2003) Maintenance of health behavior change in preventive cardiology. Internalization and self-regulation of new behaviors.Behavior Modification 27(1): 103-31.

Benowitz NL, Kuyt F, Jacob P. (1984) Influence of nicotine on cardiovascular and hormonal effects of cigarette smoking. Clin Pharmacol Ther 36: 74-81.

Berglund G, Wilhelmsen L, Sannerstedt R, Hansson L, Andersson O, Sivertsson R, Wedel H, Wikstrand J. (1978). Coronary heart disease after treatment of hypertension. Lancet 1:1-5.

Berkman LF. (1984) The relationship between social network and social support in morbidity and mortality. In J Cohen & L Syme (Eds.), Social support and health. New York: Academic Press.

Berkman LF, Blumenthal J, Burg M, Carney RM, Catellier D, Cowan MJ, Czajkowski SM, DeBusk R, Hosking J, Jaffe A, Kaufmann PG, Mitchell P, Norman J, Powell LH, Raczynski JM, Schneiderman N; Enhancing Recovery in Coronary Heart Disease Patients Investigators(ENRICHD) (2003) Effects of treating depression and low perceived social support on clinical events after myocardial infarction: the Enhancing Recovery in Coronary Heart Disease Patients (ENRICHD) Randomized Trial. JAMA 289(23): 3106-16.

Berlin JA, Colditz GA. (1990) A meta analysis of physical activity in the prevention of coronary heart disease. Am J Epidemiol 132: 612-628.

Bondjers G, Hansson G, Olsson G, Petterson K. (1990) Smoking and catecholamines and their effects on endothelial integrity. Adv Exp Med Biol 273: 51-59.

Breslow JL. (1991) Lipoprotein transport gene abnormalities underlying coronary heart disease susceptibility. Ann Rev Med 42: 357-371.

Brindley DN, McCann BS, Niaura R, Stoney CM, Suarez EC. (1993) Stress and lipoprotein metabolism: modulators and mechanisms. Metabolism 42(9 Suppl 1): 3-15.

Burke AP, Farb A, Malcolm GT, Liang Y-H, Smialek J, Virmani R. (1997) Coronary risk factors and plaque morphology in men with coronary disease who died suddenly. New Engl J Med 336: 1276-1282.

Campbell N, Thain J, Deans H, Ritchie L, Rawles J, Squair J. (1998) Secondary prevention clinics for coronary heart disease: A randomized trial of effect on health. BMJ 316: 1434-1437.

Castelli WP. (1984) Epidemiology of coronary heart disease: The Framingham study. Am J Med 76: 4-12.

Cavender JB, Rogers WJ, Fisher LD, Gersh BJ, Coggin CJ, Myers WO. (1992) Effects of smoking on survival and morbidity in patients randomized to medical or surgical therapy in the coronary artery surgery study (CASS): 10 year follow-up. JAm College Cardiol 20: 287-294.

Cheitlin MD. (1988) Finding the high risk patient with coronary artery disease. JAMA 259: 2271-2277.

Chrousos GP. (1995) The hypothalamic-pituitary-adrenal axis and immune-mediated inflammation. New Engl J Med 332(20): 1351-1362.

Craig WY, Palomaki GE, Haddow JE. (1989) Cigarette smoking and serum lipid and lipoprotein concentrations: An analysis of published data. BMJ 298: 784-788.

de Lorgeril M, Salen P, Martin JL, Monjaud I, Delaye J, Mamelle N (1999) Mediterranean diet, traditional risk factors, and the rate of cardiovascular complications after myocardial infarction: Final report of the Lyon diet heart study. Circulation 99: 779-785.

Epstein LH, Perkins KA. (1988) Smoking, stress and coronary heart disease. J Consult Clin Psychol 56: 342-349.

Expert Panel. (1988) Report of the national cholesterol education program experts panel on detection, evaluation and treatment of high cholesterol in adults. Arch Int Med 148: 142-152.

Gaziano JM. (2001) Global burden of cardiovascular disease. In E Braunwald, DP Zipes and P Libby: Heart Disease. Philadelphia, Pennsylvania: WB Saunders Company

Gersh BJ, Braunwald E, Bonow RO.(2001 Chronic coronary artery disease. In E Braunwald, DP Zipes & P Libby (Eds.), Heart Disease. Philadelphia, PA: WB Saunders.

Gordon NF, Haskell WL. (1997) Comprehensive cardiovascular disease risk reduction in a cardiac rehabilitation setting. Am J Cardiol 80: 69H-73H.

Gould KL, Ornish D, Scherwitz L, Brown S, Edens RP, Hess MJ, Mullani N, Bolomey L, Dobbs F, Armstrong WT, et al. (1995) Changes in myocardial perfusion abnormalities by positron emission tomography after long-term, intense risk factor modification. JAMA, 274(11): 894-901

Gould KL, Ornish D, Kirkeeide R, Brown S, Stuart Y, Buchi M, Billings J, Armstrong W, Ports T, Scherwitz L. (1992) Improved stenosis geometry by quantitative coronary arteriography after vigorous risk factor modification. Am J Cardiol 69: 845-853.

Grundy SM, Balady GJ, Criqui MH, Fletcher G, Greenland P, Hiratzka LF, Houston-Miller N, Kris-Etherton P, Krumholz HM, LaRosa J, Ockene IS, Pearson TA, Reed J, Washington R, Smith SC Jr. (1998) Primary prevention of coronary heart disease: Guidance from Framingham: A statement for health care professionals from the AHA task force on risk reduction. Circulation 97:1876-1887.

Hambrecht R, Niebauer J, Marburger C, Grunze M, Kalberer B, Hauer K, Schlierf G, Kubler W, Schuler G. (1993) Various intensities of leisure time physical activity in patients with coronary artery disease: effects on cardiorespiratory fitness and progression of coronary atherosclerotic lesions. J Am College Cardiol 22(2): 468-77.

Haskell WL, Alderman EL, Fair JM, Maron DJ, Mackey SF, Superko HR, Williams PT, Johnstone IM, Champagne MA, Krauss RM et al. (1994) Effects of intensive multiple risk factor reduction on coronary atherosclerosis and clinical cardiac events in men and women with coronary artery disease. The Stanford Coronary Risk Intervention Project (SCRIP). Circulation 89: 975-990.

Haynes SG, Matthews KA. (1988) The association of type A behavior with cardiovascular disease – update and critical review. In BK Houston & CR Snyder (Eds.), Type A behavior pattern (pp . 51-82). New York: Wiley

Hennekens CH, Rosner B, Cole DS. (1978) Daily alcohol consumption and fatal coronary heart disease. Am J Epidemiol 107: 196-200.

Hofman-Bang C, Lisspers J, Nordlander R, Nygren A, Sundin O, Ohman A, Ryden L. (1999a) Two-year results of a controlled study of residential rehabilitation for patients treated with percutaneous transluminal coronary angioplasty. A randomized study of a multifactorial programme. Eur Heart J 20: 1465-1474.

Hofman-Bang C, Svane B, Lisspers J, Nordlander R, Nygren Å, Sundin Ö, Öhman A. Rydén L. (1999b) Effects of a multifactorial lifestyle program on progression of atherosclerotic lesions assessed by quantitative coronary arteriography - A randomized controlled study. In: Hofman-Bang. C. Evaluation of a multifactorial rehabilitation programme on lifestyle behaviour and secondary prevention in patients with coronary artery disease (Study IV). Dissertation: Department of Clinical Neuroscience, Karolinska institute (ISBN 91-628-3552-1).

Hubert HB, Feinlieb M, McNamara PM, Castelli WP. (1983) Obesity as an independent risk factor for cardiovascular disease: A 26 year follow-up of participants in the Framingham Heart Study. Circulation 67: 968-977.

Hunink MG, Goldman L, Tosteson ANA, Mittleman MA, Goldman PA, Williams LW, Tsevat J, Weinstein MC. (1997) The recent decline in mortality from coronary heart disease, 1980-1990. the effects of secular trends in risk factor and treatment. JAMA 227:535-542.

Janz NK, Backer MH. (1984) The health belief model: A decade later. Health Education Quart 11(1): 1-47.

Janz NK, Champion VL,Strecher VJ. (2002) The health belief model. In: Glanz, K, Rimer, BK & Lewis, FM (Eds.) Health behavior and health education: Theory, research, and practice (pp 45-66). San Francisco, CA: Jossey-Bass

Jones DA, West RR. (1996) Psychological rehabilitation after myocardial infarction: A multicentre randomized controlled trial. BMJ 313: 1517-1521.

Jolly K, Bradley F, Sharp S, Smith H, Thompson S, Kinmonth A-L, Mant D. (1999) Randomized controlled trial of follow up care in general practice of patients with myocardial infarction and angina: final results of the Southampton heart integrated care project (SHIP). BMJ 318: 706-711.

Kannel WB. (1987) New perspectives on cardiovascular risk factors. Am Heart J 114: 213-219.

Kaplan RM, Atkins CJ. (1984) Specific efficacy expectations mediate exercise compliance in patients with COPD. Health Psychol 3(3): 223-242.

Karasek RA, Theorell T, Schwartz J, Pieper C, Alfredsson L. (1982) Job, psychological factors, and coronary heart disease. Swedish prospective findings and U.S. prevalence using a new occupational influence method. Adv Cardiol 29: 62-67.

Krantz DS, Kop WJ, Santiago HT, Gottdiener JS. (1996) Mental stress as a trigger of myocardial ischemia and infarction. Cardiol Clin 14: 271-287.

Kop WJ, Appels AWM, Mendes de Leon CF, de Swart HB, Bär FW. (1994).Vital exhaustion predicts new cardiac events after successful coronary angioplasty. Psychosomatic Med 56: 281-287.

Koertge J, Wamala SP, Janszky I, Blom M, Al-Khalili F, Sundin Ö, Chesney M, Svane B, Schenck-Gustafsson K. (2002) Vital Exhaustion as predictor of poor prognosis in women with acute myocardial infarction. Psychol Health Med 7: 117 - 126.

Lane D, Carrol D, Lip GYH. (1999) Psychology in coronary care. Q J Med, 92: 425-431.

Lees LA, Dygdon JA. (1988) The initiation and maintenance of exercise behavior: A learning theory conceptualization. Clin Psychol Rev 8: 345-353.

Liebson PR, Amsterdam EA. (1999) Prevention of coronary heart disease. Part I. Primary prevention. Disease-a-month, 45: 497-571.

LIPID study group. (1998) The long term intervention with pravastatin in ischaemic disease. Prevention of cardiovascular events and death with pravastatin in patients with coronary heart disease and a broad range of initial cholesterol levels. New Engl J Med 339: 1349-1357.

Lisspers J, Sundin O, Ohman A, Hofman-Bang C, Ryden L, Nygren A. (2005) Long-term effects of lifestyle behavior change in coronary artery disease: effects on recurrent coronary events after percutaneous coronary intervention. Health Psychol 24(1): 41-8.

Lisspers J, Hofman-Bang C, Nordlander R, Ryden L, Sundin O, Ohman A. Nygren A. (1999a) Multifactorial evaluation of a program for lifestyle behavior change in rehabilitation and secondary prevention of coronary artery disease. Scan Cardiovasc J 33: 9-16.

Lisspers J, Sundin O, Hofman-Bang C, Nordlander R, Nygren A, Ryden L, Ohman A. (1999b) Behavioral effects of a comprehensive, multifactorial program for lifestyle change after percutaneous transluminal coronary angioplasty: a prospective, randomized controlled study. J Psychosom Res 46: 143-154.

Manchanda SC, Narang R, Reddy KS, Sachdeva U, Prabhakaran D, Dharmanand S, Rajani M, Bijlani R. (2000) Retardation of coronary atherosclerosis with yoga lifestyle intervention. J Assoc Phys India 48: 687-694.

McCann BS, Warnick GR, Knopp RH. (1990) Changes in plasma lipids and dietary intake accompanying shifts in perceived workload and stress. Psychosom Med 52: 212-219.

Niebauer J, Hambrecht R, Marburger C, Hauer K, Velich T, von Hodenberg E, Schlierf G, Kubler W, Schuler G. (1995) Impact of intensive physical exercise and low-fat diet on collateral vessel formation in stable angina pectoris and angiographically confirmed coronary artery disease. Am J Cardiol 76(11): 771-5.

Niebauer J, Hambrecht R, Velich T, Hauer K, Marburger C, Kalberer B, Weiss C, von Hodenberg E, Schlierf G, Schuler G, Zimmermann R, Kubler W. (1997) Attenuated progression of coronary artery disease after 6 years of multifactorial risk intervention: role of physical exercise. Circulation 96:2534-2541.

Nunes EV, Frank KA, Kornfeld DS. (1987) Psychological treatment for the type A behavior pattern and for coronary heart disease: a meta-analysis of the literature. Psychosom Med 48: 159-173.

O'Connor GT, Buring JE, Yusuf S, Goldhaber SZ, Olmstead EM, Paffenbarger RS et al. (1989) An overview of randomized trials of rehabilitation with exercise after myocardial infarction. Circulation 80:234–44.

Oldridge NB. (1988) Compliance with exercise in cardiac rehabilitation. In: R.K. Dishman (Ed.), Exercise adherence: It's impact on public health. Champaign, IL: Human Kinetics Books, 283-304.

Oldridge NB, Guyatt GH, Fischer ME, Rimm AA. (1988) Cardiac rehabilitation after myocardial infarction. Combined experience of randomized clinical trials. JAMA 260: 945–50.

Ornish D, Scherwitz LW, Billings JH, Brown SE, Gould KL, Merritt TA, Sparler S, Armstrong WT, Ports TA, Kirkeeide RL, Hogeboom C, Brand RJ. (1998) Intensive lifestyle changes for reversal of coronary heart disease. JAMA 280(23): 2001-7

Ornish D, Brown SE, Scherwitz LW, Billings JH, Armstrong WT, Ports TA, McLanahan SM, Kirkeeide RL, Brand RJ, Gould KL. (1990) Can lifestyle changes reverse coronary heart disease? The Lifestyle Heart Trial. Lancet 336: 129-133.

Paffenbarger RS. (1985) Physical activity is a defense against coronary heart disease.

In WE Connor & JD Bristow (Eds.), Coronary Heart Disease: Prevention, complications and treatment (pp 135-155). Philadelphia, PA: Lippincott.

Paffenbarger RS, Hyde RT, Wing AL, Lee IM, Jung DI, Kamper JB. (1993) The association of changes in physical-activity level and other life style characteristics with mortality among men. New Engl J Med 328: 538-545.

Paul O. (1989) Background of the prevention of cardiovascular disease: II: Arteriosclerosis, hypertension, and selected risk factors. Circulation 80: 206-214.

Prochaska JO, DiClemente CC. (1983) Stages and processes of self-change of smoking: Toward a more integrative model of change. J Consult Clin Psychol 5: 390-395.

Prochaska JO, Redding CA, Evers KE. (2002) The transtheoretical model and stages of change. In: Glanz, K, Rimer, BK & Lewis, FM (Eds.) Health behavior and health education: Theory, research, and practice (pp 99-120). San Francisco, CA: Jossey-Bass.

Öhman A, Sundin Ö. (1995) Emotional factors in cardiovascular disorder. Cur Opin Psychiatr 8, 410 - 413.

Quinn TG, Alderman EL, McMillan A. Haskell W. (1994) Development of new coronary atherosclerotic lesions during a 4-year multifactor risk reduction program: the Stanford Coronary Risk Intervention Project (SCRIP). J Am College Cardiol 24,:900-908.

Richardson PD, Davies MJ, Born GVR. (1989) Influence of plaque configuration and stress distribution on fissuring of coronary atherosclerotic plaques. Lancet 2: 941-944.

Rigotti NA, Pasternak RC. (1996). Cigarette smoking and coronary heart disease. Risks and management. Cardiol Clin 14: 51–68.

Robertson, D, Tseng CJ, Appalsamy, M (1988) Smoking and mechanisms of cardiovascular control. Am Heart J 115: 258-263.

Rosenberg L, Palmer JR, Shapiro S. (1990) Decline in the risk of myocardial infarction among women who stop smoking. N Engl J Med 322(4): 213-7.

Rosengren A, Hawken S, Ounpuu S, Sliwa K, Zubaid M, Almahmeed WA, Blackett KN, Sitthi-amorn C, Sato H, Yusuf S; INTERHEART investigators. (2004) Association of psychosocial risk factors with risk of acute myocardial infarction in 11119 cases and 13648 controls from 52 countries (the INTERHEART study): case-control study. Lancet 364: 953-62.

Rosenstock IM. (1974) Historical origins of the health belief model. Health Education Monographs 2(4): 1-9.

Rosenstock IM, Strecher VJ, Becker MH. (1988) Social learning theory and the health belief theory. Health Education Quart 15: 175-183.

Sansone C, Harackiewicz JM. (2000) Looking beyond rewards: The problem and promise of intrinsic motivation. In: Sansone, C. (Ed.): Intrinsic and Extrinsic Motivation. The Search for Optimal Motivation and Performance. London, USA: Academic Press, 2000, 1-6.

Scandinavian Simvastatin Survival Study Group. (1994) Randomised trial of cholesterol lowering in 4444 patients with coronary heart disease: the Scandinavian Simvastatin Survival Study (4S). Lancet 344: 1383-89.

Schuler, G, Hambrecht, R, Schlierf, G, Niebauer, J, Hauer, K, Neumann, J, Hoberg, E, Drinkmann, A, Bacher, F, Grunze M et al. (1992) Regular physical exercise and low-fat diet. Effects on progression of coronary artery disease. Circulation 86: 1-11.

Sebregts EH, Falger PR, Bar FW. (2000) Risk factor modification through nonpharmacological interventions in patients with coronary heart disease. J Psychosom Res 48: 425-41.

Shekelle RB, Shyrock AM, Paul PO, Lepper M, Stamler J, Liu S, Raynor WJ. (1981) Diet, serum cholesterol, and death from coronary heart disease - The Western Electric Study. New Engl J Med 304: 65-70.

Sheperd RJ, Balady GJ. (1999) Exercise as Cardiovascular therapy. Circulation 99: 963-972.

Singh RB, Rastogi SS, Verma R, Laxmi B, Singh R, Ghosh S, et al. (1992) Randomised controlled trial of cardio-protective diet in patients with recent acute myocardial infarction: results of one year follow up. BMJ 304: 1015–9.

Skinner BF. (1977) Why I am not a cognitive psychologist. Behaviorism 5(2): 1-10.

Skinner BF. (1985) Cognitive science and behaviourism. Brit J Psychol 76(3): 291-301.

Skinner BF. (1988) Whatever happened to psychology as the science of behavior? Counsel Psychol Quart 1(1): 111-122.

Skinner BF. (1989) The origins of cognitive thought. Am Psychol 44(1): 13-18.

Strawn WB, Bondjers G, Kaplan JR, Clarkson TB, Manuck SB, Weingard KW, Shively CA, Adams MR. (1991) Endothelial dysfunction in response to psychological stress in monkeys. Circulation Res 68: 1270-1279

Sundin Ö. (1993) Psychophysiological reactivity, type A behaviour, and rehabilitation after myocardial infarc-tion. Acta Univ Ups., Comprehensive summaries of Uppsala Dissertation from the faculty of Social Sciences, 36.

Sundin Ö, Öhman A, Palm T, Ström G (1995) Cardiovascular reactivity, type A behavior, and coronary heart disease. Psychophysiol 32: 28-36

Sundin Ö, Lisspers J, Hofman-Bang C, Öhman A, Rydén L. (2003) Comparing Multi-factorial Lifestyle Interventions and Stress-management in Coronary Risk Reduction. Int J Behav Med 10: 191-204.

Taylor RS, Brown A, Ebrahim S, Jolliffe J, Noorani H, Rees K, Skidmore B, Stone JA, Thompson DR, Oldridge N. (2004) Exercise-based rehabilitation for patients with coronary heart disease: systematic review and meta-analysis of

BEHAVIORAL AND LIFESTYLE INTERVENTIONS FOR THE TREATMENT OF HYPERTENSION

Thomas Pickering

INTRODUCTION

Hypertension affects 65 million individuals in the United States, and is a major risk factor for coronary heart disease and stroke, which are the first and third most common causes of death in the US. The relationship between blood pressure and risk is a continuous one, and the risk increases steadily above a systolic pressure of 115 mmHg. The level of blood pressure above which treatment (usually but not necessarily with medications) is recommended is 140/90 mmHg. The recent guidelines for the detection and treatment of hypertension (JNC 7, 2003) introduced a new classification of hypertension. A truly normal blood pressure is defined as less than 120/80 mmHg, and if the pressure is in the high normal range (120-130/80-89 mmHg) it is called prehypertension. Stage 1 hypertension is a pressure between 140 and 159/90-99 mmHg, and stage 2 is defined as a pressure above 160/100 mmHg.

Numerous studies using antihypertensive drugs have demonstrated that treating hypertension can reverse the risk of cardiovascular events of stroke by about 50% and heart attacks by about 25%. A meta-analysis of the drug trials shows that a 5mmHg reduction of blood pressure would lower cardiovascular events by about 20%. (Turnbull et al., 2003). There has been considerable debate as to whether it matters which type of antihypertensive drug is used to lower the pressure, but the consensus is that it is the reduction of blood pressure that is the critical factor. Given that drug trials suggest that it does not matter which mechanism is used to lower blood pressure, it is reasonable to suppose that non-drug methods of lowering blood pressure should also help to reduce cardiovascular events. Thus far, non-drug trials of treating hypertension have not shown any reduction of cardiovascular events because they have been insufficiently powered to do so. Nevertheless, several non-drug interventions for hypertension show promise. In this chapter we will examine research into behavioral and lifestyle interventions for the treatment of hypertension, focusing on studies of biofeedback, relaxation techniques, dietary modification, exercise and medication adherence. These behavioral methods could be used either alone or in conjunction with antihypertensive drugs to reduce overall blood pressure while potentially requiring less medication. Because a large number of randomized controlled trials have been conducted on these topics, we will focus on the results of recent metaanalyses.

TRAINING PATIENTS TO CONTROL BLOOD PRESSURE

Historical Foundations of Relaxation and Biofeedback Therapies for Hypertension

Patients frequently seek to treat hypertension in a way that does not sentence them to a lifetime of taking drugs. Since there is a common perception that hypertension is one of the results of the stressful lifestyles, techniques that lead to stress reduction might be expected to lower blood pressure. Although procedures such as autogenic training and progressive muscular relaxation have been practiced for more than 50 years, the idea really took off in the early seventies with the popularization of two forms of treatment, one ancient and the other novel-transcendental meditation and biofeedback.

The former was championed by Herbert Benson, M.D., in Boston (Benson et al., 1974), and the latter by Dr. Chandra Patel in the UK (Patel et al., 1981; Patel & Marmot, 1988). Both groups published dramatic results which suggested that these behavioral treatments could produce decreases of blood pressure of the same magnitude as seen with drug treatment, without the expense and side effects of drugs. Moreover, Benson reported a reduction of 10.5/4.9 mmHg in patients on antihypertensive drugs who practiced the relaxation response regularly (Benson et al., 1974). Thirty years later, neither procedure has established a place in the routine treatment of hypertension, although both are used for other purposes. Despite the medical profession's lack of enthusiasm for behavioral treatments, the public are still interested. In a survey of the use of unconventional medicine in the United States, Eisenberg and colleagues (1993) indicated that 11% of hypertensive patients reported using unconventional therapy in the past 12 months, mostly relaxation techniques and homeopathy.

Biofeedback

The idea of biofeedback originated with the work of Dr. Neal Miller, a renowned experimental psychologist, who first developed the concept of "visceral learning" (Miller, 1974). It was based on a series of animal experiments which showed that rats could be trained to raise and lower their blood pressure using psychological conditioning techniques. Biofeedback was applied to human studies, where subjects were instructed to learn voluntary blood pressure control by attempting to keep a tone sounding, which was triggered by changes of blood pressure in the appropriate direction. The rationale was that one reason why we cannot normally control our autonomic functions voluntarily is that we lack the conscious perception of them, and that if this is provided (by biofeedback)

we can learn to "drive our own bodies", as one of the early enthusiasts put it.

In addition to the direct measurement of blood pressure through biofeedback, other somatic indices have been used to reduce blood pressure including muscle tension as measured through electromyography and skin temperature as measured through thermal feedback (e.g., hand-warming). Studies using only biofeedback, while initially encouraging, were less likely to show significant changes in blood pressure when measurements were made out of the office (see Blanchard et al., 1996) and thermal biofeedback (training subjects to warm their hands and feet) had no measurable effect on home or ambulatory blood pressure. A meta-analysis (Eisenberg et al., 1993) included six groups (n=90) that received only biofeedback therapies. The blood pressure reduction was minimal (-2.6/0.2 mmHg) in comparison with patients who were waitlist controls or who underwent sham therapies (-2.9/-1.2 mmHg), and in whom the baseline blood pressure measurements had extended beyond one day. Even in the studies that reported reductions in blood pressure with direct biofeedback, long term follow-up data beyond a six month period has been inconsistent or lacking.

A more recent meta-analysis (Yucha et al., 2001) concluded that when biofeedback was compared against an active control group (such as relaxation training, cognitive behavioral therapy, or self-monitoring) the changes were not clinically significant, but when compared against an "inactive" control (wait list control, or sham biofeedback), significant effects on clinic blood pressure were achieved. These changes are summarized in Table 1. These data are for blood pressure measured in the clinic setting, so they should be interpreted with caution. As will be discussed in more detail later, clinic blood pressure readings are often biased by mood and anxiety related to the clinic setting.

Table 1: Meta-analysis of effects of biofeedback (BFB) on clinic blood pressure (Yucha et al., 2001)

Comparison	Mean change (mmHg)	95% CI	Number of studies
Systolic pressure			
BFB vs active control	-2.1	-7.0, 2.9	6
BFB vs. inactive control	-6.7*	-10.2, -3.2	14
Diastolic pressure			
BFB vs active control	-3.4	-7.4, 0.6	6
BFB vs inactive control	-4.8*	-7.2, -2.3	13

- $p < 0.05$ for comparison between experimental and control groups

The same meta-analysis reviewed the different types of biofeedback to determine if any one appeared to be superior. The authors concluded that thermal and electrodermal activity (EDA) biofeedback were superior to combined EMG and blood pressure feedback (Table 2), but the numbers of studies are too small to allow any definitive conclusions.

Table 2: Meta-analysis of effects of different types of biofeedback (BFB) on clinic blood pressure (Yucha et al., 2001)

Comparison	Mean change (mmHg)	95% CI	Number of studies
Systolic pressure			
Thermal BFB vs inactive control	-5.0*	-9.1, -0.9	5
EDA BFB vs. inactive control	-7.1	-14.3, 0.2	3
EMG/BP BFB vs. inactive control	0.2	-5.6, 6.1	2
Diastolic pressure			
Thermal BFB vs inactive control	-6.3*	-9.9, -2.7	4
EDA BFB vs inactive control	-3.8*	-7.0, -0.6	3
EMG/BP BFB vs. inactive control	1.3	-1.6, 4.3	2

EDA = electrodermal activity (skin resistance); EMG/BP = combined electromyogram and blood pressure feedback.
* $p < 0.05$ for comparison between experimental and control groups

A novel method has been used by Hunyor, to monitor blood pressure continuously from a finger (Hunyor et al., 1997). This technique uses a method similar to the Finapres device, which monitors blood pressure noninvasively on a beat-to-beat basis. One of the attractive features of this method is that it is possible to provide false feedback, so that the placebo effect produced by the expectation that the impressive equipment will improve blood pressure can be eliminated. Subjects in the true feedback condition can be trained to raise and lower their blood pressure by attempting to move a line on a computer screen, whose position is determined by the blood pressure. However, patients in the placebo group were able to produce similar changes in clinic blood pressure, and there were no significant effects on ambulatory pressure in either group. A second study using this technique (Henderson et al., 1998) extended the training to include practice at home, and it was demonstrated that people can learn to improve their ability to lower blood pressure with repetition. Despite this technical sophistication, the clinical effectiveness of this procedure remains equivocal. Although clinic blood pressures fell more in the treatment group (154/98 to 144/91mm Hg, as compared to 152/96 to 147/93 mmHg in the control group), the differences between the two groups were not statistically or clinically significant. In summary, although perhaps capable of producing reductions in clinic blood pressure, there is little evidence that biofeedback produces clinically meaningful reductions in ambulatory blood pressure and no standardized method of biofeedback is currently recommended as a therapy for hypertension.

Relaxation techniques

In 1938, Edmund Jacobson proposed that patients with hypertension were hypermetabolic and had excessive muscle tension, and that a reduction in this muscle tension would lead to a corresponding decrease in blood pressure (Jacobson, 1938). His technique, known as Progressive Muscle Relaxation, has been used for many years and involves a procedure in which patients are instructed to tense and then relax different sets of muscles.

Jacobson reasoned that since relaxation methods induce a state of physiologic hypometabolism described by Hess (Hess, 1957), which in cats is associated with decreased sympathetic activity, these were protective responses that countered excessive stress or flight or fright responses.

In practice, relaxation therapies may range from a physician's simple advice to his patient to "relax" to more formal structured techniques. These may include meditative techniques like Yoga and Zen based on eastern traditions, progressive relaxation developed by Jacobson, or autogenic training as developed by Luthe (Luthe, 1969). The common elements in all these techniques appears to be mental focusing, task awareness, sitting quietly, and relaxing all muscle groups. Mental focusing involves directing attention to a constant or repetitive internal or external stimulus such as the feeling accompanying relaxation or a silently repeated word or phrase.

Several relaxation methods have been identified by Shapiro for the treatment of hypertension (Shapiro et al., 1978) as follows:

- Progressive relaxation: a technique directed at relaxation of major skeletal muscle groups
- Autogenic training: standard "auto-suggestive" exercises for inducing altered physiologic and mental states.
- Hypnotic relaxation: hypnosis and post-hypnotic suggestion to induce physiologic and mental relaxation.
- Zen meditation: methods of meditation involving passive concentration on respiration and exercise to elicit relaxation.
- Hatha yoga: relaxation elicited via bodily postures and exercises, breath control and meditation.
- Transcendental meditation: a cognitive technique derived from vedic practices in which individuals assume a comfortable position, breathe peace-fully, close the

eyes, and repeat a "mantra" as each breath is exhaled.

Since the early 1970s several studies have reported statistically significant reductions in both systolic and diastolic blood pressures with relaxation therapy as a sole intervention (Benson et al., 1974; Benson, 1982). As mentioned above, Benson's group (Caudill et al., 1987) showed that practice of a standardized meditation technique for one month resulted in reduction of blood pressure in 22 untreated borderline hypertensives (average reduction of 7 mm Hg systolic and 4 mm Hg diastolic) and 14 treated hypertensive patients (average blood pressure reduction of 11 mm Hg systolic and 5 mm Hg diastolic) which persisted for a five month period. Brady et al. (1974) used a metronome-conditioned relaxation therapy and achieved a reduction of up to 10 mm Hg diastolic blood pressure in four hypertensive patients.

Most of the early studies were limited by weaknesses in methodology, including small sample size, absence of control groups, confounding factors such as pharmacological treatment or placebo response, statistical artifacts including regression to the mean, and reliance on clinic or laboratory blood pressure measurements (Jacob et al., 1991). Later studies that measured ambulatory blood have produced mixed results. Two have reported positive findings. Southam et al. (1982) studied the effects of relaxation therapy on forty-two patients with diastolic pressures of greater than 90 mm Hg who were randomized to either relaxation training or no intervention. At six months there was a clinically significant reduction in the daytime ambulatory blood pressure in the treatment group (mean change of –6.0/–12.1 as compared to +1.3/–2.2 mm Hg in the control group). The changes in the pressure measured in the clinic were somewhat larger than the changes in ambulatory pressures. In a study of 39 subjects randomized to either a meditation group or a cognitive stress education control group, Wenneberg et al. (1997) reported a mean reduction of 9 mmHg in ambulatory diastolic pressure in the meditation group.

Other studies have found no effect on ambulatory blood pressure. A study by Jacob et al. (1986) on the effect of relaxation therapy as compared with antihypertensive medications (atenolol and chlorthalidone) indicated a modest but marginally statistically significant reduction in clinic blood pressure (2 to 3 mm Hg decrease in systolic and diastolic blood pressures), but no effect on ambulatory blood pressure. In contrast, the effects of the drugs were substantial and significant for both measures of blood pressure A later study by van Montfrans et al. (1990) found a modest reduction of clinic pressure (2 mm Hg), but no change in intra-arterial 24 hour pressure following relaxation training. This issue is thus still unresolved.

As with biofeedback studies, one of the problems with relaxation studies has been that similar decreases in blood pressure are often seen in both the active treatment and control groups. A good example of this phenomenon was reported by Irvine and Logan (1991) in 100 untreated hypertensives, who were randomized to a 12 week course of relaxation training (with a little biofeedback included in some sessions) or a non-specific support group. Both groups received weekly sessions with the same therapists. Blood pressure fell by the same amount (5/5 mmHg) in both groups. The same thing occurred in an industry-based study by Chesney et al. (1987), who found marked reduction of clinic blood pressure of 7.4/4.5 mmHg in the treatment group (relaxation plus biofeedback), but this was also observed in the control (blood pressure monitoring) group, where the fall was 9.0/5.9 mmHg. This study measured blood pressure in the clinic and the worksite, where the changes were less pronounced, but virtually identical for the two groups (Figure 1).

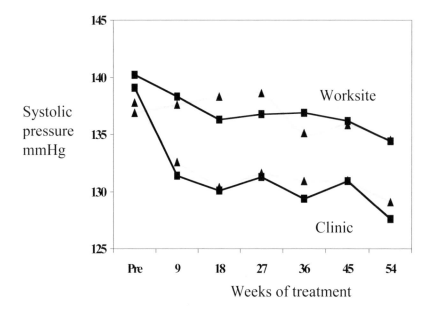

Figure 1:
Decline of blood pressure measured both at the worksite and in the clinic during a controlled trial of relaxation therapy. Black lines show changes in the active treatment group, and grey lines the control group (Chesney et al., 1987).

One factor that appears to be very important in determining the magnitude of the effects of any of these techniques on blood pressure is the pretreatment level of pressure, as shown by a meta-analysis conducted by Jacob et al. (1991). Thus many of the negative studies have included subjects whose initial pressures were essentially normal. One example is the Trial of Hypertension Prevention, phase I (TOHP-I) (Batey et al., 2000), in which 562 healthy participants (diastolic blood pressures of 80-89 mm Hg) were randomized to either stress management intervention or an assessment only (control) group. The interventions included training in relaxation techniques in addition to cognitive techniques, anger management, improvement of communication skills and time management. Intention to treat analysis showed an absence of blood pressure lowering efficacy of the intervention. A second example is a study by Fiedler et al. (1989), that investigated the effects of a stress management program in 66 hazardous waste workers. The study utilized a combination of progressive muscular relaxation and meditation techniques, and found no changes of ambulatory blood pressure in either the experimental or control groups. This is hardly surprising since the pretreatment work blood pressures were normal: 124/80 mmHg and 124/79 mmHg in the experimental and control groups. The Jacob meta-analysis included 75 treatment groups and 41 control groups (Jacob et al., 1991) and showed that the reduction of blood pressure after treatment was directly related to the height of the pressure before treatment. The analysis also established that the treatment effect was related to the number of pre-treatment baseline readings. Thus the expected decrease of systolic pressure with a pre-treatment pressure of 140 mmHg and one baseline session was 9.4 mmHg, whereas if there were four baseline visits the expected decrease would be only 3.3 mmHg. This analysis suggests that regression to the mean could explain much of the change in blood pressure over time. If regression to the mean was responsible for treatment effects, one would expect the same decrease of pressure to be seen in both the treatment and control groups (as was observed, for example in the Irvine and Logan study). These results suggest that relaxation techniques are not effective therapies for hypertension control.

Several studies have compared different varieties of biofeedback and relaxation techniques, but with the exception of the controlled breathing device described later, none have shown any consistent superiority over the others (McCaffrey & Blanchard, 1985). Linden et al. (2001) reported substantial reductions of ambulatory blood pressure (6/4 mmHg) as a result of a stress management program that utilized a variety of interventions including autogenic training, biofeedback, cognitive therapy, and anxiety management. In this study, the exact mode of treatment was individualized, which makes it very difficult to generalize these results.

Effects of Relaxation Training on Cardiovascular Events

One analysis has examined whether the use of transcendental meditation (TM) might affect survival (Schneider et al., 2005). The results of two randomized controlled studies of TM in elderly patients whose original goal was reduction of blood pressure and for which long-term follow-up was available were pooled. Both compared the effects of TM against other behavioral forms of treatment (mindfulness training, mental relaxation, and progressive muscle relaxation) and usual care. In the combined studies there were 202 subjects, and 101 deaths during the 7.6 year follow-up. Although the authors found that TM was associated with a marginally (p<0.04) significant reduction in overall mortality when compared with the active controls, there was no effect when it was compared with usual care on either total or cardiovascular mortality.

Can the effects of biofeedback and relaxation be attributed to placebo effects?

One source of variability in the results of these studies is the procedure used to measure blood pressure. The early trials used clinic measurements (Patel et al. 1981; Patel & Marmot, 1988; Benson et al., 1974), which are known to be very susceptible to the placebo effect. It is now clearly recognized that blood pressure tends to increase just before a clinic visit, a phenomenon commonly called the *white coat effect* and attributed to the anxiety associated with the visit. Thus any intervention which reduces anxiety may lower the clinic blood pressure, without necessarily affecting blood pressure at other times. As shown in Figure 2, a reduction in the pressure measured in the clinic could reflect a similar reduction in the pressure measured outside the clinic, or it could simply be the result of a reduction of the white coat effect (the difference between the clinic and ambulatory pressure) without any change in the pressure outside the clinic. The former would be regarded as a therapeutic effect, while the latter may be a placebo effect, specifically, an acute reduction in blood pressure induced by beliefs about or the context of the treatment. Antihypertensive drugs lower the clinic and the ambulatory pressures, but the reduction of clinic pressure is typically greater, so that the white coat effect is reduced, but not eliminated.

One of the most dramatic demonstrations of the powers of the placebo effect and the effectiveness of reassurance was provided by an ingenious experiment designed by Dr.

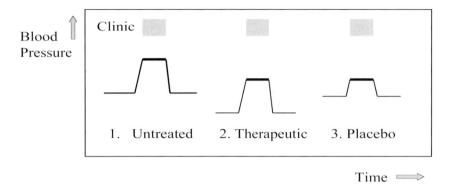

Figure 2: Shows how the white coat effect (the increase of blood pressure at the time of a clinic visit (shaded bar) may confuse the measurement of treatment response. Panel 1 shows pattern before treatment; panel 2, a sustained reduction of blood pressure (a therapeutic response), and panel 3, a reduction of the clinic pressure without a change of the pressure outside the clinic (a transient placebo response).

William Goldring and his colleagues (1956). They made an impressive-looking device which they called "the electron gun," which consisted of a large metal coil mounted by a conical "gun" and an oscilloscope. The patient was seated in a darkened room, with the gun pointing at his or her chest. When it was turned on the nozzle of the gun began to glow as if it was red hot, and to emit sparks and crackling sounds. At the same time a series of sinusoidal waves was displayed on the oscilloscope. The treatment was carried out by a sympathetic nurse twice a week for several months, and then discontinued. In about half of the patients the clinic blood pressure decreased during the treatment period, with an average drop of 36/27 mm Hg- a very impressive change. In addition, the patients all reported an improvement in their symptoms, and several were able to return to work. However, once the treatment was discontinued, the pressure gradually

climbed back to pretreatment levels. This study only evaluated blood pressure measured in the clinic.

One critical aspect of the placebo effect on blood pressure is the expectancy of the patients, and it has been suggested that an expectancy of positive results is a necessary, if not sufficient condition for placebo effects (Chesney & Black, 1986). Two lines of evidence support the notion that at least some of the benefits of behavioral forms of treating hypertension derive from placebo effects. First, Agras et al. (1982) studied the effects of relaxation training on blood pressure, and divided patients into two groups. One was informed that the relaxation would not have an immediate effect on blood pressure, while the other was told that it would. The group with the more positive expectations showed the biggest fall of pressure. The second line of evidence comes from the control groups of these studies. In general, it has been found that the more closely the control procedure resembles the "active" treatment the more likely it is to show a fall of blood pressure (Wadden et al., 1984).

Another problem with the meditation and biofeedback studies has been that other investigators were unable to replicate the dramatic early results. Some of the individual studies were quite small, which limited their generalizability, and this led the National Heart, Lung, and Blood Institute to form a Hypertension Intervention Pooling Project (Kaufmann et al., 1998) which collected data from 733 patients in nine randomized studies, all of which used various types of biofeedback or relaxation training. The results, published in 1988, were disappointing: there was no effect of the interventions in treated patients, and in untreated patients there was a modest reduction of diastolic pressure, but no change in systolic pressure. A few years later (1993) further doubt about these behavioral forms of treatment was the result of a meta-analysis by Eisenberg et al. (1993). The authors reviewed studies using a variety of behavioral techniques, which included biofeedback, relaxation, and stress management, and identified only 26 which satisfied the selection criteria for scientific rigor. The results, while generally negative, were of interest. Studies which used only a single day's readings to measure the baseline pressure, and then compared the effects of the intervention with wait list controls, achieved an average reduction of 13.4/9.0 mmHg more than the controls, while those that used a longer baseline period achieved a smaller reduction (4.1/4.0 mmHg), and those that used a placebo-treated control group did not achieve any net reduction of blood pressure. One interpretation of this analysis is that the positive reports of the behavioral interventions may have been attributable to regression to the mean and the placebo

effect. However, most of the studies had sample sizes that may have been too small to be able to demonstrate a significant difference between the groups.

It could be argued that it does not matter whether the reduction of blood pressure is specific to the type of treatment or to a placebo effect, since any reduction is therapeutic. The important thing is whether the reduction is sustained over 24 hours, as opposed to merely during the clinic visit (a diminution of the white coat effect). The solution to the placebo question is to use 24 hour ambulatory monitoring, which is the ultimate determinant of therapeutic efficacy. Any intervention that lowers blood pressure throughout the day and night can be regarded as therapeutically effective, while one that merely lowers the clinic pressure is ineffective. In general, placebos have been found to lower clinic pressure but not 24-hour pressure. Most of the studies of biofeedback and relaxation used clinic pressure, but there were some early ones that claimed a reduction of ambulatory pressure (Southam et al., 1982).

Controlled Breathing Technique

A promising new behavioral technique in managing hypertension combines features of biofeedback and relaxation training using a novel device that trains patients to lower their breathing rate to about 6 breaths per minute. The device, which is marketed as the RespeRate, comprises a belt that goes round the chest to record breathing movements. This belt is linked to a battery-operated monitor that detects the movements, and emits a series of musical tones which have a different pitch for expiration and inspiration. The patients are instructed to synchronize their breathing to the music, and after a few breaths the device gradually begins to prolong the expiratory phase notes, so that the patient gradually slows the breathing rate to a minimum of about

6/minute. The device also has a data logger that records the duration of use on a daily basis, and the breathing rates achieved. Patients are encouraged to practice this for about 15 minutes a day. Several studies based on the use of the device have been published, and suggest that the effects on blood pressure are both sustained and substantial. It takes about 4 weeks for the full effects to be realized. One study has used 24-hour blood pressure monitoring (Rosenthal et al., 2001), and reported that in 13 hypertensive patients the average reduction was 7.2/2.3 mmHg during the day, but smaller at night. Similar changes were seen in both home and clinic pressures. The effects were greatest in older patients. Another study used a randomized controlled study design (Schein et al., 2001), with a walkman tape player which played relaxing music as the control condition. At the end of 8 weeks there was a larger reduction in clinic pressure in the treated group (15.2/11.3 mmHg) than in the Walkman control group (11.3/5.6 mmHg), but note that the reduction was still substantial in the latter, underscoring the need for placebo controls in studies of this nature.

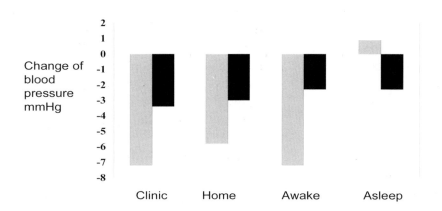

Figure 4: Blood pressure response to treatment with RespeRate, measured in the clinic, at home (self-monitoring), and by ambulatory monitoring (awake and asleep). Grey bars indicate systolic, and black bars diastolic pressure (Rosenthal et al. 2001).

Cost effectiveness of relaxation and biofeedback

A general problem facing any type of behavioral or lifestyle intervention is that it typically involves a series of training sessions between the patient and the therapist. A typical example would be 12 weekly session of 45 minutes each (Jacob et al., 1991). This means that such interventions are not cheap. A major determinant of the cost-effectiveness of such interventions would be the duration of the effects. Most studies have not included long-term follow-up, but one that did was conducted by Agras et al. (1987) in a worksite setting. The patients all had uncontrolled hypertension at entry (diastolic pressures above 90 mmHg despite taking antihypertensive therapy), and the treatment consisted of 8 relaxation training sessions over 8 weeks, done either singly or in small groups. After that there were monthly follow-up sessions. As shown in Figure 5, both groups showed a marked improvement in the rate of blood pressure control, but immediately post-treatment the rate was much higher in the treatment group than in the control group (69.4% versus 41.5%). Over the next 2½ years, however, the difference between the two groups was gradually eroded, probably because the physicians changed the patients' medications. This would indicate that the cost-effectiveness of the relaxation training was low.

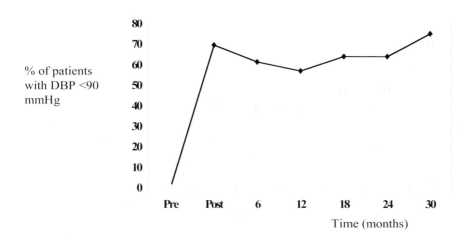

Figure 5: Shows the rates of blood pressure control in patients with initially uncontrolled hypertension, who were in the active treatment (relaxation) group (solid lines) or control group (hatched lines). Immediately after the treatment the blood pressure was better in the treated group (59 versus 41% with blood pressure in the target range), but these differences gradually disappeared. Medications were changed during the follow-up period (Agras et al., 1987).

An exception to the necessity for intensive and prolonged personal contacts may be provided by the RespeRate device. This sells for about $400, and requires virtually no personal training by a skilled therapist. In addition, it can be used for an indefinite period. Thus, if the encouraging early work is confirmed, it may be the first really cost-effective modality for the use of biofeedback/relaxation treatment of hypertension.

Current Guidelines on Biofeedback and Relaxation Techniques

These emerging research findings on relaxation and biofeedback have been reflected in the Joint National Committee (JNC) recommendations over the years. In 1980, the committee concluded that "these methods are still experimental and cannot yet be recommended for sustained control of hypertension" (JNC, 1980). The 1984 report (JNC, 1984) was more optimistic: "various relaxation and biofeedback therapies may consistently produce modest but significant blood pressure reduction...and that they "should be considered in the context of a comprehensive treatment program that may include both pharmacologic and nonpharmacologic therapeutic approaches." In 1988 the pendulum had begun to swing the other way: "these promising methods have yet to be subjected to rigorous clinical trial evaluation and should not be considered as definitive treatment for patients with high blood pressure" (JNC, 1988). The sixth report, published in 1997 (JNC, 1997) stated: "Relaxation therapies and biofeedback have been studied in multiple controlled trials with little effect beyond that seen in control groups...the available literature does not support the use of relaxation therapies for definitive therapy or prevention of hypertension". The latest report (JNC, 2003) published in 2003, does not mention the topic.

LIFESTYLE INTERVENTIONS
Exercise

Both observational and longitudinal studies have demonstrated an inverse relationship between physical fitness and blood pressure, and there have been a substantial number of interventional studies examining the effects of exercise training on blood pressure. Most have used regular aerobic exercise, such as walking, jogging, or cycling performed in group sessions once or twice a week. A meta-analysis of 39 randomized studies of at least 4 weeks of exercise concluded that aerobic exercise training reduced blood pressure by 4.7/3.1 mmHg. Increasing exercise intensity to more than 70% of maximum oxygen uptake or increasing the frequency to more than 3 sessions per week did not appear to confer any additional benefit (Halbert, 1997). This analysis was based on changes of clinic blood pressure, but as shown by the examples quoted above, there were often also decreases in the control groups. In 2004, the American College of Sports Medicine issued a position paper on Exercise and Hypertension (Pescatell et al., 2004). They reviewed a number of meta-analyses of randomized controlled trials of endurance exercise, the largest of which included 54 studies, and found an average reduction of resting blood pressure of 3.8/2.8 mmHg. Seals et al (1997) found that exercise training in post-

menopausal women produced "clinically important reductions" of clinic pressure, but ambulatory blood pressure was unchanged. Nevertheless, the American College of Sports Medicine review reported that 11 studies had evaluated changes of ambulatory blood pressure, and concluded that the average reduction of daytime blood pressure was 3/3.2 mmHg. There appears to be a greater effect on daytime than nighttime pressure. Table 3 reports recommendations, including the strength of evidence supporting them, from the American College of Sports Medicine report.

One of the undisputed effects of exercise on blood pressure is the phenomenon of post-exercise hypotension, which is a reduction of blood pressure to a level below the baseline value that may last for several hours after the period of exercise. The duration of the exercise does not influence the extent of the blood pressure fall, and it is seen even after exercise lasting only 10 minutes (Mac-Donald et al., 2000). The amount of muscle mass used in the exercise is also not critical. There is also evidence that this reduction of blood pressure may persist during normal daily activities (MacDonald et al., 2001). The effects are greater in subjects with higher baseline pressures, and are generally more pronounced with exercise of moderate intensity (60% of maximum oxygen uptake or higher) than light exercise (40% of maximum) (Pescatello et al., 2004).

Another meta-analysis concluded that walking lowers blood pressure by a small amount (3/1 mmHg) (Kelley et al., 2001). One small study found that swimming for 45 minutes, 3 days per week lowered blood pressure in hypertensives without any change of body weight (Tanaka,, 1997). A meta-analysis of 11 studies of the effects of resistance exercise on blood pressure concluded that progressive resistance exercise lowers resting blood pressure by 3/3 mmHg (Kelley & Kelley, 2000).

Table 3: American College of Sports Medicine Position statements on exercise in hypertensive patients

	Evidence Statement	Evidence Category
Benefits	• Higher levels of physical activity and greater fitness at baseline are associated with a reduced incidence of hypertension in white men; however, the paucity of data precludes definitive conclusions regarding the role of sex and ethnicity	C
	• Dynamic aerobic training reduces resting BP in individuals with normal BP and in those with hypertension	A
	• The decrease in BP with aerobic training appears to be more pronounced in those with hypertension	B
	• Aerobic training reduces ambulatory BP and BP measured at fixed submaximal work load	B
	• Dynamic exercise acutely reduces BP among people with hypertension for a major portion of the daytime hours	B
	• Resistance training performed according to the ACSM guidelines reduces BP in normotensive and hypertensive adults	B
	• There are currently no studies available to provide a recommendation regarding the acute effects of static exercise on BP in adults	None
Recommendations	• For persons with high BP an exercise program that is primarily aerobic based is recommended	A
	• Resistance training should serve as an adjunct to an aerobic-based program	B
	• The evidence is limited regarding frequency, intensity, time, and type recommendation	C

Evidence category A: randomized controlled trials provide a consistent pattern of findings; B: limited data from randomized controlled trials; C: non-randomized trials or observational data

There may be subsets of individuals in whom exercise training does not lower blood pressure. A meta-analysis of studies in children did not show any significant decrease, but the authors concluded that there were insufficient data in hypertensive children to be sure about this (Kelley et al., 2003). Stewart et al. (2005) found a negligible effect of exercise training in older patients with systolic hypertension despite evidence of weight loss and increased maximal oxygen consumption. Aortic stiffness was unchanged.

Thus, exercise training appears to produce a modest reduction of blood pressure, although the results have been somewhat inconsistent. A lack of a true control group limits the conclusions that can be made from some of these studies, however, and better controlled studies would be helpful to confirm these effects. Some of the inconsistency in study results may stem from the variable efficacy of interventions to increase adherence to an exercise program (see Volume II, Chapter 16). Patients prescribed an exercise program rarely show perfect adherence to the intended program; thus efforts to improve interventions to increase physical activity amongst patients with chronic disease may secondarily improve the effects of exercise interventions on hypertension.

Weight Loss

The association between obesity and blood pressure is clearly established by both cross-sectional and longitudinal studies. In addition, intervention trials using low calorie diets have, for the most part, shown reductions of blood pressure. For example, Singh et al. (1990) randomized 416 patients in 2X2 design to 1) a low or normal calorie diet and 2) a high fiber, high potassium diet low in saturated fats or 3) their usual diet. After 3 months, they found a significant decrease in blood pressure in all of the groups except the normal calorie usual diet, suggesting that either reducing obesity by reducing daily caloric intake or improving nutrition can reduce blood pressure. It is often stated that there is roughly a 1:1 relationship between the change in blood pressure (in mmHg) and the change in weight (in kg) (Neter et al., 2003), based on the results of randomized trials. In a metaanalysis of 25 randomized controlled trials examining the effects of weight reduction on blood pressure, Neter and colleagues (2003) found that a weight reduction of 5.1 kg was associated with a reduction in systolic blood pressure of 4.44 mm and of diastolic blood pressure by 3.57 mm. Studies which produced greater weight loss found greater reductions in blood pressure. Additionally, decreases in diastolic blood pressure were greater in populations taking anti-hypertensive medications, suggesting that weight loss may provide

benefits on top of those produced by medications, A more recent meta-analysis looked at the long term results of weight loss (2 years or more). Eleven randomized trials satisfied the inclusion criteria, and concluded that a 10kg weight loss (22 pounds) would on average result in a long-term decrease of diastolic pressure of 4.6 mmHg, and systolic pressure of 6 mm Hg.

Thus, effective weight loss interventions are associated with significant reductions in blood pressure, and interventions to prevent or reduce obesity are recommended to reduce hypertension. Unfortunately, no consistently effective behavioral therapies for treatment of obesity have been identified (see Volume I, Chapters 15 and 16), and only a minority of patients are able to lose weight and maintain weight loss. The lack of effective behavioral treatments for the management of obesity limits the usefulness and effectiveness of weight loss interventions for the treatment of hypertension. Nevertheless, if patients are able to reduce obesity, weight loss is expected to reduce hypertension.

Salt Restriction

The most controversial and widely studied association between diet and blood pressure is undoubtedly salt consumption. Epidemiological studies have shown a reasonably consistent but not very strong association between salt intake and blood pressure, culminating in the INTERSALT study, conducted in 52 sites in 32 countries (Stamler, 1997). This study demonstrated significant associations between urinary sodium excretion and median blood pressure values, prevalence of hypertension and the slope of change in blood pressure with age. Within populations, however, it has been difficult to show a relationship, probably because salt intake varies greatly from day to day in many people. Trials of sodium restriction have generally confirmed that reducing salt intake does lower blood pressure, although not in everyone, leading to the concept of individual differences in salt sensitivity. Unfortunately, no reliable test has been devised to identify who is and who is not salt sensitive. As a general rule, however, people who are older, African-American, or obese are more likely to be salt sensitive (Luft et al., 1991).

Some recent meta-analyses have examined the randomized trials of sodium restriction for lowering blood pressure. Midgley et al. (1996) found 28 trials in hypertensive patients, in whom sodium excretion was reduced by 95 mmol/day (a reduction of about 50% of usual salt intake), and concluded that the average blood pressure reduction was 3.7/0.9 mmHg. In another 28 trials performed in normotensive subjects with a similar reduction of salt intake, the average blood pressure fall was 1/0 mmHg. The reviewers commented that decreases of blood pressure were larger in older hypertensives.

Other Dietary Interventions

A large number of other dietary interventions have been investigated for lowering blood pressure, which include changing the intake of other minerals (potassium, calcium, and magnesium), and other dietary components such as fish and omega-3 fatty acids. A high potassium diet is generally thought to be beneficial for blood pressure, and a meta-analysis by Whelton et al (1997) of 33 randomized trials found that potassium supplementation lowered blood pressure by 3/2 mmHg. Treatment effects appeared to be enhanced in studies in which participants concurrently consumed high levels of sodium. Based on these results, potassium supplementation should be considered for hypertensive patients, especially for those with high sodium diets.

Other minerals which have been thought to be related to blood pressure are calcium and magnesium. Like potassium, the intake both have been reported to be inversely related to blood pressure in epidemiological studies, but it has been difficult to sort out their precise correlation, because they tend to coexist in commonly eaten foods such as fruits and vegetables. Meta-analyses of intervention studies where calcium and magnesium were given individually (typically as tablets) have shown weak and inconsistent effects on blood pressure. Sacks et al. (1995) performed a well-designed study in which 125 mildly hypertensive patients (mean blood pressure:139/90 at baseline) were randomized to 4 groups-Potassium plus calcium; potassium plus magnesium; calcium plus magnesium; or placebo pills, all of which were taken daily. There was no difference in the change in blood pressure seen in the placebo group versus any of the supplement groups. Contrary to predictions from the correla-ional data, this study provided little evidence to support the effectiveness of mineral supplements for the management of mild hypertension.

The DASH diet

One of the most important advances in the no-drug treatment of hypertension in the past few years was the introduction of the DASH (Dietary Approaches to Stop Hypertension) diet. The diet was designed to increase the intake of certain minerals-potassium, calcium, and magnesium, while reducing the intake of saturated fats. Unlike other diets for treating hypertension, it was not originally designed to restrict either sodium or calories. There are two compon-ents to it: first, a Mediterranean type of diet that is high in fruits, grain, and vegetables, and second, low fat dairy products, which were included to increase calcium intake. These two components were tested separately in the original study, in which subjects were randomized to either a usual American diet, the fruits, vegetables and grains, or the full DASH diet. The fruits and vegetables diet lowered blood pressure by 2.8/1.1 mmHg, while the addition of the dairy products produced a reduction of 5.5/3.0 mmHg in subjects with borderline blood pressure, and 11.4/5/5 mmHg in hypertensive subjects. These reductions in blood pressure are comparable to those obtained with drugs (Appel et al., 1997). A second study (DASH Sodium) combined the DASH diet with sodium restriction, and reported a reduction of 5.9/2.9 mmHg with the DASH diet in subjects with borderline hypertension, and 8.9/4.5 mmHg with a combination of the DASH diet and sodium restriction (Sacks et al., 2001). A subsequent study (DEW-IT) (Miller et al., 2002) of drug-treated and overweight hypertensives reported a net change of 9.5/5.3 mmHg in ambulatory pressure and 7.4/5.7 mmHg in clinic pressure using a low calorie version of the DASH diet in combination with weight loss. In all of these three studies the participants were provided with ready prepared meals, so compliance with the diet was not an issue.

More recently a fourth study (PREMIER) (Appel et al., 2003) has investigated the effects of combining the DASH diet with "Established" recommendations, comprising weight loss, exercise, and restriction of sodium and alcohol. Since all these interventions have been shown to lower blood pressure individually, it might be anticipated that the effects of combined interventions on blood pressure would be additive. The changes were smaller than expected: for the Established group the reduction was 3.7/1.7 mmHg, and for the group that followed the Established recommendations and the DASH diet it was 4.3/2.6 mmHg. Thus the addition of the DASH diet in PREMIER produced an incremental fall of blood pressure of a mere 0.6/0.9 mmHg (1.7/1.6 mmHg in the hypertensives). What happened?

There are several explanations that need to be considered. The first is that the subjects in PREMIER were not following the DASH diet as closely as in the three earlier DASH studies, which provided the subjects with prepared meals. PREMIER was the first study to investigate the effects of the DASH diet when subjects actually purchased their food. Thus in the original DASH study subjects were provided with an average of 9.6 daily servings of fruits and vegetables, whereas in PREMIER the intake increased from a baseline level of 4.8 to 7.8 servings. In the original DASH study, urine potassium increased by 105% with the change of diet, whereas in the combined group of PREMIER it increased by only 28%. The same explanation could account for the results of the DASH sodium study, where the effects of sodium restriction (a reduction of blood pressure of 6.7/3.5 mmHg) greatly exceeded the changes seen in almost all other studies where subjects prepared their own low salt meals.

A second possibility is that the beneficial effects of the interventions were masked by parallel reductions of blood pressure in the control group. In PREMIER the control group was given advice on diet and lifestyle changes in a single 30 minute session, but they showed a surprisingly large fall of blood pressure (6.6/3.8 mmHg), which was actually larger than the net changes in the combined intervention group. In the original DASH study subjects eating the control diet showed no significant change of blood pressure (Appel et al., 1997). Likewise in DEW-IT the control group showed no change of ambulatory blood pressure (Miller et al., 2002). This would not explain the lack of effect of adding the DASH diet, however.

Another explanation is what the authors term subadditivity, by which they mean that a combination of two or more interventions has a smaller effect on blood pressure than the sum of the effects of the individual interventions. Thus in the DEW-IT study, where a hypocaloric DASH diet was fed to obese hypertensive subjects, the net reduction of clinic blood pressure was 7.4/5.7 mmHg, comparable to the effects of the DASH diet alone. However, these subjects lost 5.5 kgs of body weight, which might have been expected to result in a further blood pressure decrease of around 6/5.5 mmHg (the decrease reported in TOHP II, where the weight loss was 4.4 kgs) (Stevens et al., 2001). And in TOHP II the effect of adding sodium restriction to weight loss produced no further decrease of blood pressure, even though sodium restriction alone produced a modest but significant decrease. Similarly, in the DASH sodium study the combined effects of the DASH diet and sodium restriction were less than the effects of either intervention on its own (Sacks et al., 2001). So far, therefore, no study has shown any additive effect of combining lifestyle interventions on blood pressure.

Why should this be so? Two possibilities must be considered. First, it may be that most people are not capable of changing more than one lifestyle factor at a time. This explanation does not pass muster, however. In TOHP II there were three groups- weight loss, sodium restriction, and both in combination. The decreases of body weight and sodium excretion were only marginally smaller in the combined group than in the two individual intervention groups, but the reduction of blood pressure was no greater than with weight loss alone (Pickering, 1997). And since the DASH sodium trial was a feeding study it seems unlikely that the participants were not consuming the diets they were prescribed (this was verified by measuring urinary excretion of key minerals).

A second possibility is that the different lifestyle interventions may act through the same physiological mechanism, and that as with antihypertensive drugs, the dose-response relationship is non-linear. For most drugs, doubling the dose produces only a small further decrement of blood pressure. In contrast, combining two different drugs often has a genuinely additive effect (Abernethy, 1997), unless the two drugs have a similar mechanism of action. Thus adding a diuretic to the treatment of patients not controlled on a combination of amlodipine and lisinopril is more effective than adding a beta blocker (Antonios et al., 1996. Unfortunately, we know relatively little about the mechanisms by which lifestyle factors such as obesity raise blood pressure (Hall, 2003; Rumantir et al., 1999).

The final issue is how these results should be interpreted and put into practice. While it is often stated that non-drug treatment is cheaper and has fewer side effects than drug treatment, this is not necessarily the case. Studies such as PREMIER require numerous counseling sessions to achieve their results, which are not feasible in everyday practice. Nevertheless, the Advice only group of PREMIER did show a substantial fall of blood pressure, and physicians should certainly continue to give the type of advice advocated in JNC VI (JNC, 1997). Beyond this, it may be worth focusing on the risk factor which is likely to be contributing most to the patient's level of risk. Weight loss has many benefits other than lowering blood pressure, and the same probably applies in non-obese patients who consume the DASH diet. An excellent book is available which gives practical and detailed advice about the diet (Moore et al., 2001).

Medication Adherence

Although antihypertensive medications are highly effective for reducing blood pressure, lack of adherence to medication regimens prevents many patients from achieving hypertension control. *Fully 47% of patients prescribed antihypertensives do not meet target blood pressure* (US DHHS, 2003), and poor adherence to medication prescriptions is a major cause of treatment failure (Feldman et al., 1998). In addition to behavioral and lifestyle interventions that directly lower blood pressure, behavioral interventions that improve adherence to antihypertensive medication prescriptions may improve blood pressure management. Behavioral interventions to improve medication adherence are extensively reviewed in Chapter 14, and the majority of the studies included in that review examine adherence to blood pressure lowering drugs. Nevertheless, because of the importance of the topic, we will briefly review key findings of these studies.

A recent metaanalysis examined results of 58 different interventions for improving antihypertensive adherence conducted between 1975 and 2000 (Schroder et al., 2004). The review reported that no single intervention was clearly superior. Patient education did not significantly improve medication adherence. In contrast, simplifying dosing regimens improved medication adherence in 7 of 9 trials with adherence increasing by 8-19%. Interventions that focused on increasing patient motivation or support increased medication adherence from 5-10%. These included telephone calls from nurses, family-member support, telephone-linked computer counseling, and training in self-determination. Patient reminders, such as daily drug reminder charts, packaging improvements, and electronic medication aid caps, also produced small increases in medication adherence.

Multicomponent interventions produced somewhat greater improvements in adherence. In the 8 of 18 studies in which multicomponent interventions improved adherence, increases in adherence rates ranged from 5-41%. These interventions generally combined patient education, reminders and brief counseling. Several recent studies have tested a patient-centered pharmaceutical care model, which used pharmacists to counsel, educate, remind and support patients as needed. The patient-centered research studies indicated improvement of about 15%. Because these studies tested complex interventions it is impossible to determine the relative importance of the various included components. Nevertheless, a mix of simplified dosing, reminders, social support, counseling and possibly education is most likely to improve medication compliance.

A second metaanalysis of 16 randomized trials reported similar findings, and concluded that, because no single intervention improves adherence to blood pressure lowering medication more than others, a patient-centered approach should be modeled (Takiya et al., 2004). Individual tailoring of use of the above approaches to a patients needs (e.g. reminders for persons with memory problems, counseling for those who lack motivation) is suggested, under the assumption that each of the interventions is helpful only in so far as they address an individual's personal barriers to adherence.

CONCLUSION

Despite early positive results, relaxation and biofeedback therapies have not proven effective for the management of hypertension and are no longer recommended in evidence-based guidelines. Continued research into the techniques may improve effectiveness, but currently, research does not support general implementation of these treatments for blood pressure control. Lifestyle interventions show more promise. Weight loss, exercise and dietary modifications have all demonstrated effectivenss for reducing hypertension. The primary weakness of these strategies is a lack of interventions that consistently reduce obesity, increase physical activity and maintain a healthful diet in individuals over the long-term. Increasing potassium intake and decreasing sodium intake may be helpful for subpopulations of patients, but data supporting the general effectiveness of these interventions are weak. Behavioral strategies may effectively improve medication adherence and improve blood pressure control.

REFERENCES

Abernethy DR. (1997) Pharmacological properties of combination therapies for hypertension. Am J Hypertens 10(3): 13S-16S.

Agras S, Horne M, Taylor CB. (1982) Expectation and the blood pressure lowering effects of relaxation. Psychom Med 44:389-395.

Agras WS, Taylor CB, Kraemer HC, Southam MA, Schneider JA. (1987) Relaxation training for essential hypertension at the worksite: II. The poorly controlled hypertensive. Psychosom Med 49: 264-273.

Andersson B, Elam M, Wallin BG, Bjorntorp P, Andersson OK. (1991) Effect of energy-restricted diet on sympathetic muscle nerve activity in obese women. Hypertension 18: 783-9.

Antonios TF, Cappuccio FP, Markandu ND, Sagnella GA, MacGregor GA. (1996) A diuretic is more effective than a beta-blocker in hypertensive patients not controlled on amlodipine and lisinopril. Hypertension 27(6): 1325-8.

Appel LJ, Moore TJ, Obarzanek E, Vollmer WM, Svetkey LP, Sacks FM, Bray GA, Vogt TM, Cutler JA, Windhauser MM, Lin PH, Karanja N. (1997) A clinical trial of the effects of dietary patterns on blood pressure. DASH Collaborative Research Group. N Engl J Med 336: 1117-24.

Appel LJ, Champagne CM, Harsha DW, Cooper LS, Obarzanek E, Elmer PJ, Stevens VJ, Vollmer WM, Lin PH, Svetkey LP, Stedman SW, Young DR; Writing Group of the PREMIER Collaborative Research Group. (2003) Effects of comprehensive lifestyle modification on blood pressure control: main results of the PREMIER clinical trial. JAMA 289: 2083-9.

Barnes VA, Treiber FA, Turner JR, Davis H, Strong WB. (1999) Acute effects of transcendental meditation on hemodynamic functioning in middle-aged adults. Psychosom Med 61:525-531.

Batey DM, Kaufmann PG, Raczynski JM, Hollis JF, Murphy JK, Rosner B. (2000) Stress management intervention for primary prevention of hypertension: detailed results from Phase I of Trials of Hypertension Prevention (TOHP-I). Ann Epidemiol 10:45-58.

Benson H. (1982) The relaxation response: history, physiological basis and clinical usefulness. Acta Med Scand 660: 231-237.

Benson H, Rosner BA, Marzetta BR, Klemchuk HM. (1974) Decreased blood-pressure in pharmacologically treated hypertensive patients who regularly elicited the relaxation response. Lancet 1: 289-291.

Blanchard EB, Eisele G, Vollmer A, Payne A, Gordon M, Cornish P. (1996) Controlled evaluation of thermal biofeedback in treatment of elevated blood pressure in unmedicated mild hypertension. Biofeedback Self Regul 21: 167-190.

Blumenthal JA, Siegal WC, Appelbaum M. (1991) Failure of exercise to reduce blood pressure in patients with mild hypertension. Results of a randomised controlled trial. JAMA 266: 2098-2104.

Blumenthal JA, Sherwood A, Gullette EC, Babyak M, Waugh R, Georgiades A,

Craighead LW, Tweedy D, Feinglos M, Appelbaum M, Hayano J, Hinderliter A. (2000) Exercise and weight loss reduce blood pressure in men and women with mild hypertension: effects on cardio-vascular, metabolic and hemodynamic functioning. Arch Intern Med 160(13): 1947-58.

Brady JP, Luborski L, Kron RE. (1974) Blood pressure reduction in patients with essential hypertension through metro-nome-conditioned relaxation: a prelim-inary report. Behav Ther 5:203-209.

Caudill MA, Friedman R, Benson H. (1987) Relaxation therapy in the control of blood pressure. Bibl Cardiol 106-119.

Chesney MA, Black GW. (1986) Behavioral treatment of borderline hypertension: an overview of results. J Cardiovasc Pharmacol 8:S57-S63.

Chesney MA, Black GW, Swan GE, Ward MM. (1987) Relaxation training for essential hypertension at the worksite: I. The untreated mild hypertensive. Psychosom Med 49:250-263.

Cooper AR, Moore LA, McKenna J, Riddoch CJ. (2000) What is the magnitude of blood pressure response to a programme of moderate intensity exercise? Randomised controlled trial among sedentary adults with unmedi-cated hypertension. Br J Gen Pract 50: 958-62.

Eisenberg DM, Kessler RC, Foster C, Norlock FE, Calkins DR, Delbanco TL. (1993) Unconventional medicine in the United States. Prevalence, costs, and patterns of use. N Engl J Med 328:246-252.

Eisenberg DM, Delbanco TL, Berkey CS, Kaptchuk TJ, Kupelnick B, Kuhl J, et al. (1993) Cognitive behavioral techniques for hypertension: are they effective? Ann Intern Med 118:964-972.

Fagard RH, Staessen JA. (1999) Treatment of isolated systolic hypertension in the elderly: the Syst-Eur trial. Systolic Hypertension in Europe (Syst-Eur) Trial Investigators. Clin Exp Hypertens 21: 491-497.

Feldman R, Bacher M, Campbell N. (1998) Adherence to pharmacologic manage-ment of hypertension. Can J Public Health 89: 16-18.

Fiedler N, Vivona-Vaughan E, Gochfeld M. (1989) Evaluation of a work site relaxation training program using ambulatory blood pressure monitoring. J Occup Med 31:595-602.

Goldring W, Chasis H, Schreiner GE, Smith HW. (1956) Reassurance in the management of benign hypertensive disease. Circ 14:260-264.

Gordon NF, Scott CB, Levine BD. (1997) Comparison of single versus multiple lifestyle interventions: are the antihyper-tensive effects of exercise training and diet-induced weight loss additive? Am J Cardiol 79(6): 793-7.

Halbert JA, Silagy CA, Finucane P, Withers RT, Hamdorf PA, Andrews GR. (1997) The effectiveness of exercise training in lowering blood pressure: a meta-analysis of randomised controlled trials of 4 weeks or longer. J Hum Hypertens 11: 641-9.

Hall JE. (2003) The kidney, hypertension, and obesity. Hypertension 41:625-33.

Henderson RJ, Hart MG, Saroj KL, Hunyor SN. (1998) The effect of home training with direct blood pressure biofeedback of hypertensives: a placebo-controlled study. J Hypertens 16:771-778.

Hess WR. (1957) The functional organiza-tion of the diencephalon. New York: Grune & Stratton.

Hunyor SN, Henderson RJ, Lal SK, Carter NL, Kobler H, Jones M. (1997) Placebo-controlled biofeedback blood pressure effect in hypertensive humans. Hypertension 29: 1225-1231.

Irvine MJ, Logan AG. (1991) Relaxation behavior therapy as sole treatment for mild hypertension. Psychosom Med 53:587-597.

Jacob RG, Chesney MA, Williams DM, Ding Y, Shapiro AP. (1991) Relaxation therapy for hypertension: design effects and treatment effects. Ann Behav Med 13:5-17.

Jacob RG, Shapiro AP, Reeves RA, Johnsen AM, McDonald RH, Coburn PC. (1986) Relaxation therapy for hypertension. Comparison of effects with concomitant placebo, diuretic, and beta-blocker. Arch Intern Med 146:2335-2340.

Jacobson E. (1938) Progressive Muscular Relaxation. Chicago: University of Chicago Press.

Jalkanen L. (1991) The effect of a weight reduction program on cardiovascular risk factors among overweight hypertensives in primary health care. Scand J Soc Med 19(1): 66-71.

Joint National Committee. (1980) The 1980 report of the Joint National Committee on prevention, detection, evaluation, and treatment of high blood pressure. Arch Int Med 140:1280-1285.

Joint National Committee. (1984) The 1984 report of the Joint National Committee on prevention, detection, evaluation, and treatment of high blood pressure. Arch Int Med 144:1045-1057.

Joint National Committee. (1988) The 1988 report of the Joint National Committee on detection, evaluation, and treatment of high blood pressure. Arch Int Med 148:1023-1038.

Joint National Committee. (1997) The sixth report of the Joint National Committee on prevention,detection, evaluation,and treatment of high blood pressure. Arch Intern Med 157:2413-2446.

Joint National Committee. (2003) The seventh report of the Joint National Committee on Prevention, Detection, Evaluation and Treatment of High Blood Pressure: the JNC 7 report. JAMA 289: 2560-2572.

Kaufmann PG, Jacob RG, Ewart CK, Chesney MA, Muenz LR, Doub N. (1988) Hypertension Intervention Pooling Project. Health Psychol 7:209-224.

Kawamua M, Akasaka T, Kasatsuki T, Nakajima J, Onodera S, Fujiwara T, Hiramori K. (1993) Blood pressure is reduced by short-time calorie restriction in overweight bypertensive women with a constant intake of sodium and potassium. J Hyertens 5: S320-1.

Kelley GA, Kelley KS. (2000) Progressive resistance exercise and resting blood pressure : A meta-analysis of random-ized controlled trials. Hypertension 35(3):838-43.

Kelley GA, Kelley KS, Tran ZV. (2001) Walking and resting blood pressure in adults: a meta-analysis. Prev Med 33:120-7.

Kelley GA, Kelley KS, Tran ZV. (2003) The effects of exercise on resting blood pressure in children and adolescents: a meta-analysis of randomized controlled trials. Prev Cardiol 6(1):8-16.

Linden W, Lenz JW, Con AH. (2001) Individualized stress management for primary hypertension: a randomized trial. Arch Intern Med 161:1071-1080.

Luft FC, Miller JZ, Grim CE, Fineberg NS, Christian JC, Daugherty SA, Weinberger MH. (1991) Salt sensitivity and resistance of blood pressure. Age and race as factors in physiological responses. Hypertension 17:I102-8.

Luthe W. (1969) Autogenic therapy. New York: Grune and Stratton.

MacDonald JR, MacDougall JD, Hogben CD. (2000) The effects of exercising muscle mass on post exercise hypo-tension. J Hum Hypertens 14:317-20.

MacDonald JR, Hogben CD, Tarnopolsky MA, MacDougall JD. (2001) Post exercise hypotension is sustained during subsequent bouts of mild exercise and simulated activities of daily living. J Hum Hypertens 15(8):567-71.

Martin JE, Dubbert PM, Cushman WC. (1990) Controlled trial of aerobic exercise in hypertension. Circulation 81(5): 1560-7.

McCaffrey RJ, Blanchard EB. (1985) Stress management approaches to the treatment of essential hypertension. Ann Behav Med 7:5-12.

Midgley JP, Matthew AG, Greenwood CM, Logan AG. (1996) Effect of reduced dietary sodium on blood pressure: a meta-analysis of randomized controlled trials. JAMA 275(20):1590-7.

Miller NE. (1974) Editorial: Biofeedback: evaluation of a new technic. N Engl J Med 290:684-685.

Miller ER 3rd, Erlinger TP, Young DR, Jehn M, Charleston J, Rhodes D, Wasan SK, Appel LJ. (2002) Results of the Diet, Exercise, and Weight Loss Intervention Trial (DEW-IT). Hypertension 40:612-8.

Moore TJ, Karanja N, Svetkey LP, Jenkins M. (2001) The DASH Diet for Hypertension. New York: The Free Press.

Moreira WD, Fuchs FD, Ribeiro JP, Appel LJ. (1999) The effects of two aerobic training intensities on ambulatory blood pressure in hypertensive patients: results of a randomized trial. J Clin Epidemiol 52(7): 637-42.

Nakao M, Nomura S, Shimosawa T, Fujita T, Kuboki T. (2000) Blood pressure biofeedback treatment of white-coat hypertension. J Psychosom Res 48:161-169.

Neter JE, Stam BE, Kok FJ, Grobbee DE, Geleijnse JM. (2003) Influence of weight reduction on blood pressure: a meta-analysis of randomized controlled trials. Hypertension 42(5):878-84.

Patel C, Marmot MG, Terry DJ. (1981) Controlled trial of biofeedback-aided behavioural methods in reducing mild hypertension. Br Med J 282:2005-2008.

Patel C, Marmot MG, Terry DJ, Carruthers M, Hunt B, Patel M. (1985) Trial of relaxation in reducing coronary risk: four year follow up. Br Med J 290: 1103-1106.

Patel C, Marmot M. (1988) Can general practitioners use training in relaxation and management of stress to reduce mild hypertension? Br.Med J 296:21-24.

Pescatello LS, Guidry MA, Blanchard BE, Kerr A, Taylor AL, Johnson AN, Maresh CM, Rodriguez N, Thompson PD. (2004) Exercise intensity alters postexercise hypotension. J Hypertens 22(10):1881-8.

Pescatello LS, Franklin BA, Fagard R, Farquhar WB, Kelley GA, Ray CA; American College of Sports Medicine. (2004) American College of Sports Medicine position stand. Exercise and hypertension. Med Sci Sports Exerc 36(3):533-53.

Pickering TG. (1997) Lessons from the Trials of Hypertension Prevention, phase II. Energy intake is more important than dietary sodium in the prevention of hypertension. Arch Intern Med 157:596-7.

Rosenthal T, Alter A, Peleg E, Gavish B. (2001)Device-guided breathing exercises reduce blood pressure: ambulatory and home measurements. Am J Hypertens 14:74-76.

Rumantir MS, Vaz M, Jennings GL, Collier G, Kaye DM, Seals DR, Wiesner GH, Brunner-La Rocca HP, Esler MD. (1999) Neural mechanisms in human obesity-related hypertension. J Hypertens 17(8):1125-33.

Sacks FM, Brown LE, Appel L, Borhani NO, Evans D, Whelton P. (1995) Combinations of potassium, calcium and magnesium supplements in hypertension. Hypertension 26: 950-6.

Sacks FM, Brown LE, Appel L, Borhani NO, Evans D, Whelton P. (1995) Combinations of potassium, calcium, and magnesium supplements in hypertension. Hypertension 26:950-6.

Sacks FM, Svetkey LP, Vollmer WM, Appel LJ, Bray GA, Harsha D, Obarzanek E, Conlin PR, Miller ER 3rd, Simons-Morton DG, Karanja N, Lin PH; DASH-Sodium Collaborative Research Group. (2001) Effects on blood pressure of reduced dietary sodium and the Dietary Approaches to Stop Hypertension (DASH) diet. DASH-Sodium Collaborative Research Group. N Engl J Med 344(1):3-10.

Schein MH, Gavish B, Herz M, Rosner-Kahana D, Naveh P, Knishkowy B. (2001) Treating hypertension with a device that slows and regularises breathing: a randomised, double-blind controlled study. J Hum Hypertens 15:271-278.

Schneider RH, Alexander CN, Staggers F, Orme-Johnson DW, Rainforth M, Salerno JW, Sheppard W, Castillo-Richmond A, Barnes VA, Nidich SI. (2005) A randomized controlled trial of stress reduction in African Americans treated for hypertension for over one year. Am J Hypertens 18(1):88-98.

Schroeder K, Fahey T, Ebrahim S. (2004) How can we improve adherence to blood pressure-lowering medication in ambulatory care? Arch Intern Med 164: 722-732.

Seals DR, Silverman HG, Reiling MJ, Davy KP. (1997) Effect of regular aerobic exercise on elevated blood pressure in postmenopausal women. Am J Cardiol 1: 80(1):49-55.

Shapiro AP, Schwartz GE, Redmond DP, Ferguson DC, Weiss SM. (1978) Non-

pharmacologic treatment of hypertension. Ann NY Acad Sci 304:222-235.

Singh RB, Ratogi SS, Mehta PJ, Mody R, Garg V. (1990) Effect of diet and weight reduction in hypertension. Nutrition 6(4): 297-302.

Singh RB, Sircar AR, Rastogi SS, Singh R. (1990) Dietary modulators of blood pressure in hypertension. Eur J Clin Nutr 44(4):319-27.

Singh RB, Niaz MA, Bishnoi I, Singh U, Begum R, Rastogi SS. (1995) Effect of low energy diet and weight loss on major risk factors, central obesity and associated disturbances in patients with essential hypertension. J Hum Hypertens 9: 355-62.

Southam MA, Agras WS, Taylor CB, Kraemer HC. (1982) Relaxation training. Blood pressure lowering during the working day. Arch Gen Psychiatry 39:715-717.

Stamler J. (1997) The INTERSALT Study: background, methods, findings, and implications. Am J Clin Nutr 65(2 Suppl):626S-642S.

Stevens VJ, Obarzanek E, Cook NR, Lee IM, Appel LJ, Smith West D, Milas NC, Mattfeldt-Beman M, Belden L, Bragg C, Millstone M, Raczynski J, Brewer A, Singh B, Cohen J; Trials for the Hypertension Prevention Research Group. (2001) Long-term weight loss and changes in blood pressure: results of the Trials of Hypertension Prevention, phase II. Ann Intern Med 134(1):1-11.

Stewart KJ, Bacher AC, Turner KL, Fleg JL, Hees PS, Shapiro EP, Tayback M, Ouyang P. (2005) Effect of exercise on blood pressure in older persons: a randomized controlled trial. Arch Intern Med 165(7):756-62.

Takiya LN, Peterson AM, Finley RS. (2004) Meta-analysis of interventions for medication adherence to antihypertensives. Ann Pharmacotherapy 38: 1617- 1624.

Tanaka H, Bassett DR Jr, Howley ET, Thompson DL, Ashraf M, Rawson FL. (1997) Swimming training lowers the resting blood pressure in individuals with hypertension. J Hypertens 15:651-7.

Turnbull F; Blood Pressure Lowering Treatment Trialists' Collaboration. (2003) Effects of different blood-pressure-lowering regimens on major cardio-vascular events: results of prospectively-designed overviews of randomised trials. Lancet 362(9395):1527-35.

US Department of Health and Human Services, National Heart, Lung and Blood Institute. National High Blood Pressure Education Program. Available at:
Http://www.nhlbi.nih.gov/about/nhbpep/index.htm

van Montfrans GA, Karemaker JM, Wieling W, Dunning AJ. (1990) Relaxation therapy and continuous ambulatory blood pressure in mild hypertension: a controlled study. BMJ 300:1368-1372.

Wadden T, Luborski L, Greer S, Crits-Christoph P. (1984) The behavioral treatment of essential hypertension: an update and comparison with pharm-acological treatment. Clin Psychol Rev 4:403-429.

Wenneberg SR, Schneider RH, Walton KG, Maclean CR, Levitsky DK, Salerno JW. (1997) A controlled study of the effects of the Transcendental Meditation program on cardiovascular reactivity and ambulatory blood pressure. Int J Neurosci 89:15-28.

Whelton PK, Appel LJ, Espeland MA, Applegate WB, Ettinger WH Jr. Kostis JB, Kumanyika S, Lacy CR, Johnson KC, Folmar S, Cutler JA. (1998) Sodium reduction and weight loss in the treatment of hypertension in older persons: a randomized controlled trial of nonpharmacologic interventions in the elderly (TONE). TONE Collaborative Research Group. JAMA 279: 839-46.

Whelton PK, He J, Cutler JA, Brancati FL, Appel LJ, Follmann D, Klag MJ. (1997) Effects of oral potassium on blood pressure. Meta-analysis of randomized controlled clinical trials. JAMA 277: 1624-32.

Young DR, Appel LJ, Jee S, Miller ER 3rd. (1999) The effects of aerobic exercise and T'ai Chi on blood pressure in older people: results of a randomized trial. J Am Geriatr Soc 47(3): 277-84.

Yucha CB, Clark L, Smith M, Uris P, LaFleur B, Duval S. (2001) The effect of biofeedback in hypertension. Appl Nurs Res 14:29-35.

BEHAVIORAL MANAGEMENT OF HEART FAILURE

Valerie Emery and Michael W. Rich

While taking a case of chronic disease one should carefully examine and weigh the particular conditions of the patient's day-to-day activities, living habits, diet, domestic situation, and so on.
Dr. Samuel Hahnemann
-Organon of Medicine, 1842

Heart failure (HF) is a complex cardiovascular disorder that has become a major public health concern. Recent data indicate that HF affects nearly five million Americans, and approximately 550,000 new cases are diagnosed each year (American Heart Association, 2001). In addition, due to the aging of the population, the number of Americans with HF is expected to double over the next 20 years (Rich, 1997). Chronic HF is characterized by recurrent exacerbations; as a result, HF is one of the most frequent causes for hospital admission. In 1996, there were 870,000 hospitalizations with a primary diagnosis of HF, representing a 2.3-fold increase from the 377,000 admissions in 1979 (O'Connell, 2000). In addition, although the true economic impact of HF is difficult to ascertain, total expenditures in 1991 were estimated at $38 billion (O'Connell, 2000). Approximately two-thirds of these costs were for hospitalizations, which averaged approximately $11,000 per admission. These figures substantiate the emergence of HF as a significant concern for health care providers, not only in terms of the large number of people afflicted, but also in terms of the tremendous economic burden attributable to this condition.

CLINICAL FEATURES

The syndrome of HF occurs when the heart is unable to pump a sufficient quantity of blood to meet the metabolic requirements of the body (Hunt, 2001). The most common cause of HF is left ventricular systolic dysfunction resulting from coronary heart disease, hypertension, cardio-myopathy, or valvular abnormalities. Left ventricular diastolic dysfunction is another important etiology of HF that is most often related to long-standing hypertension or age-related changes in the structure and function of the heart muscle (Rich, 1997). In either case, the resultant syndrome produces similar symptoms, signs, and outcomes.

The most prominent symptoms of HF are shortness of breath and impaired exercise tolerance associated with clinical signs of fluid retention, such as pulmonary rales, elevated jugular venous pressure, hepatic congestion, and lower extremity edema (Hunt, 2001). Although persons with mild HF may feel relatively well between exacerbations, HF is nonetheless a chronic condition requiring daily attention to diet, medications and activities in order to reduce the risk of clinical deterioration, recurrent hospitalizations, and premature death. Thus, behavioral management plays an essential role in the treatment of chronic HF.

MEDICAL MANAGEMENT

Pharmacological therapies comprise the primary treatment modality for HF, and several classes of medications have been shown to slow disease progression, reduce symptoms, and/or improve survival. Currently recommended pharmaco-therapeutic agents include angiotensin converting enzyme (ACE) inhibitors, beta-blockers, diuretics, digoxin, and spironolactone (Hunt, 2001). ACE inhibitors are the cornerstone of HF therapy because these agents decrease mortality and morbidity, improve quality of life, and reduce hospitalizations (Flather, 2000). Beta-blockers have also been shown to decrease HF symptoms, improve quality of life, and decrease mortality and hospital admissions (Brophy, 2001). Diuretics improve symptoms by relieving pulmonary and systemic venous congestion, but with the exception of spironolactone, which reduces mortality in patients with advanced HF (Pitt, 1999), diuretics have not been shown to improve clinical outcomes. Digoxin improves symptoms, quality of life, and exercise tolerance. Digoxin also reduces HF hospitalizations, but does not affect mortality (The Digitalis Investigation Group, 1997). Optimal medical therapy for patients with symptomatic HF thus involves a minimum of 3 to 5 drugs, and the majority of patients are taking additional medications for other common conditions, such as hypertension, diabetes, and coronary heart disease. Management of such complex medication regimens is often challenging for physicians and patients alike, and mandates a systematic approach to ensure appropriate prescribing practices and maximum patient adherence.

In addition to medications, diet plays an important role in the management of chronic HF. Excess dietary salt intake contributes to fluid retention and is an important cause of recurrent HF exacerbations (Ghali, 1988; Vinson, 1990). For this reason, moderate dietary salt restriction is an integral component of effective HF therapy. Patients with advanced HF or significant renal insufficiency also need to avoid excess fluid intake, and additional dietary restrictions may apply in patients with diabetes, hyperlipidemia, or coronary heart disease.

Another important aspect of HF management relates to physical activity. Obesity and physical inactivity increase the risk for developing HF, and persistent physical inactivity contributes to the progressive functional decline that occurs in HF patients. Conversely, regular exercise has been associated with enhanced functional capacity and sense of well-being in patients with HF (McKelvie, 2002; Pina, 2003).

In summary, several aspects of caring for patients with chronic HF are suitable for behavioral intervention.

HEART FAILURE DISEASE MANAGEMENT

Over the past 10 years, numerous studies have evaluated the effects of various HF disease management strategies for improving quality of care and clinical outcomes in HF patients. Most of these programs rest on a foundation that is in the domain of behavioral management. Central elements of successful HF management programs include education of the patient and/or care providers, discussion of behavioral strategies to increase adherence to dietary guidelines and medications, recommendations regarding symptom management and physical activities, and monitoring HF signs and symptoms (Moser, 2000; Moser and Mann, 2002).

The accompanying Table 1 summarizes randomized controlled trials of HF disease management interventions in chronological sequence according to publication date. In each of these studies, the control group received "usual care", as prescribed by the appropriate health care provider. In 1995, Rich et al published the results of a study in which 282 patients were randomized to receive usual care or usual care plus a nurse-directed multidisciplinary intervention. The intervention consisted of comprehensive

Table 1: Randomized controlled trials of heart failure disease management

Study	Subjects/ Group	Intervention	Duration of Inter-vention	Length of Follow-up	Primary Outcomes
Rich et al (1995)	282 T=142 C=140	Nurse-directed education regarding self-management with enhanced follow-up after discharge by home visits and regular phone contacts	3 months	3 months with limited 1-year data	Improved event-free survival and quality of life at 3 months, 56% reduction in heart failure admissions, cost of care $460 less per pt in the intervention group
Cline et al (1998)	190 T=110 C=80	Education about self-management along with access to a nurse-directed outpatient clinic	8 months	1 year	Longer time to readmission (141 days vs. 106 days) and fewer days in hospital (4.2 days vs. 8.2 days) for the treatment group at 1-year
Stewart et al (1998)	97 T=49 C=48	Home-based intervention consisting of initial contact by study nurse prior to discharge and a home visit 1-2 weeks after discharge by the nurse and a pharmacist	Varied, dependent upon findings from initial home visit	6 months	Intervention group had fewer unplanned readmissions (36 vs. 63) and deaths (1 versus 5) than the control group
Ekman et al (1998)	158 T=79 C=79	Nurse-monitored outpatient clinic with individualized care plans and goals developed by pt and nurse along with telephone contacts	6 months	Mean follow-up of 5 months	No definite reduction in the number of readmissions, mortality, number of hospital days, or survival without readmission; both groups experienced slight improvement in New York Heart Association functional class
Serxner et al (1998)	109 T=55 C=54	Planned mailings (4) of educational material regarding heart failure self-management every 3-4 weeks following hospitalization	3 months	6 months	44% reduction in hospital re-admissions, fewer total re-admissions in intervention group, non-significant improvement in self-report scales
Jaarsma et al (1998)	179 T=84 C=95	Supportive-education intervention consisting of planned education regarding self-management of heart failure, including inpatient contact along with a post-discharge home visit	10 days from hospital discharge	9 months after hospital discharge	No significant impact on readmissions; improvement in self-care behaviors at 3-months for intervention group vs. control, improvement not seen until 9-months in the control

Study	Subjects/ Group	Intervention	Duration of Inter-vention	Length of Follow-up	Primary Outcomes
Stewart et al (1999)	200 T=100 C=100	Home-based intervention consisting of a structured home visit by a cardiac nurse 7-14 days after discharge that included assessment and education; phone contact at 3 and 6 months post discharge	6 months	6 months	40% reduction in primary events (out-of-hospital death or unplanned readmission) during the 6-month period for the home-based intervention group compared to controls
Stewart et al (1999)	97 T=49 C=48	Home-based intervention (see above)	Varied	18 months	18-month follow-up of original cohort showing fewer unplanned readmissions and out-of-hospital deaths, fewer hospital days, and decreased frequency of multiple admissions in intervention group
Blue et al (2001)	165 T=81 C=84	Planned home visits of decreasing frequency along with telephone contacts for 1-year after discharge; pts also given heart failure self-management guidelines	1 year	1 year	28% reduction in all-cause readmission or death in the intervention group at 1-year; risk of heart failure readmission reduced by 62% in the intervention group
Krumholz et al (2002)	88 T=44 C=44	Education and support intervention consisting of face-to-face interactions and planned telephone follow-up with tapering frequency	1 year	1 year	Fewer pts in the intervention group readmitted (57% vs. 82%), 39% reduction in the total number of readmissions (49 vs. 80), lower costs ($7,515 per pt) for readmissions in the intervention group
Kasper et al (2002)	200 T=102 C=98	Inpatient multi-disciplinary team (cardiologist, heart failure nurse, telephone nurse, and primary care physician) along with outpatient telephone contacts	6 months	6 months	Reduced heart failure readmissions from 59 in the control group to 43 in the treatment group; quality of life scores improved in both groups with greater improvement in the treatment group; intervention costs were $90 per pt with no significant difference in resource use between groups
Riegel et al (2002)	358 T=130 C=228	Telephone case management and monitoring post-discharge	6 months	6 months	46% fewer heart failure admissions at 3-months and 48% fewer at 6-months; average cost savings ~$600 over 6-month intervention period

Study	Subjects/ Group	Intervention	Duration of Intervention	Length of Follow-up	Primary Outcomes
Stewart et al (2002)	297 T=149 C=148	Long-term follow-up of home-based intervention cohorts (see above)	6 months	4.2 years (median)	Persistent benefit in terms of reduced out-of-hospital deaths and unplanned readmissions
Doughty et al (2002)	197 T=100 C=97	Outpatient heart failure clinic visits and group education sessions	6 months	1 year	No difference in primary endpoint of hospitalization or death, but 26% decrease in hospital readmission rate; improved physical functioning scores in the intervention group (-5.8 point change vs. +11.1)

patient education prior to hospital discharge accompanied by intensive post discharge follow-up to reinforce self-management behaviors and to monitor for signs and symptoms of worsening HF. During a 90-day follow-up period, hospital readmissions were reduced by 44% in the intervention group, and HF readmissions were reduced by 56% (Rich, 1995). In 1998, Cline et al reported a randomized trial involving 190 patients. The intervention included inpatient education, a nurse visit after discharge, and easy access to a nurse-directed outpatient clinic. Patients in the intervention group also received guidelines for adjusting diuretic dosages based upon symptoms and daily weights. The intervention was associated with 36% fewer hospitalizations and a trend toward fewer hospital days.

Also in 1998, Stewart et al described the effects of a home-based intervention on unplanned readmissions in a study involving 762 medical and surgical patients. The intervention, which consisted of a pre-discharge evaluation by a nurse and a single home visit by a nurse and pharmacist, reduced unplanned readmissions, out-of-hospital deaths, total deaths, emergency room visits, and total hospital days. In subsequent papers, Stewart et al (1998, 1999) reported beneficial effects of the home-based intervention on unplanned readmissions and death among 297 patients

hospitalized for acute HF. More recently, long-term follow-up of these patients has been reported (Stewart, 1999, 2002). At 18-months follow-up, patients receiving the home-based intervention had fewer unplanned admissions and out-of-hospital deaths compared to the usual care group (Stewart, 1999). Furthermore, after a median follow-up of 4.2 years, the beneficial effects of the home-based intervention persisted, and a significant increase in survival was demonstrated (Stewart, 2002).

Serxner et al. (1998), Jaarsma et al. (1998), and Ekman et al. (1998) have also reported their experiences with HF disease management interventions. Serxner et al found that mailing educational materials every 3 to 4 weeks to patients discharged following a hospitalization for HF resulted in improved health behaviors, a 44% reduction in the number of patients readmitted, and a 51% reduction in the total number of readmissions during 6 months of follow-up. Jaarsma et al found that an intervention involving patient education during the index hospitalization and a home visit within 10 days after discharge led to increased self-care behaviors in the early months following discharge, although the benefits waned during the ensuing 9 months. In this study, the intervention did not reduce readmission rates. Ekman et al evaluated an intervention that consisted of enhanced post-discharge follow-up. An individualized plan was developed for each patient based on an assessment of that patient's medical and psychosocial needs. The plan included a prescribed number of outpatient visits and patient-specific goals. Patients were also contacted by telephone on a regular basis to reinforce information provided during the outpatient visits. Phone calls were made at least once a month for those patients unable to visit the clinic. A total of 158 patients were enrolled in the trial, but there were no significant differences between groups with respect to readmissions, mortality, or survival without readmission.

In another study, Blue et al (2001) enrolled 165 patients into a randomized trial evaluating a nurse specialist intervention. The treatment group received patient education prior to discharge and home visits for up to 1 year. Nurse specialists were educated in HF management and were guided by written medication protocols as well as supervision by a cardiologist. During one year of follow-up, fewer patients in the intervention group died or had an admission for HF compared to the usual care group. There were also fewer admissions for any reason, fewer admissions for HF, and fewer hospital days for HF in the intervention group.

In 2002, four additional trials added to the growing body of evidence attesting to the benefits of HF disease management programs. Krumholz et al (2002) found that an education and support intervention resulted in a significant reduction in the number of patients who died or were readmitted for HF during one year of follow-up. Kasper et al (2002) examined the impact of multidisciplinary care in patients admitted with a HF exacerbation and followed for 6 months post discharge. These authors found that their intervention was associated with fewer HF readmissions and deaths, as well as improvements in quality of life scores, compliance with dietary recommendations, and medication dosages. Riegel et al (2002) reported similar results using a telephone-based intervention initiated shortly after a HF discharge. These authors found a 45.7% lower HF hospitalization rate in the intervention group at 3 months post-discharge, and a 47.8% lower rate at 6 months. Finally, Doughty et al (2002) utilized a cluster randomization of primary care physicians to enroll 197 patients into a trial of integrated HF care. The intervention comprised outpatient HF clinic visits with a cardiologist, HF self-management education, and a series of 3 group-learning sessions conducted by a cardiologist and nurse. Although there was no difference between groups in the combined end-point of death or hospitalization at one year, there were fewer HF admissions and fewer patients with multiple readmissions in the intervention group. There was also a significant improvement in the physical functioning component of the Minnesota Living with Heart Failure quality of life questionnaire at one year in the intervention group.

In aggregate, these 12 randomized trials involving 2223 HF patients provide strong evidence that HF disease management programs improve clinical outcomes. The greatest benefit is a reduction in HF readmissions; additional benefits include reductions in all-cause readmissions and hospital days, as well as improved quality of life. Most studies have also shown reductions in the cost of care (McAlister, 2001). Although mortality data are limited, long-term follow-up of the patients treated by Stewart et al (2002) indicates that such programs may have a favorable impact on survival. Based on these studies, HF disease management programs are now recommended as an integral component of optimal HF care (Grady, 2000; Krumholz, 2000; Hunt, 2001).

ELEMENTS OF SUCCESSFUL DISEASE MANAGEMENT PROGRAMS

An important limitation of the existing evidence base is the lack of uniformity of the interventions tested in the various trials. The question therefore arises as to what characteristics or components of these programs are essential to their success. In analyzing the published trials, several commonalities can be identified. First, in most of the studies a current or recent hospitalization initiated enrollment into the program. As noted by Konstam (2001), hospitalization represents either failure of treatment or progression of disease. As such, hospitalization represents an opportunity to identify deficiencies in care and implement corrective measures. Since these deficiencies often include a failure of patient self-management (i.e., noncompliance with medications or diet), hospitalization provides an excellent opportunity to initiate or reinforce patient education about HF and its management, with particular emphasis on the important role that the patient plays in day-to-day disease management through lifestyle adjustments and behavioral changes. Hospitalization may also serve as a "wake-up call" to patients regarding the chronicity of their disease, and hospitalized patients may therefore be more receptive to educational and behavioral interventions than when they are feeling relatively well and "disease-free". Finally, studies have shown that hospitalization for HF is a strong predictor of subsequent readmission, and that readmission rates are highest during the first 3 months following hospital discharge (Vinson, 1990). Therefore, initiating treatment at the time of hospital discharge, or shortly thereafter, is likely to produce the greatest benefit in terms of reducing the number of rehospitalizations.

Another common element of successful HF disease management programs is the dissemination of health care information, usually in the form of direct interactions between the patient and/or family and a nurse educator, often supplemented by printed materials. The goal of the educational process is to provide patients with knowledge and skills that will enable them to better manage their illness. This typically includes patient-specific information about dietary restrictions, exercise, daily monitoring of weights, and recognition and management of HF symptoms. In several studies, the initial educational intervention was reinforced through home visits or telephone contacts. The importance of patient education is perhaps best exemplified by the studies of Serxner (1998) and Riegel (2002). In both of these studies, the primary focus of the intervention was education, and both demonstrated significant reductions in readmission rates. Thus, focused and individualized education regarding self-management of HF with special attention to health behaviors is a critical component of successful HF disease management programs.

Enhanced contact following hospital discharge is another characteristic of HF disease management interventions that contributes to improved clinical outcomes. Most of the randomized trials included regular follow-up contacts by telephone, clinic visits, or home visits, with follow-up durations ranging from 3 months to 1 year. An apparent exception to this approach is the home-based intervention described by Stewart et al (Stewart, 1997, 1998), which consisted of a single home visit 1 to 2 weeks following hospital discharge. However, patients who exhibited poor medication knowledge or compliance at the initial visit received an expanded intervention that included remedial counseling and regular monitoring. Although further details regarding the intensity of this followup program have not been reported, it seems likely that enhanced follow-up was critical to the long-term efficacy of the intervention (Stewart, 1999, 2002).

A final element common to all but one of the randomized clinical trials of HF disease management programs is the pivotal role of a specialized nurse case manager or advanced practice nurse as the person who directs the intervention. In the single exception (Serxner, 1998), personalized mailings of educational material were sent to patients following hospital discharge, but routine follow-up by a nurse was not a standard component of the intervention. Nonetheless, the authors found that providing at least one home visit increased the efficacy of the educational intervention. All of the other studies featured a designated nurse who coordinated the care of the patients and assumed responsibility for the overall implementation of the intervention.

In summary, there are four characteristics that are consistently present in successful HF disease management programs. These include: entry into the program either during or shortly after an admission for HF; emphasis on the behavioral aspects of HF management and on improving self-management skills through meaningful, patient-centered education; enhanced follow-up contacts beyond physician office visits through the use of telephone support, outpatient clinic visits, or home visits; and utilization of a nurse specialist to coordinate and facilitate patient care. Although the relative importance of each of these components cannot be determined from existing data, the evidence strongly supports the view that HF disease management programs that include all 4 elements substantially improve outcomes beyond those achieved through usual care (Moser and Mann, 2002). Moreover, there is evidence that a well-integrated, disease-specific, patient-focused plan is essential for

success. Thus, as demonstrated by Weinberger et al (1996), simply providing increased access to the primary care provider without emphasizing self-management skills or incorporating regularly prescribed follow-up into the care plan is ineffective in reducing hospitalizations or improving clinical outcomes. As suggested by Moser and Mann (2002), providing increased access to usual care, which is typically characterized by overly brief encounters that do not adequately address the multidimensional needs of patients with chronic illness, would not be expected to favorably modify patient behaviors, and would therefore not be expected to improve clinical outcomes.

FUTURE DIRECTIONS

While these studies provide strong support for behaviorally oriented HF disease management interventions, additional research is clearly needed. First, there is a need for studies designed to delineate the optimal HF disease management intervention in terms of intensity, critical elements, and duration. There is also a need for studies to define which patients derive the most benefit from these interventions, so that interventions may be tailored to meet individual patient needs and to maximize cost-effectiveness. In this regard, despite the fact that HF disease management interventions have been repeatedly shown to improve clinical outcomes, there is currently no viable mechanism of financial support for these programs. Further analysis of reimbursement methodologies is needed to ensure that cost-effective disease management strategies and behavioral interventions are made widely available to the growing number of patients with chronic HF. There is also a need for studies that evaluate methods for translating the beneficial effects of HF disease management into routine clinical practice. Finally, there is a need for studies to develop and test behaviorally oriented interventions for the primary prevention of HF among individuals at high risk for developing this disorder, such as persons with hypertension, diabetes mellitus, or coronary artery disease.

RESOURCES FOR HEALTH PROFESSIONALS

American College of Cardiology (web site: www.acc.org)

American Heart Association (web site: www.americanheart.org)

Heart Failure Online (web site: www.heartfailure.org)

Heart Failure Society of America (web site: www.hfsa.org)

Heart Failure Society of America Practice Guidelines. (1999) HFSA Guidelines for management of heart failure caused by left ventricular systolic dysfunction-pharmacological approaches. J Cardiac Failure 5:357-382.

Hunt SA, Baker DW, Chin MH, Cinquegrani MP, Feldman AM, Francis GS, Ganiats TG, Goldstein S, Gregoratos G, Jessup ML, Noble RJ, Packer M, Silver MA, Stevenson LW. ACC/AHA guidelines for the evaluation and management of chronic heart failure in the adult: a report of the American College of Cardiology/American Heart Association Task Force on Practice Guidelines (Committee to Revise the 1995 Guidelines for the Evaluation and Management of Heart Failure). 2001. Available at www.acc.org

Konstam M, Dracup K, Baker D, et al. (1994) Heart Failure: Management of Patients With Left Ventricular Systolic Dysfunction: Clinical Practice Guidelines for Clinicians No. 11. Rockville, Md: Agency for Health Care Policy and Research, Public Health Service, US Department of Health and Human Services.

Moser D, Riegel B. eds. (2001) An Interdisciplinary Approach to Improving Outcomes in Heart Failure. Gaithersburg, Md: Aspen Publishers.

REFERENCES

American Heart Association. (2001) 2002 Heart and Stroke Statistical Update. Dallas, Tex: American Heart Association.

Blue L, Lang E, McMurray JV, Davie AP, McDonagh TA, Murdoch DR, Petrie MC, Connolly E, Norrie J, Round CE, Ford I, Morrison CE. (2001) Randomised controlled trial of specialist nurse intervention in heart failure. BMJ 323:715-718.

Brophy JM, Joseph L, Rouleau JL. (2001) Beta-blockers in congestive heart failure. A Bayesian meta-analysis. Ann Intern Med 134:550-560.

Cline CMJ, Israelsson BYA, Willenheimer RB, Broms K, Erhardt LR. (1998) Cost effective management programme for heart failure reduces hospitalisation. Heart 80:441-446.

Doughty RN, Wright SP, Pearl A, Walsh HJ, Muncaster S, Whalley GA, Gamble G, Sharpe N. (2002) Randomized, controlled trial of integrated heart failure management. Eur Heart J 23:139-146.

Ekman I, Andersson B, Ehnforst M, Matejka G, Persson B, Fagerberg B. (1998) Feasibility of a nurse-monitored, outpatient-care programme for elderly patients with moderate-to-severe chronic heart failure. Eur Heart J 19:1254-1260.

Flather MD, Yusuf S, Kober L, Pfeffer M, Hall A, Murray G, Torp-Pedersen C,

Ball S, Pogue J, Moye L, Braunwald E. (2000) Long-term ACE-inhibitor therapy in patients with heart failure or left-ventricular dysfunction: a systematic overview of data from individual patients. Lancet 355:1575-1581.

Ghali JK, Kadakia S, Cooper R, Ferlinz J. (1988) Precipitating factors leading to decompensation of heart failure. Traits among urban blacks. Arch Intern Med 148:2013-2016.

Grady KL, Dracup K, Kennedy G, Moser DK, Piano M, Stevenson LW, Young JB.(2000) Team management of patients with heart failure: A statement for healthcare professionals from the cardiovascular nursing council of the American Heart Association. Circulation 102:2443-2456.

Hunt SA, Baker DW, Chin MH, Cinquegrani MP, Feldman AM, Francis GS, Ganiats TG, Goldstein S, Gregoratos G, Jessup ML, Noble RJ, Packer M, Silver MA, Stevenson LW. (2001) ACC/AHA guidelines for the evaluation and management of chronic heart failure in the adult: a report of the American College of Cardiology/ American Heart Association Task Force on Practice Guidelines (Committee to Revise the 1995 Guidelines for the Evaluation and Management of Heart Failure). www.acc.org/clinical/guidelines/failure/ hf_index.htm

Jaarsma T, Halfens R, Huijer Abu-Saad H, Dracup K, Gorgels T, van Ree J, Stappers J. (1999) Effects of education and support on self-care and resource utilization in patients with heart failure. Eur Heart J 20:673-682.

Kasper EF, Gerstenblith G, Hefter G, Van Anden E, Brinker JA, Thiemann DR, Terrin M, Forman S, Gottlieb SH. (2002) A randomized trial of the efficacy of multidisciplinary care in heart failure outpatients at high risk of hospital readmission. J Am Coll Cardiol 39:471-480.

Konstam MA. (2001) Relating quality of care to clinical outcomes in heart failure: In search of the missing link. J Cardiac Failure 4:299-301.

Krumholz HM, Amatruda J, Smith GL, Mattera JA, Roumanis SA, Radford MJ, Crombie R, Vaccarino V. (2002) Randomized trial of an education and support intervention to prevent readmission of patients with heart failure. J Am Coll Cardiol 39:83-89.

Krumholz HM, Baker DW, Ashton CM, Dunbar SB, Friesinger GC, Havranek EP, Hlatky MA, Konstam M, Ordin DL, Pina IL, Pitt B, Spertus JA. (2000) Evaluating quality of care for patients with heart failure. Circulation 101: E122-E140.

McAlister FA, Lawson FME, Teo KK, Armstrong PW. (2001) A systematic review of randomized trials of disease management programs in heart failure. Am J Med 110:378-384.

McKelvie RS, Koon KT, Roberts R, McCartney N, Humen D, Montague T, Hendrican K, Yusuf S. (2002) Effects of exercise training in patients with heart failure: The Exercise Rehabilitation Trial (EXERT). Am Heart J 144:23-30.

Moser DK. (2000) Heart failure management: Optimal healthcare delivery programs. Annu Rev Nurs Res 18:91-126.

Moser DK, Mann DL. (2002) Improving outcomes in heart failure: It's not unusual beyond usual care. Circulation 105:2810-2812.

O'Connell JB. (2000) The economic burden of heart failure. Clin Cardiol 23:III-6-III-10.

Pina IL, Apstein CS, Balady GJ. Belardinelli R. Chaitman BR, Duscha BD, Fletcher BJ, Fleg JL, Myers JN, Sullivan MJ.

(2003) Exercise and heart failure. A statement from the American Heart Association Committee on Exercise, Rehabilitation, and Prevention. Circulation 107:1210-1225.

Pitt B, Zannad F, Remme WJ, Cody R, Castaigne A, Perez A, Palensky J, Wittes J. (1999) The effect of spironolactone on morbidity and mortality in patients with severe heart failure. N Engl J Med 341:709-717.

Rich MW. (1997) Epidemiology, pathophysiology, and etiology of congestive heart failure in older adults. J Am Geriatr Soc 45:968-974.

Rich MW. (1999) Heart failure disease management: A critical review. J Cardiac Failure 5:64-75.

Rich MW, Beckham V, Wittenberg C, Leven CL, Freedland KE, Carney RM. (1995) A multidisciplinary intervention to prevent the readmission of elderly patients with congestive heart failure. N Engl J Med 333:1190-1195.

Riegel B, Carlson B, Kopp Z, LePetri B, Glaser D, Unger A. (2002) Effect of a standardized nurse case-management telephone intervention on resource use in patients with chronic heart failure. Arch Intern Med 162:706-712.

Serxner S, Miyagi M, Jeffords J. (1998) Congestive heart failure disease management: A patient education intervention. Congest Heart Failure 4:23-28.

Stewart S, Horowitz JD. (2002) Home-based intervention in congestive heart failure: Long-term implications on readmission and survival. Circulation 105:2861-2866.

Stewart S, Marley JE, Horowitz JD. (1999) Effects of a multidisciplinary, home-based intervention on unplanned readmissions and survival among patients with chronic congestive heart failure: A randomised controlled study. Lancet 354:1077-1083.

Stewart S, Pearson S, Horowitz JD. (1998) Effects of a home-based intervention among patients with heart failure discharged from acute hospital care. Arch Intern Med 158:1067-1072.

Stewart S, Pearson S, Luke CG, Horowitz JD. (1998) Effects of home-based intervention on unplanned readmission and out-of-hospital deaths. J Am Geriatr Soc 46:174-180.

Stewart S, Vandenbroek AJ, Pearson S, Horowitz JD. (1999) Prolonged beneficial effects of a home-based intervention on unplanned readmissions and mortality among patients with congestive heart failure. Arch Intern Med 159:257-261.

The Digitalis Investigation Group. (1997) The effect of digoxin on mortality and morbidity in patients with heart failure. N Engl J Med 336:525-533.

Vinson JM, Rich MW, Sperry JC, Shah AS, McNamara T. (1990) Early readmission of elderly patients with congestive heart failure. J Am Geriatr Soc 38:1290-1295.

Weinberger M, Oddone EZ, Henderson WG. (1996) Does increased access to primary care reduce hospital readmissions? N Engl J Med 334:1441-1447.

MEDICAL THERAPY FOR COPD

Claudia G. Cote and Bartolome R. Celli

COMPREHENSIVE MANAGEMENT OF COPD

The Global Obstructive Lung Disease Initiative, sponsored by the World Health Organization and the National Institutes of Health, have defined chronic obstructive pulmonary disease (COPD) as a disease state characterized by airflow limitation that is not fully reversible. The airflow limitation is usually progressive and associated with an abnormal response of the lungs to noxious particles or gases (Pawels et al., 2001). This chapter will review the management of COPD, excluding smoking cessation as this topic is covered in other chapters of this textbook. Likewise, this chapter will not deal with surgical issues related to COPD because they comprise a large body of work that will require its own chapter.

The airflow obstruction of COPD, as defined by the forced expiratory volume in one second (FEV_1), is thought to be largely irreversible (ATS, 1995; Pawels et al., 2001). This physiologic fact has generated an unjustifiably pessimistic therapeutic attitude in many health care providers. The evidence suggests otherwise, and an optimistic attitude towards patients with COPD goes a long way in relieving a patient's fears and misconceptions. In contrast to many other diseases, some forms of interventions, such as smoking cessation (Anthonisen, 1994; Kottke 1988), long-term oxygen therapy in hypoxemic patients (NOTT, 1980; MRC, 1981) and mechanical ventilation in acute respiratory failure (Brochard, 1990) improve survival, while interventions such as pharmacological therapy, pulmonary rehabilitation and surgery can improve symptoms and quality of life. Table 1 summarizes the available therapeutic options for patients with COPD. The overall goals of treatment of COPD are to prevent further deterioration in lung function, alleviate symptoms, and treat complications as they arise. Once diagnosed, the patient should be encouraged to actively participate in disease management. This concept of *collaborative management* may improve self-reliance and esteem. All patients should be encouraged to lead a healthful lifestyle and exercise regularly. Preventive care is extremely important at this time and all patients should receive appropriate immunizations, including pneumococcal vaccine and yearly influenza vaccines. An algorithm detailing this comprehensive approach is shown in Figure 1.

Table 1. Therapy of Patients with Symptomatic Stable COPD

Interventions that improve survival	Interventions that improve symptoms
Smoking Cessation	Pharmacotherapy
Oxygen therapy if hypoxemic	Rehabilitation Education, Training and exercise, Nutrition
	Surgery Pneumoplasty (LVR), Lung Transplant

Figure 1: Algorithm describing the comprehensive management of patients with chronic obstructive pulmonary disease.

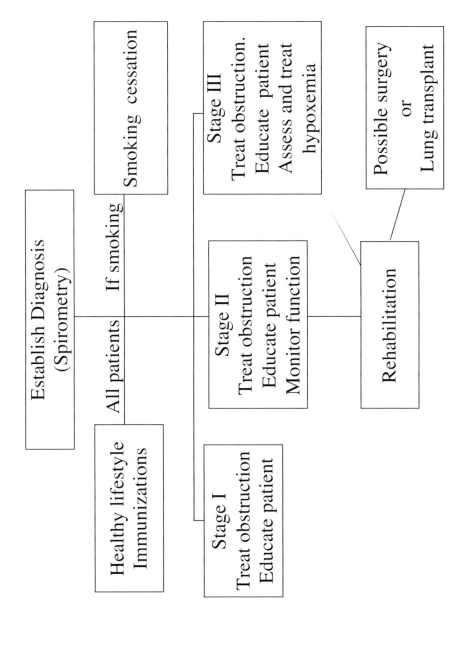

Smoking Cessation

As smoking is the major cause of COPD, smoking cessation is the most important component of therapy for patients who still smoke (ATS, 1995; Pawels, 2001). For a more comprehensive review, the reader is referred to the appropriate chapters of this book (Volume I, Chapters 8,9). However, a short paragraph addressing some basic concepts is necessary. A patient who smokes should be strongly encouraged to stop. Because second-hand smoking is known to damage lung function, limitation of exposure to involuntary smoke, particularly in children, should be encouraged. While most patients agree that smoking is risky, many seem unaware of its true significance. The factors that cause patients to smoke include the addictive potential of nicotine; conditional responses to stimuli surrounding smoking; psychosocial problems such as depression, poor education and low income; and forceful advertising campaigns. As the causes that drive the patient to smoke are multi-factorial, smoking cessation programs should also involve multiple interventions. The clinician should always actively support smoking cessation because a physician's advice to quit smoking can discriminate successful from unsuccessful results (Fiore et al., 2000; Chapman, 1991; Chalker and Celli, 1993).

Pharmacological therapy of airflow obstruction

The pharmacological therapy of COPD should be organized according to the severity of the disease and the tolerance of the patient for specific drugs (ATS, 1995, Ferguson and Cherniack, 1993; Pawels et al., 2001, Chapman, 1991, Chalker and Celli, 1993). In the outpatient setting, a step-wise approach (Table 2) similar in concept to that developed for asthma and systemic hypertension may be helpful. There is no current evidence that the regular use of any pharmacological agent alters the progressive deterioration of lung function in COPD. However, bronchodilators alleviate symptoms, improve exercise tolerance and improve quality of life, all worthwhile goals in COPD.

Bronchodilators

Several important concepts guide the use of bronchodilators. First, in some patients the changes in airflow limitation as expressed by the FEV_1 may be insignificant, although symptomatic benefit may arise through a decrease in the hyperinflation of the lung consequent to increased ventilatory demand experienced during exercise (Belman et al., 1996, O'Donnell et al., 1998, Tantucci et al., 1998). Second, older patients with COPD may have poor tolerance for sympathomimetic-induced tremor, nervousness and cardiac side effects produced by these drugs (Chalker and Celli, 1993). Third, some older COPD patients cannot effectively activate metered dose inhalers (MDIs); health providers should recognize this limitation and work with the patient to achieve mastery of the MDI. Most patients will learn the correct use of inhalers if taught by qualified persons. If this is not possible, use of a spacer to facilitate inhalation of the medication will help to achieve the desired results. Mucosal deposition in the mouth will result in local side effects (i.e. thrush with inhaled steroids) or general absorption and its consequences (i.e. tremor after beta-agonists). Fourth, the inhaled route is preferred over oral administration (Pawels 2001). Fifth, longer acting bronchodilators may improve compliance and provide symptom relief of longer duration (Mahler et al., 1999). The currently available bronchodilators are:
Beta-agonists

These drugs increase cyclic adenosine monophosphate (cAMP) within many cells and promote airway smooth muscle relaxation.

Table 2. Pharmacological Step Care of COPD

1. For mild variable symptoms:	**Selective Beta 2-agonist MDI aerosol**	1-2 puffs every 2-6h prn. (Not to exceed 8-12 puffs/24 h)
2. For mild to moderate continuing symptoms:	**Ipratropium MDI aerosol** *plus* **Selective beta-agonist MDI aerosol** *or* **Long acting beta-agonist MDI aerosol** *or* **Long acting anticholinergic**	2-6 puffs every 6-8 h. (Not to be used more frequently) 1-4 puffs prn qid. (For rapid relief, when needed or as regular supplement) 1 puff bid 1 capsule each day
4. If control of symptoms is suboptimal:	Consider a course of : **oral steroids (e.g., prednisone)** - if improvement occurs, wean down to low daily or alternate day dosing, e.g., 7.5 mg - if no improvement occurs, stop - if steroid appears to help, consider possible use of aerosol MDI, particularly if patient has evidence of bronchial hyperreactivity and repeated exacerbations	up to 40 mg/d for 10-14 days;
5. For severe exacerbation:	**Increase beta2-agonist dosage** **Increase iprotropium dosage** and **Provide theophylline dosage** And **Provide methylprednisolone dosage** Add **An antibiotic, if indicated.**	e.g MDI with spacer 4-6 puffs every 1/2-2 hours, or inhalent solution, unit dose every 1/2-2 hours e.g. MDI with spacer 6-8 puffs every 3-4 hours or inhalent solution of ipratropium 0.5 mg every 4-8 hours i.v. with amount calculated to bring serum level to 10-12 mcg/ml i.v. giving 50-100 mg immediately, then every 6-8 hours. Taper as soon as possible (2 weeks)

Other non-bronchodilator effects have been observed but their significance is uncertain. In patients with intermittent symptoms, it is reasonable to initiate drug therapy with an MDI of a short acting beta-agonist, prescribed as needed for relief of symptoms (ATS, 1995). Albuterol, (preferable to the less selective drugs epinephrine, isoproterenol or ephedrine) should be taken up to a maximum of 4-6 times a day or as prophylaxis. The rapid onset of action of beta-agonist aerosols may lead to dyspneic patients favoring them for regular use. Beta-agonist therapy decreases dyspnea and dynamic hyperinflation, and improves exercise tolerance in COPD (Belman et al., 1996). The potential for arrhythmias necessitates careful dosing in patients with probable or known cardiac disease, although serious cardiac complications are rare with conventional doses. In more advanced disease, it is appropriate to use long-acting beta-agonists (Dahl et al., 2001; Mahler et al., 1998; Rennard et al., 2001), at a dose of 1 or 2 puffs twice daily. They have been shown to prevent nocturnal bronchospasm, increase exercise endurance and improve quality of life. These agents may improve compliance, which can result in an improved outcome in some patients. A novel $beta_2$-receptor agonist with simultaneous dopaminergic-2-receptor activity (Ind et al., 2003) improved cough, phlegm production and dyspnea during the first 6 weeks of a randomized trial. However, it failed to maintain its effect over the next 6 months. Its role as an effective agent remains to be determined.

Anticholinergics

Once the patient suffers from persistent symptoms, an alternative to $beta_2$-agonists is regular use of anticholinergics by MDI. These drugs act by blocking muscarinic receptors that are known to be functional in COPD. The drug has a slower onset and longer action than short acting $beta_2$-agonists such as albuterol, and thus is less suitable for as-needed use (ATS, 1995; Karpel et al., 1994; Pawels et al., 2001; Rennard et al., 1996). The appropriate dosage is 2-4 puffs three or four times a day, but some patients require and tolerate larger dosages. It has been shown that ipratropium is effective in increasing exercise tolerance and decreasing dyspnea. The therapeutic effect is a consequence of a decrease in exercise-induced increased lung inflation or dynamic hyperinflation (O'Donnell et al., 1999). A large multi-center controlled trial of therapy with ipratropium bromide documented a significant bronchodilator effect, but there was no alteration in the rate of decline in lung function in the patients receiving the medication (Anthonisen et al., 1994). As is true for beta agonists, there is no substantial evidence to suggest that regular use of anticholinergic therapy, with or without a $beta_2$-agonist, leads to a worsening of spirometry or to exacerbation of COPD. Thus, it is appropriate to use regular therapy with ipratropium and to add a $beta_2$-agonist as often as needed for up to four treatments a day (Pawels et al., 2001). A new long-acting quaternary ammonium compound (Tiotropium) has been very effective in inducing long-term bronchodilation in patients with severe COPD (Casaburi et al., 2002). In addition, Tiotropium shows a beneficial effect on dyspnea, recurrence of exacerbations, and health-related quality of life when compared to placebo and even to ipratropium bromide (Vincken et al., 2002). Where available, Tiotropium may become the first line bronchodilator for patients with persistent symptoms. The results of further clinical trials evaluating its potential role as a disease-modifying agent will determine its place in the array of treatments for patients with COPD.

Currently, there is an available inhaled combination of ipratropium and a beta-agonist that has proven effective in the management of COPD (Combivent trial group, 1994). Furthermore, recent analysis of prospectively collected data shows that the combination of beta-agonists and ipratropium may decrease the incidence of acute COPD exacerbation and hospitalizations, and in that way decrease overall therapy cost (Friedman et al., 1999).

Phosphodiesterase inhibitors

The third line agent in the therapy of COPD is theophylline (ATS, 1995). This drug is a non-specific phosphodiesterase inhibitor that increases intracellular cAMP within airway smooth muscle. The bronchodilator effects of this drug are best seen at high doses where there is also a higher risk of toxicity. Its potential for toxicity has led to a decline in its popularity. Theophylline is of particular value for less compliant or less capable patients who cannot use aerosol therapy optimally because it can be taken once or twice a day (Pawels et al., 2002). Theophylline has been shown to improve the function of the respiratory muscles, stimulate the respiratory center, decrease dyspnea and enhance activities of daily living (McKay et al., 1993, Thomas et al., 1992). The drug also improves cardiac output, reduces pulmonary vascular resistance and improves the perfusion of ischemic myocardial muscle. Recent evidence suggests an anti-inflammatory role for this drug, thereby expanding its potential indications. It follows that there are several advantages to theophylline therapy in patients with cardiac disease or right ventricular failure, but its use should be carefully followed and intermittent serum levels should be monitored. The previously recommended therapeutic serum levels of 15 to 20 mg/dL are too close to the toxic range and are frequently associated with side effects. Therefore, a lower target range of 8 to 13 mg/dL is safer and still therapeutic in nature. The regular use of theophylline has not been shown to have a detrimental effect on the course of COPD. The combination of two or more bronchodilators (theophylline, albuterol and ipratropium) has some logical rationale as they seem to have additive effects and can result in maximum benefit in stable COPD (Thomas et al., 1992). A recent large, randomized prospective trial indicated that a combination of theophylline with salmeterol (a long-acting beta-agonist) was a significantly better bronchodilator than either agent alone (ZuWallack et al., 2001). This study supports the use of a combination of different classes of bronchodilators in the management of COPD.

There are other phosphodiesterase inhibitors in developmental phase. Specifically, a phosphodiesterase E4 inhibitor with an anti-inflammatory and bronchodilator effect, but less gastrointestinal irritation, could prove extremely useful if its theoretical advantages are clinically confirmed.

Anti-inflammatory therapy

In contrast to their value in asthma management, anti-inflammatory drugs have not been documented to have a significant role in the routine treatment of patients with stable COPD (ATS, 1995). Cromolyn and nedocromil have not been established as useful agents, although they could possibly be helpful if the patient has associated respiratory tract allergy. The groups of leukotriene inhibitors that have proven useful in asthma have not been adequately tested in COPD so that a final conclusion about their potential use in COPD cannot yet be drawn.

Corticosteroids

Corticosteroids could be considered in individual patients who fail to improve on adequate bronchodilator therapy (Callahan et al., 1991, Dompeling et al., 1993). Glucocorticoids act at multiple points within the inflammatory cascade. Their effects in COPD are more modest than their effects in bronchial asthma. Data from large patient studies suggest that inhaled corticosteroids can produce a small increase in post-bronchodilator FEV_1 and a small reduction in bronchial reactivity in stable COPD. In outpatients, exacerbations necessitate a course of oral steroids (Albert et al., 1980) but it is important to wean patients quickly, since the older COPD population is susceptible to complications such as skin damage, cataracts, diabetes, osteoporosis and secondary infection. These risks do not accompany standard doses of inhaled corticosteroid aerosols, which may cause thrush but pose a negligible risk for causing pulmonary infection. Most studies suggest that only 10-30% of patients with COPD improve if given chronic oral steroid therapy (Callahan et al., 1991). The dangers of steroids require careful documentation of the effectiveness of such therapy before a patient is placed on prolonged daily or alternate day dosing. The latter regimen may be safer, but its effectiveness has not been adequately evaluated in COPD. Several recently reported large multi-center trials decreased rate of exacerbations. Finally, recent retrospective analyses of large databases suggest a possible effect of inhaled corticosteroids on increased mortality (Sin and Tu, 2001; Soriano et al., 2002). This has prompted the initiation of a large prospective trial to explore the effect of inhaled corticosteroids on mortality. Results of this trial could influence how and when to use corticosteroids. The concurrent use of inhaled steroids with albuterol and ipratropium must be evaluated on an individual basis. Patients with moderate to severe COPD who have had repeated episodes of acute exacerbation may be the best candidates for this form of therapy.

Mucokinetic drugs

This loosely defined group of drugs aims to decrease sputum viscosity and adhesiveness in order to facilitate expectoration. The only controlled study in the US suggesting a value for these drugs in the chronic management of bronchitis was a multi-center evaluation of organic iodide (Petty and Finegan, 1968). This study demonstrated symptomatic benefits. The values of other agents, including water, have not been clearly demonstrated. Some agents (such as oral acetylcysteine) are favored in Europe for their anti-oxidant effects in addition to their mucokinetic properties. Several small controlled trials have shown some effect of these agents on FEV_1 and in recurrence of acute exacerbations of the disease (Poole and Black, 2001). A large trial now under way, may help define the possible role of these agents.

Genetically engineered ribonuclease seems to be useful in cystic fibrosis, but is of no value in COPD.

Antibiotics

Antibiotics are of unproven value in the prevention of exacerbations of COPD. However in patients with evidence of respiratory tract infection, such as fever, leukocytosis and a change in the chest radiograph, antibiotics have proven effective (Anthonisen et al., 1987). If recurrent infections occur, particularly in winter, continuous or intermittent prolonged courses of antibiotics may be useful. When an acute bacterial infection is believed to be present, antibiotic therapy may be justified, but the decision is usually made clinically since culture of sputum is not of cost-effective value. In prescribing treatment, fiscal concerns should be a consideration since older less costly agents are often effective; e.g., tetracycline, doxycycline, amoxicillin or erythromycin (ATS, 1995). The major bacteria to be considered are *Streptococcus pneumoniae*, *Hemophilus influenzae* and *Moraxella catarrhalis*. The antibiotic choice will depend on local experience, supported by sputum culture and sensitivities if the patient is moderately ill or needs to be admitted to hospital. The recent introduction of oral fluoroquinolones and macrolides has increased our capacity to effectively treat patients with acute respiratory tract infections. Quinolones may be favored in the more severely ill patient for whom highly resistant Gram-negative bacteria seem to be a growing problem (Adams et al., 2000; Miratvilles, 2002).

Alpha-1 antitrypsin

Although supplemental weekly or monthly administration of the enzyme alpha-1 antitrypsin may be indicated in non-smoking, younger patients with genetically determined emphysema, in practice such therapy is difficult to initiate. There is evidence that the administration of alpha-1 antitrypsin is relatively safe, but the appropriate selection of the candidate for such therapy is not clear (ATS, 1995; Dirksen et al., 1999). Patients with very severe and crippling COPD or those with good lung function are not good candidates for therapy. Likewise enzyme-deficient non-smoking patients are at low risk to develop airflow obstruction. Therefore, the most likely candidates for replacement therapy would be smoking patients with mild to moderate COPD. The cost of therapy is prohibitive, especially considering that its safety and long-term effects remain unknown.

Respiratory stimulants and depressants

Respiratory stimulants such as doxapram are currently not favored, although they are used in some countries (ATS, 1995; Pawels et al., 2001). Psychoactive drugs that have potential depressant effects on the respiratory centers are often sought by older patients to treat depression, anxiety, insomnia or pain. In general, these agents can be given with appropriate care, and with particular awareness of their depressant effect on the respiratory center. Benzodiazepines do not have a marked effect on respiration in mild or moderate COPD, but can be suppressive in severe disease, particularly during sleep. The safer hypnotics for use in insomnia include sedating antihistamines or chloral hydrate. Antidepressants may also have the advantage of improving sleep. Concomitant use of cardiovascular drugs may be needed in severe COPD and congestive heart failure; e.g., diuretics, angiotensin-converting enzyme inhibitors and calcium channel blockers. Digoxin is occasionally useful, while beta-adrenergic blockers are generally contraindicated. These drugs must be used cautiously to avoid dehydration, hypotension, myocardial ischemia and arrhythmias. Since

most patients requiring such therapy are elderly or have impaired drug clearance, all potential side effects must be carefully sought and responded to by modifying the drug regimen.

Vaccination

Ideally, infectious complications of the respiratory tract should be prevented in patients with COPD by using effective vaccines (Nichol et al., 1999a, Nichol et al., 1999b). Although the currently available vaccines are not totally effective and are not utilized widely, there is evidence that COPD patients benefit from their use, and thus routine prophylaxis with pneumococcal and influenza vaccines is recommended (Pawels et al., 2001).

Antiviral agents

Amantadine and rimantadine selectively inhibit the ion-channel function of the M2 protein of influenza A viruses. Even though these agents have proven useful as prophylactic agents in households of infected patients, no benefit has been shown in ill members of the household. Furthermore, rapid emergence of resistance has been documented. A new family of inhibitors of viral neuraminidase, inhaled zanamivir and oral oseltamivir, is effective in the treatment of early-phase influenza A and B infections in healthy adults and children. However, they are no substitute for prophylactic vaccination and while their role in the treatment of patients with COPD has not been well studied, they likely offer some potential value.

Management of Acute Exacerbations

An exacerbation of COPD is characterized by a change in the patient's baseline dyspnea, cough and/or sputum production beyond day-to-day variability that is sufficient to warrant a change in management. In the case of an acute exacerbation the pharmacological therapy is initiated with the same therapeutic agents available for its chronic management (ATS, 1995; Pawels et al., 2001). Care must be taken to rule out heart failure, myocardial infarction, arrhythmias and pulmonary embolism, all of which may present with clinical signs and symptoms similar to exacerbation of COPD.

The most important agents for acute exacerbation of COPD are anticholinergic and beta-agonists aerosols. Ipratropium may be administered via MDI, sometimes with a spacer if the administration is erratic or as an inhalant solution by nebulization. Although the upper limit of dosage has not been established, the drug is safe, and higher dosages can be given to a poorly responsive patient. However, the prolonged half-life means that repeat doses should not be given more often than every 4 to 8 hours. Beta-2-agonists should also be administered using the same techniques. These drugs have a reduced functional half-life in exacerbations of COPD, and thus may be given every 30 to 60 minutes if tolerated. The safety and value of continuous nebulization have not been established, but in selected cases this may be worth a trial. Subcutaneous or intramuscular dosing is only recommended if aerosol use is not feasible; intravenous administration is not an acceptable practice. Careful administration of theophylline may be useful. The drug can be given as intravenous aminophylline in a severe exacerbation. Serum levels are needed as a guide to avoid toxicity, and in most patients a serum level of 8-12 mg/mL is appropriate. When the patient improves, oral long-acting theophylline can be substituted, using 80% of the daily dose of aminophylline.

Combination therapy is often needed, and systemic corticosteroids should be added to the regimen. Two small (Davies et al., 1999; Thompson et al., 1996) and one large randomized trial (Nieweohner et al., 1999) have demonstrated the usefulness of corticosteroids. It is important to avoid prolonged (over 2 weeks) or high-dose therapy since older patients are susceptible to severe complications such as psychosis, fluid retention and a vascular necrosis of bones. In addition, data from the large randomized trial in which 2 versus 8 weeks of steroids were compared, showed no benefits from the longer administration of the medication (Nieweohner et al., 1999). Weaning must be accomplished as soon as possible.

Antibiotics such as amoxicillin, doxycycline, erythromycin, quinolones and macrolides (clarithromycin and azithromycin) have been helpful in exacerbations of COPD (Noira et al., 2001). Mucokinetic agents, such as iodides, given systemically have not been shown to be effective in exacerbations of COPD, although some patients report subjective improvement when given these agents.

Pulmonary Rehabilitation

Pulmonary rehabilitation is increasingly recognized as an important component of the comprehensive management of patients with symptomatic lung disease. A somewhat pessimistic view of rehabilitation became widespread when multiple studies evaluating this therapeutic tool in patients with severe lung disease failed to show any improvement in conventional pulmonary function tests. Fortunately, thanks to the perseverance of many investigators from multiple disciplines, research studies have shown that pulmonary rehabilitation offers the best treatment option for patients with symptomatic lung disease (ACCP/AACVPR 1997). This section reviews the fundamental concepts of pulmonary rehabilitation, its different components and its effect on several outcomes.

Definition

Pulmonary rehabilitation has recently been redefined by an American Thoracic Society (ATS) statement (Pulmonary Rehabilitation ATS, 1999) as a "A multi-disciplinary program of care for patients with chronic respiratory impairment that is individually tailored and designed to optimize physical and social performance and autonomy." The most important concept in the definition is that any program must attempt to treat each patient enrolled as an "individual." This definition is similar to others that have been proposed over the years (ACCP/AACVPR, 1998; Research NIH, 1994). In these reviews, it is clear that because pulmonary rehabilitation is multi-disciplinary and utilizes different therapeutic components, it is difficult to attribute improved global outcomes to the effect of individual elements of a program. However, certain concepts are based on significant evidence (Celli, 1995). Independent of the study design used, conventional pulmonary function tests do not change after pulmonary rehabilitation. Nevertheless, well-controlled studies (Table 3) have shown significant improvement in different outcomes including increased exercise

capacity, improved health-related quality of life, decreased dyspnea and fewer hospital admissions (Bendstrup et al., 1997; Cockcroft et al., 1981; Goldstein et al., 1994; Griffiths et al., 2000; Guell et al., 2000; Reardon et al., 1994; Ries et al., 1995; Wedzicha et al., 1998; Wykstra et al., 1994).

Objectives and Goals

Pulmonary rehabilitation has two major objectives.

a. Control, alleviate and reverse as much as possible the symptoms and pathophysiological processes leading to respiratory impairment.

b. Improve the quality of and attempt to prolong the patient's life.

In a practical sense, comprehensive care may be best provided using a multi-disciplinary approach via a structured rehabilitation program. The practical goals are shown in Table 4.

Table 3. Outcomes of Pulmonary Rehabilitation in patients with COPD.

Outcome	Effect	Grade of Evidence
Exercise Endurance	Large and significant increase	A
Exercise Work Capacity (Watt or VO2)	Modest Increase	A
Biochemical Muscle Enzyme Changes	Controversial	B
Dyspnea	Large and Significant Improvement	A
Quality of life	Improvement	A
Health related cost	Improvement	B

Evidence is graded according to these guidelines.
Grade A. Evidence obtained from well controlled randomized studies.
Grade B. Evidence obtained from well designed controlled trials, small numbers.
Grade C. Evidence obtained from multiple time series.

Table 4. Practical Goals of a Pulmonary Rehabilitation Program

Reduce Work of Breathing
Improve Pulmonary Function
Normalize Arterial Blood Gases
Alleviate Dyspnea
Increase Efficiency of Energy Utilization
Correct Nutrition
Improve Exercise Performance and Activities of Daily Living
Restore a Positive Outlook in Patients
Improve Emotional State
Decrease Health Related Costs
Improve Survival

Patient Selection

Any patient symptomatic from respiratory disease is a candidate for rehabilitation. Patients with moderate to moderately severe disease are preferred targets for treatment to prevent the disabling effects of end-stage respiratory failure. This is an important issue because patients with minimal functional limitations may benefit little from programs designed to improve function. Although some patients with advanced disease may be considered unlikely to benefit from rehabilitation, patients with the most severe degree of lung disease, such as those awaiting for lung transplantation and lung volume reduction surgery, have shown significant functional improvement and increased exercise endurance after pulmonary rehabilitation (Cooper et al., 1995; Gelb et al., 1996).

Mild disease may not justify the intense effort needed to maintain a viable program. Other factors that may hinder the ultimate success of rehabilitation for an individual are: presence of disabling diseases such as severe heart failure or arthritis, a very low educational level, lack of support and above all, lack of motivation (Petty et al., 1969, Pulmonary Rehabilitation ATS, 1999). Although it is customary to not consider patients with cancer as candidates for rehabilitation, we have treated selected patients with limited exercise performance who would otherwise be candidates for surgery. There are recent reports of simultaneous resection of lung nodules in patients with severe COPD who were until now deemed inoperable because of very severe airflow obstruction. The findings of improved outcome in such patients suggests that pulmonary rehabilitation may be indicated even for patients with the most severe disease, as long as they are willing and able to participate in the rehabilitation program (Pulmonary Rehabilitation ATS, 1999).

The rehabilitation program should have resources available to teach and supervise respiratory therapy techniques (oxygen, use of inhalers, nebulizers, etc.), physical therapy (breathing techniques, chest physical therapy, postural drainage), exercise conditioning (upper and lower extremity), and activities of daily living (work simplification, energy conservation). Also desirable are services to evaluate and advise on nutritional needs, psychological evaluation and vocational counseling (Hodgkin et al., 2001, Petty et al., 1969). The ideal system is one that provides an in-hospital arm for patients who may benefit from the program while recovering from acute exacerbations, and an outpatient arm (including home therapy) that could complete the program started in the hospital. This assures good continuity of care.

Exercise conditioning

Exercise conditioning is based on three physiological principles (Casaburi, 1993, Hodgkin et al., 2001):

1. Specificity of training, which attributes improvement only to the type of exercise that is practiced. This means that if the training is limited to the lower extremities, such as bicycling, exercise performance will only accrue for ergometry.

2. Intensity of training, which establishes that only a load higher than baseline will induce a training effect.

3. Reversal of the training effect, which states that once discontinued, the training effect will disappear.

Lower Extremity Exercise

Several recent controlled trials demonstrate that pulmonary rehabilitation is better than regular treatment in the symptomatic COPD patient. Goldstein *et al.* (Goldstein et al., 1994) randomized 89 patients to either inpatient rehabilitation for 8 weeks followed by 16 weeks of outpatient treatment, or to conventional care as provided by their physician. At the end of the study, the patients in the rehabilitation group (n=45) significantly improved their exercise endurance and sub-maximal cycle time compared to controls (n=44). This was associated with a decrease in dyspnea, and improvements in emotional function and the mastery domain of the chronic respiratory disease-specific health status questionnaire. Wijkstra and coworkers reported the results of 12 weeks of rehabilitation in 28 COPD patients that were compared to 15 patients who received no treatment and served as controls (Wykstra et al., 1994). This study is unique in that the rehabilitation was conducted at home, with the program supervised by non-specialists. The

treated patients improved their exercise endurance, perception of dyspnea and health-related quality of life compared with controls. This suggests that pulmonary rehabilitation could be conducted at home if the program is well structured and implemented.

Exercise training is the most important component of a pulmonary rehabilitation program. Casaburi reviewed 36 uncontrolled studies that evaluated the effect of exercise training on exercise performance in over 900 patients with COPD (Casaburi, 1993). Exercise training improved exercise endurance in these patients. This has been confirmed by controlled trials which have shown that a rehabilitation program that includes lower extremity exercise is better than other forms of therapy, such as optimization of medication, education, breathing retraining and group therapy (Bendstrup et al., 1997; Crockcroft et al., 1981; Goldstein et al., 1994; Griffiths et al., 2000; Guell et al., 2000; Wedzicha et al., 1998; Wykstra et al., 1994).

All of these studies have demonstrated an increase in exercise endurance, a modest but significant improvement in work or oxygen uptake and a decrease in the perception of dyspnea with the therapy.

It has been suggested that with exercise, patients with COPD become desensitized to the dyspnea induced by the ventilatory load. This concept was supported by studies such as the one by Belman and Kendregan (Belman and Kendregan, 1981), who randomized patients to upper or lower extremity exercise and obtained muscle biopsies of the trained limbs before and after training. In spite of a significant increase in exercise endurance, there were no changes in the oxidative enzyme content of the trained muscle. In contrast, Maltais *et al.* document evidence for a true training effect (Maltais et al., 1996). In this study the muscle biopsies of trained patients, but not controls, manifested significant increases in all enzymes responsible

175

for oxidative muscle function.

The effect of rehabilitation on 6-minute walking distance is shown in Figure 2. There was a significant improvement in 6-minute walking distance in patients with severe COPD (mean FEV_1 of 0.82 L) who underwent preoperative pulmonary rehabilitation before lung volume reduction surgery at our institution. Overall, it is safe to state that some training is required and that the intensity should be the highest possible, taking into account the patient's tolerability and specific goals (Casaburi et al., 1997; Clark et al., 1996; Normandin et al., 2000; O' Donnell et al., 1998; Spruit et al., 2002).

Upper Extremity Exercise

Most of our knowledge about exercise conditioning is derived from programs emphasizing leg training. This is unfortunate, because the performance of many everyday tasks requires not only the hands, but also the concerted action of other muscle groups in the upper torso for arm positioning. Some of these serve a dual function (respiratory and postural), and arm exercise will decrease their capacity to participate in ventilation (Celli, 1994). These observations suggest that if the arms are trained to perform more work, or if the ventilatory requirement for the same work is decreased, the capacity to perform activities of daily living could improve. Arm training results in improved performance that is for the most part task-specific. Two studies (Martinez et al., 1993; Ries et al., 1988) have concluded that unsupported arm exercise may be useful for training patients in activities that resemble those of daily living.

Figure 2. Timed (6 minutes) walking distance (meters) in 24 patients with advanced lung disease (COPD) before and after 24 sessions of preoperative pulmonary rehabilitation for Lung Volume Reduction Surgery at St. Elizabeth's Medical Center.

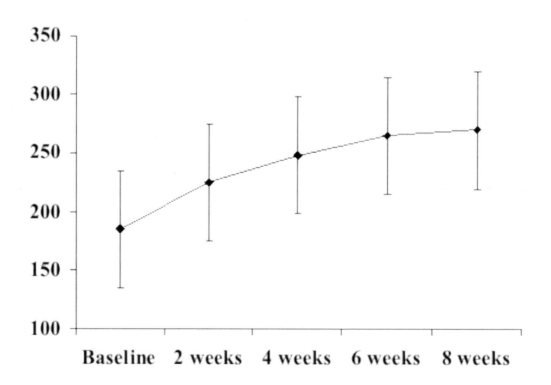

Physical modalities of ventilatory therapy

There are two types of physical modalities of ventilatory therapy (Faling, 1986): Controlled breathing techniques (diaphragmatic breathing exercise, pursed lip breathing and bending forward) and chest physical therapy (postural drainage, chest percussion and vibration position). The former are aimed at decreasing dyspnea and the latter should enhance drainage of secretions. The benefits of these therapies include less dyspnea, a decrease in anxiety and panic attacks and improvement in the sensation of well being. These therapies require careful instruction by specialists who are familiar with the techniques. They should be initiated as soon as possible and repeated often with close supervision until the patient shows thorough understanding of the technique. It is often necessary to involve relatives since many of these modalities require the help of another person (e.g. chest percussion).

Breathing training is aimed at controlling the respiratory rate and breathing pattern to decrease air trapping. Pursed lip breathing and diaphragmatic breathing attempt to decrease the work of breathing and improve the position and function of the respiratory muscles (Faling, 1986). These maneuvers result in a decrease in dyspnea in some patients with severe COPD, both at rest and during exercise. The improvement in the position of the respiratory muscles can also be obtained in the supine or Trendelenburg position. This may be the reason why many patients with COPD perceive less dyspnea when supine compared to standing, a finding that is in sharp contrast to the increased perception of dyspnea that is frequently described by patients with congestive heart failure when they adopt the supine position.

Ventilatory Muscle Training

Respiratory muscles can be specifically trained to improve their strength or their endurance. Since reduced inspiratory muscle strength is evident in patients with COPD, considerable efforts have been made to determine the effectiveness of respiratory muscle training in these patients. Strength training has limited clinical significance. Controlled trials of endurance training have shown an increase in the time that the ventilatory muscles could tolerate a known load (Lisboa et al., 1997; Sanchez et al., 2001; Scherer et al., 2000; Weiner et al., 1992). Some have shown a significant increase in strength and a decrease in dyspnea during inspiratory load and during exercise. In the studies where systemic exercise performance was evaluated, there was an increase in walking distance and cardiopulmonary exercise endurance. The extensive data available indicate that ventilatory muscle training (VMT) with resistive breathing results in improved ventilatory muscle strength and endurance, and has a beneficial effect on overall exercise performance. It is not clear whether this effort results in changes in important clinical outcomes such as health status or functional dyspnea, although the results in some recent small studies are encouraging (Lisboa et al., 1997; Sanchez et al., 2001). Whether respiratory muscle training has a positive impact on morbidity or health care resource utilization remains unexplored. Given the relative complexity of this form of therapy, it is currently only recommended for rehabilitation of patients with respiratory muscle weakness associated with significant dyspnea (ATS, 1995; ACCP/AACVPR, 1997).

Respiratory muscle resting

When the respiratory muscles have to work against a large enough load, they may become fatigued. Experimentally, this has been shown to occur both in normal volunteers and in patients with COPD. Clinically, it seems that respiratory muscle fatigue plays an important role in the acute respiratory failure seen in patients with COPD. It seems logical that noninvasive ventilation (NIV) may be helpful in cases of acute or chronic respiratory failure with impending respiratory muscle fatigue. Several randomized trials have confirmed this assumption (Bott et al., 1993; Brochard et al., 1995; Kramer et al., 1995). These trials evaluated different outcomes, including rate of intubation, length of intensive care unit (ICU) and hospital stays, dyspnea and mortality. The patients with the best outcomes were those with elevated $PaCO_2$, who were able to cooperate with care givers and who had no other important co-morbid problems (sepsis, severe pneumonia). Because positive pressure non-invasive ventilation is potentially dangerous, patients considered for this therapy should be closely monitored and treated by individuals familiar with these ventilatory techniques.

The possibility that the respiratory muscles of patients with stable severe COPD were functioning close to the fatigue threshold, led numerous investigators to explore the role of resting the muscles using non-invasive negative and positive pressure ventilation. All but one of the controlled trials (Casanova et al., 2000; Meecham-Jones et al., 1995) using both forms of ventilation have shown no benefit in most of the outcomes studied. Therefore, the routine use of NIV in stable COPD is currently not justified.

Nutritional Evaluation

Many patients with emphysema appear thin and emaciated. It has recently been shown that they may suffer from protein-calorie malnutrition. Although evidence is lacking as to the type of diet that would result in unequivocal benefits for the respiratory system, most authorities agree that an attempt should be made to correct deficiencies that may be present (Hodgkin et al., 2001). Correction of factors such as anemia (to improve oxygen-carrying capacity) or electrolyte imbalances (sodium,

potassium, phosphorus and magnesium) could result in improved cardiopulmonary performance. Similarly, simple measures such as encouraging the patient to take small amounts of food at more frequent intervals results in less abdominal distention and decreases dyspnea after meals. We also recommend evaluating oxygen saturation during meals. If dyspnea during eating is present, it may be alleviated by supplementing the patient with O_2 at meal time.

Psychological Support

Most patients with advanced lung disease have psychological problems, mainly disease-related depression and anxiety (Hodgkin et al., 2001). Fortunately, these problems are likely to improve as the patients become involved in a rehabilitation program that improves activity performance (Pulmonary Rehabilitation ATS, 1999). Simple measures such as being able to exercise under the supervision of supportive specialists frequently results in a desensitization to symptoms, including dyspnea and fear. It has been shown that for patients with COPD, rehabilitation sessions that include education, exercise, modalities of physical therapy, breathing techniques and relaxation are more effective in reducing anxiety than a similar number of psychotherapy sessions (Celli, 1995). Occasional patients will have major psychological problems that will require primary psychiatric evaluation and treatment.

Pulmonary rehabilitation has gradually become the gold standard treatment for patients with severe lung disease, especially chronic obstructive pulmonary disease. The positive results on outcome, in several well-conducted randomized trials, have documented the effectiveness of pulmonary rehabilitation. This therapeutic modality should be made available to all patients with symptomatic respiratory disease.

Home Oxygen Therapy

Therapeutic oxygen has been used systematically since the association between hypoxemia and right heart failure was recognized, and the benefit of continuous oxygen delivery to patients with severe COPD had come to be appreciated (Barach, 1922; Petty and Finegan, 1968). Since then much has been learned about the effects of oxygen and hypoxemia, and progress has been made in the area of mechanical oxygen delivery devices.

The results of the Nocturnal Oxygen Therapy Trial (NOTT) and Medical Research Council (MRC) studies have established that continuous home oxygen improves survival in hypoxemic COPD and that survival is related to the number of hours of supplemental oxygen per day (NOTT, 1980; MRC, 1981). Other beneficial effects of long-term oxygen include reduction in high red cell count or polycythemia (a phenomenon perhaps related more to lowered carboxy-hemoglobin levels than improved arterial saturation), and reductions in pulmonary artery pressures, dyspnea and rapid-eye movement-related hypoxemia during sleep (Zielinsky et al., 1998). Oxygen also improves sleep and may reduce nocturnal arrhythmias. Importantly, oxygen can also improve neuropsychiatric outcomes (Grant et al., 1987; Prigatani et al., 1983). Oxygen supplementation improves exercise tolerance (Criner and Celli, 1987), which has been attributed to 1) central mechanisms causing reduced minute ventilation at the same workload thereby delaying the time until ventilatory limitations are reached; 2) improved arterial oxygenation, enabling greater oxygen delivery and reversal of hypoxemia-induced bronchoconstriction; and 3) the effect of oxygen on respiratory muscle recruitment (Bradley et al., 1978; Criner and Celli, 1987; Bye et al., 1985; Dean et al., 1992; Vyas et al., 1974).

Prescribing Home Oxygen

Patients are evaluated for long-term oxygen therapy (LTOT) by measuring the PaO_2. It is therefore recommended that measurement of PaO_2, not pulse oximetry (SaO_2), be the clinical standard for initiating LTOT particularly during rest (ATS, 1995). Oximetry SaO_2 may be used to adjust oxygen flow settings over time. If elevated concentrations of carbon dioxide (hypercapnia) or acid pH in the blood (acidosis) are suspected, an arterial blood gas (ABG) must be performed. Some COPD patients who were not hypoxemic before the events leading to their exacerbation will eventually recover to the point that they will no longer need oxygen. It is therefore recommended that the need for long-term oxygen be reassessed in 30-90 days when the patient is clinically stable and receiving adequate medical management. Oxygen therapy can be discontinued if the patient does not meet blood gas criteria. To prescribe long-term oxygen therapy, a certificate of medical necessity must be completed. The Health Care Financing Administration (HCFA) form evolved in an attempt to insure that the physician, not the home medical equipment (HME) supplier, was in charge of decisions concerning therapy. HCFA requires the physician or an employee of the physician, rather than the home medical equipment supplier, to complete the form. Like any drug, oxygen has potential deleterious effects that may be particularly relevant to older patients. The hazardous effects of oxygen therapy can be considered under three broad headings (Tiep, 1990, West and Primeau, 1983).

First, there are physical risks such as fire hazard or tank explosion, trauma from catheters or masks and drying of mucous membranes owing to high flow rates and inadequate humidification. Second, there are functional effects related to increased carbon dioxide retention and absorptive collapse of portions of lung segments (atelectasis) Elevated $PaCO_2$ in response to supplemental oxygen is a well-recognized complication in a minority of patients. The mechanism has traditionally been ascribed to reductions in hypoxic ventilatory drive. However, in many patients the decrease in minute ventilation is minimal. The most consistent finding is a worsening of the ratio of pulmonary ventilation to blood perfusion distribution with a resulting decrease in oxygen level (Aubier et al., 1980). This presumably results from oxygen's blockage of local hypoxic vasoconstriction, thereby increasing perfusion of poorly ventilated areas.

Administration Devices

Oxygen is typically administered with continuous flow by nasal cannula; however, because alveolar delivery occurs during a small portion of a spontaneous respiratory cycle (approximately the first one-sixth), the rest of the cycle being used to fill dead space and for exhalation, the majority of continuously flowing oxygen is not used by the patient and is wasted into the atmosphere (Hoffman, 1994; Kory et al., 1962). To improve efficiency and increase patient mobility, several devices are available that focus on oxygen conservation and delivery during early inspiration. These devices include reservoir cannulas, demand-type systems and transtracheal catheters (Hoffman, 1994).

Reservoir nasal cannulas and pendants store oxygen during expiration and deliver a 20-mL bolus during early inspiration. Because more alveolar oxygen is delivered, flows may be reduced proportionally. This has been shown to result in a 2:1 to 4:1 oxygen savings at rest and with exercise. Cosmetic considerations have traditionally limited patient acceptance of these devices. Reservoir cannulas have been utilized for patients with a high flow oxygen requirement.

Demand valve systems have an electronic or pneumatic sensor that delivers oxygen specifically during early inspiration (Tiep, 1990). By restricting or accentuating oxygen delivery during inspiration, wasted delivery into dead space or during exhalation is minimized. This results in a 2:1 to 7:1 oxygen savings. Demand systems sometimes fail to provide adequate oxygenation during exercise. This deficiency has been addressed with larger pulses and higher delivery settings (Tiep et al., 2002). The effect of mouth-breathing on efficacy is not yet clear.

Transtracheal oxygen (TTO) therapy employs a thin flexible catheter placed into the lower trachea for delivery of continuous or pulsed oxygen (Benditt et al., 1993; Kampelmacher et al., 1997). Because oxygen is delivered directly into the trachea, dead space is reduced and the upper trachea serves as a reservoir of undiluted oxygen. This provides a 2:1 to 3:1 oxygen savings over nasal cannula and improves compliance. In summary, oxygen therapy has been shown to prolong survival in patients with COPD and hypoxemia. The development of simple portable and well-accepted devices has helped many patients lead a life with quality and few limitations.

CONCLUSION

Over the years, our knowledge about COPD has increased significantly. Smoking cessation campaigns have resulted in a significant decrease in smoking prevalence in the USA. Similar efforts in the rest of the world should have the same impact. The consequence should be a drop in incidence of COPD in the years to come. The widespread application of long-term oxygen therapy for hypoxemic patients has resulted in increased survival. Over time we have expanded our drug therapy armamentarium and have used medications to effectively improve dyspnea and quality of life. Recent studies have documented the benefits of pulmonary rehabilitation. Non-invasive ventilation has offered new alternatives for the patient with acute or chronic failure. The revival of surgery for emphysema, although still experimental, may serve as an alternative to lung transplant for those patients with severe COPD who are still symptomatic on maximal medical therapy. With all these options, an optimistic attitude toward the patient with COPD is certainly justified.

REFERENCES

ACCP/AACVPR. (1997) Pulmonary rehabilitation: Joint evidence based guidelines. J Cardiopulm Rehab 17:371-405.

Adams SG, Melo J, Luther M, Anzueto A. (2000) Antibiotics are associated with lower relapse rates in outpatients with acute exacerbations of COPD. Chest 117:1345-52.

Albert R, Martin T, Lewis S. (1980) Controlled clinical trial of methyl-prednisolone in patients with chronic bronchitis and acute respiratory insufficiency. Ann Int Med 92:753-75.

American Thoracic Society. (1995) Standards for the diagnosis and case of patients with chronic obstructive pulmonary disease. Am J Respir Crit Care Medicine 152:78-121.

Anthonisen NR, Manfreda J, Warren CPW, Hershfield ES, Harding GKM, Nelson NA. (1987) Antibiotic therapy in exacerbations of chronic obstructive pulmonary disease. Ann Int Med 106:196-204.

Anthonisen NR, Connett JE, Kiley JP, Altose MD, Bailey WC, Buist AS, Conway WA, Enright PL, Kanner RE, O'Hara P, Scanlon PO, Tashkin DP, Wise RA, for the Lung Health Study Group. The effects of smoking intervention and the use of an inhaled anticholinergic bronchodilator on the rate of decline of FEV_1: The Lung Health Study. JAMA 272:1497-1505.

Aubier M, Murciano D, Milie-Emili M. (1980)

Effects of the administration of oxygen therapy on ventilation and blood gases in patients with chronic obstructive pulmonary disease during acute respiratory failure. Am Rev Respir Dis 122:747-754.

Barach AL. (1922) The therapeutic uses of oxygen. JAMA 79: 693-98

Belman M, Kendregan BE. (1981) Exercise training fails to increase skeletal muscle enzymes in patients with chronic obstructive pulmonary disease. Am Rev Respir Dis 123:256-261.

Belman MJ, Botnick WC, Shin JW. (1996) Inhaled bronchodilators reduce dynamic hyperinflation during exercise in patients with chronic obstructive pulmonary disease.Am J Respir Crit Care Med 153:967-975.

Benditt, J, Pollock M, Roa MJ, Celli B. (1993) Transtracheal delivery of gas decreases the oxygen cost of breathing. Am Rev Respir Dis 147: 1207-1210

Bendstrup KE, Ingenman Jensen J, Holm S, Bengtsson B. (1997) Out-patient rehabilitation improves activities of daily living, quality of life, and exercise tolerance in chronic obstructive pulmonary disease. Eur Repir J 10:2801-2806

Bott J, Caroll P, Conway J et al. (1993) Randomized controlled trial of nasal ventilation in acute ventilatory failure due to obstructive lung disease. Lancet 341:1555-1559

Bradley BL, Garner AE, Billiu D, Mestas JM, Forman J. (1978) Oxygen-assisted exercise in chronic obstructive lung disease. The effect on exercise capacity and arterial blood gas tension. Am Rev Respir Dis 118:239-43

Brochard L, Isabey D, Piquet J, Amaro P, Mancebo J, Messadi,A, Brun-Buisson C, Rauss A, Lemaire F, Harf A. (1990) Reversal of acute exacerbations of chronic obstructive lung disease by inspiratory assistance with a face mask. N Engl J Med 323:1523-30.

Brochard L, Mancebo J, Wysocki M, et al. (1995) Noninvasive ventilation for acute exacerbation of chronic obstructive pulmonary disease. N Engl J Med 333:817-822.

Burge PS, Calverley PM, Jones PW, Spencer S, Anderson JA, Maslen TK. (2000) Randomised, double blind, placebo controlled study of fluticasone propionate in patients with moderate to severe chronic obstructive pulmonary disease: the ISOLDE trial. B M J 320:1297-303.

Bye PTP, Esau SA, Levy RD, Shriner RJ, Macklem PT, Martin JG, Pardy RL. (1985) Ventilatory muscle function during exercise in air and oxygen in patients with chronic air-flow limitation. Am Rev Respir Dis 132:236-40

Callahan C, Dittus R, Katz BP. (1991) Oral corticosteroids therapy for patients with stable chronic obstructive pulmonary disease: a meta-analysis. Ann Int Med 114:216-223.

Casaburi R, Mahler DA, Jones PW et al. (2002) A long-term evaluation of once-daily inhaled tiotropium in chronic obstructive pulmonary disease. Eur Respir J 19:217-224

Casaburi R, Porszasz J, Burns M, Carithers E, Chang R. Cooper C. (1997) Physiologic benefits of exercise training in rehabilitation of patients with severe chronic obstructive pulmonary disease. 155:1541-1551.

Casaburi R. (1993) Exercise training in chronic obstructive lung disease. Casaburi R, Petty TL, eds. Principles and practice of pulmonary rehabilitation. W. B. Saunders Co., Philadelphia 1993.

Casanova C, Celli B, Tost L, Soriano E, Abreu J, Velasco V, Santolaria F. (2000) Long-term controlled trail of nocturnal nasal positive pressure ventilation in patients with severe COPD. Chest 118:1582-1590

Celli BR. (1995) Pulmonary Rehabilitation. Am J Respir Crit Care Med 152:861-864.

Celli BR. (1994) The clinical use of upper extremity exercise. Clin Chest Med 15:339-349

Chalker R, Celli B. (1993) Special considerations in the elderly. Clin Chest Med 14:437-452.

Chapman KR. (1991) Therapeutic algorithm for chronic obstructive pulmonary disease. Am J Med 91(4A):17S-23S.

Clark CJ, Cochrane L, Mackay E. (1996) Low intensity peripheral muscle conditioning improves exercise tolerance and breathlessness in COPD. Eur Respir J 2590-2596.

COMBIVENT Inhalation Aerosol Study Group. (1994) In chronic obstructive pulmonary disease, a combination of ipratropium and albuterol is more effective than either agent alone. An 85-day multicenter trial. Chest 105:1411-1419

Cooper J, Trulock E, Triantafillou A, et al. (1995) Bilateral pneumectomy (volume reduction) for chronic obstructive pulmonary disease. J Thorac Cardiovas Sur 109:106-113

Criner GJ, Celli BR. (1987) Ventilatory muscle recruitment in exercise with O_2 in obstructed patients with mild hypoxemia. J Appl Physiol 63:195–200

Crockoft AE, Saunders MJ, Berry G. (1981) Randomized controlled trial of rehabilitation in chronic respiratory disability. Thorax. 36:2003-2005.

Dahl R, Greefhorst LA Nowak D, Nonikov V, Byrne AM, Thomson MH, Till D, Della CG. (2001) Inhaled Formoterol Dry Powder Versus Ipratropium Bromide in Chronic Obstructive Pulmonary Disease. Am J Respir Crit Care Med 164:778-784.

Davies L, Angus RM, Calverley PM. (1999) Oral corticosteroids in patients admitted to hospital with exacerbations of chronic obstructive pulmonary disease: a prospective randomized controlled trial. Lancet 345:456-60

Dean NC, Brown JK, Himelman RB, Doherty JJ, Gold WM, Stulbarg MS. (1992) Oxygen may improve dyspnea and endurance in patients with chronic obstructive pulmonary disease and only mild hypoxemia. Am Rev Respir Dis 146:941-45

Dirksen A, Dijkman JH, Madsen F, Stoel B,Hutchison DC, Ulrik CS, Skovgaard LT, Kok-Jensen A, Rudolphus A, Seersholm N,Vrooman HA, Reiber JH, Hansen NC, Heckscher T, Viskum K, Stolk J. (1999) A randomized clinical trial of alpha(1)-antitrypsin augmentation therapy. Am J Respir Crit Care Med 160:1468-1472

Dompeling E, van Schayck CP, van Grunsven PM, van Herwaarden CLA, Akkermans R, Molema J, Folgering H, van Weel C. (1993) Slowing the deterioration of asthma and chronic obstructive pulmonary disease observed during bronchodilator therapy by adding inhaled corticosteroids: a 4-year prospective study. Ann Int Med 118:770-778.

Faling LJ. (1986) Pulmonary rehabilitation. Physical Modalities. Clin Chest Med 7:599.

Ferguson GT, Cherniack RM. (1993) Management of chronic obstructive pulmonary disease. N Eng J Med 328:1017-1022.

Fiore M, Bailey W, Cohen S, Dorfman S, Goldstein M, Gritz E, Heyman R, Jaen C, Kottke T, Lando H, Mecklenburg R, Mullen P, Nett L, Robinson L, Sistzer M, Tommasello A, Villejo L, Wewers M. (2000) Treating Tobacco Use and Dependence. Rockville, MD: U.S. Department Of Health and Human Services.

Friedman M, Serby C, Menjoge S, Wilson D, Hilleman D, Witek T. (1999) Pharmacoeconomic evaluation of a combination of ipratropium plus albuterol compared with ipratropium alone and albuterol alone in COPD. Chest 115:635-641.

Gelb A, Mc Kenna R, Brenner et al. (1996) Contribution of lung and chest wall mechanics following emphysema resection. Chest 110:11-16.

Goldstein RS, Gork EH, Stubbing D et al. (1994) Randomized controlled trial of respiratory rehabilitation. Lancet 344:1394-1397

Grant I, Prigatano GP, Heaton RK, McSweeny AJ, Wright EC, Adams KM. (1987) Progressive neuropsychologic impairment and hypoxemia. Relationship in chronic obstructive pulmonary disease. Arch Gen Psychiatry 44:999–1006.

Griffiths TL, Burr ML, Campbell IA, Lewis-Jenkins V, Mullins J, Shields K, Turner-Lawlor PJ, Pyne N, Newcombe RG, Lonescu AA, Thomas J, Turnbridge J. (2000) Results at 1 year of outpatient multidisciplinary pulmonary rehabilitation: a randomized controlled trial. Lancet 355:362-368.

Guell R, Casan P, Belda J, Sangenis M, Morante F, Guyatt G, Sanchis J. (2000) Long-term effects of outpatient rehabilitation of COPD: A randomized trial. Chest 117:976-983.

Hodgkin JE, Celli B, Connors GL. (2001) Pulmonary Rehabilitation. Guidelines to success. 3rd Ed. Lippincott, Philadelphia.

Hoffman LA. (1994) Novel strategies for delivering oxygen: Reservoir cannula, demand flow, and transtracheal oxygen administration. Respir Care 39:363-376

Ind PW, Laitinen L, Laursen L, Wenzel S, Wouters E, Deamer L, Nystrom P. (2003) Early clinical investigation of Viozan (sibenadet HCl), a novel D2 dopamine receptor agonist for the treatment of chronic obstructive pulmonary disease symptoms. Respir Med 97:S9- S21.

Jones PW, Bosh TK. (1997) Quality of life changes in COPD patients treated with salmeterol. Am J Respir Crit Care Med 155:1283-1289.

Jorenby DE, Leischow SG, Nides MA, et al. (1999) A controlled trial of sustained release buproprion, a nicotine patch or both for smoking cessation. N Engl J Med 340:685-691.

Kampelmacher MJ, Deenstra M, van Kesteren RG, Melissant CF, Douze JMC, Lammers JWJ. (1997) Transtracheal oxygen therapy: An effective and safe alternative to nasal oxygen administration. Eur Respir J 10:828-833

Karpel JP, Kotch A, Zinny M, Pesin J, Alleyne W. (1994) A comparison of inhaled ipratropium, oral theophylline plus inhaled -agonist, and the combination of all three in patients with COPD. Chest 105:1089-1094.

Kory RC, Bergmann JC, Sweet RD et al. (1962) Comparative evaluation of oxygen therapy techniques. JAMA 179:123-128.

Kottke TE, Battista RN, DeFriese GH. (1988) Attributes of successful smoking cessation interventions in medical practice: A meta-analysis of 39 controlled trials. JAMA 259:2882-2889.

Kramer N, Meyer T, Meharg J et al. (1995) Randomized prospective trial of non-invasive positive pressure ventilation in acute respiratory failure. Am J Respir Crit Care Med 151:1799-1805

Lisboa C, Villafranca C, Leiva A, Cruz E, Pertuze J, Borzone G. (1997) Inspiratory muscle training in chronic airflow limitation: effect on exercise performance. Eur Respir J 10:537-542

Mahler DA, Donohue JF, Barbee RA, Goldman MD, Gross NJ, Wisniewski ME, Yancey SW, Zakes BA, Rickard KA, Anderson WH. (1999) Efficacy of salmeterol xinafoate in the treatment of COPD. Chest 115:957-965.

Maltais F., LeBlanc P, Simard C et al. (1996) Skeletal muscle adaptation to endurance training in patients with Chronic Obstructive Pulmonary Disease. Am J Respi Crit Care Med 154:436-44.

Martinez FJ, Vogel PD, Dupont DN et al. (1993) Supported arm exercise vs. unsupported arm exercise in the rehabilitation of patients with chronic airflow obstruction. Chest 103:1397-1402

McKay SE, Howie CA, Thomson AH, Whiting B, Addis GJ. (1993) Value of theophylline treatment in patients handicapped by chronic obstructive lung disease. Thorax 48:227-232.

Meecham-Jones DJ, Paul EA, Jones PW et al. (1995) Nasal pressure ventilation plus oxygen compared with oxygen therapy alone in hypercapnic COPD. AM J Respir Crit Care Med 152:538-544

Miravitlles M. (2002) Epidemiology of chronic obstructive pulmonary disease exacerbations. Clin Pulm Med 9(4):191-97

Nichol KL,Baken L, Nelson A. (1999a) Relation between influenza vaccination and outpatient visits, hospitalization, and mortality in elderly persons with chronic lung disease. Ann Intern Med 130:397-403.

Nichol KL, Mendelman PM, Mallon KP, Jackson LA, Gorse GJ, Belshe RB, Glezen WP, Wittes J. (1999b) Effectiveness of live, attenuated intranasal influenza virus vaccine in healthy, working adults: a randomized controlled trial JAMA 282:137-144.

Nieweohner DE, Erbland ML, Deupree RH, et al. (1999) Effect of glucocorticoids on exacerbations of chronic obstructive pulmonary disease. N Engl J Med 340:1941-1947.

Nocturnal Oxygen Therapy Trial Group.

(1980) Continuous or nocturnal oxygen therapy in hypoxemic chronic obstructive lung disease. Ann Intern Med 93:391-398.

Normandin EA, McCusker C, Connors M, Vale F, Gerardi D, ZuWallack RL. (2002) An evaluation of two approaches to exercise conditioning in pulmonary rehabilitation. Chest 121:1085-91

Nouira S, Marghli S, Belghith M, Besbes L, Elatrous S, Abroug F. (2001) Once daily oral ofloxacin in chronic obstructive pulmonary disease exacerbation requiring mechanical ventilation: a randomized placebo-controlled trial. Lancet 358:2020-2035

O'Donnell DE, McGuire M, Samis L, Webb KA. (1998) General exercise training improves ventilatory and peripheral muscle strength and endurance in chronic airflow limitation 157:1489-1497.

O'Donnell DE, Lam M, Webb KA. (1999) Spirometric correlates of improvement in exercise performance after anticholinergic therapy in chronic obstructive pulmonary disease. Am J Respir Crit Care Med 160:542-549.

O'Donnell DE, Lam M, Webb KA. (1998) Measurement of symptoms, lung hyperinflation, and endurance during exercise in chronic obstructive pulmonary disease. Am J Respir Crit Care Med 158(5 Pt 1): p. 1557-65.

Pauwels RA, et al., (2001) Global strategy for the diagnosis, management, and prevention of chronic obstructive pulmonary disease. NHLBI/WHO Global Initiative for Chronic Obstructive Lung Disease (GOLD) Workshop summary. Am J Respir Crit Care Med 163(5): p. 1256-76.

Pawels R, Lofdahl C, Laitinen L, Schouten J, Postma D, Pride N, Ohlson S. (1999) Long-term treatment with inhaled budesonide in persons with mild chronic obstructive pulmonary disease who continue smoking. N. Engl J Med 340:1948-1953.

Petty T, Nett LM, Finigan MM et al. (1969) A comprehensive program for chronic airway obstruction: methods and preliminary evaluation of symptomatic and functional improvement. Ann Int Med 70:1109-1119

Petty TL. (1990) The National Mucolytic Study: results of a randomized, double-blind, placebo-controlled study of iodinated glycerol in chronic obstructive bronchitis. Chest 97:75-83.

Petty TL, Finigan NM. (1968) Clinical evaluation of prolonged ambulatory oxygen therapy in chronic airway obstruction Am J Med 45:242-252.

Poole P, Black P. (2001) Oral mucolytic drugs for exacerbations of chronic obstructive pulmonary disease: systematic review. BMJ 322:1271-1274.

Poole PJ, Black PN. (2000) Mucolytic agents for chronic bronchitis or chronic obstructive pulmonary disease. Cochrane Database of Systematic Reviews: CD001287.

Prigatano GP, Parsons OA, Wright E, Levin DC, Hawryluk G. (1983) Neuro-psychologic test performance in mildly hypoxemic patients with chronic obstructive pulmonary disease. J Consult Clin Psychol 51:108–16

Puente-Maestu L, Sanz M, Ruiz de Ona JM, Rodriguez-Hermosa JL, Whipp BJ. (2000) Effects of two types of training on pulmonary and cardiac responses to moderate exercise in patients with COPD. Eur Respir J 15:1026-1032.

Pulmonary Rehabilitation – 1999. (1999) Statement of the American Thoracic Society. Am J Respir Crit Care Med 159:1666-1682.

Reardon J, Awad E, Normandin E. et al. (1994) The effect of comprehensive outpatient pulmonary rehabilitation on dyspnea. Chest 105:1046-1052.

Rennard SI, Serby CW, Ghafouri M, Johnson PA, Friedman M. (1996) Extended therapy with Ipratropium is associated with improved lung function in patients with COPD. Chest 110:62-70.

Rennard SI, Anderson W, ZuWallack R, Broughton J, Bailey W, Friedman M, Wisniewski M, Rickard K. (2001) Use of a long-acting inhaled beta2-adrenergic agonist, salmeterol xinafoate, in patients with chronic obstructive pulmonary disease. Am J Respir Crit Care Med 163:1087.-92.

Report of the Medical Research Council Working Party. (1981) Long-term domiciliary oxygen therapy in chronic hypoxic cor pulmonale complicating chronic bronchitis and emphysema. Lancet 1:681-685.

Research N.I.H. Workshop Summary. (1994) Am Rev Respir Dis 49:825-893.

Ries AL, Ellis B, Hawkins RW. (1988) Upper extremity exercise training in chronic obstructive pulmonary disease. Chest 93:688-692

Ries AL, Kaplan R, Linberg T et al. (1995) Effects of pulmonary rehabilitation on physiologic and psychosocial outcomes in patients with chronic obstructive pulmonary disease. Ann Intern Med 122;823-832

Sanchez Riera H, Montemayor T, Ortega F, Cejudo P, Del Castillo D, Elias T, Castillo J. (2001) Inspiratory muscle training in patients with COPD. Chest 120:748-756.

Scherer T, Spengler C, Owassapian D, Imhof E, Boutellier U. (2000) Respiratory muscle endurance training in chronic obstructive pulmonary disease. Impact on exercise capacity, dyspnea, and quality of life. Am J Respir Crit Care J 162:1709-1714

Sin DD, Tu JV. (2001) Inhaled corticosteroids and the risk for mortality and readmission in elderly patients with chronic obstructive pulmonary disease Am J Respir Crit Care Med 164:580-584

Soriano JB, Vestbo J, Pride N, Kin V, Maden C, Maier WC. (2002) Survival in COPD patients after regular use of fluticasone propionate and salmeterol in general practice. Eur Respir J 20:819-824

Spruit MA, Gosselink R, Tooster T, De Paepe K, Decramer M. (2002) Resistance versus endurance training in patients with COPD and peripheral muscle weakness. Eur Respir J 19:1072-1078

Tantucci C, Duguet A, Similowski T., Zelter M., Derenne J-P, Milic-Emili J. (1998) Effect of salbutamol on dynamic hyperinflation in chronic obstructive pulmonary disease patients. Eur Respir J 12:799-804.

The Lung Health Study Research Group. (2000) Effect of inhaled triamcinolone on the decline in pulmonary function in chronic obstructive pulmonary disease. New Engl J Med 343:1902-1909.

Thomas P, Pugsley JA, Stewart JH. (1992) Theophylline and salbutamol improve pulmonary function in patients with irreversible chronic obstructive pulmonary disease. Chest 101:160-165.

Thompson WH, Nielson CP, Carvalho P, et al. (1996) Controlled trial of oral prednisone in outpatients with cute COPD exacerbation. Am J Respir Crit Care Med 154:407-12

Tiep BL. (1990) Long-term home oxygen therapy. Clin Chest Med 11:505–21

Tiep BL, Barnett J, Schiffman G, Sanchez O, Carter R. (2002) Maintaining oxygenation via demand oxygen delivery during rest and exercise. Respir Care 47(8):887-892

Vestbo J, Sorensen T, Lange P, Brix A, Torre P, Viskum K. (1999) Long-term effect of inhaled budesonide in mild and moderate chronic obstructive pulmonary disease: a randomised trial. Lancet 353:1819-1823.

Vincken W, van Noord JA, Greefhorst AP et al. (2002) On behalf of the Dutch/Belgian Tiotrpium Study Group. Improved health outcomes in patients with COPD during 1-year treatment with tiotropium. Eur Respir J 19:209-216.

Vyas MN, Banister EW, Morton JW, Grzybowski S. (1971) Response to exercise in patients with chronic airway obstruction. II. Effects of breathing 40 percent oxygen. Am Rev Respir Dis 103:401–12.

Wedzicha JA, Bestall JC, Garrod R, Garnham R, Paul EA, Jones PW. (1998) Randomised controlled trial of pulmonary rehabilitation in severe chronic obstructive pulmonary disease patients, stratified with the MRC dyspnoea scale. Eur Respir J 12:363-369

Weiner P, Azgad Y, Ganam R. (1992) Inspiratory muscle training combined with general exercise conditioning in patients with COPD. Chest 102: 1351-1356

West GA, Primeau P. (1983) Nonmedical hazards of long-term oxygen therapy. Respiratory Care 28:906-912.

Wykstra PJ, Van Altens R, Kraan J et al. (1994) Quality of life in patients with chronic obstructive pulmonary disease improves after rehabilitation at home. Eur Respir J 7:269-273.

Zielinski J, Tobiasz M, Hawrylkiewicz I, Sliwnski P, Palasiewicz G. (1998) Hemodynamics in COPD patients: A 6-years prospective study. Chest 113:65-70.

Zuwallack RL, Mahler DA, Reilly D, Church N, Emmett A, Rickard K, Knobil K. (2001) Salmeterol plus theophylline combination therapy in the treatment of COPD. Chest 119:1661-1670.

PREVENTION AND TREATMENT OF VIRAL HEPATITIS

Jane N. Zuckerman and Arie J. Zuckerman

INTRODUCTION AND DEFINITIONS

Viral hepatitis is a major public health problem throughout the world affecting several hundreds of millions of people. Viral hepatitis is a cause of considerable morbidity and mortality in the human population both from acute infection and chronic sequelae which include, with hepatitis B and hepatitis C infection, chronic active hepatitis, cirrhosis and primary liver cancer, and acute and chronic liver disease with hepatitis D.

The hepatitis viruses include a range of unrelated and, at times, unusual human pathogens:

Hepatitis A virus (HAV), a small unenveloped symmetrical RNA virus which shares many of the characteristics of the picornavirus family. This virus has been classified as <u>hepatovirus</u> within the heparnavirus genus and is the cause of infectious or epidemic hepatitis transmitted by the fecal-oral route.

Hepatitis B virus (HBV), a member of the <u>hepadnavirus</u> group, double-stranded DNA viruses which replicate by reverse transcription. Hepatitis B virus is endemic in the human population and hyperendemic in many parts of the world. This virus is transmitted essentially by blood to blood contact and by the sexual route. Mutations of the surface coat protein of the virus and of the core and other proteins have been identified in recent years. Natural hepadnavirus infections occur in other animals including woodchucks, beechy ground squirrels and ducks.

Hepatitis C virus (HCV), an enveloped single-stranded RNA virus which is related (possibly in its evolution) to flaviviruses, although hepatitis C is not transmitted by arthropod vectors. Seroprevalence studies confirm the importance of the parenteral route of transmission and transmission by blood and blood products, but in as many as 50% of patients the origin of the infection has not been identified. Several genotypes have been described. Infection with this virus is common in many countries. Hepatitis C is associated with chronic liver disease and also with primary liver cancer, at least in some countries.

Hepatitis D virus (HDV) is an unusual single-stranded circular RNA virus with a number of similarities to certain plant viral satellites and viroids. This virus requires hepadnavirus helper functions for propagation in hepatocytes, and is an important cause of acute and severe chronic liver damage in some regions of the world. The modes of transmission of HDV are similar to the transmission of hepatitis B.

Hepatitis E virus (HEV), is an enterically-transmitted non-enveloped, single-stranded RNA virus, which shares many biophysical and biochemical features with caliciviruses. Hepatitis E virus is an important cause of large epidemics of acute hepatitis in the subcontinent of India, Central and south-east Asia, the Middle East, parts of Africa and elsewhere. Infection with this virus is responsible for high mortality during the third trimester of pregnancy.

Over the years, evidence became available for additional hepatitis viruses – the so-called non-A-E hepatitis. The evidence was based on the observation of short and long incubation periods in post-transfusion hepatitis and in experimental transmission studies; multiple bouts of hepatitis in the same patient; chronic hepatitis not due toHBV, HCV or HDV; chloroform-resistant non-ABC hepatitic virus, and cross-challenge experiments in susceptible primates. The search for new hepatitis viruses continues.

The clinical expression of infection with any of the hepatitis viruses is similar and varies considerably from subclinical infection, anicteric and mild illnesses in young children, to the full range of symptoms with jaundice in adolescents and adults. The ratio of anicteric to icteric illnesses varies considerably both in individual cases and during outbreaks.

HEPATITIS A

Outbreaks of jaundice have been described frequently for many centuries and the term infectious hepatitis was coined in 1912 to describe the epidemic form of the disease. Hepatitis A virus (HAV) is spread by the faecal-oral route and continues to be endemic throughout the world and hyperendemic in areas with poor standards of sanitation and hygiene. The seroprevalence of antibodies to HAV has declined since World War II in many countries and infection results most commonly from person to person contact, but large epidemics do occur. For example, an outbreak of hepatitis A associated with the consumption of clams in Shanghai in 1988 resulted in almost 300,000 cases.

Pathogenesis

Hepatitis A virus enters the body by ingestion. The virus then spreads, probably by the bloodstream, to the liver, a target organ. Large numbers of virus particles are detectable in feces during the incubation period, beginning as early as 10-14 days after exposure and continuing, in general, until peak elevation of serum aminotransferases (Figure 1). Virus is also detected in feces early in the acute phase of illness, but relatively infrequently after the onset of clinical jaundice. IgG antibody to hepatitis A virus that persists is also detectable late in the incubation period, coinciding approximately with the onset of biochemical evidence of liver damage.

Hepatitis A viral antigen has been localised by immunofluorescence in the cytoplasm of hepatocytes after experimental transmission to chimpanzees. The antigen has not been found in any tissue other than the liver following experimental intravenous inoculation in susceptible non-human primates.

Pathological changes induced by hepatitis A appear only in the liver. These include marked focal activation of sinusoidal lining cells; accumulations of lymphocytes and more histiocytes in parenchyma often replacing hepatocytes, lost cytolytic necrosis predominantly in the periportal areas; occasional coagulative necrosis resulting in the formation of acidophilic bodies; and focal degeneration.

Epidemiology

Viral hepatitis type A (infectious or epidemic hepatitis) occurs endemically in all parts of the world, with frequent reports of minor and major outbreaks. The exact incidence is difficult to estimate because of the high proportion of subclinical infections and infections without jaundice, differences in surveillance and differing patterns of disease. The degree of under-reporting is very high.

The development of specific serological tests for hepatitis A made possible the study of the incidence and distribution of hepatitis A. These studies have shown that infections with hepatitis A virus are widespread and endemic in all parts of the world, chronic excretion of hepatitis A virus does not occur, the infection is rarely transmitted by blood transfusion although transmission by blood coagulation products has been reported. There is not evidence of progression to chronic liver disease.

The incubation period of hepatitis A is 3-5 weeks, with a mean of 28 days. Subclinical and anicteric cases are common and, although the disease has, in general, a low mortality rate (before the age of 49 years), patients may be incapacitated for many weeks. There is no evidence of persistent infection, nor progression to chronic liver damage.

Hepatitis A virus is spread by the fecal-oral route, most commonly by person-to-person contact; infection occurs readily under conditions of poor sanitation and overcrowding. Common source outbreaks are initiated most frequently by fecal contamination of water and food, but waterborne transmission is not a major factor in maintaining this infection in industrialised communities. On the other hand, many foodborne outbreaks have been reported. This can be attributed to the shedding of large quantities of virus in the feces during the incubation period of the illness in infected food handlers; the source of the outbreak often can be traced to uncooked food or food that has been handled after cooking. Although hepatitis A remains endemic and common in the developed countries, the infection occurs mainly in small clusters, often with only few identified cases.

Figure 1: Electron micrograph of hepatitis A virus. Note the vast number of virus particles present in a fecal extract. x 200 000 (From a series by Anthea Thornton and Arie J. Zuckerman)

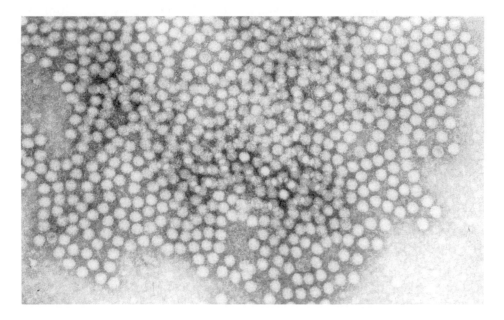

Diagnosis

Various serological tests are available for hepatitis A, including immune electron microscopy, complement-fixation, immune adherence haemagglutination, radioimmuno-assay and enzyme immunoassay. Sensitive enzyme immunoassays are now the serological tests of choice.

Only one serotype of hepatitis A virus has been identified in volunteers infected experimentally with the MS-1 strain of hepatitis A, in patients from different outbreaks of hepatitis in different geo-graphical regions, and in random cases of hepatitis A. Several genotypes of the virus are recognised. Isolation of virus in tissue culture requires prolonged adaptation and it is, therefore, not suitable for diagnosis (reviewed by Harrison et al., 2000).

Prevention and Control of Hepatitis A

In areas of high prevalence, most children are infected early in life and such infections are generally asymptomatic. Infections acquired later in life are of increasing clinical severity. Less than 10% of cases of acute hepatitis A in children up to the age of 6 are icteric, but this increases to 40-50% in the 6-14 age group and to 70-80% in adults. Of 115,551 cases of hepatitis A in the USA between 1983 and 1987, only 9% of the cases, but more than 70% of the fatalities, were in those aged over 49. It is important, therefore, to protect those susceptible to this risk because of personal contact with infected individuals or because of travel to a highly endemic area. Other groups at risk of hepatitis A infection include staff and residents of institutions for the mentally-handicapped, day care centres for children, semi-closed institutions such as prisons, sexually active male homosexuals, intravenous drug abusers, sewage workers, health care workers in countries where hepatitis A is common, military personnel and certain low socio-economic groups in defined community settings.

Patients with chronic liver disease, especially if visiting an endemic area, should be immunised against hepatitis A. In many developing countries, the incidence of clinical hepatitis A is increasing as improvements in socio-economic conditions result in infection later in life and immunisation against hepatitis A has not been introduced.

Passive Immunisation

Control of hepatitis A infection is difficult. Since fecal shedding of the virus is at its highest during the late incubation period and the prodromal phase of the illness, strict isolation of cases is not a useful control measure. Spread of hepatitis A is reduced by simple hygienic measures and the sanitary disposal of excreta.

Normal human immunoglobulin, containing at least 100 international units (IU)/ml of anti-hepatitis A antibody, given intramuscularly before exposure to the virus or early during the incubation period will prevent or attenuate a clinical illness. The dosage should be at least 1 IU of anti-hepatitis

A antibody/kg body weight, but in special cases such as pregnancy or it patients with liver disease that dosage may be doubled (Table 1). Immunoglobulin does not always prevent infection and excretion of hepatitis A virus, and inapparent or subclinical hepatitis may develop. The efficacy of passive immunisation is based on the presence of hepatitis A antibody in the immunoglobulin and the minimum titre of antibody required for protection is believed to be about 10 IU/l.

HAV antibody titres vary among batches of pooled normal human immunoglobulin and are decreasing in batches obtained from pooled plasma of donors in industrialised countries, resulting in clinical cases despite prophylaxis with immunoglobulin. Immunoglobulin is used most commonly for close personal contacts of patients with hepatitis A and for those exposed to contaminated food. Immunoglobulin has also been used effectively for controlling outbreaks in institutions such as homes for the mentally-handicapped and in nursery schools. Prophylaxis with immunoglobulin is recommended for persons without hepatitis A antibody visiting highly endemic areas. After a period of six months the administration of immunoglobulin for travellers needs to be repeated since passive protection is temporary, unless it has been demonstrated that the recipient had developed hepatitis A antibodies.

Active Immunisation against Hepatitis A

In areas of high prevalence, most children have antibodies to hepatitis A virus by the age of 3 years and such infections are generally asymptomatic. Infections acquired later in life are of increasing clinical severity, as noted above. It is important, therefore, to protect those at risk because of personal contact or because of travel to highly endemic areas and the other groups of at risk of hepatitis A infection listed above. In some developing countries, the incidence of clinical hepatitis A is increasing as improvements in socio-economic conditions result in infection later in life and protection by immunisation would be prudent, but strategies are yet to be agreed upon.

Table 1: Passive immunisation with normal immunoglobulin for travellers to highly endemic areas

Person's Body Weight	Period of Stay <3 Months	Period of Stay >3 Months
< 25 kg	50 IU anti-HAV (0.5 ml)	100 IU anti-HAV (1.0 ml)
25-30 kg	100 IU anti-HAV (1.0 ml)	250 IU anti-HAV (2.5 ml)
< 50 kg	200 IU anti-HAV (2.0 ml)	500 IU anti-HAV (5.0 ml)

Killed (Inactivated) Hepatitis A Vaccines

The foundations for a hepatitis A vaccine were laid in 1975 by the demonstration that formalin-inactivated virus extracted from the liver of infected marmosets induced protective antibodies in susceptible marmosets on challenge with virus. Subsequently, hepatitis A was cultivated after a serial passage in marmosets, in a cloned line of fetal rhesus monkey kidney cells (FRhK6), thereby opening the way to the production of hepatitis A vaccines. Later is was demonstrated that prior adaptation in marmosets was not a prerequisite to growth of the virus in cell cultures and various strains of virus have been isolated directly from clinical material using several cell lines, including human diploid fibroblasts and various techniques have been employed to increase the yield of virus in cell culture (Koff, 1998). Several formalin inactivated hepatitis A vaccines are available commercially.

Combined Hepatitis A Vaccines

Combined hepatitis A and hepatitis B vaccines are also available, and hepatitis A combined with other vaccines, e.g. typhoid.

Treatment

There is no specific treatment for acute hepatitis A infection.

Other Interventions

The epidemiology of hepatitis A dictates immunisation as the single most important preventive measure, particularly in the developing countries. Nevertheless, the introduction of behavioural interventions based upon strict personal hygiene, improvement in socio-economic conditions, the provision of safe water and food supplies e.g. chlorination of water, safe disposal of sewage, avoiding the consumption of raw seafood, clean water for the cultivation of oysters and shell fish, thorough washing and cooking of food, and strict hygienic measures in closed and semi-closed institutions, have contributed much to the marked reduction of the burden of this common and important infection in the industrialised countries, and more recently in developing countries.

HEPATITIS B

Hepatitis B virus was recognised originally as the agent responsible for "serum hepatitis", an important and frequent cause of acute and chronic infection of the liver. The incubation period of hepatitis B is variable, with a range of 1 to 6 months. The clinical features of acute infection resemble those of the other viral hepatitides. Acute hepatitis B is frequently anicteric and asymptomatic, although a severe illness with jaundice can occur and occasionally acute liver failure may develop.

More than a third of the world's population has been infected with hepatitis B virus and the World Health Organisation estimates that hepatitis B virus infection results in 1-2 million deaths every year.

The virus persists in approximately 5-10% of immunocompetent adults and in as many as 90% of infants infected perinatally. Persistent carriage of hepatitis B defined by the presence of hepatitis B surface antigen (HBsAg) in the serum for more than 6 months, has been estimated to affect about 350 million people world-wide. The pathology is mediated by the responses of the cellular immune response of the host to the infected hepatocytes. Long term continuing virus replication may lead to progression to chronic liver disease, cirrhosis and hepatocellular carcinoma.

In the first phase of chronicity, virus replication continues in the liver and replicative intermediates of the viral genome may be detected in DNA extracted from liver biopsies. Markers of virus replication in serum include HBV DNA, the surface proteins (HBsAg) and a soluble antigen, hepatitis B e antigen (HBeAg) which is secreted by infected hepatocytes. In those infected at a very young age, this phase may persist for life, but more usually, virus levels decline over time. Eventually, in most individuals, there is immune clearance of infected hepatocytes associated with seroconversion from HBeAg to anti-HBe.

During the period of replication, the viral genome may integrate into the chromosomal DNA of some hepatocytes and these cells may persist and expand clonally. Rarely, seroconversion to anti-HBs follows clearance of virus replication, but more frequently, HBsAg persists during a second phase of chronicity as a result of the expression of integrated viral DNA.

Structure and Organization of the Virus

The hepatitis B virion is a 42 nm particle comprising an electron-dense core (nucleocapsid) 27 nm in diameter surrounded by an outer envelope of the surface protein (HBsAg) embedded in membraneous lipid derived from the host cell (Figure 2). The surface antigen, originally referred to as Australia antigen, is produced in excess by the infected hepatocytes and is secreted in the form of 22 nm particles and tubular structures of the same diameter.

The nucleocapsid of the virion consists of the viral genome surrounded by the core antigen (HBcAg). The genome is approximately 3.2 kilobases in length. One of the two DNA strands is incomplete and is associated with a DNA polymerase molecule which is able to complete that strand in the presence of deoxynucleoside triphosphates.

Analysis of the coding potential of the genome reveals four open reading frames (ORFs). The first ORF encodes the various forms of the surface protein S, pre-S1 and pre-S2. The core open reading frame has two in-phase initiation codons. The "pre-core" region is highly conserved, has the properties of a signal sequence and is responsible for the secretion of HBeAg.

The third ORF, which is the largest and overlaps the other three, encodes the viral polymerase.

The fourth ORF was designated "x" because the function of its small gene product was not known. However, "x" has now been demonstrated to be a transcriptional transactivator (Figure 3).

Figure 2: Electron micrograph of a serum from a patient with hepatitis B. The double-sided particle is the complete virion. Tubular structures and 22 nm HBsAg particles are present in small numbers.   x 200 000

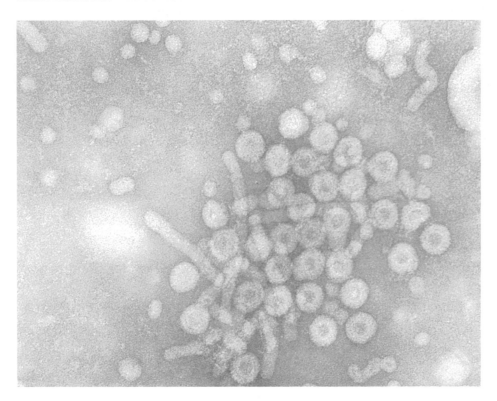

Figure 3: The molecular structure of the genome of hepatitis B virus

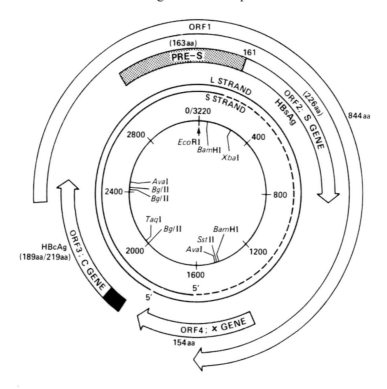

Immune Responses

Antibody and cell-mediated immune responses to various types of antigens are induced during the course of the infection; however, not all these are protective and, in some instances, may cause autoimmune phenomena that contribute to disease pathogenesis. The immune response to infection with hepatitis B virus is directed toward at least three antigens: hepatitis B surface antigen, the core antigen and the e antigen. The view that hepatitis B exerts its damaging effect on hepatocytes by direct cytopathic changes is inconsistent with the persistence of large quantities of surface antigen in liver cells of many apparently healthy persons who are carriers. Additional evidence suggests that pathogenesis of liver damage in hepatitis B virus is related to the immune response by the host.

The surface antigen appears in the sera of most patients during the incubation period, 2-8 weeks before biochemical evidence of liver damage or the onset of jaundice. The antigen persists during the acute illness and usually clears from the circulation during convalescence. Next to appear in the circulation is the virus-associated DNA polymerase activity, which correlates in time with damage to liver cells as indicated by elevated serum transaminases. The polymerase activity persists for days or weeks in acute cases and for months or years in some persistent carriers with active viral replication. Antibody of the IgM class to the core antigen is found in the serum 2-10 weeks after the surface antigen appears and persists during replication of the virus. Core antibody of the IgG class is detectable for many years after recovery. Finally, antibody to the surface antigen component, anti-HBs, appears.

During the incubation period and during the acute phase of the illness, surface antigen-antibody complexes may be found in the sera of some patients. Immune complexes have been found by electron microscopy in the sera of all patients with fulminant hepatitis, but are seen only infrequently in non-fulminant infection. Immune complexes also are important in the pathogenesis of other disease syndromes characterised by severe damage of blood vessels (for example, polyarteritis nodosa, some forms of chronic glomerulonephritis and infantile papular acrodermatitis).

Immune complexes have been identified in variable proportions of patients with virtually all the recognised chronic sequelae of acute hepatitis B. Deposits of such immune complexes have also been demonstrated in the cytoplasm and plasma membrane of hepatocytes and on or in the nuclei; who only a small proportion of patients with circulating complexes develop vasculitis or polyarteritis is, however, not clear. It is possible that complexes are critical pathogenic factors only if they are of a particular size and of a certain antigen-to-antibody ratio.

Cellular immune responses are important in determining the clinical features and course of viral infections. The occurrence of cell-mediated immunity to hepatitis B antigens has been demonstrated in most patients during the acute phase of hepatitis B and in a significant proportion of patients with surface-antigen-positive chronic active hepatitis, but not in asymptomatic persistent hepatitis B carriers. These observations suggest that cell-mediated immunity is important in terminating the infection and, under certain circumstances, in promoting liver damage and in the genesis of autoimmunity. Evidence also suggests that progressive liver damage may result from an autoimmune reaction directed against hepatocyte membrane antigens, initiated in many cases by infection with hepatitis B virus.

Epidemiology

Although various body fluids (blood, saliva, menstrual and vaginal discharges, serous exudates, seminal fluid and breast milk) have been implicated in the spread of infection, infectivity appears to be especially related to blood and to body fluids contaminated with blood. The epidemiological propensities of this infection are therefore wide; they include infection by inadequately sterilised syringes and instruments, transmission by unscreened blood transfusion and blood products, by close contact and by sexual contact. Antenatal (rarely) and perinatal (frequently) transmission of hepatitis B infection from mother to child may take place; in some parts of the world (south-east Asia and Japan), perinatal transmission is very common.

Diagnosis

Hepatitis B surface antigen first appears during the late stages of the incubation period and is easily detectable by radioimmunoassay or enzyme immunoassay. Enzyme immunoassay is specific and highly sensitive and is used widely in preference to radioisotope methods. The antigen persists during the acute phase of the disease and sharply decreases when antibody to the surface antigen becomes detectable. Antibody of the IgM class to the core antigen is found in the serum after the onset of the clinical symptoms and slowly declines after recovery. Its persistence at high titer suggests continuation of the infection. Core antibody of the IgG class persists for many years and provides evidence of past infection (reviewed by Harrison *et al.*, 2000).

Protection against Hepatitis B

The discovery of variation in the epitopes presented on the surface of the virions and subviral particles identified several subtypes of HBV which differ in their geographical distribution. All isolates of the virus share a common epitope, a, which is a domain of the major surface protein which is believed to protrude as a double loop from the surface of the particle. Two other pairs of mutually exclusive antigenic determinants, d or y and w or r, are also present on the major surface protein. These variations have been correlated with single nucleotide changes in the surface ORF which lead to variation in single amino acids in the protein. Four principal subtypes of HBV are recognised: adw, adr, ayw and ayr. Subtype adw predominates in Northern Europe, the Americas and Australasia and also is found in Africa and Asia. Subtype ayw is found in the Mediterranean region, Eastern Europe, Northern and Western Africa, the near East and the Indian subcontinent. In the Far East, adr predominates, but the rarer ayr occasionally may be found in Japan and Papua New Guinea.

Passive Immunisation

Hepatitis B immunoglobulin (HBIG) is prepared specifically from pooled plasma with high titer of hepatitis B surface antibody (anti-HBs) and may confer temporary passive immunity under certain defined conditions. The major indication for the administration of hepatitis B immunoglobulin is a single acute exposure to hepatitis B virus, such as occurs when blood containing surface antigen is inoculated, ingested or splashed onto mucous membranes and the conjunctiva.

The optimal dose has not been established, but doses in the range of 250-500 IU have been used effectively. It should be administered as early as possible after exposure and preferably with 48 hours, usually 3 ml (containing 200 IU of anti-HBs per ml) in adults. It should not be administered 7 days following exposure. It is generally recommended that two doses of hepatitis B immunoglobulin should be given 30 days apart.

Results with the use of hepatitis B immunoglobulin for prophylaxis in neonates at risk of infection with hepatitis B virus are encouraging if the immunoglobulin is given as soon as possible after birth or within 12 hours of birth. The risk of the baby developing the persistent carrier state is reduced by about 70%. More recent studies using combined passive and active immunisation indicate an efficacy approaching 90%. The dose of hepatitis B immunoglobulin recommended in the new-born is 1-2 ml (200 IU of anti-HBs per ml).

Active Immunisation

The major response of recipients of hepatitis B vaccine is to the common a epitope with consequent protection against all subtypes of the virus. First generation vaccines were prepared from 22 nm HBsAg particles purified from plasma donations from asymptomatic (healthy) chronic carriers. These preparations are safe and immnogenic, but have been superseded in many countries by recombinant vaccines produced by the expression of HBsAg in yeast cells. The expression plasmid contains only the 3' portion of the HBV surface ORF and only the major surface protein, without pre-S epitopes, is produced. Vaccines containing pre-S2 and pre-S1 as well as the major surface proteins expressed by recombinant DNA technology are available.

In many areas of the world with a high prevalence of HBsAg carriage, such as China and south-east Asia, the predominant route of transmission is perinatal. Although HBV does not usually cross the placenta, the infants of viraemic mothers have a very high risk of infection at the time of birth.

Administration of a course of vaccine with the first dose immediately after birth is effect-ive in preventing transmission from an HBeAg-positive mother in approximately 70% of cases and this protective efficacy rate may be increased to greater than 90% if the vaccine is accompanied by the simultaneous administration of hepatitis B immune globulin (HBIG).

Immunisation against hepatitis B is now recognised as a high priority in preventive medicine in all countries and strategies for immunisation are being revised. Universal vaccination of infants and adolescents is recommended as a possible strategy to control the transmission of this infection. More than 150 countries now offer hepatitis B vaccine to all children, including the United States, Canada, Italy, France and most Western European countries (Kane, 1996; Van Damme and Vorsters, 2002).

However, immunisation against hepatitis B is at present recommended in a number of countries with a low prevalence of hepatitis B only to groups which are at an increased risk of acquiring this infection. These groups include individuals requiring repeated transfusions of blood or blood products, prolonged in-patient treatment, patients who require frequent tissue penetration or need repeated circulatory access, patients with natural or acquired immune deficiency and patients with malignant diseases. Viral hepatitis is an occupational hazard among health care personnel and the staff of institutions for the mental retarded and in some semi-closed institutions. High rates of infection with hepatitis B occur in narcotic drug addicts and intravenous drug abusers, sexually active male homosexuals and prostitutes. Individuals working in high endemic areas are, however, at an increased risk of infections and should be immunised.

Young infants, children and susceptible persons (including travellers) living in certain tropical and sub-tropical areas where present socio-economic conditions are poor and the prevalence of hepatitis B is high should also be immunised. It should be noted that in about 30% of patients with hepatitis B the mode of infection is not known and this is, therefore, a powerful argument for universal immunisation.

Site of Injection for Vaccination and Antibody Response

Hepatitis B vaccination should be given in the upper arm or the anterolateral aspect of the thigh and not in the buttock. There are over 100 reports of unexpectedly low antibody seroconversion rates after hepatitis B vaccine using injection into the buttock. In one center in the United States a low antibody response was noted in 54% of healthy adult health care personnel. Many studies have since shown that the antibody response rate was significantly higher in centers using deltoid injection than centers using the buttock. On the basis of antibody tests after vaccination, the Advisory Committee on Immunisation Practices of the Centers of Disease Control, USA recommended that the arm be used as the site for hepatitis B vaccination in adults, as have the Departments of Health in the United Kingdom.

Apart from the site of injection, there are several other factors which are associated with a poor or no antibody response to currently licensed vaccines. Indeed, all studies of antibody response to plasma-derived hepatitis B vaccines and hepatitis B vaccines prepared by recombinant DNA technology have shown that between 5% and 10% or more of healthy immunocompetent subjects do not mount an antibody response (anti-HBs) to the surface antigen component (HBsAg) present in these preparations (non-responders) or that they respond poorly (hypo-responders). The exact proportion depends partly on the definition of non-responsiveness or hypo-responsiveness, generally less than 10 IU/l or 100 IU/l respectively against an international antibody standard.

Non-response to Current Hepatitis B Vaccines

All studies of the antibody response to the plasma-derived and recombinant DNA vaccines containing the single antigen only have shown that between 5 and 10% or more of health immunocompetent subjects do not mount an anti-HBs antibody response to the surface antigen component (HBsAg) present in these preparations (non-responders) or that they respond poorly (hyporesponders) (Zuckerman, 1996; Zuckerman et al., 1997).

Non-responders remain susceptible to infection with HBV. While several factors are known to adversely affect the antibody response to HBsAg including: the site and route of injection, gender, advancing age, body mass (overweight), immunosuppression and immunodeficiency.

Evidence is accumulating that there is, at least in part, an association between immuno-genetics and specific low responsiveness in different populations. Considerable experimental evidence is available suggesting that the ability to produce antibody in response to specific protein antigens is controlled by dominant autosomal class II genes of the major histocompatibility complex (MHC) in the murine model and in humans. Other mechanisms underlying non-responsiveness to current hepatitis single antigen vaccines remain largely unexplained (McDermott et al., 1997, 1999).

The Kinetics of Anti-HBs Response to Immunisation and Booster Doses

The titer of vaccine-induced anti-HBs declines, often rapidly, during the months and years following a complete course of primary immunisation. The highest anti-HBs titers are generally observed one month after booster vaccination followed by rapid decline during the next 12 months and thereafter more slowly. Mathematical models have been designed and an equation was derived consisting of several exponential terms with different half-life periods. It is considered by some researchers that the decline of anti-HBs concentration in an immunised subject can be predicted accurately by such antibody kinetics with preliminary recommendations on whether or not booster vaccination is necessary (see review by Zuckerman, 1996).

If the minimum protection level is accepted at 10 IU/l, consideration should be given to the diversity of the individual immune response and the decrease in levels of anti-HBs as well as to possible errors in quantitative anti-HBs determinations. It would then be reasonable to define a level of >10 IU/l and <100 IU/l as an indication for booster immunisation. It has been demonstrated that a booster inoculation results in a rapid increase in anti-HBs titres within 4 days. However, it should be noted that even this time delay might permit infection of hepatocytes.

Several options are therefore under consideration for maintaining protective immunity against hepatitis B infection:

- Relying upon immunological memory to protect against clinical infection and its complications, a view which is supported by *in vitro* studies showing immunological memory for HBsAg in B cells derived from vaccinated subjects who have lost their anti-HBs, but not in B cells from non-responders, and by post-vaccination surveys.

- Providing booster vaccination to all vaccinated subjects at regular intervals without determination of anti-HBs. This option is not supported by a number of investigators because non-responders must be detected. While an anti-HBs titer of about 10 IU/l may be protective, this level is not protective from a laboratory point of view, since many serum samples may give non-specific reactions at this antibody level.

- Testing anti-HBs levels one month after the first booster and administering the next booster before the minimum protective level is reached.

No empirical data are available for the anti-HBs titer required for protection against particular routes of infection or the size of the infectious inoculum. The minimum protective level has been set at 10IU/l against an international standard. However, the international standard is a preparation of immunoglobulin prepared from pooled plasma of individuals recovered from infection rather than immunised subjects and the antibody avidity is likely to be different. Furthermore, studies carried out in the 1980s indicated asymptomatic infection after immunisation in subjects and health care workers who had antibody titres below 50 IU/l.

There are studies that hepatitis B vaccine provides a high degree of protection against clinical symptomatic disease in immunocompetent persons despite declining levels of anti-HBs (reviewed by Zuckerman and Zuckerman, 1998). These studies encouraged the Immunization Practices Advisory Committee of the United States, the National Advisory Committee on Immunisation of Canada and the European Consensus Group (2000) to recommend that routine booster immunisation against hepatitis B is not required. Caution, however, dictates that those at high risk of exposure, such as cardio-thoracic surgeons and gynaecologists would be prudent to maintain a titer of 100 IU/l of anti-HBs by booster inoculations, more so in the absence of an appropriate international antibody reference preparation. Breakthrough infections have been reported and, whereas long term follow-up of children and adults indicated that protection is attained for at least nine years after immunisation against <u>chronic</u> hepatitis B infection, even though anti-HBs levels may have become low or declined below detectable levels (reviewed by the European Consensus Group, 2000), brief periods of viraemia may not have been detected because of infrequent testing. Longer follow-up studies of immunised subjects is required to guide policy, as is well illustrated by a study carried out in Gambian children (Whittle *et al.*, 2002). Whittle *et al.* (2002) found, by a cross-sectional study of hepatitis B infection in children in The Gambia, that the efficacy of hepatitis B vaccination against chronic carriage of HBV

14 years after immunisation was 94%, and the efficacy against infection was 80% and lower (65%) in those vaccinated at the age of 15-19 years. Further and longer follow-up studies of immunised subjects are therefore required to guide policy.

Hepatitis B Surface Antigen Mutants

Hepatitis B virus has been classified into six genotypes, designated A to F, based on phylogenetic analysis of complete viral genomes. Genotypes A and D are disseminated widely throughout the Old World, while genotypes B and C are confined to the east Asian populations, and genotype E to sub-Saharan Africa. Genotype F is more divergent from the other genotypes and is found in aboriginal American populations. All six genotypes share a common immunodominant region on the surface antigen, termed the a determinant, spanning amino acids 124-147.

Neutralising antibodies induced by immunisation are targeted principally to the conformational epitopes of the a determinant, and there is evidence (reviewed below) that amino acid substitutions within this region of the surface antigen can allow replication of HBV in vaccinated persons, since antibodies induced by current vaccine do not recognise critical changes in the surface antigen domain.

The emergence of variants of hepatitis B virus, possibly due to selection pressure associated with extensive immunisation in an endemic area, was suggested by the findings of hepatitis B infection in individuals immunised successfully (Zanetti et al., 1988). These studies were extended subsequently by the finding of non-complexed HBsAg and anti-HBs and other markers of hepatitis B infection in 32 of 44 vaccinated subjects, and sequence analysis from one of these cases revealed a mutation in the nucleotide encoding the a determinant, the consequence of which was a substitution from glycine to arginine at amino acid position 145 (G145R) (Carman et al., 1990).

Various mutations and variants of HBsAg have since been reported from many countries, including Italy, the UK, Holland, Germany, the USA, Brazil, Singapore, Taiwan, China, Japan, Thailand, India, West and South Africa and elsewhere (reviewed by Zuckerman and Zuckerman, 1999; Francois et al., 2001). However, the most frequent and stable mutation was reported in the G145R variant. A large study in Singapore of 345 infants born to carrier mothers with HBsAg and HBeAg, who received hepatitis B immunoglobulin at birth and plasma-derived hepatitis B vaccine within 24 hours of birth and then one month and 2 months later, revealed 41 breakthrough infections with HBV despite the presence of anti-HBs. There was no evidence of infection among 670 immunised children born to carrier mothers with HBsAg and anti-HBe, nor in any of 107 immunised infants born to mothers without HBsAg. The most frequent variant was a virus with the G145R mutation in the a determinant. Another study in the USA of serum samples collected between 1981 and 1993 showed that 94 (8.6%) of 1092 infants born to carrier mothers became HBsAg positive despite post-exposure prophylaxis with hepatitis B immunoglobulin and hepatitis B vaccine. Following amplification of HBV DNA, 22 children were found with mutations of the surface antigen, most being in amino acids 142-145; five had a mixture of wild-type HBV and variants and 17 had only the 145 variant (Nainan et al., 1997).

A report from Taiwan (Hsu et al., 1999) noted the increase in the prevalence of mutants of the a determinant of HBV over a period of 10 years in immunised children, from eight of 103 (7.8%) in 1984 to 10 of 51 (19.6%) in 1989, and 9 of 32 (28.1%) in 1994. This is of particular concern. The prevalence of HBsAg mutants among those fully immunised was higher than among those not vaccinated (12/33 vs. 15/153, P=0.0003). In all 27 children with detectable mutants, the mean age of those vaccinated was lower than of those not vaccinated, and mutation occurred in a region with greatest hydrophilicity of the surface antigen (amino acids 140-149) and more frequently among those vaccinated than among those not vaccinated. More mutations to the neutralizing epitopes were found in the 1994 survey in Taiwan (Hsu *et al.*, 1999).

Another important aspect of the identification of surface antigen variants is the evidence that HBsAg mutants may not be detected by all of the blood donor screening tests and by existing diagnostic reagents. Such variants may therefore enter the blood supply or spread by other means. This is emphasised by the finding in Singapore, between 1990 and 1992, of 0.8% of carriers of HBV variants in a random population survey of 2001 people (Oon *et al.*, 1995, 1996). These findings add to the concern expressed in a study of mathematical models of HBV vaccination, which predict, on the assumption of no cross-immunity against the variant by current vaccines, that the variant will not become dominant over the wild-type virus for at least 50 years – but the G145R mutant may emerge as the common HBV in 100 (or more) years' time (Wilson *et al.*, 1999).

It is important, therefore, to institute epidemiological monitoring of HBV surface mutants employing test reagents which have been validated for detection of the predominant mutations, and consideration should be given to incorporating into current hepatitis B vaccines antigenic components which will confer protection against infection by the predominant mutant(s) (Zuckerman, 2000).

Pre-core/core Variants

The nucleotide sequence of the genome of a strain of HBV cloned from the serum of a naturally infected chimpanzee was reported by Vaudin *et al.* (1988). A surprising feature was a point mutation in the penultimate codon of the precore region which changed the tryptophan codon (TGG) to an amber termination codon (TAG). The nucleotide sequence of the HBV precore region from a number of anti-HBe-positive Greek patients and others was investigated by direct sequencing PCR-amplified HBV DNA from serum (Carman *et al.*, 1989). An identical mutation of the penultimate codon of the precore region to a termination codon was found in 7 of 8 anti-HBe-positive patients who were positive for HBV DNA in serum by hybridization. In most cases there was an additional mutation in the preceding codon. Similar variants were found by amplification of HBV DNA from serum from anti-HBe-positive patients in other countries (Nakahori, 1995). In many cases precore variants have been described in patients with severe chronic liver disease and who may have failed to respond to therapy with interferon. This observation has raised the question of whether some mutants may be more pathogenic than the wild-type virus.

Mutations have also been described in the X gene of HBV and in the gene coding for the polymerase. More data on these mutants are anticipated (reviewed by Francois *et al.*, 2001).

The Pre-S1 and Pre-S2 Domains and Third Generation Vaccines

There is evidence that the pre-S1 and pre-S2 domains of the surface antigen have an important immunogenic role in augmenting anti-HBs responses, preventing the attachment of the virus to hepatocytes and eliciting antibodies which are effective in viral clearance, stimulating cellular immune responses and circumventing genetic non-responsiveness to the S antigen.

These observations led to the development of a new triple antigen hepatitis B vaccine (Hepacare), a third generation recombinant DNA vaccine containing pre-S1, pre-S2 and S antigenic components of hepatitis B virus surface antigen of both subtypes <u>adw</u> and <u>ayw</u>. All three antigenic components are glycosylated, closely mimicking the surface protein of the virus itself, produced in a continuous mammalian cell line, the mouse c127 clonal cell line, after transfection of the cells with recombinant HBsAg DNA. The vaccine is presented as an aluminium hydroxide adjuvant preparation of purified antigenic protein.

Animal studies showed that the vaccine was well tolerated and a viral challenge study in chimpanzees demonstrated protective efficacy.

This vaccine was evaluated for reactogenicity and immunogenicity in a number of clinical trials (reviewed by Zuckerman and Zuckerman, 2002). The major conclusions from these studies were that the vaccine was safe and immunogenic and overcame the non-responsiveness to the single S antigen vaccines used widely in some 70% of non-responders, and that even a single dose of 20mcg of the triple antigen provided significant seroprotection levels of antibody.

However, the anticipated high costs of the triple antigen vaccine will limit the use of the triple antigen vaccine initially to the following groups:
- Vaccination of non-responders to the current single antigen(s) vaccines, who are at risk of exposure to HBV infection
- Subjects with inadequate humoral immune response to single antigen hepatitis B vaccines, e.g. those over the age of 40 years, males, obese, smokers and other hyporesponders, and
- Persons who require protection rapidly, e.g. healthcare employment involving potential exposure to parenteral procedures involving blood-to-blood contact (current schedules of immunisation with single antigen hepatitis B vaccines involve three doses at 0, 1 and 6 months).

Studies are required to determine the efficacy of the triple antigen in patients who are immunocompromised and also to determine whether the inclusion of pre-S1 and pre-S2 antigenic components in this new vaccine will protect against the emergence of HBV surface antigen mutants (see below).

HBV and Hepatocellular Carcinoma

When tests for HBsAg became widely available, regions of the world where the chronic carrier state is common were found to be coincident with those where there is high prevalence of primary liver cancer. Furthermore, in these areas, patients with this tumor are almost invariably seropositive for HBsAg. A prospective study in Taiwan revealed that 184 cases of hepatocellular carcinoma (HCC) occurred in 3,454 carriers of HBsAg at the start of the study, but only 10 such tumors arose in the 19,253 control males who were HBsAg negative (Beasley and Hwang, 1991).

Other case-control and cohort studies and laboratory investigations indicate that there is a consistent and specific causal association between hepatitis B virus, chronic liver disease, cirrhosis and HCC and that up to 80% of such cancers are attributable to this virus. Hepatitis B is thus second only to tobacco (cigarette smoking) among the known human carcinogens (World Health Organisation, 1983).

Southern hybridisation of tumor DNA yields evidence of chromosomal integration of viral sequences in at least 80% of HCCs from HBsAg carriers. There is no similarity in the pattern of integration between different tumors and variation is seen both in the integration site(s) and in the number of copies or partial copies of the viral genome. Sequence analysis of the integrants reveals that the direct repeats in the viral genome often lie close to the virus/cells junctions, suggesting that sequences around the ends of the viral genome may be involved in recombination with host DNA. Integration seems to involve microdeletion of host sequences and rearrangements and deletions of part of the viral genome also may occur. When an intact surface gene is present, the tumor cells may produce and secrete HBsAg in the form of 22 nm particles. Production of HBcAg by tumours is rare, however, and the core ORF is often incomplete and modifications such as methylation may also modulate its expression. Cytotoxic T cells targeted against core gene products on the hepatocyte surface seem to be the major mechanism of clearance of infected cells from the liver. Thus, there may be immune selection of cells with integrated viral DNA which are incapable of expressing HBcAg.

The mechanisms of oncogenesis by HBV remain uncertain. HBV may act non-specifically by stimulating active regeneration and cirrhosis which may be associated with long-term chronicity. However, HBV-associated tumors occasionally arise in the absence of cirrhosis and such hypotheses do not explain the frequent finding of integrated viral DNA in tumors. In rare instances, the viral genome has been found to be integrated into cellular genes such as cyclin A and a retinoic acid receptor. Translocations and other chromosomal rearrangements also have been observed. Although insertional mutagenesis of HBV remains an attractive hypothesis to explain its oncogenicity there is insufficient supportive evidence.

Like many other cancers, development of hepatocellular carcinoma is likely to be a multifactorial process. The clonal expansion of cells with integrated viral DNA seems to be an early stage in this process and such clones may accumulate in the liver throughout the period of active virus replication. In areas where the prevalence of primary liver cancer is high, virus infection usually occurs at an early age and virus replication may be prolonged although the peak incidence of tumor is many years after the initial infection.

It follows, therefore, that if integration of viral DNA can be prevented then cell transformation and neoplastic changes will not occur. This crucial step has been described by Chang *et al.* (1997), providing, at the same time, evidence for a direct causal relationship between HBV and HCC. Immunisation against hepatitis B in Taiwan reduced carriage of hepatitis B in children aged 6 years from about 10% between 1981 and 1986 to between 0.9% and 0.8% between 1990 and 1994. This highly significance reduction in the prevalence of carriage of hepatitis B surface antigen was accompanied by a sharp decline in the average annual incidence of HCC in children and adolescents. Similar observations have been described since from Hong Kong, Singapore and The Gambia.

Treatment of Hepatitis B

At present, specific treatment for acute hepatitis B infection is not available. Symptomatic treatment of nausea, anorexia, vomiting and other clinical symptoms may be required.

The primary aim of treatment of chronic hepatitis B infection is to prevent progressive liver damage, including chronic hepatitis and longer term complications such as cirrhosis and hepatocellular carcinoma, by elimination of the virus, stopping its replication and suppressing inflammatory processes in the liver. A secondary goal is to terminate the chronic carrier state of HBV and thereby reduce transmission of infection and the reservoir of carriers in the population.

There are two types of treatment:
- Immune modulators which assist the immune system, and
- Antiviral drugs which suppress or inhibit replication of the virus.

It should be noted, before reviewing current therapy of chronic hepatitis B, that corticosteroids, which induce enhanced expression of virus and viral antigens and a suppression of T-lymphocyte function, nor adenine arabinoside, acyclovir or dideoxyinosine, are not effective in the treatment of chronic hepatitis B.

At present, only interferon alpha-21a and interferon alpha-2b are licensed for the treatment of chronic hepatitis B. Interferon alpha is a cytokine with properties which include antiviral, immunostimulatory and antiproliferative properties. The interferons enhance T-cell helper activity, induce maturation of B lymphocytes, inhibit T-cell suppressors and enhance HLA type I expression. Any patient with compensated HBV-related liver disease and markers of active viral replication, elevated ALT levels and histological biopsy evidence of liver damage is a candidate for treatment with interferon alpha. This treatment has a dose-dependent efficacy and the currently recommended doses range from 4.5 to 5 million units (MUI) three times weekly for 6 months, or from 5 MUI to 10 MUI three times weekly for 4 months. The results of treatment are best in patients with low levels of circulating HBV DNA, ALT levels two to four times the normal value, wild type HBV (not those with pre-core or core mutants), and absence of both liver decompensation and cirrhosis (reviewed by Merle and Trepo, 2001). Sustained remission of the disease occurs in about 35% of patients with normalisation of liver enzymes and loss of three markers of active infection (HBeAg, HBV DNA and HBsAg), but complete elimination of the virus is achieved only rarely (Gow and Mutimer, 2001; World Health Organisation, 2002). The efficacy of interferon is lower in Chinese patients than in Caucasians, because of the acquisition of the infection in early childhood (usually perinatally) in the Chinese (Yuen and Lai, 2001).

Treatment with interferon of patients with HBV-related compensated cirrhosis decreased significantly the rate of progression to hepatocellular carcinoma, particularly in patients with high serum HBV DNA (World Health Organisation, 2002). Note that in decompensated cirrhosis, administration of interferon alpha is not recommended in most patients because of severe side-effects.

Side effects of treatment with interferon, particularly with high doses can be significant and severe including fever, fatigue, malaise, depression and suppression of white blood cells and platelets.

Combination therapy of interferon with specific antiviral drugs is considered below.

The most promising results of specific treatment of chronic hepatitis B have been obtained with second generation nucleoside analogues (reviewed by Dusheiko, 1999; Zuckerman, 1999; Schiff, 2000; Farrell, 2000).

Lamivudine is a 2', 3'-dideoxy cytosine analogue which has potent inhibitory effects on the HBV polymerase and therefore on replication of the virus and the process of reverse transcription. Lamivudine is given as a tablet by mouth, usually 100 mg once daily and is generally well tolerated and effective.

Typically, 80% (or more) of patients have a hundred-fold decline in the level of HBV DNA to almost undetectable levels by very sensitive techniques, after treatment for one year. A relapse usually occurs when treatment is stopped because supercoiled HBV DNA intermediates within the hepatocytes are not affected by treatment. The emergence of drug-resistant HBV polymerase (YMDD) mutants is a significant risk.

The key variant with lamivudine therapy involves the highly conserved tyr-met-asp-asp polymerase. Although experimental studies have shown that such YMDD variants confer resistance of lamivudine *in vitro*, they also have reduced replication competence both *in vitro* and in the clinical setting. As such, their emergence is not a signal to stop treatment with lamivudine. In patients with HBsAg,

14% of patients develop the variant. While this was associated in one study with elevation of HBV DNA and ALT, these had not reached baseline levels by week 52 and the variant was not associated with any reduction in the histological response. The YMDD variants also emerged in anti-HBe patients and, while 40% of such patients have lost HBV DNA by 52 weeks, about 25% have the variant. In either case, the emergence of the variants is not a signal to stop treatment with lamivudine. Indeed, HBeAg seroconversion van still occur in patients with the YMDD variant (see reviews by Lai and Yuen, 2000; Schiff, 2000).

Lamivudine is, at present, the drug of choice for patients with decompensated hepatitis B-related cirrhosis, and recurrent HBV infection after transplantation (Keeffe, 2000).

Other drugs are under evaluation. These include famciclovir, a guanosine analogue, but it appears to be less effective therapeutically than lamivudine, and drug resistant viral variants have been described with a genetic profile indicating potential cross-resistance with lamivudine. Adefovir dipivoxil is an oral prodrug of an adenine nucleotide, which appears promising in phase II studies. Lobucavir, a guanosine analogue, reduces HBV DNA levels, but toxicity reports have led to suspension of clinical studies. Other nucleoside analogues are under investigation.

Studies on combination therapy of lamivudine and other antiviral drugs and interferon alpha are in progress.

Preliminary studies indicate that in liver transplant patients, lamivudine in combination with hepatitis B immunoglobulin is useful for prevention of reinfection of the graft with HBV.

Other Interventions and Behaviour Modifications

Additional measures which have been employed to reduce the prevalence of hepatitis B infection include needle and syringe exchange programs for intravenous drug users, education on the need to use effective barrier methods i.e. condoms, in particular in non-stable sexual relationships, modification of sexual contact among male homosexuals (condoms, unprotected oro-genital contact), multiple use of instruments contaminated with blood, strict avoidance of tattooing, scarification, ear and body piercing with non-sterile instruments and other common sense procedures dictated by the epidemiology of hepatitis B as described above, including as an obvious example the imperative need to screen all blood and blood products for evidence of hepatitis B markers by the most sensitive techniques available, the use of voluntary blood donors and avoiding replacement donors (who are usually paid or commercial donors). Other measures recommended include the control of blood and blood products across national borders and strict control of, and preferably avoiding, the use of commercial plasma.

One further note on needle and syringe exchange programs designed in the mid-1980s to reduce and prevent the transmission of hepatitis B in intravenous drug abusers. While there was initial objection by law enforcement agencies to this practise on the grounds that this may encourage the use of addictive substances by drug abusers, there was some evidence that the needle exchange programme was of some success initially. However, there is now evidence in the United Kingdom that more than one in five intravenous drug abusers share injection equipment and that there is some socio-cultural reasons for this practice among this population. Obviously targeted active hepatitis B immunisation is the solution, but it is difficult to reach drug abusers for a full course of three injections of the vaccine.

HEPATITIS C

Transmission studies in chimpanzees established that the main agent of parenterally acquired non-A, non-B hepatitis was likely to be an enveloped virus some 30 to 60 nm in diameter. These studies made available a pool of plasma which contained a relatively high titer of the virus. In order to clone the genome, the virus was pelleted from the plasma. Because if was not known whether the genome was DNA or RNA, a denaturation step was included prior to the synthesis of complementary DNA so that either DNA or RNA could serve as a template. The resultant cDNA was then inserted into the bacteriophage expression vector lambda gt 11 and the libraries screened using serum from a patient with chronic non-A, non-B hepatitis. This approach led to the detection of a clone (designated 5-1-1) which was found to bind to antibodies present in the sera of several patients infected with non-A, non-B hepatitis. This clone was used as a probe to detect a larger, overlapping clone in the same library. It was possible to demonstrate that these sequences hybridised to a positive-sense RNA molecule of around 10,000 nt which was present in the livers of infected chimpanzees but not in uninfected controls. No homologous sequences could be detected in the chimpanzee or human genomes. By employing a "walking" technique, it was possible to use newly detected overlapping clones as hybridisation probes in turn to detect further virus-specific clones in the library. Thus, clones covering the entire viral genome were assembled and the complete nucleotide sequence determined (reviewed by McGarvey *et al.*, 1998).

Properties of HCV

The genome of HCV resembles those of the pestiviruses and flaviviruses in that it comprises around 10,000 nt of positive sense RNA, lacks a 3' polyA tract and has a similar gene organisation. It has been proposed that HCV should be the prototype of a third genus in the family Flaviviridae. All of these genomes contain a single large open reading frame which is translated to yield a polyprotein (of around 3000 amino acids in the case of HCV) from which the viral proteins are derived by post-translational cleavage and other modifications (Figure 4).

Figure 4: The structure of the genome of hepatitis C virus

Hepatitis C Viral Genome

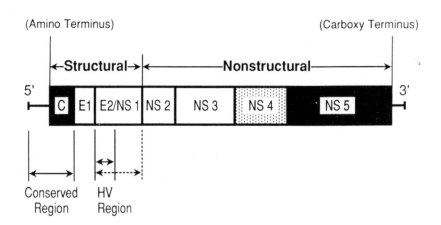

The amino acid sequence of the nucleocapsid protein seems to be highly conserved among different isolates of HCV. The next domain in the polyprotein also has a signal sequence at its carboxyl-terminus and may be processed in a similar fashion. The product is a glycoprotein which is probably found in the viral envelope and is variably termed E1/S or gp35. The third domain may be cleaved by a protease within the viral polyprotein to yield a second surface glycoprotein, E2/NS1 or gp70. These proteins are the focus of considerable interest because of their potential use in tests for the direct detection of viral proteins and for HCV hypervariable regions. It is possible that this divergence has been driven by antibody selection pressure and that these regions specify important immunogenic epitopes.

The non-structural region of the HCV genome is divided into regions NS2 to NS5. In the flaviviruses, NS3 has two functional domains, a protease which is involved in cleavage of the non-structural region of the polyprotein and a helicase which is presumably involved in RNA replication. Motifs within this region of the HCV genome have homology to the appropriate consensus sequences, suggesting similar functions.

Hepatitis C virus consists of a family of highly related, but nevertheless, distinct genotypes, numbering at present 6 genotypes and various subtypes with differing geographical distribution and with a complex nomenclature. The C, NS3 and NS4 domains are the most highly conserved regions of the genome, and therefore these proteins are the most suitable for use as capture antigens for broadly reactive tests for antibodies to HCV. The sequence differences observed between HCV groups suggest that virus-host interactions may be different, which could result in differences in pathogenicity and in response to antiviral therapy.

In addition to the sequence diversity observed between HCV groups, there is considerable sequence heterogeneity among almost all HCV isolates in the N-terminal region of E2/NS1, implying that this region may be under strong immune selection. Indeed, sequence changes within this region may occur during the evolution of disease in individual patients and may play an important role in progression to chronicity.

Diagnosis of HCV Infection

Successful cloning of portions of the viral genome permitted the development of new diagnostic tests for infection by the virus. Since the 5-1-1 antigen was originally detected by antibodies in the serum of an infected patient it was an obvious candidate as the basis of an ELISA to detect anti-HCV antibodies. A larger clone, C100, was assembled from a number of overlapping clones and expressed in yeast as a fusion protein using human superoxide dismutase sequences to facilitate expression. This fusion protein formed the basis of first generation tests for HCV infection. The 5-1-1 antigen comprises amino acid sequences from the non-structural, NS4, region of the genome and C100 contains both NS3 and NS4 sequences.

It is now known that antibodies to C100 are detected relatively late following an acute infection. In addition, the first generation ELISAs were associated with a high rate of false positive reactions when applied to low incidence populations and there were additional problems with some retrospective studies on stored sera.

Second generation and subsequent tests include antigens from the nucleocapsid and further non-structural regions of the genome. The former antigen (C22) is particularly useful and antibodies to the HCV core protein appear relatively early in the course of infection.

Positive reactions by ELISA require confirmation by supplementary testing using, for example, a recombinant immunoblot assay

207

(RIBA). Nevertheless, indeterminant results obtained by ELISA represent a significant problem. It should also be noted that the time for seroconversion is variable.

The presence of antibodies to specific antigen components is variable and may or may not reflect viraemia and, in the case of interferon treatment, a correlation between response and loss of specific antibodies to the E2 component.

Detection and monitoring of viraemia are important for management and treatment. Sensitive techniques are available for the measurement of HCV RNA based on reverse-transcribed PCR amplification, nested-PCR, signal amplification using branched DNA analytes and others.

The identification of specific types and subtypes is becoming increasingly important with observations indicating an association between response to interferon and particular genotypes, and the possibility, still under investigation, that different types may differ in the pathogenicity. A line probe assay, in which reverse transcribed PCR products are hybridized to strips containing type-specific oligonucleotide probes, is generally available. Types and subtypes can also be identified by priming and sequencing RT-PCR products within the NS5, the E1 or other regions. Immunoabsorbent assays (ELISA) are also becoming available.

Epidemiology of Hepatitis C

Infection with hepatitis C virus occurs throughout the world, currently estimated at 170 million people. Much of the seroprevalence data are based on blood donors, who represent a carefully selected population in many countries. The prevalence of antibodies to HCV in blood donors varies from 0.02% in different countries. Almost 4 million Americans (1.8% of the population of the USA) have antibody to HCV, indicating ongoing or previous infection with this virus. Higher rates have been found in southern Italy, Spain, central Europe, Japan and parts of the Middle East, with as many as 19% in Egyptian blood donors. Until screening of blood donors was introduced hepatitis C accounted for the vast majority of non-A, non-B post-transfusion hepatitis. However, it is clear that while blood transfusion and the transfusion of blood products are efficient routes of transmission of HCV, these represent a small proportion (about 15%) of cases of acute clinical hepatitis in the USA and a number of other countries (with the exception of patients with haemophilia). Current data indicate that in some 40-50% of patients in industrialised countries the source of infection cannot be identified; 35% or more of patients have a history of intravenous drug misuse; household contact and sexual exposure do not appear to be major factors in the epidemiology of this common infection, and occupational exposure in the health care setting accounts for about 2% of cases. Transmission of HCV from mother to infant occurs in about 10% of viraemic mothers and the risk appears to be related to the level of viraemia. The possibility of transmission *in utero* is also being investigated.

Clinical Features

Most acute infections are asymptomatic, with about 20% of acute infections with jaundice. Fulminant hepatitis has been described. Extrahepatic manifestations include mixed cryoglobulinaemia, membraneous proliferative glomerulone-phritis and porphyria cutanea tarda.

Current data suggest that about 60-80% of infections with HCV progress to chronicity and chronic infection with HCV affects at present between 1-2% of the world population. Histological examination of liver biopsies from asymptomatic HCV-carriers (blood donors) reveals that none has normal histology and that up to 70% have chronic active hepatitis and/or cirrhosis. Whether the virus is cytopathic or whether there is an immunopathological element remains unclear.

HCV infection is also associated with progression to primary liver cancer. For example, in Japan, where the incidence of hepatocellular carcinoma has been increasing despite a decrease in the prevalence of HBsAg, HCV is now the major risk factor. In the USA, hepatitis C virus accounts for 60-70% of chronic hepatitis, up to 50% of cirrhosis, end-stage liver disease and liver cancer. Hepatitis C virus causes an estimated 8.000 to 10,000 deaths annually in the USA (Alter and Seeff, 2000).

Vaccine Development

Difficulties in vaccine development include the sequence diversity between viral groups and the substantial sequence heterogeneity among isolates in the N-terminal region of E2/NS1. Neutralising antibodies have not been clearly defined. The virus has not been cultivated *in vitro* to a sufficient degree to permit the development of inactivated or attenuated vaccines (cf. yellow fever vaccines). Much work is in progress employing recombinant DNA techniques. Preliminary experimental protection studies in chimpanzees have been undertaken.

Behavioural Interventions

Since the epidemiology of hepatitis C is similar to that of hepatitis B, the same intervention strategies apply, particularly with respect to the screening of blood and blood products, needle and syringe exchange programmes among intravenous drug abusers and other measures outlined for the prevention of "blood-to-blood" contact including the imperative use of sterile needles and instruments for all parenteral and skin piercing procedures.

The urgent need for the development of a hepatitis C vaccine is obvious.

One final comment on behavioural modification is merited. Alcohol consumption is an important factor in exacerbating liver damage in the case of infection with any of the hepatitis viruses, and particularly among persistently infected carriers of hepatitis B, C and D. Careful counselling is essential.

Treatment of Chronic Hepatitis C Infection

Early treatment and eradication of hepatitis C virus infection is important in order to reduce the risk of progressive liver disease and also to prevent the spread of infection. There is now continuing development and progress in the treatment of patients with HCV infection and clinical guidelines on the management of hepatitis C are available (see for example Booth *et al.*, 2001; NIH publication, 2002). Sustained virological response can now be achieved in over 50% of patients with chronic hepatitis C, who meet the clinical criteria for treatment. Viral clearance is associated with a reduction of hepatic inflammation and fibrosis and presumably to reduction in morbidity and mortality (reviewed by Davis, 2001).

Treatment of chronic hepatitis C has evolved over the last decade or so from the use of alpha interferon to the current optimal regimen of a combination of pegylated alpha interferon and the antiviral drug ribavirin.

The several forms of recombinant alpha interferon (alpha-2a, alpha-2b, consensus interferon) which are available for treatment of hepatitis C are being replaced by pegylated interferons (peginterferons). Peginterferon alpha-2B is available for general use, while peginterferon alpha-2a is still under clinical trial. These two peginterferons are approximately equivalent in efficacy and safety, but have differing doses: peginterferon alpha-2a is given subcutaneously in a dose of 180 mcg per week, whereas peginterferon alpha-2b is given subcutaneously weekly in doses of 1.5 mcg per kg per week (range of 75-150 mcg per week).

Ribavirin is an oral nucleoside analogue with activity against a wide range of viruses, although on its own it has little or no effect on HCV. However, combination of ribavirin with alpha interferon results, for reasons which are not understood, in much improved and sustained biochemical, virological and histological response rates. Ribavirin is given by mouth twice daily in a total daily dose of 800-1200 mg based on body weight and the form of peginterferon (NIH, 2002). When combined with peginterferon alpha-2a, the dose of ribavirin is 1000 mg for patients who weigh less than 75 kg and 1200 mg for those who weigh more than 75 kgs. Ribavirin is given in two divided doses daily.

The optimal duration of treatment depends on whether interferon monotherapy or combination therapy is used, and also on the genotype of HCV.

A 48-week course is recommended for patients treated with peginterferon monotherapy, irrespective of the HCV genotype.

The optimal duration of treatment of patients with combination therapy depends on the viral genotype. Patients infected with genotype 2 and 3 respond well (70-80% response rate) and a 24-week course of treatment is sufficient. Patients infected with genotype 1 have a lower response rate (40-45%) and a 48-week course is recommended.

Indications for Treatment

Patients who should be treated are those with anti-HCV, HCV RNA, elevated serum aminotransferase levels and histological evidence in liver biopsy of chronic hepatitis, and with no contraindications (see below). Consideration should not be based on the presence or absence of symptoms, the genotype of the virus or the level of serum HCV RNA.

Patients with cirrhosis can be treated provided there are no signs of decopensation.

Patients over 60 years old should be managed on an individual bases, since side-effects appear to be worse and the effectiveness of treatment has not been evaluated fully.

The role of interferon treatment in children with chronic hepatitis C and the use of ribavirin are uncertain and have not been evaluated sufficiently.

Treatment outside controlled trials is inadvisable in patients with decompensated cirrhosis; normal aminotransferase levels; organ transplants, and in patients with specific contraindications to either interferon or combination therapy.

Alcohol consumption should not be allowed since it appears to hasten progression of the disease. In addition, interferon therapy can be associated with an increased risk of relapse in patients with a previous history of drug or alcohol abuse.

HEPATITIS D

Delta hepatitis (reviewed in Gerin et al., 1991) was first recognised following detection of a novel protein, delta antigen (HDAg), by immunofluorescent staining in the nuclei of hepatocytes from patients with chronic active hepatitis B (Rizzetto et al., 1977). Hepatitis delta virus (HDV) is now known to require a helper function of HBV for its transmission. HDV is coated with HBsAg which is needed for release from the host hepatocyte and for entry in the next round of infection.

Two forms of delta hepatitis infection are known. In the first, a susceptible individual is co-infected with HBV and HDV, often leading to a more severe form of acute hepatitis caused by HBV. In the second, an individual chronically infected with HBV becomes superinfected with HDV. This may cause a second episode of clinical hepatitis and accelerate the course of the chronic liver disease, or cause overt disease in asymptomatic HBsAg carriers. HDV itself seems to be cytopathic and HDAg may be directly cytotoxic (reviewed by Monjardino and Lai, 1998).

Delta hepatitis is common in some areas of the world, with a high prevalence of HBV infection, particularly the Mediterranean region, parts of Eastern Europe, the Middle East, Africa and South America. It has been estimated that 5% of HBsAg carriers world-wide (approximately 18 million people) are infected with HDV. In areas of low prevalence of HBV, those at risk of hepatitis B, particularly intravenous drug abusers, are also at risk of HDV infection (reviewed by Di Bisceglie, 1998).

Properties and Structural Organisation of HDV

The HDV particle is approximately 36 nm in diameter and composed of an RNA genome associated with HDAg, surrounded by the envelope of hepatitis B virus (HBsAg). The HDV genome is a closed circular RNA molecule of 1679 nucleotides and resembles those of the satellite viroids and virusoids of plants and similarly seems to be replicated by the host RNA polymerase II with autocatalytic cleavage and circularisation of the progeny genomes via trans-esterification reactions. Consensus sequences of viroids which are believed to be involved in these processes also are conserved in HDV.

Unlike the plant viriods, HDV codes for a protein, HDAg. This is encoded in an open reading frame in the antigenomic RNA, but four other open reading frames which are also present in the genome, do not appear to be used. The antigen, which contains a nuclear localisation signal, was detected originally in the nuclei of infected hepatocytes and may be detected in serum only after stripping off the HBsAg outer envelope of the virus with detergent.

Pathogenesis

Hepatitis B virus provides a helper function to HDV, which is a defective virus.

The histopathological pattern in the liver is suggestive of a direct cytopathic effect. Pathological changes are limited to the liver and histological changes are those of acute and chronic hepatitis with no particular distinguishing features apart from severity, and, in tropical areas in particular, microvesicular steatosis.

Diagnosis

Laboratory diagnosis in acute infection is based on specific serological tests for anti-HDV IgM or HDV RNA or hepatitis delta antigen in serum. Acute infection is usually self-limited and markers of HDV infection often disappear within a few weeks.

Superinfection with HDV in chronic hepatitis B may lead to suppression of HBV markers during the acute phase. Chronic infection with HDV (and HBV) is the usual outcome in non-fulminant disease.

Other Features of HDV

The modes of transmission of HDV are similar to those for HBV, although sexual transmission of HDV is less efficient than for HBV and perinatal transmission of HDV is rare. Antibody to delta hepatitis has been found in most countries, commonly among intravenous drug abusers, patients with haemophilia and those requiring treatment by blood and blood products. A high prevalence of infection has been found in Italy and the countries bordering the Mediterranean, Eastern Europe and particularly Romania; the former Soviet Union; South America, particularly the Amazon basin, Venezuela, Columbia (hepatitis de Sierra Nevada de Santa Marta), Brazil (Labrea black fever) and Peru; and parts of Africa, particularly West Africa.

The ratio of clinical to subclinical cases of HDV and superinfection is not known. However, the general severity of both forms of infection suggests that most cases are clinically significant. A low persistence of infection occurs in 1-3% of acute infections and about 80% or higher in superinfection of chronic HBV carriers. The morality rate is high, particularly in the case of superinfection ranging from 2-20%. In the Amazon basin, epidemics of HDV have occurred among chronic HBV carriers in isolated communities with rapid progression to fulminant hepatitis and fatality rates of 10-20%.

Prevention and Control

Prevention and control for HDV are similar to those for hepatitis B. Immunisation against hepatitis B protects against HDV. The difficulty is protection against super-infection of the many millions of established carriers of hepatitis B. Studies are in progress to determine whether specific immunisation against HDV based on hepatitis D antigen is feasible.

Treatment of Hepatitis D Infection

The unusual structure of HDV and its replication make this pathogen difficult to treat specifically with antiviral drugs.

Medical treatment of chronic hepatitis D, although not entirely satisfactory, depends on high doses of interferon-alpha (9-10 MIU three times weekly) as soon as diagnosis of chronic HDV disease is reached. Treatment should be continued for 12 months, but the results are not generally good. Sustained response is accompanied by clearance of HBsAg from the serum. Available antiviral drugs, including nucleoside analogues, are ineffective.

Patients with decompensated liver disease should be considered for transplantation. Transplantation is associated with a high risk of reinfection, which is reduced considerably with adequate prophylaxis against reinfection with hepatitis B virus.

Behaviour Intervention

The epidemiology of hepatitis D infection is very similar to that of hepatitis B, and identical intervention programmes are indicated, including those introduced for intravenous drug abusers.

Immunisation against hepatitis B protects against infection with hepatitis D. A case has been made for the need to develop a vaccine against hepatitis D in carriers of hepatitis B only.

HEPATITIS E

Retrospective testing of serum samples from patients involved in various epidemics of hepatitis associated with contamination of water supplies with human feces indicated that an agent other than HAV (or hepatitis B) was involved. Epidemics of enterically transmitted non-A, non-B hepatitis in the Indian subcontinent were first reported in 1980, but outbreaks involving tens of thousands of cases have also been documented in the USSR, South-East Asia, Northern Africa, Mexico and previously in India. Infection has been reported in returning travellers. The average incubation period is slightly longer than for hepatitis A, with a mean of six weeks. The epidemiological features of the infection resemble those of hepatitis A. The highest attack rates are found in young adults and high mortality rates of 20% or more have been reported in women infected during the third trimester of pregnancy, but the reasons for the progressively higher mortality rate in each succeeding trimester are not known.

Virus-like particles have been detected in the feces of infected individuals by immune electron microscopy using convalescent serum. However, such studies have often proved inconclusive and a large proportion of the excreted virus may be degraded during passage through the gut. Bile was shown to be a rich source and the particles have a mean diameter of 32-34 nm. Cross reaction studies between sera and virus in feces associated with a variety of epidemics in several different countries suggests that a single serotype of virus is involved, although two distinct isolates were recognised designated as the Burma (B) strain and the Mexico (M) strain. Two other isolates were sequenced more recently, so that there are four recognised genotypes, of which two contain viruses isolated from humans and swine.

Studies on hepatitis E virus (HEV), have progressed following transmission to susceptible non-human primates. HEV was first transmitted to cynomologous macaques and a number of other species of monkeys including chimpanzees also have been infected.

Properties of the Virus

Physicochemical studies have shown that the virus is very liable and sensitive to freeze-thawing, caesium chloride and pelleting by ultracentrifugation. Full virions have a buoyant density of 1.29 g/cm^3 in potassium tartrate/glycerol gradients and a sedimentation coefficient of 183 S in neutral sucrose gradients, with empty particles of 165 S under the same conditions.

Confirmation that the virus has been propagated in cell culture is awaited. All these properties suggest that hepatitis E virus is similar to the caliciviruses. However, detailed morphological studies and the lack of similarities in genome sequence between HEV and recognised caliciviruses suggest that HEV is a single member of a novel virus genus. However, HEV resembles most closely the sequences of rubella virus and a plant virus, beet necrotic yellow vein virus. It has therefore been proposed that these three viruses should be placed in separate, but related, families. The virus is unclassified at present.

Genomic Organisation

HEV was cloned in 1991 and the entire 7.5 Kb sequence is known. The genome is a single-stranded, positive sense polyadenylated RNA molecule, with three overlapping open reading frames, which express different proteins.

Epidemiology

All epidemics of hepatitis E reported to date have been associated with fecal contamination of water, with the exception of a number of foodborne outbreaks in China. Sporadic hepatitis E has been associated with the consumption of uncooked shellfish and in travellers returning from endemic areas. Epidemics of hepatitis E and a high prevalence of antibody determined by serological tests have occurred in the subcontinent of India, South-East Asia and Central Asia, the Middle East, North and West Africa and outbreaks in East Africa and Mexico.

Unexpectedly, the highest prevalence of antibody to hepatitis E virus is found in young adults and not in infants and children, and more frequently in males in some epidemics, but equal distribution between males and females in young adults in most outbreaks. However, the prevalence of antibody to HEV in endemic regions is much lower at 3-26% than expected.

Recently, an HEV-like virus has been isolated from chickens. Although there is 48-60% of nucleotide homology with human HEV strains, antibodies of the avian HEV cross-react with the capsid protein of human and swine strains. The avian virus causes liver disease in chickens (reviewed by Emmerson and Purcell, 2003).

Hepatitis E virus has also been isolated from patients with sporadic acute hepatitis in countries not considered to be endemic for HEV such as the USA, Italy and other European countries and in individuals who had not travelled abroad. There is now evidence that HEV may have an animal reservoir and there are HEV isolates from swine with high sequence identity to human HEV strains isolated from pigs in areas without HEV epidemics. There is recent evidence of a higher prevalence of HEV antibodies among swine farmers, particularly in those with an occupational history of cleaning barns or assisting sows at birth, and also a history of drinking raw milk. Most swine isolates are of genotype 3, except the virus strain in Taiwan which belongs to genotype 4.

There is recent evidence of widespread HEV or HEV-like infection in rodents in the USA (60% in rats), which may be a reservoir of infection in industrialised countries.

It is also of interest that in endemic areas, antibody to HEV acquired naturally has been found in 40-67% of cows, sheep and goats (World Health Organisation, 2001).

Clinical Features

Individual cases cannot be differentiated on the basis of clinical features from other cases of hepatitis, although cholestatic jaundice is more common. In epidemics, most clinical cases will have anorexia, jaundice and hepatomegaly. Serological tests indicate, however, that clinically inapparent cases occur. The severity of the infection and high mortality during pregnancy have been noted above. Co-infection of young children with HEV and HAV may lead to severe illness, including acute liver failure. Hepatitis E does not progress to chronicity.

Diagnosis

Serological tests are necessary to establish the diagnosis. The tests available at present commercially detect anti-HEV IgM in up to 90% of acute infections if serum is obtained 1-4 weeks after the onset of illness and IgM remains detectable for about 12 weeks. Anti-HEV IgG appears early and reaches a maximum tier 4 weeks after the onset of illness, falling rapidly thereafter.

Tests for HEV-RNA by the polymerase chain reaction are available in specialised laboratories.

Prevention and Control

The provision of safe public water supplies, public sanitation and hygiene, safe disposal of feces and raw sewage and personal hygiene are essential measures.

Passive immunisation with immune globulin derived from endemic areas has not been successful.

Vaccines using various recombinant vaccines are under development. Extensive studies have been carried out with truncated recombinant capsid proteins expressed in insect cells using baculovirus vectors, and one such preparation is in phase II/III efficacy trial in Nepal.

REFERENCES

Alter H J, Seeff LB. (2000) Recovery, persistence, and sequelae in hepatitis C virus infection: a perspective on long-term outcome. Sem Liver Disease 20:17-35.

Beasley RP, Hwang L-Y. (1991) Overview of the epidemiology of hepatocellular carcinoma. In: Viral Hepatitis and Liver Disease (Hollinger FB, Lemon SM, Margolis HS, eds).., pp 532-535. Baltimore: Williams and Wilkins.

Booth JCL, O'Grady J, Neuberger J. (2002) Clinical guidelines on the management of hepatitis C. Gut 49(Suppl. 1):11-121.

Bowden S. (2001) New hepatitis viruses: Contenders and pretenders. J Gastro Hepatol 16:124-131.

Carman WF, Jacyna MR, Hadziyannis S, Karayiannis P, McGarvey MJ, Markis A, Thomas HC. (1989) Mutation preventing formation of hepatitis B e antigen in patients with chronic hepatitis B infection. Lancet 2:588-591.

Carman WF, Zanetti AR, Karayiannis P, Waters J, Manzillo G, Tanzi E, Zuckerman AJ, Thomas HC. (1990) Vaccine-induced escape mutant of hepatitis B virus. Lancet 336:325-329.

Davis GL. (2001) Treatment of chronic hepatitis C. Brit Med J 323:141-1142.

Di Bisceglie AM. (1998) Hepatitis D virus: epidemiology and diagnosis. In: Viral Hepatitis (Zuckerman AJ, Thomas HC, eds), pp371-378. Churchill Livingstone, London.

Dusheiko G. (1999) A pill a day, or two, for hepatitis B? Lancet 353:1032-1033.

Emmerson S, Purcell R. (2003) Hepatitis E. Rev Med Virol. In Press.

European Consensus Group on Hepatitis B Immunity (2002) Are booster immune-isations needed for lifelong hepatitis B immunity? Lancet 355:561-565.

Farrell G. (2000) Hepatitis B e antigen seroconversion: effects of lamivudine alone or in combination with interferon alpha. J Med Virol 61:374-379.

Francois G, Kew M, Van Damme P, Mphahlel J, Meheus A. (2001) Mutant hepatitis B viruses: a matter of academic interest only or a problem with far-reaching implications? Vaccine 19:3799-3815.

Gerin JL, Purcell RJ, Rizzetto M (eds) The Hepatitis Delta Virus.

Gow PJ, Mutimer D. (2001) Treatment of chronic hepatitis. Brit Med J 323:1164-1167.

Harrison TJ, Dusheiko GM, Zuckerman AJ. (2000) Hepatitis viruses. In: Principles and Practice of Clinical Virology 4th Edition (Zuckerman AJ, Banatvala JE, Pattison JR, eds), pp187-234. Wiley and Sons, Chichester.

Hsu HY, Chang MH, Liaw SH, Ni YH, Chen HL. (1999) Changes of hepatitis B surface antigen variants in carrier children before and after universal vaccination in Taiwan. Hepatology 30:1312-1317.

Kane MA. (1996) Global status of hepatitis B immunisation. Lancet 348:696-698.

Keeffe EB. (2000) End-stage liver disease and liver transplantation: role of lamivudine therapy in patients with chronic hepatitis B. J Med Virol 61:403-408.

Koff RS. (1998) Hepatitis A. Lancet 351:1643-1649.

Lai CL, Yuen MF. (2000) Profound sup-pression of hepatitis B virus replication with lamivudine. J Med Virol 61:367-373.

McDermott AB, Zuckerman JN, Sabin CA, Marsh SGE, Madrigal JA. (1997) Contribution of human leukocyte antigens to the antibody response to hepatitis B vaccination. Tissue Antigens 50:8-14.

McDermott A, Cohen SBA, Zuckerman JN, Madrigal JA. (1999) Human leukocyte antigens influence the immune response to a pre-S/S hepatitis B vaccine. Vaccine 17:330-339.

McGarvey MJ, Houghton M, Weiner AJ. (1998) Hepatitis C virus: structure and molecular virology. In: Viral Hepatitis (Zuckerman AJ, Thomas HC, eds), pp 253-270. Churchill Livingstone, London.

Merle P, Trepo C. (2001) Therapeutic management of hepatitis B-related cirrhosis. J Viral Hep 8:391-403.

Monjardino J, Lai MMC. (1998) Hepatitis D virus: structure and molecular virology. In: Viral Hepatitis (Zuckerman AJ, Thomas HC, eds), pp 359-370. Churchill Livingstone, London.

Mushahwar IK. (2000) Recently discovered blood-borne viruses: Are they hepatitis viruses or merely endosymbionts? J Med Virol 62:399-404.

Nainan OV, Stevens CE, Taylor PE, Margolis HS. (1997) Hepatitis B virus (HBV) antibody resistant mutants among mothers and infants with chronic HBV infection. In: Viral Hepatitis and Liver Disease (Rizzetto M, Purcell RH, Gerin JL, Verme G, eds) pp 132-134. Minerva Medica, Torino.

Nakahori S. (1995) Detection of hepatitis B virus pre-core stop codon mutant by selective amplification methods: frequent detection of mutants in pre-core hepatitis B e antigen positive healthy carriers. J Gastroenterol Hepatol 70:7056-7061.

NIH Publication No. 02-4230. (2002) Chronic hepatitis C: current disease management. Available on: http://www.niddk.nih.gov/health/digest/pubs/chrnhepc/chrnhepc.htm

Oon C-J, Lim G-K, Zhao Y, Goh K-T, Tan K-L, Yo S-L, Hopes E, Harrison TJ, Zuckerman AJ. (1995) Molecular epidemiology of hepatitis B virus vaccine variants in Singapore. Vaccine 13:699-702.

Oon C-J, Tan K-L, Harrison TJ, Zuckerman AJ. (1996) Natural history of hepatitis B surface antigen mutants in children. Lancet 348:1524.

Rizzetto M, Canese MG, Arico S, Crivelli O, Bonino F, Trepo CG, Verme G. (1977). Immunofluorescence detection of a new antigen-antibody system (delta/anti-delta) associated with hepatitis B virus in the liver and in the serum of HBsAg carriers. Gut 18:997-1003.

Schiff ER. (2000) Lamivudine for hepatitis B in clinical practice. J Med Virol 61:386-391.

Van Damme P, Vorsters A. (2002) Hepatitis B control in Europe by universal vaccination programmes: the situation in 2001. J Med Virol 67:433-439.

Vaudin M, Wolstenholme AJ, Tsiquaye KN, Zuckerman AJ, Harrison TJ. (1988) The complete nucleotide sequence of the genome of a hepatitis B virus isolated from a naturally infected chimpanzee. J gen Virol 69:1383-1389.

Whittle H, Jaffar S, Wansborough M, Mendy M, Dumpis U, Collinson A, Hall A. (2002) Observational study of vaccine efficacy 14 years after trial of hepatitis B vaccination in Gambian children. Brit Med J 325:569-572.

Wilson JN, Nokes DJ, Carman WF. (1999) The predicted pattern of emergence of vaccine-resistant hepatitis B: a cause for concern? Vaccine 17:973-978.

World Health Organisation. (1983) Prevention of Liver Cancer. Tech Rep Series No. 691. Geneva.

World Health Organisation. (2001) Hepatitis E. Previsani N, Lavanchy D. Geneva. Available on: http://www.who.int/emc/disease/hepatitis/index.html

World Health Organisation. (2002) Hepatitis B. Previsani N, Lavanchy D. Geneva. Available on: httpl://www.who.int/emc/diseases/hepatitis/index.html

Yuen MF, Lai CL. (2001) Treatment of chronic hepatitis B. Lancet Infect Dis 1:232-241.

Zanetti AR, Tanzi E, Manzillo G, Maio G, Shreglia C, Caporaso N, Thomas H, Zuckerman AJ. (1988) Hepatitis B variant in Europe. Lancet 2:1132-1133.

Zuckerman AJ, ed. (1999) Hepatitis B in the Asian-Pacific Region. Volume 3: New insights into managing and treating patients. Pp 1-50. Royal College of Physicians, London.

Zuckerman AJ. (2000) Effect of hepatitis B virus mutants on efficacy of vaccination. Lancet 355:1382-1384.

Zuckerman AJ, Zuckerman JN. (1999) Molecular epidemiology of hepatitis B virus mutants. J Med Virol 58:193-195.

Zuckerman JN. (1996) Non-response to hepatitis B vaccines and the kinetics of anti-HBs production. J Med Virol 50:283-288.

Zuckerman JN, Zuckerman AJ. (1998) Is there a need for boosters of hepatitis B vaccines? Viral Hepatitis Rev 4:43-46.

Zuckerman JN, Zuckerman AJ. (2002) Recombinant hepatitis B triple antigen vaccine: Hepacare. Expert Rev Vaccine 1:141-144.

Zuckerman JN, Sabin C, Craig FM, Williams A, Zuckerman AJ. (1997) Immune response to a new hepatitis B vaccine in healthcare workers who had not responded to standard vaccine; randomised double blind dose-response study. Brit Med J 314:315-318.

TYPE 1 DIABETES MELLITUS

Tim Wysocki

INTRODUCTION

This chapter provides a summary and evaluation of clinical health psychology practices in the area of type 1 or insulin-dependent diabetes mellitus and considers whether these practices have sufficiently strong empirical support to justify a designation as "Best Practices". Consistent with the objectives of this book, clinical practices are recommended only if there is sound empirical support for their adoption. The chapter begins with a brief discussion of the diagnosis and treatment of type 1 diabetes mellitus to provide the context for understanding this research and its public health significance. Then, several empirically-validated psychological practices for patients with diabetes are described and evaluated. In each case, discussion of the recommended practice is prefaced by a brief discussion of the history of research that has culminated in the body of sound scientific data that now supports clinical adoption of that practice. In some cases, critical gaps in the existing research are identified.

DIAGNOSIS AND TREATMENT OF DIABETES MELLITUS

Treatment of diabetes mellitus and its complications account for 12-14% of annual health care costs in the U.S. (National Diabetes Data Group, 1995). Type 1, or insulin-dependent, diabetes mellitus (DM1), which accounts for less than 10% of all cases of diabetes, results from autoimmune destruction of the pancreatic insulin-producing cells, resulting in insulin deficiency. DM1 often has its onset in childhood and has been referred to as insulin-dependent diabetes mellitus or juvenile-onset diabetes mellitus, although its onset can occur at any age through middle adulthood. Prevalence of DM1 is variable around the world, but is estimated at 1-2 cases per 1,000 population in North America. Treatment consists of multiple daily insulin injections or use of an insulin pump, daily blood glucose testing, a constant carbohydrate diet and exercise. Short-term complications of DM1 are episodes of hypoglycemia that can require emergency care, and diabetic ketoacidosis that is the most common reason for hospitalization. Type 2 diabetes mellitus (DM2), the far more common form with a prevalence of about 60 cases per 1,000 population, often has its onset in adulthood and results from insulin resistance rather than insulin deficiency. It is estimated that about 5.4 million affected people in the United States are unaware that they have the disease. Treatment may consist of exercise and diet alone, oral hypoglycemic drugs or insulin injections. In many patients with DM2, insulin resistance early in the disease tends to evolve into insulin deficiency and their treatment then becomes indistinguishable from that for DM1. All forms of diabetes mellitus increase risks of damage to the heart, kidneys, nerves, eyes and other organs. The incidence of DM2 has become epidemic in the pediatric population, especially among racial and ethnic minorities, possibly owing to increases in obesity and sedentary lifestyle among children and adolescents in the past few decades. Currently, as many as 20% of all newly diagnosed cases of diabetes in children and adolescents consist of DM2. Russell Glasgow and Diane King provide an excellent overview of the behavioral medicine literature on DM2 elsewhere in this book.

Important Intervention Studies

The Diabetes Control and Complications Trial (DCCT Research Group,1993) was a major NIH study to determine if long-term maintenance of near-normal blood glucose concentrations decreased the onset and progression of diabetic complications. A sample of 1,441 patients with DM1 (including 195 adolescents) was randomized to either Intensive or Conventional Therapy and followed for an average of about 7 years. Intensive Therapy was an effort to keep blood glucose near normal through more frequent insulin injections or use of an insulin pump, more frequent blood glucose monitoring, use of blood glucose data for insulin and diet adjustments. Patients had free access to the consultative services of a diabetes nurse, dietitian and psychologist to help them to achieve optimal adaptation to this regimen. Intensive Therapy yielded significantly better diabetic control than did Conventional Therapy in each year of the study. Intensive Therapy reduced the onset and progression of diabetic complications by 50-75%, even though few patients achieved consistent normoglycemia during the study. There was a linear relationship between average glycosylated hemoglobin (HbA_{1C}) and complication rates; <u>any</u> improvement in diabetic control reduced complications. Although adolescents maintained consistently higher HbA_{1C} throughout the trial, their overall results were similar to those achieved with adults. Since the benefits of Intensive Therapy were achieved with extant medical tools, a key factor mediating its success was the capacity of patients, with the support of diabetes teams, to achieve and maintain long term change in self-care behaviors. Although intensive therapy as implemented in the DCCT is three to four times more expensive than conventional therapy in the short-term, cost-effectiveness analyses indicate that this investment is returned amply in the long run due to cost savings resulting from prevention of long-term complications of the disease (DCCT Research Group, 1996).

The recent United Kingdom Prospective Diabetes Study, using a multidisciplinary intervention similar to that employed in the DCCT (UKPDS Group, 1998), yielded results for DM2 similar to the DCCT findings for DM1. Thus, maintenance of tight glycemic control reduces the onset and slows the progression of long-term complications in both forms of diabetes.

It is difficult to exaggerate the profound influence that these two major studies have had on modern clinical management of diabetes mellitus. Since the DCCT and UKPDS studies were published, diabetes management has evolved toward more intensive and aggressive treatment of patients of all ages except for very young children. Notably, though, the samples in both of these studies were comprised predominantly of adults. The DCCT enrolled adolescents as young as 14 years of age, but these patients were in early adulthood by the conclusion of the study. Since the self management of diabetes is almost entirely a behavioral endeavor, it is likely that there will be greater need for the skills of health psychologists in helping patients to integrate this demanding regimen into their lives. Health psychologists should therefore be familiar with the vast diabetes research literature and its clinical implications.

This chapter has been preceded by several excellent literature reviews in the past few years. Glasgow et al. (1999) summarized key contributions of behavioral science to our understanding of the psychosocial aspects of diabetes and discussed barriers to the widespread clinical application of these research findings. Delamater et al. (2001), Glasgow et al. (2001) and Wing et al. (2001) provided working group reports on psychosocial therapies, health care delivery, and lifestyle changes, respectively, that resulted from a National Institutes of Health conference on behavioral science research in diabetes. Hampson et al. (2000; 2001) published a meta-analytic review of more than 60 studies of psychological and psychoeducational interventions for adolescents with diabetes. They reported that the most careful randomized controlled trials of such interventions had a median effect size of 0.36 standard deviations for psychosocial outcomes and 0.18 standard deviations for metabolic outcomes. Gonder-Frederick et al. (2002) contributed a summary of recent advances in behavioral diabetes research published in the decade following their publication of a similar, earlier review (Cox and Gonder-Frederick, 1992). Rubin and Peyrot (2001) contributed a review of the research on concomitant psychopathology in patients with diabetes and on the psychological burden endured by most patients in trying to cope with the disease and its treatment. Wysocki (in press) summarized the empirical support for behavioral assessment and intervention strategies for children and adolescents with DM1. These reviews are excellent sources of additional information and more detailed treatment of several of the topics discussed in this chapter.

Empirically Validated Clinical Practices in Type 1 Diabetes Mellitus

As is evident from these many thorough review articles that have been published about behavioral and psychosocial issues in the management of diabetes mellitus, there is a very large and growing body of research that can guide clinical health psychologists and other diabetes professionals in their clinical work with these patients. There are many topics and practices that have received a reasonable degree of empirical support in this literature, but only a subset of these will be discussed in detail here. The chapter emphasizes three broad domains of behavioral medicine research in diabetes that enjoy the strongest empirical support:

1. Studies demonstrating the long-term effectiveness of behavioral and psychological interventions targeting improvement in self-management behaviors such as treatment adherence, diabetes problem solving, patient motivation and empowerment, blood glucose discrimination training and therapeutic use of blood glucose test results.
2. Evaluations of the merits of stress management interventions targeting diabetes outcomes and of assessment and intervention for concurrent psychopathology (e.g. depression and anxiety disorders) that occur with increased incidence among patients with diabetes.
3. Studies of the neuropsychological sequelae of diabetes and risk factors for diabetes-related cognitive impairments.

Selection of the specific studies chosen for more detailed discussion in this chapter was driven by their methodological rigor and scientific or public health significance. The studies that received greater emphasis are more likely than not to have randomized treatment designs, larger sample sizes, pertinent control groups, well-validated measures, appropriate statistical analyses, clearly articulated theoretical or conceptual frameworks and a background of several related previous investigations. In instances in which the requisite data was provided in the original paper, effect size estimates have been calculated and reported here. While interventions targeting obesity and sedentary lifestyle play important roles in both the prevention and treatment of type 2 diabetes (see Wing et al., 2001 for a review), these health behaviors are reviewed comprehensively elsewhere in this book and so are not discussed here. Also, the research summarized in this chapter has been accompanied by the development and validation of many excellent diabetes-specific assessment instruments and methods (see Bradley, 1994 for a review), but a comprehensive summary of these tools is beyond the scope of this chapter.

Diabetes Self Management Interventions

At its core, the management of DM1 consists almost entirely of behavioral self-regulation processes. Consequently, the largest segment of the behavioral medicine research on DM1 is concerned with such issues as acquisition and maintenance of diabetes knowledge and skills, patient motivation, self-efficacy and empowerment, treatment adherence, diabetes-specific coping skills, and problem solving related to the prevention, detection and correction of blood glucose fluctuations.

Diabetes Self-Management Education

The management of DM1 perhaps places a greater proportion of responsibility for treatment and monitoring tasks directly on the patient or family than is true of other diseases. Patients with DM1 play a central and active role in determining their own health status. The centrality of DM1 patients in day-to-day medical decision-making has stimulated considerable research and discourse recognizing this basic fact and searching for ways to structure the clinical practice of diabetes management and education that acknowledge and capitalize on this fundamental reality (Anderson et al., 1996; Glasgow et al., 2001; Rubin et al., 1989, 1993; Williams et al., 1998). Rather than viewing the patient with DM1 as a passive recipient of medical care and education, these approaches emphasize that clinical and educational encounters should equip patients with the knowledge, skills and support needed to make active, informed choices about their daily diabetes self-management.

Clement (1995) provided a thorough and compelling review of studies demonstrating the effectiveness of diabetes self-management education programs on such outcomes as diabetes knowledge, treatment adherence, attitudes about diabetes, and health outcomes. Clement concluded that diabetes self-management education programs with the following characteristics are most effective: 1.) Didactic instruction augmented with extensive incorporation of behavior change strategies such as individualized goal-setting, training in problem solving and coping skills, behavioral contracting, frequent monitoring, etc. 2.) Integration of education with expert adjustment of medication and reinforcement of learned behaviors by the health care provider; and 3.) Instruction in the use of blood glucose data to enable patients to optimize the insulin regimen. Several of the more rigorous studies in this area are summarized below to illustrate these points.

Rubin, Peyrot, and Saudek (1989; 1993) evaluated the educational, psychosocial and glycemic effects of participation in a 5-day outpatient diabetes education program attended by 165 adults (63 DM1; 102 DM2). The program was delivered by a multidisciplinary team and incorporated a substantial emphasis on the teaching of diabetes-specific coping skills. Measures of diabetes knowledge, self-care behaviors, and emotional wellbeing were obtained at the beginning and end of the program and at 6-month and 12-month follow-ups. HbA$_{1C}$ was measured at study entry and at 6-month and 12-month follow-up. Measures of diabetes knowledge, self-management behaviors and emotional wellbeing showed significant improvement from study entry to program completion. Effects on measures of emotional wellbeing (self-esteem, anxiety, depression and self-efficacy) remained significant at 6-month follow-up. HbA$_{1C}$ dropped from 11.5% at entry to 9.5% at 6-month follow-up (effect size = 0.72; p < .001), but 12-month results were not reported. There were no differences in treatment effects between patients with DM1 and DM2.

Anderson et al. (1995) reported the results of a randomized, controlled trial of a patient empowerment approach to diabetes patient education consisting of 6 weekly 2-hour sessions. The empowerment program addressed six objectives for participants : 1. Enhance ability to set realistic goals; 2. Apply a systematic problem-solving strategy to eliminate barriers to those goals; 3. Cope with circumstances that cannot be changed; 4. Manage stress associated with diabetes and with life in general; 5. Identify and obtain helpful social support; and 6. Improve their ability to motivate themselves for better self-care. A sample of 64 adults with diabetes (23 DM1 and 41 DM2) were assigned to either complete the patient empowerment education program immediately or to a waiting list who would complete the program after a 6-week delay. Measures that were evaluated at baseline and at 6-week intervals thereafter included 8 self-efficacy scales, 5 diabetes attitude scales and HbA_{1C}. Results showed that the patient empowerment program yielded immediate and sustained improvements on 4 of the 8 self-efficacy scales and 2 of the 5 diabetes attitude scales. HbA_{1C} declined from 11.8% to 11.0% for program participants ($p < .05$; effect size = .25) and showed no significant change for control patients (10.8% at both measurements).

Williams, Freedman, and Deci (1998) applied the self-determination theory of human motivation to study whether patients' perceptions of the supports for patient autonomy from their health care providers were related to changes in glucose control over a 12 month interval. Briefly, self-determination theory holds that autonomous motivation, as contrasted with motivation that has an extrinsic source, is more likely to lead to durable, clinically meaningful behavior change. A sample of 128 adults with diabetes (47 DM1; 81 DM2) completed questionnaires on three occasions during a 12-month period to provide measures of autonomy support versus controlled motivation for diabetes management and their perceived self-competence for managing diabetes. HbA_{1C} was measured at these same three occasions. Multiple regression analyses of change in HbA_{1C} during the study period supported the tenets of self-determination theory. Autonomy support was significantly negatively related to HbA_{1C} at all three time points (average r = -.32; $p < .001$) as was perceived self-competence (average r = -.32; $p < .01$). These associations did not differ as a function of diabetes type.

These studies illustrate the important role of attending to psychological factors in the planning, implementation and evaluation of diabetes education programs. Since it is unethical to deprive patients of diabetes education, future studies can advance this literature by randomizing patients to educational programs that differ in substantial and systematic ways in order to determine the type of curricula that achieve optimal outcomes in terms of patient knowledge, self-management behavior, emotional wellbeing, empowerment and motivation. For example, a purely didactic educational program could be contrasted with programs that emphasize patient empowerment or that provide specific instruction and practice of diabetes-specific coping skills. In any event, the studies summarized above, and others reviewed by Clement (1995) indicate that effective diabetes self-management education reflect careful attention to psychological considerations such as those illuminated by these researchers.

Promotion of treatment adherence

The diabetes regimen may include administration of daily insulin or an oral hypoglycemic agent, blood glucose testing, a constant carbohydrate diet, and regular exercise. Patients must also recognize and correct unwanted fluctuations in blood glucose by engaging in appropriate actions to either raise the blood glucose level (e.g. consume carbohydrates) or lower the blood glucose level (e.g. take more insulin, get exercise, defer eating). Extensive research on adherence with this regimen has yielded several broad conclusions. First, adherence with the diabetes regimen is not a global or stable personality trait. Adherence with the various regimen components varies within and between patients and there is often a weak association between measures of adherence with the various aspects of care (Glasgow et al., 1987; Johnson et al., 1986). Second, perfect adherence with the regimen is rare; most patients have at least moderate difficulty integrating all of these treatment and monitoring demands into their daily lives (Anderson, 1996). Third, treatment adherence is particularly difficult to maintain during adolescence (Johnson, 1995; Weissberg-Benchell, 1995) and this may be a common cause of preventable hospitalizations. Finally, efforts to find a robust link between treatment adherence and diabetic control have often failed (Johnson, 1995). Although this seems counter-intuitive, there are plausible explanations. Poor adherence with one treatment task can be offset by good adherence with another. Existing measures of adherence rely heavily on self-report, possibly resulting in inaccurate measurement. If a patient's treatment regimen is not optimal, adherence with that regimen may not yield good glycemic control.

Wysocki (in press) has reviewed studies that evaluated behavior modification approaches targeting improvements in diabetes treatment adherence among children and adolescents with DM1. Such approaches typically include selecting one or more observable target behaviors for improvement, regular monitoring of the target behavior(s), frequent positive reinforcement for fulfilling negotiated behavior change goals, periodic refinement of reinforcement contingencies as needed, and gradual withdrawal of positive reinforcement as behavior change is maintained. Although there has not been a large-scale randomized, controlled trial of behavior modification conducted with this specific clinical problem, there are more than 30 peer-reviewed publications that have reported positive effects of such procedures on treatment adherence in pediatric DM1 (e.g. Lowe and Lutzker, 1978; Schafer et al., 1982; Wysocki et al.,1989) and glycemic control (e.g. Carney et al.,1983; Epstein, et al., 1981; Matam et al., 2000; Mendez and Belendez, 1997). It would therefore appear appropriate to recommend that the clinical practice of behavioral medicine in pediatric DM1 should include the application of skills and expertise in designing, implementing, monitoring, evaluating and refining behavior modification interventions for medical treatment adherence.

Diabetes Problem Solving

The demands of diabetes pervade daily life and the maintenance of good glycemic control depends substantially on the patient's response to unwanted fluctuations in blood glucose levels and the efficacy of their coping with frequent intrusions of diabetes demands into other aspects of their daily lives. There has consequently been much research done in this area (e.g. Peyrot and Rubin, 1990; Delamater et al., 1989; Wysocki et al., 1992), including a number of well-controlled randomized trials of pertinent interventions.

Anderson et al. (1989) demonstrated that a peer group intervention designed to promote adolescents' skills in diabetes problem solving and decision making based on blood glucose test results was effective in improving glycemic control compared with standard medical care. Over the 18 months of follow-up, 50% of standard care patients showed a deterioration in HbA_{1C} levels of $\geq 1.0\%$, compared with only 23% of those in the intervention group. At 18-month follow-up, mean HbA$_{1C}$ for the intervention group (10.1%) was significantly lower than that for the standard care group (11.04%), yielding an estimated effect size on HbA$_{1C}$ of approximately 0.47 standard deviations. Cost effectiveness of the intervention was not evaluated.

Delamater et al. (1990) randomized 36 children with newly diagnosed DM1 to conventional medical therapy (CT), supportive counseling (SC) or a self management training intervention (SMT) and followed them prospectively for 2 years. The SMT intervention was a 7 session program during the first 4 months after diagnosis that included parent training in behavior modification specifically related to family diabetes management and an emphasis on teaching parents and youths how to use blood glucose test results effectively to guide adjustments to insulin doses, eating choices and exercise in order to optimize glycemic control. Booster sessions occurred at 6 and 12 months after diagnosis. The results showed that the SMT group maintained significantly lower HbA$_{1C}$ at 1-year and 2-year follow-ups compared with CT, but not when compared with SC. Hampson et al. (2001) calculated an effect size of 0.18 standard deviations on HbA$_{1C}$ for both the SC and SMT interventions in this study.

Grey, Boland, Davidson, Li and Tamborlane (2000) reported one year follow-up data from a randomized trial of a coping skills training intervention (CST) for 77 adolescents who initiated intensive therapy for DM1. The CST intervention was delivered in a 6-session, monthly, small group format in which specific coping skills were taught during sessions and practiced between sessions in the areas of social problem solving, cognitive behavior modification and conflict resolution. Outcome assessments showed that, compared with control patients, the SMT group had significantly lower HbA$_{1C}$, (effect size = 0.31) better diabetes self-efficacy, and less impact of DM1 on their quality of life at immediate post-treatment and 12-month follow-ups (effect size = 0.44). Girls also realized significant and persistent benefits in terms of less weight gain and less frequent severe hypoglycemia over this interval. The results indicated that the addition of a behavioral intervention to intensive diabetes management yielded improved outcomes that persisted over 12 months.

Taken together, these three studies suggest that behavioral interventions that target specific DM1-related problem solving and coping skills can yield persistent benefits to children and adolescents, including lasting improvement in HbA$_{1C}$ levels and psychosocial outcomes.

There have been few similar studies conducted with adults with DM1. Snoek et al. (2001) recently reported one such study. A sample of 24 adults with poorly controlled DM1 participated in a 4-week cognitive-behavioral group intervention. Repeated measures analysis of variance revealed a significant effect on HbA$_{1C}$ from baseline (9.3%) to 6-month follow-up (8.5%), yielding an effect size estimate of 0.67. Replication of this study with random assignment to control or intervention conditions and long-term follow-up would be a valuable contribution since it could clarify whether these effects are specific to this intervention.

Blood Glucose Awareness Training

Most patients with DM1 believe that they are able to identify specific, idiosyncratic subjective physical symptoms that are reliable indicators of their prevailing blood glucose levels, yet only a minority are consistently correct in these beliefs (Cox et al., 1983). Since blood glucose testing is not always available or convenient, improvement in the accuracy of patients' estimates of their blood glucose levels based on subjective physical symptoms and other cues, coupled with appropriate responses to these signals, could enhance their ability to maintain better glycemic control.

In an elegant series of studies, Cox and colleagues have developed and validated a Blood Glucose Awareness Training (BGAT) program (Cox et al., 1989) and later refined the program elements to create BGAT-2 (Cox et al., 2001). BGAT incorporates both behavioral and cognitive strategies to improve self-management and decision-making in patients with DM1. The program targets self-regulation behaviors such as empirically identifying and recognizing idiosyncratic relationships between subjective symptoms and blood glucose levels, identifying treatment decisions that may contribute to glucose dysregulation and employing problem solving strategies to increase the probability of adequate glycemic control. The BGAT-2 curriculum places comparatively greater emphasis on self-management behaviors that could prevent severe hypoglycemia. Cox et al. (1994; 1995; 2001) verified that the BGAT-2 program yields less extreme daily blood glucose excursions, fewer episodes of severe hypoglycemia, fewer motor vehicle accidents and improved psychosocial status compared with usual DM1 management and education. Further, many of these benefits are maintained over at least 12 months (Cox et al., 1994; Cox et al., 2001), and the effects have been replicated in multi-center studies (Cox et al., 1995, Cox et al., 2001), and with adolescents (Nurick and Johnson, 1991). At present, research on blood glucose awareness training is the best example of the programmatic development, validation and refinement of a diabetes-specific behavioral intervention.

Interventions targeting the social context of diabetes

Most events that affect diabetic control occur during patients' daily lives at home, work, and school. Not surprisingly, many studies have found that social variables can influence patients' psychological adjustment to diabetes, the effectiveness of diabetes self-care and diabetic control (e.g. Anderson, 1996; Hanson et al., 1995; Hanson et al., 1987; Lorenz and Wysocki, 1991). The social context of diabetes carries the potential to enhance or to impede adaptation to diabetes. A number of well-controlled intervention studies have targeted aspects of this problem.

Satin, La Greca, Zigo, and Skyler (1989) reported the results of a controlled trial in which 32 families of adolescents with DM1were randomized to either a control group (C), 6 weekly sessions of a multi-family support group (MF) or a multifamily support group augmented with parental simulation of living with diabetes (MF+S). Both the MF and MF+S groups yielded more positive parental attitudes toward their adolescents with DM1. The MF+S group had lower HbA_{1C} and better treatment adherence immediately after treatment and at 6-month follow-up compared with the C and MF groups. A very large effect size of 2.00 was obtained for HbA_{1C}., the magnitude of which contrasts with that of most other psychological intervention studies with this population (Hampson et al., 2000; Hampson et al., 2001). Given the relatively small sample size employed in this study, a larger randomized controlled trial of the MF+S intervention would be a valuable contribution.

Historically, clinical and educational management of pediatric DM1 has emphasized the importance of children achieving autonomy in diabetes self-management (McNabb et al., 1994). Several recent studies have questioned this assumption and these studies cumulatively lead to the conclusion that excessive self care autonomy may be associated with adverse metabolic and behavioral outcomes (Allen et al., 1983; Anderson et al., 1990; Ingersoll et al., 1986; La Greca et al., 1990; Weissberg-Benchell et al., 1995; Wysocki et al., 1996).

Consequently, the maintenance of helpful parental involvement in diabetes management during adolescence is now a more commonly advocated therapeutic and educational objective. However, until recently there have been no studies that tested methods of accomplishing this. Anderson, Brackett, Ho and Laffel (1999) developed and evaluated an office-based intervention designed to promote and maintain constructive diabetes teamwork between parents and adolescents. A sample of 85 families of 10-15 year old youth with DM1 was randomized to Standard Care, Attention Control or Teamwork conditions for the 24-month study period. Families in the Teamwork condition received written plans and counseling from a research assistant that identified multiple causes of hypoglycemia and hyperglycemia, extended realistic expectations for blood glucose levels and self-management behaviors during adolescence and stressed the importance of helpful, constructive and positive parental involvement in insulin injections and blood glucose monitoring. Families were assisted in developing a written responsibility-sharing plan and this was reviewed and refined at subsequent diabetes clinic visits. Outcomes consisted of measures of parental involvement in insulin administration and blood glucose monitoring, measures of diabetes-related family conflict and HbA_{1C}. Results showed that the Teamwork condition yielded significantly greater parental involvement in diabetes management and significantly lower levels of diabetes-related family conflict compared with the other conditions. Although mean HbA_{1C} levels did not differ among the groups at 12-months, at 24-month follow-up, change in HbA_{1C} levels was -.20% for the Teamwork group and 0.11% for the other groups. Among the Teamwork group, 68% of patients realized an improvement of at least 1.0% in HbA_{1C} levels, compared with 47% in the other groups, an effect that approached statistical significance (p < .07). This model

therefore merits further investigation as it could lead to a practical, disseminable and economical intervention.

Extensive research has shown that family conflict and ineffective parent-adolescent communication are associated with poor treatment adherence and inadequate glycemic control on both a cross-sectional (Anderson et al., 1990; Bobrow et al., 1985; Miller-Johnson et al., 1994; Wysocki, 1993) and longitudinal basis (Gustafsson et al., 1987; Hauser et al., 1990; Koski et al., 1976). Robin and Foster (1989) summarized evidence supporting their Behavioral Family Systems Therapy (BFST) model for improving parent-adolescent relationships in a variety of clinical populations of adolescents without chronic medical conditions. We reasoned that this therapeutic model might be beneficial for families in which cooperation between parents and adolescents in diabetes management was impeded by excessive conflict and poor communication and problem solving. We were able to complete a controlled treatment outcome study in which families of 119 adolescents with DM1, who reported moderate or greater parent-adolescent conflict, were randomized to remain in their current medical therapy (CT) alone or augmented by 3 months of participation in either BFST or attendance at a multifamily educational support (ES) group (Wysocki et al., 2000). Outcome measures included questionnaire and direct-observation measures of parent-adolescent communication and problem-solving, DM1-related family conflict, diabetes treatment adherence and HbA_{1C}, each of which were measured at Baseline, end of treatment and at 6-month and 12-month post-treatment follow-ups. Results showed significant treatment benefits from BFST relative to one or both comparison groups on paper and pencil measures of parent-adolescent relationships (Wysocki et al., 2000), directly observed family communication and problem solving skills

(Wysocki et al., 1999), parent and adolescent social validity ratings of the acceptability, applicability and effectiveness of BFST compared to ES (Wysocki et al., 1997) and maintenance of most of these changes over the 12-month follow-up (Wysocki et al, 2001). Combined effect size for the psychosocial variables in this study was 0.38. While BFST did not yield significant improvement in HbA_{1C} levels (effect size = -0.03), delayed improvement in treatment adherence did result (Wysocki et al, 2001). A second trial of BFST, incorporating several refinements designed to enhance its impact on treatment adherence and health outcomes, is in progress.

In addition to adult caregivers, siblings and peers of youth with DM1 also stand to influence the child's diabetes self-management behaviors and psychosocial adjustment to diabetes. A few intervention studies have targeted peer influences on these outcomes in children with DM1. Gross, Heimann, Shapiro, and Schultz (1983) and Gross, Magalnick, and Richardson (1985) showed that training in diabetes-specific assertiveness enhanced the ability of children with diabetes to cope effectively with peer influences that were contrary to optimal diabetes self-management. Kaplan, Chadwick, and Schimmel (1985) demonstrated that a brief social skills training program for youth with DM1 not only improved their social skills, but also yielded statistically significant reductions in HbA_{1C} relative to a control group. Greco, Shroff-Pendley, and McDonnell (2001) took a different approach to the same issue in their pilot evaluation of a peer group intervention for 21 adolescents with diabetes and their best friends. Their group intervention targeted the identification and promotion of diabetes-specific social support behaviors that friends could demonstrate in order to be helpful to the youth with DM1. Results of the study showed significant effects on friends' diabetes

knowledge, diabetes support and self-perceptions. Youth with DM1 reported a significantly higher proportion of peer support relative to family support and parents reported significantly less family conflict about diabetes. This study did not include measurement of glycemic control. The social support and social skills interventions used in these studies merits further evaluation in randomized controlled trials.

Summary

Efforts to affect health outcomes by influencing intermediate mechanisms such as coping skills, family communication, problem solving, social support, empowerment and other such variables must have very robust effects in order to achieve a meaningful therapeutic impact on health outcomes. It is not surprising, therefore, that many tested interventions have stronger effects on psychosocial and behavioral mediators than on the health outcomes they are expected to influence. Although some of these intervention studies yielded statistically significant effects on measures of diabetic control (e.g. Kaplan et al., 1985; Satin et al., 1989), typically such effects fell short of significance. This extensive list of psychological and behavioral intervention studies, many of which demonstrate impressive methodological rigor, indicates that clinically meaningful improvements in a wide range of diabetes self management behaviors, measures of psychosocial wellbeing and health outcomes can be achieved. At the same time, it is clear that additional research needs to be done to maximize the therapeutic benefits of these techniques and to identify the characteristics of patients and target behaviors that are predictive of treatment outcomes. Further evaluation of social support interventions with siblings and friends would be a particularly valuable contribution.

Stress, Coping and Psychopathology

Patients who experience a great deal of psychological stress or who cope ineffectively are at risk of poor diabetic control (Surwit et al., 1992). This may be a consequence of two different mechanisms that are not mutually exclusive. Stress may directly increase secretion of counter-regulatory hormones that block insulin action or transform stored glycogen into glucose for release into the bloodstream (Aikens et al.,1992; Chase and Jackson, 1981; Frenzel et al., 1988; Hanson et al., 1987). Stress may impede diabetic control indirectly through interference with diabetes self-management by distracting the patient from careful monitoring and proactive self-care (Hanson et al., 1987; Hanson and Pichert, 1986). The health psychologist must appreciate the influence of stress and coping on the patient's adjustment to diabetes. Evaluation of patients who have difficulty coping with diabetes should include assessment of the frequency and severity of recent stressful life events and minor daily stresses and the patient's ability to cope effectively with them.

Surwit et al. (2000) reported that a five session group diabetes education program with stress management training was effective in improving long term glycemic control in patients with type 2 diabetes. Participants were followed for 1 year, at the end of which experimental patients had mean HbA_{1C} levels about 0.5% lower than those in the control group. Surwit, Schneider, and Feinglos (1992) postulated that patients with type 2 diabetes may be more physiologically reactive to stress than are those with type 1 diabetes. There have been few rigorously controlled evaluations of stress management interventions with either adults or youth with DM1. A few studies with adolescents have suggested some promise for stress management interventions.

Boardway, Delamater, Tomakowsky and Gutai (1993) contributed an evaluation of a stress management intervention for adolescents with DM1. Nine patients were randomized to Stress Management Training (SMT) and ten to the control group (C). A 6-month, 13-session treatment program preceded a 3-month follow-up period. Results showed significant reductions in diabetes-specific stress for the SMT group but not the C group with an estimated effect size of 0.10. Neither group, however, realized significant improvement in glycemic control, regimen adherence, coping styles or diabetes self-efficacy. The authors concluded that the SMT intervention may be effective in reducing DM1-specific stress, but that other intervention approaches are needed to address the other types of outcomes. Rose, Firestone, Heick, and Faught (1983) reported positive psychological effects and minimal metabolic benefit from a similar intervention. Hains, Davies, Parton, Totka, and Amoroso-Camarata (2000) reported that a stress management training program for adolescents in poor glycemic control was ineffective in improving measures of coping, anxiety, stress or metabolic control. The intervention evaluated by Mendez and Belendez (1997) incorporated elements of coping skills and problem solving training in addition to stress management. The significant effects of this intervention on glycemic control may indicate that stress management interventions must target additional behavioral outcomes in order to yield sufficiently robust effects as to improve glycemic control.

Fowler, Budzynski and Vandenbergh (1978) evaluated biofeedback-assisted relaxation training with several adults with poorly controlled DM1. Glycemic benefit from this approach was small and inconsistent. While the results demonstrated some promise for this approach, the small sample limits the generality of the findings.

In summary, there is ample evidence that psychosocial stress may impair DM1 self-management and glycemic control. But, there is little evidence that typical stress management interventions alone are sufficient in protecting patients from these deleterious effects of stress. Further research is needed to determine if the outcomes of more comprehensive interventions can be bolstered with the addition of stress management components.

Perhaps related to the high levels of psychological stress experienced by patients with DM1, there is an increased incidence of certain psychiatric disorders in this population. Diabetes appears to increase the risks of depression, anxiety disorders and eating disorders in both the pediatric and adult age groups. Kovacs, Goldston, Obrosky, and Bonar (1997) showed prospectively that 27% of youths had an episode of major depression during the 10 years after onset of diabetes and 13% had anxiety disorders. Youth with these disorders were more likely to demonstrate pervasive noncompliance with medical treatment and poorer health status (Kovacs et al., 1996). There is also an increased risk of depression in adults with diabetes (Lustman et al., 1992; Peyrot and Rubin, 1997). Depression may impede treatment adherence and its treatment may improve diabetic control (Lustman et al., 1996). Anxiety disorders also occur more commonly among adults with diabetes (Lustman, 1988; Peyrot and Rubin, 1997) and the presence of such a disorder is predictive of worse treatment adherence and higher HbA_{1C}. Anorexia nervosa and bulimia also appear to more common in young women with Type 1 diabetes than in the general population (Rodin and Daneman, 1992) and, again, these disorders are associated with less favorable diabetes outcomes (Affenito et al., 1997). Patients who suffer from diabetes and a psychiatric disorder are at increased risk of poorer diabetes outcomes than are those without such disorders. Patients with diabetes may also suffer from subclinical depression and anxiety that warrant treatment. Polonsky

et al. (1995) have validated the Problem Areas in Diabetes Scale, which can be used to evaluate diabetes-specific distress.

There is thus a fairly extensive research literature documenting the increased incidence of psychopathology among patients with DM1 at all ages. Additional studies show that patients who suffer from depression, anxiety disorders and eating disorders, even at subclinical levels, tend to be in poorer health status, to demonstrate worse treatment adherence and appointment-keeping and to be over-represented among patients who are hospitalized or seen for emergency room care. In contrast to this rather broad literature, there have been very few well-controlled treatment outcome studies that have evaluated any types of psychological or pharmacological interventions with patients who have both DM1 and a comorbid psychiatric disorder. The most notable exceptions to this generalization are studies contributed by Lustman and his colleagues.

Lustman, Griffith, Freedland, Kissel, and Clouse (1998) conducted a randomized controlled trial of cognitive behavior therapy (CBT) with adults who had concomitant depression and type 2 diabetes. Patients received 10 weeks of individualized CBT or were assigned to a control condition with no specific antidepressant treatment. Immediately after treatment, 85% of CBT patients had realized remission of depression as measured by the Beck Depression Inventory, compared with 27% of control patients (p < .001). At follow-up 6 months after treatment, depression remission rates were 70% for CBT and 33% for controls (p < .03). HbA_{1C} did not differ between groups at baseline or end of treatment, but at 6 month follow-up, the CBT group had significantly lower (p < .03) mean HbA_{1C} (9.5%) compared with controls (10.9%). CBT appeared to be of comparable effectiveness for the treatment of depression in this sample of patients with diabetes as it is in the general population.

This same group has reported the results of a series of 8-week, randomized, placebo-controlled trials of pharmacologic agents for the treatment of depression and anxiety disorders in adults with diabetes. These have included studies of alprazolam in patients with diabetes and anxiety disorders (Lustman et al., 1995), nortriptyline for depression (Lustman et al., 1997), and fluoxetine for depression (Lustman et al., 1997). In each case depressive or anxious symptoms were significantly reduced with drug compared with placebo, although the various medications appeared to have differing effects on glycemic control. To date, no study has been reported in which CBT and medication have been used together and separately in the treatment of depression or anxiety disorders in patients with diabetes.

No rigorous randomized controlled trials of pharmacological or behavioral interventions for the treatment of eating disorders in patients with DM1 could be located. Nor have comparable rigorous treatment outcome studies been published with children or adolescents with DM1 who have depression, anxiety disorders or eating disorders. These are obviously important omissions from the research literature.

Independent of whether rigorous randomized, controlled trials of psychological interventions have been conducted with patients who have both DM1 and one of these psychiatric disorders, it is still important for health psychologists to be sensitive to the occurrence of these disorders in their patients with DM1. At this time there is no evidence to suggest that patients with DM1 respond differently to established treatments for depression, anxiety disorders or eating disorders than do patients in general. Consequently, patients with DM1 and one of these other psychiatric disorders should be involved in an appropriate combination of cognitive behavior therapy, pharmacotherapy

inpatient psychiatric treatment or a partial hospitalization program.

Summary

Health psychologists and other behavioral medicine clinicians must be familiar with the types of stressors, coping problems and psychopathology that may affect patients with diabetes, sensitive to evidence that patients are exhibiting these symptoms, skilled in administration and interpretation of appropriate assessment tools and capable of implementing interventions that have been empirically validated for these disorders. Completion of randomized trials of treatment for depression or anxiety disorders in which pharmacotherapy and cognitive behavior therapy are implemented separately and in combination would be especially valuable, particularly in the pediatric age group.

Neuropsychological Sequelae of Diabetes

Substantial research shows that diabetes may have adverse cognitive effects on an acute and chronic basis. Children with early diabetes onset (about 5-7 years of age) are at risk of learning disabilities, although various neuropsychological changes have been reported (Rovet and Fernandes, 1998; Ryan, 1997). Since diabetes duration, frequency of hypoglycemia, frequency of ketoacidosis and chronicity of hyperglycemia are inter-correlated, it has been difficult to confirm that any of these etiological factors is causative. Even mild hypoglycemia leads to acute deterioration in mental acuity. Decreased cognitive function may be the first sign of hypoglycemia for some patients. Deterioration in cognitive function may persist for several days following severe hypoglycemia. Several prospective investigations support the contention that severe hypoglycemia may play an etiologic role in cognitive decline among youth with DM1 (Deary et al., 1992; Golden et al., 1989; Hershey et al., 1999; Hershey et al., 1997;

Northam , 2001; Rovet and Erlich, 1999). Other investigators have reported no such association (Austin and Deary, 1999; Kramer et al., 1997; Reichard et al., 1991; Snoek et al., 1998; Wysocki et al., in press).

To illustrate this controversy further, four studies of the link between severe hypoglycemia and cognitive decline in children with DM1 are considered in greater detail. Each of these studies evaluated children who were tested on two or more occasions over relatively long intervals while the occurrence of severe hypoglycemia was measured. Hershey, Barghava, Sadler, White, and Craft (1999) administered a battery of 18 neuropsychological tests to 16 nondiabetic children, 12 children on conventional DM1 regimens and 13 children on intensive DM1 regimens at diagnosis and again after an average interval of 2.3 years. Intensively treated children had about triple the risk of severe hypoglycemia during the study than conventionally treated children. Although intensively treated children showed deficits in spatial declarative memory and processing speed compared with conventional patients, the paper did not explicitly compare cognitive function among those who did and did not experience severe hypoglycemia after DM1 diagnosis. Rovet and Erlich (1999) evaluated 16 children with DM1 at diagnosis and 1, 3 and 7 years later with the same neuropsychological battery. They reported that the 9 youth who had experienced episodes of severe hypoglycemia that included seizures or loss of consciousness during a 7-year period had significantly lower scores on measures of perceptual, motor, memory and attention tasks than did the 7 youth without a history of such episodes. Cognitive function of the four children with hypoglycemic seizures before age 7 did not differ from those with later episodes. Notably, neither Verbal IQ nor Full Scale IQ were affected by hypoglycemic seizures. Northam, et al. (2001) reported results of a comparison of neuropsychological functioning of 90 children with DM1 and 84 matched healthy controls over the 6 years since the diagnosis of DM1. Among children with DM1, those who had episodes of severe hypoglycemia had significantly lower Verbal IQ and Full Scale IQ scores at the 6-year follow-up. Most recently, Wysocki et al. (2003) reported that neither the presence/absence nor the frequency of severe hypoglycemia experienced by 6 to 15 year old children (n = 142) over an 18-month interval were associated with decline in either global measures of cognitive function or subtest scores on the Das-Naglieri Cognitive Assessment System (Das and Naglieri, 1997). Obviously, severe hypoglycemia should be avoided in all patients with DM1. However, the existing research has not proven conclusively that severe hypoglycemia causes persistent cognitive decline in school-aged children and no studies have carefully explored the sequelae of such episodes in earlier childhood.

Older patients with diabetes may suffer accelerated cognitive declines. Diabetes may, in effect, hasten aging, such that the types of cognitive impairments that have been identified tend to be typical of much older persons (Perlmuter et al., 1984).

Summary

Some patients with diabetes merit evaluation of cognitive functioning. These include those patients who are at risk of diabetes-associated cognitive impairment (younger children, youth diagnosed before age 7, patients with frequent episodes of severe hypoglycemia and the elderly). These same patients warrant special efforts to minimize the frequency of hypoglycemia and of prolonged hyperglycemia. Health psychologists should consider cognitive impairment as a possible factor contributing to ineffective diabetes self-management.

DIABETES RESOURCES FOR BEHAVIORAL MEDICINE CLINICIANS

The following section provides a brief summary of the primary practical implications of this extensive body of research for behavioral medicine clinicians who provide clinical services to patients with type 1 diabetes mellitus. Recommendations are offered with respect to each of the major domains of clinical research surveyed in this chapter.

Similarly, the last section of this chapter lays out some of the crucial research questions that remain to be answered regarding these same issues. Recognizing the limits of existing knowledge is at least as important as being able to identify and deliver those services that have been empirically validated.

Behavioral medicine clinicians who wish to expand or refine their expertise in the assessment and treatment of diabetes-related clinical problems can take advantage of multiple resources. These opportunities include:

- Become a member of the American Diabetes Association and its Council on Behavioral Medicine and Psychology. Attend the annual meetings of the American Diabetes Association and the American Association of Diabetes Educators.
- Subscribe to diabetes-related journals such as Diabetes Care, Diabetes Spectrum, The Diabetes Educator, Diabetic Medicine, Diabetes Self Management or Pediatric Diabetes.
- Read recent books on psychology and diabetes such as Anderson and Rubin (2002), Bradley (1994), Snoek and Skinner (2000), Polonsky (1999) and Wysocki (1997). These books appear in the reference list following this chapter.
- Read the other recent review articles that were cited in the introduction to this chapter.

- Utilize the National Diabetes Information Clearinghouse (http://ndic.nih.gov) to search for diabetes-related information, publications, educational materials and other resources.
- Use other reputable internet websites about diabetes, including diabetes.org (American Diabetes Association) childrenwithdiabetes.com, aade.net (American Association of Diabetes Educators)

SUMMARY OF CLINICAL RECOMMENDATIONS

- Clinicians who see patients with type 1 diabetes mellitus should maintain current familiarity with the extensive clinical research literature that is summarized in this chapter.
- Interventions targeting self-management behaviors such as treatment adherence, diabetes problem solving, blood glucose awareness, patient motivation and empowerment, and therapeutic use of blood glucose data have been researched most extensively. These tools should be part of the therapeutic repertoire of all clinicians working with this population of patients.
- Patients with diabetes have a heightened need for effective stress management since stress can impede diabetic control and since they face an inordinate risk of depression, anxiety disorders and eating disorders. Clinicians should therefore be prepared to offer effective stress management interventions and to detect and treat these types of psychopathology that are common in this population.
- Patients with diabetes face an increased risk of neuropsychological and cognitive impairments, although the etiology of these problems remains to be specified conclusively. Nonetheless, clinicians should be alert to this possibility, be prepared to administer and interpret

appropriate test batteries for the detection of these disorders and recognize that cognitive impairments may limit the effectiveness of behavioral or psychoeducational interventions.

REMAINING RESEARCH QUESTIONS

- What intervention components are critical to maximizing the likelihood that changes in self-management behaviors will be translated into improvements in diabetic control? How can health care policy be influenced in order to support the incorporation of such practices into routine diabetes care?
- What strategies can be used to prevent or minimize the effects of depression, anxiety disorders, and eating disorders in this population?
- Under what specific conditions do certain people experience cognitive impairments secondary to diabetes? Are these impairments clinically significant and do they interfere with diabetes self-management?

REFERENCES

Affenito G, Backstran, JR, Welch GW, Lammi-Keefe CF. (1997) Subclinical and clinical eating disorders in IDDM negatively affect metabolic control. Diabetes Care 20: 182-184.

Aikens J, Wallander J, Bell D, Cole J. (1992) Daily stress variability, learned Resourcefulness, regimen adherence and metabolic control in Type 1 diabetes mellitus: Evaluation of a path model. J Consult Clin Psychol 60: 113-118.

Allen DA, Tennen H, McGrade BJ, Affleck G, Ratzan S. (1983) Parent and child perceptions of the mangement of juvenile diabetes. J Pediatr Psychol 8: 29-41.

Anderson BJ. (1996) Involving family members in diabetes treatment. Practical psychology for diabetes clinicians. (Anderson BJ, Rubin RR eds.) pp. 43-52.

Alexandria VA: American Diabetes Association.

Anderson BJ, Auslander WF, Jung KC, Miller JP, Santiago JV. (1990) Assessing family sharing of diabetes responsibilities. J Pediatr Psychol 15: 477-492.

Anderson BJ, Brackett J, Ho J, Laffel L. (1999) An office-based intervention to maintain parent-adolescent teamwork in diabetes management: impact on parent involvement, family conflict, and subsequent glycemic control. Diabetes Care 22: 713-721.

Anderson BJ, Ho J, Brackett J, Finkelstein D, Laffel L. (1997). Parental involvement in diabetes management tasks: relationships to blood glucose monitoring adherence and metabolic control in young adolescents with insulin-dependent diabetes mellitus. J Pediatr 130 257-265.

Anderson BJ, Rubin R. (1996) Practical psychology for diabetes clinicians. Alexandria, VA: American Diabetes Association.

Anderson BJ, Rubin R. (2002). Practical psychology for diabetes clinicians (2nd edition). Alexandria, VA: American Diabetes Association.

Anderson BJ, Wolf FM., Burkhart MT, Cornell RG, Bacon GE. (1989) Effects of peer-group intervention on metabolic control of adolescents with IDDM: Randomized outpatient study. Diabetes Care 12: 179-183.

Anderson RM, Funnell MM, Arnold MS. (1996) Using the patient empowerment approach to help patients change behavior. In: Practical psychology for diabetes clinicians. (Anderson BJ, Rubin RR, eds.) pp. 163-172. Alexandria VA: American Diabetes Association,.

Anderson RM, Funnell MM, Butler P, Arnold MS, Fitzgerald JT, Feste C. (1995) Patient empowerment: Results of a randomized, controlled trial. Diabetes Care 18: 943-949.

Austin EJ, Deary IJ. (1999) Effects of repeated hypoglycemia on cognitive function: A psychometrically validated reanalysis of the Diabetes Control and Complications Trial data. Diabetes Care 22: 1273-1277.

Boardway RH, Delamater AM, Tomakowsky J, Gutai JP. (1993) Stress management training for adolescents with diabetes. J Pediatr Psychol 18: 29-45.

Bobrow ES, AvRuskin TW, Siller J. (1985) Mother-daughter interaction and adherence to diabetes regimens. Diabetes Care 8: 146-151

Bradley C. (1994) Handbook of psychology and diabetes. Amsterdam: Harwood Academic Publishers.

Bryden KS, Peveler RC, Stein A, Neil A, Mayou R., Dunger DB. (2001) Clinical and psychological course of diabetes from adolescence to young adulthood: a longitudinal cohort study. Diabetes Care 24: 1536-1540.

Carney RM, Schechter K, Davis T. (1983) Improving adherence to blood glucose testing in insulin-dependent diabetic children. Behav Therapy 14: 247-254.

Chase HP, Jackson G. (1981) Stress and sugar control in children with insulin-dependent diabetes mellitus. J Pediatr 98: 1011-1013.

Clement S. (1995). Diabetes self-management education. Diabetes Care 18: 1204-1214.

Cox DJ, Clarke WL, Gonder-Frederick LA. (1985). Accuracy of perceiving blood glucose in IDDM. Diabetes Care 8: 529-536.

Cox DJ, Gonder-Frederick LA. (1992) Major developments in behavioral diabetes research. J Consult Clin Psychol 60: 628-638.

Cox DJ, Gonder-Frederick LA, Julian DM, Clarke WL. (1994) Long-term follow-up evaluation of blood glucose awareness training. Diabetes Care 17: (1), 1-5.

Cox DJ, Gonder-Frederick, LA, Polonsky W, Schlundt D, Julian D, Clarke WL. (1995) A multicenter evaluation of blood glucose awareness training. Diabetes Care 18: 523-528.

Cox DJ, Gonder-Frederick LA, Polonsky WH, Schlundt DG, Kovatchev B, Clarke WL. (2001) Effects and correlates of blood glucose awareness training (BGAT-II): Long-term benefits. Diabetes Care 24: 637-642.

Daneman D, Olmsted M, Rydall A, Maharaj S, Rodin G. (1998) Eating disorders in young women with type 1 diabetes: Prevalence, problems and prevention. Horm Res 50: 79-86.

DCCT Research Group. (1993) Diabetes Control and Complications Trial: The effect of intensive treatment of diabetes on the development and progression of long-term complications in insulin-dependent diabetes mellitus. N Engl J Med 329: 977-986.

DCCT Research Group. (1996) Lifetime benefits and costs of intensive therapy as practiced in the Diabetes Control and Complications Trial. JAMA 276: 1409-1415.

Deary IJ, Langan SJ, Graham KS, Hepburn D. (1992) Recurrent severe hypoglycemia, intelligence, and speed of information processing. Intelligence 16: 337-359.

Delamater A.M, Bubb J, Davis SG, Smith JA, Schmidt L, White NH, Santiago JV. (1990) Randomized prospective study of self management training with newly diagnosed diabetic children. Diabetes Care 13: 492-498.

Delamater AM, Jacobson AM, Anderson BJ, Cox DJ, Fisher L, Lustman P, Rubin R, Wysocki T. (2001) Psychosocial therapies in diabetes: Report of the Psychosocial therapies working group. Diabetes Care 24: 1286-1292.

Delamater AM, Kurtz SM, Bubb J, White NH, Santiago JV. (1987) Stress and coping in relation to metabolic control of adolescents with type 1 diabetes. J Dev Behav Pediatr 8: 136-140.

Delamater AM, Smith JA, Kurtz SC., White NH. (1988) Dietary skills and adherence in children with Type I diabetes mellitus. The Diabetes Educator 14: 33-36.

Delamater AM, Davis SG, Bubb J, Smith JA, White NH, Santiago JV. (1989) Self monitoring of blood glucose by adolescents with diabetes: Technical skills and utilization of data. The Diabetes Educator 15: 56-61.

Epstein LH, Beck S, Figueroa J, Farkas G, Kazdin AE, Daneman D, Becker DJ. (1981) The effects of targeting improvement in urine glucoe on metabolic control in children with insulin-dependent diabetes mellitus. J Appl Behav Anal 14: 365-375.

Feinglos MN, Hastedt P, Surwit RS. (1987) Effects of relaxation therapy on patients with type 1 diabetes mellitus. Diabetes Care 10: 72-75.

Fosbury JA, Bosley CM, Ryle A, Sonksen PH, Judd SL. (1997) A trial of cognitive analytic therapy in poorly controlled type 1 patients. Diabetes Care 20: 959-964.

Fowler JE, Budzynski TH, Vandenbergh RL. (1978) Effects of an EMG biofeedback relaxation program on the control of diabetes. Biofeedback and Self-Regulation 1: 105-112.

Frenzel MP, McCaul KD, Glasgow RE, Schafer LC. (1988) The relationship of stress and coping to regimen adherence and glycemic control of diabetes. J Soc Clin Psychol 6: 77-87.

Glasgow RE, Chance P, Toobert DJ, Brown J, Hampson SE, Riddle MC. (1997) Long term effects and costs of brief behavioral dietary intervention for patients with diabetes delivered from the medical office. Patient Education and Counseling 32: 175-184.

Glasgow RE, Fischer EB, Anderson BJ, La Greca AM, Johnson SB, Rubin R, Cox DJ. (1999) Behavioral science in diabetes: Contributions and opportunities. Diabetes Care 22: 832-843.

Glasgow RE, Hiss RG, Anderson RM, Friedman NM, Hayward RA, Marrero DG, Taylor CB, Vinicor F. (2001) Report of the health care delivery work group: Behavioral research related to the establishment of a chronic disease model for diabetes care. Diabetes Care 24: 124-130.

Glasgow RE, McCaul KD, Schaefer LC. (1987) Self care behaviors and glycemic control in Type I diabetes. J Chronic Diseases 40: 399-412.

Glasgow RE, Toobert DJ. (2000) Brief, computer-assisted diabetes dietary self management counseling: effects on behavior, physiologic outcomes and quality of life. Med Care 38: 1059-1061.

Golden M, Ingersoll GM, Brack CJ, Russell BA, Wirht JC, Huberty TJ. (1989) Longitudinal relationship of asymptomatic hypoglycemia to cognitive function in type 1 diabetes. Diabetes Care 12: 89-93.

Gonder-Frederick LA, Carter W, Cox DJ, Clarke WL. (1990) Environmental stress and blood glucose change in insulin-dependent diabetes mellitus. Health Psychol 9: 503-515.

Gonder-Frederick LA, Cox DJ. (2002) Diabetes and behavioral medicine: The second decade. J Consult Clin Psychol 70: 611-625.

Gonder-Frederick, L.A., Cox DJ, Kovatchev B, Schlundt D, Clarke WL. (1997) A biopsychobehavioral model of risk of severe hypoglycemia. Diabetes Care 20: 661-669.

Greco P, Shroff-Pendley J, McDonell K. (2001) A peer group intervention for adolescents with type 1 diabetes and their friends. J Pediatr Psychol 26: 485-490.

Grey M, Boland E, Davidson M, Li J, Tamborlane WV. (2000) Coping skills training for youth on intensive therapy ahs long-lasting effects on metabolic control and quality of life. J Pediatr 137: 107-113.

Gross A, Heimann L, Shapiro R, Schultz RM. (1983) Children with diabetes: Social skills training and HbA$_{1C}$ levels. Behav Modif 7: 151-163.

Gross AM, Magalnick LJ, Richardson P. (1985) Self-management training with families of insulin-dependent diabetic chidlren: Controlled long-term investigation. Child and Family Behavior Therapy 7: 35-50.

Gustafsson P, Cederblad M, Ludvigsson J, Lundin B. (1987) Family interaction and metabolic balance in juvenile diabetes mellitus: A prospective study. Diabetes Res Clin Pract 4: 7-14.

Halford WK, Cuddihy S, Mortimer RH. (1990) Psychological stress and blood glucose regulation in type 1 diabetic patients. Health Psychol 9: 516-528.

Hampson SE, Skinner TC, Hart J, Storey L, Gage H, Foxcroft D, Kimber A, Cradock S, McEvilly EA. (2000) Behavioral interventions for adolescents with type 1 diabetes: How effective are they? Diabetes Care 23: 1416-1422.

Hampson SE, Skinner TC, Hart J, Storey L, Gage H, Foxcroft D, Kimber A, Shaw K, Walker J. (2001) Effects of educational and psychological interventions for adolescents with diabetes mellitus: A systematic review. Health Technol Assess 5: 1-77.

Hanson CL, De Guire MJ, Schinkel AM, Kolterman OG. (1995) Empirical validation of a family-centered model of care. Diabetes Care 18: 1347-1356.

Hanson CL, Henggeler SW, Burghen GA. (1987) Social competence and parental support as mediators of the link between stress and metabolic control in adolescents with insulin-dependent diabetes mellitus. J Consult Clin Psychol 55: 529-533.

Hanson S, Pichert J. (1986) Perceived stress and diabetic control in adolescents. Health Psychol 5: 439-452.

Hauser ST, Jacobson AM, Lavori P, Wolfsdorf JI, Herskowitz RD, Milley JE, Wertlieb D. (1990) Adherence among children and adolescents with insulin-dependent diabetes mellitus over a four year follow-up. II: Immediate and long term linkages with the family milieu. J Pediatr Psychol 15: 527-542.

Hershey T, Bhargava N, Sadler M, White NH, Craft S. (1999) Conventional versus Intensive diabetes therapy in children with type 1 diabetes: Effects on memory and motor speed. Diabetes Care 22: 1318-1324.

Hershey T, Craft S, Bhargava N,White NH. (1997) Memory and insulin-dependent diabetes: Effects of childhood onset and severe hypoglycemia. J Int Neuropsychol Soc 3: 509-520.

Ingersoll G, Orr DP, Herrold AJ, Golden MP. (1986) Cognitive maturity and self-management among adolescents with insulin-dependent diabetes mellitus. J Pediatr 108: 620-623.

Johnson SB. (1995) Insulin-dependent diabetes mellitus in childhood. In: Handbook of pediatric psychology (2nd Edition). (Roberts MC, ed.) pp 286-309. New York: Guilford Press.

Johnson SB, Freund A, Silverstein JH, Hansen CA,Malone JI. (1990) Adherence-health status relationships in childhood diabetes. Health Psychol 9: 606-631.

Johnson SB, Pollak J, Silverstein J, Rosenbloom A, Spillar R, McCallum M, Harkavy J. (1982) Cognitive and behavioral knowledge about insulin-dependent diabetes among children and parents. J Pediatr 69: 708-713.

Johnson SB, Silverstein JH, Rosenbloom A, Carter R, Cunningham W. (1986) Assessing daily management of childhood diabetes. Health Psychol 5: 545-564.

Kaplan RM, Chadwick MW, Schimmel LE. (1985) Social learning intervention to improve metabolic control in Type 1 diabetes mellitus: Pilot experiment results. Diabetes Care 8: 152-155.

Koski M, Ahlas A, Kumento A. (1976) A psychosomatic follow-up study of juvenile diabetics. Acta Paedopsychiatrica 42: 12-25.

Kovacs M, Goldston D, Obrosky DS, Bonar LK. (1997) Psychiatric disorders in youths with IDDM: Rates and risk factors. Diabetes Care 20: 36-44.

Kovacs M, Murkerji P, Iyengar, S, Drash A. (1996) Psychiatric disorder and metabolic control among youths with IDDM: A longitudinal study. Diabetes Care 19: 318-323.

Kramer L, Fasching P, Madl C, Schneider B, Damjancic P, Waldhausl W,

Irsigler K, Grimm G. (1997) Previous episodes of hypoglycemic coma are not associated with permanent brain dysfunction in IDDM patients on intensive insulin treatment. Diabetes 47: 1909-1914.

La Greca AM, Auslander WF, Greco P, Spetter D, Fisher EB, Santiago JV. (1995) I get by with a little help from my friends: Adolescents' support for diabetes care. J Pediatr Psychol 20: 449-476.

La Greca AM, Follansbee DM, Skyler JS. (1990) Developmental and behavioral aspects of diabetes management in youngsters. Children's Health Care 19: 132-139.

Lorenz RA, Wysocki T. (1991) From research to practice: The family and childhood diabetes. Diabetes Spectrum, 4, 260-292.

Lowe K., Lutzker JR. (1979) Increasing compliance to a medical regimen with a juvenile diabetic. Behavior Therapy 10: 57-64.

Lustman P. (1988) Anxiety disorders in adults with diabetes mellitus. Psychiat Clin North Am 11: 419-432.

Lustman P, Anderson R, Freedland K, DeGroot M, Carney RM, Clouse R. (2000) Depression and poor glycemic control: a meta-analytic review of the literature. Diabetes Care 23: 934-942.

Lustman P, Clouse RE, Freedland KE. (1998) Management of major depression in adults with diabetes: Implications of recent clinical trials. Semin Clin Neurospychiatry 2: 15-23.

Lustman PJ, Freedland KE, Griffith LS, Clouse RE. (2000) Fluoxetine for depression in diabetes: a randomized, double-blind, placebo-controlled trial. Diabetes Care 23: 618-623.

Lustman P, Griffith LS, Clouse RE. (1996). Recognizing and managing depression in patients with diabetes. In Practical psychology for diabetes clinicians. (B.J. Anderson BJ; Rubin RR, eds.), pp. 143-152. Alexandria VA: American Diabetes Association.

Lustman PJ, Griffith LS, Clouse RE, Freedland KE, Eisen SA, Rubin EH, Carney RM, McGill JB. (1995) Effects of alprazolam on glucose regulation in diabetes. Results of a double-blind, placebo-controlled trial. Diabetes Care 18: 1133-1139.

Lustman PJ, Griffith LS, Clouse RE, Freedland KE, Eisen SA, Rubin EH, Carney RM, McGill JB. (1997) Effect of nortriptyilne on depression and glycemic control in diabetes: results of a double-blind, placebo-controlled trial. Psychosom Med 59: 241-250.

Lustman PJ, Griffith LS, Gavard JA, Clouse RE. (1992) Depression in adults with diabetes. Diabetes Care 15: 1631-1639.

Marteau TM, Bloch S, Baum JD. (1987) Family life and diabetic control. Journal of Child Psychol Psychiatry 28: 823-833.

Matam P, Kumaraiah V, Munichoodappa C, Kumar KM, Aravind S. (2000). Behavioural intervention in the management of compliance in young type

1 diabetics. J Association Physicians India 48: 967-971.

McGrady A, Bailey BK, Good MP. (1991) Controlled study of biofeedback-assisted relaxation in type 1 diabetes. Diabetes Care 14: 360-365.

McNabb W, Quinn M, Murphy D, Thorp F, Cook S. (1994) Increasing children's responsibility for self-care: The in-control study. The Diabetes Educator 20: 121-124.

Mendez F, Belendez M. (1997) Effects of a behavioral intervention on treatment adherence and stress management. Diabetes Care 20: 1370-1375.

Miller-Johnson S, Emery RE, Marvin RS, Clarke W, Lovinger R, Martin M. (1994) Parent-child relationships and the management of insulin-dependent diabetes mellitus. J Consult Clin Psychol 62: 603-610.

National Diabetes Data Group. (1995) Diabetes in America (2nd Edition). Bethesda, MD: National Institutes of Health and National Institutes of Diabetes, Digestive and Kidney Diseases. NIH Publication # 95-1468.

Northam EA, Anderson PJ, Jacobs R, Hughes M, Warne GL, Werther GA. (2001) Neuropsychological profiles of children with type 1 diabetes 6 years after disease onset. Diabetes Care 24: 1541-1546.

Nurick M, Johnson SB. (1991) Enhancing blood glucose awareness in adolescents and young adults with IDDM. Diabetes Care 14: 1-7.

Perlmuter LC, Hakami MK, Hodgson-Harrington C, Gingsberg J, Katz J, Singer DE, Nathan, DM. (1984) Decreased cognitive function in aging, non-insulin dependent diabetic patients. Am J Med 77: 1043-1048.

Peveler RC, Fairburn CG. (1989) Anorexia nervosa in association with diabetes mellitus - a cognitive behavioral approach. Behav Res Ther 27: 95-99.

Peyrot M, Rubin RR. (1988) Insulin self-regulation predicts better glycemic control. Diabetes 37: 53A.

Peyrot M, Rubin RR. (1997) Levels and risks of depression and anxiety symptomatology among diabetic adults. Diabetes Care 20: 585-590.

Polonsky WH. (1999) Diabetes burnout. Alexandria, Virginia: American Diabetes Association.

Reichard P, Britz RP, Rosenqvist U. (1991) Intensified conventional insulin treatment and neuropsychological impairment. BMJ 303: 1439-1442.

Robin AL, Foster SL. (1989) Negotiating parent-adolescent conflict: a behavioral family systems approach. New York: Guilford Press.

Rodin GM, Daneman D. (1992) Eating disorders and IDDM: A problematic association. Diabetes Care 15: 1402-1412.

Rose MI, Firestone P, Heick HMC, Faught AK. (1983) The effect of anxiety management training on the control of juvenile diabetes. J Behav Med 6: 381-395.

Rovet F, Alvarez M. (1997) Attentional functioning in children and adolescents with IDDM. Diabetes Care 20: 803-810.

Rovet JF, Ehrlich RM. (1999) The effect of hypoglycemic seizures on cognitive function in children with diabetes: A 7-year prospective study. J Pediatr 134: 503-506.

Rovet J, Fernandes C. (1998) Insulin-dependent diabetes mellitus. In Cognitive aspects of chronic illness in children. (Brown RT, ed). pp. 142-171. New York: Guilford Press.

Rubin RR, Peyrot M. (1989) Effect of diabetes education on self care, metabolic control and emotional well-being. Diabetes Care 12: 673-679.

Rubin RR, Peyrot M. (2001) Psychological issues and treatments for people with diabetes. J Clin Psychol 57: 457-478.

Rubin RR, Peyrot M, Saudek CD. (1993) The effect of a comprehensive diabetes education program incorporating coping skills training on emotional well-being and diabetes self-efficacy. The Diabetes Educator 19: 210-214.

Ryan CM. (1997) Effects of diabetes mellitus on neuropsychological function: A lifespan perspective. Sem Clin Neuropsychiatry 2: 4-14.

Ryden O, Nevander L, Johnsson P, Hansson K, Krovvall P, Sjoblad S, Westbom L. (1994) Family therapy in poorly controlled juvenile IDDM: effects on diabetic control, self-evaluation and behavioral symptoms. Acta Paediatrica 83: 285-291.

Satin W, La Greca AM, Zigo M, Skyler JS. (1989) Diabetes in adolescence: Effects of multifamily support group intervention and parent simulation of diabetes. J Pediatr Psychol 14: 259-275.

Schafer LC, Glasgow RE, McCaul KD. (1982) Increasing the adherence of diabetic adolescents. J Behav Med 5: 353-362.

Snoek FJ, Skinner TC. (2000) Psychology in diabetes care. London: Wiley Inc.

Snoek FJ, van der Veer N, Heine RJ, de Haan EH. (1998) No differences in attentional functioning between type 1 diabetic patients with and without a history of severe hypoglycemia. Diabetes Care 21: 1568-69.

Snoek FJ, van der Ven NC, Lubach CH, Ader HJ, Heine RJ, Jacobson AM. (2001) Effects of cognitive behavioural group training (CBGT) in adult patients with poorly controlled insulin-dependent (type 1) diabetes: a pilot study. Patient Education and Counseling 45: 143-148.

Surwit R, Schneider M, Feinglos M. (1992) Stress and diabetes mellitus. Diabetes Care 15: 1413-1422.

Surwit RS, van Tilburg MA, Zucker N, McCaskill CC., Parekh P, Feinglos MN,

Edwards CL, Lane JD. (2002) Stress management improves long-term glycemic control in type 2 diabetes. Diabetes Care 25: 30-34.

UK Prospective Diabetes Study (UKPDS) Group. (1998) Intensive blood glucose control with sulphonylureas or insulin compared with conventional treatment and risk of complications in patients with Type 2 diabetes (UKPDS 33). Lancet 352: 837-853.

Weissberg-Benchell J, Glasgow AM, Tynan WD, Wirtz P, Turek J, Ward J. (1995) Adolescent diabetes management and mismanagement. Diabetes Care 18: 77-82.

Williams GC, Freedman ZR, Deci EL. (1998) Supporting autonomy to motivate glucose control in patients with diabetes. Diabetes Care 21: 1644-1651.

Wing RR, Goldstein MG, Acton KJ, Birch L, Jakicic JM, Sallis JF, Smith-West D, Jeffrey RW, Surwit RS. (2001) Behavioral science research in diabetes: Lifestyle change related to obesity, eating behavior and physical activity. Diabetes Care 24: 117-123.

Wysocki T. (1993) Associations among teen-parent relationships, metabolic control and adjustment to diabetes in adolescents. J Pediatr Psychol 18: 443-454.

Wysocki T. (1997) The ten keys to helping your child grow up with diabetes. Alexandria, VA: American Diabetes Association.

Wysocki T. (in press). Behavioral assessment and intervention in pediatric diabetes. Behav Modif.

Wysocki T, Greco P, Harris MA, Harvey LM, Danda CE, White NH. (2001) Behavior Therapy for families of adolescents with IDDM: Maintenance of treatment effects. Diabetes Care 24.

Wysocki T, Green LB, Huxtable K. (1989) Blood glucose monitoring by diabetic adolescents: Compliance and metabolic control. Health Psychol 8: 267-284.

Wysocki T, Harris MA, Greco P, Bubb J, Danda CE, Harvey LM, White NH. (2000) Randomized controlled trial of behavior therapy for families of adolescents with IDDM. J Pediatr Psychol 25: 22-33.

Wysocki T, Harris MA, Greco P, Harvey LM, McDOnell K, Danda CE, Bubb J, White NH. (1997) Social validity of support group and behavior therapy interventions for families of adolescents with insulin-dependent diabetes mellitus. J Pediatr Psychol 22: 635-650.

Wysocki T, Harris MA, Mauras N, Fox LA, Taylor A, Jackson SC, White NH. (2003) Absence of adverse effects of severe hypoglycemia on cognitive function in school-aged children with diabetes mellitus over 18 months. Diabetes Care 26: 1100-1105.

Wysocki T, Hough BS, Ward KM, Allen A, Murgai N. (1992) Use of blood glucose data by families of children and adolescents with IDDM. Diabetes Care 15: 1041-1044.

Wysocki T, Miller KM, Harvey LM, Taylor A, Elder-Danda C, McDonell K, Greco P, Harris MA, White NH. (2000) Behavior therapy for families of adolescents with diabetes: Effects on directly observed family interactions. Behav Ther 30: 507-525.

Wysocki T, Taylor A, Hough B, Linscheid TR, Yeates KO, Naglieri JA. (1996a) Deviation from developmentally appropriate self care autonomy: Association with diabetes outcomes. Diabetes Care 19: 119-125.

Wysocki T, Taylor A, Meinhold PA, Barnard MU, Clarke WL, Bellando BJ, Bourgeois MJ. (1996b) Normative data for the Diabetes Independence Survey – Parent Version. The Diabetes Educator 22: 587-591.

BEHAVIORAL SELF-MANAGEMENT OF TYPE 2 DIABETES: KEY ISSUES, EVIDENCE-BASED RECOMMENDATIONS AND FUTURE DIRECTIONS

Diane K. King and Russell E. Glasgow

If we are neither cured when we are ill nor well cared for when we are disabled, what is the role of medicine in which so much has been invested, in hope and resources? (McKeown, 1979)

As the U.S. population ages, human health needs take on a different emphasis. Many, if not most, of the acute ailments associated with childhood or with inadequate sanitation have been conquered and are now overshadowed by ailments associated with increased age and/or affluence, i.e., heart disease, hypertension, cancer, diabetes, arthritis, and Alzheimer's disease (McKeown, 1979; Brownson et al., 1998). Even infectious diseases that were recently considered acute, mortal ailments, such as HIV/AIDS, are no longer considered an automatic death sentence, but can be "managed" as chronic conditions that require lifelong attention. Western medicine's role is evolving from "cure" to "chronic care," which brings new challenges, as patients struggle to adhere to lifelong regimens with varying degrees of impact on their activities of daily life.

Diabetes serves as a model for chronic illness management as research continues to show the benefits of a lifestyle or "self-management" approach. The term "self-management" refers to the daily decisions and behaviors that patients make to manage their chronic illness. Self-management is especially critical for persons with diabetes and the terminology has been adopted by the American Diabetes Association as well as other diabetes organizations (American Diabetes Association, 1995; Glasgow and Anderson, 1999). The role of the health care provider is to provide self-management

support to the patient, as explained below. With approximately seventeen million Americans affected (American Diabetes Association, 2001; Centers for Disease Control and Prevention, 2002; National Institute of Diabetes, 2000), including an estimated 5.9 million that live with the disease but are not diagnosed, effective interventions that can be readily adopted into the patient's lifestyle are critical. At present, most clinical interventions focus on patient education that promotes adherence to a healthy diet, regular moderate physical activity, medication adherence, blood glucose testing, and quarterly medical surveillance; changes that impact major components of human daily life (American Diabetes Association, 2001; DQIP, 2002; Clement, 1995). Many of these approaches consist of a class or written materials that may not resonate with the patient's unique lifestyle, family demands, work setting, physical health, culture, or values. Thus, long-term adherence is often not accomplished using traditional didactic patient education techniques alone (Glasgow and Anderson, 1999; Piette and Glasgow, 2001; Clement, 1995; Brown, 1992). Consequently, diabetes remains the seventh leading cause of death in this country and is a major contributor to serious health problems such as heart disease, stroke, blindness, hypertension, kidney disease, and amputations (Centers for Disease Control and Prevention, 2002). Estimates of direct and indirect costs related to diabetes range from $57 to $98 billion dollars, due to medical costs, complications and loss of productivity (American Diabetes Association, 1998; DQIP, 2002; National Institute of Diabetes, 2000). Thus, while many of the complications associated with diabetes can be prevented or reduced with moderate changes in lifestyle behaviors, lifelong adoption of these regimens is the larger challenge.

In light of the increased concern about the growing prevalence of diabetes, a number of excellent evidence-based reviews of behavior-based clinical trials have been conducted (Boule et al, 2002; Clement, 1995; Glasgow and Eakin, 2000; Gonder-Frederick et al., 2002; Norris et al, 2002a; Norris et al, 2002b; Piette and Glasgow, 2001; Renders et al., 2001). This chapter will discuss their conclusions and highlight the findings of four exemplary studies that focus on self-management interventions for people living with type 2 diabetes. Barriers to sustaining lifelong behavior change will be discussed, as well as outcomes-based recommendations for clinical practice and directions for future study.

SELF-MANAGEMENT AND THE CHRONIC CARE MODEL

. . . the body is one possession that cannot be left under the care of the server while the client goes about his other business. (Goffman, 1961)

Evidence from the Diabetes Control and Complications Trial (DCCT Research Group, 1993) promoted the benefits of patient adherence to a strict treatment regimen in order to achieve tight metabolic control. However, patients' ability to stick to inflexible lifelong regimens and a physician's ability to provide the level of surveillance and support required for patients to achieve these goals is a difficult and impractical proposition (Gonder-Frederick et al., 2002). As an increasing number of individuals live with ailments for which there are no cure, only care, the role of health care must shift from one of absolute authority of the physician over the patient to shared authority and decision-making. Patients with diabetes and

other chronic conditions need to be equipped to make informed choices with regard to managing their disease 24 hours a day for the rest of their lives (Frosch and Kaplan, 1999). To address these changes, Wagner, et al. (Wagner et al., 1996) developed a multi-dimensional model for effective chronic illness care (Wagner, 2000) that incorporates major tenets of the social-ecological perspective. The social-ecological perspective purports that there are multiple domains that influence health behavior and that these various dimensions may also interact with each other to directly or indirectly influence individual behaviors (Brown, 1999; Sallis and Owen, 1996). Thus, multi-level, multi-dimensional approaches may be needed to maximize the success of health behavior interventions. Four key domains of focus within the Chronic Care Model include communities, health care organizations, practice teams and patients. These domains exist within an *environment* in which patients live, work and manage their diabetes, and thus represent venues where resources for health support should be placed. For example, community resources that would benefit individuals living with a chronic disease would include information on local health resources as well as structural elements to promote healthful lifestyles, such as grocery stores with fresh fruits and vegetables or safe, well-lighted walking paths. *Health systems* could better support chronic care by providing reimbursement for patient self-management education, and developing and disseminating information on practice guidelines for chronic disease. *Practice teams* could support chronic illness care by delivering effective self-management interventions that promote patient autonomy and empowerment, delegating patient care management to mid-level practitioners, following evidence-based guidelines and protocols, and establishing registries to allow for follow-up with patients to assure their ongoing medical needs are met.

Patients could become better managers of their own health if they were equipped with information, skills and strategies to allow them to integrate management of their chronic condition into their daily routines and lifestyles. The Chronic Care Model recommends the adoption of evidence-based interventions within each of these arenas (Glasgow et al., 2002; Wagner et al., 2001) (Figure 1).

Figure 1. Chronic Care Model

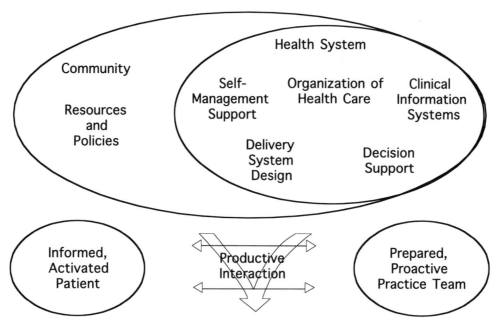

www.improvingchroniccare.org

While communities, health care organizations, practice teams and patients all play an important role in assuring effective chronic care, the key to successful chronic disease management lies with the patient. That is not to say that chronically ill patients should shoulder the blame for lack of adherence to recommended health activities or behavior change. What it is saying is that patients need to be equipped and supported in their efforts to manage their illness, and that the role of health care should evolve to meet this need. To accomplish these goals, a variety of "disease management" programs have been developed for use in primary care. The problem with many of these programs is they are often separate, short–term programs that are not integrated into daily practice, thus may risk being seen as "flavor of the month" type interventions that are soon forgotten. In addition, many such programs are targeted towards one specific chronic illness as opposed to providing a means for improving health practices across a broad range of chronic conditions. Such broad applicability of self-care practices is extremely important, particularly for older adults who may be living with multiple chronic conditions (Glasgow et al., 2002; Piette et al., 2001).

The self-management model proposed by Glasgow and colleagues. (Glasgow et al., 2002) is congruent with an effective methodology that was developed by the National Cancer Institute to guide physicians in counseling their patients to quit smoking (Glynn and Manley, 1989), now called the Five A's: assess, advise, agree, assist, arrange (Whitlock et al., 2002). Each "A" corresponds to a brief behavioral intervention that together has been shown to be effective in smoking cessation in particular. The 5 A's are now included as part of the Public Health Service Clinical Practice Guideline (Fiore, et al., 2000; Morgan and Fox, 2000). The self-management model is analogous to the Five A's model, with each "A" corresponding to a key step (see *Figure 2)*. Although this model has worked well in facilitating various health care professionals to understand and improve their self-management support offered to diabetes patients (Glasgow et al, 2002; Glasgow et al, 2003), it has not been explicitly tested in diabetes. It is included as a heuristic to convey in a meaningful, and easy-to-remember way, the various behavior change strategies that have individually been found to be effective.

Figure 2.

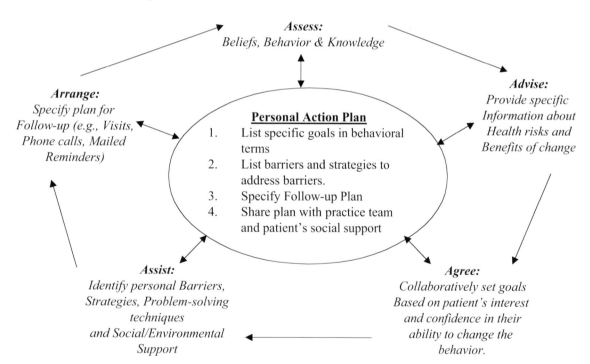

Self-Management Model with 5 A's (Glasgow, et al, 2002; Whitlock, et al, 2002)

In addition, the self-management model integrates concepts from Lorig, et al. (Lorig et al., 1999) on self-management education and from Anderson, et al. (Anderson et al., 1995) on patient empowerment. The model differs from stand alone, one-size-fits-all patient education programs in several key ways. First, it illustrates key activities or principles, rather than a specific instrument, procedure or method of intervention. Thus, these principles should apply across practices, but the specific way in which they are implemented should vary across office settings. Second, the model promotes collaborative goal setting, and identification of specific behaviors to be adopted or changed. It emphasizes that patients are responsible for making choices that affect their health with regard to diet, physical activity, monitoring, and medications. Third, successful self-management programs use standardized patient assessment tools to determine patients' level of knowledge, skills and performance with regard to the behaviors necessary to manage their condition, and also provide a mechanism for determining patients' level of confidence or self-efficacy. Such programs encourage patients to identify barriers to accomplishing their goals as well as strategies for avoiding or overcoming barriers, and follow-up support to maintain long-term adoption of these health behaviors. Fourth, the model is an iterative, life-long collaborative process of change focused on integration into patients' lives. Fifth, the model is designed for integration into the overall health care system design and practice philosophy, as opposed to being an isolated activity that is divorced from primary care (such as a one-time referral for "patient education"). The role of healthcare, therefore, is one of educating, empowering, and providing patients with realistic options for managing their health, as well as providing emotional support and encouraging continuous surveillance of their illness with regular diabetes office visits that incorporate tests and procedures in concordance with the most recent medical guidelines for diabetes care.

CONCLUSIONS FROM STUDY REVIEWS

A number of excellent evidence-based reviews of behavior-based clinical trials have been conducted of diabetes self-management education and behavioral interventions. What follows is a brief discussion of the conclusions drawn from the evidence presented. Since diabetes is a multi-faceted chronic condition that impacts not only the physical, but also the psychological, emotional, social and spiritual domains of an individual's life (Anderson et al., 1995; Gonder-Frederick et al., 2002), the reviews discussed include studies that represent a broad range of outcome variables, specifically, glycemic control where regulating blood glucose levels was a primary goal, with "tight" control typically corresponding to an index measure, such as a glycated hemoglobin test that is less than 8% (Clement, 1995; Boule et al., 2002; Norris et al., 2002a; Norris et al., 2002b; Glasgow et al., 2000), lipid levels (Norris et al., 2002a; Norris et al., 2002b; Glasgow et al., 2000), foot ulcers and amputations (Clement, 1995; Norris et al., 2002a; Norris et al., 2002b; Glasgow et al., 2000), lifestyle health behaviors including healthy eating practices, regular physical activity and smoking cessation (Clement, 1995; Norris et al., 2002a; Norris et al., 2002b; Glasgow et al., 2000; Gonder-Frederick et al., 2002), insulin self-adjustment (Clement, 1995), healthcare utilization for diabetes-related problems, reduction in diabetes-related healthcare costs (Clement, 1995; Norris et al., 2002a; Norris et al., 2002b), body mass (Boule et al., 2002; Norris et al., 2002a; Norris et al., 2002b), patient knowledge and self-efficacy, patient perceived quality of life (Norris et al., 2002a; Norris et al., 2002b; Glasgow et al., 2000;

Gonder-Frederick et al., 2002), and health care professionals' delivery of care (Renders et al., 2001). These are just some of the many outcome variables investigated. Studies included in these reviews have focused primarily on the patient and consist of clinical trials to evaluate the effectiveness of diabetes self-management education programs and targeted behavioral programs for specific patient behaviors such as foot care, nutrition or physical activity. In addition, some interventions reviewed also included the practice team or elements of the healthcare delivery system, and a few focused on the environment or context of program delivery. These studies are summarized below using the framework of the Chronic Care Model (CCM) and according to different intervention levels following social-ecological theory (see Table 1).

Table 1. Summary of Conclusions from Study Reviews using Social-Ecological and Chronic Care Models

CCM Domain	Application	Significant Outcomes	Lessons Learned	Future Considerations
Patient	Self-Management Education Programs Targeted behavioral interventions	- Improved glycemic control. - Reduced diabetes-related hospitalization.	- Successful programs use adult learning models (non-didactic techniques) to actively engage participants.	- Multiple dimensions of self-care. - Patient activation and engagement in self-management
Practice Team	Physician training Physician involvement in patient education Combined patient education w/physician prompts	- Increased patient and provider surveillance (SMBG and foot exams) - Improved glycemic control and foot health. - Reduced diabetes-related health care costs.	- Successful programs involve patients, physicians, nurses, and other members of the healthcare team in the learning process.	- Incorporate diabetes self-management education into post-graduate education for health professionals. - Adopt a public health approach to disseminate cost-effective self-management interventions on diet and physical activity.
Health Systems	Disease Management Case Management Chronic care guidelines implementation	- Improved provider monitoring of care. - Decreased foot lesions and decreased HbA1c.	- Targeted interventions that involve heightened surveillance lead to improved results. - At the clinic level, interventions need to be integrated into the care delivery system with multiple disciplines involved in patient assessment, coaching and follow-up.	- More study of whether extremely focused interventions translate to long-term adoption of behavior change. More study of computerized, Internet, or other systematic delivery methods to help assure consistent patient assessment, feedback, and reinforcement.

Table 1 continued

Environ-ment	Context of Program Delivery	- Improved provider screening. - Improved glycemic control.	- Disease Management combined with Case Management most effective.	- More study of delivery in non-clinic settings such as community, home and worksite.

Patient Interventions: "Doing" Self-management

Since patient behavior is extremely variable across regimen areas (e.g., medication adherence versus diet and exercise behavior), studying how patients "do" self-management is not a small problem (Gonder-Frederick et al., 2002). Most studies reviewed focused on very specific patient behaviors, attempting to intervene in a targeted way while controlling for other behaviors. While there is much to be learned from efficacy studies of isolated behaviors and reliably measuring the behaviors; generalizing these results to real-world situations, where patient circumstances, values, and goals are variable and dynamic, is not always possible (Glasgow et al 2002). Furthermore, studying a single patient behavior in a controlled environment is generally impractical and cost prohibitive within the context of clinical health care.

It is therefore not surprising that outcomes were variable among the many studies that evaluated targeted patient behavioral interventions. Boule et al. (2002) reviewed 14 controlled clinical trials that focused on the impact of regular moderate physical activity on glycemic control and body mass for persons with type 2 diabetes. Using meta-analysis techniques, they concluded that regular moderate physical activity reduced blood glucose levels by a statistically and clinically significant level. Body mass was not significantly impacted in these studies; thus it appears that improvements in metabolic outcome can be achieved without significant weight loss or BMI change. However, the authors point out that in one study where MRI techniques were used to measure abdominal adiposity, a significant decrease in adipose tissue was associated with increased physical activity. Since most studies used more conventional techniques to measure body mass including BMI, waist circumference and waist-to-hip ratio, or skin-fold measures, more research using sophisticated measurement tools is needed before any definitive conclusions can be drawn.

Studies of the impact of patient self-monitoring of blood glucose (SMBG) on patient health behaviors and outcomes also yielded contradictory results. Clement (Clement, 1995) reviewed several studies that looked at the benefit of SMBG on insulin self-adjustment. The conclusions from these studies were that SMBG is useful for both type 1 and type 2 diabetes patients with regard to optimization of the insulin regimen. Piette and Glasgow (Piette et al., 2001) reviewed 13 studies of SMBG's impact on glycemic control for both type 1 and type 2 diabetes patients. They concluded that while it is essential for type 1 patients to monitor themselves for dysregulation, the evidence did not support an overall effect of improved glycemic control for any diabetes patients, regardless of type. The reasons suggested included inaccurate readings, equipment, recording or interpretation of data, poor technique, lack of communication with the doctor, and lack of adjustment of patient behavior in response to their readings. Thus, it may be possible that interventions that strictly control measurement techniques, interpretation, and appropriate behavioral response to information may result in better patient outcomes. On the other hand, in the real world, it may be extremely difficult to implement the controls necessary to yield a significant benefit from SMBG for type 2 patients.

Intensity of the intervention offered may also be relevant to achieving sustained health behavior change, but raises health policy implications with regard to current reimbursement constraints. The effectiveness of a 16-session weight loss intervention was compared with a medically reimbursable 4-session program during a randomized controlled trial conducted in two rural community health centers. One-hundred-eighty-seven adults with type 2 diabetes participated. The more intensive intervention proved to be significantly more effective with 49% versus 25% of participants losing 2kg or more at 12 months (Mayer-Davis, et al, 2004).

Diabetes self-management education programs that addressed a variety of behaviors simultaneously yielded a variety of promising results (Clement, 1995; Piette et al., 2001; Gonder-Frederick et al., 2002). In a review of several long-term prospective studies (Clement, 1995), it was found that programs using specific behavior change strategies that focused on individual beliefs about diabetes, barriers to self-care, coping skills and the patient's social environment showed significant improvements in glycemic control and reduced hospitalizations for diabetes-related problems. Interventions that targeted problem-solving skills, patient-physician communication enhancement techniques such as negotiation and information-seeking skills, also resulted in decreased HbA1c, reduced absenteeism from work and better quality of life in comparison with controls (Piette et al., 2001; Grey et al. , 2000). No program that used didactic methods of education alone showed positive results (Clement, 1995). Thus, *interventions targeting skill building that can be applied to a wider range of self-management behaviors show more consistent, positive outcomes, provided the patient is actively engaged in the learning process.*

Practice-Team: Adopting The Facilitation Role

The physician-patient relationship plays a key role in adherence and behavior change. Brief advice from the physician has been shown to result in significantly higher quit rates among smokers, and even better results when the message is echoed repeatedly by other members of the health care team (Fiore et al, 2000; Piette et al., 2001; Whitlock et al., 2002). Other complex lifestyle behaviors, such as eating habits and physical activity, have been shown to benefit from a public health approach to intervention, with behavioral interventions conducted by primary care professionals, as opposed to psychologists. In this way large numbers of individuals can be reached in a more cost effective manner (Wing et al., 2001). Primary care is one of the settings in which self-management education will need to be conducted to produce a population-wide impact. For instance, studies that coupled patient education on foot care with physician and office environment prompts to perform foot exams showed significant reductions in foot ulcers (Clement, 1995; Litzelman et al., 1993).

A group visit approach, where patients are brought together with their physician and other health care team members for a combined primary care visit and educational session have yielded reduced health services utilization and costs and improved patient satisfaction and self-efficacy (Scott et al, 2004). This approach may be an especially effective and efficient way to deliver concurrent education, routine assessment, and social support to adults with type 2 diabetes. Trento et al (2004) conducted a 5-year randomized controlled clinical trial that compared group medical visits with matched controls who received traditional one-on-one care. Significant improvements for group visit patients included improved knowledge of diabetes, problem solving ability and self-reported quality of life (Trento et al, 2004). In addition, HbA1c levels were stable over the 5-year period for the group care patients but progressively increased for the controls.

In general, self-management programs that provide physician training in diabetes self-management along with patient training, involve the physician, nurse and others as part of an integrated education team, combine patient education with physician prompts, and include follow up visits or phone calls as part of routine care, show significant improvements in glycemic control, foot health, and major reductions in diabetes-related costs (Clement, 1995; Renders et al., 2001). *A key conclusion for patients and health professionals is that successful interventions should involve patients, physicians, and other members of the practice team in order to reinforce messages and integrate care into both patient lives and practice team protocols.*

Health Systems: Improving Processes To Support Patient Care

Just as literature on behavior change indicates that effective strategies need to be tailored to individuals, practice-change strategies also will likely need to be tailored to the particular office environment to be most effective. Norris et al (Norris et al., 2002a) looked at the effectiveness and economic efficiency of 27 studies focused on disease management and 15 studies focused on case management. *Disease management* was defined as an organized, proactive, multi-faceted approach, where care is integrated across the entire spectrum of the disease and prevention of comorbidities and relevant aspects of the delivery system are emphasized (consistent with the chronic care model). Such interventions were effective in improving provider screening for hyper-glycemia, lipids, retinopathy, foot lesions, and urine protein, leading to significant improvements in glycated hemoglobin.

Case management was defined as providing individual attention to patients to educate, assess, develop individual care plans, and monitor outcomes (e.g., follow-up phone calls from a nurse and follow-up visits with a physician). There is strong evidence that case management interventions were effective in improving glycemic control as well as in improving provider monitoring of glycated hemoglobin when they were combined with disease management, and when they were delivered with one or more educational, reminder, or support interventions. These findings further underscore the importance of involving the physician and other clinical staff in the reinforcement of self-management behaviors. The vast majority of these interventions were conducted by nurse care managers, but it remains an open question as to the qualifications of the most effective intervention agents.

Interventions that focused on health systems innovations at the office visit level were more commonly aimed at specific adherence to chronic care guidelines. These are often focused on solving a specific problem and consequently reap focused results, such as in one study where physician performance of foot exams yielded a 59% reduction in serious foot lesions (Litzelman et al., 1993). However, maintaining focus over the long term may be challenging unless the behaviors are integrated into the patient and practitioners' routines. On the other hand, structural innovations such as using computers, automated telephone systems, or other systematic methods to assess patients, provide feedback and reinforcement and generate patient and provider reminders and follow-up materials, have been shown to improve professional performance as well as patient health outcomes. Thus, *structural innovations that include use of technology to reinforce self-management may be a way to assure that successful interventions are consistently performed and institutionalized over time* (Renders et al., 2001; Glasgow et al., 2000; Piette et al., 2001; Funnell and Anderson, 2003).

Environment Or Context: Method of Program Delivery

How and where self-management education programs are delivered appears to be as important to successful patient outcomes as the content of the program. Renders et al. (Renders et al., 2001) reviewed 41 studies targeted at improvement of care for persons with type 1 and type 2 diabetes. They found that effective interventions included interdisciplinary delivery of care with special emphasis on the role of a nurse to deliver patient education, follow-up, and facilitate physician adherence to chronic care guidelines. Glasgow and Eakin (Glasgow et al., 2000) echo these findings in their review of office-based interventions. Patient education and reinforcement can occur at several critical points starting with mailed reminders prior to patient's office visit to bring self-care materials such as blood glucose, physical activity, and/or eating logs; waiting room materials that emphasize the importance of diabetes self-care; nurse education and instruction for the patients to remove their shoes, and physician messages that emphasize the seriousness of diabetes and the importance of patient behavior in diabetes management. Successful interventions combine the physician's ability to influence patients in their care with reinforcement of the patient's goals shared among all members of the health care team.

Outside of the clinic setting, diabetes self-management education has been conducted in community settings such as libraries, social centers, faith institutions, home settings and worksites. The advantages of such interventions include potentially enhanced participation rates, cultural relevance, convenience, increased involvement of family members and support. The disadvantages of such interventions are that they are often highly self-selected and could jeopardize privacy, particularly in community and worksite settings. Norris et al. (Norris et al., 2002b) reviewed a small number of studies that evaluated the success of such programs and found sufficient evidence for successful glycemic control interventions conducted in community settings, but insufficient evidence for successful interventions that focused on diet, physical activity, weight loss, blood pressure, and lipid outcomes. Similarly, insufficient evidence was available for home and worksite interventions. This does not mean that these interventions are ineffective, but it does mean that more evidence is needed to draw conclusions. *More study of the effectiveness of community, home or workplace settings for delivering diabetes self-management education interventions is critical.*

EXEMPLARY STUDIES
The RE-AIM Framework

To enhance the potential of studies for public health impact, our research group has developed a framework that we call the RE-AIM model. Specifically, the five components of the RE-AIM model are: 1) **Reach**, or the percent and representativeness of patients who are willing to participate in a given program; 2) **Efficacy** or **Effectiveness** (depending on the study), or the impact of an intervention on important outcomes, including potential negative effects, quality of life, and economic outcomes. There are also three less often studied, but equally important factors, which concern impact at the level of the organizational setting. These "AIM" dimensions are: 3) **Adoption**, or the percent and representativeness of settings that are willing to adopt or try a health promotion program; 4) **Implementation**, or how consistently various elements of a program are delivered as intended by different intervention agents, and the time/cost requirements of intervention;

and 5) **Maintenance**, or the extent to which a program or policy becomes institutionalized or part of the routine practices and policies of an organization. Maintenance in the RE-AIM framework also has referents at the individual level. At the individual level, Maintenance refers to the long-term effects of a program on outcomes 6 months or more following the most recent intervention contact. The RE-AIM framework can be applied in several capacities including planning studies to maximize understanding of both internal and external validity characteristics, comparing the effectiveness of several interventions for policy decisions, and judging the level of "transferability" of findings to other settings and populations (Glasgow et al., 1999; Glasgow et al., 2001; Glasgow et al., 2002) (www.re-aim.org). What follows are some examples of studies that are illustrative of key aspects of RE-AIM (Table 2).

Improving Foot Care, A Health Systems Approach *(Efficacy, Adoption, Implementation & Maintenance)*

A study conducted by Litzelman, et al. (Litzelman et al., 1993) focused on reducing lower extremity clinical abnormalities in 352 patients with type 2 diabetes, demonstrated impressive outcomes using an intervention design that included 3 major elements of the Chronic Care Model and illustrates four key aspects of RE-AIM This randomized control trial focused simultaneously on the patient, practice team and health care system. Intervention patients received a risk assessment, foot care education, behavioral contracts for specific foot care activities and tailored phone and postcard follow-up reminders from the practice team. The program was integrated into the health care system by instituting colorful folders with foot decals that were designed to "prompt" practice team members to take specific action with these patients. Patients were directed to remove shoes and socks when they entered

the exam room to provide the care provider with a visual cue to perform a foot exam. Informational flow sheets that provided information on specific risk factors and foot care practice guidelines were also clipped to the patient charts, in addition to diagnostic work-up, treatment and referral guidelines for the care provider to follow. These patients were compared to similar "controls" who received the risk assessment followed by their usual care. The *reach* of the study was respectable, with 48% of those eligible to participate completing the study. Representativeness however, is limited, since the study took place at one health center, but did include participants who reflected the general patient population at that site, consisting primarily of underserved, minority females (i.e., 76% African American, 81% Female, and a majority low income, low education, and medically indigent). *Efficacy* was very impressive with regard to the desired outcomes. Patients receiving the intervention significantly reduced prevalence of lower extremity abnormalities including serious foot lesions at 12-month follow-up relative to controls. There was also a trend toward fewer fungal skin infections and significantly higher self-report of desired foot care behavior. Thus, this simple, very brief intervention simultaneously improved patient and practice team foot care practices resulting in intervention patients with significantly lower relative risk of serious foot lesions (baseline prevalence, 2.9%; odds ratio, 0.41 [95% CI, 0.16 to 1.00]; p=0.05). Unfortunately the study did not include quality of life or measures of any potential negative impacts. *Adoption* of the intervention program was not discussed in this study, however, it was demonstrated that this simple, low cost intervention was easily integrated into a routine patient visit. Subsequently, similar protocols have been adopted by other facilities, and the practice and patient foot care activities that were the focus of the

Table 2. Evaluation of Exemplary Studies using RE-AIM

Study	Participants	Method and Intervention	Outcome Per Group	Results using RE-AIM Criteria
Litzelman et al (1993) Reduction of lower extremity clinical abnormalities in patients with NIDDM.	352 patients w/ NIDDM; 76% AA, 81% F, low income, low education, indigent.	Randomized control trial. Focus on 3 major elements of the CCM: patient, practice team, health care system. **Intervention (I) Pts:** - Risk Assessment; - Foot care education, behavioral contracts; - Phone and mail follow-up reminders. **Health Care System:** - Physician prompts (e.g., colorful folders, foot decals). **Practice Team:** - Footwear removal. - Informational flow sheets; foot care practice guidelines; diagnostic, treatment, and referral guidelines. **Control (C) Pts:** - Risk Assessment; - Usual care	**I - Patients:** - Significantly reduced prevalence of LE abnormalities including serious foot lesions at 12 months (baseline prevalence, 2.9%; odds ratio, 0.41 [95% CI, 0.16 to 1.00]; p=0.05); - Trend toward fewer fungal skin infections; - Significantly higher self-report for desired foot-care behavior; **I - Practice Team:** - Significant increase in foot exams; education recording of patient symptoms, and referrals to podiatry clinics.	**Reach:** 48% of those eligible to participate completed the study. Generalizability limited to minority, female patients. **Efficacy:** Highly efficacious in reducing lower extremity abnormalities and increasing patient and physician foot care practices. **Adoption:** Intervention easily integrated into a routine visit. **Implementation:** Simple and low cost. **Maintenance:** Patients and practices followed for 12 months. Longitudinal studies needed to assess longer-term outcomes.
Glasgow et al (1997) Long term effects and costs of brief behavioral dietary intervention for patients with diabetes delivered from the medical office.	206 patients with DM1 and DM2, 62% F, mean age 63, moderate income and education levels	12-month randomized controlled trial, to test the effect of a brief, primary care-based, dietary self-management program. **Intervention (I) Pts:** - Detailed dietary assessments; BMI[a], serum cholesterol and HbA1c[b]; patient satisfaction w/visit questionnaire. - Tailored printouts on dietary barriers, video reinforcement of strategies for overcoming barriers; 20 minute interventionist self-management counseling; telephone follow-up to reinforce goals. - 3-month follow up visit.	**I - Patients:** - Significant improvement at 12 months in dietary behaviors (2.2% less calories from fat, p=.023) and serum cholesterol levels (15 mg/dl: p=.002) - Significant improvement in patient satisfaction. - No significant differences in HbA1c or BMI. - Cost of intervention above U/C was modest ($137/patient).	**Reach:** 60% of those who scheduled an outpatient visit completed the study. **Efficacy:** Achieved long-term impacts on dietary behaviors and serum cholesterol levels. **Adoption:** Needs further testing with intervention delivery by practice team. **Implementation:** Relatively low-cost, simple design. **Maintenance:** Patients and practices followed for 12 months. Sustained improvements in dietary behavior and serum cholesterol

Study	Sample	Design / Conditions	Results	RE-AIM Evaluation
		Practice Team: - Brief physician reinforcement. **Control (C) Pts:** - Same assessments as I; - Usual care		levels. Extended studies with intervention conducted by clinic staff needed to assess possibility of life-long behavior change.
Diabetes Prevention Program Group (2002)	3234 persons with elevated glucose levels. Highly-screened, 68% F, 55% White, Mean age = 50.6	Randomized Control Trial, 3 conditions: **Intervention (I):** - Lifestyle treatment 16 initial sessions covering diet and exercise. Individualized follow-up sessions. Intervention materials available on website: www.preventdiabetes.com - Metformin[c] in treatment **Control (C):** - Placebo	- Consistent effects favoring Lifestyle treatment on all key outcomes: fat intake, weight loss, physical activity and incidence of diabetes (29% placebo, 22% metformin, 14% lifestyle). - Effects equally strong among various ethnic and racial groups, and both men and women.	**Reach:** little data provided in this article. Participants were heavily screened for motivation. Good proportion of minorities included. **Effectiveness:** No measures of QOL reported. **Adoption:** Conducted in specialty research centers. No measures reported. **Implementation:** High but by paid research staff. **Maintenance:** Individual level was good over a four year period of study follow up.
Cox et al. (1994) Long-term follow-up evaluation of blood glucose awareness training (BGAT)	28 participants who had been randomized to BGAT and 12 previous control subjects. Mean Age + 40-47; diabetes history = 14-18 years; all require insulin.	**Intervention (I):** - BGAT alone - 7 weekly classes to teach participants how to identify symptoms specific to their personal hyper- and hypoglycemia; and to anticipate extreme blood glucose levels. - BGAT with "Booster" - 50% BGAT participants randomized to booster session that was delivered via hand-held computer and 2-week diary plotted actual-estimated blood glucose.	- BGAT with booster superior to other two conditions on BG estimation accuracy. No between group differences in A1c. - BGAT versus control resulted in fewer automobile crashes (42% vs. 15% over 4 years).	**Reach:** NA. Contacted 52 of 64 previous subjects. **Efficacy:** Intervention achieved improved blood glucose estimation accuracy. **Adoption:** Not reported. **Implementation:** Not reported. 12% of participants provided unreliable data. **Maintenance:** Individual level shows long-term effects on socially important outcome such as reduced automobile crashes.

a **BMI, Body Mass Index, is a measure of body fat based on height and weight.**
b **HbA1c, also termed glycosylated hemoglobin A1c test, is a lab test which reveals average blood glucose over a period of 2-3 months and is expressed as a percentage with 4-6% considered "normal".**
c **Metformin is an oral antihyperglycemic drug used for treatment of type 2 diabetes.**

intervention (patient foot care regimen, regular foot exams, diagnosis, treatment and referral guidelines) are recommended by the American Diabetes Association as part of the National Committee for Quality Assurances Diabetes Physician Recognition Program (National Committee for Quality Assurance (NCQA), 2002). *Implementation* of the intervention was simple and low cost, thus did not pose a problem for the intervention teams to perform. The practice team also demonstrated a significant increase in the percent of patients who were asked by nurses to remove their shoes and socks, and in physicians performing foot exams (68% versus 28%; $p<0.001$), and providing education on proper foot care (42% versus 18%; $p<0.001$). Physicians were also significantly more likely to record patient symptoms of neuropathy and examinations of feet, and to also refer patients to podiatry clinics (10.6% versus 5.0%; $p=0.04$). *Maintenance* of the intervention was good, with patients followed for a period of 12 months. More longitudinal studies should be conducted to assess long-term reduction in serious foot problems and amputations for patients and practices that follow the described protocol throughout their lifespan.

Computer-Assisted Dietary Change (*Reach, Efficacy, Implementation*)

A study of the long-term effects and costs of a brief behavioral dietary intervention for patients with both type 1 and type 2 diabetes was conducted by Glasgow et al. (Glasgow et al., 1997) and incorporated two key aspects of the chronic care model: the patient and the practice team. Two hundred and six patients (62% female, average age 63, moderate income and education levels) participated in this 12-month randomized controlled trial designed to test the effect of a brief primary care-based dietary self-management program. The program took place in a primary care office with two participating internists, however, with the exception of the

physicians, the primary interventionists were research staff employees as opposed to clinical staff members. All participants received detailed dietary assessments including a 4-day food record, dietary behavioral questionnaires, and computerized assessment of barriers to healthy eating habits. Physiological measures included BMI, serum cholesterol, and HbA1c. Patient satisfaction information was also collected. Intervention group patients received tailored printouts on their dietary barriers, a video to reinforce strategies for overcoming these barriers (two versions were provided, based on the patient's self-reported self-efficacy), brief physician reinforcement of the importance of working on managing their diet, and 20-minute interventionist counseling that included patient-centered dietary goal setting, problem-solving, and self-help materials. The patient's goals were reinforced at intervals by the interventionist via telephone follow-up calls, and patients returned for a follow-up office visit at three months. Control group patients received the same assessments as the intervention group, followed by usual care.

Reach for the study was good, with 60% of those who scheduled an outpatient visit completing the study, and participants being similar to non-participants on all measures collected. However, representativeness is again limited due to the use of only one health center, and patients with a scheduled visit. The authors suggested that participation rates could be improved by including the program as part of a routine office visit. *Efficacy* was evidenced by the long-term impact on dietary behaviors (2.2% less calories from fat, $p=.023$) and serum cholesterol levels (15 mg/dl: $p=.002$). HbA1c and BMI were not significantly affected, due possibly to the inclusion of both type 1 and type 2 patients, and the fact that a majority of subjects used insulin. Because of these factors, baseline glycemic and weight control were already good. Patient satisfaction with their visit was significantly higher for intervention patients compared with controls (p<.02). *Adoption* of this cost effective, simple intervention seems feasible, however, this would need to be tested with clinic staff delivering the intervention versus research staff. *Implementation* of the intervention was relatively low-cost (i.e., $137/patient over usual care), with an impressive long-term effect on dietary behavior and serum cholesterol. However authors were unable to collect enough information on the intervention process to fully evaluate its applicability and ease of implementation. *Maintenance* of the intervention effect looked promising with patients and practices followed for 12 months. Sustained improvements in dietary behavior and serum cholesterol levels during this period suggest that the outcomes could be maintained, but longitudinal studies that focus on the life-long impact of ongoing support and relapse prevention strategies are needed to assess patient burn out, depression and other factors that are associated with non-adherence to chronic illness regimens. Anecdotal data from follow-up contact with the clinic revealed that after the study concluded, the office staff were continuing to use the touchscreen computer and brief counseling, but were not doing the follow-up phone calls.

A similar intervention conducted by regular clinic staff in clinics across the state of Colorado was recently completed by Glasgow and colleagues (Amthauer et al., 2003; Glasgow et al., 2004; Glasgow et al., 2005). This program took place in 30 primary care clinics settings, with an interactive computerized self-management program as the primary intervention tool. Clinic staff were trained to provide counseling and follow-up in support of the patient's self-management action plan goals, that were set via the computerized program. *Adoption* results were less favorable than hoped, with only 5% of physicians invited opting to

participate in the study. Those that participated were representative of all those invited with regard to physician age and gender, practice tenure, practice size and other measures collected in a preliminary survey of over 1,000 Colorado primary care providers. *Implementation* of the office intervention and follow-up activities over the course of their twelve month participation in the study was high, especially given that they were conducted by regular clinic staff. The intervention resulted in significant increases in diabetes-related laboratory assays and self-management support activities compared to those clinics that were randomized to the control condition (Glasgow et al., 2005). *Maintenance* data is currently being collected from clinics and patients, to determine if any of the key program elements were institutionalized.

Diabetes Prevention Project (*Reach and Efficacy*)

The Diabetes Prevention Project (DPP), while conducted with adult participants with elevated glucose levels rather than those who had been previously diagnosed with diabetes, is one of the most important diabetes studies conducted in the past 5-10 years. This study provides a good illustration of *Reach* and *Efficacy*. The size of the study (n = 3,234), the careful documentation of the intervention process, the demonstration of clinically significant outcomes (58% reduction in the incidence of diabetes during the observation period) for the lifestyle intervention versus control condition, and the collection of data on negative side effects were exemplary. While the screening and exclusion procedures employed resulted in a highly motivated sample, there were a large percentage of minority and low-income participants. On the other hand, the intensity of the intervention in this prospective efficacy study (16 individual sessions followed by later contacts, etc.) raises questions about how widely this intervention will be adopted (no adoption data were reported).

The DPP has probably done more to demonstrate the importance and potential of lifestyle change interventions for healthy eating and regular physical activity than any other single study. There is active discussion of the implications of this project for dissemination that has attracted participants from around the world.

Long-term Follow-up of Blood Glucose Awareness Training (*Implementation & Maintenance*)

The follow-up report by Cox and colleagues (Cox et al., 1994) is a good example of both how a self-management intervention can have important and lasting impact, and also of collecting long-term maintenance data on program effects. They followed up with 28 participants who had previously received their Blood Glucose Awareness Training (BGAT, see Table 2) program compared to 12 control participants from previous randomized trials.

The follow-up was conducted a mean of 4.9 years following BGAT study training, and the results revealed that BGAT participants had significantly fewer automobile accidents over this interval than control participants. In addition, half of the previous BGAT participants were randomly assigned to receive a "booster" intervention that consisted of completing a BGAT self-monitoring diary for 2 weeks. These participants were more accurate at estimating their blood glucose levels and more aware of hypoglycemia than BGAT participants who did not receive the booster. Demonstrating the specificity of treatment effects, there were no differences at long term follow-up between conditions on Hemoglobin A1c levels: all conditions demonstrated improvements on A1c relative to baseline of 1.5 to 2%.

From a RE-AIM perspective, this study provides important data on *implementation*

and *maintenance*. The BGAT training process followed a specified protocol, and it was found that the simple booster exercise enhanced BG estimation and hypoglycemia awareness. It is rare to see a 5-year follow-up and the demonstration of results translating into the clinically meaningful reduction in automobile accidents was exemplary. The Reach of the study (52 of 64 previous participants) was reasonably good, but adoption issues were not addressed in this paper. Other studies of BGAT including a multi-center study by Cox, et al. (Cox et al., 1995) have shown that BGAT can be successfully implemented by different research teams.

BARRIERS TO SELF-MANAGEMENT: WHY DOES MY PATIENT IGNORE MY ADVICE?

To dodge a prescription can be to dodge an identity (Goffman, 1961).

Adherence to medication and lifestyle regimens has long been a challenge in treating chronic illness (Singh et al., 1999; Miller, 1997). Medical non-adherence in the United States is extremely costly, contributing to 10% of all hospitalizations, 25% of all nursing home admissions, with an overall estimated cost of over 100 billion dollars per year (Miller, 1997). Patients who are living with a chronic disease may choose NOT to adhere to prescribed regimens because they may 1) wish to avoid or deny being labeled as ill and so avoid taking medications or following restrictive dietary plans; 2) be dealing with so many co-morbidities, all with complex or conflicting regimen demands, they just give up or simply forget; 3) be unable to overcome social or environmental barriers to prescribed self-care regimens; or 4) weigh the cost/benefits of following prescribed regimens with regard to their impact on perceived quality of life.

"I don't think of myself as a 'diabetic'". Impact of self-identity and coping

Studies of patients with diabetes and other diseases that warrant lifelong medical treatment as well as significant lifestyle changes, show a disconnect between the medical perspective on patient "compliance" and the patient's perspective. Physicians and other health care providers prescribe regimens that they believe will help the patient if only they will follow the "doctor's orders." Patients, on the other hand, may or may not fully understand the importance of adherence or may not believe they really need to make the recommended changes. Health regimens that greatly interfere with the patient's routine may be followed in the short-term, but the behavior may not be sustained if required over a long period or lifetime. While many studies focus on non-adherence to complicated medication regimens, for patients with diabetes, studies have shown that patients report the greatest number of barriers when trying to follow dietary and exercise programs and the fewest barriers to medication taking (Glasgow et al., 1986; Glasgow, 1994).

A patient's coping style may also impact perceptions of his or her ability to take charge of a health condition. Coping behavior serves as a way to control, avoid or reduce emotional distress. Specific coping strategies are considered adaptive so long as they are successful at reducing distress. When they are no longer successful they are considered maladaptive. Taylor (Taylor, 1983) discussed how adjustment centers around three domains: 1) the search for meaning or significance of the illness; 2) the attempt to regain mastery over the illness as well as one's life; 3) the effort to restore self-esteem through self-enhancement. These three areas are colored by a coping mechanism that Taylor refers to as "illusion". In other words, individuals will find their own explanation for why their illness occurred, believe they can regain control over their body, their treatment or their life, and believe

that they are doing as well or better than others who are in the same boat. Taylor suggests that illusion may actually serve to preserve mental health. Thus, the patient who is on a long-term diabetes regimen may choose to not comply in order to retain his or her self identify as a "normal" healthy individual.

Self-determination may influence how one chooses to adjust to a long-term threat, and whether or not one rejects a prescribed identity as a "diabetic" or chooses to define his or herself in another way. Related to self-determination are the concepts of autonomous self-regulation and self-efficacy, which have both been positively associated with adherence and life satisfaction (Senecal et al., 2000; Williams et al., 1998; Williams et al., 1998). However, if the individual chooses to reclaim their "pre-diagnosis" identity by ignoring the realities of their illness, it will obscure the fact that the disease, left unmanaged, will ultimately be in control.

"I have so many things wrong with me; I don't know where to begin!" Impact of co-morbidities

One of the challenges for diabetes patients, their family and clinicians is that most older patients have to cope with not only diabetes but also with other chronic illnesses such as hypertension, high cholesterol levels, arthritis, etc. This sets up the situation for very complex and at times competing or incompatible medication or lifestyle regimen recommendations. Frequently, patients end up being overwhelmed or confused, especially if they get different messages from different health professionals. Thus, it is often helpful to provide a written record of mutually agreed upon goals for the patient, and to provide a copy for other health care team members, to make sure that everyone is "on the same page." Another recommendation is to empathize with patients concerning the complexity of their regimen, and to ask specifically how you can help to make this more manageable. Finally, it can reduce the magnitude of the challenges faced by patients to focus on only one or two primary goals between each visit, and to use the longitudinality of primary care to address different issues over time in a sequential manner, rather than overwhelming patients with too much at once.

"I don't have…(time, money, transportation, support from my family, support from my workplace)…to take care of myself."
Social and environmental impact

Understanding patients' barriers to self-management and the resources and supports available to them, is key to helping achieve a successful self-management plan (Glasgow et al., 2000). Health care providers should ask their patients directly about factors that may interfere with their self-management goals, and work with them to develop specific strategies for overcoming these obstacles. Integral to a patient's ability to communicate relevant information to the practice team is the individual patient's confidence or self-efficacy regarding specific behaviors and factors that influence self-management activities. Thus, by helping patients develop clear, specific strategies that they can use to avoid or overcome obstacles, patients will develop greater confidence or self-efficacy, in their ability to actually carry out their self-management plan. In a study by Anderson (Anderson, 1995) to enhance patient empowerment, participants in a six-week patient empowerment education program showed significant increases in self-efficacy along with significant reductions in glycated hemoglobin. The need for patients to feel knowledgeable enough to make informed behavioral choices that will affect their diabetes is key. During the six weekly 2-hour empowerment sessions, participants and their family or friends developed skills in the area of goal-setting; systematic problem-solving; coping with the "daily hassles" of living with diabetes; stress management; attaining social support; and making cost/benefit decisions with regard to specific routine health behaviors (e.g., dietary choices). While *reach* for this study was limited (participants were recruited via advertisements, so information about non-participants is unknown), the results are worth noting. The intervention group showed significant gains over the comparison group in their ability to set goals, manage stress, obtain support and make decisions. They also showed a significant decline in negative attitudes toward living with diabetes, and significantly greater reductions in glycated hemoglobin than controls (intervention $11.75 \pm 3.01\%$ to $11.02 \pm 2.89\%$; control $10.82 \pm 2.94\%$ to $10.78 \pm 2.59\%$; p= 0.05). Participants did state that they had either made or intended to make changes in self-management behaviors such as diet, SMBG, or exercise. Patient empowerment is an area that deserves further attention to determine whether empowered patients are better equipped to adopt positive self-management behaviors and sustain them over the long run (Anderson and Funnell, 2000).

"What's the point of living if I can't eat anything?"
Impact of perceived quality of life

Patients with diabetes report the greatest number of barriers to following strict eating and exercise regimens, undoubtedly due to the fundamental role that food and activity plays in quality of life. Thus many people would probably prefer to take a pill as opposed to eliminating their favorite foods or incorporating daily exercise into their routine. Quality of life is multi-faceted and includes: physical and social function, role preservation, mental health, and avoidance of complications (Rubin and Peyrot, 1994; Glasgow et al., 2000). Polonsky (Polonsky, 2002) argues that the patient's perceived quality of life may be the single most important clinical and research outcome. Identifying whether patient adherence is a function of perceived identity, coping skills, self-efficacy, or socio-environmental factors, may take a back seat to identifying the source of a patient's distress. Once this source is identified, its impact on other related variables can be addressed. It is presumed that a bi-directional relationship exists between perceived quality of life and the impact of diabetes on the physical, emotional, and social aspects of the individual's life. Perceived distress in any of these areas, whether it is related to diabetes or more generic aspects of the patient's life, will impact the patient's ability to self-manage, and to make and sustain changes in life activities.

Polonsky (Polonsky, 2002) presents a model that could help clinicians identify the relevant psychosocial variables for each individual patient so that a pattern of impaired health-related quality of life (HRQOL) could emerge and clinicians could focus interventions appropriately. The model assesses individuals across 3 dimensions, physical, emotional, and social, for both diabetes-related and generic aspects of HRQOL. For example, diabetes-specific physical aspects of HRQOL would include short and long-term complications that impact life activities (e.g., work, leisure, or self-care). Generic physical aspects would similarly look at how non-diabetes related medical issues (e.g., arthritis) play a role. Diabetes-specific emotional aspects of HRQOL would include major depression, anxiety, hopelessness, guilt, fatigue, anger, and the like. Generic emotional aspects may include chronic stress due to other lifestyle factors beyond those caused by diabetes. Diabetes-specific social aspects of HRQOL would consider the quality of relationships when it comes to diabetes-related social situations (e.g., eating patterns, self-monitoring of blood glucose, and adherence to medication, and whether family or friends sabotage the patient's efforts or set

themselves up as the "diabetes police"). Generic social aspects may include general roles and expectations within a family or community setting, and quality and quantity of social support. Assessment of all these various domains is probably impractical for busy clinical practices given the need for multiple instruments, each with a different scale and scoring method. To address this, Polonsky developed the *Problem Areas in Diabetes Survey* (PAID), a brief 20-item questionnaire on areas of diabetes-related psychosocial distress that could easily be administered in a busy office environment (Polonsky et al., 1995). This instrument was tested on 451 female patients with type 1 and type 2 diabetes. All patients received HbA1 within 30 days of survey completion and again 1-2 years later. The PAID was positively associated with other measures of psychosocial distress including general emotional distress, disordered eating, fear of hypoglycemia, short- and long-term diabetes-related complications, and HbA1c, and negatively associated with self-care behaviors. The PAID accounted for approximately 9% of the variance in HbA1. Diabetes-related emotional distress was found to contribute significantly to adherence to self-care behaviors after adjustment for age, duration since diagnosis, and general emotional distress. Thus, this brief, easy-to-administer and score instrument, may be a useful tool for clinicians to assess diabetes-related emotional distress that may impact quality of life, self-care and health outcomes.

OUTCOMES-BASED RECOMMENDATIONS FOR CLINICAL PRACTICE

A summary of recommendations for clinical practice is provided in Table 3. While these recommendations are consistent with four of the major domains contained in the Chronic Care Model, many of the recommendations overlap, as do the opportunities for implementation. For example, while perceived quality of life may largely reside in the patient domain, assessing and addressing patient distress and quality of life concerns could be accomplished by members of the health care team as well as by resources and support that exist in the patient's environment.

Table 3. Summary of Outcomes-Based Recommendations

Chronic Care Model Domain	Common barriers	Outcomes-Based Recommendations
Patient:	- Self-Identity/Coping - Co-Morbidities - Social-Environment - Perceived Quality of Life	- Patient empowerment through targeted skill-building and engagement in learning and goal-setting; - Identify barriers, resources and support including family, friends, workplace, organizations, media resources. - Patient quality of life addressed during office visits by using PAID or other tool to identify areas of patient distress.
Practice Team:	- Lack of time - Lack of skills and information - Competing demands	- Provide resources through pre-visit mailed materials and waiting room information or CD-ROM for self-management. - Share the responsibility by involving physicians and other members of the practice team to integrate and reinforce diabetes self-management messages. - Physicians emphasize the seriousness of diabetes and the important role that patients play in controlling it.
Health System:	- Lack of guidelines and protocols - Lack of reimbursement - Competing priorities	- Establish patient registries to better target chronic care programs. - Use technology such as computerized assessments and interactive goal-setting programs to standardize and institutionalize self-management interventions. - Redesign practice structure to ensure that important patient-centered and proactive prevention activities receive priority - Implement population-based management strategies and centralize resources.
Environ-ment:	Accessibility of: - information, - resources, - social support, - safe places for engaging in physical activity, - availability of supermarkets staurants that offer nutritious	- Identify and develop socio-environmental resources for nutrition, exercise and general wellness. - More study of community-based diabetes education, where family and friends are encouraged to participate. - Collaborate with local organizations and programs having similar goals (e.g., senior citizen and community centers)

FUTURE DIRECTIONS FOR MANAGING CHRONIC CONDITIONS

We cannot solve our problems with the same thinking we used when we created them (Albert Einstein).

The evolution of medicine from "cure" to "care" calls for a different paradigm and a new set of tools for health professionals (Anderson et al., 1995; Glasgow et al., 1999; Wagner et al., 1996). The chronic care model provides a picture of what medicine is moving towards as the population ages. Activated patients, involved clinicians, supportive health systems and environments provide a means for patients to maximize their health and prevent complications from chronic diseases such as diabetes. To accomplish these goals, a number of factors need to be present:

1. Standards of care need to be established and communicated, so that health care teams (and patients) have up-to-date best practices to guide patient treatment.

2. Registries that allow physicians to identify and provide proactive planned care to patients with diabetes and other chronic conditions will ensure that practices are targeted correctly.

3. Problem-based and patient-centered education that includes patients and their health care team members to assure patients and practitioners have the same information and learn how to work together as a team.

4. Behavioral focus, so that patients understand and receive support for lifestyle changes that are of prime importance to managing diabetes but are also usually the most challenging (e.g., diet and exercise).

5. Tools, such as online or CD-ROM based interactive technology that allows patients to receive information, set goals, develop action plans and identify resources and support, and automatic telephone systems that provide patient follow-up, can help to assure that patients receive tailored care in an efficient manner.

6. Continued research on self-management interventions that are applied in a variety of venues and with diverse populations, such as community-based and lay educator programs to reach underserved groups.

7. Incentives, regulations and policies that reinforce both patients and clinicians for "doing the right thing," rather than waiting until a crisis emerges

In this way, care for the chronically ill will evolve to be flexible, delivered and reinforced by a variety of professionals and lay people in a variety of settings, and personalized to the individual who is living with the condition, to maximize health in a cost-effective manner.

REFERENCES

American Diabetes Association. (1995) American Diabetes Association: Clinical practice recommendations. Diabetes Care 18: 1-96.

American Diabetes Association.(1998) Economic consequences of diabetes mellitus in the U.S. in 1997. Diabetes Care 21: 296-309.

American Diabetes Association (2001) Facts and Figures. http://www.diabetes.org/main/application/commercewf?origin=*.jspandevent=link(B1)

Amthauer H, Gaglio B, Glasgow RE, King DK. (2003) Strategies and lessons learned in patient recruitment during a diabetes self-management program conducted in a primary care setting. The Diabetes Educator 29: 673-681.

Anderson RM. (1995) Patient empowerment and the traditional medical model. Diabetes Care 18: 412-415.

Anderson RM, Funnell MM. (2000) The art of empowerment. Alexandria, VA: American Diabetes Association.

Anderson RM, Funnell MM, Butler PM, Arnold MS, Fitzgerald JT, Feste CC. (1995) Patient empowerment: Results of a randomized controlled trial. Diabetes Care 18 : 943-949.

Boule NG.et al. (2002) Effects of exercise on glycemic control and body mass in type 2 diabetes mellitus: A meta-analysis of controlled clinical trials. Scand J Med Sci Sports 12: 60-61.

Brown S. (1992) Meta-analysis of diabetes patient education research: Variations in intervention effects across studies. Res Nurs Health 15: 409-419.

Brown KM (1999). Ecological Models of Health Behavior and Health Promotion. University of South Florida, Community and Family Health. Available at: http://www.med.usf.edu/~kmbrown/Ecological_Models_Overview.htm

Brownson RC, Remington PL, Davis JR. (1998) Chronic disease epidemiology and control. (2nd ed.) Baltimore, MD: Port City Press.

Centers for Disease Control and Prevention. (2002) 2002 Diabetes Surveillance System: Number and percent of U.S. population with diagnosed diabetes. http://www.cdc.gov/diabetes/statistics/prev/national/index.htm

Clement S. (1995) Diabetes self-management education. Diabetes Care 18: 1204-1214.

Cox D, Gonder-Frederic L, Polonsky W, Schlundt D, Julian D, Clarke W. (1995) A multi-center evaluation of Blood Glucose Awareness Training-II. Diabetes Care 18: 523-528.

Cox DJ, Gonder-Frederick L, Julian DM, Clarke W. (1994) Long-term follow-up evaluation of blood glucose awareness training. Diabetes Care 17: 1-5.

DCCT Research Group (1993) The effect of intensive treatment of diabetes on the development and progression of long-term complications in insulin-dependent diabetes mellitus. N Engl J Med 329: 977-986.

DQIP. (2002) The Diabetes Quality Improvement Project. http://www.dquip.org

Fiore MC, Bailey WC, Cohen SJ, et al (2000) Treating tobacco use and dependence: Clinical practice guideline (Rep. No. June). Rockville, MD: U.S. Department of Health and Human Services, Public Health Service.

Frosch DL, Kaplan RM. (1999) Shared decision making in clinical medicine: Past research and future directions. Am J Prev Med 17: 285-294.

Funnell MM, Anderson RM. (2003) Changing office practice and health care systems to facilitate diabetes self-management. Current Diab. Rep, 3(2): 127-33.

Glasgow RE. (1994) Social-environmental factors in diabetes: Barriers to diabetes self-care. In C.Bradley (Ed.), Handbook of psychology and diabetes research and practice (pp. 335-349). Berkshire, England: Hardwood Academic.

Glasgow RE, Anderson RM. (1999) In diabetes care, moving from compliance to adherence is not enough: Something entirely different is needed. Diabetes Care 22: 2090-2092.

Glasgow RE, Davis C, Funnell MM, Beck A (2003) Implementing practical interventions to support chronic illness self-management in health care settings: lessons learned and recommendations. The Joint Commission Journal on Quality & Safety 29:563-574.

Glasgow RE, Eakin EG. (2000) Medical office-based interventions. In F.J.Snoek and C. S. Skinner (Eds.), Psychological aspects of diabetes care (pp. 142-168). London: John Wiley and Sons, Ltd.

Glasgow RE, Funnell MM, Bonomi AE, Davis C, Beckham V, Wagner EH. (2002) Self-management aspects of the improving chronic illness care. Breakthrough Series: Implementation with diabetes and heart failure teams. Ann Behav Med 24, 80-87.

Glasgow RE, La Chance P, Toobert DJ, Brown J, Hampson SE, Riddle MC. (1997) Long term effects and costs of brief behavioral dietary intervention for patients with diabetes delivered from the medical office. Patient Ed Counsel 32: 175-184.

Glasgow RE, Lichtenstein E, Marcus AC. (2003) Why don't we see more translation of health promotion research to practice? Rethinking the efficacy to effectiveness transition. Am J Pub Health, 93(8): 1261-1267.

Glasgow RE, McCaul KD, Schafer LC. (1986) Barriers to regimen adherence among persons with insulin-dependent diabetes. J Behav Med 9: 65-77.

Glasgow RE, McKay HG, Piette JD, Reynolds KD. (2001) The RE-AIM framework for evaluating interventions: What can it tell us about approaches to chronic illness management? Patient Education and Counseling 44: 119-127.

Glasgow RE, Nutting PA, King DK, Nelson CC, Cutter G, Gaglio B, Kulchak Rahm A, Whitesides H, Amthauer H. (2004) Results from a practical randomized trial of the Diabetes Priority Program: Improvements in care and patient outcomes using RE-AIM criteria. Journal of General Internal Medicine, 19(12): 1167-1174.

Glasgow RE, Nutting PA, King DK, Nelson CC, Cutter G, Gaglio B, Kulchak Rahm A, Whitesides H. (2005) Randomized effectiveness trial of a computer-assisted intervention to improve diabetes care. Diabetes Care, 28(1): 33-39.

Glasgow RE, Vogt TM, Boles SM. (1999) Evaluating the public health impact of health promotion interventions: The RE-AIM framework. Am J Pub Health 89: 1322-1327.

Glasgow RE, Wagner E, Kaplan RM, Vinicor F, Smith L, Norman J. (1999) If diabetes is a public health problem, why not treat it as one? A population-based approach to chronic illness. Ann Behav Med 21: 159-170.

Glynn TM, Manley MW. (1989) How to help your patient stop smoking: A manual for physicians (Rep. No. NIH Publication #89-3064). Bethesda, MD: National Cancer Institute.

Goffman E. (1961) Asylums: Essays on the social situation of mental patients and other inmates. New York: Doubleday, Anchor.

Gonder-Frederick LA, Cox DJ, Ritterband LM. (2002) Diabetes and behavioral medicine: The second decade. J Counsel Clin Psychol 70: 611-625.

Grey M, Boland EA, Davidson M, Li J,Tamborlane WV. (2000) Coping skills training for youth with diabetes mellitus has long-lasting effects on metabolic control and quality of life. J Pediatr 137: 107-113.

Litzelman DK, Slemenda CW, Langefeld CD, Hays LM, Welch MA, Bild DE, Ford ES, Vinicor F. (1993) Reduction of lower extremity clinical abnormalities in patients with non-insulin-dependent diabetes mellitus: A randomized, controlled trial. Ann Intern Med 119: 36-41.

Lorig KR, Sobel DS, Stewart AL, Brown BW, Bandura A, Ritter P, Gonzalez VM, Laurent DD, Holman HR. (1999) Evidence suggesting that a chronic disease self-management program can improve health status while reducing hospitalization. Med Care 37: 5-14.

Mayer-Davis EJ, D'Antonio AM, Smith Sm, Kirkner G, Martin SL, Parr-Medina D, Schultz R. (2004) Pounds off with empowerment (POWER): a clinical trial of weight management strategies for black and white adults with diabetes who live in medically underserved rural communities. American Journal of Public Health, 94: 1736-1742.

McKeown T. (1979) The role of medicine: Dream, mirage, or nemisis? Princeton, NJ: Princeton University Press.

Miller NH. (1997) Compliance with treatment

regimens in chronic asymptomatic diseases. Am J Med 102: 43-49.

Morgan GD, Fox BJ. (2000) Promoting Cessation of Tobacco Use. *http://www.physsportsmed.com/issues/2000/12_00/tobacco.htm*

National Committee for Quality Assurance (NCQA) (2002) Diabetes Physician Recognition Program (DPRP) Frequently Asked Questions: Measures for Adult Patients. http:www.ncqa.org/dprp/dprpfaz.htm#adultmeasures

National Institute of Diabetes, Digestive, and Kidney Diseases. (2000) National diabetes statistics: General information on diabetes in the United States, 2000. National Diabetes Information Clearinghouse.

Norris SL. and et al (2002a) Increasing diabetes self-management education in community settings. A systematic review. Am J Prev Med 22: 39-66.

Norris SL. and et al (2002b) The effectiveness of disease and case management for people with diabetes. A systematic review. Am J Prev Med 22: 15-38.

Piette JD, Glasgow RE. (2001) Strategies for improving behavioral and health outcomes among patients with diabetes: Self-management education. In H.C.Gerstein and R.B.Haynes (Ed.), Evidence-based diabetes care Ontario, Canada: B.C. Decker.

Polonsky W. (2002) Emotional and quality-of-life aspects of diabetes management. Curr Diabetes Rep 2 : 153-159.

Polonsky WH, Anderson BJ, Lohrer PA, Welch G, Jacobson AM, Aponte JE, Schwartz CE. (1995) Assessment of diabetes-related distress. Diabetes Care 18: 754-760.

Renders CM, Valk GD, Griffin SM, Wagner EH, Eijk JT, Assendelft WJ. (2001) Interventions to improve the management of diabetes in primary care, outpatient, and community settings. Diabetes Care 24: 1821-1833.

Rubin RR, Peyrot M. (1994) Implications of the DCCT: Looking beyond tight control. Diabetes Care 17: 235-236.

Sallis JF, Owen N. Ecological models. In: Glanz K, Lewis FM, Rimer BK, eds. (1996) Health Behavior and Health Education: Theory, Research, and Practice. second ed. San Francisco: Jossey-Bass; 403-424.

Scott JC, Conner DA, Venohr I, Gade G, McKenzie M, Kramer AM, Bryant L, Beck A. (2004) Effectiveness of a group outpatient visit model for chronically ill older health maintenance orbanization members: a 2-year randomized trial of the cooperative health care clinic. J American Geriatric Society; 52:1463-1470.

Senecal C, Nouwen A, White D. (2000) Motivation and dietary self-care in adults with diabetes: Self-efficacy and autonomous self-regulation complementary or competing constructs? Health Psychol 19: 452-457.

Singh N, Berman SM, Swindells S, Justis JC, Mohr JA, Squier C, Wagener MM. (1999) Adherence of human immunodeficiency virus-infected patients to antiretroviral therapy. Clin Infect Dis 29: 824-830.

Taylor SE. (1983) Adjustment to threatening events: A theory of cognitive adaptation. Am Psychol 1161-1173.

Trento M, Passera P, Borgo E, Tomalino M, Bajardi M, Cavallo F, Porta M. (2004) A 5-year randomized controlled study of learning, problem solving ability, and quality of life modifications in people with type 2 diabetes managed by group care. Diabetes Care, 26: 670-675.

Wagner EH. (2000) The role of patient care teams in chronic disease management. BMJ 320: 569-572.

Wagner EH, Austin B, Von Korff M. (1996) Improving outcomes in chronic illness. Managed Care Quarterly 4: 12-25.

Wagner EH, Glasgow RE, Davis C, Bonomi AE, Provost L, McCulloch D, Carver P,

Sixta C. (2001) Quality improvement in chronic illness care: A collaborative approach. J Joint Commission on Health Care Quality 27: 63-80.

Whitlock EP, Orleans CT, Pender N, Allan J. (2002) Evaluating primary care behavioral counseling interventions: An evidence-based approach. Am J Prev Med 22: 267-284.

Williams GC, Deci EL, Ryan RM. (1998) Building health-care partnerships by supporting autonomy: Promoting maintained behavior change and positive health outcomes. In P.Hinton-Walker, A. L. Suchman, and R. Botelho (Eds.), Partnerships, power and process: Transforming health care delivery Rochester: University of Rochester Press.

Williams GC, Freedman ZR, Deci EL. (1998) Supporting autonomy to motivate patients with diabetes for glucose control. Diabetes Care 21: 1644-1651.

Wing RR, Goldstein MG, Acton KJ, Birch LL, Jakicic JM, Sallis JF Jr, Smith-West D, Jeffery RW, Surwit RS. (2001) Behavioral science research in diabetes. Diabetes Care 24: 117-123.

BEHAVIORAL MANAGEMENT OF CHRONIC DENTAL DISORDERS: METHODOLOGICAL AND RESEARCH ISSUES

Julie Wagner and Susan Reisine

INTRODUCTION

The recent Surgeon General's Report on Oral Health in America (U. S. Department of Health and Human Service, 2000) describes the high prevalence of oral conditions in the US populations. Nearly all adults experience some form of either dental caries or periodontal disease in their lifetime making oral health problems the most pervasive chronic condition in the US. Oral cancer, although one of the less prevalent neoplasms, accounting for about 2-3% of all cancer diagnoses, has one of the worst five year survival rates with only 52% still living after five years (American Cancer Society, 2003). Temporomandibular joint disorders (TMD) occur in 10 million Americans (Lipton et al., 1993) affecting between 5-15% of adults. TMD pain is most common among adults ages 20-40, during the most productive work and family years. The Surgeon General's Report goes on to describe the large social and psychological impacts of oral conditions, direct and indirect economic costs of oral conditions and the effect of oral health on well-being and quality of life.

Most oral health conditions, particularly the two most common diseases, dental caries and periodontal diseases, can be prevented and managed with effective behavioral strategies, such as good oral hygiene practices, use of fluoride, the use of regular professional treatment and proper nutrition. However, many barriers to the initiation and maintenance of these behaviors prevent individuals from establishing and continuing behaviors that assure good oral health. The goals of this chapter are to describe and critically evaluate the literature on behavioral management of chronic oral health conditions, focusing on randomized controlled trials. Our emphasis will be on studies that assess the efficacy of interventions to initiate, increase or maintain methods of known efficacy to prevent, control or manage oral health problems. We will primarily address the two most common oral health conditions, dental caries and periodontal diseases. Bruxism and cancer will not be addressed.

The introduction section provides an orientation to the concept of oral health, measures of health status, prevalence estimates and risk factors for the incidence and prevalence of common oral health conditions. This section offers a description of key terms in oral health that may be unfamiliar to some readers.

WHAT IS ORAL HEALTH?

The literature evaluating oral health status has followed the movement in general health status assessment in that oral health is more than the absence of disease. Oral health is a multidimensional construct that includes physical, social, psychological and economic well-being (Reisine and Locker, 1995). "Oral" health became separated from general health by historical accident as medicine as a discipline separated from dentistry as a health profession in the late 19th and early 20th centuries. Contemporary thinking, however, strives to reunite the concepts of general health and oral health such that people cannot be considered healthy without good oral health.

Oral health refers to a fairly circumscribed craniofacial complex that includes the face, oral cavity, teeth and gums as well as salivary glands, jaws, tongue and esophagus. Our discussion of interventions will be limited to these structures, although the craniofacial complex houses a complicated network of nerves and organ systems that are responsible for numerous sensory, cognitive and affective processes, including taste, smell, touch, temperature, speaking, chewing, swallowing, hearing, etc. The craniofacial complex contains salivary glands, including parotid, submandibular and sublingual glands. These glands secret a mucous fluid and with tiny salivary glands found throughout the lips, cheeks and mouth secrete mucinous saliva. Saliva, like other exocrine secretions, has antimicrobial properties that inhibit the growth of infectious microbes, fungi and some viruses. Saliva also prevents oral mucosa from drying and from chemical irritants, helps maintain healthy pH levels, promotes wound healing and protects against dental caries (Surgeon General's Report on Oral Health in America, U. S. Department of Health and Human Service, 2000).

The face and craniofacial complex occupy a central role in maintaining general physical health and in social interactions. The mouth and teeth are necessary for breathing, eating, chewing and swallowing. The mouth and face also can serve as "mirrors" of health and disease (see Surgeon General's Report, p. 98-100). Conditions such as primary HIV infection, sexually transmitted diseases, and chicken pox can be detected by the presence of oral mucosal lesions. The mouth reflects nutritional status, such as vitamin deficiencies, as well as the effects of tobacco use.

Although saliva offers considerable protection from infectious diseases, the mouth can be a portal for infection that can have negative consequences for general health. Recent studies of periodontal diseases have shown associations between periodontal infections and diabetes, heart disease, stroke and premature delivery during pregnancy. Preliminary studies of diabetes have shown that periodontal disease is more prevalent among people with both Type I and Type II diabetes and that the presence of periodontal disease affects glycemic control (Surgeon General's Report on Oral Health in America, 2000). These studies are either case-control or descriptive studies. Several prospective cohort studies have demonstrated an increase risk of heart attack and stroke associated with the presence of periodontal diseases. However, few studies have the methodological rigor to unequivocally support the relationship between periodontal disease and cardiovascular diseases (Loesche, 2000; Grossi, 2001). Human and animal studies of preterm birth and periodontal diseases suggest that periodontitis as a gram negative infection, may be associated with premature birth and low birth weight babies (Offenbacher et al., 1996). More longitudinal studies with large samples are needed to support these findings from these early studies (Jeffcoate and Geurs, 2001).

STATUS OF ORAL HEALTH IN THE UNITED STATES

This section provides a brief overview of the major oral health problems, including the pathology of the major diseases, the prevalence of these conditions in the United States and a description of the major risk factors. Data are presented for the two major dental diseases, dental caries and periodontal diseases, for facial injuries and for acute and chronic pain.

Dental caries

Dental caries is a multifactorial infectious process that involves bacteria, diet and host factors (Burt and Eklund, 1999). Bacteria that colonize on teeth form a biofilm called dental plaque. Bacteria in dental plaque consume and ferment sugars and carbohydrates to produce acids that dissolve tooth enamel causing cavities in the teeth. If unchecked, infection of the pulp tissue, abscess, destruction of bone and systemic infections can occur. Bacteria are transmitted from caregiver to child some time after birth during childhood through intimate contact, such as kissing and food sharing. Knowledge of when transmission and establishment of bacteria colonies occurs is not well-established (Caufield et al., 1993; Karn et al., 1998). The consumption of sugar and starches plays an essential role in the etiology of dental caries but is probably most important among individuals who are susceptible (Burt et al., 1988; Rugg-Gunn et al., 1984). Dental caries can occur any time after the eruption of teeth and at any age.

Prevalence and incidence of dental caries is measured in several ways (Burt and Eklund, 1999). As caries prevalence has declined, presence/absence of caries has become an important indicator of oral health, particularly when caries occurs among children. The most common index for children, def, is based on the DMF index for adults developed by Klein, Palmer and Knutson (1938). D stands for decay, M for missing due to caries and F for filled permanent teeth or surfaces on permanent teeth. The DMF score is the sum of these individual measures for either teeth (T) or surfaces (S) and can range from 0-32 for DMFT or 0-160 for DMFS. The def index stands for d, decayed, e, extracted and f for filled teeth/surfaces. Small letters denote primary teeth/surfaces. There are numerous limitations to the def and DMF indexes (Burt and Eklund, 1999). The DMF index is not linked to the number of teeth at risk or age; the index gives equal weighting to each of the constituent indicators; does not differentiate between teeth lost due to caries, trauma or other oral health problems; cannot account for sealants; and finally, the index represents a lifetime of accumulated disease. Other caries measures have been developed and some investigators suggest that the pattern of caries incidence is more important than the total DMF/def index (Poulsen and Horowitz, 1974; Douglass et al., 2001). A commonly used measure of untreated need is D or d divided by total DMFS (def) or by the number of filled surfaces. Dental caries that occur on the root surfaces of teeth (root surface caries) often are treated separately from the DMFS index for adults. The Root Caries Index (RCI) (Katz, 1980) is measured by the total number of decayed and filled root surfaces divided by the number of root surfaces at risk that have loss of periodontal attachment times 100. In addition to controversies about the indexes to measure caries prevalence and incidence, there is considerable debate about the diagnostic criteria for caries (see Horowitz et al., 2001). However, the DMF and def indexes are the most commonly used measures of caries in epidemiological studies.

Dental caries is a highly prevalent condition in the United States and the most common childhood disease affecting 50% of children ages 5-9 years and 78% of 17 year olds (Kaste et al., 1996; Winn et al, 1996). Caries also is highly prevalent among adults with the average number of decayed, missing and filled surfaces (DMFS) increasing with age from a mean of 10 DMFS for 15-24 year olds to more than 60 DMFS for 55-64 year olds to approximately 80 DMFS for those 75 years and older (Winn et al., 1996). There has been a dramatic decline in the prevalence and severity of dental caries in the US between two national oral health surveys conducted in 1979-80 (US Public Health Service, 1981) and 1988-91 (Winn et al., 1996) as well as in other economically developed countries (Burt and Eklund, 1985). The exact cause of this decline is unknown, but may be attributable to a natural rise and fall in an infectious disease process. Most investigators recognize the increased use of fluoride as the most important factor contributing to this decline (Burt and Eklund, 1985).

Risk Factors for Dental Caries
Sociodemographic Characteristics

The incidence and prevalence of dental caries increases with age as primary teeth and permanent teeth erupt and more surfaces are exposed to infection. This trend continues as individuals age into adulthood and as teeth continue to be exposed to the infectious process. Aging also may be associated with increased host susceptibility. Females generally have higher DMFS scores than males, but this is most likely a treatment effect as females have higher rates of dental services utilization. Race/ethnicity has been found to be a significant factor in differences in caries experience with ethnic minorities experiencing higher rates of unmet treatment needs compared to whites. Most recent studies show that these differences are largely due to socioeconomic differences.

A substantial body of literature exists which documents the relationship between socioeconomic status (SES) and health (Marmot et al., 1995). Most studies of acute and chronic health problems in the United States and other industrialized countries consistently find an inverse relationship between SES and the incidence and prevalence of disease: as socioeconomic status increases, disease, illness and their impacts decrease. This is especially true of health conditions related to lifestyle factors, such as cardiovascular disease and some cancers (National Center for Health Statistics, 2000) as well as for infectious diseases (Famer, 1999). A comprehensive review of the relationship between SES and caries (Reisine and Psoter, 2001) demonstrates an inverse relationship between caries incidence and prevalence and socioeconomic status with the lowest SES groups being at the greatest risk for disease. Furthermore, the greatest declines in caries rates over the past thirty years have been observed among the most advantaged SES groups. Data on SES and caries suggest that dental caries is a disease of poverty.

Health Conditions as Risk Factors

As previously mentioned, saliva plays an important protective role in preventing dental caries. People with reduced salivary flow have increased risk of developing dental caries (Spak et al., 1994; Papas et al. 1993; Leone and Oppenheim, 2001). Certain systemic diseases, such as primary and secondary Sjogren's Syndrome, and medications for the treatment of common general health conditions such as hypertension and major depression, are the primary causes of xerostomia (or dry mouth symptoms) and limitations in salivary flow rates (Atkinson and Baum, 2001). Talal (1992) estimates that there are one to two million people in the United States with Sjogren's Syndrome, with a ratio of nine females to every male with the diagnosis. More that 400 medications (Sreenby and Schwataz, 1997) have dry mouth as a side effect. Additionally, individuals with some types of oral cancers who are treated with radiation therapy that destroys salivary glands also have reduced levels of salivary flow rates. Head and neck cancer affects more than 30,000 patients each year, and most of them receive some radiation therapy. There are two FDA approved drugs to increase salivary flow for patients who still have functional saliva producing cells.

Behavioral Risk Factors

Two types of behaviors influence risk of developing caries and progression of disease, including those that promote health and prevent caries and those that increase the risk of disease. Preventive behaviors include use of fluoride, tooth brushing and professional application of dental sealants and fluoride. Behaviors that increase risk are the excessive consumption of sugar and inappropriate use of the baby bottle (Burt and Eklund, 1999;

Reisine and Psoter, 2001; Reisine and Douglas, 1998; Tinanoff et al., 2002).

Preventive Behaviors

It is well-established that fluoride reduces the incidence and progression of carious lesions (Surgeon General's Report on Oral Health in America, 2000; Truman et al., 2002). Community water fluoridation represents one of the major triumphs of public health in the last century (Milgrom and Reisine, 2000) in the prevention of dental caries, a major public health problem. However, only 62% of the US population is exposed to fluoridated water, although 43 of the 50 largest cities in the US have fluoridated water supplies. It is particularly important for individuals not exposed to fluoridated drinking water and for those at high risk of developing caries to initiate and maintain individual behaviors that assure optimal fluoride exposure. The US Preventive Services Task Force of the Centers for Disease Control strongly recommend (Code A) the use of fluoridated dentifrices for all people and the use of mouth rinses (Leverett, 1989), use of fluoride supplements for children ages 6-16, and fluoride gels and varnishes for high risk individuals.

A recent review of the efficacy of tooth brushing as a preventive strategy in dental caries (Reisine and Psoter, 2001; Kay and Locker, 1998) found weak evidence that tooth brushing reduced rates of dental caries. Furthermore, the preventive effects of tooth brushing are largely due to the effects of fluoride toothpaste rather than the mechanical removal of plaque. Plaque measures are frequently used as an outcome measure in caries intervention trials as a measure of oral hygiene. Although mechanical removal of plaque is not considered the effective intervention, it is considered a reliable and valid measure of oral hygiene practices. The Simplified Oral Hygiene Index (OHI-S) (Green and Vermillion, 1964) measures the presence of plaque and calculus on six index teeth. Scores can range from 0-6.

Use of professional dental services, such as fissure sealants (National Institutes of Health, 1984; Rozier, 2001) and professional fluoride treatments and antimicrobial agents (Rozier, 2001; Truman et al., 2002) also have been shown to be effective in reducing the incidence of dental caries (Burt and Eklund, 1999). Factors associated with professional dental services are discussed below.

Behaviors Enhancing Risk of Caries

As previously mentioned, sugar consumption is a necessary but not sufficient cause of dental caries and may be most important among individuals with demonstrated susceptibility to disease. Burt and Pai (2001) conducted a systematic review of the literature on sugar consumption and caries risk and concluded that the association between sugar consumption and caries has become attenuated in the context of the effects of fluoride in preventing dental caries. However, reducing the intake of sugar is important in reducing caries risk, especially among children and adults susceptible to this disease.

The American Academy of Pediatric Dentistry (2003) recommends that children not be put to bed with a bottle, children drink from a cup as they approach the age of 12 months and children be weaned from the bottle or breast at 12 to 14 months. The consumption of juices from a bottle should be avoided. Oral hygiene should begin at tooth eruption, including a visit to the dentist 6 months after the eruption of the first tooth and assessment of the primary caregivers mutans levels to decrease the transmission of bacteria. The evidence (Reisine and Poster, 2001; Reisine and Douglas, 1998) on the relationship between nursing, use of the baby bottle and early childhood caries is equivocal but not strong enough to alter current recommendations about baby bottle usage or breast feeding. As with sugar consumption, feeding patterns and exposure to cariogenic substances in the baby bottle and breast milk probably have their greatest effect among those with greater susceptibility to disease.

Periodontal Diseases

Periodontal diseases are highly prevalent and consist of a group of diseases rather than one discrete entity (Ranney, 1977). The two most common periodontal diseases are gingivitis and periodontitis. As with dental caries, these diseases result from bacteria in dental plaque and involve host susceptibility, as well. Gingivitis is an "inflammatory process of the gingiva in which the junctional epithelium, although altered by the disease, remains attached to the tooth at its original level. Periodontitis also is an inflammatory condition of the gingival tissues, characterized by the loss of attachment of the periodontal ligament and bony support of the tooth." (Burt and Eklund, 1999, p. 237). Gingivitis is associated with periodontitis, but gingivitis does not always progress to periodontitis. Loss of periodontal attachment (LPA) is considered to be the best measure of periodontitis (Goodson, 1990). It is the extent to which the periodontal ligament has detached from the tooth measured in millimeters.

Recent national surveys of gingivitis and periodontitis in the US (Burst and Eklund, 1999) show that ginigivits occurs at all ages, affecting 40-60% of school children and 47% of males and 39% females. There is some evidence that the prevalence of gingivitis in the US has declined since the 1960s, most likely associated with improved oral hygiene practices.

Risk Factors for Periodontitis
Sociodemographic Characteristics

Women have a slight tendency to have lower prevalence of periodontitis than men (Brown et al., 1996), which has been attributed to better oral hygiene practices among women. As with dental caries, African Americans and other ethnic minorities in the US tend to have higher levels of attachment loss compared to Whites, but, as with dental caries, these differences also have been ascribed to socioeconomic factors. Cross-sectional surveys consistently demonstrate an increasing prevalence of attachment loss with increasing age (Brown et al., 1996), but this most likely a reflection of accumulating effects of disease. The few longitudinal studies of periodontitis suggest that attachment loss increases rapidly among those who are most susceptible to disease as they age. Others who are less susceptible experience modest increases in disease as they age (Burt and Eklund, 1999). Socioeconomic status is strongly associated with periodontitis as those of low SES have severe attachment loss and more sites of attachment loss than those of middle or high SES. This association persists even when controlling for the effects of age.

Behavioral Risk Factors

Several behavioral factors contribute to the incidence and progression of gingivitis and periodontitis, including oral hygiene practices and tobacco use. Considerable data on the association between gingivitis and oral hygiene demonstrate a straightforward causal relationship between plaque levels and gingivitis (Loe et al., 1965). The relationship between oral hygiene, plaque and periodontitis is less clear. The presence of plaque and periodontal pathogens may be a necessary, but not sufficient cause of periodontitis. Host factors and susceptibility to disease play an important role in the onset and severity of disease. However, most clinicians suggest that patients treated for periodontitis maintain good oral hygiene as a way of preventing future disease progression (Nevins et al., 1990).

Plaque and calculus indexes are often used as outcomes measures in intervention studies. The OHI-S Index (Greene and Vermillion, 1964) and the Plaque Index (PlI) (Silness and Loe, 1964) are widely used measures of plaque that are associated with gingivitis. The OHI-S Index is less frequently used because it does not distinguish between plaque above and below the gum line or calculus. The PlI improved upon the OHI-S Index by measuring plaque thickness at the gum line. In 1977, the WHO developed a measure of oral hygiene based on the presence of calculus below the gum line because of the importance of calculus in the etiology of periodontitis.

Aside from other deleterious effects, smoking tobacco also increases the risk of periodontitis adjusting for other factors including age, sex and oral hygiene (Ismail et al., 1983). Bergstrom and Preber (1994) found that smoking independently increased the risk of periodontitis among smokers 2.5 to 6 times that of non-smokers.

Facial Injuries

Data on the incidence and prevalence of injuries to the head, face and mouth are limited. As reported in the Surgeon General's report on oral health, in 1993 and 1994 there were 20 million emergency room visits each year for craniofacial injuries. The NHANES III survey (Kaste et al., 1996) found that 25% of Americans six to 50 years of age reported having had an injury to one or more anterior tooth. In 1991 (Gift and Bhat, 1993), there were 5.9 million injuries treated in private dental practices. Taken together, these studies indicate that facial injuries are highly prevalent and are associated with economic costs and negative impacts on well-being. The most common causes of facial injuries are falls, assaults, sports injuries and motor vehicle accidents. There have been substantial efforts on the part of government agencies and professional health and sports organizations to increase the use of helmets and other protective equipment to reduce the incidence of sports-related injuries. Studies of helmet use among bicycle and motorcycle users have shown that use of helmets reduces the incidence of facial trauma although a study by Rivera et al. (1997) indicates that helmets alone are not sufficient to prevent more serious injuries. A recent report from the CDC Task Force on Community Preventive Services on use of helmets, faceguards and mouthguards in contact sports concluded that there is insufficient evidence on the effectiveness of these measures to reduce risk of injury (Truman et al., 2002).

Incidence and Prevalence of Acute and Chronic Oral Pain

A common symptom associated with oral/dental problems is acute and chronic pain. Acute pain conditions are often associated with specific dental or oral diseases, are brief in duration and can be treated effectively. Chronic pain conditions are defined as conditions persisting for six months or more. The most common chronic oral pain conditions are temporomandibular disorders (TMD). The etiology of these disorders are not well understood and the treatment approach for these pain conditions, like that of most chronic pain syndromes, is aimed at the management of the symptoms, rather than cure.

Lipton et al. (1993) published a national study of the prevalence of self-reported orofacial pain. More than 39 million people, or 22% of the US population, reported having one or more of five types of oral pain in the previous six months. The most common pain was toothache, followed by oral sores and pain in the jaw joint. Van Korf (1995) conducted a community based study of TMD problems and found that between five and 15% of those surveyed had self-reported pain or clinical signs of TMD.

Risk Factors for Chronic Facial Pain
Sociodemographic Characteristics

A review of the epidemiology of TMD (Carlsson and LeResche, 1995) reported that several demographic characteristics were associated with a higher prevalence of signs and symptoms of this disorder. Some controversy exists about whether women have a higher risk of TMD compared to men and whether increased risk for women is associated with biological factors related to sex or whether increased risk is due to gender differences associated with social roles, pain tolerance and illness behaviors. Most studies of clinic populations demonstrate a higher prevalence of TMD among women, but several community based studies show few differences between men and women. However, a recent systematic review (Drangsholt and LeResche, 1999) identified gender as an important risk factor for TMD. Age seems to be negatively associated with incidence of TMD, as one longitudinal study found that the prevalence of TMD declines with age.

Behavioral Factors

Behaviors, such as bruxism (Moss and Garrett, 1984; Rugh et al., 1993) have been associated with increased risk of TMD as those with higher levels of nocturnal bruxing (or tooth clenching) seem to be at greater risk for muscle hyperactivity and subsequent TMD (Moss and Garrett, 1984). Rugh, Woods and Dahlstrom (1993) also argue that psychological factors may predispose people to development of TMD. These include anxiety, depression and stressful life events. A state-trait analysis of the role of distress and personality factors in TMD pain (Zautra et al., 1995) found that stressful events were associated with distress, but not pain. However, distress was associated with increased pain levels. A recent systematic review of TMD that included only studies that adjusted for age and gender (Drangsholt and LeResche, 1999) identified depression and pre-existing pain conditions as the only credible risk factors in addition to gender. A recent report on risk factors for TMD diagnostic subgroups (Huang et al., 2002) showed that those with myofascial pain only were characterized by being more likely to report clenching, to have third molars removed, to be prone to somatization and to be female. Myofascial pain accompanied by arthralgia was associated with the same factors with the additional risk of having experienced trauma.

UTILIZATION OF PROFESSIONAL DENTAL SERVICES

Use of professional preventive dental services is a prominent factor in preventing dental caries and periodontal diseases and should be considered in the behavioral management of oral diseases. A substantial literature exists on models predicting utilization of professional dental services (Petersen and Holst, 1995). Andersen's model of predisposing, enabling and need factors offers a useful paradigm for understanding the process of dental services utilization in the United States. Predisposing factors consist of beliefs and attitudes about oral diseases and treatments and sociodemographic characteristics; enabling factors are financial ability to pay for care and availability of professional services; need factors include the perceived need for care and clinical oral health status. This model considers dental services to be elective because most dental conditions are not life threatening and because of this characteristic, use of dental services is more sensitive to financial barriers to care.

The recent National Health Interview Survey (US Public Health Service, 2003) indicates that in 2000 66.2% of those two years of age and older had a visit to the dentist in the past year. Children ages two to 17 had the highest percentage with 74.1%

having a visit in the past year. Sixty-five percent of adults 18-64 years old and 56% of adults over 64 years had a visit. More females had dental visits than males, more Whites had dental visits than non-Whites and more non-poor had dental visits than poor. However, when ethnicity and poverty were examined together, of those of poor economic status, fewer non-Hispanic and Whites had dental visits (63%) compared to poor Black or African Americans (67.5% with a dental visit).

IMPACTS OF ORAL HEALTH CONDITIONS – ECONOMIC COSTS, PAIN AND WELL-BEING

Direct and Indirect Economic Costs of Oral Conditions

Oral health problems and their treatment incur both direct and indirect economic costs. The direct costs refer to the costs associated with treatment of disease, including professional health care services, medications and over the counter pharmaceuticals. Indirect costs are associated with the consequences of oral health problems including lost productivity from paid work, the estimated value of unremunerated work in the household and lost time from school. There is considerable complexity to estimating the value of unremunerated family work, limitations in activity among adults who are retired or not employed and time lost from school, in addition to the need to discount these costs to allow for analysis of lost opportunity to invest these expenditures in other areas of the economy (Reisine andLocker, 1995).

Total national health care expenditures in the United States in 2000 were $1.3 trillion of which $60 billion were for professional dental services (Centers for Medicare and Medicaid Services, 2003). Unlike other health care expenditures, dental services are reimbursed primarily through private sources. Of the total of $60 billion, $26.9 billion (45%) were paid out of pocket, $30.1 billion (50%) from private insurance, $0.2 billion from other private sources and only $2.8 billion (5%) from public sources. In contrast, 33% of physician services and 45% total health care expenditures were reimbursed in the year 2000 through public funds.

Indirect costs of oral health problems and their treatments are difficult to estimate. The Surgeon General Report on oral health in America states that in 1996 (2000), 2.44 millions days were lost from work, 1.61 million days were lost from school and there were 9.71 million days when individuals had to cut down on their normal activities or visited a dentist or physician because of acute dental conditions.

Oral Health Conditions and Well-Being

Oral health can have important effects on quality of life and well-being (Coulter et al., 1994; Gift and Atchison, 1995; Gift et al., 1997). As Gift and Atchison (1995) state, measuring health-related quality of life allows assessment of "the trade-off between how long and how well people live." This is particularly the case for oral health conditions as most are not life threatening but influence those aspects of life that make it enjoyable, such as eating favorite foods and communicating through speech and facial expression.

The literature on oral health and well-being has tended to focus on the negative impacts of oral health problems (Surgeon General's Report, 2001). These negative impacts of oral health problems are considerable and range from acute and chronic pain and chewing dysfunction, to limitations in social functioning and psychological distress. Few studies, however, have addressed the benefits or enjoyment individuals derive from a healthy dentition.

A critical advance in recent years in assessing oral health and well-being has been the development and evaluation of multidimensional indicators of oral health. These patient-based outcome measures are guided by the theoretical orientation that oral health is a multidimensional concept, consisting of social, psychological and economic well-being as well as physical symptoms. Most of these scales are in the early stages of evolution and more work is needed to evaluate their sensitivity and specificity, patient acceptance and ease of administration. Nevertheless, epidemiological studies that have used these scales provide a fairly consistent picture of the clinical health care factors associated with diminished oral health related quality of life. They include tooth loss, untreated decay, advancing periodontal disease and infrequent or problem-based dental visits. These measures of oral health related quality of life may serve as important outcome measures when assessing the efficacy of behavioral management strategies in chronic oral health conditions.

Barriers to the Adoption of Oral Health Promotion Behaviors

Barriers to the adoption of oral health promotion behaviors are similar to those in general health promotion practices, including access to and availability of health services, beliefs and attitudes about oral diseases and fear and anxiety about dental care. Additionally, the characteristics of periodontal diseases and dental caries that involve host susceptibility and a long term rather than proximal relationship between health promotion behaviors and disease onset, create barriers to the adoption of desired preventive behaviors.

A BIOPSYCHOSOCIAL MODEL AS A PARADIGM FOR BUILDING INTERVENTIONS IN ORAL HEALTH PROMOTION

Engel (1977) first introduced the concept of the biopsychosocial model as a new paradigm for understanding the etiology and progression of disease. He suggested that disease represented a complex interplay among biological vectors, host factors and environment. This model is in contrast to the Medical Model of disease that suggests that diseases have a medically defined cause and course with known treatments and outcomes. Limitations in the Medical Model have been discussed at length (Kleinman, 1989). The Biopsychosocial (BPS) model has been applied to a host of medical and psychological health problems and offers a useful paradigm for understanding oral health conditions. As discussed previously, there is a relatively poor understanding of the role of host factors, particularly the effects of socioeconomic factors, beliefs/attitudes and stress, in the onset and progression of caries and periodontal diseases. The BPS provides a conceptual framework and rationale for developing interventions that will improve oral health based on environmental and psychosocial factors.

The BPS has been used in the context of predicting caries among preschool children in the US (Reisine et al., 1994; Litt et al., 1995). Studies of biological predictors of caries are equivocal in identifying biological markers that have both high sensitivity and specificity in assessing caries risk (Horowitz et al., 2001). Several investigators have shown the importance of self-efficacy, locus of control, knowledge and socioeconomic status on caries risk (Reisine et al.,1994; Sogaard, 1992; Gift, 1992). The following review, based on a BPS approach, highlights individual, organizational and community based interventions that incorporate multiple levels of understanding of how to improve oral health through health promotion and disease prevention activities.

METHODS

The social sciences in general, and the technology of behavior change specifically, have the potential to provide the foundation for interventions that are of direct benefit to the dental care provider. Areas of application include dental fears and phobias, appointment keeping, chronic non-malignant oral pain, pediatric disruptive behavior, gag reflex, oral habits such as thumbsucking, use of helmets and protective gear, wearing orthodontic headgear, as well as lifestyle changes to improve oral health including tobacco use, alcohol consumption, and eating habits. Interested readers are referred to Dworkin (2001), Schou (2000), and Stetson (2000) for examples of these applications. While it is important to acknowledge the potentially broad benefit of the behavioral sciences to dentistry, each of these areas warrants its own specific review and will not be covered in this chapter. This review specifically focuses on interventions designed to improve patient dental self-care behaviors and/or subsequent oral outcomes.

The dental literature from 1980 to 2002 was searched using the Medline and Cochrane databases. The search terms used included 'dental', 'oral', 'behavior', 'self care', 'adherence', 'compliance', 'psychosocial', 'intervention', 'treatment', and 'outcome'. Reference lists from papers retrieved by this search were reviewed and any relevant references were also obtained. The following were excluded: case studies, reviews, qualitative analyses, articles written in languages other than English, public policy interventions designed to increase access to care, and educational interventions with neither behavioral nor oral outcomes (i.e., educational interventions with knowledge as the only dependent variable). Also excluded were studies in which the main intervention was dental treatment (e.g., fissure sealant or regular prophylaxis) with only a minor educational or behavioral focus (e.g., Pavi et al., 1991; Brown et al., 1990; Petersen, 1989; Ashley and Sainsbury, 1981).

To indicate the degree to which the results of each study were subject to bias, each article was scored according to a set of criteria. These criteria were based on the work of Kay and Locker (1996), and adapted to reflect the specific content area of this review. Twenty criteria were established (see table 1). Studies were scored dichotomously yes=1 or no=0 for each criterion. Thus, each study could obtain a total score of 20, with higher scores indicating more rigorous studies. Cases for which it was unclear whether a particular criterion was met were scored no=0 (e.g., no mention of whether all subjects completed study or whether there was some attrition; no mention of whether examiners were blinded). There were some studies for which all 20 criteria were not relevant (e.g., measured only oral, but not behavioral, outcomes). For these cases, the total score and the number of relevant criteria are indicated in the table (e.g., 17/19). Converting this proportion to a percentage allows for easier comparison across studies, and these percentages are also reported. Studies with a score of >50% were retained. Originally, only randomized controlled trials were to be included in this review. However, a considerable number of interventions in dental behavior change have been implemented as non-randomized public health interventions in schools. Thus, non-randomized trials with a score of 50% or greater have also been included. Also, some studies with particularly innovative interventions were included despite low scores (e.g., Harrison and White, 1997). Studies are listed in tables 2-4 first by their raw score, then alphabetically by first author, then by publication year.

State of the Literature

The search produced approximately 250 journal articles, technical reports, and book chapters. One hundred and eight studies were retained for review (see Table 2-4). Sixty

Table 1. Study review criteria.

1.	Research aims clearly defined?
2.	Criteria for inclusion/exclusion given?
3.	Random allocation to groups?
4.	Control or reference group included?
5.	N for each group given?
6.	Sample adequately described?
7.	Precise details of intervention provided?
8.	Details of drop-outs given?
9.	Examiners blinded?
10.	Outcome measures clearly defined?
11.	Behavioral outcome measures valid and reliable?
12.	Oral outcome measures valid and reliable?
13.	Baseline measures administered to both groups?
14.	Means and SD's for baseline and final treatment and control provided?
15.	Follow up period clearly defined?
16.	Appropriate statistical analysis?
17.	Results section written clearly and thoroughly?
18.	Clinical significance of findings considered?
19.	Type I error considered in discussion of results?
20.	Type II error considered in discussion of results?

four of these were controlled, randomized investigations. The volume of published studies in this area has decreased over time, however, the rigor of the studies has generally improved. We found 62 studies published in the 1980's that met conditions for inclusion, with an average score of 66%. We found 37 studies published in the 1990's, with an average score of 72%. From 2000-2002 we found 9 studies, with an average score of 81%.

The studies tended to fall into two categories, program evaluations and systematic trials of theoretically based experimental treatments. The first category could be considered program evaluations, wherein an existing program (usually oral health education) is evaluated in terms of acceptability, cost, and effectiveness in modifying attitude, knowledge, behavior, and/or clinical outcomes. These studies tend to have several components that are tested in concert, have larger Ns, be less well controlled in terms of comparison groups and randomization, and have less intervention integrity. They are in some ways difficult to analyze because of their various components. That is, it is difficult to assess whether any effect was due to, say, curriculum or to, say, provision of dentifrice. An example is Blinkhorn, McIntyre, MacPhail and Shove (1981). The studies that fall into the second category are more systematic trials of theoretically based experimental treatments. These studies tend to be better controlled and have more structured interventions. However, what these studies gain in experimental rigor they tend to lose in sample size and generalizability. An example is Stewart, Jacob-Schoen, Padilla, Maeder, Wolfe and Hartz (1991).

The studies reported here have used a variety of designs and populations. Outcomes vary and include proximal variables such as oral health knowledge and behavior to intermediate measures such as plaque and

Table 2. Clinic Based Interventions.

Study	Sample	Comparison Group	Randomized	Intervention	Outcome	Raw Quality Score	Percentage of Criteria met
Little, Hollis, Stevens, Mount, Mullooly, Johnson (1997)	107 patients from a U.S. dental HMO aged 50-70 years with moderate PD	Yes	Yes	Experimental: usual care plus five 90-minute oral hygiene classes with skills training, behavior change strategies, and feedback Control: usual care	After 4 months, experimental group showed significant improvements relative to the controls on plaque, gingival bleeding, bleeding on probing, and pocket depth	18/20	90%
Stewart, Jacob-Schoen, Padilla, Maeder, Wolfe, Hartz (1991)	100 male U.S. veterans	Yes	Yes	Group 1: two 25-minute cognitive-behavioral sessions w/ thought restructuring, self-monitoring, feedback, problem solving, and stimulus control Group 2: two 20-minute dental education sessions w/ OHI Group 3: attention control with non-disease lectures on dentistry Group 4: no tx control	After 5 weeks, no group differences. All 3 treatment groups showed increased brushing frequency and decreased plaque compared to controls.	17/20	85%
Tedesco, Keffer, Davis, Christersson (1992)	108 adults with mild to moderate gingivitis in U.S.	Yes	Yes	Experimental: viewed slides of active, mobile bacteria taken from their mouths, plus OHI on 5 successive visits. Control: standard OHI.	Both experimental and control groups improved on plaque and gingival indices, with no group differences. No group differences for cognitive or behavioral measures. Slight advantage for experimental group on "zero bleeding on probing".	16/20	80%
Lee, Friedman, McTigue, Carlin, Cline, Flintom (1981)	30 pediatric patients, aged 8-9 years, receiving care at a university dental clinic in US	Yes	Yes	Experimental: OHI by hygienist plus daily charting of home brushing behavior, turned the chart in to clinic weekly Control: OHI only	At 2, 3, 4, and 7 weeks, no group differences for plaque or gingival index. Experimental group had higher self-reported brushing frequency	15/20	75%
Glavind, Christensen, Pedersen, Rosendahl Attstrom (1985)	55 adult patients of a general dentistry practice in Denmark, w/ plaque on > 30% of teeth surfaces	Yes	Yes	Experimental: Self-instruction manual regarding self-examination and OHI Control: One session of chairside OHI	3 and 6 months after treatment, no group differences for plaque or bleeding on probing. Both groups improved equally on both measures.	14/20	70%
Iwata, Becksfort (1981)	42 U.S. adults	Yes	No	Group 1: OHE Group 2: OHE plus fee reduction for improved plaque Group 3: no tx control	All groups improved, but fee reduction group showed most improvement at posttreatment and 6 month follow-up	14/20	70%
McGlynn et al., (1987)	59 orthodontic patients at a U.S. university dental clinic, aged 12-31	Yes	No	Experimental: charting and patient administered contingency management. Ss given TB, TP, and mouthrinse. Control: 2-minute persuasive speech about self-care; given TB, TP, and mouthrinse.	After 8 weeks, no group differences for plaque, gingival inflammation, or frequency of brushing or rinsing. Both groups improved equivalently on all outcomes.	14/20	70%

PD=periodontal disease TB=toothbrush TP=toothpaste DA=disclosing agent MM=mouthmirror OHI=oral hygiene instruction OHE=oral health education

277

Study	Population		Intervention	Results		
Persson, Persson, Powell, Kiyak (1998)	297 low income U.S. adults >60 years old, with no recent preventive care	Yes	Group 1=Usual care (UC) Group 2=UC+self-monitroing (SM) Group 3=UC+SM+weekly chlorhexidine (C) Group 4=UC+SM+C+semi-annual fluoride varnish (F) Group 5=UC+SM+C+F+ semi-annual prophylaxis	After 3 years, no differences in gingival inflammation; no differences in probing depth; no differences in clinical attachment loss; however, tooth loss favored groups 3,4, and 5 over groups 1 and 2.	13/20	65%
Walsh, Heckman, Moreau-Dettinger (1985)	36 patients in U.S. with gingival inflammation and bleeding on probing	Yes	Group1: instructed in TB use Group 2: instructed in toothpick use Group 3: instructed to use toothpick to self-assess bleeding on probing at home	After 3 months, groups 2 and 3 showed significantly less gingival bleeding compared to group 1.	13/20	65%
Moltzer, Hoogstraten (1986)	82 new patients of a group practice in the Netherlands	Yes	Group 1: 6 min film on dental hygiene Group 2: film plus 30-min hygienist led group discussion Group 3: 30-min standard verbal information and OHI from hygienist	6 months after treatment, no group differences for knowledge, attitude toward care, fear, self-care behaviors, or oral cleanliness	12/20	60%
Rinchuse, Rinchuse, Zullo (1992)	70 consecutively treated orthodontic patients, aged 6-17, in private practice in U.S.	Yes	Group 1: OH evaluated by orthodontist Group 2: evaluated by orthodontist and parents Group 3: evaluated by orthodontist and patient Group 4: evaluated by orthodontist, parents, and patient All groups received OHI	After 5 monthly appointments, no group differences. No gains in oral cleanliness over time for any group. Parents and patients tended to rate oral cleanliness higher than did orthodontists.	12/20	60%
Glavind, Zeuner (1985)	24 periodontal patients in Denmark	Yes	Experimental: scaling, manualized OHI plus 12-minute videotaped OHI. Control: scaling, manualized OHI only.	After 8 weeks, no group differences for plaque, gingival bleeding, or ability to properly clean teeth in an observed 'toothbrushing test'.	11/20	55%
Baab, Weinstein (1986)	31 adult periodontal recall patients in U.S.	Yes	Group 1: instructed over 4 visits to use at-home DA Group 2: shown disclosure during 4 office visits	After 6 months, no group differences for bleeding on probing or oral hygiene skills. Group 1 showed decreased plaque over time, but this may reflect regression to the mean.	16/19	84%
Blinkhorn, Downer, Mackie, Bleasdale (1981)	178 socially deprived, urban children aged 11-13 receiving routine dental care in Scotland	Yes	Experimental: Three visits, 6 months apart, with chairside instruction on diet, fluoride tablets, and OHI. Fluoride tablets provided for home use. Control: No tx control.	No effect for periodontal measures, no overall effect for caries increment. When girls were analyzed separately, a small decrease in caries was found in favor of experimental group. Girls more compliant w/ home fluoride tablets.	16/19	84%
Bullen, Rubenstein, Saravia, Mourino (1988)	Parents of 50 preschool children who were patients at dental clinics in U.S.	Yes	Experimental: Parents shown how to brush childs teeth, practiced on the child to proficiency Control: Parents shown how to brush child's teeth, but did not practice to proficiency.	At 4 weeks, experimental children had significantly decreased plaque scores relative to controls. Results favored new patients over recall patients. No group differences for gingival index.	16/19	84%

Study	Sample			Intervention	Results		
Feil, Grauer, Gadbury-Amyot, Kula, McCunniff (2002)	40 adolescent orthodontic patients with poor oral hygiene in U.S.	Yes	Yes	Experimental: asked to participate in a study of 'experimental' TP, but this was a placebo and aim of study was to observe the Hawthorne effect. Control: not asked to participate in any study	At 3 and 6 months, experimental Ss showed significant decreases in plaque relative to controls.	16/19	84%
Ambjornsen, Rise (1985)	138 elderly edentulous denture wearers in Norway	Yes	Yes	Group 1: five-min of verbal information from dentist on cleaning dentures. Group 2: verbal information plus demonstration of plaque disclosure. Group 3: no tx control	14 days after treatment, groups 1 and 2 had significantly less plaque than group 3. At 180 days, group 1 showed significantly less plaque than groups 2 and 3.	15/19	79%
Glavind, Zeuner, Attstrom (1983)	63 adult periodontal patients at a university dental clinic in Denmark	Yes	No	Group 1: brochure on brushing technique; given oral hygiene kit (TB, interdental aids, DA, MM). Group 2: manualized OHI and oral hygiene kit. Group 3: same as group 2, plus feedback re: plaque. Group 4: same as group 2, plus feedback re: brushing	After 3 months, plaque scores were significantly lower for the 2 groups that received feedback relative to those without feedback. Differences disappeared by 7 and 13 months. No group differences for gingival bleeding.	15/19	79%
Glavind, Zeuner, Attstrom (1981)	37 adult Danish dental patients	Yes	No	Group 1: manualized self-instruction OHI. Group 2: individual OHI from a dental hygienist. Group 3: brief brochure on brushing technique	No group differences. All groups improved on plaque scores after week 2, but no additional improvement was seen at 3 or 6 month follow up. All groups showed improved bleeding on probing from baseline to 6 weeks.	15/19	79%
Glavind, Zeuner and Attstrom (1984)	74 patients with periodontal disease at a university dental clinic in Denmark	Yes	Yes	Group 1: manualized gingival self-assessment, followed by manualized OHI; given TB, TA, MM, and interdental aids. Group 2: OHI only; TB, TA, MM, and interdental aids. Group 3: received OHI 6 weeks after groups 1 and 2	At 3 months, group 2 showed significant improvements in plaque and bleeding on probing, with no additional benefits found due to self-assessment in group 1 or delay in OHI in group 3. Improvements were maintained for an additional 4 months.	14/19	74%
Alcouffe (1988)	26 adult periodontal patients w/ poor oral hygiene at a university clinic in France	Yes	Yes	Experimental: one-hour of 'exploratory listening' with a psychologist regarding oral hygiene adherence. Control: no tx control	After 3 months, experimental Ss showed significant decrease in plaque relative to controls. Group differences maintained at 2 years.	13/19	68%
Baab, Weinstein (1983)	18 adult periodontal recall patients in U.S.	No	No	Manualized oral self-inspection plaque index. Given a lighted mouth mirror and DA for home use.	Before-brushing plaque scores decreased by week 2 and were maintained at 6 weeks. After-brushing plaque scores decreased more slowly, but reached significance by week 6.	13/19	68%
Richter, Nanda, Sinha, Smith (1998)	144 pediatric orthodontic patients in U.S.	Yes	Yes	Group 1: standard orthodontic OHI. Group 2: standard orthodontic OHI plus monthly compliance report cards. Group 3: standard orthodontic OHI plus small rewards for compliance and entry into raffle for prizes	At 6 months, a particularly noncompliant subset of Ss in group 3 showed significant improvements in oral hygiene compared to group 1. No treatment effects were detected for appointment punctuality, appliance wear, or appliance maintenance.	13/19	68%

Study	Sample			Intervention	Results		
Soderholm, Nobreus, Attstrom, Egelberg (1982)	69 adults in Sweden	Yes	Yes	Group 1: received five consecutive 30 min OHI sessions over 14 days Group 2: same educational components given in two 60-minute sessions Group 3: no treatment	Groups 1 and 2 both improved on plaque, gingival bleeding, and pocket scores. No differences between groups 1 and 2. Control group also showed improvements for plaque and gingival bleeding.	13/19	68%
Tan, Wade (1980)	38 adult periodontal patients in England	Yes	Yes	Group 1: OHI, scale and polish, TB provision Group 2: OHI, scale and polish, given TB and DA and lighted MM for home use Crossover design so that both groups eventually got treatment.	No treatment differences. After 2 weeks, both groups showed significantly improved plaque scores.	13/19	68%
Boyd (1983)	24 orthodontic patients aged 9-14 in U.S. who were scheduled to receive full banded orthodontic appliances	Yes.	Yes	Group 1: prophylaxis and three 15-minute brushing lessons Group 2: prophylaxis and three 15-minute brushing instruction sessions, plus DA for home use. Group 3: prophylaxis, no specific plaque control	At 10 months, group 1 showed temporary improvement followed by a return to baseline levels. Group 3 showed significantly increased gingivitis scores compared to baseline.	12/19	63%
Weinstein, Tosolin, Ghilardi, Zanardelli (1996)	20 adult patients with periodontic problems	Yes	Yes	Group 1: chairside OHI, and twice weekly professional exam w/ verbal praise contingent upon plaque score Group 2: same as group 1 plus charting self-care behaviors Group 3: chairside OHI Group 4: chairside OHI plus weekly phone reports to dentist of self-assessed plaque scores	After 2 months of treatment, group 2 showed the greatest reduction in full mouth plaque.	11/19	58%
Goodkind, Loupe, Clay, Di Angelis (1988)	92 edentulous patients of a university prosthodontics clinic in U.S.	Yes	No	Experimental: 7 chairside sessions and 2 small group seminars on proper care of dentures Control: routine care	4-6 months after dentures were inserted, experimental group showed modest benefits for denture knowledge and self-care relative to controls, but no skill improvement.	10/19	53%
Holst, Ek (1988)	5173 pediatric patients of 127 dentists in Sweden	Yes	No	Experimental: Dentists trained in behavior shaping via manual and videotape Control: No tx control dentists	Acceptance of procedures higher among children of experimental dentists. Effect was strongest for youngest children, and those receiving restoration/extraction.	10/19	53%
Stewart, Wolfe, Maeder, Hartz (1996)	123 male U.S. veterans	Yes	Yes	Group 1: four weekly forty-min OHEsessions Group 2: four weekly forty-min sessions of stage-based, motivational behavior change Group 3: no tx control	Both groups showed significant gains in knowledge relative to controls. Group 2 showed significant gains in flossing self –efficacy relative to groups 1 and controls.	16/18	89%
Primosch, Balsewich, Thomas (2001)	300 U.S. Medicaid children <6 yo needing follow up after procedures w/ general anesthesia	Yes	No	Consultation appointment with parents re: importance of follow-up care; appointment cards; written OHE materials	No differences in attendance at follow-up appointments. Lack of follow up still extremely problematic.	13/18	72%

Study	Sample			Treatment	Results		
Hoogstraten Moltzer (1983)	108 adult patients of a group private practice in the Netherlands	Yes	Yes	Group 1: 30-min of standard chairside OHI from hygienist; Group 2: same as group 1 plus 10-minute videotape covering the same material; Group 3: no treatment control	Groups 1 and 2 showed some benefits for self-care behaviors and attitude toward dental hygiene and behavior relative to controls. No differences between experimental groups.	12/18	67%
Gross, Sanders, Smith, Samson (1990)	12 pediatric orthodontic patients beginning treatment w/ headgear at a univ. dental clinic	Yes	Yes	Experimental: parents instructed in contingency management procedure for headgear use at home; Control: no tx control	After approximately 5 months of treatment, experimental Ss showed significantly greater headgear use compared to controls. Effect maintained at 2 month follow up.	11/18	61%
Cureton, Regenmitter, Yancey (1993)	28 adolescent orthodontic patients in U.S.	Yes	No	Experimental: Ss charted their headgear use on a calendar; Control: no tx control	Charting daily headgear use significantly increased amount of time that headgear was worn.	10/18	56%
Rantanen, Shrila, Lehvila (1980)	89 denture-wearing patients at a university clinic in Denmark	Yes	Yes	Group 1: four-page denture-related OHE brochure; Group 2: same as group 1, plus pictures, plus individual education and motivation at each visit; Group 3: no tx control	After 1 year of treatment, group 1 showed small but significant benefits for knowledge. No differences for oral self-care.	10/18	56%
Stewart, Wolfe (1989)	33 adult male patients in U.S.	No	No	Two 30-minute OHI sessions w/ return demonstration of proper brushing and flossing technique and corrective feedback.	At 3 weeks, brushing and flossing skills improved significantly, and plaque decreased significantly. At 1 year, skills remained good, but plaque had increased to baseline levels.	10/18	56%
West, Pendergrast (1993)	162 U.S. low SES, Black adolescent medical patients in need of a dental appointment	Yes	Yes	Appointment reminder card. vs. no card. Appointment scheduled by patient vs. by health professional.	No effect on appointment keeping for reminder card. No effect for person scheduling appointment. No interaction.	12/17	71%
Weinstein et al. (1989)	71 'high plaque' patients in state dental practices in U.S.	No	No	Baseline: oral health status assessed at home visit. 2 weeks: prophylaxis and chairside OHI by either periodontists or general dentists. Oral health status assessed at home again at 6 and 24 weeks.	Fewer than 1 in 3 patients had plaque scores below 1.0 at 6 weeks, and only 1 in 7 at 24 weeks. No differences for type of provider.	10/17	59%
Hujoel, Powell, Kiyak (1997)	Adults >60 years receiving care at low cost community clinics in U.S.	Yes	Yes	Group 1: Usual care (UC); Group 2: UC + cognitive behavioral treatment (CBT); Group 3: UC + CBT + chlorhexidine rinse (CHX); Group 4: UC + CBT + CHX + semi-annual fluoride varnish (F); Group 5: UC + CBT + CHX + F + scaling	Tooth mortality after first year of treatment was 45% lower in groups 3,4, and 5 than in groups 1 and 2. After 2 years of treatment, difference increased to 59%. Group 5 showed most improvement.	14/15	3%
Cohen, Weinstein, Wurster (1980)	306 patients of a community dental clinic in U.S.	No	No	Group 1: phone call to remind patients of next appointment; Group 2: postcard mailed to patient, requesting patient call to confirm next appointment; Group 3: postcard given at first appt., requesting patient call to confirm	Each treatment was run in sequence for 2 months. Group 3 showed a significantly lower missed appointment rate relative to other groups and to baseline.	10/15	67%

Table 3. School Based Interventions.

Reference	Population		Randomization	Intervention	Results	Score	%
Julien (1994)	403 Canadian schoolchildren from 16 classes	Yes	Schools randomized	Experimental: 1-2 parent workshops w/ OHI and contingency management contract made between child, parent, and project director; TB, DA, floss, and monitoring chart. 15 months periodic schoolbased OHE. Control: no tx control	After 4 months of intensive intervention, experimental Ss showed lower plaque and gingival scores relative to controls. One year after full 15-month program, effect for plaque scores remained, but not for gingival scores.	17/20	85%
Pine, McGoldrick, Burnside, Curnow, Chesters, Nicholson, Huntington (2000)	461 5-year-old children in a materially deprived area of Scotland	Yes	Yes	Experimental: supervised daily toothbrushing at school w/ variable reinforcement; home charting of toothbrushing; TB provision Control: no tx control	After 2 years, no group differences for frequency of home brushing. However, experimental Ss showed 56% less dentinal caries in first permanent molar teeth than controls, indicating benefit of school brushing.	17/20	85%
Kallio, Uutela, Nordblad, Alvesalo, Murtomaa (1997)	328 adolescents attending public school in Finland	Yes	Yes	Group 1: single session dental office based self-assessment of gingival bleeding w/ toothpicks; given TB, toothpicks, MM Group 2: single session dental office based self-assessment of plaque with DA; given TB, toothpicks, MM	After 9 months, both groups showed comparable, significant improvement in bleeding on probing relative to baseline. Higher SES was related to better outcomes.	16/20	80%
Worthington, Hill, Mooney, Hamilton, Blinkhorn (2001)	>288 ten-year olds in England	Yes	Schools randomized	Four, 1-hour interactive school-based educational sessions with a dental facilitator	Treatment group had slightly lower plaque scores and greater knowledge about how to use TB and DA. Effects remained at 7 months	16/20	80%
Wight, Blinkhorn (1988)	1067 Scottish adolescent schoolchildren	Yes	No	Group 1: four small-group sessions per year of schoolbased dental education and OHI delivered by a visiting dental hygienist; topical fluoride gel 2X/year given by hygienist Group 2: three lessons per year of schoolbased dental education delivered by teachers 7 OHI by visiting hygienist; fluoride tablets given daily by teachers. Group 3: no tx control	After 2 years, group 1 showed modest benefit for DMFT increment, probably due to fluoride gel administration. Both experimental groups showed small benefits for knowledge and gingival inflammation relative to controls.	15/20	75%
Melsen, Agerbaek (1980)	164 adolescent schoolchildren in Denmark	Yes	Classes randomized	Experimental: biweekly 20-minute sessions of OHE, games, and activities Control: no tx control	After 2 years, no group differences for knowledge, plaque, or DMFS scores.	14/20	70%
Redmond, Blinkhorn, Kay, Davies, Worthington, Blinkhorn (1999)	School children (M=12 years) in England	Yes	Schools randomized	Experimental: Three 20-min sessions of school based, small group, interactive OHE; TB, TP and DA; letter to parents encouraging children's self-care. Control: No tx control	After 6 months of treatment, experimental group showed increased knowledge, longer brushing times, and lower plaque scores than controls. Differences in plaque maintained at 12 months.	14/20	70%

Citation	Sample			Intervention	Results		
Craft, Croucher, Blinkhorn (1984)	410 Scottish schoolchildren aged 13-14 years	Yes	Schools randomized	Experimental Group: Three 75-min sessions OHE integrated into biology curriculum including lessons, experiments, and activities re etiology of dental disease; homework including experiments and activities. Control Group: No tx control.	5 weeks from baseline experimental group showed improvements in knowledge, attitude toward self-care, and plaque compared to controls. At 6 months follow up, experimental group still showed some plaque benefits. No differences for gingival inflammation.	13/20	65%
Olsen, Brown, Wright (1986)	310 students, aged 6-9 years, from 4 schools in Australia	Yes	Schools randomized	Group 1: One home-visit by a health worker; individualized, need based OHE Group 2: mailed notification of child's dental status and standard oral health information	Group 1 showed small benefit for DMFT scores.	13/20	65%
Tan, Ruiter, Verhey (1981)	85 Dutch royal military academy students	Yes	No	Experimental: OHI and prophylaxis by hygienist plus a 4-6 month follow up group discussion of problems with oral hygiene. Control: no tx control.	Experimental Ss showed improvements in dental knowledge, attitude, reported behavior, and ability to detect gingivitis. Effects replicated in a second experiment.	13/20	65%
Craft, Croucher, Dickinson (1981)	1491 English schoolchildren randomly sampled from 4500 who received intervention	Yes	No	Experimental: 3-week, schoolbased OHE curriculum package, including behavioral concepts, delivered by teachers Control: no tx control	At posttest, experimental Ss showed benefits for knowledge, attitude toward self-care, and self-care behaviors. Re-examination of a subset of Ss at 6-9 months follow up shows some benefit for plaque and gingival health.	11/20	55%
Mazzocchi, Moretti (1997)	397 eight-year-old schoolchildren in Italy	Yes	Yes	Experimental: in –school exposure to a children's dental education book Control: no tx control	Authors report a significant reduction in plaque for experimental group.	10/20	50%
McIntyre, Wight, Blinkhorn (1985)	400 Scottish schoolchildren	Yes	No	Compared a random sample of 209 children who received OHE according to Blinkhorn, McIntyre, MacPhail, Shove (1981) to 101 control children.	Results difficult to interpret, but experimental children showed some benefit for plaque and self-reported eating habits compared to controls.	10/20	50%
Rayner (1992)	349 Scottish nursery school children from deprived urban neighborhoods	Yes	No	Group 1: supervised daily brushing in school Group 2: same as group 1 plus 2 sessions of home OHI for parents Group 3: two sessions of home OHI for parents only Group 4: no tx control	After 1 year, groups 2 and 3 showed significant improvements in plaque levels and gingivitis. However, parental compliance with home visits was poor, with >30% refusal rate.	16/19	84%
Walsh (1985)	639 adolescent public middle school students in U.S.	Yes	Yes	Experimental: Four 1-hour classroom dental health sessions including didactics on caries, PD, fluoride and plaque, and supervised brushing and flossing. Control: no tx control	At posttest, experimental group showed significant benefits for knowledge relative to controls. No group differences for attitude toward self-care. Girls in the experimental group showed improvement for frequency of brushing and flossing.	16/19	84%
Bentley, Cormier, Oler (1983)	1,452 rural children aged 5-13 in U.S.	Yes	Grades randomized	Private practice in community vs. school based dental practice with a standard treatment protocol. Standard school-based health education vs. enriched school-based dental education. All children received free dental care and school-based fluoride treatment.	After three years of treatment, children in the combined school based practice + enriched dental education used dental services more regularly than the other 3 groups. Moreover, these children were more likely to receive appropriate intervention at time of service.	14/19	74%

Study	Sample			Intervention	Results		
Buischi, Axelsson, Oliveria, Mayer, Gjermo (1994)	186 13 year old Brazilian private schoolchildren	Yes	Yes	Group 1: comprehensive OHI with group discussion for children and parents Group 2: standard child OHI Group 3: no tx control from same school as groups 1 and 2 Group 4: no tx control from a different school	After 3 years, group 1 showed improvements in knowledge and self-reported sugar consumption and flossing compared to all other groups. Group 2 showed more knowledge than groups 3 or 4.	14/19	74%
Nowjack-Raymer, Ainamo, Suomi, Kingsman, Driscoll, Brown (1995)	336 14-15 year olds in U.S. public school	Yes	Yes	Group 1: group, individual, and written instruction for gingival bleeding assessment Group 2: group, individual, and written instruction for plaque assessment. Both groups received oral hygiene kits (e.g., interdental aids and MM)	After 24 months, no group differences. Both groups showed significant and steadily decreasing bleeding on probing from baseline to follow-up.	14/19	74%
Nylander, Kumlin, Martinsson, Twetman (2001)	874 7th graders in Sweden	Yes	No	School based, yearly OHI and feedback on lactobacillus count, emphasis on healthy eating	After 5 years of treatment, no differences	14/19	74%
Albandar, Buischi, Mayer, Axelsson (1994)	227 Brazilian 13-year olds attending private school	Yes	Yes	Group 1: Comprehensive, individualized OHI including home plaque disclosure and plaque and gingivitis charting Group 2: Conventional OHI Group 3: No tx control	After 3 years, group 1 had significantly less plaque and gingival bleeding than groups 2 and 3. No differences between groups 2 and 3.	13/19	68%
Hodge, Buchanan, O'Donnell, Topping, Banks (1987)	273 schoolchildren aged 10-11 years, in England	Yes	No	Experimental: four 1-hour weekly dental education lessons emphasizing brushing and decreasing sugar intake Control: no tx control	One week posttreatment, experimental Ss showed significantly better knowledge and plaque levels. Middle income children benefited more than low income children.	13/19	68%
Blinkhorn, McIntyre, MacPhail, Shove (1981)	201 Scottish schoolchildren sampled from 4 schools in working class areas	No	No	One-week program w/ supervised brushing at school; TB, TP, and DA for home use; posters, wall charts, and informational pamphlets given to Ss.	Six months posttreatment, 24% decrease in number of children w/ gingivitis, improvement in caries knowledge, and uptake of dental treatment such that unmet needs decreased. No change in plaque.	12/19	63%
Torpaz, Noam, Anaise, Sgan-Cohen (1984)	180 Israeli schoolchildren aged 11-14 years	Yes	Yes	Assigned to either no tx control, or to one of 10 experimental groups, each a permutation of OHI lecture, OHI group instruction, individual OHI, and TB provision.	After one month, all experimental groups showed improved hygiene relative to controls, with groups receiving TBs showing the most improvements. Differences increased at 3 months, but by 10 months, all groups deteriorated.	11/19	58%
Arnold, Doyle (1984)	124 English schoolchildren, 13 and 14-years old	Yes	No	Replication of Craft, Croucher, Dickinson (1981). Compared children who completed that program to a control group who had not.	At posttest and 6 months, experimental group showed very small gains in knowledge relative to controls; no group differences for plaque.	10/19	53%
Howat, Craft, Croucher, Rock, Foster (1985)	169 schoolchildren aged 8-9 years and 13-14 years from 8 schools in U.K.	No	No	Two sessions of school-based OHE sessions of 2.5 hours each, 4-6 months apart. OHE delivered by dental students.	At posttest, there was a small decrease in plaque for anterior, but not posterior teeth. No changes in frequency of brushing or snacking habits,	10/19	53%

Study	Sample	Control	Randomized	Intervention	Results	Score	%
Sogaard, Tuominen, Holst, Gjermo (1987)	1038 15-year old Norwegians in 15 public schools	Yes	Classrooms randomized	Group 1:one-shot standard gingival health education Group 2: Standard education w/ visualization and parental involvement Group 3: no tx control	At 1 week post-treatment all groups improved on bleeding on probing. Children with worst baseline status improved most, and benefited more from enhanced treatment	10/19	53%
Towner (1984)	34 elementary schoolchildren (randomly sampled from 1533 English schoolchildren who had received the interventions)	No	No	Using a core manual as a guide, teachers designed their own school based dental curricula that emphasized accurate, consistent dental health messages and promoted positive aspects of oral health. Parental involvement and child participation and activity were encouraged.	After 2 semesters, the subset of children sampled showed some improvements plaque, gingival condition, and self-reported brushing frequency.	10/19	53%
ter Horst, Hoogstraten (1989)	452 Dutch adolescent public school children	Yes	Schools randomized	Experimental: 20-min film on the causes, consequences, and prevention of PD was shown during regular class time Control: no film	Substantial increases in knowledge and small increases in attitudes were detected immediately after film and maintained at 2 months. No differences in self reported behavior.	14/18	78%
Holund (1990)	114 adolescent schoolchildren in Denmark	Yes	No	Experimental: 14-year olds participate in 25 dietary lessons, and then delivered a healthy eating presentation to classrooms of 10-year olds Control: no tx control	Eating behavior of the 14-year olds was the treatment target. Relative to controls, experimental Ss showed significant decreases in between meal sugar consumption and overall sugar consumption. Benefits maintained at 2-month follow up.	12/18	67%
Sogaard, Holst (1988)	1167 fifteen-year old schoolchildren in 15 Norwegian public schools	Yes	No	Group 1: comprehensive school-based gingival health education w/ active involvement, visualization, and parental support Group 2: traditional gingival health education Group 3: no tx control	After 3 weeks, group 1 showed benefits for brushing rate, knowledge, self-efficacy, communication with parents re: dental health, and openness to media dental messages. No effect for caries knowledge or use of interdental aids.	12/18	67%
Cooke, Graham, Sadles (1983)	31 7th graders in parochial school in U.S.	Yes	No	Experimental: two 45-minute school-based dental health education sessions, yearly for 5 years Control: no tx control	Experimental Ss showed significantly better plaque scores, fewer decayed surfaces, and more use of dental treatment, and more dental knowledge, relative to controls.	11/18	61%
McGlynn, Mings, Marks, Goebel (1985)	52 dental students in U.S.	Ss served as own controls	No	Ss trained in goal setting, monitoring, and contingency management. Implemented these strategies sequentially across brushing and flossing for 1 semester.	Behavioral self-management generally increased targeted behaviors. Adherence self-reports confirmed with measurement of unused floss/TP.	10/18	56%
Russell, Horowitz Frazier (1989)	284 sixth-grade students in U.S.	Yes	No	Experimental: Four years of one of the six National Preventive Dentistry Demonstration Program treatment regimens; included yearly school-based OHE and supervised brushing/flossing. Control: No treatment control	16 months after the end of the intervention there were no group differences for knowledge or self-reported oral self-care behaviors.	10/18	56%
Truin, Plasschaert, Konig, Vogels (1981)	800 schoolchildren exposed to a city-wide oral public health campaign in the Netherlands	No	No	OHE materials given to mothers at birth, 6-10 weeks after birth, and well-baby checks. Children 4-6 years exposed to OHE materials 1-2X/year. Children 6-9 years exposed to variety of posters and learning materials.	9 years after implementation, significant reduction in caries experience for all age groups. Higher SES children benefited most.	10/18	56%

Laiho, Honkala, Nyyssonen, Milen (1993)	357 7th graders in three schools in Finland	Yes	No	Group 1: 45 min of standard OHE given by a dentist to groups of 25 pupils. Group 2: 45 min of OHE delivered by trained pupils to groups of 20 of their peers. Group 3: pupils attended an oral health exhibit for 30 min and gathered information	At posttest, Ss in groups 1 and 2 endorsed significantly greater need for improvement in their oral self-care.	12/17	71%
Cipes, Miraglia (1985)	224 second-graders in 4 public U.S. schools	Yes	Yes	Group 1: OHE slide show; 14 day supply fluoride mouthrinse for home use. Group 2: same as group 1 plus at home charting of mouthrinsing. Group 3: same as group 1 plus parent controlled contingency management of mouthrinsing. Group 4: same as group 1 plus charting and contingency management.	After 14 weeks of treatment, group 2 showed significantly more doses of mouthrinsing, returned more bottles, and used more doses per bottle relative to other groups.	11/17	65%
Swain, Allard, Holborn (1982)	45 elementary schoolchildren in Canada	Subjects served as their own controls	No	Baseline: in-school plaque disclosure Treatment: Students divided into teams who competed daily in a 'cleanest teeth' contest with DA for 2 weeks. Winners names posted in classroom, and won stickers.	Toothbrushing game substantially lowered plaque scores relative to baseline. 9-month follow up continued to show decreased plaque score relative to baseline levels.	10/17	59%
Albandar, Buischi, Oliveira, Axelsson (1995)	227 sixth-grade Brazilian schoolchildren	Yes	Yes	Group 1: standard OHI 3 times/year; TB, TP, and tape. Group 2: Individualized OHI w/ plaque disclosure and flossing instruction, plus feedback and motivation 3 times per year; given TB, TP, tape, and DA. Group 3: Given TP only.	After 3 years, no group differences for alveolar bone loss. All groups showed significant bone loss over time.	13/15	87%

Table 4. Community Based Interventions.

Study	Sample			Intervention	Results		
McCaul, Glasgow, O'Neill (1992)	181 U.S. college students, divided into 3 experiments	Yes	Yes	Experiment 1: three sessions of flossing instruction vs. flossing instruction w/ social support. Experiment 2: Similar to experiment 1, except Ss received no- minimal- or intensive-contact from a dental hygienist during a 10 week maintenance period. Experiment 3: similar to experiment 2, except all Ss had mild gingivitis, and were assigned to either a flexible maintenance plan, a difficult to achieve maintenance plan, or no maintenance plan.	Experiment 1: at posttreatment, Ss w/ social support significantly increased flossing; but, by 2-month follow up flossing dropped dramatically across groups. Experiment 2: at posttreatment and during 10 week maintenance, flossing increased equivalently across all groups; but, by 2 month follow up flossing dropped dramatically across groups; by 9 months, no Ss flossed regularly. Experiment 3: difficult to achieve maintenance plan, or no maintenance plan only. No group differences found during treatment or at 2- or 6-month follow up.	17/20	85%
Price, Kiyak (1981)	60 independent living members of 2 senior centers in the U.S., serving European- and Japanese- Americans	Yes	Yes	Group 1: 6 OHI group lectures over 3 weeks; TB and TP. Group 2: same as group 1 plus daily charting of oral self care behaviors and verbal reinforcement of performance during the lectures. Group 3: given TB and TP only	After treatment, groups 1 and 2 both showed decreased plaque scores relative to group 3. However, only group 2 maintained these benefits at 3 week follow up. Group 2 also showed the strongest benefits for self-care behaviors and beliefs about importance and control of oral health.	16/20	80%
Holt, Winter, Fox, Askew (1985)	324 mothers of young children in U.K.	Yes	Yes	Group 1: Three home visits before child 18 months old, w/ need based oral health information and free fluoride drops. Group 2: mothers received dental health literature through the mail as per group 1's schedule. Group 3: no tx control	When children reached 5 years, mothers in group 1 were significantly more likely to administer fluoride to children, had fewer caries, and less gingivitis. Lowest caries were found in mothers who administered fluoride drops for the longest duration. No group differences for plaque or eating habits.	15/20	75%
Schou, Wight, Clemson, Douglas, Clark (1989)	201 institutionalized elderly in Scotland	Yes	Yes	Group 1: three 1-hour oral health sessions w/ active involvement of residents only. Group 2: same as group 1, but w/ active involvement of staff. Group 3: same as group 1, but w/ active involvement of both staff and residents. Group 4: no tx control	Six months after the beginning of the program, no group differences for oral hygiene behaviors. About50% of the sample could not remember having participated.	15/20	75%
Ekman, Perrson (1990)	Immigrant Finnish and native Swedish families, in Sweden	Yes	Yes	Group 1: Finnish families; oral health education in Finnish when child was 6 and then 18 months old. Group 2: Finnish families; education in Swedish as per group 1's schedule. Group 3: Finnish families, no treatment control. Group 4: Swedish families, education in Swedish as per group 1's schedule	At 36 months, children whose immigrant parents received education in their own language were more likely to be caries free and have lower DFS scores than parents who received education in non-native language. All immigrant groups had worse oral outcomes than the native Swedish group.	14/20	70%
Hetland, Midtun, Kristoffersen (1981)	71 adult employees of a single worksite in Norway	Yes	Yes	Group 1: prophylaxis. Group 2: OHI. Group 3: prophylaxis and OHI	After 24 weeks, groups 2 and 3 showed significantly more improvement on plaque, gingival index, and pocket depth compared to group 1.	14/20	70%

Study			Intervention	Results	Score	%
Mojon, Rentsch, Budtz-Jorgensen, Baehni, (1998)	Yes	Wards randomized	Experimental: 45 minute dental education presentation to caregivers of residents, OHI, plus as-needed on-site prophylaxis; TB and TP. Control: standard care	After 18 months, experimental group showed significantly fewer active root caries and lower streptococci count relative to control. No group differences for plaque.	17/19	89%
Bagley, Low 1992	Yes	Yes	Experimental: Shown pictures of the progression of PD; discussion of the importance of flossing. Control: Flossing instruction only.	No group differences. After 24 days, self-reported flossing increased and plaque scores decreased for both groups.	15/19	79%
Fishwick, Ashley, Wilson (1998)	Yes	Worksites randomized	Experimental: feedback regarding clinical status, written information, plus TB, DA, and floss. Control: no tx control	After 6 weeks, experimental Ss showed a significant reduction in bleeding on probing and pocket depth, relative to controls.	15/19	79%
Lim, Davies (1996)	Yes	Yes	Group 1: OHI only Group 2: scaling only Group 3: OHI + scaling Group 4: no tx control	At 16 months, all treatment groups had significantly lower plaque and bleeding scores compared to baseline and compared to the control group. OHI+scaling showed the best and most consistent response.	14/19	74%
Lim , Davies, Yuen (1996)	Yes	Yes	Group 1: personal OHI instruction Group 2: video OHI instruction Group 3: written OHI manual Group 4: combination of 1, 2 and 3	No group differences.At 2 weeks, 4 months, and 10 months, all groups showed significant reductions in bleeding and plaque scores.	14/19	74%
Vigild (1990)	Yes	No	Experimental: Staff given OHI, plus on site, part time dentist available for consultation, treatment, and preventive measures. Control: Routine care	After 1 year, 50% of experimental group received care from a dentist compared to 16% of controls. Emergency dental care decreased by 56% in experimental group, but increased by 20% in controls. Per resident cost for dental care was actually slightly less for experimental group than controls.	14/19	74%
Bruerd, Kinmey, Bothwell (1989)	No	No	Each community used a core manual to flexibly design their own culturally appropriate intervention to reduce early child caries (ECC). Individual and public health approaches were used. All Ss received sippee cups.	After 3 years, prevalence of ECC decreased an average of 25% across all sites (range 18%-33%).	13/19	68%
Shaw, Shaw (1991)	Yes	Yes	Group 1: supervised daily brushing and 6-monthly OHI by hygienist Group 2: supervised daily brushing and 3-monthly OHI plus prophylaxis Group 3: supervised daily brushing and monthly OHI plus prophylaxis Group 4: no tx control	All treatment groups showed benefits for plaque, calculus, and pocket depth relative to control. 3-monthly treatment was equivalent to monthly treatment	13/19	68%
Kallio, Ainamo, Dusadeepan (1990)	Yes	Yes	Experimental: manualized instruction for the assessment of gingival bleeding; given TB, toothpicks, and MM Control: written OHI	At 1 and 3 months, experimental group who had high levels of gingival bleeding at baseline showed significant improvement compared to controls. Differences lost by 6 months.	12/19	63%
Soderholm, Egelberg (1982)	Yes	Yes	Group 1: three 30-min OHI sessions over 14 days Group 2: three 15-minute OHI sessions over 14 days Group 3: no tx control	At 12 weeks, no group differences. Both treatment groups improved on plaque relative to controls from baseline.	12/19	63%

Author (Year)	Sample		Health centers randomized	Intervention	Results	Ratio	%
Sgan-Cohen, Mansbach, Haver, Gofin (2001)	Parents of 6-12 month old infants in Jerusalem	Yes	Yes	Nurse education (15 min per visit of OHI, video on pacifying infants without bottle, and brochures on child oral health) vs. no education. Free TB and TP vs. none.	No differences in bottle drinking practices. Increases in brushing were greatest in education + dentifrice group.	15/18	3%
Hamilton, Davis, Blinkhorn (1999)	500 mothers of nursing babies who had never received oral health promotion, in England	Yes	No	Experimental: when children aged 8 months, home health visitors gave mothers dental package of sippee cup, baby TB, baby TP, and literature re: weening and ECC, during routine health visit. Control: no dental package given during health visit.	Compared to controls, experimental mothers recalled advice regarding sippee cups, brushing with fluoride, restricting sugar intake, and registering the child with a dentist. Experimental mothers also more likely to bring children to clinic for a routine hearing check.	12/18	67%
Holt, Winter, Fox, Askew (1989)	126 children out of an original 1321 English children.	Yes	Yes	Group 1: three home visits when child <16 months; given fluoride drops and OHE. Group 2: pamphlets through the mail providing same information as group 1; offered fluoride droplets from local clinic, but required to pick them up themselves Group 3: no tx control.	10-year follow-up shows no group differences for caries. However, group 1 showed less plaque and better gingival health than groups 2 or 3.	12/18	67%
Lunn, Williams (1990)	84 mentally disabled children attending special school in England	No	No	Staff trained in OHI; supervised daily brushing w/ assistance as needed.	At 3, 9, and 14 months Ss showed decreased debris score relative to baseline. Most severely disabled Ss benefited most.	11/18	61%
Benitez, O'Sullivan, Tinanoff (1994)	Caretakers of 17 children, aged 21-36 months, with evidence of ECC, at community pediatric dental clinics in U.S.	No	No	During routine clinic visit, caretakers instructed to brush w/ fluoride, and to wean children or substitute water for sweet liquid. Instructions reinforced with phone call between visits.	After 3 months, the 2 children weaned and using fluoride showed no caries progression and decreased streptococci count. However, most not weaned, not using the fluoride, and carious lesions increased in number and severity for most children.	10/18	56%
Holt, Winter, Fox, Askew, Lo (1983)	314 mothers of young children in U.K.	No	No	As part of a larger study, mothers received 3 home visits before child 18 months old, w/ need based OHE and free fluoride drops.	Virtually all mothers accepted the free fluoride drops, and at 16 months, 65% reported using them. Use of sweetened comforters decreased.	9/18	50%
Bruerd, Jones (1996)	1319 three-to-five year old American Indian/Alaska Native children enrolled in 12 Head Start centers in 10 states	No	Yes	8-year follow up to Bruerd, Kinney and Bothwell (1989)	Five sites that continued the program during the 8-year follow up showed significant decrease in ECC of 38%. Seven sites that did not continue the program during the 8-year follow-up showed a non-significant increase in ECC.	11/17	65%
Croucher, Rodgers, Humpherson, Crush, (1985)	Families of 73 schoolchildren in U.K.	Yes	No	Experimental: Families of schoolchildren had participated in "natural nashers" as per Craft, Croucher and Blinkhorn (1984) Control: Families of schoolchildren who had not participated	Experimental group reported receiving significantly more new dental information, and making more changes in oral self-care behaviors. For 80%, the child was reported to be the agent for information and change.	11/17	65%
Nicolaci, Tesini (1982)	118 institutionalized developmentally delayed persons in U.S.	No	No	Select staff received 12-hours dental education including special care OHI. Monthly resident oral hygiene reports used to flag for need for professional consultation.	At 6, 12, and 18 months there were significant differences in the oral hygiene index, debris, and calculus in a decreasing linear relationship. Variability between Ss also decreased over time.	11/16	69%

Author (year)	Population			Intervention	Results/Comments		
Harrison, White (1997)	Mothers of children in a British Columbia First Nations community	Yes	No	Experimental: culturally relevant ECC intervention traditional means of comforting babies, nurse counseling, and print materials. Control: no tx control	Compared to baseline and to a control community, there were trends for weaning at an earlier age and decreased rates of ECC. Small sample size limits conclusions.	9/16	56%
Friel, Hope, Kelleher, Comer, Sadlier (2002)	1534 seven- to twelve-year olds in Ireland	No-TV campaign Yes-dental nurse	Schools randomized to receive interactive talk	Television campaign, smile of the year contest, one-time school-based interactive OHI with dental nurse	TV campaign alone, no differences. OHI alone showed some improvements in oral health behaviors. TV campaign + OHI showed most improvement in oral health behaviors.	14/15	93%
Faulks Hennequin (2000)	25 care facility residents with special needs; 28 caretakers of those residents in France	No	No	Series of 3 oral hygiene workshops over 1 year, to educate caretakers about oral health and disease of residents, plus OHI protocols specific to their resident's needs and limitations.	Posttests showed caretaker improvement in frequency of brushing, time spent on oral hygiene, and reaching posterior teeth. However, caretakers continued to care for own teeth better than those of residents.	10/15	67%
Rise, Sogaard (1988)	Norwegians >15 years old	No	No	3-month long mass media campaign via print, TV, and radio to increase brushing and interdental aids; increased courses/information on periodontics for dentists	No short-term effects on knowledge nor behaviors; however, significant improvement in knowledge and behavior 2, 3, and 4 years later. Lag in effect difficult to interpret.	10/14	71%
Bakdash, Lange, McMillan (1983)	Representative cross section of 1,000 adults from Minnesota	No	No	30-second TV message about seeking preventive dental care; aired 1280 times over 2 six-week periods on 17 TV stations.	79% of those surveyed recalled the message; of them, 90% correctly recalled the content and 10% indicated an intention to increase preventive dental visits. Those who recalled the message had more dental knowledge and more regular dental visits than those who did not.	9/14	64%

gingival bleeding to endpoints such as DMFS and pocket depth. Some studies also considered dental service utilization and cost. While these are all important outcomes, their range makes comparison across studies difficult. Additionally, duration of follow up ranges widely, from immediate posttest to several weeks to several years.

Each study had its own strengths and weaknesses, however some weaknesses were so pervasive that they warrant particular discussion. Measurement issues, atheoretical interventions, lack of attention to statistical power, and poor reporting of results were all problems in many (though certainly not all) of the studies. Each of these will be discussed next in order to provide a context for interpreting results.

Measurement

As was discussed in the introduction, plaque removal per se is important for the prevention of periodontal disease. Furthermore, while plaque removal per se is not key to caries prevention, it is an indicator of toothbrushing behavior, and this toothbrushing likely supplies the fluoride that is key to caries prevention. Thus, plaque has been used as an outcome measure in many of the studies reviewed here. However, this approach of using plaque as an indicator of behavior is not without limitations. This review did not reveal any data that addressed the relationship between oral hygiene behaviors (i.e., brushing) per se and oral cleanliness (i.e., plaque scores). In the absence of such data, it is only possible to guess that this relationship is imperfect, that is to say, has a correlation coefficient <1.0. Furthermore, we know that host susceptibility contributes to plaque levels. Thus, although oral hygiene behaviors are no doubt extremely important in the removal of plaque for periodontal disease and the application of topical fluoride for caries, they are not a perfect measure of behavior. One could argue

that behavior and plaque should both be measured, and their unique contributions to disease be assessed. Any difference in the amount of variance in disease risk that they account for could reveal clues about other, as yet unknown, risk factors. Many studies did, in fact, measure both oral hygiene behavior and plaque, however their measurement of behavior was so problematic as to render it of little use.

A few studies have measured oral hygiene behavior by means of comparing the amount of a product (e.g., mouthrinse, floss) given to a patient to the amount still remaining at the end of the study period. However, most studies have measured behavior by means of a subject self-report questionnaire. Currently, no valid and reliable questionnaire of patient oral self-care behaviors exists in the literature. When no adequate scale exists, it is sometimes necessary to design one's own scale for the measurement of a particular variable. However, this is an important undertaking and should be approached according to the published and well-established steps for measurement development. Interested readers are encouraged to refer to writings on psychometric theory (e.g., Nunally, 1978) and to practical guidelines for scale development (e.g., de Vellis, 1991). When designing a scale to measure adherence behavior, it is especially important to address issues of social desirability, because it is well documented that patients tend to overreport adherence to health care regimens. At the very least, even if formal measurement development is not undertaken, authors should describe the construct that was thought to be measured, the process by which items were developed, the method for scoring, and reliability coefficients which are easily calculable with current statistical packages. Virtually none of the studies reviewed in this chapter have followed the established guidelines. One exception was Richter,

Nanda, Sinha and Smith (1998) who used the Orthodontic Patient Cooperation Scale (Slakter et al., 1980) which has published internal consistency and test-retest reliability data, albeit on a small, homogenous sample. Only a handful made any attempt to describe the items or the process by which they were developed and scored. For example, McCaul, Glasgow and O'Neill (1992) reported the actual items and reported coefficient alphas for the scale, Walsh (1985) described the item response format, and Arnold and Doyle (1984) provided a test-retest coefficient.

It appears that some researchers, not being able to find adequate scales in the literature, simply wrote some questions and administered them to subjects. Some went on to compound the problem by analyzing single items, which in even a well-designed scale, are less reliable than total scores. Measurement is always a difficult issue, in both the basic and behavioral sciences. ter Horst and de Wit (1993) have already addressed the difficulties of measuring adherence to dental recommendations, and the need for more standardized measures. To have any confidence whatsoever that the null hypothesis has been correctly rejected or accepted, measurement of the phenomenon of interest must be accurate. This is usually, and mistakenly, regarded as an issue reserved for the social sciences, wherein the constructs of interest are thought to be abstract, latent, or otherwise difficult to measure. This is all the more reason to approach measurement of these constructs with as much rigor and precision as science and statistics can currently offer.

This same issue applies to the measurement of oral health knowledge. No measure of knowledge has been thoroughly developed. Some authors have further compounded the problem by including what appear to be adherence items (e.g., "Did you brush your teeth this morning?") and oral health status items (e.g., "Did your gums bleed the last time you brushed your teeth?") in what were reported as knowledge questionnaires. For the field to progress, researchers first need reliable, validated measures of oral health behavior and knowledge.

Atheoretical Interventions

Many studies tested effectiveness of education programs on self-care behavior change and oral health outcomes. These education only interventions were published in the 80s, 90s, and since 2000. It is widely accepted that information is a necessary but insufficient condition for meaningful behavior change. There is a need for more sophisticated, multivariate interventions. And even when theoretical models are expanded to include knowledge, attitudes, and behaviors, there is still considerable unexplained variance in health outcomes. The bio- and the psycho- domains of the biopsychosocial model are being measured, however, the social (contextual) domain has been somewhat ignored. Contextual variables that interact with the social level, including socioeconomic status (related to income), socioeconomic position (related to social class), race, ethnicity, and health beliefs are all potentially important variables. When they are measured, these variables should be treated as naturally occurring independent variables, like sex, rather than controlled as covariates. This contextual approach to health behavior change is especially important given what is already known about oral health disparities. The studies that did look at some of these variables produced very interesting findings. For example, the studies that investigated SES tended to find that higher SES subjects benefited more from treatment than lower SES subjects (e.g. Kallio et al., 1997). Studies that investigated culture and language found that those variables were very important not only for the tailoring of programs and feasibility of implementation

(Bruerd and Jones, 1996) but also community use of the programs and subsequent outcomes (Ekman and Persson, 1990).

Furthermore, when educational programs are investigated, not all of the information taught is necessary for improved outcomes. For example, one intervention taught children that the first permanent molar erupts at approximately age six. Another asked children to differentiate the parts of the teeth (cementum, dentin, enamel, pulp). While this information is accurate, it is not particularly relevant to increasing toothbrushing frequency. Furthermore, there was considerable attempt in several studies to promote eating sweets as quickly as possible in order to avoid prolonged exposure of bacteria to its energy source. While this may be beneficial for teeth, it is generally not an eating habit that should be promoted. Only one program, "Natural Nashers" (Craft et al., 1981), qualified this advice with the statement that although this strategy is good for teeth, it is not good for general health. So too, while the qualification is accurate, the result of combining both statements does not suggest a proper course of action and may be confusing even for adults. Blinkhorn (1998) addressed this issue and reinforced the need for simple, straightforward health messages. The British Health Education Authority has agreed on the following four simple oral health messages 1) reduce the consumption and frequency of intake of sugar containing food and drink 2) clean the teeth and gums thoroughly every day with a fluoride toothpaste 3) seek dental advice and early treatment on a regular basis, and 4) support water fluoridation (Levine, 1995).

Perhaps one reason that some of the interventions were cumbersome and exhibited limited effectiveness is that they were for the most part atheoretical. Several studies described their interventions as based on social cognitive theory, but upon closer inspection seemed to simply be educational interventions without any specific theoretical underpinning. There are many promising and exciting models and theories that are appropriate for studies of oral health behavior change, including the health belief model (Maiman and Becker, 1974), theory of reasoned action (Ajzen and Fishbein, 1980) and planned behavior (Ajzen, 1985), transtheoretical model (Prochaska and DiClemente, 1983), self efficacy theory (Bandura, 1977) as well as many others. Dentistry has in fact incorporated some of these models, as well as others, into its conceptualization of patient behavior (e.g., Stillman-Lowe and Crossley, 2001; Kallio, 2000; Ramsay, 2000; Calley et al., 2000; Tedesco et al., 1991). However, its clinical trials do not reflect these theoretical considerations. Multidisciplinary studies that promote collaboration between the social and dental sciences would promote such theoretically based intervention studies.

Statistical Power

The vast majority of studies reviewed did not acknowledge issues of statistical power and only a very few actually performed a power analysis. Power surveys of articles in journals of behavioral and psychosocial phenomena have generally reported low power, in the range of 50% likelihood of detecting a statistical significance (Cohen, 1988). A recent review of 3 health behavior journals showed some improvement within the last few years, with power generally being adequate for detecting medium or large effect sizes. However, studies were seriously underpowered to detect small effect sizes. This is especially relevant to the literature reviewed in this chapter, given that most health behavior interventions result in only small effect sizes (Maddock and Rossi, 2001). Thus, statistical power is an issue for oral self-care interventions, but has not been addressed in the majority of studies. As Lipsey (1990) notes, experimental designs that lack sensitivity and, correspondingly, statistical comparisons that lack power, make for treatment effectiveness research that cannot accomplish its central purpose – to determine the effects of treatment.

Statistical Analysis

Some of the larger interventions were limited by the chosen unit of analysis. For example, most of the pediatric interventions took place in schools, and designated the school or the class, rather than the child, as the unit of analysis. That is to say that schools, rather than children in those schools, were randomized to experimental conditions. While not inappropriate per se, this type of design has limitations. First, it decreases the number of units being analyzed, decreasing statistical power. Second, it tends to decrease the likelihood of equivalent groups and underestimates standard errors. When randomizing larger units of analysis (e.g., schools, community health centers, nursing homes), there are corrections that can be made to mitigate these potential problems. Specifically, adjustments should be made for correlations within the unit of randomization. Redmond, Blinkhorn, Kay, Davies, Worthington and Blinkhorn (1999) and Worthington, Hill, Mooney, Hamilton and Blinkhorn (2001) provide examples of appropriate management of these issues. Statistical packages are also available to handle these analyses, including SUDANN published by RTI, and hierarchical linear modeling, available through Scientific Software.

Two studies referred to 'multivariate' analyses, when the context of the study called for repeated measure univariate analyses. It was unclear from the manuscript if these were analytical flaws or errors in reporting.

Some findings that were reported as significant may have been attributable to type I error due to lack of correction for multiple comparisons. Very few studies, even those that analyzed multiple items on a questionnaire one at a time, reported having corrected for multiple comparisons.

Reporting

There were several issues with the results sections of the studies included in this review. First, several studies reported significance without even reporting what analysis had been performed. Second, there was considerable attention paid to statistical trends and near significance. Significance is a probability statement, that is, it is a dichotomous yes or no phenomenon and should be reported as such. Further, given the lack of attention to statistical power, it is unclear if any lack of significance is due to low power (type II error) or true lack of effect. A shift from reporting statistical significance to reporting effect size has been suggested for just this reason (Rossi, 1997; Rossi, 1990). Effect sizes were virtually never reported in this literature. Doing so would address this problem and better allow for comparison across studies.

Third, the description of samples was generally poor. Some articles described the sample's dental history in considerable detail, but few described demographics. Many were missing basic demographics such as age, sex, race/ethnicity, and SES. These data are necessary for generalization of results. One study even analyzed race, but did not describe how it was measured, nor gave the racial breakdown of the sample. The description of interventions was also sometimes lacking. Many articles referred to "behavioral intervention" or "dental health education" as though those terms referred to a single, universally defined construct.

Fourth, there was a tendency to overreport sample size. That is, the n reported in the abstract referred to how many people were enrolled in the study when in fact far fewer were included in outcome analysis due to attrition. One of several exceptions is Wight and Blinkhorn (1988) who correctly reported in the abstract the number of subjects who were used in the analyses.

Fifth, in most of the studies attrition was not adequately addressed. The few studies that mentioned attrition only mentioned it, but even most of them did not investigate whether attrition was systematic or randomly distributed among groups. Julien (1994) and Vigild (1990) were exceptions, both of which analyzed the effects of attrition.

RESULTS

For ease of interpretation, the results of the studies included in this review have been divided into clinic based interventions, community based interventions, and school based interventions. While these distinctions are somewhat arbitrary and at times blurred (for example, providing dental treatment in schools is both school based and clinic based), some discrimination between them is helpful in drawing conclusions.

Forty of the studies we identified attempted to stimulate behavior change using clinic based approaches. These primarily relied upon the dental office personnel, and in some cases the patient's family, to act as behavior change agents to the patient. Two studies attempted to increase headgear use by pediatric orthodontic patients (Cureton et al., 1993; Gross et al., 1990). Both had positive findings, the first using home charting and the second using a parent implemented contingency management procedure. The small samples (n=28 and n=12, respectively), limit generalization of these results. Three studies attempted to improve clinic attendance (Primosch et al., 2001; West et al., 1993; Cohen et al., 1980). Overall, there was no effect for the use of appointment cards, reminder phone calls, having the patient (as opposed to the provider) make the follow up appointment, or even a separate consultation appointment stressing the importance of follow up care. Some benefit was found,

however, for the intervention designed by Cohen et al., requesting that the patient call the clinic to confirm the follow up appointment. Although this study had a relatively large sample (n=306), it was not well controlled, so these findings must be interpreted cautiously.

Thirty-two studies attempted to increase frequency of brushing and/or flossing, with a goal of improving oral cleanliness and/or gingival health. Of them, 2 interventions showed no effect when compared to a no treatment control condition (Rinchuse et al., 1992; Soderholm et al., 1982). Fourteen studies showed a positive overall effect, but no differences among treatment groups. This appears to be largely due to the relatively good performance of the comparison groups, rather than the poor performance of the treatment in question per se. The remaining 16 studies showed a positive effect for a particular treatment condition. One group of these found the best effect when preventive dental treatment (e.g., fluoride, chlorhexidine rinse) was combined with behavioral strategies (Perrson et al., 1998; Hujoel et al., 1997; Blinkhorn et al., 1981). Another subset of studies found positive effects from using traditional behavior modification techniques including skills training (Bullen et al., 1988), charting (Weinstein et al., 1996), observation (Feil et al., 2002), contingency management (Iwata and Becksforth, 1981; Richter et al., 1998), and provision of objective feedback (Little et al., 1997; Glavind et al., 1983; Stewart and Wolfe, 1989). Furthermore, acceptance of dental procedures is higher among children whose dentists are trained in behavior modification (Holst and Ek 1988). Readers interested in learning more about these techniques are directed to readings such as Martin and Pear (1992). Follow up periods typically ranged from 2 weeks to 18 months, with one study following patients for 3 years (Persson et al., 1998). Generally, effects were difficult to maintain over time. Similar types of interventions have been used successfully in senior centers (Price and Kiyak, 1981), and with college students (McCaul et al., 1992; Bagley andLow, 1992; Tan et al., 1981). Results have been similar to those found in clinic based studies, with behavioral interventions initiating change in self-care behaviors, but producing poor maintenance of these behaviors over time. There was no clear difference in relapse among age groups. This phenomenon of relapse, or lack of maintenance, is certainly not unique to dentistry, but in fact is pervasive among health behaviors (see Health Psychology volume 19 [2001] for a review of this topic). However, one-hour of exploratory listening, wherein patients are encouraged to talk about their perceptions of their oral condition and their provider with a supportive, nonjudgmental person, can produce meaningful change in oral hygiene behaviors up to 2 years later (Alcouffe, 1988).

A number of clinic based studies have investigated the use of home self-inspection techniques to provide feedback about hygiene performance. Studies on self-inspection for gingival bleeding show either no effect on gingival health (Glavind et al., 1984), no added benefit (Walsh et al., 1985) or only short-term effects with a subsample (Kallio et al., 1990). Studies specifically investigating home plaque self-inspection techniques, including disclosing agents, show either no added benefit (Ambjornsen and Rise, 1985; Glavind et al., 1985; Boyd, 1983; Tan and Wade, 1980) or equivocal results (Baab and Weinstein, 1986). On the other hand, Kallio, Uutela, Nordblad, Alvesalo and Murtomaa (1997) and Nowjack-Raymer, Ainamo, Suomi, Kingsman, Driscoll and Brown (1995) found a good effect for self-assessment of both plaque and bleeding. These newer studies may have benefited from much larger sample sizes (on the order of 1.5 to 10 times as many subjects) and subsequent increased statistical power.

Studies that have investigated the source of oral health information show that the source of the information is generally unimportant to patients' uptake of the information. Weinstein, Milgrom, Melnick, Beach and Spadafora (1989) showed that general dentists and specialists are equally effective. Soderholm, Nobreus, Attstrom and Egelberg (1982) found no difference between five 30-minute or two 60-minute sessions of OHI. Type of media has also been investigated, and written manuals, videotapes, face-to-face instructions, and group discussion have not shown differences on patient uptake of information (e.g., Lim and Davies, 1996; Moltzer and Hoogstraten, 1986; Hoogstraten and Moltzer, 1983; Glavind and Zeuner, 1985; Glavind et al., 1981), although no one study has compared all approaches. However, these various methods have not been explored with diverse populations, such as those for whom English is a second language, those with low literacy, or patients who are difficult to engage in the educational endeavor. It would seem that differences would be more likely to emerge if these methods were compared in such populations. What does appear to make a difference, however, is the degree to which students are actively involved in the curriculum, with more involvement yielding better results (Sogaard and Holst, 1988; Laiho et al., 1993; Schou, 1985).

We found 30 articles that employed community based approaches. By 'community' we mean any setting that is neither the school nor the dental office, such as care facilities, worksites, college campuses, or the general public in their own neighborhoods. Six studies implemented interventions in care facilities. The only one of these studies that met with poor results had made the residents, rather than the staff, the primary target of intervention (Schou et al., 1989). In that study, after 6 months about half of the elderly residents (or 100 participants) could not remember having received the lengthy intervention, and the authors reported confusion (perhaps dementia) among the subjects. The remainder of the studies produced good results in outcomes such as plaque, calculus, pocket depth, and time spent on oral hygiene behaviors (Faulks and Hennequin, 2000; Nicolaci and Tesini, 1982). These interventions targeted the staff on the premise that they would in turn train residents who were trainable, and provide direct care to those who were not. While maintaining the autonomy of residents is of extreme practical and ethical importance, it is possible that institutional staff is best able to determine who is trainable to perform self-care and who should receive direct oral hygiene care. Two studies implemented on-site dental treatment. Mojon, Rentsch, Budtz-Jorgensen and Baehni (1998) found fewer active root caries and lower streptococci counts. Vigild (1990) showed an increase in overall dental care, with a simultaneous decrease in emergent dental treatment. Futhermore, because of this shift from emergent to routine care, net cost for dental care was actually lower for the group receiving on-site care. The longest period of follow up for these interventions was 18 months, so the longer term outcomes are unknown.

Ten community interventions were aimed at the caretakers (usually mothers) of infants and young children. Information-only interventions produced only minimal results (Sgan-Cohen et al., 2001) or equivocal results (Truin et al., 1981). Other studies investigated differences between mothers who received home visits for child OHE vs those who did not. In the studies showing improvement with home care, visits were typically made by nurses or health educators. Home visit programs can be expensive, and are not always well received. For example, Rayner (1992) had >30% refusal rate for home visits. However, when they were completed, home visits were found to be superior in the short term for plaque and gingivitis (Rayner, 1992), caries experience and gingivitis (Holt et al, 1985), parental knowledge of oral health behaviors and subsequent health clinic attendance (Hamilton et al., 1999), and in the long term for plaque and gingival health, but not caries (Holt et al., 1989).

Olsen, Brown and Wright (1986) provided a single home visit to immigrant parents speaking languages other than English, and found a small effect for DMFT, but not service utilization. Ekman and Perrson (1990) also found that when delivering OHE to parents of young children, it was beneficial to deliver it in their native language, even when parents claimed to be bi-lingual. There has also been an effort to create culturally relevant interventions for American Indian/Alaska Native families with young children, since rates of ECC are particularly high in those populations. While the studies are not tightly controlled, they have produced a considerable effect, with a 25% decrease in ECC at 3 years (Bruerd et al., 1989) and a 38% decrease at 8 years (Bruerd and Jones, 1996). The success of these programs may lie in the fact that they arise from existing community institutions and relationships, and employ traditional means of comforting babies. Indeed, the non-tailored interventions described above emphasized earlier weaning, but did not mention educating mothers about alternatives to bottles for comforting fussy babies. Providing subjects with alternatives for problem behaviors is key to behavior change.

Worksite interventions were the focus of five studies. Many other worksite interventions have been published, but most of them primarily investigate the provision of worksite professional dental care, rather than worker self-care behavior, and thus have not been included in this review. Hetland, Midtun and Kristoffersen (1981) showed that

OHI alone produced more improvement for plaque, gingival index, and pocket depth than prophylaxis alone, and that the combination was most effective. Similar results were found by Fishwick, Ashley and Wilson (1998) and Lim and Davies (1996). The longest period of follow up for any of these studies was 16 months, so the longer term effect of such programs is unknown.

A final group of community interventions targeted the general population through public health campaigns. Rise and Sogaard (1988) found no short-term effects of a mass media campaign, but some improvements in knowledge and behavior several years later. Bakdash, Lange and McMillan (1983) also used a mass media campaign, and found that although much of the campaign's message was recalled correctly, only 10% of respondents indicated any intention to make changes based on the message. Friel, Hope, Kelleher, Comer and Sadlier (2002) found no effect for a media campaign alone, but some success in changing behaviors when the media campaign was paired with schoolbased OHI.

Thirty-eight of the articles we found used school-based approaches. Most of these programs were combinations of several components, including OHE curriculum, supervised brushing during the schoolday, parental involvement, and on-site dental care. Because of these multicomponent designs, it is difficult to compare programs, and it is difficult to determine the effectiveness of any given component. For example, six studies incorporated supervised brushing programs into comprehensive programs, with conflicting results. Russell, Horowitz and Frazier (1989) showed no differences for out of school self-care behaviors. Walsh (1985) showed improvements for brushing frequency in girls. Swain, Allard and Hoborn (1982) showed a decrease in plaque. Blinkhorn, McIntyre, MacPahil and Shove (1981) showed no change in plaque but a decrease in

the number of children with gingivitis. Rayner (1992) showed positive results for plaque and gingivitis. However, the most rigorous and straightforward test of supervised brushing (Pine et al., 2000) showed a large difference in caries despite no change in brushing patterns at home, suggesting that supervised brushing caused the caries difference.

Twelve of the school based studies entailed either explicit parental involvement or they entailed activities to be performed at home that would presumably involve parents, such as plaque disclosure, contingency management, or charting of brushing. Overall, programs that included parental involvement showed positive outcomes. Benefits include effects for plaque (Julien, 1994; Redmond et al., 1999; Albandar et al., 1994; Towner, 1984), gingival health (Julien, 1994; Albandar et al., 1994; Blinkhorn et al., 1981; Towner, 1984), knowledge (Redmond et al., 1999; Blinkhorn et al., 1981), and brushing (Redmond et al., 1999; Blinkhorn et al., 1981). And in designs that allow for a specific test of parent involvement, parental involvement was found to improve outcomes including knowledge, sugar consumption, and flossing (Buischi et al., 1994) as well as brushing, self-efficacy, openness to mass media dental messages, and communication with parents about dental health (Sogaard and Holst, 1988). The level of parent involvement in these studies was not entirely clear and the dose response relationship between parent involvement and child outcomes remains an interesting empirical question.

Several of the school based interventions tested the effectiveness of OHE only. Observed benefits have generally been short term, of small magnitude, and for some but not all outcomes. Benefits of education only interventions include reductions in plaque (Mazzocchi and Moretti, 1997; Worthington et al., 2001; Hodge et al., 1987; Torpaz et al. 1984; Howat et al., 1985; McIntyre et al., 1985; Cooke et al., 1983). Increases in knowledge have also been observed by Worthington, Hill, Mooney, Hamilton and Blinkhorn (2001) Hodge, Buchanan, O'Donnell, Topping and Banks (1987), Torpaz, Noam, Anaise and Sgan-Cohen (1984) and ter Horst and Hoogstraten (1989). Changes in self-reported eating habits were found by McIntyre, Wight and Blinkhorn (1985), and decrease in decayed surfaces was found by Cooke, Graham and Sadles (1983).

On the other hand, several research reports have not identified differences for knowledge or DMFS (Melsen and Agerbaek, 1980), DFS (Nylander et al., 2001), posterior plaque, brushing, eating habits (Howat et al., 1985), oral hygiene behaviors (ter Horst and Hoogstraten, 1989), or bone loss (Albandr et al., 1995). These contradictory finding are likely due to differences in the intensity and type of education provided, the level of learner involvement, as well as vast differences in measurement of outcomes.

CONCLUSIONS

In spite of limitations with respect to the interventions, the methods used, and the reporting of results, some conclusions about these studies can be drawn. The conclusions of this review are not substantially different from previous reviews (Sprod et al., 1996; Kay and Locker 1998, Kay and Locker, 1996; Schou and Locker, 1994; Brown, 1994). First, knowledge and behavior can be modified, and their modification can result in improvements in oral health outcomes. Second, maintenance of these behaviors is more difficult than their initiation. Third, not all groups benefit to the same degree, with lower SES and minority groups benefiting less.

Education alone can be effective in changing knowledge, but is only minimally effective in changing behavior. Mass media campaigns are ineffective in promoting knowledge or behavior change, although they may increase awareness. At least for general,

not special populations, the medium through which dental health information is delivered does not make a significant difference. However, active involvement on the part of the learner is helpful. There is good evidence for behavioral interventions including skills training, charting, contingency management, and provision of feedback. These interventions are enhanced when combined with preventive dental care. There is good evidence for including caretakers (parents, nursing home staff) in the oral care of their charges. There is some evidence that tailoring oral health information to meet the linguistic and cultural needs of the target group is beneficial.

RECOMMENDATIONS FOR CLINICIANS

The research reviewed here gives direction for those delivering clinical oral health care. The good news is that patients can, and do, modify their oral self-care behaviors. Oral outcomes are especially good when behavior change interventions are delivered in conjunction with dental procedures, so dental clinicians are in a uniquely powerful position to intervene on these behaviors. Providing some relevant information, either chairside or at home, written or videotaped, can improve knowledge. Keep the dental health messages short, relevant, and to the point. However, do not expect dental education alone to change patients' behavior. Combining behavior modification techniques with standard dental care appears to be the best way to change behavior. Setting clear goals, having patients chart their own behaviors, and praising them for successful approximations of the desired behavior is key. Emphasizing what to do, and what benefits will be gained from the target behavior is better than telling patients what not to do, and what bad things will happen if they do not change their behavior. Teaching these techniques to children's families and helping caretakers implement reward systems also helps.

While working with patients on these goals, it may be helpful to take an exploratory listening approach. This means listening to and validating patients' experiences with barriers to self-care behaviors. Remember, if you are listening, you cannot be talking. Pay attention to what the patient is ready to address and follow the patient's lead. If the patient is ready to reduce sweets, but you think that it's more important that they start flossing, consider tackling the eating habits first. Meeting with some short term success may help your patient feel more confident and increase their willingness to try the flossing at a later time. If you are unsure about any of these strategies, consult with someone trained in this area. A one-time consultation with a health psychologist or providing an inservice for you and your staff could greatly improve your practice.

Bear in mind that not all patients will improve at the same rate, to the same degree, or at all. Patients who speak a language other than your own will have difficulty, and an interpreter can be helpful. Lower SES patients may have difficulty and you may need to spend more time with these patients. So, to keep from getting discouraged, look for incremental changes. Also bear in mind that patients may have trouble maintaining their new, positive behavior. Your nonjudgmental support will be central to their getting back on track.

RECOMMENDATIONS FOR RESEARCHERS

Issues of evaluation should be considered well in advance of actually implementing and testing an oral health promotion program. Watt, Fuller, Harnett, Treasure and Stillman-Lowe (2001) give clear guidelines for these considerations. Based on our review, additional recommendations can be made for future research in promotion of oral self-care.

Some are general recommendations that might be made to most health care researchers, including the implementation of randomized controlled trials, using larger and more diverse samples, with longer follow up periods. While these are obviously important guidelines, their implementation requires large, well funded research programs. There are also several recommendations specific to this field that can be implemented by virtually all oral health researchers that do not depend upon funding. First, measurement issues need to be addressed. Reliable and valid means of assessing knowledge and self-care behaviors need to be developed. The relationship between self-care behaviors and oral health status (i.e., plaque levels and gingival health) needs to be elaborated more carefully. Second, collaboration between dental and social scientists should be promoted so that interventions are theoretically driven and therefore make meaningful contributions to the behavior change literature. They should incorporate the 'social' domain of the biopsychosocial model, and include contextual variables such as SES and culture. Third, analytical issues should be addressed. Specifically, power analyses should be performed, corrections for multiple comparisons should be made, nested designs should use appropriate analytic strategies, and effect sizes should be reported. Fourth, reporting should improve with regard to accurate sample sizes, characteristics of the sample, details of the intervention, and systematic attrition. Progress in these areas will not only help promote oral health, but will also help push forward the field of health behavior change more generally which can have even wider public health implications.

REFERENCES

Ajzen I. (1985) From intentions to actions: A theory of planned behavior. In: Action-Control: From Cognitions to Behavior (Kuhland J and Beckman J, eds), (pp. 11-

39). Heidelberg, Bermany: Springer.

American Academy of Pediatric Dentistry website (2003), http://www.aapd.org/media/policies.asp

Ajzen I, Fishbein M. (1980) Understanding attitudes and predicting social behavior. Englewood Cliffs, NJ: Prentice Hall.

Albandar JM, Biushi YA, Mayer MP, Axelsson P. (1994) Long-term effect of two preventive programs on the incidence of plaque and gingivitis in adolescents. J Periodontol 65:605-610.

Albandar JM, Buishi YA, Oliveria LB, Axelsson P. (1995) Lack of effect of oral hygiene training on periodontal disease progression over 3 years in adolescents. J Periodontol 66:255-60.

Alcouffe F. (1988) Improvement of oral hygiene habits: A psychological approach. J Clin Periodontol 15:49-52.

Ambjornsen E, Rise J. (1985) The effect of verbal information and demonstration on denture hygiene in elderly people. Acta Odontol Scand, 43, 19-24.

American Cancer Society website, (2003) http://www.acs.org

Arnold C, Doyle AJ. (1984) Evaluation of the dental health education program "Natural Nashers". Community Dent Health 1:141-7.

Ashley FP, Sainsbury RH. (1981) The effect of a school-based plaque control progamme on caries and gingivitis. A 3-year study in 11 to 14 year old girls. Br Dent J 150:41-5.

Atkinson JC and Baum BJ. (2001) Salivary enhancement: Current status and future therapies. J Den Edu 65:1096-1101.

Atlkinson JC, Baum BJ. (2001) Salivary enhancement: current status and future therapies. J Dent Edu 65:1096-1101.

Baab D Weinstein P. (1986) Longitudinal evaluation of a self-inspection plaque index in periodontal recall patients. J Clin Periodontol 13:313-8.

Baab DA, Weinstein P. (1983) Oral hygiene instruction using a self-inspection plaque index. Community Dent Oral Epidemiol 11:174-9.

Bagley JG, Low KG. (1992) Enhancing flossing compliance in college freshmen. Clin Prev Dent 14:25-30.

Bakdash MB, Lange AL, McMillan, DG. (1983) The effect of a televised periodontal campaign on public periodontal awareness. J Periodontol 54:666-70.

Bandura A. (1977) Toward a unifying theory of behavioral change. Psychol Rev 84:191-215.

Benitez C, O'Sullivan D, Tinanoff N. (1994) Effect of a preventive approach for the treatment of nursing bottle caries. Journal of Dentistry in Children 1:46-9.

Bentley JM, Cormier P, Oler J. (1983) Rural dental health program: The effect of a school based dental health education program on children's utilization of dental services. Amer J Public Health 73:500-5.

Bergstrom J, Preber H. (1994) Tobacco use as a risk factor. J Periodontol 65:545-50.

Blinkhorn AS. (1998) Dental health education: What lessons have we ignored? Br Dent J 184:58-9.

Blinkhorn AS, Downer MC, Mackie IC, Bleasdale RS. (1981) Evaluation of a practice based preventive programme for adolescents. Community Dent Oral Epidemiol 9:275-9.

Blinkhorn AS, McIntyre J, MacPhail K, Shove CM. (1981) An evaluation of the Lothian 1979/80 "Mind Your Teeth Week" dental health programme. Health Bull 39:287-95.

Boyd RL. (1983) Longitudinal evaluation of a system for self-monitoring plaque control effectiveness in orthodontic patients. J Clin Periodontol 10:380-8.

Brown CPM, Lennon MA, Crosland WE. (1990) A dental care programme for occasional dental attenders. Community Dent Health 7:407-12.

Brown LF. (1994) Research in dental health

education and health promotion: A review of the literature. Health Educ Q 21:83-102.

Brown LJ, Brunelle JA, Kingman A. (1996) Periodontal status in the United States, 1988-91: Prevalence, extent, and demographic characteristics. J Dent Res 75 (Special Issue):672-683.

Bruerd B, Jones C. (1996) Preventing baby bottle tooth decay: Eight year results. Public Health Rep, 111, 63-5.

Bruerd B, Kinney MB, Bothwell E. (1989) Preventing baby bottle tooth decay in American Indian and Alaska Native communities: A model for planning. Public Health Rep 104:631-40.

Buischi Y, Axelsson P, Oliveira L, Mayer M, Gjermo P. (1994) Effect of two preventive programs on oral health knowledge and habits among Brazilian school-children. Community Dent Oral Epidemiol 22:41-6.

Bullen C, Rubenstein L, Saravia ME et al. (1988) Improving children's oral hygiene through parental involvement. Journal of Dentistry in Children 55:125-8.

Burt B, EklundSA. (1999) Dentistry, Dental Practice and the Community (5th Edition) Philadelphia: W B Saunders Co.

Burt B, Ismail AI, Eklund SA. (1988) Diet, nutrition and food cariogenicity. J Dent Res 67:1422-9.

Burt B, Pai S. (2001) Sugar consumption and caries risk: A systematic review. J Dent Edu 1017-27.

Burt BA. (1985) The future of the caries decline J Public Health Dent 45:261-9.

Calley KH, Rogo E, Miller DL, Hess G, Eisenhauer L. (2000) A proposed client self-care commitment model. J Dent Hyg 74:24-35.

Carlsson GE, Le Resche L. (1995) Epidemiology of temporomandibular disorders in Temporomandibular Disorders and Related Pain Conditions, Progress in Pain Research and Management Vol 4, (Sessle BJ, Bryant PS, Dionne RA, eds), pp. 211-235. Seattle: IAASP Press.

Caufield PW Cutter GR, Dasanayake AP. (1993) Initial acquisition of mutans streptococci by infants: evidence for a discrete window of infectivity. J Dent Res 72:37-45.

Center for Medicare and Medicaid Services website. (2003) http://www.hcfa.gov/stats/nhe/projections-2001/t2.asp.

Chen MS. Oral health status and its inequality among education groups: comparing seven international study sites.

Cipes M, Miraglia M. (1985) Monitoring versus contingency contracting to increase children's compliance with home fluoride mouthrinsing. Pediatr Dent 9:247-50.

Cohen AJ, Weinstein P, Wurster C. (1980) The effects of patient-initiated phone confirmation on appointment keeping at a hospital dental clinic. J Public Health Dent 40:64-8.

Cohen, J. (1988) Statistical power analysis for the behavioral sciences. Hillsdale, NJ: Lawrence Erlbaum Associates.

Cooke V, Graham SR, Sadles MC. (1983) Evaluation of a reinforced school-based dental health education program as provided by dental hygiene students. Educ Dir 8:18-23.

Coulter ID, Marcus M, Atchison KA. (1994) Measuring oral health status: theoretical and methodological challenges. Soc Sci Med 38:1531-41.

Craft M, Croucher R, Dickenson J. (1981) Preventive dental health in adolescents: Short and long term pupil response to trials of an integrated curriculum package. Community Dentistry and Oral Epidemiology 9:199-206.

Craft N, Croucher R, Blinkhorn A. (1984) 'Natural Nashers' dental health education programme: The results of a field trial in Scotland. Br Dent J 156:103-5.

Croucher R, Rodgers AI, Humpherson WA, Crush L. (1985) The 'spread effect' of a school based dental health education project. Community Dent Oral Epidemiol 13:205-7.

Cureton SL, Regennitter FJ, Yancey JM. (1993) The role of headgear calendar in headgear compliance. Amer J Orthodont Dentofac Orthop 104:387-94.

De Vellis RF. (1991) Scale development: Theory and applications. Newbury Park, CA: Sage.

Douglass JM, Tinanoff N, Tang JM, Altman DS. (2001) Dental caries patterns and oral health behaviors in Arizona infants and toddlers. Community Dent Oral Epidemiol 29:14-22.

Drangsholt M, LeResche L. (1999) Temporomandibular disorder pain. in The Epdimiology of Pain Crombie IK (ed). Seattle: IASP Press.

Dworkin SF. (2001) The dentist as bio-behavioral clinician. J Dent Educ 65: 1417-29.

Ekman A, Persson B. (1990) Effect of early dental health education for Finnish immigrant families. Swed Dent J 14:43-1151

Engel GL. (1977) The need for a new medical model: a challenge for biomedicine. Science 196:129-36.

Famer, P. (1999) Infections and Inequities. Berkley: University of California Press.

Faulks D, Hennequin M. (2000) Evaluation of a long-term oral health program by careers of children and adults with intellectual disabilities. Spec Care Dentist 20:199-208.

Feil PH, Grauer JS, Gacbury-Amyot CC, Kula K, McCunniff MD. (2002) Intentional use of the Hawthorne effect to improve oral hygiene compliance of orthodontic patients. J Dent Educ 66:1129-35.

Fishwick MR, Ashley FP, Wilson RF. (1998) Can a workplace preventive programme affect periodontal health? Br Dent J 184:290-3.

Friel S, Hope A, Kelleher C, Comer S, Sadlier D. (2002) Impact evaluation of an oral health intervention amongst primary school children in Ireland. Health Promot Int 17:119-126.

Gift H, Bhat M. (1993) Dental visits for orofacial injury: Defining the dentist's role. J Am Dent Assoc 124:92-96.

Gift H. (1993) Social factors in health promotion. in Oral Health Promotion (Schou L and Blinkhorn, eds), pp 65-81.Oxford: Oxford University Press.

Gift H. (1996) Quality of life-an outcome of oral health care? J Public Health Dent 56:67-8.

Gift HC, Atchison KA, Dayton CM. (1997) Conceptualizing oral health and oral health-related quality of life. Soc Sci Med 44:601-608.

Gift HC, Atchison KA. (1995) Oral health, health, and health-related quality of life. Med Care 33:NS57-NS77.

Glavind L, Christensen H, Pedersen E, Rosendahl H, Attstrom R. (1985) Oral hygiene instruction in general dental practice by means of self-teaching manuals. J Clin Periodontol 12:27-34.

Glavind L, Zeuner E. (1985) Evaluation of a television tape demonstration for the reinforcement of oral hygiene instruction. J Clin Periodontol 13:201-4.

Glavind L, Zeuner E, Attstrom R. (1981) Oral hygiene instruction of adults by means of a self-instruction manual. J Clin Periodontol 8:1657-76.

Glavind L, Zeuner E, Attstrom R. (1983) Evaluation of various feed back mechanisms in relation to compliance by adult patients with oral home care instruction. J Clin Periodontol 10:57-68.

Glavind L, Zeuner E, Attstrom R. (1984) Oral cleanliness and gingival health following oral hygiene instruction by self-educational programs. J Clin Periodontol 11:262-73.

Goodkind RJ, Loupe MJ, Clay DJ, Diangelis AJ. (1988) Modifying the knowledge, skills, and habits of denture patients. Gerodontics 4:95-100.

Goodson JM. (1990) Selection of suitable indicators of periodontitis. in Risk Assessment in Dentistry. (Bader JD, ed) pp. 69-70 Chapel Hill: University of North Carolina.

Greene JC, Vermillion JR. (1964) The simplified oral hygiene index. J Am Dent Assoc 1964; 68:7-13.

Gross A, Sanders S, Smith C, Samson G. (1990) Increasing compliance with orthodontic treatment. Child and Family Behavior Therapy 12:13-23.

Grossi, SG. (2001) Dental plaque attack: The connection between periodontal disease, heart disease, and diabetes mellitus. Compendium of Cont Edu in Dent 22:13-21.

Hamilton FA, Davis KE, Blinkhorn, AS. (1999) An oral health promotion programme for nursing caries. Int J Pediatr Dentist 9:195-200.

Harisson R, White L. (1997) A community-based approach to infant and child oral health promotion in a British Colombia first nations community. Can J Community Dent 12:7-14.

Hetland L, Midtun N, Kristoffersen T. (1981) Effect of oral hygiene instructions given by para professional personnel. Community Dent Oral Epidemiol 10:8-14.

Hodge H, Buchanan M, O'Donnell P, Topping B, Banks I. (1987) The evaluation of the junior dental health education programme developed in Sefton, England. Community Dent Health 4:223-9.

Holst A, Ek L. (1988) Effect of systematized 'behavior shaping' on acceptance of dental treatment in children. Community Dent Oral Epidemiol 16:349-55.

Holt RD, Winter GB, Fox B, Askew R. (1985) Effects of dental health education for mothers with young children in London. Community Dent Oral Epidemiol 13:148-51.

Holt RD, Winter GB, Fox B, Askew R. (1989) Second assessment of London children involved in a scheme of dental health education in infancy. Community Dent Oral Epidemiol 17:180-2.

Holt RD, Winter GB, Fox B, Askew R, Lo GL. (1983) Dental health education through home visits to mothers with young children. Community Dent Oral Epidemiol 11:98-101.

Holund U. (1990) Promoting change of adolescent's sugar consumption: The 'learning by teaching' study. Health Educ Res 5:451-8.

Hoogstraten J, Moltzer G. (1983) Effects of dental care instruction on knowledge, attitude, behavior, and fear. Community Dent Oral Epidemiol 11:278-82.

Horowitz AM, Selwitz RH, Kleinman DV, Ismail AI, Bader JD (eds). (2001) NIH Consensus Development Conference on Diagnosis and Management of Dental Caries throughout Life, J Dent Edu 65.

Howat AP, Craft M, Croucher R, Rock WP, Foster TD. (1985) Dental health education: A school visit program for dental students. Part 1:The school visits project. Community Dent Health 2:23-32.

HuangGJ, LeResche L, Critchlow CW, Martin MD, Drangsholt MT. (2002) Risk factors for diagnostic subgroups of painful temporomandibular disorders (TMD). J Dent Res 81:284-8.

Hujoel PP, Powell LV, Kiyak HA. (1997) The effects of simple interventions on tooth mortality: Findings in one trial and implications for future studies. J Dent Res 76:867-74.

Ismail AI, Burt B, Eklund SA. (1983) Epidemiological patterns of smoking and periodontal disease in the United States. J Am Dent Assoc 106:617-21.

Iwata BA, Becksfort CM. (1981) Behavioral research in preventive dentistry: Educational and contingency management approaches to the problem of patient compliance. Journal of Applied Behavior Analysis 14:111-20.

Jeffcoat MJ, Geurs N. (2001) Oral bone loss, osteoporosis, and preterm birth: What do we tell our patients ? Compendium of Cont Edu in Dent 22:22-27.

Julien MG. (1994) The effect of behavior modification techniques on oral hygiene and gingival health of 10-yeaqr old Canadian children. Int Paediatr Dentist 4:3-11.

Kallio P, Ainamo J, Dusadeepan A. (1990) Self-assessment of gingival bleeding. Int Dent J 40:231-6.

Kallio P, Uutela A, Norblad A, Alvesalo I, Murtomaa H. (1997) Self-assessed bleeding and plaque as methods for improving gingival health in adolescents. Int Dent J 47:205-12.

Kallio PJ. (2000) Health promotion and behavioral approaches in the prevention of periodontal disease in children and adolescents. Periodontol 26:135-45.

Karn TA, O'Sullivan DM, Tinanoff N. (1998) Colonization of mutans streptococci in 8- to 15-month-old children. J Public Health Dent 58:248-9.

Kaste LM, Gift HC, Bhat M, Sango PA. (1996) Prevalence of incisor trauma in persons 6-50 years of age: United States, 1988-91. J Dent Res 75:631-41.

Katz RV. (1980) Assessing root caries in populations: The evolution of the Root Caries Indes. J Public Health Dent 40:7-16.

Kay EJ, Locker D. (1996) Is dental health education effective? Community Dent Oral Epidemiol 244:231-5.

Kay EJ, Locker D. (1998) A systematic review of the effectiveness of health promotion aimed at improving oral health. Community Dent Health 15:132-44.

Klein H, Palmer CE, Knutson JW. (1983) Studies on dental caries: I. Dental status and dental needs of elementary school children. Public Health Rep 68:768-72.

Kleinman A. (1989) The Illness Narratives, Suffering, Healing and the Human Condition. New York: Basic Books.

Laiho M, Honkala E, Nyyssonen V, Milen A. (1993) Three methods of oral health education in secondary schools. Scand J Dent Res 101:422-7.

Lee MM, Friedman CM, McTigue DJ, Carllin SA, Cline VN, Flintom CJ. (1981) Affecting oral hygiene behaviors in children: Use of a chart as a motivational device. Clin Prev Dent 3:28-31.

Leone CW, Oppenheim FG. (2001) Physical and chemical aspects of saliva a indicators of risk for dental caries in humans. J Dent Edu 65:1054-1062.

Leverett DH. (1989) Effectiveness of mouthrinsing with fluoide solutions in preventin coronal and root caries. J Public Health Dent 49 (Special Issue): 310-16.

Levine R. (1995) The scientific basis of dental health education, a policy document. 4th ed. London: Health Education Authority.

Lim LP, Davies WI. (1996) Comparison of various modalities of "simple" periodontal therapy of oral cleanliness and bleeding. J Clinical Periodontol 23:595-600.

Lim LP, Davies WI, Yuen KW, Ma MH. (1996) Comparison of modes of oral hygiene instruction in improving gingival health. J Clin Periodontol 23:693-7.

Lipsey MW. (1990) Design sensitivity: Statistical power for experimental research. Newbury Park, CA: Sage.

Lipton J, Ship J, Larch-Robinson D. (1993) Estimated prevalence and distribution of reported orofacial pain the United States. J Am Dent Assoc 124:115-21.

Litt MD, Reisine S, Tinanoff N. (1995) Multidimensional causal model of dental caries development in low-income preschool children. Public Health Rep 110:607-17.

Little SJ, Hollis JF, Stevens VJ, Mount K, Mullooly JP, Johnson BD. (1997) Effective group behavioral intervention for older periodontal patients. J Periodont Res 32:315-25.

Locker D. (2000) Deprivation and oral health: a review. Community Dent Oral Epidemiol. 28:161-9.

Loe H, Theilade E, Jensen SB. (1965) Experimental gingivitis in man. J Periodontol 36:177-87.

Loesche WJ. (2000) Periodontal disease: Link to cardiovascular disease. Compend Contin Educ Dent 21:463-70.

Lunn HD, Williams AC. (1990) The development of a toothbrushing programme at a school for children with moderate and severe learning difficulties. Community Dent Health 7:403-6.

Maddock JE, Rossi JS. (2001) Statistical power analysis of articles published in three health psychology related journals. Health Psychol 20:76-8.

Maiman LA, Becker MH. (1974) The Health Belief Model: Origins and correlates in psychological theory. Health Educ Monogr 2:336-53.

Marmot, MG, Bobak M, Smith, GD. (1995) Explanations for social inequalities in health in Society and Health (Amick BC, Levine S, Tarlov AR, Walsh DC eds). New York:Oxford University Press.

Martin, G. and Pear, J. (1992). Behavior Modification: What it is and how to do it. Prentice Hall, Englewood Cliffs, NJ

Mazzocchi AR, Moretti R. (1997) Effectiveness of a dental preventive program on plaque index results in 8-year-old children of Bergamo, Italy. Community Dent Oral Epidemiol 25:332-3.

McCaul KD, Glasgow RE, O'Neill HK. (1992) The problem of creating habits: Establishing health protective dental behaviors. Health Psychol 11:101-11.

McGlynn FD, Le Compte EJ, Thomas RG, Courts FJ, Melamed BG. (1987) Effects of behavioral self-management on oral hygiene adherence among orthodontic patients. Amer J Orthod Dentofacial Orthop 91:15-21.

McGlynn FD, Mings EL, Marks G, Goebel G. (1985) Behavioral self-management of oral hygiene activities for student dentists. J Dent Educ 49:718-20.

McIntyre J, Wight C, Blinkhorn AS. (1985) A reassessment of Lothian health board's dental health education program for primary school children. Community Dent Health 2:99-108.

Melsen B, Agerbaek N. (1980) Effect of an instructional motivation program on oral health in Danish adolescents after 1 and 2 years. Community Dent Oral Epidemiol 8:72-8.

Milgrom P, Reisine S. (2000) Oral health in the United States: the post-fluoride generation. Annu Rev Public Health 21:403-36.

Moss RA, Garrett JC. (1984) Temporomandibular joint dysfuncton syndrome and myofascial pain dysfunction syndrome: a critical review. J Oral Rehabil 11:3-28.

Mojon P, Rentsch A, Budtz-Jorgensen E, Baehni PC. (1998) Effects of an oral health program on selected clinical parameters and salivary bacteria in a long-term care facility. European Journal of Oral Science 106, 827-34.

Moltzer G, Hoogstraten J. (1986) The effect of three methods of dental health care instruction and dental knowledge, attitude, behavior, and fear. Community Dent Health 3:83-9.

National Institutes of Health Consensus Development Conference Statement. (1984) Dental sealants in the prevention of tooth decay. J Dent Edu 48:126-31.

Nevins M, Becker W, Kornman K (eds). (1999) Proceedings of the World Workshop in Clnical Periodontics. Chicago: American Academy of Periodontology, 123-31.

Nicolaci AB, Tesini DA. (1982) Improvement in the oral hygiene of institutionalized mentally retarded individuals through training of direct care staff: A longitudinal study. Spec Care Dentist 2;217-21.

Nowjack-Raymer R, Ainamo J, Suomi JD, Kingman A, Driscoll WS, Brown LD. (1995) Improved periodontal status through self-assessment: A 2-year longitudinal study in teenagers. J Clin Perdiodontol 22:603-8.

Nunnally JC. (1978) Psychometric Theory. New York, NY: McGraw Hill.

Nylander A, Kumlin I, Martinsson M, Twetman S. (2001) Effect of a school based preventive program with salivary lactobacillus counts as sugar-motivating tool on caries increment in adolescents. Acta Odontol Scan 59:88-92.

Offenbacher S, Katz V, Fertik G., et al. (1996) Periodontal infection as a possible risk factor for preterm low birth weight. J periodontal 67:1103-1113.

Olsen CB, Brown DF, Wright FAC. (1986) Dental health promotion in a group of children at high risk to dental disease. Community Dent Oral Epidemiol 14:302-5.

Papas AS, Joshi A, MacDonald SL, Maravelis-Spangounias L, Pretara-Spanedda P, Curro FA. (1993) Caries prevalence in xerostomic individuals. J Can Dent Assoc 59:171-4, 177-9.

Petersen PE, Holst D. (1995) Utilization of dental health services. In Cohen L and Gift HC (eds) Disease Prevention and Oral Health Promotion, Socio-Dental Sciences in Action Copenhagen: Munksgaard pp 341-86.

Pavi E, Kay EJ, Murray K, Stephen KW. (1991) A programme of preventive dentistry in field conditions carried out in Glasgow, Scotland. Community Dent Health 9:249-59.

Persson RE, Persson GR, Powell LV, Kiyak HA. (1998) Periodontol effects of a biobehavioral prevention program. J Clinl Periodontol 25:322-9.

Petersen PE. (1989) Evaluation of dental preventive programmes for Danish chocolate workers. Community Dent Oral Epidemiol 17:53-9.

Pine, CM, McGoldrick PM, Burnside G, Curnow MM, Chesters RK, Nicholson J, Huntington E. (2000) An intervention program to establish regular tooth-brushing: Understanding parents' beliefs and motivating children. Int Dent J suppl., pp 312-23.

Poulsen S, Horowitz H. (1974) An evaluation of a hierarchical method of describing the pattern of dental caries attack. Community Dent Oral Epidemiol 2:7-11.

Price S, Kiyak HA. (1981) A behavioral approach to improving oral health among the elderly. Spec Care Dentist 1:267.

Primosch RE, Balsewich CM, Thomas CW. (2001) Outcomes assessment an intervention strategy to improve parental compliance to follow-up evaluations after treatment of early childhood caries using general anesthesia in a Medicaid population. J Dent Children March-April 102-8.

Prochaska JO, DiClemente CC. (1983). Stages and processes of self-change of smoking: Toward a integrative model of change. J Consult Clin Psychol 5:390-5.

Ramsay DS. (2000) Patient compliance with oral hygiene regimens: A behavioral self-regulation analysis with implications for technology. Int Dent J, suppl, 304-11.

Ranney RR. (1977) Pathogenesis of periodontal disease. In: International Conference on Research in the Biology of Periodontal disease pp 223-300 Chicago: University of Illinois School of Dentistry.

Rantanen T, Siirila HS, Lehvila P. (1980) Effect of instruction and motivation on dental knowledge and behavior among wearers of partial dentures. Acta Odontologica Scand 38:9-15.

Rayner JA. (1992) A dental health education programme, including home visits, for nursery school children. Br Dent J 172:57-62.

Redmond CA, Blinkhorn FA, Kay EJ, Davies RM, Worthington HV, Blinkhorn AS. (1999) A cluster randomized controlled trial testing the effectiveness of a school-based dental health education program for adolescents. J Public Health Dent 59:12-17.

Reisine S, Douglass J. (1998) Psychosocial and behavioral issues in early childhood caries. Comm Dent Oral Epidemiol 26 (Supplement 1):32-44.

Reisine S, Litt M, Tinanoff N. (1994) A biospsychosocial model to predict caries in preschool children. Pediatric Dent 16:413-418.

Reisine, S. and D. Locker. (1995) Social, Psychological and Economic Impacts of Dental Problems and Treatments, in Oral Health Promotion (Cohen L and Gift H, eds) pp. 33-108 Copenhagen: Munksgaard.

Reisine, S., W. Psoter. (2001) Socioeconomic status and selected behavioral determinants as risk factors for dental caries. J Dent Edu, 65:1009-16.

Richter DD, Nanda NS, Sinha PK, Smith DW. (1998) Effect of behavior modification on patient compliance in orthodontics. Angle Orthod 68:123-32.

Rinchuse DJ, Rinchuse DJ, Zullo TG. (1992) Oral hygiene compliance; A clinical investigation. J Clin Orthod 26:33-8.

Rise J and Sogaard AJ. (1988) Effect of a mass media periodontal campaign upon preventive knowledge and behavior in Norway. Community Dent Oral Epidemiol 16:1-4.

Rivara FP, Thompson DC, Tompson RS. (1997) Epidemiology of bicycle injuries and risk factors for serious injury. Inj Prev 3:110-4.

Rossi JS. (1990) Statistical power of psychological research: What have we gained in 20 years? J Consult Clin Psychol 58:646–656.

Rossi JS. (1997) A case study in the failure of psychology as a cumulative science: The spontaneous recovery of verbal learning. In: What if There Were No Significance Tests? (Harlow LL, Mulaik SA and Steiger JH, eds), pp. 175–197. Hillsdale, NJ: Lawrence Erlbaum.

Rozier G. (2001) Effectiveness of methods used by dental professionals for the primary prevention of dental caries J Dent Edu 1063-73.

Rozier RG. (2001) Effectiveness of methods used by dental professionals for the primary prevention of dental caries. J Dent Edu 65:1063-72.

Rugg-Gunn AJ Hackett AF, Appleton DR., et al. (1984) Relationship between dietary habits and caries increment assessed over two years in 405 English adolescent school children. Arch Oral Biol 29:983-92.

Rugh JD, Woods BJ, Dahlstrom L. (1993) Temporomandibular disorders: assessment of psychological factors. Adv Dent Res. 7:127-36.

Russell BA, Horowitz AM, Frazier PJ. (1989) School-based preventative regimens and oral health knowledge and practices of sixth graders. J Public Health Dent 49, 192-200.

Schou L. (1985) Active-involvement principle in dental health education. Community Dent Oral Epidemiol 13, 128-32.

Schou L. (2000) The relevance of behavioural sciences in dental practice. Int Dental J 50:324-32.

Schou L, Locker D. (1994) Oral health: A Review of the Effectiveness of Health Education and Health Promotion. Utrecht: Landelijk Centrum GVO.

Schou L, Wight C, Clemson N, Douglas S, Clark C. (1989) Oral health promotion for institutionalized elderly. Community

Dent Oral Epidemiol 17:2-6.

Sgan-Cohen HD, Mansbach I, Haver D, Gofin R. (2001) Community-oriented oral health promotion for infants in Jerusalem: Evaluation of a program trial. J Public Health Dent 61:107-113.

Shaw MJ, Shaw L. (1991) The effectiveness of differing dental health education programmes in improving the oral health of adults with mental handicap attending Birmingham adult training centers. Community Dent Health 8:139-45.

Silness J, Loe H. (1964) Periodontal disease in pregnancy. II. Correlation between oral hygene and periodontal condition. Acta Odontol Scand 22:112-35.

Slakter M, Albino JE, Fox RN, Lewis EA. (1980) Reliability and stability of the orthodontic patient cooperation scale. Amer J Orthod 78:559-63.

Soderholm CL, Nobreus N, Attstrom R, Egelgerg J. (1982) Teaching plaque control. A five visit versus a two-visit program. J Clin Periodontol 9:203-13.

Soderholm G, Egelberg J. (1982) Teaching plaque control II. 30-minue vs. 15-minute appointments in a three-visit program. J Clin Periodontol 9:214-22.

Sogaard AJ, Holst D. (1988) The effect of different school based dental health education programmes in Norway. Community Dent Health 5:169-84.

Sogaard AJ, Tuominen R, Holst D, Gjermo P. (1987) The effect of 2 teaching programs on the gingival health of 15-year old schoolchildren. J Clin Periodontol 14:165-70.

Sogaard AJ. (1993) Theories and models of health behavior in Oral Health Promotion (Schou L and Blinkhorn, eds) Oxford: Oxford University Press pp 25-57.

Spak CJ, Johnson G, Ekstrand J. (1994) Caries incidence, salivary flow rate and efficacy of fluoride gel treatment in irradiated patients. Caries Res. 28:388-93.

Sprod A, Anderson R, Treasure E. (1996) Effective oral health promotion. Technical Report 20. Cardiff, Wales: Health Promotion Wales.

Sreenby LM, Schwartz SS. (1997) A reference guide to drugs and dry mouth 2nd edition. Gerodontology 14:33-47.

Stetson BA. (2000) Influence of behavioral science research on oral health promotion. Compendium on Continuing Education Dental Supplement 30:24-30.

Stewart JE, Jacobs-Schoen M, Padilla MR, Maeder LA, Wolfe GR, Hartz GW. (1991) The effect of a cognitive behavioral intervention on oral hygiene. J Clin Periodontol 18:219-22.

Stewart JE, Wolfe GR. (1989) The retention of newly-acquired brushing and flossing skills. J Clin Periodontol 16:331-2.

Stewart JE, Wolfe GR, Maeder L, Hartz GW. (1996) Changes in dental knowledge and self-efficacy scores following interventions to change oral hygiene behavior. Patient Educ Counsel 27:269-77.

Stillman-Lowe C, Crossley ML. (2001) Application of Prochaska and DiClemente's model to dental health related behaviors. Community Dent Health 18:263.

Swain JJ, Allard GB, Holborn SW. (1982) The good toothbrushing game: A school-based dental hygiene program for increasing the toothbrushing effectiveness of children. J Appl Behav Anal 15:171-6.

Talal N. (1992) Sjogren's Syndrome: historical overview and clinical spectrum of disease. Rheum Dis Clin North Am 18:507-15.

Tan AES, Wade B. (1980) The role of visual feedback by a disclosing agent in plaque control. J Clin Periodontol 7:140-8.

Tan HH, Ruiter E., Verhey H. (1981) Effect of repeated dental health care education on gingival health, knowledge, attitude, behavior and perception. Community Dent Oral Epidemiol 9:15-21.

Tedesco LA, Keffer MA, Davis EL,

Christersson LA. (1992) Effect of a social cognitive intervention on oral health status, behavior reports, and cognitions. J Periodontol 63:567-75.

Tedesco LA, Keffer MA, Fleck-Kandeth C. (1991) Self-efficacy, reasoned action, and oral health behavior reports: Social cognitive approach to compliance. J Behavior Med 14:341-55.

ter Horst G, de Wit CA. (1993) Review of behavioural research in dentistry 1987-1992:Dental anxiety, dentist-patient relationship, compliance and dental attendance. Int Dent J 43:265-78.

ter Horst G, Hoogstraten J. (1989) Immediate and delayed effects of a dental health education film on periodontal knowledge, attitudes, and reported behavior of Dutch adolescents. Community Dent Oral Epidemiol 17:183-6.

Tinanoff N, Kanellis MJ, Vargas CM. (2002) Current understanding of the epidemiology mechanisms, and prevention of dental caries in preschool children. Pediatr Dent 24:543-51.

Torpaz E, Noam Y, Anaise JZ, Sgan-Cohen HD. (1984) Effectiveness of dental educational program on oral cleanliness of schoolchildren in Israel. Dent Hyg 58:384-7.

Towner EML. (1984) The "Gleam Team" programme:Development and Evaluation of a dental health education package for infant schools. Community Dent Health 1:181-91.

Truin GJ, Plasschaert AJ, Konig KG, Vogels AL. (1981) Dental caries in 5-,6-, 9- and 11-year-old schoolchildren during a 9-year dental health campaign in the Hague. Community Dent Oral Epidemiol 9:55-60.

Truman BI, Gooch BF, Sulemana I, Gift HC, Horowitz AM, Evans CA, Griffin SO, Carande-Kulis VG. (2002) The Task Force on Community Preventive Services. Reviews of evidence on interventions to prevent dental caries, oral and pharyngeal cancers, and sport-related craniofacial injuries. Am J Prev Med 23:21-54.

U.S. Department of Health and Human Service. Oral health in America: A Report of the Surgeon General. Rockville, MD: U. S. Department of Health and Human Service, National Institute of Dental and Craniofacial Research, National Institutes of Health; 2000.

United States Public Health Service, National Center for Health Statistics. (2003) Health, United States, 2002 website http://www.cdc.gov/nchs/hus.htm.

United States Public Health Service, National Center for Health Statistics. (1981) Decayed, Missing and Filled Teeth among Persons 1-74 years, United States. DHHS Publ No (PHS) 81-1673, Series 11 No 223 Washington DC: Government Printing Office.

Vargas CM, Ronzio CR. (2002) Relationship between children's dental needs and dental care utilization: United States, 1988-1994. Am J Public Health. 92:1816-21.

Winn DM, Brunelle JA, Selwitz RH, Kaste LM,Olsdakowski RJ, Kingman A, Brown LJ. (1996) Coronal and root caries in the dentition of adults in the Unites States, 1988-91. J Dent Res 75(Special Issue): 642-51.

Vigild M. (1990) Evaluation of an oral health service for nursing home residents. Acta Odontol Scand 48:99-105.

Von Korff M. (1995) Health Services research and temporomandibular pain in Temporomandibular Disorders and Related Pain Conditions, Progress in Pain Research and Management Vol 4, (Sessle BJ, Bryant PS, Dionne RA, eds), pp. 227-36. Seattle: IAASP Press.

Walsh MM. (1985) Effects of school-based dental health education on knowledge, attitudes, and behavior of adolescents in San Fransisco. Community Dent Oral Epidemiol 13:143-7.

Walsh MM, Heckman BH, Moreau-Diettinger

R. (1985) Use of gingival bleeding for reinforcement of oral home care behaviour. Community Dent Oral Epidemiol 13:133-5.

Watt R, Fuller S, Harnett R, Treasure E, Stillman-Lowe C. (2001) Oral health promotion evaluation: Time for development. Community Dent Oral Epidemiol 29:161-6.

Weinstein P, Milgrom P, Melnick S, Beach B, Spadafor A. (1989) How effective is oral hygiene instruction: Results after 6 and 24 weeks. J Public Health Dent 32-38.

Weintstein R, Tosolin F, Ghilardi L, Zanardelli E. (1996) Psychological intervention in patients with poor compliance. J Clin Periodontol 23:283-88.

West KP, DuRant RH, Pendergrast R. (1993) An experimental test of adolescents' compliance with dental appointments. J Adolesc Health 14:384-9.

Wight C, Blinkhorn A. (1988) An assessment of two dental health education programmmes for schoolchildren in the Lothian region of Scotland. J Pediatr Dent 4:1-7.

Worthington HV, Hill KB, Mooney J, Hamilton FA, Blinkhorn AS. (2001) A cluster randomized controlled trial of a dental health education program for 10-year-old children. J Public Health Dent 61:22-7.

Zautra AJ, Marbach JJ, Raphael KG, Dohrenwend BP, Lennon MC, Kenny DA. (1995) The examination of myofascial face pain and its relationship to psychological distress among women. Health Psychol 14:223-31.

A SYSTEMATIC REVIEW OF INTERVENTIONS FOR IMPROVING ADHERENCE WITH LONG-TERM PHARMACOTHERAPY

Cynthia Willey and Brian J. Quilliam

INTRODUCTION

Medication non-adherence is common in most conditions for which medication is prescribed. Sub-optimal adherence is associated with unfilled prescriptions (Monane et al., 1994), overly aggressive prescribing of medications, and most importantly worse outcomes (Feldman et al., 1998; Andrade et al., 1999; Hepke et al., 2004; Krapek et al., 2004; Pladevall et al., 2004). The extent to which a person's behavior coincides with the clinical prescription (in terms of taking medications, following diets, or executing other life-style changes) has been defined as 'compliance' (Sackett, 1976), but in recent years the term 'adherence' has been preferred. The terms 'compliance' and 'adherence' will be used interchangeably in this document, in accord with the publications reviewed. A person who is non-adherent with their medication may skip doses, take "drug holidays" for short time periods, forget to take the medication, discontinue the medication completely, or take the medication inappropriately.

How big is the problem?

Adherence with medication is low for many chronic diseases including cardiovascular disease, diabetes, HIV, depression, and others (Dunbar-Jacob et al., 2000; DiMatteo, 2004). Early studies reported low rates of non-compliance, but these studies were clinical trials that enrolled carefully selected participants, and studied them for very short periods of time (Andrade et al., 1995). Large population based studies with longer follow-up times show much higher rates of non-compliance with medication (Table 1).

Hypertension

Survey results in the United States, Canada, France and the United Kingdom indicate that at best only 30% of hypertensive patients maintain target blood pressure levels of 140/90 mm Hg and inadequate treatment adherence is believed to be a major cause (Sclar, 1991). Several studies have shown that within the first year of treatment 16-57% of hypertensives stop taking their anti-hypertensive medication (Andrade et al., 1995). Patients with newly diagnosed hypertension, i.e. new users of medication, are most likely to discontinue therapy (Caro et al., 1999), while those with established hypertension have higher rates of adherence. Lack of adherence to pharmacologic therapy for hypertension has important implications both for blood pressure control and cardiovascular complications (Feldman et al., 1998).

Hyperlipidemia

Large population based studies have shown that patients prescribed medication for high cholesterol do not fill their prescriptions for at least a third of the year; in a large, cross-national study approximately 7300 older patients with prescription coverage failed to fill their prescriptions for cholesterol lowering medication for 40% of the study year (Avorn et al., 1998). After 5 years, about half (48%) of the surviving original cohort in the United States had stopped using cholesterol lowering medication altogether. Other studies of managed care populations show similar results; a cohort study of approximately 2400 new users of cholesterol lowering medication showed that during the first year, about 40 percent of patients discontinued their medication (Andrade et al., 1995).

Diabetes

Several trials have now demonstrated a strong correlation between intensive glycemic control and reduction in risk for various complications encountered in patients with diabetes mellitus, (UK Prosrective Diabetes Study (UKPDS) Group 1998a; 1998b) however, long-term compliance with drug therapy remains poor with compliance to oral agents ranging from 30-80% (Paes et al., 1997). In a recent Scottish study of 2,920 patients with type 2 diabetes, only 34% of patients receiving metformin and 31% of patients receiving a sulfonylurea medication adhered to therapy over the course of 12 months, and compliance among patients receiving both agents in combination was only 13% (Morris et al., 2000). In a study of 9875 patients in a large managed care organization, the pro-portion of patients who continued metformin therapy at 12 months was approximately 55% (Selby et al., 1999).

Improving medication-taking behavior is one area where there is wide agreement about the need for new strategies to predict and improve adherence with prescribed regimens. The extent of medication non-adherence in general populations is sizeable, and because adherence is a principal determinant of treatment effectiveness, poor adherence prevents optimal clinical outcomes in a large number of treated patients, and reduces the efficiency of health care resources. The purpose of our study was to review current knowledge about how to improve adherence with long-term pharmacotherapy, and make recommendations for future research.

Table 1: Adherence Rates Reported in Large, Population-Based Studies by Disease Area

Disease State	*Estimated Adherence*	*References*
Hypertension	50-70% of prescribed doses actually taken	(Feldman et al., 1998)
Hyperlipidemia	50-60% of prescribed doses actually taken	(Andrade et al., 1995) (Andrade, 1998) (Avorn et al., 1998) (Simons et al., 1996) .
Congestive Heart Failure	50-60% of prescribed doses actually taken	(Monane et al., 1994).
Diabetes	55% remain on therapy after 12 months	(Selby et al., 1999)

METHODS

Data Sources

MEDLINE, CINAHL and PSYCHLIT were searched in December 2004 for English language papers including the terms patient compliance or patient adherence or patient non-compliance or patient non-adherence and drug therapy or medication, and intervention study or intervention. The resulting citations (n=527) were searched for primary research articles focusing upon interventions to improve patients' adherence with medication. The bibliographies of relevant articles were also searched for additional studies.

Criteria for Inclusion

We included only randomized, controlled trials (RCT) that focused on interventions to improve adult patients' medication taking behavior. Studies that used a pre-post design or other quasi-experimental design strategy were excluded. Studies that included only cognitively impaired adults were not included. We did not include studies that focused on interventions to improve adherence with medications for HIV because a separate chapter in this volume deals specifically with that topic.

In contrast to previous reviews (Haynes et al., 1996), we did include studies that used self-report of medication adherence as a primary outcome measure. Although self-report is known to overestimate medication compliance (Cramer et al., 1989; Cramer, 1995; Urquhart and De Klerk, 1998), differential over-estimation between treatment and control groups is unlikely. Thus, although self-report of medication adherence is biased toward higher levels, comparison of treatment and control groups should not be distorted.

Studies with methodologic problems that would bias results were excluded from the review. These problems included: excessive loss to follow-up (defined as >=20%), failure to control for baseline differences in analyses of outcome measures, inadequate power to detect an intervention effect, failure to apply corrections for multiple statistical tests, or

using a non-replicable definition for adherence outcome measures.

RESULTS

Of the 527 research articles identified, 35 satisfied the inclusion criteria (Table 2). The primary reason for exclusion was study design: many studies used quasi-experimental designs or were small pilot studies. Also, many studies were not primary research articles, but either literature review studies or studies describing possible intervention strategies. The studies reviewed used various measures and definitions of adherence including self-reported adherence, obtaining refills on time as measured by insurance claims, pill counts, and continuing versus discontinuation of therapy. Most studies focused upon a single disease or condition, and these included: hypertension, hyperlipidemia, non-insulin dependent diabetes (NIDDM), tuberculosis, asthma, chronic obstructive pulmonary disease, or organ transplant. In addition, a few studies focused upon multiple diseases or conditions, such as polypharmacy among the elderly.

Types of Intervention Strategies

We separated intervention types into the following ten categories:

Type of Intervention Strategy	Definition
Single Focus Interventions	
Education-Only	Patients were educated about their disease and/or their medication
Reminders-Only	Patients were reminded via telephone or mail to take their medication as directed
More Convenient Access to Nurse or Physician	Extended work-site care by nurses or physicians
More Convenient Medication Packaging	Providing medication in more convenient packaging units such as labeled blister packs
More Convenient Medication Dosing	Simplifying dosing by reducing the frequency of oral doses to once daily or using once per week transdermal dosing

Counseling on Specific Behavioral Objectives	Patients were counseled on specific behavioral strategies for taking medication as directed such as pill-taking and appointment keeping
Multiple Focus Interventions	
Education Plus Reminders	Patients were educated/counseled about their disease, their medication, or strategies for taking medication as directed AND were reminded via telephone or mail to take their medication
Education Plus Monitoring	Patients were educated about their disease, their medication, or strategies for taking medication as directed AND they were routinely monitored for medication related problems, such as side effects, and provided opportunities to ask medication related questions
Pharmaceutical Care	Provision of clinical pharmacy services including review of medications, education regarding medication use, minimizing adverse drug effects and follow-up for detection of medication related problems
Intensive Multi-Component Intervention	Multi-faceted interventions that minimally included: education, counseling, extended health care provider support, and social support enhancement

SINGLE FOCUS INTERVENTIONS
Education-Only

The most common intervention strategy in these randomized, controlled trials was education about medication and encouraging responsibility for one's own care. However, this strategy was very often used in combination with other strategies, rather than as a single, tested intervention. Only 2 studies tested education-only as a single intervention strategy (Gonzalez-Fernandez et al., 1990; Lowe et al., 1995). Both of these studies were performed in hospital settings and evaluated whether education provided in the hospital setting was related to improved medication adherence after discharge; both studies found that patients who received education while in the hospital setting had higher adherence rates after discharge, however long-term follow-up was not performed. These studies suggest that hospitalized patients may benefit from education about medication use, but cannot be generalized to patients with less serious conditions and do not provide information about long-term medication adherence.

Reminders Only

Only two studies investigated reminders-only as an intervention strategy (McKenney et al., 1992; Park et al., 1992). Park et al. gave patients organizational charts and medication organizers and compared adherence after two weeks; the intervention was only effective for patients over 70 years old, suggesting that reminders may be helpful for elderly patients. McKenney et al. also studied older patients (>50) and found that a container that beeped

Table 2: Studies of Interventions to Improve Adherence with Long-Term Pharmacotherapy

STUDY	SUBJECTS / GROUP	INTERVENTION STRATEGY	OUTCOME
Single Focus Interventions : Education only			
Gonzalez-Fernandez et al. (1990) Usefulness of a systemic hypertension in-hospital program	N=24 patients aged 50-70 years, with systemic hypertension, admitted to hospital with a non-hypertension related diagnosis	C) No Intervention E) Educational programs related to BP, diet, exercise and medication compliance were delivered on the fourth day after admission	Eight weeks after the intervention, both SBP and DBP were significantly lower in the treatment group.
Lowe et al. (1995) Effects of self medication program on compliance with treatment in elderly patients	N=44 elderly patients at a district general hospital in the UK	C) Usual hospital care E) A hospital self medication program in which patients are educated about their medicines and given increasing responsibility for taking them in hospital.	10 days post-discharge pill count revealed that the mean compliance score was significantly higher in the intervention group (95% vs. 83%, p<.02).
Park et al. (1992) Medication adherence behaviors in older adults: effects of external cognitive supports	N=15 community dwelling elderly in the southern U.S.	C) No intervention E1) Organizational chart E2) Over-the-counter medication organizer E3) Both the chart and organizer	After 2 wks, bar code technology used for pill counts indicated that the intervention was only effective for those >70 years. Young-old subjects showed high adherence (94%) and no improvement with the addition of interventions. Omission errors were lower in the condition in which subjects received both chart and organizer (p=.007).
Single Focus Interventions : Reminders only			
McKenney et al. (1992) Impact of an electronic medicaton compliance aid on long-term blood pressure control	N=35 patients over 50 years of age, treated for hyper-tension > 12 months and randomly allocated to 2 groups	C) Standard medication vials E) Prescript TimeCap, a device that displays day and time when container was last opened), and beeps when dose is due	% doses taken at 12 weeks was 95% for the treatment group vs. 79% for standard vials (p=.006)

STUDY	SUBJECTS / GROUP	INTERVENTION STRATEGY	OUTCOME
Single Focus Interventions : More Convenient Access to Nurse or Physician			
Logan et al. (1979) Work-site treatment of hypertension by specially trained nurses. A controlled trial	n=228 employees in metropolitan Toronto whose blood pressure was screened	C) Management by family physician E) Work site care by nurses who were allowed to prescribe and change drug therapy at the work site without prior physician approval	Patients who received E were significantly more likely to be prescribed antihypertensive medications (94.7% vs 62.7%), to reach goal blood-pressure in the first 6 months (48.5% vs 27.5%), and to take the drugs prescribed (67.6% vs 49.1%).
Sackett et al. (1975) Randomized clinical trial of strategies for improving medication compliance in primary hypertension	N=115 Canadian steelworkers with hypertension	C) Usual practice with visits to family physicians outside working hours E) Augmented convenience for hypertensive care via follow-up by industrial physicians during working hours	Convenience of follow-up at work had no effect upon compliance with antihypertensive drug regimens at 6 months
Single Focus Interventions : More Convenient Medication Packaging			
Becker et al. (1986) A randomized trial of special packaging of antihypertensive medications	n=90 patients with demonstrated poor blood pressure control	C) Traditional pill vials E) 28-day plastic blister packets containing each day's medication. The day and time of dosing was printed on each plastic blister.	At the 3 month follow-up, no difference was found in average diastolic blood pressure, self-reported compliance or pill counts.
Single Focus Interventions : More Convenient Medication Dosing			
Burris et al. (1991) Therapeutic adherence in the elderly: transdermal clonidine compared to oral verapamil for hypertension	N=29 elderly patients with mild hypertension, average age=67	C) Oral sustained-release verapamil (verapamil-SR) taken once daily E) Treatment with transdermal clonidine patches to be changed once per week	After 2 months, transdermal clonidine was worn as directed during > 96% of patient-weeks of treatment. Verapamil-SR was taken as directed during approximately 50% of patient-weeks of therapy (p<.01)
Single Focus Interventions : Specific Behavioral Objectives			
Zismer et al. (1982) Improving hypertension control in a private	N=20 hypertensive patients receiving drug therapy from a private,	C) Usual care E) The intervention program focused on three behavioral objectives: pill	After 6 months, BP fell in the E group (-13 mm Hg, systolic; -8 mm Hg, diastolic) but rose slightly in the

STUDY	SUBJECTS / GROUP	INTERVENTION STRATEGY	OUTCOME
medical practice	solo medical practice	taking, appointment keeping, and dietary sodium reduction while stressing the need for taking responsibility for one's own care	C group (3 mm Hg, systolic 0.5 mm Hg, diastolic). The difference was significant for both systolic and diastolic BP.

Multiple Focus Interventions: Education Plus Reminders

STUDY	SUBJECTS / GROUP	INTERVENTION STRATEGY	OUTCOME
Raynor et al. (1993) Effects of computer generated reminder charts on patients' compliance with drug regimen	N=49 elderly patients being discharged from a UK hospital who were regularly taking 2 or more drugs, average age=69	C1 & C2) Counseling, either from a nurse or from a pharmacist E1) Medication reminder chart and counseling from a nurse E2) Medication reminder chart and structured counseling from a pharmacist, which included an explanation of the reminder chart.	After 10-12 days, The mean compliance score was 86% in both groups not given the reminder chart; 91% in the group given the chart without an explanation; and 95% in the group given the chart and an explanation. A mean compliance score of > 85% was achieved by 63% of patients without a reminder chart and by 86% of those receiving the chart ($p < 0.001$).
Rehder et al. (1980) Improving medication compliance by counseling and special prescription container	n=25 patients attending a hypertension clinic, prescribed 2+ medi-cations per day, assigned to 4 groups	C) No intervention E1) Counseling only E2) Medication container only E3) Medication container plus counseling	95% compliance based on pill counts was significantly greater in the medication container and container plus counseling groups, but at 6 months most patients were no longer using the medication containers regularly.

STUDY	SUBJECTS / GROUP	INTERVENTION STRATEGY	OUTCOME
Rosen et. al. (2003) Electronic monitoring and counseling to improve medication adherence	N=33 patients attending a VA primary care clinic and taking metformin	C) No Intervention E) Medication container plus counseling	After 16 weeks, mean metformin adherence improved to 80% in the E group compared to 60% in the C group (p<0.02).
Sclar et al. (1991) Effect of health education in promoting prescription refill compliance among patients with hypertension	N=226 patients with mild to moderate hypertension enrolled in a staff model HMO, all prescribed a once a day regimen of atenolol	C) No intervention E) Educational materials regarding the importance of compliance and information regarding nutrition and lifestyle, and mailed refill reminders	Days supply of medication at 180 days of follow-up was increased by 27 in existing patients and 40 days in new patients in the health education group (p<.001)
Wandless & Davie (1977) Can drug compliance in the elderly be improved?	N=15 elderly patients in two rehabilitation units in the UK, aged 64 to 93	C) Each group was instructed verbally on the nature and amount of their medication E1) One group was also given a tear-off calendar E2) A second group also received a tablet identification card as a memory aid	After 14 days, those with calendars made fewer errors than those with cards, and those with either a card or a calendar made significantly fewer errors than those given only standard instructions as determined by pill count (p<.01).

Multiple Focus Interventions: Education Plus Monitoring

STUDY	SUBJECTS / GROUP	INTERVENTION STRATEGY	OUTCOME
Cargill (1992) Medication compliance in elderly people: influencing variables and interventions	N=23 elderly patients attending a general medicine clinic, average age=72	C) No intervention E1) In-home 20-minute teaching session, including review of medications E2) In-home teaching session plus a follow-up phone call 1-2 wks post-visit	After 4-6 weeks, pill counts showed that patients in the group with the follow-up phone call showed greater improvement in adherence (p<.01)
Friedman et al. (1996) A telecommunications system of monitoring and counseling patients with hypertension: Impact on medication adherence and blood pressure control	n=134 patients who were >=60 years of age, recruited from community sites, currently taking antihypertensive medication	C) Usual care E) Usual care plus a Telephone-Linked Computer (TLC) system that could answer questions using the patients' touch tone keypad	Mean percent adherence improved 17.7% in the E group versus 11.7% in the C group (p=.03) at 6 months follow-up

STUDY	SUBJECTS / GROUP	INTERVENTION STRATEGY	OUTCOME
Katon et al. (2001) A randomized trial of relapse prevention of depression in primary care	N=192,194 patients with recurrent major depression or dysthymia who had recovered after 8 weeks of antidepressant treatment	C) Usual care E) A multi-faceted relapse prevention intervention that included patient education, 2 visits with a depression specialist, and telephone monitoring and follow-up	E group patients were more likely to refill prescriptions during the 12 month follow-up (OR=1.91, p<.001).
Katon et al. (2004) The Pathways Study. A randomized trial of collaborative care in patients with diabetes and depression	N=329 patients with diabetes and concomitant major depression and/or dysthymia with or without antidepressant treatment in the previous 3 months.	C) Usual Care E) A stepped intervention beginning with regular in-person educational visits, followed by monthly telephone follow-up	Using automated antidepressant refill data, the E patients was more likely than the C to be adherent at 3 (OR=3.20, p<0.05), 6 (OR=2.29, p<0.05), 9 (OR=2.78, p<0.05) and 12 months (OR=2.18, p<0.05) of follow-up.
Piette et al. (2000) Do automated calls with nurse follow-up improve self-care and glycemic control among vulnerable patients with diabetes?	N=140 adults with diabetes using hypoglycemic medications and treated in a county health care system	C) Usual care E) Usual care plus bi-weekly automated assessment and self-care education calls with follow-up by a nurse educator	At 12 months intervention group patients reported better glycemic control (p=.005) and fewer problems with medication adherence (p<.03)
Basler et al. (1982) Psychological group treatment of essential hypertension in general practice	N=107 obese patients with essential hypertension from eight general practices	C) No Intervention E: Group therapy in 12 weekly sessions: E1) Modification of nutritional patterns E2) Modification of nutritional patterns plus self-monitoring of blood pressure E3) Modification of nutritional patterns plus relaxation training; information about the causes and consequences of high blood pressure	BP and medication compliance measured before and after intervention showed a significant reduction; no differential effect between the various group therapy procedures could be demonstrated.

STUDY	SUBJECTS / GROUP	INTERVENTION STRATEGY	OUTCOME
Multiple Focus Interventions: Pharmaceutical Care			
Chishol et al. (2001) Impact of clinical pharmacy services on renal transplant patients' compliance with immunosuppressive medications	n=12 patients who received a renal transplant from 2/97-1/99	C) No Intervention E) Clinical pharmacy services, including review of medications, education regarding medication, minimizing adverse drug effects, and provision of recommendations to nephrologists	During the 12 month post-transplant study period, E group patients had a longer duration of compliance, as measured by refill records (p<.001), and were more likely to achieve target compliance levels (p<.05)
Faulkner et al. (2000) Impact of pharmacy counseling on compliance and effectiveness of combination lipid-lowering therapy in patients undergoing coronary artery revascularization: a randomized, controlled trial	N=15 high risk patients who had undergone cardiac surgery within 7-30 days with baseline fasting low-density lipoprotein levels higher than 130 mg/dl.	C) All patients were counseled on the appropriate use of prescribed lovastatin E) Plus weekly telephone contact with a pharmacist for 12 weeks. Contact involved questions about when prescriptions were filled, potential side effects, overall well-being and reasons for non compliance.	Short- and long-term compliance was assessed by pill and packet counts and refill records. Compliance and lipid profile results were significantly better in the E group (p<0.05) up to 2 years after the intervention.
Garcao & Cabrita. (2002) Evaluation of a pharmaceutical care program for patients in rural Portugal	N=50 patients with a diagnosis of essential hypertension who had been on drug treatment for less than 6 months	C) Usual care E) Individualized health promotion by a research pharmacist involving monthly appointments for 6 months to monitor blood pressure; assess adherence to treatment; prevent, detect, and resolve drug-related problems	After 6 months, prevalence of uncontrolled blood pressure decreased by 77.4% in the E group (P < .0001) and by 10.3% in the C group (P = .48). Systolic blood pressure was significantly lower in E vs. C patients (P <.001).
McKenney et al. (1973) The effect of clinical pharmacy services on patients with essential hypertension	N=25 patients with hypertension recruited through a health plan	C) Usual care E) Monthly appointments with a pharmacist, including provision of educational materials, management of adverse reactions, recommendations to physicians, therapy changes, blood pressure monitoring and compliance assessment	Percent of prescribed doses taken was significantly higher during the time patients were seen by the pharmacist (p<.001), but after the study period compliance levels returned to pre-study levels.

STUDY	SUBJECTS / GROUP	INTERVENTION STRATEGY	OUTCOME
Park et al. (1996) Comprehensive pharmaceutical care in the chain setting	N=26 hypertensive patients who received medications from a chain pharmacy	C) Initial and final blood pressure measurements and minimal counseling E) Monthly blood pressure and heart rate assessments and counseling on lifestyle modifications and drug therapy	After 2 weeks, blood pressure control and compliance rates as measured by Videx Time wand bar coding, were significantly improved in the study group.
Skaer et al. (1993) Effect of value-added utilities on prescription refill compliance and health care expenditures for hypertension	N=76 Medicaid beneficiaries from Florida, previously untreated for mild to moderate hypertension, prescribed 240 mg of calcium channel antagonist verapamil once daily	C) Standard pharmaceutical care at each dispensing E1) Standard pharmaceutical care and medication-refill reminder E2) Standard pharmaceutical care and unit-of-use packaging E3) Standard pharmaceutical care, mailed medication-refill reminders and unit-of-use packaging	Medication possession Ratio (MPR) during 1 year was significantly different in all 3 treatment groups versus C (p<.05) (.56 vs. (.64, .67, .79) No significant difference was discerned between groups receiving either mailed prescription-refill reminders or unit-of-use packaging.
Skaer et al. (1993) Effect of value-added utilities on prescription refill compliance and Medicaid health care expenditures-- a study of patients with non-insulin-dependent diabetes mellitus	N=65 Medicaid beneficiaries from South Carolina, previously untreated for NIDDM, prescribed 5 mg of sulfonylurea glyburide twice daily	C) Standard pharmaceutical care at each dispensing E1) Standard pharmaceutical care and medication-refill reminder E2) Standard pharmaceutical care and unit-of-use packaging E3) Standard pharmaceutical care, mailed medication-refill reminders and unit-of-use packaging	After 1 year, analysis of variance revealed that patients receiving mailed prescription-refill reminders, unit-of-use packaging, or a combination of both interventions achieved a significant increase in the Medication Possession Ratio for sulfonylurea therapy relative to C.
Weinberger et al. (2002) Effectiveness of pharmacist care for patients with reactive airways disease: a randomized controlled trial	N=447 (interv), 363 (control grp 1), 303 (control grp 2)	C1) Usual care C2) Peak flow expiratory monitoring E) Pharmaceutical care with 5 components: (1) computer display of patient-specific data, (2) tailored patient education materials, (3) resource guide for pharmacists, (4) strategies to facilitate the program, and (5) pharmacist training.	There were no significant between-group differences in medication compliance or health related quality of life at 12 month follow-up.

STUDY	SUBJECTS / GROUP	INTERVENTION STRATEGY	OUTCOME
Multiple Focus Interventions: Intensive Multi-Component Intervention			
Gallefoss & Bakke (1999) How does patient education and self-management among asthmatics and patients with COPD affect medication?	N=70 patients with bronchial asthma or COPD, aged 18-70, without serious comorbidity	C) Usual care E) Educational intervention that included printed materials, two 2-hr group sessions focused upon symptom awareness, treatment plans, medication, and physiotherapy. Also 1 or 2 40-min. individual sessions with a nurse and physiotheraptist.	Refill records over a 12 month period indicated that the odds of being >75% compliant with steroid inhalers were almost twice (OR=1.8, p=.04) for the educated group of asthma patients as compared to uneducated patients. No difference between educated and uneducated groups was found for COPD patients.
Guthrie (2001) The effects of postal and telephone reminders on compliance with pravastatin therapy in a national registry: results of the first myocardial infarction risk reduction program	N=10,335 intervention group, and 2765 control group patients, all at increased risk of MI based on the First Heart Attack Risk Test, mean age=58	C) Usual care E) Postal and telephone reminders (about coronary risk reduction and medication compliance) were sent during the first 2 months of pravastatin treatment. Both groups: received reminder postcards at 4 and 5 months, in addition to counseling by physicians about coronary risk reduction.	Neither early reminders nor baseline patient characteristics were significantly associated with self report of pravastatin doses missed at 6 months. Compliance rates were approximately 79% overall.
Haynes et al. (1976) Improvement of medication compliance in uncontrolled hypertension	N=20 patients who were non-compliant with medication six months after starting treatment	C) No intervention E) Multi-component intervention including: teaching self-monitoring of BP, charting BP and pill taking, and teaching related to tailoring pill taking to daily habits	Six months later average compliance rose 21% in the E group and blood pressures were more likely to meet goal in the E group.
Kirscht et al. (1981) A test of interventions to increase adherence to hypertensive medical regimens	N=432 randomly allocated to 36 groups ranging in size from 58 to 141	C) No intervention E) Sequential series of printed messages, nurse reminder and reinforcement, self-monitoring and social support	Nurse reinforcement via phone calls and social support significantly increased adherence from 69 to 75% based on pharmacy refill data

STUDY	SUBJECTS / GROUP	INTERVENTION STRATEGY	OUTCOME
Morisky et al. (1985) Evaluation of family health education to build social support for long-term control of high blood pressure	n=400 randomly selected patients assigned to 15 different groups in 3 phases over time	C) No intervention E1) 10 minute exit interview with a health educator to reinforce physician instructions E2) Family members support E3) Small group support	Long term outcomes were assessed at 2 years; the family support group demonstrated significantly higher levels of compliance compared to C (.876 vs. 1.92, p<.01)
Morisky et al. (1990) A patient education program to improve adherence rates with antituberculosis drug regimens	N=103 patients, age 18 or older, who were newly started on antituberculosis treatment	C) Usual care E) Special Intervention (SI) subjects received monthly health education counseling, tailored educational messages, positive reinforcement for adherence, enlistment of family support, and monetary incentives to encourage appointment keeping	After 6 to 12 months of follow-up, the proportion of patients who reported that they consumed >95% of their medication was not different between C & E with active tuberculosis, but preventive therapy patients in the E group had higher adherence (68% vs. 38%, p<.001).
Nessman (1980) Increasing compliance; patient operated hypertension groups	N=26 patients with inadequately controlled essential hypertension, with evidence via history or pill counts that they were not taking their medication as prescribed	C) Nurse-operated hypertension clinic: audiotapes on hypertension and nurse adjusted drug regimens E) Patient-operated hypertension group: group program emphasizing informed self-help	At 2 & 6 month follow-up points, E patients had lower diastolic BPs, better pill counts, and better attendance (all p <.05)
Rich et al. (1996) Effect of a multidisciplinary intervention on medication compliance in elderly patients with congestive heart failure	N=80, 76 patients >=70 years of age (mean 79) hospitalized with congestive heart failure	C) Usual care E) The intervention consisted of comprehensive patient education, dietary and social service consultations, medication review, and intensive post-discharge follow-up.	Compliance was assessed by pill counts 30 days after intervention. Compliance was 87.9 +/- 12.0% in patients randomized to E, compared with 81.1 +/- 17.2% in C (P = 0.003). A compliance rate of > or = 80% was achieved by 85.0% of the E group versus 69.7% of the C (P = 0.036).

STUDY	SUBJECTS / GROUP	INTERVENTION STRATEGY	OUTCOME
Webb (1980) Effectiveness of patient education and psychosocial counseling in promoting compliance and control among hypertensive patients	N=40 low income, rural African American patients with hypertension	C) Family MD visits only E1) Vigorous treatment: regular MD visits plus individualized counseling E2) Group patient education: regular MD visits plus group patient education	Medication compliance as measured by pill count was not significantly different at 6 months

when a dose is due improved adherence in the group using the vials. These studies suggest that older individuals may benefit from reminder devices, but neither study provided data on long-term adherence outcomes.

More Convenient Access to Nurse or Physician

Some studies tested whether more convenient access to care could improve medication adherence (Sackett et al., 1975; Logan et al., 1979). These studies were performed in work-site settings and compared usual care with extended care. Sackett et al. (Sackett et al., 1975) found no improvement in compliance with antihypertensive drug therapy when care by industrial physicians during working hours was made available to Canadian steelworkers. In contrast, Logan et al. found that work-site care by nurses increased the proportion of patients who reported taking medications as prescribed (Logan et al., 1979).

More Convenient Medication Packaging

A few studies focused upon interventions that modified the medication itself to make it more convenient to administer; more convenient packaging of medications, such as blister packs containing each days medication (Becker et al., 1986) were not found to effect self-reported compliance or pill counts among patients with hypertension.

More Convenient Medication Dosing

More convenient dosage forms such as transdermal versus oral dosing (Burris et al., 1991) were found to improve compliance with medication; transdermal clonidine was worn as directed >96% of the time while oral sustained release verapamil taken once daily was taken as directed about 50% of the time (p<.01) in an elderly population.

Specific Behavioral Objectives

Only one study focused only on specific behavioral objectives such as taking pills on time and keeping appointments; (Zismer et al., 1982) After 6 months, blood pressure fell in the group taught to focus on behavioral objectives and take responsibility for their own care.

MULTIPLE FOCUS INTERVENTIONS
Education Plus Reminders

Several studies combined educational interventions with reminders to take medication as directed (Wandless and Davie, 1977; Rehder et al., 1980; Sclar et al., 1991; Raynor et al., 1993; Rosen et al., 2003). Raynor et al. found that patients who received education and a reminder chart had higher adherence rates than those who received only counseling, but adherence was assessed at 10-12 days after the intervention, without a subsequent follow-up. Similarly, Wandless et al. studied a small sample of elderly patients and found that after 14 days those who received education and a reminder calendar made fewer medication errors. Rosen et al. used an electronic monitoring device coupled with counseling. The counseling was based on the recordings of the electronic monitoring device and patients were encouraged to associate the taking of medications with external cues. After 16 weeks of follow-up, intervention patients demonstrated greater adherence than the control group. Using a similar approach, Rehder et al. provided longer term follow-up results; patients who received counseling and a container to remind them to take medication were more adherent at the initial follow-up, but at 6 months most patients were no longer using the reminder container.

Sclar et al. provided patients with hypertension with educational materials and mailed refill reminders. They found that days supply of medication at 180 days of follow-up was increased for those receiving the intervention, and that new patients had the greatest improvement in adherence (Sclar et al., 1991). These studies suggest that education plus reminders is a useful strategy for improving adherence, especially among new patients, but the studies also suggest that continued reinforcement is necessary for this strategy to remain effective.

Education Plus Monitoring

Several studies combined educational interventions with follow-up monitoring, either by health professionals, other trained personnel, or through automation (Cargill, 1992; Friedman et al., 1996; Piette et al., 2000; Katon et al., 2001; Katon et al., 2004). Studies varied in terms of the intensity of monitoring patient status, the techniques used for monitoring, and the populations studied. One of the simplest interventions was implemented by Cargill and colleagues. The intervention consisted of an in-home 20 minute educational review of medications or the in-home review combined with a single follow-up phone call one to two weeks after the visit. Only the group that received the single follow-up phone call in addition to education showed improved medication compliance as measured by pill counts (Cargill, 1992). Unfortunately, long-term adherence outcomes were not reported in this study.

Friedman et al. (1996) implemented a Telephone Linked Computer System (TLC) that could answer questions using touch tone input; patients called the system weekly in between office visits to their physician. The patients measured their blood pressure prior to their call and reported their blood pressure as well as answered questions about their understanding of their medication regimen, their adherence and whether they had any symptoms known to be medication side effects. Mean antihypertensive adherence improved 17.7% for telephone system users 11.7% for controls during a six month period.

Stronger or longer-term effects were observed in studies that combined educational interventions with monitoring by health professionals, rather than computers or

individuals who were not health care professionals (Piette et al., 2000; Katon et al., 2001; Katon et al., 2004). Katon et al. (2001) studied patients with recurrent major depression and provided a relapse prevention intervention that included patient education plus telephone monitoring and follow-up by depression specialists. Over a 12 month period intervention group patients were nearly twice as likely to refill prescriptions as control group patients. In addition, Katon et al. (2004) also conducted a similar study in patients with diabetes mellitus and concomitant major depression. In this study, a stepped approach to treatment was initiated in the intervention group with initial counseling visits with a nurse during the first 12 weeks of treatment and telephone follow-up thereafter. After 3, 6, 9 and 12 months of follow-up, the intervention group demonstrated greater adherence to antidepressant medication than did the control group. Piette et al. implemented bi-weekly automated assessment of adult diabetics with follow-up by a nurse educator. At 12 months intervention group patients reported better glycemic control and fewer problems with medication adherence (Piette et al., 2000).

Pharmaceutical care

Pharmaceutical care interventions are similar to interventions involving education and monitoring by a health care professional, but as pharmacists' roles evolve toward regular provision of pharmaceutical care, a separate literature has begun to develop. Pharmaceutical care is defined as patient-centered, outcomes-oriented pharmacy practice that requires the pharmacist to work in concert with the patient and the patient's other health care providers to promote health, to prevent disease, and to assess, monitor, initiate, and modify medication use (Turner et al., 1999).

Pharmaceutical care was compared with usual care in several efficacy studies (McKenney et al., 1973; Park et al., 1996;

Faulkner et al., 2000; Chisholm et al., 2001; Garcao and Cabrita, 2002), and all found pharmaceutical care to significantly improve medication compliance. Several of these studies included long-term follow-up of medication compliance levels. Faulkner et al. (2000) studied high-risk cardiac patients for 2 years; all patients were counseled on the appropriate use of prescribed lovastatin and then randomized to weekly telephone contact with a pharmacist for 12 weeks or no telephone contact. Contact involved questions about when prescriptions were filled, potential side effects, overall well-being and reasons for non compliance. Adherence as measured by pill counts and refill records and lipid profile results were significantly better in the intervention group (p<0.05) up to 2 years after the intervention.

Skaer et al. (Skaer et al., 1993a; 1993b) compared standard pharmaceutical care with 3 types of enhanced pharmaceutical care in two chronic disease populations. Standard pharmaceutical care was combined with refill reminders, unit dose packaging, and both mailed refill reminders and unit of dose packaging. The results of both studies were consistent; the Medication Possession Ratio during 1 year was significantly higher in patients in the enhanced pharmaceutical care groups than in the standard pharmaceutical care group. No significant difference was found between the three types of enhancements; groups receiving either mailed prescription reminders or unit of use packaging did not differ, but in both patients with hypertension and diabetes, enhanced pharmaceutical care resulted in high adherence rates after one year (79% among patients with hypertension who received pharmaceutical care plus refill reminders and unit-of-use packaging) (Skaer et al., 1993a).

Although *efficacy* studies have consistently found that pharmaceutical care improves patient adherence, one study of the *effectiveness* of pharmaceutical care in 36 community drug stores found no significant differences in medication adherence between control and treatment groups (Weinberger et al., 2002). In this study, intervention group pharmacists accessed patient-specific data only about half of the time, and documented actions about half of the time that records were accessed. Thus, pharmaceutical care interventions were implemented only a small portion of the time. The lack of effectiveness of pharmaceutical care in this study, as compared with the strong efficacy of pharmaceutical care demonstrated in other studies, indicates that barriers to the implementation of pharmaceutical care in community pharmacies are substantial.

Intensive Multi-Component Intervention

The most elaborate intervention studies combined multiple intervention strategies including education, counseling, extended health care provider support, and social support enhancement (Haynes et al., 1976; Nessman et al., 1980; Kirscht et al., 1981; Basler et al., 1982; Morisky et al., 1985; Morisky et al., 1990; Rich et al., 1996; Gallefoss and Sigvald Bakke, 1999). For example, Morisky et al. (Morisky et al., 1990) designed a Special Intervention (SI) that consisted of monthly health education counseling, tailored educational messages, positive reinforcement for adherence, enlistment of family support, and monetary incentives to encourage appointment keeping. This intervention nearly doubled self-reported adherence rates among patients prescribed preventive therapy for tuberculosis (Morisky et al., 1990), although no effect was demonstrated for patients with active tuberculosis.

All of the multi-component interventions demonstrated the ability to improve medication adherence, but studies that compared more complex with less complex interventions did not show that additional components resulted in greater efficacy. For example Basler et al. (Basler et al., 1982) compared group therapy that focused on nutritional patterns only with modification of nutritional patterns plus self-monitoring of blood pressure, plus relaxation training, and information about the causes and consequences of high blood pressure; no differential effect between the various group therapy procedures could be demonstrated. Similarly, Kirscht et al. (Kirscht et al., 1981) used a factorial design to test printed messages, nurse reminders and reinforcements, self-monitoring and social support; some participants received all interventions and some received no interventions. Nurse reinforcement and social support each increased adherence, but no benefit was demonstrated for more complex combinations of interventions. Thus, although studies in this category consistently showed significant effects, the effects were not stronger than those found with other types of interventions such as education plus monitoring or pharmaceutical care (Skaer et al., 1993a; 1993b).

SUMMARY

Simple, single focus interventions such as changing the packaging of medications or sending a reminder letter are not effective strategies for improving medication adherence (Becker et al., 1986; Guthrie, 2001). Recent reviews of interventions to enhance medication adherence have concluded that "interventions that were effective were complex, including combinations of more convenient care, information, counseling, reminders, self-monitoring, reinforcement, family therapy, and other forms of additional supervision or attention." (Haynes et al., 2002). This review also found that more complex interventions were more likely to be effective than single focus interventions with the exception of patient education. Two studies of patient education as a single intervention strategy (Gonzalez-Fernandez et al., 1990; Lowe et al., 1995) concluded that patient education in the hospital setting

improved medication adherence after discharge.

Although extensive, multi-component interventions are more likely to improve adherence (Haynes et al., 1996; Roter et al., 1998; Newell et al., 1999; Haynes et al., 2002) than single component interventions, a linear relationship between the complexity of the intervention and its effect is not apparent; interventions with more components were not more effective than less complex interventions. This is demonstrated by several studies that compared more complex with less complex interventions (Kirscht et al., 1981; Basler et al., 1982; Skaer et al., 1993a, 1993b); all found that adding intervention components did not always improve adherence. For example, Kirscht et al. (1981) used printed messages, nurse reminders, self-monitoring and social support; some participants received all interventions and some received no interventions. Nurse reinforcement and social support were found to each increase adherence based on pharmacy refill data. These results suggest that adherence interventions can be relatively simple and effective, and that additional components do not always result in higher efficacy.

Statistical significance is an important criteria for evaluating the results of intervention studies, but it should not be used as the sole criteria for identifying effective interventions. Unfortunately, because most of the studies reviewed here followed patients for only very short periods of time, many positive intervention effects may be temporary and dissipate over time (McKenney et al., 1973). When we apply additional evaluation criteria, such as demonstrating both short-term and long-term benefit upon objective adherence measures (such as refill rates), compelling evidence for improving medication adherence is limited to only 11 studies (Haynes et al., 1976; Kirscht et al., 1981; Sclar et al., 1991; Skaer et al., 1993a, 1993b;

Friedman et al., 1996; Gallefoss and Sigvald Bakke, 1999; Faulkner et al., 2000; Chisholm et al., 2001; Katon et al., 2001; Garcao and Cabrita, 2002). Nine of these studies employed either pharmaceutical care interventions or intensive multi-component interventions. Two studies (Sclar et al., 1991; Friedman et al., 1996) utilized relatively simple interventions that included educational materials and regular patient follow-up. Thus, the least common denominator for an effective medication adherence intervention may well be provision of education regarding medication use and regular contact with a health care professional or surrogate who can detect problems that might lead to discontinuation of therapy. Interventions with greater numbers of components were not more effective than interventions that included these basic components; dissemination of *efficient*, multi-dimensional interventions for medication adherence will depend upon further understanding of the essential components useful for intervening with specific patient groups.

RECOMMENDATIONS FOR FUTURE RESEARCH

Many unanswered research questions remain in the area of improving adherence with medication. A few of these areas are briefly outlined here:

1) Many studies have tested interventions that can improve medication adherence in the short term, such as immediately after hospital discharge. More studies of efforts to improve medication adherence in the long-term are needed. Can improvements in medication adherence be maintained over time, or must interventions be continued indefinitely for continued effect?
2) Many studies tested a single complex, multi-component intervention, thus making it difficult to determine which intervention components are most effective and which are not needed. Also, some patients may benefit from specific components that do not affect other patients' adherence behavior. Patient-tailored interventions that focus on the issues that are most relevant for each patient may be more efficient and effective than interventions that deliver all components to all patients.
3) Little attention has been given to studying the cost-effectiveness of interventions to enhance medication adherence. If adherence enhancing interventions are to be implemented in health care settings, they must be efficient as well as effective.
4) Nearly all studies reviewed examined the *efficacy* of adherence interventions in controlled study settings. Little is known about how to develop and apply *effective* adherence interventions, i.e. those that are feasible for use and show benefit in real world health care settings, such as community pharmacies and primary care physicians' offices.
5) Many studies have shown that older people are more likely to be adherent with their medication, but other demographic factors and type of disease are only weakly related to adherence levels (Bailey et al., 1996; Burke et al., 1997; Feldman et al., 1998). Thus it is difficult to identify specific populations at risk for non-adherence. Many studies have focused upon patient-related predictors of adherence, but more research on provider and health care systems factors and their relationship to medication adherence is needed.

USEFUL PUBLISHED RESOURCES FOR HEALTH PROFESSIONALS INTERESTED IN IMPROVING ADHERENCE WITH LONG-TERM THERAPIES

1) World Health Organization (2003). Adherence to Long-Term Therapies:

Evidence for Action. See sections on "The Role of Nurses in Improving Adherence", "The Role of Pharmacists in Improving Adherence" "General Practice/Family Medicine Guidelines for Improving Adherence". Available February, 2003.

2) Haynes RB, McKibbon KA, Kanani R. (1996) Systematic review of randomised trials of interventions to assist patients to follow prescriptions for medications. *Lancet* 348:383-6.

3) Sclar DA. (1991) Improving medication compliance: a review of selected issues. *Clin Ther* 13(4):436-40; discussion 435.

4) Roter DL, Hall JA, Merisca R, Nordstrom B, Cretin D, Svarstad B. (1998) Effectiveness of interventions to improve patient compliance: a meta-analysis. *Med Care* 36(8):1138-61.

ACKNOWLEDGEMENTS

I would like to acknowledge Zlata Cerimagic and Saurabh Mistry for their assistance in performing literature reviews, and classifying research articles used in this review.

REFERENCES

UK Prospective Diabetes Study (UKPDS) Group. (1998a) Intensive blood-glucose control with sulphonylureas or insulin compared with conventional treatment and risk of complications in patients with type 2 diabetes. Lancet 352.

UK Prosprective Diabetes Study (UKPDS) Group. (1998b) Effect of intensive blood-glucose control with metformin on complications in overweight patients with type 2 diabetes. Lancet 352: 854-65.

Andrade SE. (1998) Lipid therapy and compliance. Drug Benefit Trends 10:39-43.

Andrade SE, Saperia GM, Berger ML, Platt R. (1999) Effectiveness of antihyper-lipidemic drug management in clinical practice. Clin Ther 21:1973-1987.

Andrade SE, Walker AM, Gottlieb LK, Hollenberg NK, Testa MA, Saperia GM, Platt R. (1995) Discontinuation of anti-hyperlipidemic drugs-do rates reported in clinical trials reflect rates in primary care settings? N Engl J Med 332:1125-1131.

Avorn J, Monette J, Lacour A, Bohn RL, Monane M, Mogun H, LeLorier J. (1998) Persistence of use of lipid-lowering medications: a cross-national study. JAMA 279: 1458-1462.

Bailey JE, Lee MD, Somes GW, Graham RL. (1996) Risk factors for antihypertensive medication refill failure by patients under Medicaid managed care. Clin Ther 18: 1252-1262.

Basler HD, Brinkmeier U, Buser K, Haehn KD, Molders-Kober R. (1982) Psychological group treatment of essential hypertension in general practice. Br J Clin Psychol 21 (Pt 4):295-302.

Becker LA, Glanz K, Sobel E, Mossey J, Zinn SL, Knott KA. (1986) A randomized trial of special packaging of antihypertensive medication. J Family Practice 22:357-361.

Burke LE, Dunbar-Jacob JM, Hill MN. (1997) Compliance with cardiovascular disease prevention strategies: a review of the research. Ann Behav Med 19:239-263.

Burris JF, Papademetriou V, Wallin JD, Cook ME, Weidler DJ. (1991) Therapeutic adherence in the elderly: transdermal clonidine compared to oral verapamil for hypertension. Am J Med 91:22S-28S.

Cargill JM. (1992) Medication compliance in elderly people: influencing variables and interventions. J Adv Nurs 17:422-426.

Caro JJ, Speckman JL, Salas M, Raggio G, Jackson JD. (1999) Effect of initial drug choice on persistence with antihyper-tensive therapy: the importance of actual practice data. CMAJ 160:41-46.

Chisholm MA, Mulloy LL, Jagadeesan M, DiPiro JT. (2001) Impact of clinical pharmacy services on renal transplant patients' compliance with immuno-suppressive medications. Clin Transplant 15:330-336.

Cramer JA. (1995) Microelectronic systems for monitoring and enhancing patient compliance with medication regimens. Drugs 49:321-327.

Cramer JA, Mattson RH, Prevey ML, Scheyer RD, Ouellette VL. (1989) How often is medication taken as prescribed? A novel assessment technique. JAMA 261:3273-3277.

DiMatteo MR. (2004) Variations in patients' adherence to medical recommendations: a quantitative review of 50 years of research. Med Care 42:200-209.

Dunbar-Jacob J, Erlen JA, Schlenk EA, Ryan CM, Sereika SM, Doswell WM. (2000) Adherence in chronic disease. Annu Rev Nurs Res 18:48-90.

Faulkner MA, Wadibia EC, Lucas BD, Hilleman DE. (2000) Impact of pharmacy counseling on compliance and effectiveness of combination lipid-lowering therapy in patients undergoing coronary artery revascularization: a randomized, controlled trial. Pharmacother 20:410-416.

Feldman R, Bacher M, Campbell N, Drover A, Chockalingam A. (1998) Adherence to pharmacologic management of hypertension. Can J Public Health 89:I16-18.

Friedman RH, Kazis LE, Jette A, Smith MB, Stollerman J, Torgerson J, Carey K. (1996) A telecommunications system for monitoring and counseling patients with hypertension. Impact on medication adherence and blood pressure control. Am J Hypertens 9:285-292.

Gallefoss F, Sigvald Bakke P. (1999) How does patient education and self-management among asthmatics and patients with chronic obstructive pulmonary disease affect medication? Am J Respir Crit Care Med 160:2000-2005.

Garcao JA, Cabrita J. (2002) Evaluation of a pharmaceutical care program for hypertensive patients in rural Portugal. J Am Pharm Assoc (Wash) 42:858-864.

Gonzalez-Fernandez RA, Rivera M, Torres D, Quiles J, Jackson A. (1990) Usefulness of a systemic hypertension in-hospital educational program. Am J Cardiol 65:1384-1386.

Guthrie RM. (2001) The effects of postal and telephone reminders on compliance with pravastatin therapy in a national registry: results of the first myocardial infarction risk reduction program. Clin Ther 23:970-980.

Haynes RB, McKibbon KA, Kanani R. (1996) Systematic review of randomised trials of interventions to assist patients to follow prescriptions for medications. Lancet 348:383-386.

Haynes RB, McDonald H, Garg AX, Montague P. (2002) Interventions for helping patients to follow prescriptions for medications. Cochrane Database Syst Rev:CD000011.

Haynes RB, Sackett DL, Gibson ES, Taylor DW, Hackett BC, Roberts RS, Johnson AL. (1976) Improvement of medication compliance in uncontrolled hypertension. Lancet 1:1265-1268.

Hepke KL, Martus MT, Share DA. (2004) Costs and utilization associated with pharmaceutical adherence in a diabetic population. Am J Manag Care 10:144-151.

Katon W, Rutter C, Ludman EJ, Von Korff M, Lin E, Simon G, Bush T, Walker E, Unutzer J. (2001) A randomized trial of relapse prevention of depression in primary care. Arch Gen Psychiatry 58:241-247.

Katon W, Von Korff M, Lin E, Simon G, Ludman E, Russo J, Ciechanowski P, Walker E, Bush T. (2004) The Pathways Study. A randomized trial of collaborative care in patients with diabetes and depression. Arch Gen Psychiatry 61:1042-1049.

Kirscht JP, Kirscht JL, Rosenstock IM. (1981) A test of interventions to increase adherence to hypertensive medical regimens. Health Educ Q 8:261-272.

Krapek K, King K, Warren SS, George KG, Caputo DA, Mihelich K, Holst EM, Nichol MB, Shi SG, Livengood KB, Walden S, Lubowski TJ. (2004) Medication adherence and associated hemoglobin A1c in type 2 diabetes. Ann Pharmacother 38:1357-1362.

Logan AG, Milne BJ, Achber C, Campbell WP, Haynes RB. (1979) Work-site treatment of hypertension by specially trained nurses. A controlled trial. Lancet 2:1175-1178.

Lowe CJ, Raynor DK, Courtney EA, Purvis J, Teale C. (1995) Effects of self medication programme on knowledge of drugs and compliance with treatment in elderly patients. BMJ 310:1229-1231.

McKenney JM, Munroe WP, Wright JT, Jr. (1992) Impact of an electronic medication compliance aid on long-term blood pressure control. J Clin Pharmacol 32:277-283.

McKenney JM, Slining JM, Henderson HR, Devins D, Barr M. (1973) The effect of clinical pharmacy services on patients with essential hypertension. Circulation 48:1104-1111.

Monane M, Bohn RL, Gurwitz JH, Glynn RJ, Avorn J. (1994) Noncompliance with congestive heart failure therapy in the elderly. Arch Intern Med 154:433-437.

Morisky DE, DeMuth NM, Field-Fass M, Green LW, Levine DM. (1985) Evaluation of family health education to build social support for long-term control of high blood pressure. Health Educ Q 12:35-50.

Morisky DE, Malotte CK, Choi P, Davidson P, Rigler S, Sugland B, Langer M. (1990) A patient education program to improve adherence rates with antituberculosis drug regimens. Health Educ Q 17:253-267.

Morris A, Brennan G, MacDonald T, Donnon P. (2000) Population-Based Adherence to Prescribed Medication in Type 2 Diabetes: A Cause for Concern. Diabetes Care 49:307-PP.

Nessman DG, Carnahan JE, Nugent CA. (1980) Increasing compliance. Patient-operated hypertension groups. Arch Intern Med 140:1427-1430.

Newell SA, Bowman JA, Cockburn JD. (1999) A critical review of interventions to increase compliance with medication-taking, obtaining medication refills, and appointment-keeping in the treatment of cardiovascular disease. Prev Med 29:535-548.

Paes AH, Bakker A, Soe-Agnie CJ. (1997) Impact of dosage frequency on patient compliance. Diabetes Care 20:1512-1517.

Park DC, Morrell RW, Frieske D, Kincaid D. (1992) Medication adherence behaviors in older adults: effects of external cognitive supports. Psychol Aging 7:252-256.

Park JJ, Kelly P, Carter BL, Burgess PP. (1996) Comprehensive pharmaceutical care in the chain setting. J Am Pharm Assoc (Wash) NS36:443-451.

Piette JD, Weinberger M, McPhee SJ, Mah C, Kraemer FB, Crapo LM. (2000) Do automated calls with nurse follow-up improve self-care and glycemic control among vulnerable patients with diabetes? Am J Med 108:20-27.

Pladevall M, Williams LK, Potts LA, Divine G, Xi H, Lafata JE. (2004) Clinical outcomes and adherence to medications measured by claims data in patients with diabetes. Diabetes Care 27:2800-2805.

Raynor DK, Booth TG, Blenkinsopp A. (1993) Effects of computer generated reminder charts on patients' compliance with drug regimens. BMJ 306:1158-1161.

Rehder TL, McCoy LK, Blackwell B, Whitehead W, Robinson A. (1980)

Improving medication compliance by counseling and special prescription container. Am J Hosp Pharm 37:379-385.

Rich MW, Gray DB, Beckham V, Wittenberg C, Luther P. (1996) Effect of a multidisciplinary intervention on medication compliance in elderly patients with congestive heart failure. Am J Med 101:270-276.

Rosen MI, Rigsby MO, Salahi JT, Ryan CE, Cramer JA. (2003) Electronic monitoring and counseling to improve medication adherence. Behav Res Ther 42:409-422.

Roter DL, Hall JA, Merisca R, Nordstrom B, Cretin D, Svarstad B. (1998) Effectiveness of interventions to improve patient compliance: a meta-analysis. Med Care 36:1138-1161.

Sackett DL. (1976) The magnitude of compliance and noncompliance. In: Compliance with Therapeutic Regimens (Sacket DLH, R.B., ed), pp 9-25. Baltimore, MD: Johns Hopkins University Press.

Sackett DL, Haynes RB, Gibson ES, Hackett BC, Taylor DW, Roberts RS, Johnson AL. (1975) Randomised clinical trial of strategies for improving medication compliance in primary hypertension. Lancet 1:1205-1207.

Sclar DA. (1991) Improving medication compliance: a review of selected issues. Clin Ther 13:436-440; discussion 435.

Sclar DA, Chin A, Skaer TL, Okamoto MP, Nakahiro RK, Gill MA. (1991) Effect of health education in promoting prescription refill compliance among patients with hypertension. Clin Ther 13:489-495.

Selby JV, Ettinger B, Swain BE, Brown JB. (1999) First 20 months' experience with use of metformin for type 2 diabetes in a large health maintenance organization. Diabetes Care 22:38-44.

Simons LA, Levis G, Simons J. (1996) Apparent discontinuation rates in patients prescribed lipid-lowering drugs. Med J Aust 164:208-211.

Skaer TL, Sclar DA, Markowski DJ, Won JK. (1993a) Effect of value-added utilities on prescription refill compliance and health care expenditures for hypertension. J Hum Hypertens 7:515-518.

Skaer TL, Sclar DA, Markowski DJ, Won JK. (1993b) Effect of value-added utilities on prescription refill compliance and Medicaid health care expenditures--a study of patients with non-insulin-dependent diabetes mellitus. J Clin Pharm Ther 18:295-299.

Turner RC, Cull CA, Frighi V, Holman RR. (1999) Glycemic control with diet, sulfonylurea, metformin, or insulin in patients with type 2 diabetes mellitus: progressive requirement for multiple therapies (UKPDS 49). JAMA 281: 2005-12.

Urquhart J, De Klerk E. (1998) Contending paradigms for the interpretation of data on patient compliance with therapeutic drug regimens. Stat Med 17:251-267.

Wandless I, Davie JW. (1977) Can drug compliance in the elderly be improved? Br Med J 1:359-361.

Webb PA. (1980) Effectiveness of patient education and psychosocial counseling in promoting compliance and control among hypertensive patients. J Fam Pract 10: 1047-1055.

Weinberger M, Murray MD, Marrero DG, Brewer N, Lykens M, Harris LE, Seshadri R, Caffrey H, Roesner JF, Smith F, Newell AJ, Collins JC, McDonald CJ, Tierney WM. (2002) Effectiveness of pharmacist care for patients with reactive airways disease: a randomized controlled trial. JAMA 288:1594-1602.

Zismer DK, Gillum RF, Johnson CA, Becerra J, Johnson TH. (1982) Improving hypertension control in a private medical practice. Arch Intern Med 142:297-299.

IMPACT OF CULTURE ON TREATMENT ADHERENCE

Michael E. Lara

INTRODUCTION

What are the cultural factors that influence treatment adherence? In recent years a number of different investigations, theoretical and practical, have attempted to provide answers. The medical literature, for example, has seen a dramatic increase in the number of articles addressing cultural competence in the delivery of healthcare. This growing interest parallels, not surprisingly, the increase in diversity of the U.S. population. During the period 1990-2000 the Hispanic population grew by 56 percent, Asians, by 40.7 percent, and African-Americans grew by 13 percent. By contrast, whites grew just 1 percent during this same time period (U.S. Census Bureau, 2001). There have also been several attempts to define and codify the nature of culture in medical contexts. One of the more ambitious projects has been the development of the outline for cultural formulation and glossary of culture-bound syndromes in the Diagnostic and Statistical Manual of Mental Disorders (DSM-IV-TR, 2000). In the areas of the basic sciences, the recent completion of the Human Genome Project has invigorated the debate regarding the validity of the related terms *race* and *ethnicity* and has ushered in the era of pharmacogenetics, the study of how genetic variability affects medication metabolism and effects.

But these same inquiries have also underscored many of the problems facing researchers interested in better characterizing the complex interaction between culture and medicine. One of the most glaring omissions in the medical literature is the lack of inclusion of ethnic minorities in randomized controlled clinical trials of a number of treatment interventions (Surgeon General, 2000). Other studies have demonstrated a lack of consistent research methodology in untangling the relationship between culture, race, and ethnicity and how these variables impact treatment outcomes. When considered as a whole, it appears that the recent investigations into culture and medicine have served mainly to highlight the complexity of the problem rather than to yield any specific answers.

Nevertheless, an inquiry into the cultural factors impacting treatment adherence remains a timely and overdue task. One can begin by unpacking many of the assumptions and implications of the question. What, for example, is meant by "cultural factors"? Can these factors be examined in an empirical way through current methodologies? What culturally-informed interventions have been tried? Can they be implemented in an efficient, cost-effective manner? Are there ethnic or cultural differences in adherence rates? Finally, and perhaps most importantly, do culturally based interventions result in improved outcomes? The current chapter is an attempt to shed light on some of these questions.

Background and Key Definitions: *Culture and Adherence*

Even among those who study culture, there is no clear consensus on how to best define it. To varying degrees and at various times, culture has subsumed other demographic categories such as race, ethnicity, age, religion, language, and socioeconomic status.

Geertz has offered one of the more relevant definitions for researchers:

The concept of culture…is essentially a semiotic one…man is an animal suspended in webs of significance he himself has spun, I take culture to be those webs, and the analysis of it to be therefore not an experiential science in search of law but an interpretive one in search of meanings (Geertz, 1973)

More recent inquiries have focused on proffering definitions of culture within specific medical contexts. One of the more clinically oriented definitions of culture, put forth by the Culture and Diagnosis Group of the National Institute of Mental Health:

Meanings, values, and behavioral norms that are learned and transmitted in the dominant society and within its social groups. Culture powerfully influences cognitions, feelings, and the "self" concept as well as the diagnostic process and treatment decisions (Mezzich, 1996).

At this juncture it is worth pointing out the differences between culture and two related terms, *race* and *ethnicity*. *Race* is a concept by which individuals have been designated or grouped primarily on the basis of general physiognomy. As the recent completion Human Genome Project has made evident, biologic basis for race remains suspect. *Ethnicity*, by contrast, refers to the subjective sense of belonging to a group of people with a common origin and with shared social and cultural beliefs and practices. Culture may be therefore construed as the substratum on which individual notions of ethnic identity are constructed.

What, then, are the essential features of a working definition for culture, especially as it pertains to medical research? Most of the previously published work examining the relationship between medicine and culture has identified culture as a subjective, reproducible construct that undergoes constant revision. (Gaw, 2001) It is, in short, a highly contextual phenomenon that poses challenges to empirically based methods of research. It is not surprising therefore, that the adherence literature favors the term *ethnicity* and, to a lesser extent, *race*, as quantifiable variables evaluating the efficacy of interventions.

Adherence, also referred to as compliance or concordance, refers to the extent to which a patient's behavior (in terms of taking medication, following a diet, modifying habits, or attending clinics) coincides with medical or health advice (Haynes, 2001). Unlike the term *culture*, adherence is a concept that can be quantified. If a patient is prescribed an antibiotic for an infection to be taken as 1 tablet 4 times a day for a week but takes only 2 tablets a day for 5 days, the adherence rate would be 36% (10/28).

Estimates of patient adherence range from 20% to 90% (Becker, 1985; Sackett, 1976). As several recent meta-analyses of the literature have reported, there is no consistent definition of adherence, nor any consensus on how to measure it. McDonald and colleagues recently published the results of one of the largest meta-analyses undertaken to date. Thirty-three unconfounded randomized controlled trials assessing specific interventions aimed at improving medication compliance were identified; of these, only 17 reported statistically significant improvements in treatment outcomes. What is even more disconcerting is that even the most effective interventions had only modest effects on treatment outcome (McDonald et al., 2002) (See chapter 11 of this volume for a more in depth review). The study also reiterated the key findings of previous reviews: demographics (sex, race, age, education, and socioeconomic status) are not consistently related to adherence (Williams et al., 1997; Cramer, 1998). It is not surprising then, that not a single study to date has attempted to address the effects of specific culturally-bound interventions for improving treatment adherence in ethnically diverse populations.

Summary of Studies Examining Cultural Factors in Treatment Adherence

A MEDLINE search using the keywords "adherence" OR "non-adherence" OR "compliance" AND "culture" OR "ethnicity" OR "race" yielded more than 200 candidate studies. Studies were included if they were written in English, used U.S. populations as a reference point, and used medication adherence as their primary outcome measure. Outcomes associated with non-pharmacologic interventions, while significant, were not included in this review in an attempt to focus the already disparate database. Studies were excluded if they did not assess outcomes, did not quantify adherence rates between study groups, or if they did not sufficiently distinguish the culturally-bound variable under question. Approximately 8% of theses studies (19/217 studies) met these criteria and were reviewed in more detail. These studies are summarized in Table 1.

What is most remarkable about these studies is the lack of randomized, controlled trials aimed at assessing culturally-bound interventions to improve

adherence in diverse populations. Culturally-bound interventions might include: matching the ethnicity of the patient to the ethnicity of the clinician, providing services in the patient's native language, providing written educational material in the patient's native language, the use of translators, integrating the patient's health beliefs into the treatment plan, attempts to integrate complementary or alternative treatment models, use of herbal medications along with prescribed medications, labeling medication in the patients native language, and involving the family in the overall treatment plan. Studies identified were largely observational, non-randomized, uncontrolled comparisons of adherence rates within specific groups or between groups of patients from culturally diverse backgrounds.

Adherence rates in 11 different disease states were reported; of these, diabetes mellitus type II, tuberculosis, and HIV/AIDS were among the most frequently studied diseases. African-Americans were the group most frequently studied, followed by Hispanics and Asians. No studies included American Indians. The number of participants in the studies ranged: 41 to 3,583. Various methods of assessing adherence were used. Among the subjective methods for measuring adherence were patient self-report (most common) and semi-structured interviews. Objective measures of adherence included: electronic monitoring, prescription refill data, pill counts, plasma levels of drugs, and comprehensive reviews of pharmacy and disease registry databases. Observation periods ranged from 2 days to 2 years.

Although studies were too disparate to warrant meta-analysis, several interesting trends were identified that have been reported in other literature reviews of medication adherence. Most significant

Table 1: Studies Assessing Cultural Factors in Medication Adherence

Study	Patients	Methods	Outcome
Adherence to anti-tuberculosis meds among Latino immigrants (Ailinger, 1998)	N=65	Tracked appointment keeping, and self-reported medication adherence over six months.	Appointment adherence fell from 81% to 59% and medication adherence fell from 89% to 64% at six months.
Adherence to inhaled steroids (Apter, 1998)	N=50	Electronically monitored for 42 days, self-report. Adherence defined as using 70% of prescribed doses.	Mean adherence: 63% Correlates of non-adherence: <12 yrs formal education, poor patient-clinician communication
Failure to refill prescriptions among elderly Blacks (Bazargan, 1993)	N=571	Self-report. Non-adherence defined as not filling prescription during previous 6 months.	Adherence: 87.2% had received a prescription and filledit during the previous 6 months.
Effects of physician communication style on adherence with antidepressants (Bultman, 2000)	N=100	Self-report via telephone interview.	82% reported missing doses or stopping medication. Initial communication style predictive of adherence.
Racial difference in adherence to cardiac medications (Charles, 2003)	N=833 African American veterans; N=4436 white veterans	Self-report, computerized prescription monitoring. Adherence defined as whether patients received enough medication to take as prescribed on 80% of days. Adherence to four types of medication were evaluated: angiotensin-converting enzyme inhibitors (ACEI), beta blockers (BB), calcium channel blockers (CCB) or HMG CoA reductase inhibitors (statins).	African Americans less likely to be adherent than whites for ACEI (81.4% v 87.6%), CCBs (75.3% v. 81.7%), and statins (59.9% v. 74.1% but NOT BBs (84.8% v. 83.5%). Racial differences in adherence were found among patients younger than 55 years old.
Racial differences in adherence to antihypertensives (Daniels, 1994)	N=403 blacks	Self-report of patients in National Health and Nutrition Examination Survey (NHANES II).	Older blacks found to be more compliant than younger blacks.

Adherence to antiretroviral medications (Duong, 2001)	N=149	Adherence measured using Patient Medication Adherence Questionnaire (PMAQ) on patients taking protease inhibitors (PI), plasma levels of HIV-1 RNA and medication levels. Adherence defined as having a virologic response and/or adequate trough plasma level of PI.	Patient motivation, optimistic attitude were important determinants of adherence, but demographic background, social support, alcohol and illicit drug use, depression were NOT associated with lower medication adherence.
HIV medication adherence factors: inner-city clinic patient's self-reports (Graney, 2003)	N=57	Semi-structured interviews, visual analog scale.	Factors enhancing adherence: social support, motivation to avoid AIDS, perceiving health care practitioner as facilitator, knowledge of medications, keeping schedules.
Effect of ethnicity on adherence to diabetic regimen (Hellman, 1997)	N=215	Self-report, medical records over a two-year period.	Ethnicity did NOT show a relationship to adherence.
Predictors of adherence to treatment for latent TB infection in Latino adolescents (Hovell, 2003)	N=286 Latino teens	Baseline interview, and up to 9 monthly interviews. Adherence assessed by cumulative number of pills consumed during study period.	Adherence was positively associatedwith counseling, grades, and being bicultural.
Alcohol consumption and compliance among minority patients with Type 2 Diabetes Mellitus (Johnson, 2000)	N=392 (61% Hispanic, 29% African American)	Self-report, Summary of Diabetes Self-Care Questionnaire, Alcohol Use Disorders Identification Test.	Drinking any alcohol-containing beverage within 30 days was associated with poorer adherence to oral medication regimen.

Barriers to HIV/AIDS treatment and treatment adherence among African-American adults (Kalichman, 1999)	N=85 Males, 53 Females	Self-report	Patients with low-education or literacy were less likely to be adherent with medications over previous 2 days.
Antidepressant blood levels in Southeast Asians (Kinzie, 1987)	N=41	Measuring blood levels of tricyclic antidepressants.	61%: no detectable medicine level 15%: therapeutic blood level
Assessing medication adherence by pill count and electronic monitoring in African-Americans (Lee, 1996)	N=94	Medication Event Monitoring System (MEMS), pill counts in African American Study of Kidney Disease and Hypertension Pilot Study (AASK).	68% adherence by pill count, but MEMS indicated non-adherence at 47% of those visits.
Barriers to treatment adherence among African American and white women with system lupus erythrematosus (Mosley-Williams, 2002)	N=68 AA females, 54 white females	Self-report on "adherence behaviors".	No difference in rates of non-adherence. Whites had poorer clinic appointment adherence than African Americans. African Americans were more likely to rely on religion and were more concerned about long-term medication effects.
Role of ethnicity in predicting antipsychotic medication adherence (Opolka, 2003)	N=3583	Review of Texas Medicaid claims; examined for association between ethnicity or medication and days' use of the medication in the year following initiation.	African American and Mexican American patients were less adherent than white patients (19 d less). Patients of all ethnicities were more compliant on olanzapine, less adherent on risperidone, and least adherent on haloperidol.

Nonadherence in tuberculosis treatment (Pablos-Mendez, 1997)	N=184	Review of New York City Tuberculosis Registry, from 1991-1994. Non-adherence defined as treatment default for at least 2 months.	48% of patients were non-adherent. Greater non-adherence was noted among blacks (RR 3.0), injection drug users (RR 1.5), homeless (RR 1.4); only injection drug use and homelessness predicted non-adherence.
Predictors of medication-refill adherence in an indigent rural population (Schectman, 2002)	N=1984	Refill data for diabetes, hypertension, and hypercholesterolemia drugs from a closed pharmacy system during a 9-month period.	Mean refill adherence <80% for 33% of population; minimum refill adherence <80% for 55% of patients. Increasing age, white race, and prescription length were associated with higher mean and minimum adherence.
Association between diabetes metabolic control and drug adherence in an indigent population (Schectman, 2002)	N=810	Self-report, Hemoglobin A1c level.	Greater non-adherence among blacks. Mean HbA1c of blacks was 0.29% higher than that of whites. For each 10% increment in drug adherence, HbA1c decreased by 0.16%.

was that no single factor (ethnicity, age, socioeconomic status, education, level of acculturation, disease state, medication type) reliably predicts medication adherence. Interestingly, older age was correlated with, but not predictive of, better adherence in several studies (Schectman, 2002; Daniels, 1994). Another consistently identified correlate of adherence was level of education with higher mean level of education correlating with better adherence (Apter et al., 1998; Hovell et al., 2003; Kalichman et al., 1999). Nevertheless, other studies found no association between education and adherence.

Interethnic differences in adherence to specific medications were examined in two studies (Charles et al., 2003; Opolka et al., 2003). In the largest, with 3,583 patients, African American and Mexican American patients were found be an average of 19 days/year less adherent than white patients on antipsychotic medication. It was not reported whether fewer days resulted in poorer outcome.

Major Findings of Related Studies on Cultural Factors

As mentioned previously, a number of observational studies addressing adherence to non-pharmacologic interventions were also identified but not included in Table 1. A number of culture-bound factors were examined, such as the impact of indigenous diets on the metabolism of medication (Ruiz, 2000; Jefferson 1998); the impact of matching patient ethnicity to treatment provider (Maramba and Hall, 2002; Langer, 1999); and ethnic differences in the perception of physical characteristics of medication (Buckalew and Coffield, 1982). Taken as a whole, these studies consistently identify a number of factors that impact treatment adherence. These factors can be grouped into four general classes: 1) Patient factors; 2) Physician factors; 3) Medication factors; and, 4) Communication factors. These factors are summarized in Figure 1-1 and several are discussed below.

Figure 1: Relationship between cultural factors and treatment adherence

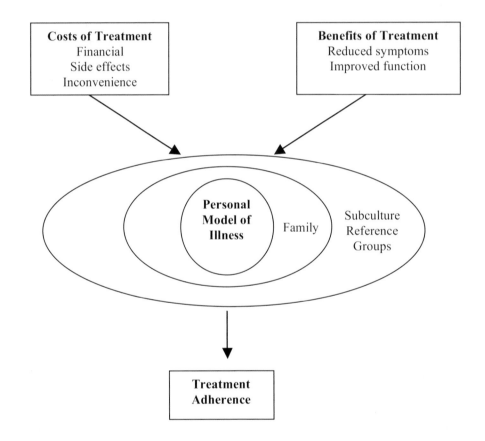

Health Beliefs

The wide-reaching influence of a patient's own explanatory models and beliefs regarding treatment are often not well appreciated among empirically-oriented investigations into treatment adherence. Indeed, incongruity between an individual's beliefs and a clinician's beliefs may well be the central feature of non-adherence. Kleinman (1988) has explored the concept of explanatory models of illness, a term which encompasses notions of etiology, timing, mode of onset, pathophysiology, natural history, severity, and appropriate treatments. Delgado (2000) has summarized the essential components of personal models of illness:

1) Beliefs about the symptoms that define an illness
2) Beliefs about the consequences of having the illness
3) Beliefs about the causes of the illness
4) Beliefs about how long it took for the illness to develop and how long it will last
5) Beliefs about what treatments are most likely to be effective.

Krippner (1995) has compared the healing models of four different cultures (Piman, Chinese, Curandero) with the Western model in attempt to reconcile key differences and guide cross-cultural treatment planning, while Becker (1985) has explored using the concept of the health belief model to guide the development of interventions that may enhance treatment adherence.

Concomitant use of herbs

The use of herbal medications, particularly among those with limited access to healthcare, has increased dramatically (Eisenberg et al., 1993). While a comprehensive review of herbals is beyond the scope of this chapter, many of the herbs currently used by traditional practitioners are biologically active. For example, valerian, a herb commonly used by Hispanics as a relaxant, is known to increase the release of the major inhibitory neurotransmitter in the central nervous system, gamma amino butyric acid (GABA). The sedative properties of valerian are enhanced when administered with medications that work directly on GABA, such as benzodiazepines or other types of anticonvulsant medications. Loera and colleagues (2001) identified mint as most commonly used herbal remedy among elderly Mexicans residing

in the US. Mint, however, has the potential to exacerbate asthma and can increase the hypotensive effects of calcium channel blockers. Ruiz (2000) and Gaw (2001) provide an overview of the pharmacologic consequences of combining herbs with prescribed medications.

Ethnic differences in response to medication

That there exist interethnic differences in the metabolism of medication is a well-recognized phenomenon. Controlled studies have demonstrated that haloperidol plasma levels are increased by as much as 50% in Asian patients as compared to Caucasians. (Lin and Shen, 1991) Other investigations have demonstrated variability in pharmaco-kinetic parameters among African Americans and Hispanics (Midha et al., 1988). While investigations continue to characterize the nature and degree of interethnic differences in the metabolism and response to medication, the predictive value of such studies remains limited. Indeed, one consistently repeated finding among these pharmacokinetic studies is that there is more variability in response to medication among members of the same ethnic group than between members of two distinct ethnic groups. Ruiz et al. (2000) explore these differences in the response to psychotropic medications among Hispanics, Blacks, and Asians.

The impact of diet on liver enzymes

Dietary practices, too, have a potential to adversely affect compliance by inducing alterations in drug metabolism. What is often not appreciated among practitioners is that certain foods have the potential to alter the activity of liver enzymes. Corn based diets, common to indigenous populations from Mexico and

Central America, are rich in quercetin, a biologically active compound that inhibits the function of one of the most active liver enzymes, 2D6. Inhibition of 2D6 may increase the likelihood having toxic plasma levels of prescribed medications. Other food products may alter the activity of other major classes of liver enzymes, resulting in a range of clinical consequences. The effects of food products on liver enzymes are summarized below and explored in more detail by Jefferson (1998).

Food	Action	Enzymes
Charcoal-broiled beef	Induction	CYP1A2
Grapefruit juice	Inhibition	CYP1A2, CYP3A4
Broccoli	Induction	CYP1A2
Cabbage	Induction	CYP1A2
Brussels sprouts	Induction	CYP1A2
Caffeine	Induction	CYP1A2
Ethanol	Induction	CYP2E1

Ethnic differences in the perception of medications.

In one of the more interesting studies undertaken, Buckalew and Coffield (1982) examined ethnic differences in response to physical characteristics of medication, including pill color. He found that Black patients tended to view white capsules as stimulants and black capsules as analgesics, while Caucasian patients tended to view black capsules as stimulants and lighter colored pills as analgesics.

SUMMARY AND DIRECTIONS FOR FUTURE RESEARCH

This review underscores several methodological challenges in the adherence literature. Most striking is the lack of empirically-based studies exploring the effects of specific interventions in ethnically diverse patient populations. Of more than 200 studies reviewed, only 19 examined interethnic differences in medication adherence rates; none of these studies examined the effects of single interventions in a randomized, controlled trial. None of the observational studies reviewed was able to demonstrate that a single intervention resulted in better treatment outcomes. And consistent with previous meta-analysis, no single demographic factor was predictive of adherence. Many studies did not specifically assess medication adherence but were included in this review because they addressed other culturally relevant factors. These factors were classified into four broad categories: patient factors, physician factors, medication factors and communication factors. Most of these studies focused on patient factors affecting adherence; very few examined the effects of patient-physician communication styles or other elements of the physician patient relationship.

Future studies will need to develop a more consistent method of assessing adherence to both pharmacologic and non-pharmacologic interventions. It is unlikely that future investigations will identify a single demographic variable that reliably predicts adherence. It remains to be seen whether any successful intervention will ultimately result in better treatment outcome.

Nevertheless, one promising area of inquiry remains the individual's health belief model, and future inquiries will need to examine ways of eliciting these beliefs and integrating them into a comprehensive plan of treatment. In the final analysis, the decision to adhere to a proposed plan of treatment often rests with the patient, who weighs perceived costs and benefits of treatments against his own personal model of illness. This personal model of illness is constructed against a background of family and other subcultural reference groups, as illustrated in Figure 1. Exactly how to prove this model and, more importantly, how to use this knowledge to enhance adherence are areas that await further inquiry.

REFERENCES

Ailinger RL, Dear MR. (1998) Adherence to tuberculosis preventive therapy among Latino immigrants. Public Health Nurs 15(1): 19-24.

American Psychiatric Association and American Psychiatric Association. Task Force on DSM-IV. (2000) Diagnostic and statistical manual of mental disorders: DSM-IV-TR. Washington, DC: American Psychiatric Association.

Applegate BW, Ames SC, Mehan DJ Jr, McKnight GT, Jones GN, Brantley PJ. (2000). Maximizing medication adherence in low-income hypertensives: a pilot study. J La State Med Soc 152(7): 349-56.

Apter AJ, Boston RC, George M, Norfleet AL, Tenhave T, Coyne JC, Birck K, Reisine ST, Cucchiara AJ, Feldman HI. (2003). Modifiable barriers to adherence to inhaled steroids among adults with asthma: it's not just black and white. J Allergy Clin Immunol 111(6): 1219-26.

Apter AJ, Reisine ST, Affleck G, Barrows E, ZuWallack RL. (1998) Adherence with Twice-daily Dosing of Inhaled Steroids . Socioeconomic and Health-belief Differences. Am J Respir Crit Care Med 157(6): 1810-242.

Bartlett SJ, Lukk P, Butz A, Lampros-Klein F, Rand CS. (2002) Enhancing medication adherence among inner-city children with asthma: results from pilot studies. J Asthma 39(1): 47-54.

Bazargan M, Barbre AR, Hamm V. (1993) Failure to have prescriptions filled among Black elderly. J Aging Health 5(2): 264-82.

Bebbington P. (1995) The content and context of compliance. Int Clin Psychopharmacol 9 Suppl 5: 41-50.

Becker MH. (1985) Patient adherence to prescribed therapies. Med Care 23(5): 539-55.

Becker MH, Maiman LA. (1980) Strategies for enhancing patient compliance. J Community Health 6(2): 113-35.

Bloom SW. (1963) The doctor and his patient; a sociological interpretation. New York: Russell Sage Foundation.

Bogart LM, Catz SL, Kelly JA, Benotsch EG. (2001) Factors influencing physicians' judgments of adherence and treatment decisions for patients with HIV disease. Med Decis Making 21(1): 28-36.

Buchanan N, Shuenyane E, Mashigo S, Mitangai P, Unterhalter B. (1979) Factors influencing drug compliance in ambulatory Black urban patients. S Afr Med J 55(10): 368-73.

Buckalew LW, Coffield KE. (1982) Drug expectations associated with perceptual characteristics: ethnic factors. Percept Mot Skills 55(3 Pt 1): 915-8.

Bultman DC, Svarstad BL. (2000) Effects of physician communication style on client medication beliefs and adherence with antidepressant treatment. Patient Educ Couns 40(2): 173-85.

Charles H, Good CB, Hanusa BH, Chang C, Whittle J. (2003) Racial differences in adherence to cardiac medications. J Natl Med Assoc 95(1): 17-27.

Cheever LW, Wu AW. (1999) Medication Adherence Among HIV-Infected Patients: Understanding the Complex Behavior of Patients Taking This Complex Therapy. Curr Infect Dis Rep 1(4): 401-407.

Chen A. (1991) Noncompliance in community psychiatry: a review of clinical interventions. Hosp Community Psychiatry 42(3): 282-7.

Connett JE, Stamler J. (1984) Responses of black and white males to the special intervention program of the Multiple Risk Factor Intervention Trial. Am Heart J 108(3 Pt 2): 839-48.

Crowley JJ, Simmons S. (1992) Mental health, race and ethnicity: a retrospective study of the care of ethnic minorities and whites in a psychiatric unit. J Adv Nurs 17(9): 1078-87.

Cuellar GEM, Ruiz AM, Monsalve MC, Berber A. (2000) Six-Month Treatment of Obesity with Sibutramine 15 mg; A Double-Blind, Placebo-Controlled Monocenter Clinical Trial in a Hispanic Population. Obes. Res. 8(1): 71-82.

Daniels DE, Rene AA, Daniels VR. (1994) Race: an explanation of patient compliance--fact or fiction? J Natl Med Assoc 86(1): 20-5.

Daratsos L, Fazekas JT, Hedlund SC, Pelusi J, Anderson LN, Mahmood F. (2000) Ethnic identification with healthcare providers and treatment adherence. Cancer Pract 8(2): 59-64.

Delgado P. (2000) Approaches to the enhancement of patient adherence to antidepressant medication treatment. J Clin Psychiatry 61 Suppl 2: 6-9.

Dolder CR, Lacro JP, Dunn LB, Jeste DV. (2002) Antipsychotic medication adherence: is there a difference between typical and atypical agents? Am J Psychiatry 159(1): 103-8.

Douglas JG, Ferdinand KC, Bakris GL, Sowers JR. (2002) Barriers to blood pressure control in African Americans. Overcoming obstacles is challenging, but target goals can be attained. Postgrad Med 112(4): 51-62.

Duong M, Piroth L, Grappin M, Forte F, Peytavin G, Buisson M, Chavanet P, Portier H. (2001) Evaluation of the Patient Medication Adherence Questionnaire as a tool for self-reported adherence assessment in HIV-infected patients on antiretroviral regimens. HIV Clin Trials 2(2): 128-35.

Eisenberg DM, Kessler RC, Foster C, Norlock FE, Calkins DR, Delbanco TL. (1993) Unconventional medicine in the United States. Prevalence, costs, and patterns of use. N Engl J Med 328(4): 246-52.

Farmer KC. (1999) Methods for measuring and monitoring medication regimen adherence in clinical trials and clinical practice. Clin Ther 21(6): 1074-90; discussion 1073.

Ferguson TF, Stewart KE, Funkhouser E, Tolson J, Westfall AO, Saag MS. (2002) Patient-perceived barriers to antiretroviral adherence: associations with race. AIDS Care 14(5): 607-17.

Fisher L, Chesla CA, Skaff MA, Gilliss C, Kanter RA, Lutz CP, Bartz RJ. (2000) Disease management status: a typology of Latino and Euro-American patients with type 2 diabetes. Behav Med 26(2): 53-66.

Flaskerud JH, Hu LT. (1994) Participation in and outcome of treatment for major depression among low income Asian-

Americans. Psychiatry Res 53(3): 289-300.

Fogarty L, Roter D, Larson S, Burke J, Gillespie J, Levy R. (2002) Patient adherence to HIV medication regimens: a review of published and abstract reports. Patient Educ Couns 46(2): 93-108.

Froehlich H, West DJ. (2001) Compliance with hepatitis B virus vaccination in a high-risk population. Ethn Dis 11(3): 548-53.

Gaw A. (2001) Concise guide to cross-cultural psychiatry. Washington, DC: American Psychiatric Press.

Golin CE, Liu H, Hays RD, Miller LG, Beck CK, Ickovics J, Kaplan AH, Wenger NS. (2002) A prospective study of predictors of adherence to combination antiretroviral medication. J Gen Intern Med 17(10): 756-65.

Gornick ME, Eggers PW, Reilly TW, Mentnech RM, Gitterman LK, Kucken LE, Vladeck BC. (1996) Effects of Race and Income on Mortality and Use of Services among Medicare Beneficiaries. N Engl J Med 335(11): 791-799.

Graney MJ, Bunting SM, Russell CK. (2003) HIV/AIDS medication adherence factors: inner-city clinic patient's self-reports. Tenn Med 96(2): 73-8.

Grant RW, Devita NG, Singer DE< Meigs JB. (2003) Polypharmacy and medication adherence in patients with type 2 diabetes. Diabetes Care 26(5): 1408-12.

Group for the Advancement of Psychiatry. Committee on Cultural Psychiatry. (2002) Cultural assessment in clinical psychiatry. Washington, DC, American Psychiatric Pub.

Halkitis PN, Parsons JT, Woltiski RJ, Remien RH. (2003) Characteristics of HIV antiretroviral treatments, access and adherence in an ethnically diverse sample of men who have sex with men. AIDS Care 15(1): 89-102.

Haynes RB, Sackett DL. (1976) Compliance with therapeutic regimens. Baltimore, Johns Hopkins University Press.

Haynes RB, Taylor DW, et al. (1979) Compliance in health care. Baltimore: Johns Hopkins University Press.

Hellman S, Baker L, Flores D, Lehman H, Bacon J. (1997) Effect of ethnicity on adherence to diabetic regimen. Ethn Dis 7(3): 221-8.

Holzemer WL, Corless IB, Nokes KM, Turner JG, Brown MA, Powell-Cope GM, Inouye J, Henry SB, Nicholas PK, Portillo CJ. (1999) Predictors of self-reported adherence in persons living with HIV disease. AIDS Patient Care STDS 13(3): 185-97.

Hovell M, Blumberg E, Gil-Trejo L, Vera A, Kelley N, Sipan C, Hofstetter CR, Marchall S, Berg J, Griedman L, Catazaro A, Moser K. (2003) Predictors of adherence to treatment for latent tuberculosis infection in high-risk Latino adolescents: a behavioral epidemiological analysis. Soc Sci Med 56(8): 1789-96.

Hwu YJ, Coates VE, Boore JR. (2001). The health behaviours of Chinese people with chronic illness. Int J Nurs Stud 38(6): 629-41.

Hyman DJ, Pavlik VN. (2002) Poor hypertension control: let's stop blaming the patients. Cleve Clin J Med 69(10): 793-9.

Ibrahim SA. (2003) Hypertension and medication adherence among African Americans: a potential factor in cardiovascular disparities. J Natl Med Assoc 95(1): 28-9.

Insull W Jr. (1985) Management of adherence to prescribed medication. Adv Exp Med Biol 183: 349-60.

Iraurgi I, Jimenez-Lerma J, Landabaso MA, Arrazola X, Gutierrez-Fraile M. (2000) Gypsies and drug addictions. Study of the adherence to treatment. Eur Addict Res 6(1): 34-41.

Ito KL. (1999) Health culture and the clinical encounter: Vietnamese refugees' responses to preventive drug treatment of inactive tuberculosis. Med Anthropol Q 13(3): 338-64.

Jefferson JW. (1998) Drug interactions-- friend or foe? J Clin Psychiatry 59 Suppl 4: 37-47.

Johnson KH, Bazargan M, Bing EG. (2000) Alcohol Consumption and Compliance Among Inner-city Minority Patients With Type 2 Diabetes Mellitus." Arch Fam Med 9(10): 964-970.

Johnson MJ. (2002) The Medication Adherence Model: a guide for assessing medication taking. Res Theory Nurs Pract 16(3): 179-92.

Kalichman SC, Catz S, Ramachandran B. (1999) Barriers to HIV/AIDS treatment and treatment adherence among African-American adults with disadvantaged education. J Natl Med Assoc 91(8): 439-46.

Ka'opua L. (2001) Treatment adherence to an antiretroviral regime: the lived experience of Native Hawaiians and kokua. Pac Health Dialog 8(2): 290-8.

Keltner NL, Folks DG. (1992) Culture as a variable in drug therapy. Perspect Psychiatr Care 28(1): 33-6.

Kinzie JD, Leung P, Boehnlein JK, Fleck J. (1987) Antidepressant blood levels in Southeast Asians. Clinical and cultural implications. J Nerv Ment Dis 175(8): 480-5.

Kleinman A. (1980) Patients and healers in the context of culture : an exploration of the borderland between anthropology, medicine, and psychiatry. Berkeley, University of California Press.

Kleinman A. (1988) Rethinking psychiatry : from cultural category to personal experience. New York London, Free Press; Collier Macmillan.

Knobel H, Alonso J, Casedo JL, Collazos J, Ruiz I, Kindelan JM, Carmona A, Juega J, Ocampo A, GEEMA study Group. (2002) Validation of a simplified medication adherence questionnaire in a large cohort of HIV-infected patients: the GEEMA Study. Aids 16(4): 605-13.

Krippner S. (1995) A Cross-Cultural Comparison of Four Healing Models. Altern Ther Health Med 1(1): 22-9.

Lacro JP, Dunn LB, Dolder CR, Leckband SG, Jeste DV. (2002) Prevalence of and risk factors for medication nonadherence in patients with schizophrenia: a comprehensive review of recent literature. J Clin Psychiatry 63(10): 892-909.

Langer N. (1999) Culturally competent professionals in therapeutic alliances enhance patient compliance. J Health Care Poor Underserved 10(1): 19-26.

Lee D, Mendes de Leon CF, Jenkins CD, Croog SH, Levine S, Sudilovsky A. (1992) Relation of hostility to medication adherence, symptom complaints, and blood pressure reduction in a clinical field trial of antihypertensive medication. J Psychosom Res 36(2): 181-90.

Lee JY, Kusek JW, Greene PG, Bernhard S, Norris K, Smith D, Wilkening B, Wright JT Jr. (1996) Assessing medication adherence by pill count and electronic monitoring in the African American Study of Kidney Disease and Hypertension (AASK) Pilot Study. Am J Hypertens 9(8): 719-25.

Lin KM, Shen WW. (1991) Pharmaco-therapy for southeast Asian psychiatric patients. J Nerv Ment Dis 179(6): 346-50.

Lin K-M, Poland RE. (1993). Psychopharmacology and psychobiology of ethnicity. Washington, DC, American Psychiatric Press.

Lip GYH, Kamath S, Hart RG. (2002) Ethnic Differences in Patient Perceptions of Atrial Fibrillation and Anticoagulation Therapy: The West Birmingham Atrial Fibrillation Project * Editorial Comment: The West Birmingham Atrial Fibrillation Project. Stroke 33(1): 238-242.

LoBue PA, Moser KS. (2003) Use of Isoniazid for Latent Tuberculosis Infection in a Public Health Clinic. Am J Respir Crit Care Med.

Loera JA, Black SA, Markides KS, Espino DV, Goodwin JS. (2001) The use of herbal medicine by older Mexican Americans. J Gerontol A Biol Sci Med Sci 56(11): M714-8.

Mac JT, Doordan A, Carr CA. (1999) Evaluation of the effectiveness of a directly observed therapy program with Vietnamese tuberculosis patients. Public Health Nurs 16(6): 426-31.

Maramba GG, Hall GC. (2002) Meta-analyses of ethnic match as a predictor of dropout, utilization, and level of functioning. Cultur Divers Ethnic Minor Psychol 8(3): 290-7.

Martinez J,Bell D. (2000). Adherence to antiviral drug regimens in HIV-infected adolescent patients engaged in care in a comprehensive adolescent and young adult clinic. J Natl Med Assoc 92(2): 55-61.

McDonald HP, Garg AX, Haynes RB. (2002) Interventions to enhance patient adherence to medication prescriptions: scientific review. Jama 288(22): 2868-79.

McNeill JA, Sherwood GD, Starck PL, Neito B. (2001) Pain management outcomes for hospitalized Hispanic patients. Pain Manag Nurs 2(1): 25-36.

Melbourne KM. (1999) The impact of religion on adherence with antiretrovirals. J Assoc Nurses AIDS Care 10(3): 99-100.

Melbourne KM, Geletko SM, Brown SL, Willey-Lessne C, Chase S, Fisher A. (1999) Medication adherence in patients with HIV infection: a comparison of two measurement methods. AIDS Read 9(5): 329-38.

Mezzich JE. (1996) Culture and psychiatric diagnosis: a DSM-IV perspective. Washington, DC, American Psychiatric Press.

Midha KK, Hawes EM, Hubbard JW, Korchinski ED, McKay G. (1988) A pharmacokinetic study of trifluoperazine in two ethnic populations. Psychopharmacology (Berl) 95(3): 333-8.

Milgrom H, Bender B. (1997) Nonadherence to asthma treatment and failure of therapy. Curr Opin Pediatr 9(6): 590-5.

Molassiotis A, Nahas-Lopez V, Chung WY, Lam SW, Li CK, Lau TF. (2002) Factors associated with adherence to antiretroviral medication in HIV-infected patients. Int J STD AIDS 13(5): 301-10.

Morisky DE, Green LW, Levine DM. (1986) Concurrent and predictive validity of a self-reported measure of medication adherence. Med Care 24(1): 67-74.

Mosley-Williams A, Lumley MA, Gillis M, Leisen J, Guice D. (2002) Barriers to treatment adherence among African American and white women with systemic lupus erythematosus. Arthritis Rheum 47(6): 630-8.

Murphy DA, Wilson CM, Durako SJ, Muenz LR, Belzer M, Adolescent Medicine HIV/AIDS Research Network. (2001) Antiretroviral medication adherence among the REACH HIV-infected adolescent cohort in the USA. AIDS Care 13(1): 27-40.

O'Brien MK, Petrie K, Raeburn J. (1992) Adherence to medication regimens: updating a complex medical issue. Med Care Rev 49(4): 435-54.

Oomen J, Owen L, Suggs LS. (1999) Culture counts: why current treatment models fail Hispanic women with type 2 diabetes. Diabetes Educ 25(2): 220-5.

Opolka JL, Rascati KL, Brown CN, Gibson PJ. (2003) Role of ethnicity in predicting antipsychotic medication adherence. Ann Pharmacother 37(5): 625-30.

Ortega AN, Gergen PJ, Paltiel AD, Bauchner H, Belanger KD, Leaderer BP. (2002) Impact of Site of Care, Race, and Hispanic Ethnicity on Medication Use for Childhood Asthma. Pediatrics 109(1): e1-.

Pablos-Mendez A, Knirsch CA, Barr RG, Lerner BH, Frieden TR. (1997) Nonadherence in tuberculosis treatment: predictors and consequences in New York City. Am J Med 102(2): 164-70.

Patel RP, Taylor SD. (2002) Factors affecting medication adherence in hypertensive patients. Ann Pharmacother 36(1): 40-5.

Peterson AM, Takiya L, Finley R. (2003) Meta-analysis of trials of interventions to improve medication adherence. Am J Health Syst Pharm 60(7): 657-65.

Post DM, Cegala DJ, Marinelli TM. (2001) Teaching patients to communicate with physicians: the impact of race. J Natl Med Assoc 93(1): 6-12.

Richter DL, Sowell RL, Pluto DM. (2002) Attitudes toward antiretroviral therapy among African American women. Am J Health Behav 26(1): 25-33.

Rose LE, Kim MT, Dennison CR, Hill MN. (2000) The contexts of adherence for African Americans with high blood pressure. J Adv Nurs 32(3): 587-94.

Rubel AJ, Garro LC. (1992) Social and cultural factors in the successful control of tuberculosis. Public Health Rep 107(6): 626-36.

Ruiz P. (2000) Ethnicity and psycho-pharmacology. Washington, DC: American Psychiatric Press.

Salabarria-Pena Y, Trout PT, Gill JK, Morisky DE, Muralles AA, Ebin VJ. (2001) Effects of acculturation and psychosocial factors in Latino adolescents' TB-related behaviors. Ethn Dis 11(4): 661-75.

Sankar A, Luborsky M, Schuman P, Roberts G. (2002) Adherence discourse among African-American women taking HAART. AIDS Care 14(2): 203-18.

Schaffer SD, Yoon SJ. (2001). Evidence-based methods to enhance medication adherence. Nurse Pract 26(12): 44-54.

Schectman JM, Bovbjerg VE, Voss JD. (2002) Predictors of medication-refill adherence in an indigent rural population. Med Care 40(12): 1294-300.

Schectman JM, Nadkarni MM, Voss JD. (2002). The Association Between Diabetes Metabolic Control and Drug Adherence in an Indigent Population. Diabetes Care 25(6): 1015-970.

Sebastian MS, Bothamley GH. (2000) Tuberculosis preventive therapy: perspective from a multi-ethnic community. Respir Med 94(7): 648-53.

Shea S, Misra D, Ehrlich MH, Field L, Francis CK. (1992) Correlates of nonadherence to hypertension treatment in an inner-city minority population. Am J Public Health 82(12): 1607-12.

Siegel K, Karus D, Schrimshaw EW. (2000) Racial differences in attitudes toward protease inhibitors among older HIV-infected men. AIDS Care 12(4): 423-34.

Singh N, Berman SM, Swindells S, Justis JC, Mohr JA, Squier C, Wagerner MM. (1999) Adherence of human immunodeficiency virus-infected patients to antiretroviral therapy. Clin Infect Dis 29(4): 824-30.

Sleath B, Rubin RH, Huston SA. (2003) Hispanic ethnicity, physician-patient communication, and antidepressant adherence. Compr Psychiatry 44(3): 198-204.

Smith SR, Rublein JC, Marcus C, Brock TP, Chesney MA. (2003) A medication self-management program to improve adherence to HIV therapy regimens. Patient Educ Couns 50(2): 187-99.

Sondik EJ, Lucas JW, Mandans JH, Smith SS. (2000) Race/ethnicity and the 2000 census: implications for public health. Am J Public Health 90(11): 1709-13.

Sorensen JL, Mascovich A, Wall TL, DePhillipps D, Batki SL, Chesney M. (1998) Medication adherence strategies for drug abusers with HIV/AIDS. AIDS Care 10(3): 297-312.

Steffensen MS, Colker L. (1982) Intercultural misunderstandings about health care. Recall of descriptions of illness and treatment. Soc Sci Med 16(22): 1949-54.

Sumartojo E. (1993) When tuberculosis treatment fails. A social behavioral account of patient adherence. Am Rev Respir Dis 147(5): 1311-20.

Svensson S, Kjellgren KI, Ahlner J, Saljo R. (2000) Reasons for adherence with antihypertensive medication. Int J Cardiol 76(2-3): 157-63.

Thompson K, Kulkarni J, Sergejew AA. (2000) Reliability and validity of a new Medication Adherence Rating Scale (MARS) for the psychoses. Schizophr Res 42(3): 241-7.

Tripp-Reimer T, Choi E. (2001). Cultural Barriers to Care: Inverting the Problem. Diabetes Spectr 14(1): 13-22.

Tucker CM, Fennell RS, Pedersen T, Higley BP, Wallack CE, Petersen S. (2002) Associations with medication adherence among ethnically different pediatric patients with renal transplants. Pediatr Nephrol 17(4): 251-6.

Tucker CM, Petersen S, Herman KC, Fennell RS, Bowling B, Pedersen T, Vosmik JR. (2001) Self-regulation predictors of medication adherence among ethnically different pediatric patients with renal transplants. J Pediatr Psychol 26(8): 455-64.

United States Public Health Service, Office of the Surgeon General, Center for Mental Health Services (U.S.). (1999). Mental health: a report of the Surgeon General. Rockville, MD.

Velligan DI, Lam F, Erseshefsky L, Miller AL. (2003) Psychopharmacology: perspectives on medication adherence and atypical antipsychotic medications. Psychiatr Serv 54(5): 665-7.

Wagner GJ, Rabkin J. (2000). Measuring medication adherence: are missed doses reported more accurately then perfect adherence? AIDS Care 12(4): 405-8.

Wagner L. (1998) Hypertension in African-American males. Clin Excell Nurse Pract 2(4): 225-31.

Walsh ME, Katz MA, Sechrest L. (2002) Unpacking cultural factors in adaptation to type 2 diabetes mellitus. Med Care 40(1 Suppl): I129-39.

Willey C, Redding C, Stafford J, GarfieldF, Geletko S, Flanigan T, Melbourne K, Mitty J, Caro JJ. (2000) Stages of change for adherence with medication regimens for chronic disease: development and validation of a measure. Clin Ther 22(7): 858-71.

Williams ML, Morris MT 2nd, Ahman U, Yousseff M, Li W, Ertel N; VANJHCS research group, Veterans Affairs of New Jersey Healthcare System. (2002). Racial differences in compliance with NCEP-II recommendations for secondary prevention at a Veterans Affairs medical center. Ethn Dis 12(1): S1-58-62.

Winkler A,Teuscher AU, Mueller B, Diem P. (2002). Monitoring adherence to prescribed medication in type 2 diabetic patients treated with sulfonylureas. Swiss Med Wkly 132(27-28): 379-85.

INCREASING AND MAINTAINING PHYSICAL ACTIVITY IN CLINICAL POPULATIONS

Janet Buckworth and Leigh Sears

INTRODUCTION

The Surgeon General's Report on Physical Activity and Health (U.S. Department of Health and Human Services, 1996) was a landmark publication supporting the physical and mental health benefits of regular physical activity. There is little doubt that a sedentary lifestyle holds a myriad of health risks. Physical inactivity is a factor in 300,000 premature deaths each year in United States, and is associated with 17 unhealthy conditions (Booth and Chakravarthy, 2002). Sedentary individuals are at greater risk for chronic diseases, such as type II diabetes and colon cancer and are more likely to have risk factors (e.g., obesity) for chronic diseases. In 1992, physical inactivity was recognized as a primary, independent risk factor for cardiovascular heart disease (Fletcher et al., 1992), and was recently listed as one of the 10 major risk factors identified in the Global Burden of Disease Study (Murray and Lopez, 1999). Level of physical activity decreases with age to the point that about 70% of adults in the United States are sedentary or active below levels recommended for health. Despite our efforts, most adults participate in no physical activity or less than the recommended 30 minutes per day. The health risks of inactivity coupled with the decrease in physical activity levels in the population highlight the importance of efforts to increase exercise adoption and maintenance.

Significant health benefits from regular exercise have been found in clinical and nonclinical populations (Flectcher et al., 1996). For example, exercise training results in reductions in resting blood pressure in approximately 75% of individuals with hypertension, and is an important adjunct treatment for mild to moderate elevations in blood pressure (Hagberg et al., 2000). Acute bouts of physical activity can favorably change abnormal blood glucose and insulin resistance and regular exercise is one of the principle therapies to treat type-2 diabetes due to its synergistic action with insulin in insulin sensitive tissues (Albright et al., 2000). Regular exercise is also associated with improvements in blood lipids and is important in a weight loss program, as well as in strengthening bones (Turner and Robling, 2003).

Rates for adherence to exercise programs, which are prescribed types and levels of regular physical activity, have ranged from 50% to 80% during the first six months, with the most precipitous dropout during the first three months. Exercise adherence tends to fall to less than 50% adherence after 12 months. The importance of physical activity as part of a treatment regimen for many chronic diseases does not necessarily bolster the compliance with exercise prescriptions in clinical populations. In a meta-analysis of interventions to increase adherence to regular exercise, the effect size (r) unweighted by sample size was lowest for patients with coronary heart disease or at high risk for the disease, r=.28 (Dishman and Buckworth, 1996). This translates into a success rate change from the typical rate of 50% without intervention to 64% after intervention, a 14% increase in exercise adherence, which was similar to the effect for healthy populations (15% increase). Increases in adherence rates were better for patients who were obese (21% increase) or suffering from a physical disability/other chronic diseases (25% increase), but few of the studies reviewed conducted follow-up assessments (Dishman and Buckworth,

1996). Over time, the physical, psychological, and social dynamics of ill health may create barriers to exercise that can be addressed by health care practitioners to increase adherence and the concomitant health benefits from a prescribed level of regular physical activity.

METHODS

This chapter describes the effectiveness of interventions on exercise adherence in randomized controlled trials with at least one-year follow-up. Studies were limited to those conducted with clinical populations (specific chronic disease or disability), although a few targeted individuals at-risk for chronic disease or considered at-risk based on being sedentary with no other measured risk factors. The outcomes of the longitudinal studies are presented in standard units of measurement when possible, that is, adherence defined as the number of sessions completed divided by the number of sessions prescribed. The effectiveness of an intervention can thus be evaluated according to the proportion of the sample that adhered at each measurement period. The percentage of participants who dropped out of a study was included when this information was reported or could be computed based on available data. Fifty-five published studies from 1981 through 2004 were located by computer searches of the literature using MEDLINE (1966 to present), CINAHL (1982 to present), PubMed, and bibliographical searches. Studies were included that had subjects who were diagnosed with a chronic disease or disability, including obesity. Sixteen studies targeted patients with cardiovascular diseases, such as coronary heart disease (7), myocardial infarction (6), angina (2), and hypertension (1). Ten studies were conducted with obese or overweight patients and five were with patients diagnosed with some form of arthritis. Patients suffering with pain, such as back pain, were targeted in four studies, and two interventions were not limited to a single

disease or disability, but reported a sample of patients suffering from "chronic diseases." Seven studies were included that targeted sedentary or physically inactive individuals specifically because they are at increased risk for chronic disease. One study of individuals with low socioeconomic status (SES) was included because the report was presented in light of low SES as a risk for disease. There were single studies reporting physical activity as an outcome variable for patients diagnosed with rheumatic disease, hemophilia, fibromyalgia, and depression, and for patients who had a kidney transplant.

Studies are categorized in Table 1 according to the predominant intervention method reported, although many included multiple strategies and/or compared different strategies or modes of exercise. The most common type of intervention was some form of exercise prescription in combination with cognitive behavioral therapy, such as goal setting or self-monitoring that was implemented in a group format. Six of the 11 cognitive behavioral interventions included structured exercise as part of the intervention. Behavioral counseling was used in four studies, all of which included group exercise sessions. Nurse-led interventions were usually conducted with individuals in a clinic setting and were more likely to be brief (e.g., as few as one contact) interventions with patients on an infrequent basis, such as every several weeks or months (e.g., Campbell et al., 1998). Interventions that were described as "lifestyle" were typically intensive group programs that targeted multiple health behaviors using multiple strategies, such as group counseling, diet modifications, supervised exercise, and educational seminars (e.g., Ornish et al., 1998). Programs that had the patients participate in physical activity in their homes were clustered together regardless of other components of the intervention. Some of these studies evaluated programs designed to support exercise outside of a supervised

Cognitive Behavioral Therapies

Study	Subjects per group	Intervention	Outcome
Effects of physical activity counseling in primary care: the Activity Counseling Trial: a randomized controlled trial. JAMA 2001 286:677-687	Inactive adults 1. Assistance (n=293) 2. Counseling (n=289) 3. Advice (n=292)	Over 2 Y, all groups: prescribed moderate intensity PA. 1. behavioral counseling based on changing social cognitive theory mediators + electronic step-counters 2. 1 + telephone counseling on decreasing frequency 3. physician advice control	6-mo total PA for women: 2 > 3 24-mo adherence to prescription Women: 1: 9.9%, 2: 25.7%, 3: 14.3% Men: 1: 29.9%, 2: 18.5%, 3: 16.4%
Intensive physical and psychosocial training program for patients with chronic low back pain. A controlled clinical trial Alaranta et al., Spine 1994: 1339-49	Adult patients with low back pain, stratified by age and sex 1. Intervention (AKSELI) (n=152) 2. UTC (n=141)	1. 3-wk inpatient intensive physical and psychosocial training program, including cognitive-behavioral disability management groups followed with 3-wk home-training 2. UTC	2% dropout at 12-mo; flexibility was better for males only in 1 vs. 2 at 3- and 12-mo follow-up; measures of strength improved more for 1 at 3-mo and 12-mo; at 3-mo, perceived performance capability increased more for 1, group difference maintained for males at 12-mo
Effects of lifestyle activity vs structured aerobic exercise in obese women: A randomized trial Anderson et al., JAMA 1999: 335-40	Adult obese women 1. Diet + Structured EX (n=20) 2. Diet + Lifestyle Activity (n=20)	16-wk both groups: cognitive behavioral weight loss program: 1. Structured EX (step aerobics classes) 2. Lifestyle Activity	Overall dropout 17.5%; ns difference in dropout between groups; Met lifestyle PA guidelines (% of last 68 weeks) 1: 48.2%, 2: 55.6%, ns dif
Comparison of lifestyle and structured interventions to increase physical activity and cardiorespiratory fitness: A randomized trial. Dunn et al., JAMA 1999: 327(1)	Sedentary and moderately overweight adults 1. PA lifestyle (n=109) 2. Structured EX (n=103)	6-mo intensive intervention and 18-mo maintenance intervention. 1. Based on Stages of Change and Social Cognitive theory; 16 weekly sessions followed by biweekly sessions for 8 wk of home-based moderate intensity PA 2. Traditional EX prescription; supervised on-site EX sessions	24-mo dropout: 1:10.6%, 2: 10.4%. Both groups: Increase in PA from BL to 6-mo & decrease from 6- to 24-mo Regularly active, moderate intensity ≥ 70% of previous 18-mo 1: 39% 2: 35%, ns

Study	Subjects per group	Intervention	Outcome
Combined exercise and motivation program: effect on the compliance and level of disability of patients with chronic low back pain: a randomized controlled trial Friedrich et al., Br Med J 1998: 475-87	Adult patients with low back pain 1. Standard EX program (n=49) 2. EX + motivation program (n=44)	1. Individual EX instruction for 10 training sessions, 2-3/wk 2. 1 + counseling and reinforcement; completed a TX contract and EX diary	Dropout 1: 28.6%, 2: 22.7% EX sessions attended (out of 10): 1: 51%, 2: 81.8% At 4-mo: Adherence to prescription 1: 69.4%, 2: 76.7% At 12-mo: Frequency of EX/wk greater in 2 compared to 1; other behavior variables not different
Multimodal cognitive behavioral treatment of patients sicklisted for musculoskeletal pain: a randomized controlled study Haldorsen et al., Scand J Rheumatol 1998: 16-25	Employed adults sick-listed 8 wk for musculoskeletal pain: 1. Intervention (n=312) 2. UTC (n=157)	1. 4-wk multimodal cognitive behavioral TX (physical TX, cognitive-behavior modification, education, and workplace-based interventions); 6 hr sessions, 5 d/wk, group & individual TX	Dropout 1: 6%, 2: 40% At 12-mo: Regular physical training (no units) greater in 1 than 2
Effect of a self-management program on patients with chronic disease Lorig et al., Eff Clin Pract 2001: 256-62	489 of 613 patients with an average of 2.3 chronic diseases (lung, heart, diabetes, arthritis) completed intervention and 1-y follow-up	Chronic Disease Self-Management Program: 2.5 h/wk for 7-wk, peer-led small group, structured format based on self-efficacy theory; problem-solving, decision making, confidence building.	Dropout 20% Significant increase of 13±97.3 min/wk of aerobic EX from baseline (87±94.7 min/wk)
The Solution Method: 2-year trends in weight, blood pressure, exercise, depression, and functioning of adults trained in development skills Mellin et al., J Am Diet Assoc 1997: 1133-38	29 obese adults	12-wk developmental skills training (2-h weekly group sessions) followed by additional 12-wk TX; subjects then completed 2nd 12-wk TX	Dropout 24.1% Baseline EX was 103±134.0 min/wk. Change from baseline: 12-mo: +140.5 min/wk 24-mo: +189.1 min/wk % reporting increased EX: 12-mo: 91% 24-mo: 68%

Study	Subjects per group	Intervention	Outcome
Effects on quality of life with comprehensive rehabilitation after acute myocardial infarction Oldridge et al., Am J Cardiol 1991: 1084-9	Patients post acute myocardial infarction with depression and/or anxiety 1. TX (n=99) 2. UTC (n=102)	1: 8-wk EX conditioning (50-min 2 times/wk) + 90-min weekly session of cognitive behavioral counseling (progressive relaxation; feelings, thoughts, attitudes, & behavior management)	Dropout 1: 12%, 2: 11.8%. Significant increase in EX tolerance from baseline to posttest for 1. No group difference in EX tolerance at 12-mo
Evaluation of a modified cognitive-behavioural programme for weight management Rapoport et al., Int J Obes Relat 2000: 1726-37	Adult obese women 1. standard (n=38) 2. modified (n=37) cognitive behavior therapy	10-wk: 1. motivational techniques to increase PA 2. 1 + non-diet, focus on lifestyle changes 2 h/wk	Dropout during intervention: 1: 15.8%, 2: 16.2% Significant increase in MET h/wk for both groups; Time effect for baseline, posttest, 24-wk and 52-wk follow-up; Maintained increased PA from posttest to 52-wk follow-up
Computerized weight loss intervention optimizes staff time: the clinical and cost results of a controlled clinical trial conducted in a managed care setting Wylie-Rosett et al., J Am Diet Assoc 2001: 1155-62	Overweight/obese adults 1. Minimal intervention control (n=116) 2. 1 + expert computer system (n=236) 3. 2 + Staff consultation (n=236)	12-mo: 1. Standalone self-help workbook 2. 1 + tailored onsite computer-determined nutrition, fitness, and psychobehavioral content 3. 2 + staff conducted CBM consultation (weekly groups 3-mo; monthly groups 9-mo)	Dropout 1: 16%, 2: 22%, 3: 17% BL – 12-mo increases ($\pm$SE): Blocks walked/day Min walked/wk 1. 5.9$\pm$1.10 5.10$\pm$1.50 2. 5.1$\pm$0.79 5.11$\pm$1.13 3. 3.9$\pm$1.10 4.96$\pm$1.09 Significant increase in PA, no difference between groups

Behavioral Counseling

Study	Subjects per group	Intervention	Outcome
Behavioral treatment of adherence to therapeutic exercise by children with hemophilia Greenan-Fowler et al., Br Med J 1987: 846-49	10 children with hemophilia	12-session behavioral physical therapy; behavior modification, reinforcement	Compliance (% of prescription followed): Baseline = 55% Post-test = 94% 1-Y = 66%

Study	Subjects per group	Intervention	Outcome
The group counseling v exercise therapy study. A controlled intervention with subjects following myocardial infarction Stern et al., Arch Intern Med 1983: 1719-25	Postmyocardial infarction patients 1. EX (n=42) 2. Counseling (n=35) 3. UTC (n=29)	12-wk: 1. supervised EX therapy, 60 min for 3d/wk 2. 60-75 min weekly group counseling sessions	Dropout: 1. 19.2%, 2. 25.7%, 3. 31% Mean compliance with intervention: 1. 81%, 2. 86% Work capacity in METs BL to 3-mo: 1. +1.53, 2. +0.52, 3. -0.28 BL to 6-mo: 1. +1.68, 2. +0.40, 3. +3.08 BL to 12-mo: No group differences 1. +1.58, 2. +1.45, 3. +1.31
Effects of aerobic exercise versus stress management treatment in fibromyalgia. A 4.5 year prospective study Wigers et al., Scand J Rheumatol 1996: 77-86	Fibromyalgia patients 90.1% female, 1. Aerobic EX (n=20), 2. Stress management (n=20) 3. UTC (n=20)	1. group EX 45 min, 3 d/wk, 14-wk 2. group TX 90 min, 2 d/wk for 6-wk, then 1 d/wk for 8-wk	Dropout from baseline Post Follow-up (4-Y) 1. 20% 25% 2. 25% 35% 3. 15% 20% At post, 1 increased work capacity, and values > 2 No differences at follow-up 1. 26.7% were exercising at follow-up 2. 69% were practicing stress management
Lifestyle intervention in overweight individuals with a family history of diabetes Wing et al., Diabetes Care 1998: 350-59	Overweight adults with parental history of diabetes 1. diet (n=37), 2. EX (n=37), 3. diet + EX (n=40) 4. control (n=40)	1-3. Weekly (0-6mo) and biweekly(6-12mo) group behavior change sessions Two 6-wk refresher courses during Y-2 2-3. Included 50-60 min walk 4. Control	Intervention sessions attended (%, mo) 0-6 6-12 Y-2 refresher 1. 70 37 36 2. 57 16 15 3. 56 29 29 6-mo improvements: 1-3. walk test 2-3. kcal/wk PA, est. VO_{2max} 12-mo improvements: 2-3. kcal/wk PA maintained 6- and 12-mo: 3 > PA than 2 24-mo: no changes maintained, no group differences in PA or

Nurse-Led

Study	Subjects per group	Intervention	Outcome
Secondary prevention in coronary heart disease: a randomized trial of nurse led clinics in primary care Campbell et al., Heart 1998: 447-52	Adults with working diagnosis of coronary heart disease 1. Intervention (n=593) 2. UTC (n=580)	Nurse run clinics in general practice; general health assessment and TX review; Feedback, goal planning, and action plan in visit #1; follow-up visits. "Stepping Out" program to promote PA	From BL to 1-Y changes in % participating in moderate PA: 1. +4.4% 2. -1.1% OR of 1.67 for effects of intervention on moderate PA
Randomized controlled trial of health promotion in general practice for patients at high cardiovascular risk Cupples and McKnight, BMJ (Clin Res Ed) 1994: 993-96	Physician identified patients with angina for ≥ 6 mo 1. UTC (n=346) 2. intervention (n=342)	1. UTC 2. 1 + Nurse implemented personal health promotion every 4-mo for 2-y	After 2-Y, % reporting daily physical EX: 1. 24% 2. 44%
Five year follow up of patients at high cardiovascular risk who took part in randomized controlled trial of health promotion Cupples and McKnight, BMJ (Clin Res Ed) 1999: 687-88	(see Cupples and McKnight, 1994)	(see Cupples and McKnight, 1994)	5-y follow-up: Dropout 1:27%, 2:32% No. of 20-min episodes of EX/wk: Baseline 2-y 5-y 1. 3.8 3.2 2.8 2. 3.6 4.0 3.0
A telephone-delivered intervention for patients with NIDDM. Effect on coronary risk factors. Kirkman et al., Diabetes Care 1994: 840-6	Non-insulin dependent diabetic older veterans: 1. Telephone delivered intervention (n=204) 2. UTC (n=71)	1. 12 monthly nurse-delivered health counseling telephone calls; focus on knowledge and barriers to compliance with diet, EX, and medications 2. UTC	EX data on obese only: % reported adherence to EX program in past wk (ns increases): BL 12-mo 1. 43.1 59 2. 45.1 51

Study	Subjects per group	Intervention	Outcome
Behavioural counselling in general practice for the promotion of healthy behaviour among adults at increased risk of coronary heart disease: randomized trial Steptoe et al., BMJ (Clin Res Ed) 1999: 943-47	Adults with 1+ modifiable risk factors for CHD and low PA 1. intervention (n=316) 2. UTC (n=567)	1. Nurse-delivered brief behavioral counseling based on the stage of change model; 3 20-min sessions (>1 risk factor) or 2 20-min sessions (1 risk factor) plus 1-2 phone contacts 2. UTC	Dropout: 4-mo 12-mo 1. 35% 46% 2. 26% 38% Increase in PA sessions greater for 1 from BL to 4-mo and 12-mo; Increase in PA at 4-mo sustained at 12-mo
Psychosocial predictors of changes in physical activity in overweight sedentary adults following counseling in primary care Steptoe et al., Prev Med 2000: 183-94	See Steptoe et al., 1999	See Steptoe et al., 1999	Odds of moving to EX action/maintenance stage for 1 vs. 2 4-mo: 1.89 12-mo: 1.68 Efficacy of intervention lower for subjects in precontemplation at baseline

Study	Subjects per group	Intervention	Outcome
		Home-Based	
Lifestyle intervention: results of the treatment of Mild Hypertension Study (TOMHS) Elmer et al., Prev Med 1995: 378-88	902 hypertensive adults 1. Placebo 2-6. One of 5 antihypertensive medications; all received the diet and PA interventions	Lifestyle program intense for first 6-mo using behavioral modification with individuals and in groups; unsupervised home-based focusing on light- to moderate-intensity PA; self-monitoring, cognitive-behavioral strategies, clinic follow-up visits every 3-mo for 4-Y	Reported leisure PA increased by 86% at Y-1 and maintained through Y-2; remained above baseline (men 57%, women 36%) at Y-4. Y-1: 70% of subjects were active above baseline Y-4: 56% of subjects remained active above baseline
A randomized trial comparing aerobic exercise and resistance exercise with a health education program in older adults with knee osteoarthritis. The Fitness Arthritis and Seniors Trial (FAST) Ettinger, et al., JAMA 1997: 25-31	Older adults with knee osteoarthritis 1. aerobic EX (n=144) 2. resistance EX (n=146) 3. health education (n=149)	1-2. 3-mo facility-based group EX program followed by 15-mo home-based program; used EX logs 3. 3 monthly group sessions to provide attention, social interaction, and education about arthritis followed by biweekly (mo 4-6) and monthly (mo 7-18) phone contact	Dropout: 1. 19%, 2. 16%, 3. 17% Mean compliance rate for interventions: 1. 68% 2. 70% Compliance overall: 3-mo 85% 9-mo 70% 18-mo 50%
Long-term effects of varying intensities and formats of PA on participation rates, fitness, and lipoproteins in men and women aged 50 to 65 years King et al., Circulation 1995: 2596-604	Sedentary older adults 1. High-intensity group-based (n=69); 2. High-intensity home-based (n=74); 3. Low-intensity home-based (n=64)	EX prescription, varied by intensity and location, self-monitoring, supervised EX or telephone contacts/program monitoring, feedback for 2-Y	Dropout 10.8% (total) % adhering to prescription: 12-mo 24-mo 1. 52.6 36.4 2. 78.7 67.8 3. 75.1 49.0 Changes in aerobic capacity and duration of graded exercise test tracked with adherence

361

Study	Subjects per group	Intervention	Outcome
A randomized trial of exercise training after renal transplantation Painter et al Transplantation 2002 74: 42-48	Adults 1-mo post renal transplantation 1. EX (n=54) 2. UTC (n=43)	1. individualized home based exercise prescription of aerobic EX up to 30 min 4x/wk at 60-65% HRmax, progressively increased to 75-80% HRmax; intensity based on baseline maximal aerobic capacity; regular phone follow up; ex logs turned in bi-weekly.	Dropout: 1. 35%, 2. 49% EX participation: 6-mo 12-mo 1. 58% 67% 2. 42% 36% VO2peak: 1 & 2: BL < 6-mo 1: 6-mo < 12-mo Increase in strength at 12-mo: 1 > 2
Effects of group- versus home-based exercise in the treatment of obesity Perri et al., J Consult Clin Psychol 1997: 278-85	Sedentary obese women 1. Weight loss TX plus group EX (n=25) 2. Weight loss TX plus home-based EX program (n=24)	1 & 2. 2-hr weekly cognitive behavioral weight loss sessions for 26 wks, biweekly group sessions for wks 27-52 focusing on adherence skills; Prescribed walking 30 min, 5 d/wk 1. 3 group-based EX sessions provided for 26 wks, then 2 sessions per wk for wks 27-52 2. Unsupervised walking 30-min, 5d/wk	Dropouts 1. 28%, 2. 4.2% No group difference in weight loss group attendance; EX compliance over 12-mo: 1. 62.1% 2. 83.8% 2 > 1 compliance at mo 7-12 (p=.04)
A randomized controlled trial comparing 2 instructional approaches to home exercise instruction following arthroscopic full-thickness rotator cuff repair surgery Roddy et al. J Orthop Sports Phys Ther. 2002: 548-559.	Adults diagnosed with full-thickness rotator cuff tear 1. Videotape instruction (n=54) 2. Individual instruction with physical therapist (PT) (n=54)	1. Videotape given post-op bedside by PT; 3 individual evaluations by PT; home-based video instruction for progressive rehabilitation 2. 4 individual instruction sessions with PT (wks 2, 6, 12, 24)	Dropouts 1. 43%, 2. 31% No difference in self-regulated patient outcomes or compliance between home-based video and PT directed methods of instruction.

Study	Population/Groups	Intervention	Results
Home exercise and compliance in inflammatory rheumatic diseases--a prospective clinical trial Stenström et al., J Rheumatol 1997: 470-76	Patients with inflammatory rheumatic disease 1. dynamic muscle training (n=27) 2. progressive muscle relaxation (n=27)	Prescribed 30-min, 5 d/wk for 3-mo, then 2-3 d/wk for 9-mo, home EX programs: 1. strength training, stretching & walking 2. 15-min progressive relaxation + 15-min quiet rest	37% of subjects in each group failed to complete study Median # EX sessions (12-mo): 1. 173; 2. 151 No change or group differences in walking speed, muscle function, strength, or endurance; Improvements in 1. Physical condition 2. Pain, emotional well-being
A comparison between an outpatient hospital-based pulmonary rehabilitation program and a home-care pulmonary rehabilitation program in patients with COPD. A follow-up of 18 mo Strijbos et al., Chest 1996: 366-72	COPD patients 1. hospital-based program (n=18) 2. home-care rehabilitation programs (n=17) 3. UTC (n=15)	Patient education, breathing & relaxation EXs, bronchial hygiene, EX reconditioning, and encouragement to continue EX daily at home; 1. TX in hospital 60-min, 2 d/wk, 12-wk 2. 24 sessions of 30-min over 12-wk in home by physiotherapist 3. UTC	Dropout: 1. 27.8%; 2. 17.6%; 3. 6.7% 1. Max work capacity increased at post & maintained for 3-6 mo; decreased at 12- and 18-mo; 2. Max work capacity increased throughout; 20.7% above baseline at 18-mo. 2. Improvements better maintained at follow-up (3-mo to 18-mo)

Lifestyle

Study	Population/Groups	Intervention	Results
The Finish diabetes prevention study (DPS): Lifestyle intervention and 3-year results on diet and physical activity Lindström et al., Diabetes Care 2003: 3230-6	Adults at high-risk of diabetes 1. lifestyle (n=265) 2. UTC (n=257)	1. Nutrition and exercise knowledge & skill development during 7 Individual consultation sessions with nutritionists tapered over 1-Y; offered supervised, individually tailored moderate intensity resistance exercise. 2. UTC	Dropout: 1. 3% 1-Y, 5.3% final; 2. 3.5% 1-Y, 7% final Min/wk mod-vigorous leisure time PA: 1. increased baseline to 1-Y and to 3-Y, p<.01 2. no change Proportion sedentary: 1. 14% 1-Y and 17% 3-Y 2. 30% 1-Y and 29% 3-Y

Study	Subjects per group	Intervention	Outcome
Secondary prevention clinics for coronary heart disease: four year follow up of a randomized controlled trial in primary care Murchie et al., BMJ 2003: 84-9	Older adults with diagnosed coronary heart disease 1. lifestyle, secondary prevention (n=673) 2. UTC (n=670)	1. Individual sessions every 2 to 6 mo for 1 yr with nurse; medical and lifestyle secondary prevention clinics 2. UTC	Dropout: 1. 1.3% at 1-Y, 4.0% at 4.7-Y; 2. 1.2% at 1-Y, 4.8% at 4.7-Y Death rate at 4.7-Y: 1 (14.5%) < 2 (18.9%), p<.05 Adequate moderate PA: BL 1-Y 4.7-Y 1. 36.3% 42.1% 34.6% 2. 30.7% 31.2% 28.1% OR 1.67 (1-Y) and 1.26 (4.7-Y); PA increase for 1 at 1-Y not sustained at 4.7-Y
Intensive lifestyle changes for reversal of coronary heart disease Ornish et al., JAMA 1998: 2001 (1)	Adults with moderate to severe coronary artery disease 1. lifestyle (n=28) 2. UTC (n=20)	1. Intensive lifestyle changes: low-fat vegetarian diet, aerobic EX (3 h/wk prescribed), stress management training, smoking cessation, group psychosocial support (2 meetings/wk) for 1 Y. 2. UTC	Available data for 1-Y and 5-Y 1. 71.4%; 2. 75% 1. increased EX times/wk from baseline to 1-Y (p=0.06). Not different from baseline at 5-Y.
A classroom mind/body wellness intervention for older adults with chronic illness: Comparing immediate and 1-year benefits Rybarczyk et al., Behav Med 2001: 15-27	Older adults with ≥ one chronic illness and psychosocial component to chronic illness, random stratification (age, primary care use) to: 1. classroom TX (n=113) 2. waiting list control (n=130)	1. 8 2-hr classes of mind/body wellness intervention (relaxation training, cognitive restructuring, problem-solving, communication, behavioral TX for insomnia, nutrition, and EX) 2. Control	Attrition at 1-y follow-up: 1. 15%; 2. 17% 1. larger increase in health behaviors (PA included with others, such as nutrition)

Study	Subjects per group	Intervention	Outcome
Behavioral and psychosocial effects of intensive lifestyle management for women with coronary heart disease Toobert et al., Patient Educ Couns 1998: 177-88	Postmenopausal women with CHD 1. TX (n=16) 2. UTC (n=12)	1. Comprehensive lifestyle self-management: diet, relaxation training, daily aerobic EX (prescribed 1/h day for 3+ d/wk), group sessions; 7-day retreat with partner followed by 4-h, 2 d/wk meetings for the next 15 mo, Intervention faded to 2-wk intervals for next 6 mo, 1/mo for final 3 mo 2. UTC	PA d/wk* Baseline 4-mo 12-mo 1. 3.8 4.8 4.5 2. 2.4 2.4 2.5 Stanford 7-Day Recall summary 1. 160 164 198 2. 137 128 128 * significant increase for 1 from baseline to 4- and 12-mo
Physiologic and related behavioral outcomes from the women's lifestyle heart trial Toobert and Glasgow, Ann Behav Med 2000: 1-9	See Toobert et al., 1998	See Toobert et al., 1998	Mean attendance for 2/wk meetings was 81%; # day EX/last 7 days increased for 1 BL to 4-mo (p<.001) and BL to 12 mo (p=.03) vs. 2

Physical Activity

Study	Subjects per group	Intervention	Outcome
Aiello et al., Menopause 2003: 382-8	Overweight post-menopausal women 1. Moderate intensity EX (n=87) 2. Stretching (n=86)	1. Prescribed 45-min 5 d/wk (225 min/wk) of moderate intensity aerobic exercise; 0-3 mo 3 d/wk supervised (group), 2 d/wk home-based; 3-12 mo 1 d /wk supervised, 4 d/wk home-based 2. 45-min 5 d/wk group stretching 0-12 mo	Dropout: 6.9% 1. Average d/wk EX = 3.7, 74% of prescribed.
Effects of sustained weight loss and exercise on aerobic fitness in obese women Ashutosh et al., J Sports Med Phys Fitness 1997: 252-57	Obese women 1. Diet only (n=6) 2. Diet + aerobics (n=8) 3. Diet + strength training (n=8) 4. Diet + aerobics + strength training (n=9)	25-wk group sessions of behavioral counseling + diet counseling (1, 2, 3, 4) and group EX (2, 3, 4); wk 27-52 all groups in weight loss maintenance program conducted by different investigators blinded to group membership	Drop-out 16.2% aerobic capacity increased in 2 and 4

Study	Subjects per group	Intervention	Outcome
Correlates of compliance in a randomized exercise trial in myocardial infarction patients Dorn, et al., Med Sci Sports Exerc 2001: 1081-89	Male myocardial infarction patients 1. TX (n=308) were included in compliance analysis	1. Structured, supervised EX 3 d/wk (first 8-wk in laboratory) for 36 mo	% compliant (attended $\geq$ 50% of possible EX sessions): End of 8-wk: 79.6% 6-mo: 55.1% 12-mo: 47% 18-mo: 40% 24-mo: 33% 30-mo: 24% 36-mo: 13%
Cognitive and psychological outcomes of exercise in a 1-year follow up study of patients with chronic obstructive pulmonary disease Emery, et al. Health Psychol 2003: 598-604	Older (> 50 yrs) adults with COPD (n=28)	0-5 wk: - Supervised EX (aerobic & strength training): 5d/wk up to 4hr/d - Lectures (stress management & psychosocial support): 4 hr/wk 6-10 wk: - Supervised EX: 3x/wk 60-90 min - Lectures: 1hr/wk At 10-wk -Individualized home-based program	EX adherence ($\geq$ 23 METS/wk) at 1-yr = 39% Adherence associated with no change in depression or anxiety; nonadherence: increased depression symptoms and increased anxiety
Jeffery et al., Am J Clin Nutr 2003: 648-9	Overweight adults 1. Standard behavior therapy (SBT) (n=93) 2. High physical activity (HPA) (n=109)	SBT for weight loss (nutrition, exercise, behavior therapy) in groups weekly for 0 to 6-mo, biweekly 6-12 mo, monthly 12-18 mo; self-monitoring and social support; plus prescribed energy expenditure (EE) goal: 1. 1000 kcal/kg/wk 2. 2500 kcal/kg/wk + exercise coaches and during 12-18 mo monetary incentive for each week EE goal met	Drop-out: 16.8% overall at 18-mo EE (kcal/kg/wk) 2>1, $p<0.01$ 6-mo 12-mo 18-mo 1. 1837±1431 1569±1309 1629±1483 2. 2399±1571 2249±1751 2317±1854 % met EE $\geq$ 2500 kcal.kg/wk 1. 28 23 20 2. 49 41 39

Study	Subjects per group	Intervention	Outcome
Hage et al., Physiotherapy Res International 2003: 13-22	See Stähle et al., Eur Heart J 1999	See Stähle et al., Eur Heart J 1999	Drop-out: 1. 11%, 2. 12% 3 – 6 yr follow-up (mean 4.4 yrs) 1. & 2. maintained self-reported level of EX compared to 12-mo post BL
Effect of two training regimens on bone mineral density in healthy perimenopausal women: a randomized controlled trial Heinonen et al., J Bone Miner Res 1998: 483-90	Middle-aged sedentary women 1. endurance training (n=32) 2. calisthenics (n=35) 3. control (n=34)	1-2. EX training 4 d/wk for 18-mo, 1 d/wk supervised of aerobic or strength-endurance. 3. stretched 1 d/wk	EX diaries estimated average compliance (completed/prescribed): 1. 80% (3.2 d/wk) 2. 66% (2.6 d/wk) 3. 72% (0.72 d/wk) Total dropout 25%, not different between groups
Retardation of coronary atherosclerosis with yoga lifestyle intervention Manchanda et al., J Assoc Physicians India 2000: 687-94	Men with coronary artery disease 1. yoga intervention (n=21) 2. UTC (n=21)	1. Patients and spouses spent 4 days at residential yoga center (yoga lifestyle methods, stress management, dietary control, moderate aerobic EX); prescribed 90 min daily yoga; visit to center every two weeks 2. UTC	Baseline to 1-Y: Overall compliance to program was 79.5%; EX duration on GXT: 1. increased 28% 2. decreased 17%
Comparison of three active therapies for chronic low back pain: results of a randomized clinical trial with one-year follow-up Mannion et al., Rheumatology 2001:772-8	Adults with chronic low back pain 1. Active physiotherapy (n=49) 2. Muscle reconditioning on devices/machines (n=50) 3. Low-impact aerobics (n=49)	Hospital based, 2 d/wk for 12-wk 1. 30-min individual instruction 2. 60-min on training devices/machines in groups of 2-3 3. 60-min low-impact aerobics in groups of 12	Dropout, post intervention 11%; at 12-mo follow-up 14% At 12-mo some EX (similar to intervention) 1. 81% 2. 79% 3. 86% No difference in adherence between groups

Study	Subjects per group	Intervention	Outcome
Exercise maintenance of persons with arthritis after participation in a class experience Minor and Brown, Health Ed Q 1993: 83-95	120 adults with rheumatoid arthritis or osteoarthritis 1. Aerobic walking 2. Aerobic aquatics 3. UTC	1-2. 60-min supervised group activity sessions 3 times per wk for 12-wk; included positive feedback, EX goal setting and problem-solving, and social support 3. UTC	Dropout, post-intervention 17%; at 3-mo & 9-mo follow-up 28% No group effects on minutes of PA per wk.
Can primary care doctors prescribe exercise to improve fitness? The Step Test Exercise Prescription (STEP) Project. Petrella, Am J Prev Med 2003: 316-322	Older adults (> 65 yrs) 1. STEP (n=131) 2. UTC (n=110)	Clinic based testing and counseling with home/community based EX 1. Brief EX counseling & prescription based on training HR (75% predicted VO_{2max}); training HR (THR) adjusted at 3 & 6-mo based on result of new step test 2. UTC: Brief EX counseling + ACSM guidelines and benefits of EX	Dropout: 1. 15% Adherence (3+ sessions at THR): 1. 76% (6 mo): 71% (12 mo) 2. 61% (6 mo): 56% (12 mo) VO_{2max} increases from BL 6-mo 12-mo 1. 11% 17% 2. 4% 3% 1. Significant changes BL to 12-mo: Exercise self efficacy: increase SBP – decrease 9 mmHg BMI – decrease 7.4%
Effects of a prescribed supervised exercise program on mortality and cardiovascular morbidity in patients after myocardial infarction. The National Exercise and Heart Disease Project. Shaw, Am J Cardiol 1981: 39-46	Adult male survivors of myocardial infarction 1. EX (n=323) 2. UTC (n=328)	1. Prescribed supervised EX in laboratory 1 h/day, 3 d/wk for 8-wk followed by aerobic activities in a gymnasium for 34-mo prescribed for 40-min for 3 d/wk 2. UTC	Total dropout through follow-ups: 1. 7%, 2. 6%; At 2-Y, 1. 23% not EX 2. 3% EX regularly

Study	Subjects per group	Intervention	Outcome
The efficacy of exercise as a long-term antidepressant in elderly subjects: a randomized, controlled trial Singh et al., J Gerontology 2001: M497-M504	Older depressed adults 1. Health Ed control (n=15) 2. EX (n=17)	0-10-wk: 1. 60 min, 2 d/wk of health ed lecture 2. 45 min, 3 d/wk supervised high intensity progressive resistance exercise training (PRT) 10-20 wk: 1 & 2. Weekly brief phone contact 2. unsupervised PRT at lab (n=9), home (n=4), health club (n=1)	Dropout at 10-wk 6% PRT at prescribed level at 20-wk: 1. 0% 2. 73% Total # exercise sessions 10-20 wk: Home (25±2.3) > Lab/health club (17.9±2.3), p=.09 At 26-mo follow-up: 1. 0% EX 2. 33% PRT regularly
Improved physical fitness and quality of life following training of elderly patients after acute coronary events - A 1 year follow-up randomized controlled study Ståhle et al., Eur Heart J 1999: 1475-84	Older adults recovering from an acute coronary event 1. EX TX (n=56) 2. UTC (n=53)	1. 50 min group-training aerobic program 3 d/wk for 3-mo; optional 1/wk training for next 3-mo 2. UTC	Dropout (after first 3-mo): 1. 9%, 2. 4% Average compliance to intervention was 87%. 1. EX capacity significantly higher than baseline at 3- and 12-mo for TX group only. Self-rated fitness and PA increased from baseline to 3-mo for both groups, increase greater for 1; Greater than baseline at 12-mo, but no group differences
A randomized controlled trial to evaluate the effectiveness of an exercise program in women with rheumatoid arthritis taking low dose prednisone Westby et al., J Rheumatol 2000: 1674-80	Women with rheumatoid arthritis 1. no steroid Rx EX TX (n=23) 2. steroid Rx EX TX (n=14) 3. UTC (n=16)	1-2. Aerobic, weight bearing EX for 45-60 min, 3 d/wk, 12-mo 3. UTC	Dropouts: 1. 20%; 2. 21%, 3. 37.5% EX log measured adherence (% prescribed) overall 71% (0-6 mo 76%; 6-12 mo 65%) 1-2. 0-12 mo increases in Caltrac (13%) and fitness score (87%)

Others

Study	Population / Groups	Intervention	Results
Effectiveness of counseling patients on physical activity in general practice: cluster randomized controlled trial Elley et al. BMJ 2003: 1-6	Sedentary patients in general practice clinics 1. TX (n=474) 2. UTC (n=446)	1. "Green Prescription" for exercise and motivational counseling from general practice clinician; ≥ 3 telephone calls from exercise specialist over next 3-mo 2. UTC	Dropouts: 1. 15%, 2. 15% Increase in % adherence to 2.5+ hr/wk moderate/ vigorous PA at 12-mo: 1 (14.8 to 32.4%) > 2 (21 to 25.9%), p=0.003 Changes from BL to 12-mo: min/wk leisure exercise – 1 (+ 43.3) > 2 (+4.8), p.0.05 kcal/kg/wk leisure PA – 1 (+4.32) > 2 (+1.29), p=0.02 Kcal/kg/wk total PA – 1 (+9.76) > 2 (+0.37), p=0.001
Patient education in arthritis: randomized controlled trial of a mail-delivered program Fries et al., J Rheumatol 1997: 1378-83	Older patients with arthritis 1. TX (n=375) 2. UTC (n=434)	1. Mail-delivered, tailored, self-management arthritis program; health assessment questionnaires mailed at 3-mo intervals for 12 mo 2. UTC	BL to 6-mo: EX frequency/wk increased for 1; no change for 2 At 6-mo: 2 received TX and both groups increased EX frequency from 6- to 12-mo
The Newcastle exercise program: A randomized controlled trial of methods to promote physical activity in primary care Harland et al., Br Med J 1999: 828-32	Socioeconomically disadvantaged adults: 1. Brief intervention (n=103) 2. Brief intervention+ 30 vouchers (n=105) 3. Intense intervention (n=106) 4. Intense intervention+ 30 vouchers (n=102) 5. UTC	12-wk intervention: 1. one motivational interview 3. six motivation interviews 2&4. One episode of aerobic activity at local facilities	Interview attendance greater in voucher groups (86% vs 77%) Voucher use greater in 4 (44% vs 27%) Proportion of subjects increasing PA greater in intervention groups than control; vouchers or intensity not factors At 12-mo, no sustained improvement in PA in any groups

Study	Subjects per group	Intervention	Outcome
Adherence in the training levels comparison trial Lee, et al., Med Sci Sports Ex 1996: 47-52	Sedentary men with coronary heart disease 1. High intensity EX (n=110) 2. Low intensity EX (n=87)	1-2. Supervised EX of high or low intensity, three 1-h sessions per wk for 2-Y; regular group meetings with subjects and their spouses	Compliance: Y-1: 1. 55.5%, 2. 64% Y-2: attendance decreased, 2 better than 1 (# not reported) Achievement of protocol defined heart rate: 6-mo: 1. 31%, 2. 55% Y-1: 1. 37%, 2. 54%
One-year followup of patients with osteoarthritis of the knee who participated in a program of supervised fitness walking and supportive patient education Sullivan et al., Arthritis Care Res 1998: 228-33	Patients with osteoarthritis of the knee 1. TX (n=47) 2. control (n=45)	1. 3 times per wk for 8-wk supervised fitness walking and patient education 2. 1/wk interviews with control group	Completed 1Y telephone follow-up 1. 62%, 2. 51% No difference between groups in estimates of distances walked/wk at 8-wk or 1-Y. Change in distance walked per wk (posttest to 1-Y): 1. -4,605 m 2. -2,450 m

Abbreviations: EX = exercise, Mo = Month, PA = Physical Activity, TX = Treatment, UTC = Usual Treatment Control or Usual Care, Wk = Week, Y = Year setting (home-based) or compared adherence between home and group based programs (on-site). One program was a mail-delivered self-management program (Fries et al., 1997). Twenty-eight of the 55 studies compared one or more interventions to a usual treatment control (UTC) group. All of the studies categorized as nurse-led, lifestyle, and most of the physical activity interventions included a UTC group in their design. Five studies had a comparison group that did not receive the intervention, but did receive some contact from researchers to equalize attention (e.g., Sullivan et al., 1998).

Sample sizes ranged from 10 to 1343; most (65%) of the studies had samples of more than 100 subjects and included both males and females unless otherwise indicated. The four studies with only males targeted men who were diagnosed with CHD or had suffered a myocardial infarction (MI). More than half of the interventions with only women targeted obesity. Subjects in almost all of the studies were adults or older individuals; one study was conducted with children (Greenan-Fowler et al., 1987). The total length of the studies ranged from one to six years, with 62% lasting a single year. Six studies lasted four or more years. Length of the reported interventions was as short as 3-weeks and as long as 5-years (i.e., an intense intervention followed by regular, although infrequent contact, such as newsletters or brief interventions via telephone). Most often, the primary intervention phase lasted 12 months (13 studies) or 12 weeks (13 studies). Most interventions were designed to last a limited numbers of weeks or months and outcome variables were measured at one or more follow-up sessions. This was considered the more traditional intervention format and was followed in 53% of the studies. However, there has been an increase in studies of interventions that begin with frequent group-based programs followed by continued patient contact that decreases over time to "fade" the intervention, such as scheduled group meetings decreasing from weekly to monthly over several months (e.g., Aiello et al., 2004).

RESULTS

Two-thirds of the interventions can be considered successful in sustaining adherence above baseline at the last follow-up, or in demonstrating significant increases in physical activity compared to a control group. A variety of interventions were effective, however, no pattern emerged to point to the "best" intervention to use with all clinical populations for enhancing exercise adherence. Studies varied in the way adherence was defined and measured, how long the intervention and follow-up lasted, sample characteristics, and intervention type and implementation, all of which can have reciprocal influences that confound comparisons of their effectiveness. These issues will be discussed and qualities of the more effective interventions will be identified. Strategies more often associated with lower adherence will also be mentioned.

Definition and Measurement of Adherence

A common outcome variable would simplify evaluating the effectiveness of these interventions, but there were multiple ways of reporting behavioral outcomes. Adherence was presented as the average percentage of prescribed therapeutic exercises performed per group, the percentage of the group who maintained the exercise prescription, the percentage of the group who increased (or maintained) the target level of exercise (or any level of exercise), the frequency of exercise per a period of time (e.g., previous 7 days, 4 weeks, 3 months), or the minutes of exercise per week. One study used estimated distance walked per week as an outcome variable (Sullivan et al., 1998). Other definitions of adherence were attending at least 50% of the possible exercise sessions (Dorn et al., 1999) and participation in regular, moderate intensity activity for at least 70% of the previous 18 months (Dunn et al., 1999). Only sixteen of the studies included adherence as the proportion of the group meeting the prescribed level of exercise. Defined this way, better adherence was found in home-based programs and in those that began with more a more intense intervention format (e.g., several sessions a week consisting of one behavior change group meeting and 2-3 supervised exercise sessions) that was faded over six or more months (Elmer et al., 1995; Ettinger et al., 1997; King et al., 1995; Perri et al., 1997; Shaw, 1981).

Adherence to the intervention in these home-based programs with an initial group-based intervention that was faded ranged from 50% to 83.8%. These interventions may have had an even greater impact on exercise behavior because the method for defining adherence can underestimate the effectiveness of the intervention. Given that adherence is defined as meeting or exceeding the pre-scribed criteria, non-adherers could include those who continued exercising throughout the measurement periods, but were below this criterion level. For example, in a study of healthy older women, Kriska et al. (1986) noted that almost half of their intervention group defined as non-compliers actually maintained a walking program during the 2-yr post intervention, but at a frequency below the defined exercise goal.

Most of the studies used self-report of physical activity as an outcome variable, and much has been written about the strengths and limitations of different instruments (e.g., Dishman et al., 2001). The validity of self-report can be challenged, particularly for groups such as obese individuals, who are more likely to over-report amount of physical activity (Lichtman et al., 1992). More objective surrogate physiological measures associated with the maintenance of a prescribed level of physical activity, such as peak oxygen consumption or work capacity in METs, can

be used to represent level of activity, and were the outcome variables in seven studies reviewed. For example, Manchanda et al. (2000) randomized men with coronary artery disease to a yoga intervention or UTC group, and reported an overall compliance with the total intervention of diet, stress management, exercise, etc. of 79.5%, but they also documented that the exercise duration on the graded exercise test increased 28% for the yoga group and decreased 17% for the UTC group from baseline to 1-yr. Petrella et al. (2003) reported significant increases in aerobic capacity in an exercise prescription plus counseling group of initially sedentary older adults compare to a UTC group. The other studies that included physiological measures also documented increases in fitness variables and maintenance of these effects in intervention groups (Alaranta et al., 1994; Ashutosh et al., 1999; Stern et al., 1983; Strijbos et al., 1996). Most of these studies reported good associations between self-report of physical activity and changes in fitness variables.

More than half of the studies included some kind of comparison group, such as a usual care group. However, a no treatment control group may, over time, adopt exercise regardless of the instructions to maintain usual level of physical activity. For example, Shaw (1981) reported that at the end of 2 years of a clinical trial with myocardial infarction patients, 23% of the treatment group had stopped exercising, while 31% of the control group reported exercising regularly. It is difficult to account for all the potential influences on level of physical activity over time in comparison groups, especially in a clinical population of individuals motivated to improve their health. Also, in this study, the most important predictor of compliance over the 36-month study was baseline work capacity, which may reflect physical inactivity present before their myocardial infarction and/or difficulties with the intensity of the exercise prescription. Other factors negatively associated with compliance were smoking, triglycerides, total cholesterol, and body mass index.

In studies of exercise adherence in nonclincial populations, dropout has been included in interpreting the effects of the intervention, assuming that something about the testing or intervention was a barrier to subjects completing the study. However, interpreting dropout data in clinical trials must be considered in light of the specific disease type and severity. For example, in one study of males who had acute myocardial infarctions (Worcester et al., 1993), 50.7% of the dropout was due to death. The longer the follow up with clinical populations with increased risk of mortality in general, the greater the chance of subject death. For example, in a 4 year follow up of individuals with CHD who had been randomized to UTC or a 1-year nurse-led lifestyle intervention, 17% of the participants had died (Murchie et al., 2003). Even though level of physical activity achieved after the intervention was not sustained, there were significantly fewer deaths than in the UTC group.

Dropout reported in the studies presented in this chapter ranged from 1.3% to 49% and tended to be higher in studies that used a traditional design, that is a time-limited intervention and no subsequent contact with the subjects except for follow-up testing. The highest dropout (46%) was reported for a brief intervention with individuals in a clinical setting (Steptoe et al., 1999). On the other hand, dropout rates were less than 10% for individual interventions for patients with CHD (4%, Muchie et al., 2003) and diabetes (5.3%, Lindstrom et al, 2003).

Study Length

Length of the studies ranged from 1 to 6 years. Two-thirds of the studies lasted 1 or 1.5 years. Improvements in exercise outcomes and adherence were better than baseline in most (~80%) of these studies with shorter follow-up periods. Adherence was greater than 55% (range 56-86%) for eight of the 10 1-yr studies for which adherence rates were reported. Generally, adherence decreased over time; the longer the follow-up, the lower the adherence. Studies that conducted follow-up assessments for longer than one year after baseline assessment and reported measures at 1-yr typically indicated greater adherence or significant treatment effects at that point, but these effects were usually not maintained for exercise at subsequent assessments. Dorn et al. (2001) reported that 47% of male MI patients attended at least 50% of possible exercise sessions at 1-yr, but this progressively decreased to 33% at 2-yr and 13% at 3-yr, the final assessment. In a study of overweight adults at risk of diabetes, Wing et al. (1998) reported significant increases in kcal/wk of physical activity at 1-yr in two of four groups that included aerobic exercise, but these changes were not maintained at 2-yr. Even though 56% of the hypertensive patients in a study by Elmer et al. (1995) were still active above baseline at 4-yr, this was still a significant decrease from 70% at 1-yr. However, in this study, health benefits, such as reductions in blood pressure and improvements in serum lipids were mostly sustained at 4-yr. These physiological outcomes were associated with multiple effects from this group-based lifestyle intervention to reduce weight, sodium, alcohol, and increase physical activity and not specifically analyzed in respect to exercise adherence.

Gender differences

Most of the studies reviewed were conducted with both males and females, and results were not compared by sex. This is unfortunate because gender differences in responses to interventions have been reported. For example, adherence was different for males and females as a function of intervention group in the Activity Counseling

Trial (2000). Inactive adults were randomized into three levels of intervention: advise (comparison), assistance, and counseling. All three groups received physician advice, written educational materials, and prescription for moderate intensity physical activity. Additional strategies were implemented with the assistance and the counseling groups, which both participated in behavioral counseling based on changing social cognitive theory mediators and received electronic step-counters. The counseling group received in addition, telephone counseling on a decreasing frequency (fading). Although adherence was poor, there were differences in adherence between assistance and counseling groups for males (assistance = 29.9%, counseling = 18.5%) and females (assistance = 9.9%, counseling = 25.7%). The addition of the counseling component was effective for females but not males. Project Primetime (Toobert et al., 1998; Toobert and Glasgow, 2000) provided an intensive intervention for women diagnosed with coronary heart disease based on the model developed by Ornish (Ornish et al., 1998). This included a counseling component and proved effective in increasing and maintaining exercise frequency for the intervention compared to the UTC group. Interestingly, all of the 10 interventions with women only were group based, and all but one reported successful (>50%) adherence rates. Interventions may need to be designed specifically for women with chronic diseases to be more effective in addressing gender related issues in exercise adoption and maintenance, such as the importance of social support in sustaining behavior change.

Disease-type Differences

Type of chronic disease was also a factor in intervention effectiveness. Motivation to begin regular exercise may be hampered in some clinical populations, such as individuals suffering with arthritis who may fear that exercise would aggravate their symptoms.

Motivation to sustain exercise is difficult with little or no immediate benefits, yet the full benefits of physical activity on clinical outcomes will not be realized unless the patients are consistent with their exercise prescriptions. Interventions were less likely to be effective for patients with musculo-skeletal disorders (e.g., arthritis, fibromyalgia). These interventions focused on physical activity alone or in combination with lifestyle or patient education techniques, and might have been more effective with the inclusion of cognitive behavioral strategies (i.e., reinforcement, self-monitoring). For individuals reporting pain, the interventions that included physical activity and cognitive behavior modification in a group format (Alaranta et al., 1994; Friedrich et al., 1998; Haldorsen et al., 1998) were successful in increasing physical activity in the intervention compared to the control group. Lifestyle interventions were most common with patients suffering from CHD, while group based exercise programs were used with patients who had had MIs. For these two populations, interventions were typically time–intensive initially and contact tapered over weeks and months, and had generally good results after 1-year. This is hopeful considering that there is a 50% recidivism for cardiac rehabilitation patients within the first six-months (Burke et al., 1997). Treatments for patients who are obese included group programs using cognitive behavior therapy, and most began with an intense intervention 10 weeks to 6 months followed by a tapering of contacts.

Patient Motivation

Limited generalizability and inflated results may occur unintentionally when the subjects are highly motivated. Intensive lifestyle programs, such as the Primetime Program (Toobert et al., 1998; Toobert and Glasgow, 2000) with women and the Ornish Program (Ornish et al., 1998) with men involve a substantial time commitment from participants and family members, such as an initial week-long retreat with spouse/ significant other followed by twice-weekly 4 hour sessions for 3-months with an eventual fading of the intervention. These programs had a unique sample of individuals who were willing to make a substantial time commitment, and are likely different from most clinical populations. Although these programs are more extensive than other interventions presented in this chapter, a more intensive, comprehensive approach may be necessary for individuals at extremely high risk, and are certainly a more cost-effective alternative than coronary bypass surgery, aside from the additional quality of life benefits (Toobert et al., 1998).

The reports on adherence are also confounded by designs that include a screening period to reduce the enrollment of subjects more likely to drop out. For example, eligibility to enroll in the study conducted by Lee et al. (1996) was limited to potential participants who attended at least four of five 1-hour educational sessions during a 2-week screening period. This was also the case for the National Exercise and Heart Disease Project (Shaw, 1981), in which a preliminary prerandomization program was used to identify individuals who would not adhere to the study. Potential subjects participated in a 6-week, low-intensity exercise program, and men who attended less than 78% of the possible 18 sessions were excluded as likely nonadherers. The good adherence in these two studies after two years (Lee et al., 1996: 64%; Shaw 1981: 67%) may be inflated by prescreening and subsequent exclusion of subjects less likely to adhere to regular exercise.

Intervention Characteristics

The primary intervention in 15 studies was the exercise program itself. Adherence was compared between the group exercise intervention and UTC group or among exercise modes or prescriptions. Heinonen et al. (1998) reported better adherence after 18 months in initially sedentary women who participated in endurance training (80%) compared to a calisthenics (66%) group. Most studies that compared type of exercise, specifically lifestyle vs. structured exercise (Anderson et al., 1999; Dunn et al., 1999) and aerobic vs. resistance exercise (Ettinger et al., 1997) did not find differences in adherence or dropout as a function of exercise mode.

The most common type of exercise prescribed was moderate intensity aerobic exercise, such as walking. Walking has the attributes of being popular, feasible for most people, and safe in respect to risk of injury. Compliance to an exercise intervention prescribing walking was demonstrated 10 years later in older women (Pereira et al., 1998), although Martin and Sinden (2001), in their review of adherence rates in 21 randomized controlled trials conducted with older adults found better adherence to strength and flexibility exercise training programs than to aerobic programs. This may be specific to older adults who can experience significant improvements in activities of daily living and functional independence from strength training. For example, very good adherence at 1 year was reported by Aiello et al. (2004) in an study comparing strength training and stretching in older obese adults. For patients with other chronic diseases, moderate aerobic activities may provide physiological improvements relevant for their condition (i.e., increased work capacity in patients with CHD) that can reinforce continuing with regular exercise.

There were several different settings for the interventions. Interventions were provided through hospitals, universities, medical clinics, or research foundations and were implemented with groups or individuals. Programs were conducted on-site or were prescribed to be implemented at home. Length of intervention varied widely, from a single health promotion counseling session during a routine health exam to the comprehensive method that began with a week-long retreat for the patients and their spouses/ significant others (Ornish et al., 1998; Toobert et al., 1998; Toobert and Glasgow, 2000). Many interventions described lifestyle counseling in which exercise prescription was part of a much broader intervention including strategies such as diet and stress management to target disease-specific outcome variables (e.g., serum cholesterol levels, blood pressure). Studies that compared a home-based approach to traditional group or site-based interventions generally found better adherence for the home-based groups, as well as fewer dropouts (King et al., 1995; Perri et al. 1997; Strijbos et al., 1996). For example, Strijbos et al. (1996) reported better adherence as measured by exercise tolerance in a home-based compared to a hospital-based exercise intervention with COPD patients. Although improvements from the 12-wk intervention were maintained in both groups at 6 months, the hospital based group showed declines while the home-based group continued to improve exercise tolerance 18 months after the start of the program. The decline in physical activity after a hospital-based intervention at 1-yr follow-up may be the consequence of losing a structured source of motivation (Sullivan et al., 1998).

Strategies to help patients apply skills they have learned in an exercise intervention after it is over should be a component of any intervention. Subjects who have been exercising at a designated location and time with a group must make many adaptations to exercising on their own when the program is over, while the transition to self-regulated exercise is easier for those participating in a home-based program. Convenience, flexibility, and attention to and resolution of barriers during the intervention are other benefits of home-based programs. A home aerobic training program in patients with systemic rheumatic disease with 6-month follow-up only, however, did not find good adherence (Daltroy et al, 1995). Again, this may be related to the type of chronic disease and the reluctance of patients to exercise for fear of aggravation of symptoms. In these cases, more supervision and support, at least initially, may be necessary to enhance exercise adherence.

Perri et al. (1997) demonstrated how a group-based behavior change intervention in combination with home-based exercise could enhance exercise adherence. This study illustrates several of the characteristics of more successful interventions discussed in this chapter. Healthy overweight women between the ages of 40 and 60 were recruited and randomized to a behavioral weight loss treatment plus home-based exercise (n=24) or to a behavioral weight loss treatment plus group-based exercise (n=25). All subjects participated in a weekly cognitive-behavioral group weight loss intervention. Specific strategies included self-monitoring and stimulus control and focused on diet and exercise. Sessions lasted for 2-hours and were held weekly for 26 weeks. For the next 26 weeks, group behavior change sessions were held biweekly and focused on problem solving and ways to overcome barriers to maintaining changes in diet and exercise. All subjects were prescribed a progressive walking program of 30 min/day, five days a week. Those randomized to the group-based program were asked to sign up and complete exercise in the clinic facility in small groups of 2 to 7 for three days per week during the first 26 weeks and two days per week for the last 26 weeks of the study. Additional days per week outside of the group setting were prescribed to reach a target goal of 150 minutes per week. Group leaders were present during each exercise session. Those in the home-based group were instructed to complete the walking program in their home or work environment, and were given personal advice at each cognitive behavioral group session for integrating the walking program into their home and work routines. Over the year of the program, 7 subjects dropped out of the group-based condition and 2 dropped out of the home-based program, one who had become pregnant. The high retention of the home-based program compared to the group-based program is a strength of this type of intervention. Adherence to the exercise program as determined by exercise logs was also greater for the home-based group. The effects of the home-based program were more meaningful during the last 6 months of the study when adherence decreased for both groups, yet remained significantly higher for patients in the home-based group compared to those in the group-based program. Home-based and group-based exercise programs coupled with a group-based behavior change component are both effective during the early stages of exercise adoption, but the home-based programs demonstrate better maintenance of behavior change.

DISCUSSION

Qualitative and quantitative reviews support the effectiveness of cognitive-behavior modification strategies in changing physical activity behavior (Dubbert, 2002), and evidence reported here provides some support for these strategies with clinical groups. There is no single intervention that will work to increase exercise adherence in all clinical populations, but there are aspects of the interventions presented in this chapter that may increase the likelihood that patients will maintain regular exercise or sustain a more active lifestyle.
1. Interventions that were faded over several months seemed to facilitate patients' ability to develop independence from the intervention structure and to implement strategies for continuing to exercise on their own.
2. Home-based programs made the transition to exercising in the subjects' natural

environment without the intervention easier. However, it is important to begin with adequate supervision and instruction, and incorporate a period of some type of follow-up supportive contact.
3. Group-based interventions generally had better adherence than individual interventions.
4. Intervention programs that lasted longer (i.e., months instead of weeks) were more effective in producing long-term exercise adherence.

REMAINING RESEARCH QUESTIONS

There are several key issues and questions that should be addressed in future research on exercise adherence in clinical populations. Fundamentally, exercise adherence should be reported according to the proportion of the subjects who were exercising at the prescribed level or more at each measurement point. Studies should also include specific information about physical activity participation, such as the absolute amount of physical activity expressed in minutes per week according to intensity and mode. Common outcome variables will aid in efforts to compare interventions and determine the best methods for enhancing exercise adherence in clinical populations. Questions based on other issues discussed in this chapter include:
1. What is the optimal intervention "dosage?" The ideal frequency, pattern (intense, faded) and length of an exercise behavior change intervention has yet to be determined. Future research should strive to determine the frequency and duration of the intervention to maximize long-term adherence.
2. Are there specific intervention strategies that work better for males or females? More research studies on exercise adherence should include in their analyses comparisons between male and female subjects. Different determinants of exercise have been identified for males and females, and the results from the Activity Counseling Trial (2001) indicate that

different types of interventions work better for males and females. This needs to be tested in other clinical populations.

3. Do different clinical populations need different types of exercise interventions? More studies need to be conducted with specific clinical populations that may have lower adherence rates, such as patients with arthritis or those struggling with chronic pain. Additional studies should be conducted with other clinical groups, such as patients with diabetes, who could certainly benefit from exercise adoption and maintenance.

4. What are the mediators of exercise adherence in clinical populations? There is a growing body of literature on mediators of physical activity behavior change (e.g., Baranowski et al., 1998; Bauman et al., 2002; Calfas et al., 1997; Pinto et al., 2001). Some of the factors that have been consistently associated with physical activity in non-clinical populations include social support, motivation, self-efficacy, enjoyment, and behavioral skills (Bauman et al., 2002). Although few of these studies addressed potential mediators of exercise adherence in clinical populations, Minor and Brown (1993) found that exercise adherence in adults with arthritis was predicted by initial aerobic capacity, anxiety, depression, and previous exercise behavior. Stenström et al. (1997) found that dropout was predicted by baseline marital status (married), low physical activity, and low exercise self-efficacy. Interventions with specific clinical populations should target purported mediators of behavior change and test for mediation to guide future intervention development.

REFERENCES

Activity Counseling Trial (2001) Effects of physical activity counseling in primary care: the Activity Counseling Trial: a randomized controlled trial. JAMA 286:677-687.

Aiello EJ, Yasui Y, Tworoger SS, Ulrich CM, Irwin ML, Bowen D, Schwartz RS, Kumai C, Potter JD, McTiernan A (2004). Effect of a yearlong, moderate-intensity exercise intervention on the occurrence and severity of menopause symptoms in postmenopausal women. Menopause 11:382-388.

Alaranta H, Rytokoski U, Rissanen A, Talo S, Ronnemaa T, Puukka P, Karppi SL, Videman T, Kallio V, Slatis P. (1994) Intensive physical and psychosocial training program for patients with chronic low back pain. A controlled clinical trial. Spine 19:1339-1349.

Albright A, Franz M, Hornsby G, Kriska A, Marrero D, Ullrich I, Verity LS. (2000) American College of Sports Medicine position stand. Exercise and type 2 diabetes. Med Sci Sports Ex 32:1345-1360.

Anderson RE, Wadden TA, Bartlett SJ, Zemel B, Verde TJ, Franckowiak SC. (1999) Effects of lifestyle activity vs structured aerobic exercise in obese women: A randomized trial. JAMA 281:335-40.

Ashutosh K, Methrotra K, Fragale-Jackson J. (1997) Effects of sustained weight loss and exercise on aerobic fitness in obese women. J Sports Med Phys Fitness 37:252-257.

Baranowski T, Anderson C, Carmack C. (1998) Mediating variable framework in physical activity interventions: How are we doing? How might we do better? Am J Prev Med 15:266-297.

Bauman AE, Sallis JF, Dzewaltowski DA, Owen N. (2002) Toward a better understanding of the influences on physical activity: the role of determinants, correlates, causal variables, mediators, moderators, and confounders. Am J Prev Med 23:5-14.

Booth FW, Chakravarthy MV. (2002) Costs and consequences of sedentary living: new battleground for an old enemy.

President's Council on Physical Fitness and Sports: Research Digest 3:1-7.

Burke LE, Dunbar-Jacob, JM, Hill, MN (1997) Compliance with cardiovascular disease prevention strategies: a review of the research. Ann Behav Med 19: 239-263.

Calfas KJ, Sallis JF, Oldenburg B, Ffrench M. (1997) Mediators of change in physical activity following an intervention in primary care: PACE. Prev Med 26:297-304.

Campbell NC, Ritchie LD, Thain J, Deans HG, Rawles JM, Squair JL. (1998) Secondary prevention in coronary heart disease: a randomised trial of nurse led clinics in primary care. Heart 80:447-452.

Cupples ME McKnight A. (1994) Randomised controlled trial of health promotion in general practice for patients at high cardiovascular risk. BMJ 309:993-996.

Cupples ME McKnight A. (1999) Five year follow up of patients at high cardiovascular risk who took part in randomised controlled trial of health promotion. BMJ (Clinical Research Ed) 319:687-688.

Daltroy LH, Robb-Nicholson C, Iversen MD, Wright EA, Liang MH. (1995) Effectiveness of minimally supervised home aerobic training in patients with systemic rheumatic disease. British J Rheumatol 34:1064-1069.

Dishman RK Buckworth J. (1996) Increasing physical activity: a quantitative synthesis. Med Sci Sports Exerc 28:706-719.

Dishman RK, Washburn RA, Schoeller DA. (2001) Measurement of physical activity. Quest 53:295-309.

Dorn J, Naughton J, Imamura D, Trevisan M. (1999) Results of a multicenter romized clinical trial of exercise and long-term survival in myocardial infarction patients. The national exercise and heart disease project (NEHDP). Circulation 100:1764-9.

Dubbert PM. (2002) Physical activity exercise: recent advances and current challenges. J Consult Clin Psychol 70:526-536.

Dunn AL, Marcus BH, Kampert JB, Garcia ME, Kohl HW, Blair SN. (1999) Comparison of lifestyle and structured interventions to increase physical activity and cardiorespiratory fitness: a randomized trial. JAMA 281:327-334.

Elley CR, Kerse N, Arroll B, Robinson E (2003). Effectiveness of counselling patients on physical activity in general practice: cluster randomised controlled trial. BMJ 326:793.

Elmer PJ, Grimm RJ, Laing B, Grandits G, Svendsen K, Van H, Betz E, Raines J, Link M, Stamler J. (1995) Lifestyle intervention: results of the Treatment of Mild Hypertension Study (TOMHS). Prev Med 24:378-388.

Emery CF, Shermer RL, Hauck ER, Hsiao ET, MacIntyre NR (2003). Cognitive and psychological outcomes of exercise in a 1-year follow-up study of patients with chronic obstructive pulmonary disease. Health Psychol 22:598-604.

Ettinger WHJ, Burns R, Messier SP, Applegate W, Rejeski WJ, Morgan T, Shumaker S, Berry MJ, O'Toole M, Monu J, Craven T. (1997) A randomized trial comparing aerobic exercise and resistance exercise with a health education program in older adults with knee osteoarthritis. The Fitness Arthritis and Seniors Trial (FAST). JAMA 277:25-31.

Fletcher GF, Balady G, Blair SN, Blumenthal J, Caspersen C, Chaitman B, Epstein S, Sivarajan F, Froelicher VF, Pina IL, Pollock ML. (1996) Statement on exercise: benefits and recommendations for physical activity programs for all Americans. A statement for health professionals by the Committee on Exercise and

Cardiac Rehabilitation of the Council on Clinical Cardiology, American Heart Association. Circulation 94:857-862.

Fletcher GF, Blair SN, Blumenthal J, Casperson C, Chaitman B, Epstein S. (1992) Statement on exercise: benefits and recommendations for physical activity programs for all Americans. Circulation 86:340-344.

Friedrich M, Gittler G, Halberstadt Y, Cermak T, and Heiller I. (1998) Combined exercise and motivation program: effect on the compliance and level of disability of patients with chronic low back pain: a randomized controlled trial. Br Med J 79:475-487.

Fries JF, Carey C, McShane DJ. (1997) Patient education in arthritis: randomized controlled trial of a mail-delivered program. J Rheumatol 24:1378-1383.

Greenan-Fowler E, Powell C, Varni JW. (1987) Behavioral treatment of adherence to therapeutic exercise by children with hemophilia. BMJ 68:846-849.

Hagberg JM, Park JJ, Brown MD. (2000) The role of exercise training in the treatment of hypertension: an update. Sports Med 30:193-206.

Haldorsen EM, Kronholm K, Skouen JS, Ursin H. (1998) Multimodal cognitive behavioral treatment of patients sicklisted for musculoskeletal pain: a randomized controlled study. Scand J Rheumatol 27:16-25.

Harland J, White M, Drinkwater C, Chinn D, Farr L, Howel D. (1999) The Newcastle exercise program: A randomized controlled trial of methods to promote physical activity in primary care. Br Med J 319:828-32.

Heinonen A, Oja P, Sievanen H, Pasanen M, Vuori I. (1998) Effect of two training regimens on bone mineral density in healthy perimenopausal women: a randomized controlled trial. J Bone Miner Res 13:483-490.

Jeffery RW, Wing RR, Sherwood NE, Tate DF (2003). Physical activity and weight loss: does prescribing higher physical activity goals improve outcome? The American journal of clinical nutrition 78:684-689.

King AC, Haskell WL, Young DR, Oka RK, Stefanick ML. (1995) Long-term effects of varying intensities and formats of physical activity on participation rates, fitness, and lipoproteins in men and women aged 50 to 65 years. Circulation 91:2596-2604.

Kirkman MS, Weinberger M, Landsman PB, Samsa GP, Shortliffe EA, Simel DL, Feussner JR. (1994) A telephone-delivered intervention for patients with NIDDM. Effect on coronary risk factors. Diabetes Care 17:840-6.

Kriska AM, Bayles C, Cauley JA, LaPorte RE, Sandler RB, Pambianco G. (1986) A randomized exercise trial in older women: increased activity over two years and the factors associated with compliance. Med Sci Sports Ex 18:557-562

Lee JY, Jensen BE, Oberman A, Fletcher GF, Fletcher BJ, Raczynski JM. (1996) Adherence in the training levels comparison trial. Med Sci Sports Ex 28:47-52.

Lichtman SW, Pisarska K, Berman ER, Pestone M, Dowling H, Offenbacher E, Weisel H, Heshka S, Matthews DE, Heymsfield SB. (1992) Discrepancy between self-reported and actual caloric intake and exercise in obese subjects. New Eng J Med 327:1893-1898.

Lindstrom J, Louheranta A, Mannelin M, Rastas M, Salminen V, Eriksson J, Uusitupa M, Tuomilehto J (2003). The Finnish Diabetes Prevention Study (DPS): Lifestyle intervention and 3-year results on diet and physical activity. Diabetes Care 26:3230-3236.

Lorig KR, Sobel DS, Ritter PL, Laurent D, Hobbs M. (2001) Effect of a self-management program on patients with chronic disease. Eff Clin Pract 4:256-262.

Manchanda SC, Narang R, Reddy KS, Sachdeva U, Prabbakaran D, Dharmanand S, Rajani M, Bijlani R. (2000) Retardation of coronary atherosclerosis with yoga lifestyle intervention. J Assoc Physicians India 48:687-694.

Mannion AF, Muntener M, Taimela S, Dvorak J (2001). Comparison of three active therapies for chronic low back pain: results of a randomized clinical trial with one-year follow-up. Rheumatology 40:772-778.

Mellin L, Croughan-Minihane M, Dickey L. (1997) The Solution Method: 2-year trends in weight, blood pressure, exercise, depression, and functioning of adults trained in development skills. J Am Diet Assoc 97:1133-1138.

Minor MA and Brown JD. (1993) Exercise maintenance of persons with arthritis after participation in a class experience. Health Ed Q 20:83-95.

Murchie P, Campbell NC, Ritchie LD, Simpson JA, Thain J (2003). Secondary prevention clinics for coronary heart disease: four year follow up of a randomised controlled trial in primary care. BMJ 326:84.

Murray CJ, Lopez AD. (1999) On the comparable quantification of health risks: lessons from the Global Burden of Disease Study. Epidemiol (Cambridge Mass) 10:594-605.

Oldridge N, Guyatt G, Jones N, Crowe J, Singer J, Feeny D, McKelvie R, Runions J, Streiner D, Torrance G. (1991) Effects on quality of life with comprehensive rehabilitation after acute myocardial infarction. Am J Cardiol 67:1084-9.

Ornish D, Scherwitz LW, Billings JH, Gould KL, Merritt TA, Sparler S, Armstrong WT, Ports TA, Kirkeeide RL, Hogeboom C, Brand RJ. (1998) Intensive lifestyle changes for reversal of coronary heart disease. JAMA 280:2001-7

Painter PL, Hector L, Ray K, Lynes L, Dibble S, Paul SM, Tomlanovich SL, Ascher NL (2002). A randomized trial of exercise training after renal transplantation. Transplantation 74:42-48.

Perri MG, Martin AD, Leermakers EA, Sears SF. (1997) Effects of group versus home-based exercise in the treatment of obesity. J Consult Clin Psychol 65:278-285.

Petrella RJ, Koval JJ, Cunningham DA, Paterson DH (2003). Can primary care doctors prescribe exercise to improve fitness? The Step Test Exercise Prescription (STEP) project. Am J Prev Med 24:316-322.

Pinto BM, Lynn H, Marcus BH, DePue J, Goldstein MG. (2001) Physician-based activity counseling: intervention effects on mediators of motivational readiness for physical activity. Ann Beh Med 23:2-10.

Roddey TS, Olson SL, Gartsman GM, Hanten WP, Cook KF (2002). A randomized controlled trial comparing 2 instructional approaches to home exercise instruction following arthroscopic full-thickness rotator cuff repair surgery. The Journal of orthopaedic and sports physical therapy 32:548-559.

Rapoport L, Clark M, Wardle J. (2000) Evaluation of a modified cognitive-behavioural programme for weight management. Int J Obes Relat 24:1726-1737.

Rybarczyk B, DeMarco G, DeLaCruz M, Lapidos S, Fortner B. (2001) A classroom mind/body wellness intervention for older adults with chronic illness: comparing immediate and 1-year benefits. Behav Med 27:15-27.

Shaw LW. (1981) Effects of a prescribed supervised exercise program on mortality and cardiovascular morbidity in patients after myocardial infarction. The National Exercise and Heart Disease Project. Am J Cardiol 48:39-46.

Singh NA, Clements KM, Singh MA (2001). The efficacy of exercise as a long-term antidepressant in elderly subjects: a randomized, controlled trial. J Gerontology 56:M497-M504.

Ståhle A, Mattsson E, Ryden L, Unden AL, Nordlander R. (1999) Improved physical fitness and quality of life following training of elderly patients after acute coronary events - A 1 year follow-up randomized controlled study. Euro Heart J 20:1475-1484.

Stenström CH, Arge B, Sundbom A. (1997) Home exercise and compliance in inflammatory rheumatic diseases--a prospective clinical trial. J Rheumatol 24:470-476.

Steptoe A, Doherty S, Rink E, Kerry S, Kendrick T, Hilton S. (1999) Behavioural counselling in general practice for the promotion of healthy behaviour among adults at increased risk of coronary heart disease: randomised trial. BMJ (Clinical Research Ed) 319:943-947.

Steptoe A, Rink E, Kerry S. (2000) Psychosocial predictors of changes in physical activity in overweight sedentary adults following counseling in primary care. Prev Med 31:183-194.

Stern MJ, Gorman PA, Kaslow L. (1983) The group counseling v exercise therapy study. A controlled intervention with subjects following myocardial infarction. Arch Intern Med 143:1719-1725.

Strijbos JH, Postma DS, van A, Gimeno F, Koeter GH. (1996) A comparison between an outpatient hospital-based pulmonary rehabilitation program and a home-care pulmonary rehabilitation program in patients with COPD. A follow-up of 18 months. Chest 109:366-372.

Sullivan T, Allegrante JP, Peterson MG, Kovar PA, MacKenzie CR. (1998) One-year followup of patients with osteoarthritis of the knee who participated in a program of supervised fitness walking and supportive patient education. Arthritis Care Res 11:228-233.

Toobert DJ, Glasgow RE, Nettekoven LA, Brown JE. (1998) Behavioral and psychosocial effects of intensive lifestyle management for women with coronary heart disease. Patient Educ Couns 35:177-188.

Toobert DJ, Glasgow RE. (2000) Physiologic and related behavioral outcomes from the women's lifestyle heart trial. Ann Beh Med 22:1-9.

Turner CH, Robling AG. (2003) Designing exercise regimens to increase bone strength. Exerc Sport Sci Rev 31:45-50.

U.S. Department of Health and Human Services. (1996) Physical activity and health: A report of the surgeon general. U.S. Depart. of Health and Human Services, Centers for Disease Control and Prevention, National Center for Chronic Disease Prevention and Health Promotion, Atlanta, GA.

Westby MD, Wade JP, Rangno KK, Berkowitz J. (2000) A randomized controlled trial to evaluate the effectiveness of an exercise program in women with rheumatoid arthritis taking low dose prednisone. J Rheumatol 27:1674-80.

Wigers SH, Stiles TC, Vogel PA. (1996) Effects of aerobic exercise versus stress management treatment in fibromyalgia. A 4.5 year prospective study. Scand J Rheumatol 25:77-86.

Wing RR, Venditti E, Jakicic JM, Polley BA, Lang W. (1998) Lifestyle intervention in overweight individuals with a family history of diabetes. Diabetes Care 21:350-359.

Wylie-Rosett J, Swencionis C, Ginsberg M, Cimino C, Wassertheil-Smoller S, Caban A, Segal-Isaacson CJ, Martin T, Lewis J (2001). Computerized weight loss intervention optimizes staff time: the clinical and cost results of a controlled clinical trial conducted in a managed care setting. J Am Diet Assoc 101:1155-1162.

BEHAVIORAL MANAGEMENT OF OSTEOPOROSIS

Deborah T. Gold and Jane G. Hertel

INTRODUCTION

Osteoporosis, a chronic metabolic bone disease, results in weakened or porous bone. Over 44 million Americans are currently affected by this disease; approximately 10 million already have osteoporosis while 34 million are at high risk and have osteopenia or low bone mass (US Department of Health and Human Services, 2004). This number is expected to increase to 64 million by 2015 (National Osteoporosis Foundation, 2002). Each year, Americans suffer over 1.5 million fractures, 700,000 of which are of the spine and 250,000 of which are of the hip (National Institutes of Health, 2000). As the population has aged, the prevalence of osteoporosis has risen, and this trend will continue over the 21st century. Osteoporosis has no cure, although pharmaceutical treatments are available.

Osteoporosis is called "a silent disease" by many health care professionals because bone loss and spinal fractures can occur without signs or symptoms. Vertebral fractures are especially likely to go unrecognized because either they are not painful, or patients attribute the pain to osteoarthritis or aging (Old & Calvert, 2004). This results in late diagnosis and treatment of bone loss. Yet, even when vertebral fractures are silent, the accumulation of fractures leads to complex negative outcomes including chronic pain and deformity. Because vertebral fractures are often silent, health care professionals may not recognize the importance and negative sequelae of multiple vertebral deformities. On the other hand, hip fractures have been recognized as having more impact than other fractures, perhaps in part because they tend to occur with increasing age. About half of people who have hip

fractures this year will never walk unaided again, and about 33% will become dependent on others for assistance with activities of daily living including dressing, toileting, and transferring. In short, hip fractures cause substantial excess morbidity and mortality globally (Johnell & Kanis, 2004). Further, the annual cost of osteoporosis in the US is staggering. Nearly $18 billion per year is spent on direct medical costs. However, the indirect costs (such as lost wages and the high cost of assistance at home) may be even higher, with some investigators estimating the total annual costs of osteoporosis in the US to be on the order of $50 billion (Melton, 2003).

However, the most distressing negative outcome of both hip and vertebral fractures is the contribution to excess mortality (Rutledge et al., 2003; Richmond et al., 2003). Between 5-40% of people with hip fractures die within 12 months, with men more likely to die than women (Fransen et al., 2002). The rate of excess mortality for vertebral fractures appears to be similar to that of hip fractures (e.g., Cauley et al., 2000). The exceptionally high levels of morbidity and mortality from osteoporotic fractures represent a serious public health problem, and the Surgeon General of the United States has recently issued the first Surgeon General's Report on Bone Health and Osteoporosis (US Department of Health and Human Services, 2004). In it, the Surgeon General wrote, "A coordinated public health approach that brings together a variety of public and private sector stakeholders in a collaborative effort is the most promising strategy for improving the bone health of Americans" (p. vi). Because osteoporosis has been on the radar screens of physicians for a relatively short time, a well developed portfolio of behavioral interventions has not yet been developed.

Osteoporosis is frequently regarded as a pediatric disease with geriatric consequences; that is, prevention needs to start early in life with appropriate calcium and vitamin D, weight bearing and strength training exercise, and the avoidance of poor health behaviors including smoking and drinking alcohol in excess. Most research, however, has been performed with postmenopausal women, with a few recent studies including men. The fact that we know little about the behaviors of childhood and adolescence that could protect bone health is indication that more research is essential.

Bone mineral density (BMD) measurement and fractures

The clinically meaningful outcomes of osteoporosis are fractures, principally of the wrist, hip and spine. Fractures cause deformity, chronic pain; functional and social limitations; and result in anxiety and depression (Gold, 2003). Thus, the ultimate goal of any osteoporosis intervention is to prevent fractures. Because people with significant loss of bone density are at a high risk of fracture, developing diagnostic tools to measure bone density has been critical to managing the disease process. Traditional radiographs could identify bone loss but only when it was severe. The gold standard for bone mineral density measurement known as dual-energy x-ray absorptiometry (DXA) was developed in the late 1980s (Kelly et al., 1998). DXA was the first major diagnostic breakthrough and allowed physicians to determine current bone mineral density without waiting for fractures to occur.

Pharmacological intervention for bone density loss

The second major challenge in the management of osteoporosis was, until recently, the absence of pharmaceutical agents able to prevent bone density loss and fractures. Two antiresorptive hormonal agents—calcitonin and estrogen—were used to treat osteoporosis in the 1960s, and sodium fluoride was used in the 1980s on an experimental basis. However, it was not until 1995 that the first bisphosphonate alendronate (a non-hormone-based antiresorptive) was approved by the FDA for the prevention and treatment of postmenopausal osteoporosis. Thereaafter, two other bisphosphonates—risedronate and ibandronate—have also been approved for these indications (Hanset & Vondracek, 2004). Another antiresorptive followed, belonging to the class of drugs called selective estrogen receptor modulators or SERMs (e.g., raloxifene) for the prevention and treatment of postmenopausal osteoporosis (Hanset & Vondracek, 2004). In 2004, a new type of pharmaceutical therapy that promotes bone formation instead of reducing bone resorption was approved by the FDA. Parathyroid hormone or teriparatide became available for the treatment of severe postmenopausal osteoporosis and fractures (Hanset & Vondracek, 2004). The development of these medications opened the way for health care professionals to first treat osteoporosis following the medical model and then to use a biopsychosocial paradigm to design and implement behavioral interventions to improve bone health. Other medications are in the pipeline and should further enhance the ability to minimize bone loss and build new bone. However, most health care professionals believe that behavioral changes must accompany a prescription for anti-resorptive or anabolic agents in the management of osteoporosis. Without fundamental behavioral modifications including maintaining sufficient calcium and vitamin D, engaging in weight-bearing and strength-training exercise, avoiding poor health habits, and complying with medication regimens, osteoporosis patients will be unable to successfully manage their chronic illness. Next, we review clinical trials investigating interventions to encourage these behavioral modifications and make recommendations for current clinical practice and future research.

BEHAVIORAL INTERVENTIONS

The primary goals of behavioral interventions for osteoporosis are to prevent fractures and improve bone health. Several important behavioral changes can help individuals achieve the desired outcome of improved bone density and reduced fractures: 1) appropriate intake of calcium and vitamin D; 2) regular and appropriate exercise; 3) avoidance of falls; 4) use of hip protectors to prevent hip fracture in the frail elderly, especially those living in nursing homes; and 5) long-term medication adherence for patients prescribed medication therapies for osteoporosis. In addition, behavioral interventions addressing the social and psychological consequences of this disease should have a central position in the armamentarium of those health care professionals who help patients manage osteoporosis. Below, each of these areas is addressed, and relevant literature is reviewed. Diagnosis and treatment of osteoporosis are relatively new phenomenon in medicine, having existed for just over a decade and therefore, behavioral interventions for osteoporosis have not been studied to as great an extent as interventions for other disorders.

Calcium and vitamin D intake

Calcium is essential for muscle and nerve function. Calcium also facilitates blood clotting and is the key mineral essential for bone health. Calcium must be provided for the body regularly for metabolism; if not, it must be taken from storage (i.e., the skeleton). Long-term depletion of skeletal calcium leads to bones that are weaker and more likely to fracture (US Department of Health and Human Services, 2004).

Calcium alone is not sufficient to prevent or treat osteoporosis. Vitamin D is also crucial to the entire process of bone remodeling. Vitamin D promotes calcium absorption and enables the body to utilize the calcium (DeLuca, 2004). Thus, an important behavior necessary for good bone health is to ingest sufficient calcium and vitamin D to maintain strong bones. The pharmaceutical agents now used to prevent and treat osteoporosis cannot work as effectively in the absence of calcium and vitamin D. Further, vitamin D and calcitriol also reduce the risk of falls, a major cause of fractures in late life (Gallagher, 2004). Randomized controlled trials have indicated that increasing calcium and vitamin D consumption improves bone density (Dawson-Hughes et al., 1990; Reid et al., 1993; Elders et al., 1994; Dawson-Hughes et al., 1997) and reduces fractures (Chapuy et al., 1992; Recker et al., 1996; Cumming & Nevitt, 1997), even in the absence of pharmaceutical intervention. But compliance with calcium and vitamin D supplementation is not reliable, and few randomized controlled studies have attempted to change calcium and vitamin D compliance through behavioral interventions (Tussing & Chapman-Novakofski, 2005).

An early observational study by Sedlak and colleagues (2000) evaluated the impact of three interventions designed to increase knowledge about osteoporosis and to change three osteoporosis-related behaviors: improving calcium intake, increasing weight-bearing exercise, and reducing caffeine intake. The groups differed mainly in the intensity and length of the educational experience: intense (3 sessions over 3 weeks), intermediate (one three-hour meeting), and brief (a 45-minute session). Unfortunately, participants were not randomly assigned to groups, nor was effort made to established respondent comparability across groups. All three groups showed increased knowledge at intervention's end when compared to baseline knowledge ($p \leq 0.01$ for all groups). However, when behavioral changes were measured 3 weeks after the study, only one behavior had significantly changed (reduction in caffeine intake, $p < 0.05$) and in only one group (the intense intervention group). These findings support the conclusion that changes in knowledge cannot be assumed to translate into behavioral changes.

Another study by Blalock and colleagues (Blalock et al., 2000) tested an educational intervention for osteoporosis designed for premenopausal women, using Prochaska's stages of change model as its theoretical base (Prochaska & Velicer, 1997). Participants were identified through the use of North Carolina driver's license records, and those who agreed to participate received a brief description of osteoporosis and calcium and exercise guidelines. They were then randomized into four groups. Group One received no packet. Group Two received an information packet. Group Three received an action plan packet. Group Four received both the information and action plan packets. Overall, having received the information packet (Groups Two and Four) was associated with changes in beliefs and knowledge about osteoporosis, regardless of individual's stage of change ($F[18,283] = 2.11$, $p < .01$). However, changed knowledge and beliefs did not translate into changed behavior. Only 307 women completed the study, a sample size that limited the ability to complete more complicated data analysis. Although knowledge was significantly changed, no increase in calcium intake or exercise were observed.

A more recent randomized controlled trial was completed by Wong and colleagues (Wong et al., 2004) to determine the effectiveness of nutritional counseling in increasing dietary calcium, protein, and caloric intake. One hundred and eighty-nine orthopedic patients with fractures at a large Hong Kong hospital were randomized. Ninety-eight patients received 3 sessions of dietary counseling as well as tailored recommendations; the other 91 patients, the control group, received usual care (pamphlets and a dietary assessment). After 4 months, the intervention group showed a significant increase in calcium intake ($p= 0.0095$ by t-test) but had no other significant changes. These findings suggest that dietary counseling can significantly improve dietary intake of calcium. In this study, positive changes in behavior resulted from a nutritional intervention.

Exercise

Exercise has been the bedrock of osteoporosis prevention, treatment, and management. Fundamentally, bone cannot remodel sufficiently (i.e., elimination of old bone and the addition of healthy bone) in the absence of exercise. Both weight-bearing and strength-training exercise are important components of any regimen designed to improve skeletal health. This has been known since Galileo first noted that there was a relationship between mechanical stress and bone mass; This finding was supported by the German anatomist Julius Wolff who found that mechanical stresses influenced bone strength (Todd & Robinson, 2000). But researchers have also learned that strength or resistance training is also essential for promoting good bone health and reducing falls (Hurley & Roth, 2000).

Most randomized controlled trials of exercise for people with osteoporosis have studied increased bone mineral density (BMD) as the primary or only outcome. Using BMD as the primary outcome is somewhat problematic given the concern that risk of falls and fractures may be greater during exercise sessions and the fact that fractures are the main cause of osteoporosis-related disability. Most exercise studies have been conducted with healthy premenopausal women, healthy postmenopausal women, and women with osteoporosis. Some of the more recent studies include men as well. For example, Vainionpaa and colleagues (Vainionpaa et al., 2005) randomized 120 healthy premenopausal women into a high-impact exercise group or a control group. After supervised exercise and a 12-month home program, they found that BMD in the exercise group was significantly greater in the hip and spine than it was in the control group. BMD was also significantly increased when compared with the exercise groups baseline levels (p=0.033, p=0.006, p=0.002, p=0.015 at various hip and spine sites). In a similar study with osteopenic postmenopausal women, Kemmler and others (Kemmler et al., 2003) studied early postmenopausal women who were osteopenic by DXA score to see if a vigorous combined high-impact, strength, and endurance exercise program could increase bone density. After 14 months of exercise training, the exercise group (n=59) increased lumbar spine BMD significantly while the control group (n=41) decreased lumbar spine BMD significantly. Differences in the hip were non-significant. High intensity exercise training seems to have positive bone density outcomes in postmenopausal osteopenic women.

Exercise trials of postmenopausal women with osteoporosis are somewhat harder to find, perhaps because the risk of fracture during the intervention is high. One trial by Yamazaki and colleagues (Yamazaki et al., 2004) tested the impact of walking exercise on bone metabolism in postmenopausal women with bone loss. Of the 50 women recruited for this study, 32 entered the exercise group (daily outdoor walking 4 times per week over 12 months) and 18 were controls who did not walk. Although there were no between-group differences in lumbar

spine BMD shown at either 6 or 12 months, the 12 month BMD measurements for the exercise group were higher than baseline. Although, as expected, the exercise group increased lumbar BMD while the control group decreased lumbar BMD, these changes from baseline were not significant in either group. In addition to bone density, urinary cross-linked N-terminal telopeptides of type I collagen (NTX) levels, a measure of bone turnover, were measured in both groups at baseline, 6 and 12 months. There was no significant correlation between bone turnover markers and BMD.

Many other randomized clinical trials have indicated that weight-bearing exercise can increase BMD in various populations, including young women and boys (Nurmi-Lawton et al,, 2004; Turner & Robling, 2005; Mein et al., 2004; MacKelvie et al., 2004) Although sample sizes are relatively small, there are some randomized controlled trials examining exercise in postmenopausal women with already reduced bone density. In a study of resistance training with older women who already had low bone mass, Liu-Ambrose and others (Liu-Ambrose et al., 2004) compared effects of resistance and agility training on BMD. They randomized 98 women, 75 to 85 years old, into one of three experimental groups: resistance training (n=32), agility training (n=34) or sham exercise (n=32). They measured total hip, femoral neck, and trochanteric BMD by DXA; peripheral quantitative computer tomography (pQCT) measurements were taken at the tibia and radius. Only 2 significant outcomes were detected at follow up 25 weeks later. The agility group had significantly increased cortical BMD at the shaft of the tibia when compared to loss in the sham exercise group (p=0.033). In addition, the resistance group showed increased cortical BMD at the radial shaft while the agility group showed a loss at this site (p=0.05). Neither the DXA or pQCT measures identified any additional significant differences between the groups. This finding is especially important in that it challenges previous beliefs about cortical bone not being as responsive as trabecular bone in terms of mechanical stimulation in aging skeletons. In this study cortical bone showed increased density with resistance exercise.

Despite the challenges of using frankly osteoporotic subjects in clinical trials of exercise (i.e., concern about adverse events), it will be virtually impossible to fully understand the role of exercise in the treatment and management of this disease unless this population is studied. Future studies should test exercise interventions in this at risk population and evaluate overall effects on fractures, disability and quality of life. Exercise effectively increases BMD when it is conducted regularly. However, more research is needed on interventions to get patients to exercise consistently over the long-term (see chapter 16), the type of exercise that is most appropriate for at risk patients, and the impact of exercise on fracture rate, disability and quality of life.

Avoiding falls

Falls increase risk of fractures in people with fragile bones, with older patients at greatest risk. The most dreaded outcome of falls is hip fracture, the cause of an inordinate proportion of institutional placements for older adults. In fact, Nyberg and colleagues (Nyberg et al., 1996) showed that approximately 95% of hip fractures are caused by falls. Thus, a reduction in falls should translate into a reduction in hip and other fractures as well. Then in 2000, Steinberg and colleagues (Steinberg et al., 2000) tested multiple fall-prevention interventions with community dwelling elders. Group #1 (n=63) participated in only an information session (usual care) and was considered the control group. Group #2 (n=69) received the same information and had a once-monthly exercise class. For Group #3 (n=61), researchers added a home safety assessment to the previous interventions. And finally, Group #4 (n=59) had these three interventions plus a clinical assessment and advice on medical risk factors for falls. Hazard ratios showed that Groups 2-4 had reductions in negative outcomes when compared with usual care. Outcomes were defined as slips, trips, and falls. There was a 58% reduction in the risk of slips, a 64% reduction in the risk of trips, and a 30% reduction in the risk of falls. However, because studies have not consistently shown that such fall prevention programs with community-dwelling elders prevent hip fractures, policymakers are generally unwilling to continue to support them.

Fall prevention interventions in nursing homes have different challenges, but there is no clear evidence to suggest that they are more successful than interventions done in the community. In a review of this literature in 2004, Vu, Weintraub, and Rubenstein (Vu et al., 2004) found mixed results in the long-term care groups. However, some interventions were successful at reducing falls in institutions. For example, Becker and colleagues (Becker et al., 2003) studied 981 residents in six community nursing homes in Germany. Residents were 60 years and older, and 79% of the sample was female. The six sites were randomized to intervention and control status. Research staff measured medical conditions, risk factors for falls, and functional status of all residents. In the intervention sites, staff and residents received various educational options on the causes and consequences of falls. Residents could choose those educational options in which they were interested; their choices included written information on fall prevention, hip protectors, environmental adaptations, and exercises. After follow up measures of risks, medical conditions, and functional status, the researchers found that the intervention group had a significantly reduced number of falls (RR: 0.55, 95% CI: 0.41–0.73). Unfortunately, the study was not powered to detect differences in the number of hip fractures, nor was there a statistically significant difference in time to first fall in the first 6 months.

The literature is replete with fall prevention interventions tested in randomized controlled trials (e.g., Suzuki et al., 2004a; Suzuki et al,, 2004b; Sze et al., 2005). Virtually all suggest some environmental changes that can make homes safer (e.g., good lighting, grab bars, non-slip mats in bathrooms). But few of these fall prevention randomized controlled trials examined secondary or tertiary prevention of osteoporotic fractures. Despite the fact that those who already have this disease are more likely to sustain a fracture from a fall, only a few of these studies have included women with osteoporosis or low bone mass.

We must not forget that the emotional consequences of falls and hip fractures are also substantial (Jorstad et al., 2005). For example, Salkeld and colleagues (Salkeld et al., 2000) embedded a quality of life survey using the time trade off technique in the context of a randomized controlled trial of hip protectors. They surveyed 194 women age 75 and older who refused to participate in a face-to-face quality of life interview, asking them to first rate the quality of their own health and then to rate three health states (fear of falling, a "good" hip fracture, and a "bad" hip fracture) using time trade offs. Eighty percent of these women chose death (utility of 0) over the loss of independence and quality of life that results from a bad hip fracture and ultimate institutionalization. These women also indicated that this scenario (bad hip fracture and nursing home placement) was less desirable than myocardial infarction or breast cancer. In other words, women who have lived beyond average life expectancy, felt that their quality of life was severely jeopardized by falls and hip fractures.

Hip protectors

Another available strategy does not prevent falls per se but can minimize fractures resulting from those falls, namely the use of hip protectors. These have always been seen as potentially most important for institutionalized elderly patients. Singh and colleagues (Singh et al., 2004) conducted a cost-effectiveness study of hip protectors by comparing three groups of institutionalized patients: (1) those using hip protectors; (2) those taking only calcium and vitamin D, and (3) those with no intervention. They found that hip protectors could save money and prevent fractures as long as they were used. Thus, compliance is a serious concern here and may be the principle reason that data on the effectiveness of hip protectors has not encouraged their use in real-life settings.

In an evidence-based review of 15 randomized controlled trials on the use of hip protectors to determine whether they do prevent hip fractures, Parker, Gillespie, and Gillespie (Parker et al., 2003) found, using pooled data from the 11 trials in nursing homes or other residential care settings, a marginally statistically significant reduction in hip fractures for those patients who wore hip protectors (relative risk (RR) 0.77, 95% confidence interval (CI) 0.62 to 0.97). The pooled data from the studies of community-dwelling older adults showed no reduction in the incidence of hip fractures in this population (relative risk (RR) 0.96, 95% confidence interval (CI) 0.54 to 1.69). Therefore, the real-world effectiveness of hip protectors remains ambiguous but in appropriate settings, hip protectors can reduce hip fractures in patients who consistently use them. The authors also comment that acceptance and adherence with hip protectors were both poor. Interventions that improve the acceptance of or adherence to hip protector use might improve outcomes with these devices.

Medication Adherence

The availability of effective medications for the prevention or management of osteoporosis raises the critical issue of medication adherence. Adherence has been well studied in other chronic disease states such as diabetes (Vermeire et al., 2005; Du Pasquier-Fediaevsky et al., 2005). A substantial literature has also been built with other "silent" chronic diseases such as hypertension (Domino, 2005; Chapman et al., 2005) and hypercholesterolemia (Burke et al., 2005; Stilley et al., 2004). Studies of medication adherence in patients across disorders are reviewed in Chapter 14, and it is assumed that effective interventions identified in this chapter may be translated to improve adherence with medication for osteoporosis. Thus far, the bulk of the adherence literature specific for osteoporosis medication has used US retail pharmacy databases' information about prescription refills to estimate adherence (Recker et al., 2005), large prospectively collected data sets (Papaioannou et al., 2003), and non-randomized studies (Turbi et al., 2004; Segal et al., 2003). The design limitations of these studies reduce the ability to generalize from them.

In one of the few randomized controlled trials of medication adherence and osteoporosis, Clowes and colleagues (Clowes et al., 2004) tested whether three monitoring interventions would improve adherence with osteoporosis medication. They randomized 75 postmenopausal women with osteopenia into one of three groups: no monitoring (usual care), nurse monitoring (attention), or marker monitoring (attention plus information on response). Adherence was measured using electronic monitoring devices that measured the date and frequency of opening the bottle; subjects did not know that there was an electric monitoring device. Adherence was increased in the monitoring groups by 57% over the no monitoring group. However, there were no significant differences between the nurse monitoring and marker monitoring groups, suggesting that simply knowing response to therapy does not make a difference in adherence. However, in *post hoc* analyses, subjects who were told they had good responses to therapy were 92% more likely to be adherent than were those in usual care. This suggests that the additional monitoring and the opportunity to ask questions may have had an impact on adherence. Contrary to their hypotheses, these researchers found that there was no increased adherence in the marker monitoring group over the nurse monitoring group. Unfortunately, the sample size was too small for more specific analyses.

DISCUSSION

As noted earlier, osteoporosis is a relatively "young" disease because the necessary technology to diagnose the disease and appropriate pharmaceutical interventions have only been recently identified. Having reliable diagnostic and treatment methods is becoming more essential as the population of the United States ages. There is clearly an association between age and bone density. If today's adolescents and young adults remain unaware of preventive actions to maintain bone health, the incidence of fractures and the costs of osteoporosis may continue to increase. Those costs are manifest in two distinct forms: the actual dollars that are spent on direct healthcare costs and the human capital that is expended on the part of family caregivers, support group members, friends, and others whose challenge is to help those afflicted with osteoporosis maintain the best possible quality of life. The dollar costs are relatively easily measured, especially for hip fractures; human capital is much more difficult to quantify. But just as we must learn about the physical outcomes associated with this disease, so too must we ascertain how the psychosocial outcomes are influenced and what we can do to improve behavioral interventions that reduce anxiety, prevent and treat depression, reintegrate fracture victims into their work or family world, and sustain important social relationships.

Isolated behavioral changes do little to prevent or manage the real problems associated with osteoporosis: fractures. As they attempt to determine what factors increase the risk of fractures, researchers are going beyond the relatively simplistic explanation of bone mineral density and focusing on such issues as bone quality and bone strength. However, improving the effectiveness of current therapies is not as much dependent on the microarchitecture of bone as it is on the behavior of those at risk of or who have clinically significant bone loss. The behaviors discussed above-using appropriate osteoporosis-specific pharmacotherapies, taking calcium and vitamin D, engaging in exercise, and avoiding falls—are essential to preventing or minimizing bone loss and fractures. Their impact is synergistic; outcomes from the combined use of these therapies are substantially more effective than those which result from the use of any therapy alone. For example, the bisphosphonates, powerful anti-resorptive therapies that can minimize bone loss, cannot work at peak effectiveness without calcium and vitamin D. Taking medicines or exercising without also using calcium and vitamin D is tantamount to trying to build a wall without bricks. Thus, persons interested in good bone health must incorporate all the strategies to reap the maximum bone rewards.

CONCLUSION

Substantial evidence exists that behavioral interventions can improve many outcomes for people with osteoporosis and fractures. Behavioral interventions have also been designed for primary prevention of osteoporosis. All of these interventions need additional research, and certain areas, such as adherence to medications and other treatments, are only beginning to be published. However, projections of the increasing incidence and prevalence of osteoporosis and fractures makes this research compelling: by 2020, 61,400,000 men and women in the US are estimated to have low bone mass or osteoporosis (National Osteoporosis Foundation, 2002). If effective behavioral interventions to prevent and treat osteoporosis can be implemented soon, the actual numbers may be substantially reduced.

At this point, it is clear that calcium and vitamin D supplementation, exercise, and osteoporosis medications can improve bone density when regimens are closely followed. While research on the best interventions to encourage these behaviors in patients with osteoporosis is in its infancy, a substantial body of research has been conducted to identify effective interventions for increasing exercise and medication adherence in other populations (see chapters 16 and 14 respectively). Until adequate research on behavioral interventions for osteoporosis is conducted, guidance on improving these behaviors must be borrowed from studies of other patient populations.

REFERENCES

Becker C, Kron M, Lindemann U, Sturm E, Eichner B, Walter-Jung B, Nikolaus T. (2003) Effectiveness of a multifaceted intervention on falls in nursing home residents J Am Geriatrics Soc 51(3):306

13.

Blalock SJ, Currey SS, DeVellis RF, DeVellis BM, Giorgino KB, Anderson JJB, Dooley MA, Gold DT. (2000) Effects of educational materials concerning osteoporosis on women's knowledge, beliefs, and behavior. Am J Health Promotion 14: 161-169.

Burke LE, Dunbar-Jacob J, Orchard TJ, Sereika SM. (2005) Improving adherence to a cholesterol-lowering diet: a behavioral intervention study. Patient Education Counsel 57(1):134-42.

Cauley JA, Thompson DE, Ensrud KC, Scott JC, Black D. (2000) Risk of mortality following clinical fractures. Osteoporosis International 11(7):556-61.

Chapman RH, Benner JS, Petrilla AA, Tierce JC, Collins SR, Battleman DS, Schwartz JS. (2005) Predictors of adherence with antihypertensive and lipid-lowering therapy. Arch Internal Med 165(10):1147-52.

Chapuy MC, Arlot ME, Duboeuf F, Brun J, Crouzet B, Arnaud S, Delmas PD, Meunier PJ. (1992) Vitamin D3 and calcium to prevent hip fractures in the elderly women. New Engl J Med 327(23): 1637-42.

Clowes JA, Peel NF, Eastell R. (2004) The impact of monitoring on adherence and persistence with antiresorptive treatment for postmenopausal osteoporosis: a randomized controlled trial. J Clin Endocrinol Metabolism 89(3):1117-23.

Cumming RG, Nevitt MC. (1997) Calcium for prevention of osteoporotic fractures in postmenopausal women. J Bone Mineral Res 12(9):1321-9.

Dawson-Hughes B, Dallal GE, Krall EA, Sadowski L, Sahyoun N, Tannenbaum S. (1990) A controlled trial of the effect of calcium supplementation on bone density in postmenopausal women. New Engl J Med 323:878-883.

Dawson-Hughes B, Harris SS, Krall EA, Dallal GE. (1997) Effect of calcium and vitamin D supplementation on bone density in men and women 65 years of age or older. New Engl J Med 337(10): 670-6.

DeLuca HF. (2004) Overview of general physiologic features and functions of vitamin D. Am J Clin Nutrition. 80(6 Suppl):1689S-96S.

Domino FJ. (2005) Improving adherence to treatment for hypertension. Am Fam Physician 71(11):2089-90.

Du Pasquier-Fediaevsky L, Chwalow AJ, Tubiana-Rufi N, PEDIAB Collaborative Group. (2005) Is the relationship between adherence behaviours and glycaemic control bi-directional at adolescence? A longitudinal cohort study. Diabetic Med 22(4):427-33.

Elders PJ, Lips P, Netelenbos JC, van Ginkel FC, Khoe E, van der Vijgh WJ, van der Stelt PF. (1994) Long-term effect of calcium supplementation on bone loss in perimenopausal women. J Bone Mineral Res 9(7):963-70.

Fransen M, Woodward M, Norton R, Robinson E, Butler M, Campbell AJ. (2002) Excess mortality or institutionalization after hip fracture: men are at greater risk than women. J Amer Geriatr Soc 50(4): 685-90.

Gallagher JC. (2004) The effects of calcitriol on falls and fractures and physical performance tests. J Steroid Biochem Molecular Biol 89-90(1-5):497-501.

Gold DT. (2003) Osteoporosis and quality of life: psychosocial outcomes and interventions for individual patients. Clin Geriatric Med 19: 271-280.

Hansen LB, Vondracek SF. (2004) Prevention and treatment of nonpostmenopausal osteoporosis. Amer J Health-System

Pharmacy 61(24):2637-54.

Hurley BF, Roth SM. (2000) Strength training in the elderly: effects on risk factors for age-related diseases. Sports Medicine 30(4):249-68.

Johnell O, Kanis JA. (2004) An estimate of the worldwide prevalence, mortality and disability associated with hip fracture. Osteoporosis Int 15(11):897-902.

Jorstad EC, Hauer K, Becker C, Lamb S, on behalf of the ProFaNE Group. (2005) Measuring the Psychological Outcomes of Falling: A Systematic Review. J Am Geriatrics Soc 53(3):501-510.

Kelly TL, Slovik DM, Schoenfeld DA, Neer RM. (1998) Quantitative digital radiography versus dual photon absorptionmetry of the lumbar spine. J Clin Endocrinol Metab 67: 839.

Kemmler W, Engelke K, Weineck J, Hensen J, Kalender WA. (2003) The Erlangen Fitness Osteoporosis Prevention Study: a controlled exercise trial in early postmenopausal women with low bone density-first-year results. Arch Phys Med Rehab 84(5):673-82.

Liu-Ambrose TY, Khan KM, Eng JJ, Heinonen A, McKay HA. (2004) Both resistance and agility training increase cortical bone density in 75-to 85-year-old women with low bone mass: a 6-month randomized controlled trial. J Clin Densitometr 7(4):390-8.

MacKelvie KJ, Petit MA, Khan KM, Beck TJ, McKay HA. (2004) Bone mass and structure are enhanced following a 2-year randomized controlled trial of exercise in prepubertal boys. Bone 34(4):755-64.

Mein AL, Briffa NK, Dhaliwal SS, Price RI. (2004) Lifestyle influences on 9-year changes in BMD in young women. J Bone Mineral Res 19(7):1092-8.

Melton LJ 3rd. (2003) Adverse outcomes of osteoporotic fractures in the general population. J Bone Mineral Res 18(6): 1139-41.

National Institutes of Health. (2000) Osteoporosis prevention, diagnosis, and therapy. Consensus Statement. Bethesda, MD: National Institutes of Health 17:1-36.

National Osteoporosis Foundation. (2002) America's Bone Health: The State of Osteoporosis and Low Bone Mass in Our Nation. Washington DC: National Osteoporosis Foundation.

Nurmi-Lawton JA, Baxter-Jones AD, Mirwald RL, Bishop JA, Taylor P, Cooper C, New SA. (2004) Evidence of sustained skeletal benefits from impactloading exercise in young females: a 3-year longitudinal study. J Bone Mineral Res 19(2):314-22

Nyberg L, Gustafson Y, Berggren D, BrŠnnstršm B, Bucht G. (1996) Falls leading to femoral neck fractures in lucid older people. J Am Geriatr Soc 44:156–60.

Old JL, Calvert M. (2004) Vertebral compression fractures in the elderly. Amer Family Physician 69(1):111-6.

Papaioannou A, Ioannidis G, Adachi JD, Sebaldt RJ, Ferko N, Puglia M, Brown J, Tenenhouse A, Olszynski WP, Boulos P, Hanley DA, Josse R, Murray TM, Petrie A, Goldsmith CH. (2003) Adherence to bisphosphonates and hormone replacement therapy in a tertiary care setting of patients in the CANDOO database. Osteoporosis International 14(10):808-13.

Parker MJ, Gillespie LD, Gillespie WJ. (2004) Hip protectors for preventing hip fractures in the elderly. Cochrane Database of Systematic Reviews (3): CD001255.

Prochaska JO, Velicer WF. (1997) The transtheoretical model of health behavior change. Am J Health Promotion 12(1):38 48.

Recker RR, Hinders S, Davies KM, Heaney RP, Stegman MR, Lappe JM, Kimmel DB. (1996) Correcting calcium nutritional deficiency prevents spine fractures in elderly women. J Bone Mineral Res 11(12):1961-6.

Recker RR, Gallagher R, MacCosbe PE. (2005) Effect of dosing frequency on bisphosphonate medication adherence in a large longitudinal cohort of women. Mayo Clinic Proceedings 80(7):856-61.

Reid IR, Ames RW, Evans MC, Gamble GD, Sharpe SJ. (1993) Effect of calcium supplementation on bone loss in post-menopausal women. New Engl J Med 329:460-464.

Richmond J. Aharonoff GB. Zuckerman JD. Koval KJ. (2003) Mortality risk after hip fracture. J Orthopaedic Trauma 17(1):53

Rutledge T, Matthews K, Lui LY, Stone KL, Cauley JA. (2003) Social networks and marital status predict mortality in older women: prospective evidence from the Study of Osteoporotic Fractures (SOF). Psychosomatic Med 65(4):688-94.

Salkeld G, Cameron ID, Cumming RG, Easter S, Seymour J, Kurrle SE, Quine S. (2000) Quality of life related to fear of falling and hip fracture in older women: a time trade off study. Brit Med J 320(7231): 341-6.

Sedlak CA, Doheny MO, Jones SL. (2000) Osteoporosis education programs: changing knowledge and behaviors. Public Health Nursing. 17(5):398-402.

Segal E, Tamir A, Ish-Shalom S. (2003) Compliance of osteoporotic patients with different treatment regimens. Israel Med Assn J 5(12):859-62.

Singh S, Sun H, Anis AH. (2004) Cost-effectiveness of hip protectors in the prevention of osteoporosis related hip fractures in elderly nursing home residents. J Rheumatology 31(8):1607-13.

Steinberg M, Cartwright C, Peel N, Williams G. (2000) A sustainable programme to prevent falls and near falls in community-dwelling older people: results of a randomised trial. J Epidemiol Community Health 54;227-232.

Stilley CS, Sereika S, Muldoon MF, Ryan CM, Dunbar-Jacob J. (2004) Psycho-logical and cognitive function: predictors of adherence with cholesterol lowering treatment. Ann Behav Med 27(2):117-24

Suzuki T, Kim H, Yoshida H, Ishizaki T. (2004) Randomized controlled trial of exercise intervention for the prevention of falls in community-dwelling elderly Japanese women. J Bone Mineral Metabolism 22(6):602-11.

Suzuki T, Kim H, Yoshida H, Ishizaki T. (2004) Randomized controlled trial of exercise intervention for the prevention of falls in community-dwelling elderly Japanese women. J Bone Mineral Metabolism 22(6):602-11.

Sze PC, Lam PS, Chan J, Leung KS.(2005) A primary falls prevention programme for older people in Hong Kong. Brit J Community Nursing 10(4):166-71.

Todd JA, Robinson RJ. (2003) Osteoporosis and exercise. Postgrad Med J 79:320-323.

Turbi C, Herrero-Beaumont G, Acebes JC, Torrijos A, Grana J, Miguelez R, Sacristan J, Marin F. (2004) Compliance and satisfaction with raloxifene versus alen-dronate for the treatment of postmeno-pausal osteoporosis in clinical practice: An open-label, prospective, nonrandom-ized, observational study. Clinical Ther 26(2):245-56.

Turner CH, Robling AG. (2005) Exercises for improving bone strength. Brit J Sports

Med 39(4):188-9.

Tussing L, Chapman-Novakofski K. (2005) Osteoporosis prevention education: behavior theories and calcium intake. J Am Dietetic Assoc 105(1):92-7.

U.S. Department of Health and Human Services. (2004) Bone Health and Osteoporosis: A Report of the Surgeon General. Rockville, MD: U.S. Department of Health and Human Services, Office of the Surgeon General.

Vainionpaa A, Korpelainen R, Leppaluoto J, Jamsa T. (2005) Effects of high-impact exercise on bone mineral density: a randomized controlled trial in premenopausal women. Osteoporosis International 16(2):191-7.

Vermeire E, Wens J, Van Royen P, Biot Y, Hearnshaw H, Lindenmeyer A. (2005) Interventions for improving adherence to treatment recommendations in people with type 2 diabetes mellitus. Cochrane Database of Systematic Reviews. (2): CD003638.

Vu MQ, Weintraub N, Rubenstein LZ. (2004) Falls in the nursing home: are they preventable?. J Am Med Directors Assoc 5(6):401-6.

Wong SY, Lau EM, Lau WW, Lynn HS. (2004) Is dietary counseling effective in increasing dietary calcium, protein and energy intake in patients with osteoporotic fractures? A randomized controlled clinical trial. J Human Nutrition Dietetics. 17(4):359-64.

Yamazaki S, Ichimura S, Iwamoto J, Takeda T, Toyama Y. (2004) Effect of walking exercise on bone metabolism in postmenopausal women with osteopenia/osteoporosis. J Bone Mineral Metabol 22(5):500-8.

CHRONIC DISEASE MANAGEMENT AND TELEMEDICINE

Richard Wootton

INTRODUCTION

The conventional health care system has evolved to deal with acutely ill patients, but is less well adapted to deal with those suffering from chronic diseases. Chronic diseases are conditions that often do not improve and are rarely cured completely, for example diabetes, dementia, congestive heart failure, hypertension and asthma. Chronic diseases represent a significant burden of ill health in society.

The term chronic disease management (CDM) describes a system of care designed to improve patient outcomes and reduce the costs associated with long-term illnesses. CDM is an approach to health care with an emphasis on helping individuals to maintain their independence and keep as healthy as possible through prevention, early detection, and management of their chronic conditions. Chronic conditions represent challenges for those affected, their families and care providers. In particular, a patient's ability to follow medical advice, to accommodate lifestyle changes, and to access appropriate resources are all factors that influence the successful management of a long-term illness.

What is telemedicine?

Telemedicine is a general term used to define health care activities carried out at a distance (Wootton, 1996). This encompasses all aspects of health care, from diagnosis and management to the continuing education of health care professionals, whenever distance is involved. Telemedicine is not a technology as such, but rather a *technique* for delivering care when the individuals concerned are located in different places. The technique involves modifying normal clinical practice to adapt to the novel circumstances of communicating at a distance, rather than in person. In using telemedicine, clinicians and other health care workers owe the same duty of care as with the conventional forms of delivery.

Other synonyms for telemedicine include the terms telehealth, online health and e-health. The use of the term telehealth is due to the perception that "health" implies a broader societal focus than the narrower focus of "medicine". The use of the term e-health is more recent and implies telemedicine activities which take place via the Internet, especially those with a commercial focus. Nonetheless, the term telemedicine remains firmly embedded in the literature. For example, a Medline search (October 2002) identified 287 articles using the term "telehealth" compared to 5219 articles using the term "telemedicine" (Fig 1). In the interests of simplicity, telemedicine is used here as a generic term encompassing all distance medicine delivery techniques.

There are essentially two types of telemedicine techniques – those that occur in real-time and those that are pre-recorded. Real-time telemedicine is interactive, requiring the presence of the specialist and the non-specialist at the same time, albeit in different locations. Real-time telemedicine can be as basic as giving health care advice over the telephone or, more advanced such as teleconsulting when one party consults with another using videoconferencing equipment. The point is that both parties are in live communication via whatever medium is in use. Thus either party can ask a question and receive an immediate reply.

In contrast, pre-recorded or store-and-forward telemedicine does not require the

Figure 1: Results of a Medline search for the keyword "telemedicine", "telehealth", "online health" etc.

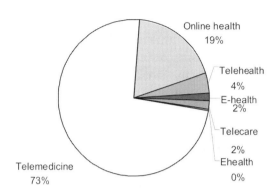

simultaneous presence of the parties concerned at each location, i.e. the health care provider and the recipient of that care do not have to be available at the same time. Information can be transmitted to a specialist health care provider, by e-mail for instance, and then viewed later at a more convenient time by the specialist. An increasingly common form of pre-recorded telemedicine is teleradiology, in which an electronic X-ray image is transmitted for reporting elsewhere by a radiologist.

The common ground between real-time and pre-recorded telemedicine is the increased accessibility to medical and health care expertise when distance is involved.

Components of a CDM program

What components of a CDM program are likely to be enhanced by telemedicine? In managing chronic diseases, experience shows that prevention, early detection and management may all be improved by suitable interventions (Weingarten et al., 2002), and in each case it is possible to deliver such interventions by an appropriate telemedicine technique, Table 1.

Table 1. Components of a CDM program and possible telemedicine interventions

Component	Telemedicine intervention
prevention	education
early detection	screening
management	monitoring

CDM involves support for health care professionals, and support for the patients themselves. For example:

professionals
- decision-support tools
- clinical information systems

patients
- information
- self-help tools

Again, telemedicine techniques can be used to provide such support. Successful CDM involves com-munication between health care professionals. It will also involve communication between health care professionals and the patient. Thus the techniques of telemedicine are likely to have an increasing role in CDM, particularly in situations where communication is difficult, such as in rural communities.

Successful CDM involves communication between health care professionals. It will also involve communication between health care professionals and the patient. Thus the techniques of telemedicine are likely to have an increasing role in CDM, particularly in situations where communication is difficult, such as in rural communities.

REVIEW OF TELEMEDICINE IN CDM

Over the last 10-20 years, technological developments have permitted the use of information and telecommunication technologies in healthcare delivery generally, but also in the healthcare of persons with chronic illnesses. Although the potential of this approach was recognized in the early 1960s, limitations of technology and cost prevented general use. However with the widespread availability of the PC and the Internet, and the decline in their costs, telemedicine now seems poised to make a major impact on chronic disease care.

The literature contains a number of reports of early work involving telemedicine and chronic disease. For example, a search of the Medline database (October 2002) for papers about various chronic diseases containing the keyword "telemedicine" re-turned a total of 190, of which the majority (45%) concerned diabetes, see Fig 2.

Diabetes

How has telemedicine been used in diabetes? The work can be classified into three main categories. First, there is remote

Figure 2: Numbers of references listed in the Medline database for papers about various chronic diseases (n=190) containing the keyword "telemedicine".

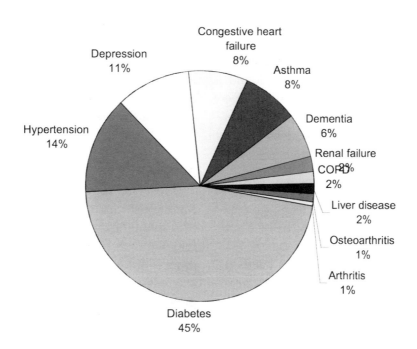

monitoring of patients in the home, in which the object is to improve management. Much of this concerns the transmission of blood glucose results from the home to a central server, so that up-to-date records can be examined easily by health care staff. Some studies have also investigated the use of video (i.e. based on low-cost videoconferencing equipment installed in the home) for real-time teleconsultations. In some trials, telephone calls have been used to improve contact with patients, either made by nursing staff or made by computerised automatic voice response systems to which patients can respond using a touch-tone phone, see Table 2a.

Second, telemedicine has been used for screening. The object is to improve diagnosis (i.e. early detection). The majority of this work concerns the transmission of image data, such as retinal photographs. There seems little doubt that – providing the appropriate equipment is employed – digital imaging can provide similar sensitivity and specificity to conventional photography, see Table 2b. Large scale trials are now required to prove the cost-effectiveness of this approach to screening.

Finally, decision support tools and clinical information systems have been employed, mainly in primary care. Although definitive trials have yet to be carried out, early results suggest that a shared-care program can improve the management of diabetes, see Table 2c.

Hypertension

In hypertension the main work has involved remote monitoring of patients in the home. This has principally concerned transmission of BP data, but there is also some experience with computerised automatic voice response systems which have been used to improve medication compliance. The object is to improve management, by providing healthcare staff with better information, so that they can intervene appropriately. A secondary benefit is that patient adherence to prescribed treatment is likely to be improved. Table 2 summarises the work.

Depression

There is a substantial literature on the use of telemedicine for mental health service delivery (see Wootton et al., 2003 for a recent multi-author review). Almost all of this work relates to the use of telemedicine in settings other than the home. However, there has been some preliminary work concerning subjects at home and telephone contact with caregivers, and self-administered psychotherapy – both have been found to be useful, see Table 2.

Congestive heart failure

Early trials of telemedicine for remote monitoring of CHF patients at home have been encouraging. Simple telephone calls have also been employed for monitoring, as they have in the context of managing other heart disease (DeBusk et al., 1994). Both techniques have shown that management can be improved, see Table 2. However, it may be the case that the additional cost of automatic monitoring equipment is unjustified. Further work will be required to establish the cost-effectiveness of the various alternatives.

Asthma

Most of the work in asthma has been remote monitoring of patients in the home, for example, transmitting spirometry data via a telephone modem to a central server. The object is to improve management. A secondary benefit is that patient adherence to prescribed treatment is likely to be improved. Early results are encouraging.

Some patient education in metered-dose inhaler (MDI) technique has also taken place by videoconferencing (in health care facilities). For subjects who have access to

Table 2a. Clinical - remote monitoring (transmission of data or telephone calls). Studies shown in italics are randomised trials

Study	Participants per group	Intervention	Results	Implications
Diabetes				
Albisser et al., 1996	204 patients	Patients used touch-tone telephone each day to report self-measured blood glucose levels or hypoglycaemic symptoms. One year open study.	Over 60,000 telephone cells were received by the computer system. The prevalence of diabetes related crises (hyperglycaemia or hypoglycaemia) fell ~ 3-fold. Glycated haemoglobin fell significantly in patients actively using the system.	Telephone contact can improve control but its cost-effectiveness remains to be demonstrated
Bangs et al., 2002	6 patients with diabetes and peripheral ulcers	Clinical information and digital photographs from home sent by email to a vascular surgeon for assessment.	Feasibility study of teleconsulting	Telemedicine clinics may be useful in primary care
Biermann et al., 2002	48 patients on insulin therapy. Randomly assigned to control (16) or telecare (27)	Four month RCT of home monitoring of blood glucose. Data transmitted via telephone modem.	Cost analysis showed savings of approximately 650 euro per year per telemedicine patient	Telemedicine may improve management and may save time and cost
Edmonds et al., 1998	35 volunteers with insulin-requiring diabetes. Randomly allocated to control(17) or intervention group(16)	Home monitoring data transmitted by telephone to a central database. Subjects received feedback summaries.	All 16 patients who began using the phone continued to do so for 6 months confirming the feasibility of the system	Feasibility study
Johnston et al., 2000	212 patients with CHF, COPD, cerebral vascular accident, diabetes etc. Randomly assigned to control (110) or intervention group (102)	Home telemedicine consultation via videophone in addition to usual home visits. The video system included peripheral equipment for assessing cardiopulmonary status.	No differences in the quality indicators, patient satisfaction, or use were seen. Total mean costs of care, excluding home health care costs, were $1948 in the intervention group and $2674 in the control group	Home teleconsulting can improve access and may produce cost savings for the provider

Study	Participants per group	Intervention	Results	Implications
Ladyzynski et al., 2001	15 pregnant type I diabetic women	Home monitoring of blood glucose date via a dial-up telephone line	Feasibility study; no major technical problems; significant improvement of metabolic control	Home monitoring may be useful in improving metabolic control
Liesenfeld et al., 2000	61 children and adolescents with type I diabetes. Intervention compared to baseline period.	Information about blood glucose, injected insulin, meals and exercise stored in a glucose meter. Data transmitted via telephone modem,	Compared to the run-in period, mean blood glucose decreased and frequency of hypoglycemia decreased	Telemedical care for intensive insulin therapy is safe, can improve glycaemic control
Piette et al., 1997	65 diabetic patients	AVM (automatic voice messaging) monitoring protocol to inquire about patients' symptoms, glucose monitoring, foot care, diet, and medication adherence. Patients responded by using their touch-tone telephone keypads.	216 AVM calls were successfully completed, an average of 3.3 out of four calls per patient. 98% of all patients reported that the calls were helpful.	Feasibility study
Piette et al., 2000a; see also Piette et al., 2000b	280 diabetic patients. Randomly assigned to control (124) or intervention group (124)	Automated telephone calls every two weeks with telephone follow-up by a diabetes nurse educator after 12 months	Positive effects on patient-centered outcomes of care, but no measurable effects on anxiety or health-related quality of life. Marginal improvements in glycaemic control.	Automated telephone calls may be useful in improving patients' ability to manage their diabetes care
Thompson et al., 1999	46 insulin-requiring diabetic patients who had poor glucose control. Randomly assigned to control (23) or intervention group (23).	Regular telephone contact with a diabetes nurse educator (3 calls per week) for advice about adjustment of insulin therapy	After 6 months, the mean HbA1c level in the intervention group was significantly lower than both the level at baseline for that group and the level for the standard-care group.	Telephone contact can improve control but its cost-effectiveness remains to be demonstrated.

Study	Participants per group	Intervention	Results	Implications
Tsang et al., 2001	20 diabetic patients randomly assigned to control then intervention, or vice versa (cross-over study).	Hand-held electronic diary used for diabetes monitoring for three months. Data transmitted via telephone modem.	Significant improvement in glycaemic control during intervention compared with control periods.	Home monitoring may be cost-effective in improving metabolic control.
Whitlock et al., 2000	28 patients with type II diabetes. Randomly assigned to control (13) or intervention group (15).	Home telemedicine consultation via videophone compared with standard outpatient care. A nurse case manager contacted the telemedicine group once a week.	Significant improvement in HbA1c in the intervention group after 3 months.	Home teleconsulting may be useful in improving metabolic control
Wojcicki et al., 2001	30 pregnant type I diabetic women. Randomly assigned to control (15) or intervention (15).	3-year randomized prospective clinical trial. Automatic transmission of blood glucose data every night.	Better glycaemic control in the study group in comparison with the control group.	Diabetes treatment during pregnancy can be improved by telemedicine; presumably other diabetic patients can also be managed better
Hypertension				
Artinian et al., 2001	26 subjects randomly assigned to control or intervention group	Home telemonitoring or nurse-managed, community-based monitoring	There were significant reductions in BP in both home monitored and community monitored groups.	Active monitoring may be preferable to usual care.
Bai et al., 1996	30 patients	Home transmission of ECG and BP data	System found to be practical	Feasibility study
Friedman et al., 1996	267 patients randomly assigned to control (134) or intervention group (133)	Automatic telephone monitoring (voice and patient-entered BP data)	Significant reduction in BP in intervention group; improved adherence.	Telemedicine may be an effective way to monitor patients with hypertension.

Study	Participants per group	Intervention	Results	Implications
Rogers et al., 2001	121 patients randomly assigned to control or intervention group	Transmission of BP data from the home, morning and evening for a minimum of 8 weeks.	Mean arterial pressure decreased significantly in the telemedicine group and increased in patients receiving usual care	Home telemonitoring may be an effective way of reducing BP in hypertension
Chronic Obstructive Pulmonary Disease				
Mair et al., 1999	6 patients	Home monitoring using analogue videophones	Feasibility of home monitoring demonstrated	
Congestive Heart Failure				
Andrews et al., 2002	6 patients	Wireless sleep monitoring compared with polysomnography	The wireless system could detect Cheyne-Stokes respiration, but there were significant respiratory sensing errors	Feasibility study
de Lusignan et al., 2001	24 patients randomly assigned to control and intervention groups	Home telemonitoring with data transmission to a web server	Telemonitoring group complied better in collecting prescriptions for their cardiac drugs	Home telemonitoring is a potentially useful technique
Jenkins et al., 2001	28 patients	Telemedicine assessment compared with in-person	Few significant differences in assessment variables	Telemedicine may be useful as a supplement to home visits
Jerant et al., 2001	37 patients randomly assigned to home telecare (13), telephone care (12) and usual care (12)	Home telecare was delivered via a 2-way videoconference device with an integrated electronic stethoscope. Telephone care was by nurse	Mean CHF-related readmission charges were lower in the telecare group and in the telephone group than in the usual care group after 6 mo	Home telecare may not offer much benefit over telephone follow-up and appears to be more expensive
Riegel et al., 2002	358 patients randomly assigned to control (228) or intervention group (130)	Telephone case management	Hospitalization rate was significantly lower in the intervention group after 3 mo. Costs were lower after 6 mo.	Telephone case management appears promising.
De Lusignan et al., 1999	20 patients randomly assigned to control (10) and intervention groups (10)	Telemedicine used to collect BP, pulse and weight daily. Also weekly videoconference with a nurse.	3 month trial demonstrated feasibility	Feasibility study

Study	Participants per group	Intervention	Results	Implications
Asthma				
Bruderman and Abboud, 1997	39 asthma patients	Home monitoring. Portable spirometer. Data transmission by telephone modem.	In 19 patients, analysis of the spirometry data detected early signs of deterioration.	Home monitoring may improve management
Finkelstein et al., 1998	10 subjects	Home monitoring - portable spirometer and palmtop computer. Data transmission by telephone modem	Average data transmission time was about 1 min by PSTN and 6 min by mobile phone	Feasibility study
Kokubu et al., 1999	High-risk patients randomly assigned to control or intervention group	Home monitoring - nurse provided instructions by telephone	Significant decrease in emergency room visits; improved PEF values in telemedicine group	Effective system for poorly-controlled asthma
Romano et al., 2001	17 patients with persistent asthma	Telemedicine (videoconferencing) follow-up visits at a school clinic	Symptom scores improved	Feasibility study
Steel et al., 2002	33 patients	Remote monitoring from home. Data transmission via telephone modem	80% compliance with monitoring; 52% compliance with transmission of results	Feasibility study
Dementia				
Lee et al., 2000	140 patients	Telemedicine assessment compared with in-person assessment over two years	Acceptance by patients and caregivers was good. Agreement between the two modalities was also good	Telemedicine appeared to be reliable and effective.
Lyketsos et al., 2001	Patients with dementia	Videoconferencing between long-term care facility to tertiary psychiatric unit.	Apparent reduction in psychiatric admissions to hospital	Telemedicine may be useful in long-term care.

Table 2b. Clinical - screening. Studies shown in italics are randomised trials

Study	Participants per group	Intervention	Results	Implications
Diabetes				
Aiello et al., 2000; also Aiello et al., 1998	18 patients (36 eyes)	Digitized retinal images transmitted and compared with conventional fundus photographs	Digital images shown to have similar diagnostic power	Feasibility study
Bjorvig et al., 2002	42 diabetic patients	Digital images sent by email to an eye specialist. Cost comparison with conventional examination.	At low workloads, for example 20 patients per annum, telemedicine was more expensive than conventional examination; at higher workloads, telemedicine was cheaper.	Telemedicine screening is economic in the right circumstances.
Bursell et al., 2001	54 patients (108 eyes) with type 1 or type 2 diabetes	Digital-video colour images compared with conventional fundus photographs.	Substantial agreement between the two techniques for clinical level of diabetic retinopathy.	Telemedicine may be useful for remotely determining the level of diabetic retinopathy.
Constable et al., 2000	27 patients (51 eyes)	Digital images compared with conventional photographs.	Sensitivity and specificity of digital imaging was satisfactory.	Telemedicine has potential for community screening for blinding eye diseases.
Cummings et al., 2001	193 volunteers with a history of diabetes	Non-mydriatic digital fundus images evaluated by a specialist.	The majority of images were rated as good or fair by the retinal specialist.	Digital imaging is a feasible screening modality in rural areas.
Liesenfeld et al., 2000	129 diabetic inpatients	Digital fundus photographs compared to conventional slit-lamp photographs in six screening centres.	Assessment of digital images resulted in a median sensitivity of 85% and a median specificity of 90% for the detection of moderate non-proliferative or sight-threatening diabetic retinopathy.	Telemedicine may be useful for remotely determining the level of diabetic retinopathy.

Study	Participants per group	Intervention	Results	Implications
Lin et al., 2002	197 patients with type I and type II diabetes	Single-field digital monochromatic nonmydriatic fundus photography compared with conventional techniques.	A single digital photograph of the disk and macula was more sensitive for diabetic retinopathy screening than mydriatic ophthalmoscopy, the currently accepted screening method.	Digital imaging may be a useful screening technique for diabetic retinopathy.
Marcus et al., 1998	17 HIV-positive (34 eyes) and 20 diabetic patients (39 eyes)	Fundus images transmitted in real-time to ophthalmologist. A second ophthalmologist performed an examination in-person.	Telemedical examination agreed with in-person examination in most cases.	Real-time telemedicine may be valuable for providing ophthalmic consultations in younger patients without lens or media opacity.
Shiba et al., 2002	61 adolescent diabetics	Digital photographs transmitted via telephone modem and compared with ophthalmological examination.	Sensitivities of examination were comparable.	Telemedicine may be a useful screening technique.
Tennant et al., 2001	121 patients (241 eyes), of whom 114 (94%) had non-insulin-dependent diabetes	Digital images for each patient were transmitted by satellite and compared to photographs on slide film.	Digital imaging had a high correlation with slide film for the identification of most features of diabetic retinopathy.	Telemedicine may be a useful screening technique.
Tennant et al., 2000	100 patients (199 eyes)	Stereoscopic digital imaging evaluated by a specialist.	Patients found to have treatable diabetic retinopathy were transferred to a tertiary eye centre for treatment.	Digital imaging of the retina appears feasible for the identification of diabetic retinopathy.
Yogesan et al., 2000	25 diabetic patients (49 eyes)	Digital images of the retina from a handheld fundus camera compared with conventional photographs.	The digital images were assessed as being of inferior quality to the conventional photographs.	Successful digital imaging requires appropriate technology.

Study	Participants per group	Intervention	Results	Implications
Dementia				
Go et al., 1997	28 patients with dementia	Telephone assessment compared with in-person clinician ratings.	Good agreement between the two modalities.	Telephone assessment is a reliable and valid screening procedure.
Monteiro et al., 1998	Elderly population with normal aging and dementia	Telephone assessment compared with in-person assessment.	Good agreement between the two modalities.	Telephone assessment appears to be a reliable procedure.

Table 2c. Clinical - information systems/decision support. Studies shown in italics are randomised trials

Study	Participants per group	Intervention	Results	Implications
Diabetes				
Branger et al., 1999	275 diabetic patients	An electronic communication network was used to link the computer-based patient records of the physicians, thus enabling electronic data interchange.	Intervention GPs received more messages per year (1.6 per patient) than control GPs. Intervention patients showed a slight but significant decrease of HbA$_{1c}$ levels.	Improved electronic communication can improve the management of diabetes.
Dinneen et al., 2000	Random sample of 200 sets of patient records from each of three primary care sites.	Diabetes management guidelines were supplemented by electronic communication, including telemedicine review.	There were significant differences between the three models of care.	Telemedicine may be useful as an adjunct to community care.
Rutten et al., 2001	770 patients with type II diabetes	Shared-care providing remote diabetologist support for 85 GPs.	Compared to baseline, there were significant improvements in biochemical variables.	A shared-care program can improve the management of diabetes.

Table 2d. Educational. Studies shown in italics are randomised trials

Study	Participants per group	Intervention	Results	Implications
Diabetes				
Earles et al., 2001	48 diabetes patients	Individual care management, aided by an Internet-based telemedicine system.	HbA$_{1c}$ levels were lower after 6 months compared with baseline values.	Telemedicine can aid a team approach to diabetes care.
Radjenovic et al., 2001	2 groups of teachers	Diabetes training material presented either on paper or via a Web-based computer system.	Subjects using the Web-based system had significantly higher knowledge scores and were significantly more satisfied with the training session than subjects who used paper documents traditionally used for teacher training.	Distance education may be cheaper.
Yip et al., 2002	41 patients with type II diabetes	4 educational sessions via videoconference at a local clinic.	Patients highly satisfied with the education.	Diabetes education by telemedicine is an acceptable technique.
Depression				
Grant et al., 2002	74 stroke survivors with an admitting diagnosis of ischemic stroke and their primary family caregivers	Initial home visit between a trained nurse and the family caregiver, followed by 4 weekly and then 4 biweekly telephone contacts.	Less depression; and significant improvement in measures of vitality, social functioning etc in the intervention group.	Telemedicine may be useful for family caregivers of stroke survivors.
Hunkeler et al., 2000	302 patients starting antidepressant drug therapy	Randomized trial comparing usual care, telehealth care, and telehealth care plus peer support.	Improved mental function and satisfaction in nurse-based telehealth patients with or without peer support.	Nurse telehealth care can improve clinical outcomes of anti-depressant drug tx.
Osgood-Hynes et al., 1998	41 patients	12-week self-help system using booklets and telephone calls to an interactive voice response system.	Depression ratings improved significantly compared to baseline values.	Computer-aided telephone self-help may be useful in depression.

Study	Participants per group	Intervention	Results	Implications
Asthma				
Bynum et al., 2001	36 subjects randomly assigned to control (21) or intervention group (15)	Metered-dose inhaler technique taught by videoconferencing.	The video group significantly improved their technique.	Videoconferencing is an effective teaching medium.
Chan et al., 2001	12 elderly subjects in a residential home	Metered-dose inhaler technique taught by videoconferencing.	Half of the subjects improved their technique after 3 months in comparison with baseline performance.	Videoconferencing is an effective teaching medium.
Dementia				
Mahoney et al., 2001	Family caregivers randomly assigned to control (51) and intervention group (49)	Telephone support for caregivers. Interactive voice response system.	Approximately half of the intervention group used the system regularly.	Overall preference was for human interaction.
Harvey et al., 1998	Callers to the telephone help line.	Telephone help line for caregivers.	In a two year study, about half the 1121 calls related to specific patients, and about half were generic requests for information.	The service became rapidly accepted by families of patients and by members of the public

facilities where high resolution videoconferencing is available, this approach seems likely to be useful.

Dementia

The main work in dementia has concerned the use of the telephone, either for screening, or to provide support for caregivers. Telephone assessment has been shown to be reliable in dementia. (In addition, there is a big literature on telephone-screening for psychiatry problems generally, rather than dementia specifically). The object is screening and to some extent, management.

Telephone help lines have been trialled, either based on automatic voice response systems or based on conventional counsellors. The object is mainly to support and educate caregivers.

Telemedicine interventions in dementia appear to be feasible, but there do not appear to have been any randomized controlled trials (RCTs) so far.

Other chronic diseases

Other chronic diseases in which telemedicine might be considered include renal failure, liver disease, osteoarthritis/arthritis and chronic obstructive pulmonary disease (COPD). Except in the latter category, there has been little telemedicine work to date. In COPD, remote (data and video) monitoring of patients at home has been tried. The results demonstrate the feasibility of the approach and encourage further work.

PROMISING DEVELOPMENTS

One potential barrier to the use of telemedicine in CDM is reimbursement, since in many countries health care providers must deal with patients face-to-face if they are to be paid for the work. In the US, a national managed care company has recently established reimbursement for Web-based Internet consultations between patients and their physicians (Smith, 2000). Privacy issues have been addressed by utilizing secure network procedures. The scheme is limited to chronic conditions such as diabetes, asthma and congestive heart failure, and will reimburse up to 24 consultations per year at a rate of $25 each. Reimbursement, when it was permitted in other areas, did not lead to a dramatic increase in telemedicine, so the effect in CDM remains to be seen.

FUTURE INTERVENTION STRATEGIES

The work on telemedicine in CDM which is summarised in Table 2 clearly shows that the technique holds promise in a number of areas. The conventional method of assessing the strength of the evidence would be a systematic review, in which each piece of work was classified according to the study design, from a meta-analysis of randomised controlled trials (strongest) to simple anecdotes or case reports (weakest). Unfortunately, in the work related to CDM – as in telemedicine generally – most of the literature refers to pilot trials and feasibility studies, with short-term outcomes, few longer than 12 months. In CDM, the strongest evidence concerns diabetes in which RCTs suggest that home monitoring will be a useful strategy to improve management. Formal studies of cost-effectiveness are awaited.

Although at present the evidence base for the use of telemedicine in CDM is weak, experience to date suggests that inter-ventions most likely to benefit from the use of telehealth are home monitoring of glucose levels in diabetes, and of blood pressure and related data in CHF and in hypertension.

UNANSWERED RESEARCH QUESTIONS

The work to date demonstrates that telemedicine is feasible in CDM, and in certain areas, it appears effectual. The fundamental research question at present is whether telemedicine is cost-effective. It is worth noting that formal studies of cost-effectiveness in telemedicine are hard to do, which may be one reason why so few have yet been attempted.

In the trials of home monitoring so far conducted it has not always been easy to discern the effect of telemedicine itself, versus the effect of increased contact with health care professionals or even the novelty effect of the technology. As always in telemedicine research, careful study design will be required.

USEFUL RESOURCES FOR HEALTH PROFESSIONALS

For those contemplating the introduction of telemedicine to support CDM, useful resources include the two peer-reviewed telemedicine journals and the Telemedicine Information Exchange (TIE) database:

- Journal of Telemedicine and Telecare. See http://www.rsm.ac.uk/pub/jtt.htm
- Telemedicine Information Exchange. See http://tie.telemed.org
- Telemedicine Journal and e-Health. See http://www.liebertpub.com/tmj/default1.asp

An introductory textbook (Wootton and Craig, 1999) may also provide useful background information.

CONCLUSION

Telemedicine looks promising for CDM, but good quality studies are scarce and the generalizability of most findings is rather limited. Much of the work to date has been pilot trials and feasibility studies. (This is true of telemedicine generally). There have been only a limited number of RCTs, e.g. in home blood glucose monitoring. The only systematic review of telemedicine shows that the value of home glucose monitoring in diabetes is equivocal (Hersh et al., 2001).

What is achieved by using telemedicine in this way? Telemedicine improves the monitoring of quantitative variables and reduces the need for a healthcare professional to visit the home so frequently. That is, there should be savings in professional time and travel, and perhaps improved clinical outcomes. Formal cost-effectiveness studies will be required to prove this.

In addition, screening and education appear to be promising areas for telemedicine in CDM, but are both at an earlier stage of examination. A recent systematic review suggests that patient education in general can significantly improve disease control (Weingarten et al., 2002).

REFERENCES

Aiello LM, Bursell SE, Cavallerano J, Gardner WK, Strong J. (1998) Joslin Vision Network Validation Study: pilot image stabilization phase. J Am Optom Assoc 69:699-710.

Aiello LM, Cavallerano A, Bursell SE, Cavallerano J. (2000) The Joslin Vision Network innovative telemedicine care for diabetes: Preserving human vision. Ophthalmol Clin North Am 13: 213-24.

Albisser AM, Harris RI, Sakkal S, Parson ID, Chao SC. (1996) Diabetes intervention in the information age. Med Inform (Lond) 21:297-316. [nb. Erratum in: Med Inf (Lond) 1997 22:205.

Andrews D, Gouda MS, Higgins S, Johnson P, Williams A, Vandenburg M. (2002) A comparative study of a new wireless continuous cardiorespiratory monitor for the diagnosis and management of patients with congestive heart failure at home. J Telemed Telecare 8:101-3.

Artinian NT, Washington OG, Templin TN. (2001) Effects of home telemonitoring and community-based monitoring on blood pressure control in urban African Americans: a pilot study. Heart Lung 30:191-9.

Bai J, Zhang Y, Dai B, Zhu Z, Cui Z, Lin J, Zhang J, Zhang P, Shen D, Yao S, Cu S, Ye D. (1996) The design and preliminary evaluation of a home electrocardiography and blood pressure monitoring network. J Telemed Telecare 2:100-6.

Bangs I, Clarke M, Hands L, Jones R, Knott M, Mahaffey W. (2002) An integrated nursing and telemedicine approach to vascular care. J Telemed Telecare 8:110-2.

Biermann E, Dietrich W, Rihl J, Standl E. (2002) Are there time and cost savings by using telemanagement for patients on intensified insulin therapy? A randomised, controlled trial. Comput Methods Programs Biomed 69:137-46.

Bjorvig S, Johansen MA, Fossen K. (2002) An economic analysis of screening for diabetic retinopathy. J Telemed Telecare 8:32-5.

Branger PJ, van't Hooft A, van der Wouden JC, Moorman PW, van Bemmel JH. (1999) Shared care for diabetes: supporting communication between primary and secondary care. Int J Med Inf 53:133-42.

Bruderman I, Abboud S. (1997) Telespirometry: novel system for home monitoring of asthmatic patients. Telemed J 3:127-33.

Bursell SE, Cavallerano JD, Cavallerano AA, Clermont AC, Birkmire-Peters D, Aiello LP, Aiello LM. (2001) Stereo nonmydriatic digital-video color retinal imaging compared with Early Treatment Diabetic Retinopathy Study seven standard field 35-mm stereo color photos for determining level of diabetic retinopathy. Ophthalmol 108:572-85.

Bynum A, Hopkins D, Thomas A, Copeland N, Irwin C. (2001) The effect of telepharmacy counseling on metered-dose inhaler technique among adolescents with asthma in rural Arkansas. Telemed J E Health 7(3):207-17

Chan WM, Woo J, Hui E, Hjelm NM. (2001) The role of telenursing in the provision of geriatric outreach services to residential homes in Hong Kong. J Telemed Telecare 7: 38-46.

Constable IJ, Yogesan K, Eikelboom R, Barry C, Cuypers M. (2000) Fred Hollows lecture: digital screening for eye disease. Clin Experiment Ophthalmol 28:129-32.

Cummings DM, Morrissey S, Barondes MJ, Rogers L, Gustke S. (2001) Screening for diabetic retinopathy in rural areas: the potential of telemedicine. J Rural Health 17:25-31.

DeBusk RF, Miller NH, Superko HR, Dennis CA, Thomas RJ, Lew HT, Berger WE 3rd, Heller RS, Rompf J, Gee D, et al.. (1994) A case-management system for coronary risk factor modification after acute myocardial infarction. Ann Intern Med 120:721-9.

de Lusignan S, Meredith K, Wells S, Leatham E, Johnson P. (1999) A controlled pilot study in the use of telemedicine in the community on the management of heart failure--a report of the first three months. Stud Health Technol Inform 64:126-37.

de Lusignan S, Wells S, Johnson P, Meredith K, Leatham E. (2001) Compliance and effectiveness of 1 year's home telemonitoring. The report of a pilot study of patients with chronic heart failure. Eur J Heart Fail 3:723-30.

Dinneen SF, Bjornsen SS, Bryant SC, Zimmerman BR, Gorman CA, Knudsen JB, Rizza RA, Smith SA. (2000) Towards an optimal model for community-based diabetes care: design and baseline data from the Mayo Health System Diabetes Translation Project. J Eval Clin Pract 6:421-9.

Earles JE, Hartung GH, Dickert JM, Moriyama HH, Coll KJ, Aiello LM, Jackson R, Polonsky W. (2001) Interdisciplinary treatment of diabetes mellitus in a military treatment facility. Mil Med 166:848-52.

Edmonds M, Bauer M, Osborn S, Lutfiyya H, Mahon J, Doig G, Grundy P, Gittens C, Molenkamp G, Fenlon D. (1998) Using the Vista 350 telephone to communicate the results of home monitoring of diabetes mellitus to a central database and to provide feedback. Int J Med Inf 51:117-25.

Finkelstein J, Hripcsak G, Cabrera M. (1998) Telematic system for monitoring of asthma severity in patients' homes. Medinfo 9:272-6.

Friedman RH, Kazis LE, Jette A, Smith MB, Stollerman J, Torgerson J, Carey K. (1996) A telecommunications system for monitoring and counseling patients with hypertension. Impact on medication adherence and blood pressure control. Am J Hypertens 9:285-92.

Go RC, Duke LW, Harrell LE, Cody H, Bassett SS, Folstein MF, Albert MS, Foster JL, Sharrow NA, Blacker D. (1997) Development and validation of a Structured Telephone Interview for Dementia Assessment (STIDA): the NIMH Genetics Initiative. J Geraitr Psychiatry Neurol 10:161-7.

Grant JS, Elliott TR, Weaver M, Bartolucci AA, Giger JN. (2002) Telephone intervention with family caregivers of stroke survivors after rehabilitation. Stroke 33:2060-5.

Harvey R, Roques PK, Fox NC, Rossor MN. (1998) CANDID - Counselling and Diagnosis in Dementia: a national telemedicine service supporting the care of younger patients with dementia. Int J Geriatr Psychiatry 13:381-8.

Hersh WR, Helfand M, Wallace J, Kraemer D, Patterson P, Shapiro S, Greenlick M. (2001) Clinical outcomes resulting from telemedicine interventions: a systematic review. BMC Med Inform Decis Mak 1:5.

Hunkeler EM, Meresman JF, Hargreaves WA, Fireman B, Berman WH, Kirsch AJ, Groebe J, Hurt SW, Braden P, Getzell M, Feigenbaum PA, Peng T, Salzer M. (2000) Efficacy of nurse telehealth care and peer support in augmenting treatment of depression in primary care. Arch Fam Med 9:700-8.

Jenkins RL, McSweeney M. (2001) Assessing elderly patients with congestive heart failure via in-home interactive telecommunication. J Gerontol Nurs 27:21-7.

Jerant AF, Azari R, Nesbitt TS. (2001) Reducing the cost of frequent hospital admissions for congestive heart failure: a randomized trial of a home telecare intervention. Med Care 39:1234-45.

Johnston B, Wheeler L, Deuser J, Sousa KH. (2000) Outcomes of the Kaiser Permanente Tele-Home Health Research Project. Arch Fam Med 9:40-5.

Kokubu F, Suzuki H, Sano Y, Kihara N, Adachi M. (1999) [Article in Japanese – Tele-medicine system for high-risk asthmatic patients] Arerugi 48:700-12.

Ladyzynski P, Wojcicki JM, Krzymien J, Blachowicz J, Jozwicka E, Czajkowski K, Janczewska E, Karnafel W. (2001) Teletransmission system supporting intensive insulin treatment of out-clinic type 1 diabetic pregnant women. Technical assessment during 3 years' application. Int J Artif Organs 24:157-63.

Lee JH, Kim JH, Jhoo JH, Lee KU, Kim KW, Lee DY, Woo JI. (2000) A telemedicine system as a care modality for dementia patients in Korea. Alzheimer Dis Assoc Disord 14:94-101.

Liesenfeld B, Kohner E, Piehlmeier W, Kluthe S, Aldington S, Porta M, Bek T, Obermaier M, Mayer H, Mann G, Holle R, Hepp KD. (2000) A telemedical approach to the screening of diabetic retinopathy: digital fundus photography. Diabetes Care 23:345-8.

Liesenfeld B, Renner R, Neese M, Hepp KD. (2000) Telemedical care reduces hypoglycemias and improves glycemic control in children and adolescents with type 1 diabetes. Diabetes Technol Ther 2:561-7.

Lyketsos CG, Roques C, Hovanec L, Jones BN 3rd. (2001) Telemedicine use and the reduction of psychiatric admissions from a long-term care facility. J Geraitr Psychiatry Neurol 14:76-9.

Mahoney DM, Tarlow B, Jones RN, Tennstedt S, Kasten L. (2001) Factors affecting the use of a telephone-based intervention for caregivers of people with Alzheimer's disease. J Telemed Telecare 7:139-148.

Mair FS, Wilkinson M, Bonnar SA, Wootton R, Angus RM. (1999) The role of telecare in the management of exacerbations of chronic obstructive pulmonary disease (COPD) in the home. J Telemed Telecare 5: 66-7.

Marcus DM, Brooks SE, Ulrich LD, Bassi FH, Laird M, Johnson M, Newman C. (1998) Telemedicine diagnosis of eye disorders by direct ophthalmoscopy. A pilot study. Ophthalmology 105:1907-14.

Monteiro IM, Boksay I, Auer SR, Torossian C, Sinaiko E, Reisberg B. (1998) Reliability of routine clinical instruments for the assessment of Alzheimer's disease administered by telephone. J Geriatr Psychiatry Neurol 11:18-24.

Osgood-Hynes DJ, Greist JH, Marks IM, Baer L, Heneman SW, Wenzel KW, Manzo PA, Parkin JR, Spierings CJ, Dottl SL, Vitse HM. (1998) Self-administered psychotherapy for depression using a telephone-accessed computer system plus booklets: an open U.S.-U.K. study. J Clin Psychiatry 59:358-65.

Piette JD, Mah CA. (1997) The feasibility of automated voice messaging as an adjunct to diabetes outpatient care. Diabetes Care 20:15-21.

Piette JD, Weinberger M, McPhee SJ. (2000a) The effect of automated calls with telephone nurse follow-up on patient-centered outcomes of diabetes care: a randomized, controlled trial. Med Care 38:218-30.

Piette JD, Weinberger M, McPhee SJ, Mah CA, Kraemer FB, Crapo LM. (2000b) Do automated calls with nurse follow-up improve self-care and glycemic control among vulnerable patients with diabetes? Am J Med. 108:20-7.

Radjenovic D, Wallace FL. (2001) Computer-based remote diabetes education for school personnel. Diabetes Technol Ther 3:601-7.

Riegel B, Carlson B, Kopp Z, LePetri B, Glaser D, Unger A. (2002) Effect of a standardized nurse case-management telephone intervention on resource use in patients with chronic heart failure. Arch Intern Med 162:705-12.

Rogers MA, Small D, Buchan DA, Butch CA, Stewart CM, Krenzer BE, Husovsky HL. (2001) Home monitoring service improves mean arterial pressure in patients with essential hypertension. A randomized, controlled trial. Ann Intern Med 134:1024-32.

Romano MJ, Hernandez J, Gaylor A, Howard S, Knox R. (2001) Improvement in asthma symptoms and quality of life in pediatric patients through specialty care delivered via telemedicine. Telemed J E Health 7:281-6.

Rutten GE, Maaijen J, Valkenburg AC, Blankestijn JG, de Valk HW. (2001) The Utrecht Diabetes Project: telemedicine support improves GP care in Type 2 diabetes. Diabet Med 18:459-63.

Shiba T, Yamamoto T, Seki U, Utsugi N, Fujita K, Sato Y, Terada H, Sekihara H, Hagura R. (2002) Screening and follow-up of diabetic retinopathy using a new mosaic 9-field fundus photography system. Diabetes Res Clin Pract 55:49-59.

Smith SP. (2002) Internet visits: a new approach to chronic disease management. J Med Pract Manage 17:330-2.

Steel S, Lock S, Johnson N, Martinez Y, Marquilles E, Bayford R. (2002) A feasibility study of remote monitoring of asthmatic patients. J Telemed Telecare 8:290-6.

Tennant MT, Greve MD, Rudnisky CJ, Hillson TR, Hinz BJ. (2001) Identification of diabetic retinopathy by stereoscopic digital imaging via teleophthalmology: a comparison to slide film. Can J Ophthalmol 36:187-96.

Tennant MT, Rudnisky CJ, Hinz BJ, MacDonald IM, Greve MD. (2000) Tele-ophthalmology via stereoscopic digital imaging: a pilot project. Diabetes Technol Ther 2:583-7.

Thompson DM, Kozak SE, Sheps S. (1999) Insulin adjustment by a diabetes nurse educator improves glucose control in insulin-requiring diabetic patients: a randomized trial. CMAJ 161:959-62.

Tsang MW, Mok M, Kam G, Jung M, Tang A, Chan U, Chu CM, Li I, Chan J. (2001) Improvement in diabetes control with a monitoring system based on a hand-held, touch-screen electronic diary. J Telemed Telecare 7:47-50.

Weingarten SR, Henning JM, Badamgarav E, Knight K, Hasselblad V, Gano A, Ofman JJ. (2002) Interventions used in disease management programs for patients with chronic illness - which ones work? Meta-analysis of published reports. BMJ 325:925-8.

Whitlock WL, Brown A, Moore K, Pavliscsak H, Dingbaum A, Lacefield D, Buker K, Xenakis S. (2000) Telemedicine improved diabetic management. Mil Med 165:579-84.

Wojcicki JM, Ladyzynski P, Krzymien J, Jozwicka E, Blachowicz J, Janczewska E, Czajkowski K, Karnafel W. (2001) What we can really expect from telemedicine in intensive diabetes treatment: results from 3-year study on type 1 pregnant diabetic women. Diabetes Technol Ther 3:581-9.

Wootton R. (1996) Telemedicine: a cautious welcome. BMJ 313: 1375-1377.

Wootton R, Craig J (eds). *(1999)* <u>Introduction to Telemedicine.</u> London: Royal Society of Medicine Press.

Wootton R, Yellowlees P, McLaren P (eds). (2003) <u>Telepsychiatry and e-Mental Health</u>. London: Royal Society of Medicine Press.

Yogesan K, Constable IJ, Barry CJ, Eikelboom RH, McAllister IL, Tay-Kearney ML. (2000) Telemedicine screening of diabetic retinopathy using a hand-held fundus camera. Telemed J 6:219-23.

Yip MP, Mackenzie A, Chan J. (2002) Patient satisfaction with telediabetes education in Hong Kong. J Telemed Telecare 8:48-51.

TELEHEALTH: A PARADIGM FOR MANAGING CHRONIC AND PREVENTABLE DISEASES BY TARGETING BEHAVIORAL RISK FACTORS

Brie Linkenhoker and William Gordon

INTRODUCTION

Telehealth seeks to adaptively change health behaviors through provider-patient interactions using distance communication technologies. Altering health behaviors can significantly improve the prevention and management of chronic and preventable diseases (CPDs). Here we describe the burden of CPDs in the US, which will grow as the population ages, and propose that chronic management of chronic diseases through telehealth programs may be the most effective approach to reducing this burden. We assess the nation's readiness for telehealth, and consider problems with existing telehealth research. We conclude by discussing remaining challenges and unanswered questions about telehealth and its future in the US.

We propose that the best solution to managing chronic diseases is distance intervention, used alone or in combination with on-site interactions. The goals of this intervention are altering health behaviors and monitoring health risks over an extended period of time. Distance intervention, which could take the form of communication by phone, email, fax, video conferencing, or contact through other personal communication devices, could have a significant impact on the incidence and management of CPDs without overburdening the health care system with soaring costs and unreasonable worker demands for face-to-face contact. We use the term telehealth to refer to the use of distance intervention coupled with communication technologies to adaptively change health-related behaviors and prevent, delay, and manage CPDs.

Chronic and Preventable Diseases: Definition and Scope

Chronic and preventable diseases result in illness, disability, and the need for treatment over a long period, and are rarely cured even with extensive medical intervention. In 2000, more than 125 million, or 45%, of Americans suffered from at least one chronic disease, and 60 million had more than one chronic condition. By 2020, the number of people living with chronic diseases in the US is expected to rise to 157 million, and nearly half of these people will have multiple chronic CPDs (Wu and Green, 2000). Chronic and preventable diseases kill more than 1.7 million Americans each year, resulting in 7 out of every 10 deaths in the United States (Centers for Disease Control and Prevention, 1999).

Direct medical care costs for people with CPDs totaled more than $510 billion in 2000, and these costs are expected to rise to $1.07 trillion annually by 2020. People with a CPD can expect twice the annual out-of-pocket expense, and five times the total annual medical costs, as a person with no chronic disorders (Partnership for Solutions, 2002). Despite the enormous cost burden CPDs pose to Americans and the American health care system, the public health expenditure targeting chronic diseases was only $1.21 per person in 1994 (Partnership for Solutions, 2002). The total indirect costs due to chronic conditions are difficult to calculate due largely to the sheer enormity of the problem, but clearly run in the trillions of dollars. Direct and indirect costs, where available, are presented along with prevalence data for individual CPDs in Table 1.

Table 1: Estimated prevalence and costs of chronic and preventable diseases.

Disease	Number of affected persons (US)	Estimated Costs (US dollars per year)	Source
Overweight/ Obesity	97.1 million (overweight); 39.8 million (obese)	51.6 billion (direct); 99.2 billion (total)	Flegal et al., 1998; Wolf and Colditz, 1998
Oral Diseases	~90 million	53.8 billion (direct)	CDC, 2000a
Cardiovascular disease	58 million	286.5 billion (total)	CDC 2000b, American Heart Association, 2001
Chronic Pain	>50 million	90 billion (total)	Louis Harris & Associates, Inc., 1999; American Chronic Pain Assn, 2002
Smoking	47 million	75 billion (direct); 155 billion (total)	CDC, 2002b
Arthritis	43 million	15 billion (direct); 65 billion (total)	CDC, 2002c
Psychiatric Disorders	~40 million	67 billion (direct); 147.8 billion (total)	Rupp et al., 1998; Rice and Miller, 1998
Drug/Alcohol Abuse	22.7 million	245.7 billion (total)	ONDCP, 2001
Asthma	17 million	8.1 billion (direct) 12.7 billion (total)	Mannino, 1998; American Lung Assn, 2003
Diabetes	17 million	44.1 billion (direct); 98.2 billion (total)	CDC, 2003c; American Diabetes Assn,1998
Sexually Transmitted Diseases (excluding HIV)	15.3 million (cases per year)	10 billion (direct)	American Social Health Association, 1998; Eng and Butler, 1997
Osteoporosis	10 million (additional 18 million at risk)	13.8 billion (direct)	National Osteoporosis, 1995
Cancer	8.9 million	56.4 billion (direct) 156.7 billion (total)	American Cancer Society, 2002
Alzheimer's Disease	>4 million	>152 billion (total)	Alzheimer's Assn, 2002
Stroke	3 million	17 billion (direct); 30 billion (total)	National Stroke Association, 2002
Epilepsy	2.3 million	12.5 billion (total)	CDC, 2003b
HIV/AIDS	800,000-900,000	6.7-7.8 billion (direct)	CDC 2001; Hellinger and Fleishman, 2000

The Importance of Targeting Health Behaviors

The development of most CPDs is strongly influenced by lifestyle factors. Many chronic conditions can be prevented, delayed, or the risk of those diseases may be substantially reduced, by modifying lifestyle variables (Gorelick et al., 1999; Knowler et al., 2000; Ornish et al., 1998). Early behavioral interventions can often significantly allay symptoms and reduce the risk of advanced disease or the development of costly comorbid disorders.

Some diseases, such as cancer, diabetes, or HIV infection, that initially may have been acute have now become chronic conditions. For example, persons infected with HIV had a life expectancy of about a year and a half in the early 1980s. With advances in antiretroviral therapy, life expectancy has dramatically increased as symptom severity decreased, but the drugs must be taken every day for the rest of an infected person's life.

Although organ transplants have enabled countless lives to be saved, organ recipients must strictly adhere to immunosuppressive drug regimens and other lifestyle changes for the rest of their lives. Advances in surgical techniques, pharmaceuticals, and cancer treatments have all improved life expectancy for a wide range of diseases, but often with the requirement of extended or lifetime medical care. It is this extended care that can be targeted by effective management programs focusing on behavioral modifications.

The one thing all CPDs have in common is that there is at least one health behavior that can be targeted to increase the chances of primary prevention, delay initial onset, or improve current or future disease status. These behaviors include, but are not limited to, the following:

> Adherence to Scheduled Health Appointments
> Avoidance of Habit-Forming Substances
> Compliance with Drug Regimens
> Dietary Changes
> Exercise
> Family Caregiving
> Regular Screening or Testing
> Routine Dental Care
> Safe Sexual Practices
> Self-monitoring
> Weight Management

Many CPDs are influenced by the same health behaviors and risk factors, and may share the best targets for interventions. Three risk factors are particularly harmful to large numbers of Americans: tobacco use, poor dietary and nutritional habits, and insufficient exercise. At least 430,000 American deaths can be attributed to smoking each year (CDC, 2002), and the total costs of caring for people with health problems due to cigarette smoking are estimated at $72.7 billion, or 11.8 % of medical payments per year (Miller et al., 1998). Because smoking can cause or

exacerbate respiratory disorders, cancers, heart disease, stroke risk, and other chronic diseases, the prevention or cessation of tobacco use represents a prime target for behavioral intervention. Poor dietary and nutritional habits and insufficient exercise have proximate deleterious effects on health, and have strong associations with obesity, type II diabetes, certain cancers, cardiovascular disease, osteoporosis, and a variety of other CPDs. Poor diet and lack of physical activity are associated with 300,000 deaths each year, second only to tobacco use(CDC, 1999). All three of these prime risk factors in health behavior can be targeted in all populations and at all ages. Although smoking prevention and lifelong good diet and exercise regimens are ideal, improving these health behaviors can have beneficial effects at any age.

Developing Problems in CPD Management

Two trends - the aging of the US population and the decrease in primary care giver-patient interactions - will seriously exacerbate the nation's problems with CPDs in the next several decades. Currently, approximately one third of total US health care expenditures is spent on older adults (65 years and older)(Centers for Disease Control and Prevention, 2002) 80% of whom suffer from at least one CPD (Marks, 1999). Nearly 40% of senior citizens living outside of institutions in 1994 were limited in some way by a chronic disorder, and a quarter of these were unable to perform daily life activities. By 2030, the number of American senior citizens will have more than doubled from current levels to 70 million, or 1 in 5, Americans (CDC, 2003). As the baby boomer generation ages and life expectancies continue to increase with advances in new medical technology, health care spending simply due to an aging population will increase by 25% by 2030, without adjusting for inflation or new technology development. Health care expenditures for older people are high due to the compounding of chronic conditions (50% of all senior citizens have more than one CPD (Stafford et al., 1999), and the high cost of common medical procedures for elderly people, which include angioplasty, bypass surgery, and hip and knee replacements. The costs of prescription drugs have also increased in recent years, and as the population ages, the amount of heath care dollars spent on medications will increase.

As CPDs have become more burdensome on a health care system that already seems stretched to capacity, face-to-face interactions between primary care physicians and patients have decreased. Between 1978 and 1994, the total number of adult visits to primary care physicians, who are most likely to be able to monitor the general health of patients over long periods of time, decreased by about 25 million per year, and the number of visits to primary care physicians as a percentage of total physician visits also decreased, from 52% of all adult visits to 41% (Stafford et al., 1999). This decrease is likely due to a true decrease in overall doctor visits, an increase in the proportion of visits made to specialists, and an increase in the number of emergency room visits in place of primary care visits. Visits to specialists may result in improved CPD outcomes, but sharing and managing information between multiple physicians, nurses, and pharmacists becomes more difficult as the number of practitioners increases, and thus presents a major challenge to the prevention and treatment of CPDs.

As visits to primary care physicians have decreased, emergency room visits have increased. Between 1992 and 1999, emergency department utilization in the United States increased 14%, from 89.8 million to 102.8 million visits, or about 38 visits per 100 persons (Cherry et al., 2003). In one study involving 56 emergency departments nationwide, admitting triage nurses classified 37% of all ED visits as

having a non-urgent condition (Young et al., 1996). As more Americans turn to acute treatments for chronic problems, poor health outcomes and increased prevalence of CPDs will ensue in the absence of effective disease management approaches.

These health care trends will exacerbate the CPD problem that already runs rampant through American society. The approach of our current health care system to managing CPDs will not be sufficient as CPDs become a larger burden on the health care system. Even if the total number of health care providers and worker hours could be increased, the costs of managing CPDs through frequent onsite contact would be too expensive to implement fully. Chronic disorders need chronic management rather than acute treatment, and both management and prevention programs need to reach those people most at risk for CPDs.

Defining Telehealth

The terms "telehealth," "telemedicine," "telematics," and "telecare" have been used to describe health care interventions occurring over a distance. Unfortunately, these terms have also been used in different or more restricted contexts, causing confusion in assessing the successes and failures of distance health intervention. "Telemedicine" is often used to describe networked computer systems that would allow doctors and health care organizations to manage patient information, and has also been applied to technological applications that allow one doctor to observe the activities of another geographically removed doctor, or permit diagnosis over a distance. "Telecare" usually connotes a specifically medical intervention that occurs via phone, internet, fax, or video transmission. "Telematics" is a term often used in European research, defined by the WHO as "health-related activities, services, and systems carried out over a distance by means of information and communications technology." This term is rarely seen in American research, however. We prefer the term "telehealth" because it is inclusive of the definition of telecare, but also includes other key services that might happen over a distance, such as case management for addiction or weight loss, phone reminders for appointments and prescription medications, preventive interventions, triage advice, and caregiver support. The term "telehealth" is the most definitionally appropriate word for the spectrum of distance interventions that we envision for the prevention and treatment of chronic disorders: "Tele-" indicates that services are exchanged over a distance, and "-health" encompasses physical, social, behavioral, and psychological aspects of a person's well-being.

Is the United States ready for Telehealth?

Current data and recent trends suggest that the United States is technologically ready for the use of telecommunications media in health care. As of March 1998, 94.1 percent of American households had telephone service (Belinfante, 2000) the medium that is most frequently used in existing telehealth programs. The number of Americans with cell phones has now surpassed 100 million, and the number is rising each year. Increased wireless usage raises the possibility for contact at home, at work, on vacation, and in transit.

The internet is likely to become more and more involved in telehealth interventions. A 2001 survey found that 65 million, or 61%, of U.S. households are actively using the Internet. Ninety percent of online households have stated that they will continue their internet service (Gartner Dataquest Survey, 2001). Individuals 50 years and older showed the largest increase (53%) as a group in internet usage between December 1998 and August of 2000 (MacDonald, 2000), an exciting trend for potential applications in telehealth given the high incidence of CPDs

in this segment of the population. Many Americans also have access to email and the internet at their offices and on their cell phones, creating even more possibilities for distance interactions using this medium. One recent study found that 70% of patients would be willing to use email to communicate with their primary care physicians, and physicians and staff were even more optimistic than patients about the potential for e-mail interactions to improve relationships between doctors and patients (Moyer et al., 2002). Thus, as internet usage increases, the potential for successful telehealth applications grows substantially.

In addition to being ready to use the media of telehealth, Americans are also in a situation to benefit from centralized delivery of telehealth services. In 1996, more than 50 million Americans received health care services through a health management organization (Agency for Health Care Policy and Research, 1996), and the trend is toward even higher enrollment. Since 1993, enrollment in America's 650+ HMOs increased by 91% (Interstudy Competitive Edge Series, 1999). Among the 74 million Americans who receive government subsidized health care in the Medicare, Medicaid, and SCHIP programs, an increasing number are choosing to receive care through an HMO rather than through the traditional fee-for service plan (Aventis Pharmaceuticals, 2001). This connection to centralized health care delivery is positive because telehealth programs in both rural and urban areas will require automated systems, specially trained workers, and management structures capable of implementing wide-scale programs. Although some telehealth applications could certainly be initiated and managed in small community settings, the economy of scale needed to efficiently operate the most efficacious and cost-effective systems will be hard to attain in a small community setting.

Targets of Telehealth

It is possible to identify certain population groups as the best potential targets of different types of interventions aimed at specific diseases, and groups that might benefit most from interventions because they are disproportionately at risk for a given set of CPDs. For example, adolescents may be the best targets of prevention programs for HIV, pregnancy, obesity, tobacco, drug, and alcohol use, and women may be best served by programs that help prevent unintended pregnancy, and encourage perinatal care, breast and cervical cancer screening, and dietary changes that will help prevent birth defects, cancers, and osteoporosis. All segments of the population may benefit from programs that counter poor nutritional habits and encourage exercise. However, not all populations may respond equally to the same types of intervention. Extensive research on representative, diverse experimental groups with appropriate controls will be needed to assess population-specific efficacy.

Although all populations in the US could benefit from telehealth interventions, chronic diseases affect women and minorities disproportionately, and these populations may benefit most from specifically targeted telehealth programs. Women account for more than half of deaths from cardiovascular disease each year, and the death rate from cervical cancer for African-American women is more than twice that for white women (CDC, 2002a). HIV disproportionately affects African-Amercian and Hispanic populations. CPDs have higher prevalence rates in those populations most disenfranchised from the traditional health care establishment. These populations may make very good targets for telehealth interventions that are less traditional and specifically targeted to their needs. Research will need to address the special needs of these populations, and take into account specific attributes of the eventual target populations when designing the initial studies.

The prevalence of many chronic and preventable diseases is higher in rural and inner city areas – regions that are notoriously behind urban and suburban areas in health care standards. The number of health care providers is lower in rural regions, and these areas are far less likely to be included in trials of new methods of treatment and prevention. In rural areas, driving distance restricts the number of contacts between patients and providers. Since the proportion of the population that is middle-aged or elderly increases as urbanization decreases, problems with health care access in rural areas are compounded by an increase in CPD incidence among older Americans. On many health care measures, rural residents fare the worst. They are the more likely than their urban and suburban counterparts to smoke, be obese, die from chronic obstructive pulmonary disease, and are less likely to have health insurance (Eberhardt et al., 2001). People living in inner city areas are more likely to develop addiction to opiates and cocaine, suffer from high infant mortality and high birthrate, and die from ischemic heart disease. This population is ethnically diverse and faces high levels of poverty, thus presenting new challenges to management of CPDs within this group.

Improving Telehealth Research

Seven recent reviews of telemedicine and telehealth research (Balas et al., 1997; Ohinmaa et al., 1999; Almazan and Gallo, 1999; Currell et al., 2000; Mair and Witten, 2000; Witten et al., 2000; Hersh et al., 2001), whether focusing primarily on improvement of health outcomes or cost-effectiveness, all found that the methodology used in the majority of studies was of poor quality, and that due to problems such as small sample sizes, short duration, and lack of follow-up at the end of the study to assess health

Table 2: Evidence for effective telehealth intervention and potential targets of future telehealth programs.

Disease	Evidence for effective telehealth intervention?	Targets of intervention
Overweight/ Obesity	Saelens et al. (2002) Delichatsios et al. (2001)	Education; emotional support; distance monitoring
Oral Diseases	Reekie & Devlin (1998)	Education and prevention; appointment compliance
Cardiovascular disease	DeBusk et al. (1994)	Distance symptom evaluation; lifestyle & drug regimen management
Chronic Pain	Ahles et al. (2001) Lorig et al. (2002)	Distance monitoring of drug regimen; emotional support
Smoking	Elder et al. (1993) Zhu et al. (2002)	Cessation support; education; prevention
Arthritis	Weinberger et al. (1989) Hughes et al. (2002)	Self-care, pain-management
Psychiatric Disorders	Simon et al. (2002)	Caregiver education; drug regimen monitoring; emotional support
Drug/Alcohol Abuse	Humphreys & Klaw (2001)	Education; prevention; emotional support
Asthma	Greineder et al. (1995)	Distance health monitoring; treatment regimen compliance, education
Diabetes	Piette et al. (2000) Turnin et al. (1992)	Self-care; in-home health monitoring; distance management; education; prevention
Sexually Transmitted Diseases (excluding HIV)	Stanton et al. (1996) Noell et al. (1997)	Prevention; education; behavior modification
Osteoporosis	Blalock et al. (2002)	Education and prevention; increased participation in testing
Cancer	Miller et al. (1997) Champion et al. (2000)	Increased participation in screening; drug regimen compliance; education
Alzheimer's Disease	Goodman & Pynoos (1990)	Caregiver education; telephone reminders for daily activities and medication
Stroke	Grant et al. (2002)	Distance diagnosis; diet and exercise counseling; caregiver support
Epilepsy	Hoch et al. (1999)	Distance monitoring; drug regimen compliance
HIV/AIDS	Tsu et al. (2002) Gustafson et al. (1999)	Drug regimen compliance; increased participation in testing and counseling

outcomes, true meta-analyses cannot be performed.

The lack of well-designed studies of telehealth interventions may make researchers less likely to make good inferences about the potential effectiveness of telehealth programs, and they may not be willing to pursue new avenues of research in the field.

Geographical biases may limit generalization of those few existing good studies as a basis for new telehealth programs. The vast majority of research on telehealth interventions comes from countries with socialized health care systems, primarily in Europe and Australia. Because the American health care system differs so fundamentally from those in Britain, Germany, and elsewhere, American health management groups may have been reluctant to draw heavily upon these data in the formation of new research questions or telehealth programs.

Before telehealth programs can be developed, optimized, and standardized, research in the field must present solid data on best practices in health behavior modification and on the efficacy and cost-effectiveness of pilot telehealth programs. Although it may be clear that targeting certain behaviors, such as smoking or inadequate exercise, will likely lead to positive health outcomes, it is in many cases unclear how to achieve the greatest change in behavior over the long term in a given population. When the best behavioral modification practices have been identified, rationally-designed telehealth programs must be tested for short- and long-term efficacy and cost-effectiveness. This second phase of research will help health care managers decide how, when, and where to implement telehealth programs for the greatest maximal benefit.

Much of the existing research on telehealth interventions is more focused on the telehealth application, rather than on the best approach to disease prevention or management. Concentrating primarily on a specific telehealth application within a highly-constrained experimental context may obscure data that can be gleaned about how well behavior-targeted approaches work in general. For example, a research group may ask, "Can automated telephone reminders increase adherence to a daily exercise regimen?" rather than, "What approaches to increasing adherence to a daily exercise regimen have been most successful? Can the best of these approaches be applied in a telehealth setting?". It will be essential to uncover the best behavioral practices used in any setting with any form of communication before new telehealth programs can be developed incorporating this data. Once we know more about what behavioral modification approaches work best for a certain population, this information can be used to design studies to test whether the same best practices are amenable to translation into the telehealth paradigm. After the techniques known to be most successful in CPD prevention and management have been translated into telehealth applications, it will be easier to more accurately assess variables underlying success and failure across types of telehealth programs, and generate a better answer to the question of telehealth's success or failure.

As best practices in behavioral medicine are being identified, research on pilot telehealth programs needs to improve. A complete study of a pilot telehealth program would include many, if not all, of the following:

- A comparison of the telehealth program with other treatments in terms of clinical efficacy
- A comparison of health outcomes and compliance within and across different populations grouped according to race, socioeconomic status, age, gender, and other factors
- The effect of the telehealth program on overall disease outcomes at multiple time points, preferably extending

through a period of at least 6 months, and optimally for several years.

- Follow-up measurements of health outcomes at time points extending beyond one year
- A measurement of patient satisfaction with the telehealth program, preferably in comparison with other treatments
- A measurement of compliance and dropout rates over the course of the telehealth program and beyond
- An assessment of the capacity to personalize the telehealth program and combine it with other behavioral modification paradigms for maximal efficacy
- A comparison of the telehealth program to other treatments in terms of overall costs, health care provider and administrator hours, patient time expenditure, and technology and training requirements
- An indication of cost-effectiveness of the telehealth program in comparison with no intervention and other treatment programs

It is unreasonable to expect that any one study should attempt to answer all of these questions. However, several groups have already attempted to combine clinical efficacy measurements with simultaneous assessments of several of the categories mentioned above (Biermann et al., 2000). These types of research approaches should form the standard that telehealth research should seek to achieve.

The need for longitudinal studies that address both clinical efficacy and cost-effectiveness creates a need for the formation of new research groups that are interdisciplinary and well-coordinated. Large HMOs and the federal government are in an ideal position to organize and fund such new research teams, and both should establish clear research goals with timelines that will allow the concurrent collection of data across disciplines in both short- and long-term study approaches. Instead of funding many small projects that cannot be maintained for long periods of time or extended beyond a restricted experimental group, HMOs and government organizations should fund coordinated smaller projects, whose data can be combined to give a well-rounded and detailed picture of the efficacy and efficiency of telehealth programs. Umbrella organizations, streamlined private grant funding, and improved communication between academia and business would also improve the efficiency of telehealth research.

In addition to the changes that need to be made in the way telehealth research is carried out, the effective implementation of telehealth systems faces four other major challenges: changing attitudes about health and medical care, dealing with the problems of comorbid disorders, developing appropriate management structures and addressing new legal concerns, and training and retraining workers to meet the specific needs of telehealth.

Challenging Attitudes about Medicine and Health

Telehealth programs will need to target attitudes and beliefs held by both health care providers and patients in order to effect behavioral changes. Recent studies have shown that many doctors are unwilling to talk to patients about making behavioral and lifestyle changes, but are more willing to prescribe medication to acutely treat chronic diseases. One study found that only 28% of sampled US adults reported receiving counseling about their physical activity levels, and of these, only 38% received help constructing an activity plan, and only 42% received any follow-up support (Glasgow et al., 2001). Another study of type 2 diabetes patients and their doctors reported that the medical and laboratory guidelines recommended by the American Diabetes

Association were followed more frequently than patient counseling about self-care guidelines (Glasgow and Strycker, 2000). Telehealth programs will require greater willingness on the parts of physicians and other health care workers to target behaviors and lifestyle factors in order to successful.

Other beliefs and attitudes that could be harmful or helpful to the aims of telehealth programs will also need to be considered in the construction of these programs. One recent study found that patients who thought that their doctor didn't order appropriate tests or referrals thought about changing doctors, and that communication problems significantly reduced trust in the doctor (Keating et al., 2002). If health care providers move more towards behavioral interventions and away from immediate medical treatment for chronic disorders, they may need to change their modes of communication in order to change patient attitudes about the necessity of medical tests and treatments when behavioral interventions may be more appropriate. Other studies have reported that patients often look at the onset of chronic disease as an inevitable part of getting older and have little understanding of what factors led to the development of disease (Rogers et al., 2000), and that many patients would often rather not know if they had a life-threatening disease, such as cancer, and believe that such a diagnosis is a "death sentence" with no viable options for curative treatment (Puschel et al., 2001). These attitudes will have to be countered with education and communication in order for telehealth interventions to be accepted. Other attitudes may be helpful to the adoption of telehealth programs. For example, a recent survey of patients' willingness to use email to communicate with their doctors found that few expressed concern about privacy and security, and that many patients and physicians were willing to communicate via email (Moyer et al., 2002). Another study reported that the number of

Americans looking to the internet for health information doubled to 98 million from 1998 to 2000 (McDonald, 2000), suggesting that Americans may be amenable to receiving health care advice, information, and interactions over the internet through telehealth programs. The number of Americans visiting alternative medicine practitioners increased 47.3% from 1990 to 629 million visits 1997 (Eisenburg et al., 1998), suggesting that Americans may be willing to welcome new types of intervention to prevent and treat chronic conditions.

The Challenge of Comorbidity

Nearly half of all people suffering from chronic disease have more than one CPD (Wu and Green, 2000). In 1999, 63 percent of aged Medicare beneficiaries had two or more chronic conditions and accounted for 95% of all Medicare spending (Partnership for Solutions, 2002a). Care for people with comorbid CPDs consumes 75% of US government health care spending, and 51% of overall public and private health care spending (Agency for Healthcare Research and Quality, 1996). As people add comorbid CPDs, their medical costs increase substantially. For example, 75% of people with cardiovascular disease have one or more additional co-morbid chronic conditions (examples include: arthritis 20.2%, eye disorders 15.5%, diabetes 15.4%, and mental illness 12.3%). Costs for caring for persons with cardiovascular disease double with two additional comorbid disorders, and triple with four comorbid disorders (Cohen et al., 1996).

Comorbid conditions cause complications that go well beyond increased medical costs. For example, rheumatoid arthritis is a chronic condition that is associated with a 5- to 15-year reduction in life expectancy, but the disease itself does not result in early death. The culprits in reduced life expectancy are the comorbid diseases associated with rheumatoid arthritis: diabetes mellitus, heart disease, and gastrointestinal bleeding (MacLean et al., 2000). The interactions between chronic diseases, and in some cases, between the treatments for one disease and the development or aggravation of another, can have a multiplicative effect on the reduction in overal health and quality of life, and can increase disability beyond what the simple addition of the disability risk for each CPD would yield.

Unfortunately, there is currently no comprehensive resource that outlines the best practices for diagnosing, treating, and managing patients with one or more comorbid disorders, nor is there a reference that documents the probability of comorbidity for each major chronic disease. Such resources are desperately needed. Specialists who treat a given CPD may be aware of certain general rates of comorbidity, but primary care givers and case managers should also be familiar with the probabilities for disease interactions. Since many sufferers of CPDs see multiple health care providers, the coordination of treatment efforts is essential to avoid ignoring, precipitating, or exacerbating comorbid chronic disorders. Centralized databases containing patient histories and current medications should be coupled with algorithms for predicting comorbidity, and professional telehealth specialists may be needed to personally coordinate care among multiple health care providers seen by the same patient.

Management and Legal Challenges

Implementing telehealth programs of any size will present a number of challenges to health care management. Developing telehealth programs will need to build up a simple and streamlined management structure and communication system that will be able to handle complex webs of information sharing and patient risk and behavior analysis. For example, developing the infrastructure for a simple automated telephone appointment

reminder system could occur while a first wave of health care professionals is being trained in case management using distance technology. When management structures are in place, these aspects of telehealth infrastructure could be combined.

Another challenge to management will be dealing with the interests of specific groups within the health care network. Patients may feel slighted if services are shifted from physicians to other health care workers; marketing of new services to health care clients will be essential to the smooth acceptance of telehealth services. Roles played by case managers, physicians, nurses, and pharmacists will likely shift as behavioral management gains importance and telehealth systems are put in place, and good management will be essential to guide these transitions. Flexibility will be needed to accommodate health care workers and their preferences for distance or face-to-face interactions, and education and new policy will be needed to encourage the most appropriate prescription and implementation of telehealth programs.

The implementation of telehealth programs will undoubtedly introduce new legal issues into a health care system that is already overburdened with litigious exercise and vexed by questions of privacy and liability. Diagnosis and treatment of patients has traditionally been carried out primarily by physicians, who must be covered by extensive malpractice insurance. Opening up diagnosis, treatment, and ongoing care recommendations to non-physician health care workers will presumably also open up new pathways for lawsuits and introduce new needs for insurance coverage. Because telehealth networks are likely to be interstate organizations, they will need to address differing standards between states on issues of licensure, accreditation, privacy and patient information sharing, informed consent, and many other legal issues (Klein and Manning,

1995). Telehealth applications such as automated reminder systems and prevention programs may create fewer initial legal quandaries, and could provide a good foundation for future, more complicated telehealth programs.

Challenging new roles for health care workers

Mature telehealth programs will require many workers trained specifically in the use of distance intervention in health care. To meet this need, health care providers practicing medicine, nursing, pharmacy, psychology, physical therapy, or social work could receive additional training and certification in telehealth. This specialization would be designed to complement existing skills and expertise, and would provide training about co-morbid disorders, successful behavioral health strategies, and applications using distance approaches that was specifically designed for a particular role in the health care network.

Another possibility is the creation of a new type of position, the personal health manager or telehealth specialist, who would be trained primarily as a case manager responsible for coordinating information flowing between the patient and her team of health care providers, but who would also have specific skills related to designing and providing behavioral intervention programs that are individually tailored based on risk factors, medical history, and other demographic factors. A nationally-credentialed personal health manager or telehealth specialist would ideally follow the same patients for many years.

Telehealth workers will require training in the use of distance communication technology. New technology and automated systems will require staff familiar with equipment and the needs of the organization to develop better software, hardware, and better software/hardware-human interactions. The application of new technology that can be used at a distance could expand job opportunities for many employees. Workers on maternity or disability leave may be able to continue work from home. Positions in which time is split between work at home and on-site may be appealing to professionals with children or elderly parents. Certain telehealth programs could be run from rural locations, providing jobs in areas with high unemployment, and health care providers with opportunities to employ workers in areas with lower costs of living and lower wage levels.

CONCLUSION

Although extensive data on patient outcomes and cost-effectiveness of telehealth programs are not yet available, the known benefits of lifestyle change and behavior modification coupled with the aging of the American population, and trends in technology use and patient-provider interactions in the US, suggest that telehealth is a sound investment. More research on cost-effectiveness, especially in the long-run, will be needed to rouse the interest of large-scale health care provider organizations. Perhaps the most important next step will be the development of a database of best practices and comorbidities in treating and preventing CPDs. However, the remaining questions surrounding telehealth are best viewed as gateways to future research, rather than barriers. The development and implementation of comprehensive telehealth programs represent the best avenue for both improving the quality of life of American residents as well as reducing the staggering and ever-expanding costs associated with chronic and preventable diseases.

REFERENCES

Agency for Health Care Policy and Research (1996) Strengthening Managed Care, Research in Action Fact Sheet, AHCPR Publication No. 96-P045, http://www.ahcpr.gov/research/managed.htm, accessed 8/27/03.

Ahles TA, Seville J, Wasson J, Johnson D, Callahan E, Stukel TA. (2001) Panel-based pain management in primary care. a pilot study. J Pain Symptom Manage 22:584-90.

Almazan C, Gallo P. (1999) Assessing Clinical Benefit and Economic Evaluation in Telemedicine. Catalan Agency for Health Technology Assessment: Barcelona, Spain.

Alzheimer's Association. (2002) Alzheimer's Disease: Statistics Factsheet. http://www.alz.org/AboutAD/Statistics.htm, accessed on 10/20/02.

American Cancer Society. (2002) Cancer facts and figures 2002, http://www.cancer.org/downloads/STT/CancerFacts&Figures2002TM.pdf, accessed on 8/27/03.

American Chronic Pain Association.(2002) What is pain?, http://www.theacpa.org/whatispain.htm, accessed on 10/20/02.

American Diabetes Association. (1998) Economic Consequences of diabetes mellitus in the U.S. in 1997. Diabetes Care 21: 296-309.

American Heart Association. (2001) Heart Disease and Stroke Statistics — 2002Update. Dallas, Tex.: American Heart Association.

American Lung Association Epidemiology and Statistic Unit. (2003) Trends in Asthma Morbidity and Mortality. http://www.lungusa.org/data/asthma/asthma1.pdf, accessed on 8/27/03.

American Social Health Association. (1998) Sexually Transmitted Diseases in America: How Many Cases and at What Cost? Menlo Park, CA: Kaiser Family Foundation.

Aventis Pharmaceuticals. (2001) Medicare/Medicaid HMO Enrollment. eManaged Care Trends Digest, http://www.managedcaredigest.com/edigests/tr2001/tr2001c01s03g01.shtml, accessed on 10/20/02.

Balas EA, Jaffrey F, Kuperman GJ, Boren SA, Brown GD, Pinciroli F, Mitchell JA. (1997) Electronic communication with patients. Evaluation of distance medicine technology. JAMA 278:152-9.

Belinfante A. (2000) Telephone subscribership in the United States (data through November 1999). Federal Communications Commission. http://www.fcc.gov/Bureaus/Common_Carrier/Reports/FCC-State_Link/IAD/subs1199.pdf, accessed on 8/27/03.

Biermann E, Dietrich W, Standl E. (2000) Telecare of diabetic patients with intensified insulin therapy. A randomized clinical trial. Stud Health Technol Inform. 77:327-32.

Blalock SJ, DeVellis BM, Patterson CC, Campbell MK, Orenstein DR, Dooley MA. (2002) Effects of an osteoporosis prevention program incorporating tailored educational materials. Am J Health Promot 16:146-56.

Centers for Disease Control and Prevention. (2003) Healthy Aging: Preventing Disease and Improving Quality of Life Among Older Americans. http://www.cdc.gov/nccdphp/aag/aag_aging.htm, accessed on 8/27/03.

Centers for Disease Control and Prevention. (2003b) Epilepsy: One of the Nation's Most Common Disabling Neurological Disorders, http://www.cdc.gov/nccdphp/epilepsy/, accessed on 8/27/03.

Centers for Disease Control and Prevention. (2003c) Diabetes: Disabling, Deadly, and on the Rise, http://www.cdc.gov/nccdphp/aag/aag_ddt.htm, accessed on 8/27/03.

Centers for Disease Control and Prevention. (2002) Chronic Disease Overview. http://www.cdc.gov/washington/overview

/chrondis.htm, accessed on 8/27/03.

Centers for Disease Control and Prevention. (2002) Targeting Tobacco Use: The Nation's Leading Cause of Death. http://www.cdc.gov/nccdphp/aag/aag_osh.htm, accessed on 8/27/03.

Centers for Disease Control and Prevention. (2002) Targeting Arthritis: Public Health Takes Action. http://www.cdc.gov/nccdphp/aag/aag_arthritis.htm, accessed on 8/27/03.

Centers for Disease Control and Prevention. (2001) HIV/AIDS Surveillance Report: Midyear edition, 13(1), http://www.cdc.gov/hiv/stats/hasr1301c.pdf, accessed on 8/27/03.

Centers for Disease Control and Prevention. (2000) Oral Health 2000: Facts and Figures. http://www.cdc.gov/OralHealth/factsheets/sgr2000-fs1.htm, accessed on 8/27/03.

Centers for Disease Control and Prevention. (2000) Preventing Cardiovascular Disease: Addressing the Nation's Leading Killer. http://www.cdc.gov/programs/chronic1.htm, accessed on 8/27/03.

Centers for Disease Control and Prevention. (1999) Chronic Diseases and Their Risk Factors: The Nation's Leading Causes of Death. http://www.cdc.gov/nccdphp/statbook/statbook.htm, accessed on 8/27/03.

Centers for Disease Control and Prevention. (1999b) National Hospital Ambulatory Medical Care Survey: 1999 Outpatient Department Summary. http://www.cdc.gov/nchs/products/pubs/pubd/ad/321-330/ad321.htm, accessed on 8/27/03.

Champion VL, Skinner CS, Foster JL.(2000) The effects of standard care counseling or telephone/in-person counseling on beliefs, knowledge, and behavior related to mammography screening. Oncol Nurs Forum 27:1565-71.

Cherry DK, Burt CW, Woodwell DA (2003) National Ambulatory Medical Care Survey: 2001 Summary. CDC Advance Data from Vital and Health Statistics 337; 1-44, http://www.cdc.gov/nchs/data/ad/ad337.pdf, accessed on 8/27/03.

Cohen JW, Monheit AC, Beauregard KM. (1996) The Medical Expenditure Panel Survey: A National Health Information Resource Inquiry. AHCPR Pub. No. 97-R043, Agency for Healthcare Research and Quality 33: 373-389.

Currell R, Urquhart C, Wainwright P, Lewis R. (2000) Telemedicine versus face to face patient care: effects on professional practice and health care outcomes. Cochrane Database Syst Rev (2):CD002098.

DeBusk RF, Miller NH, Superko HR, Dennis CA, Thomas RJ, Lew HT, Berger WE 3rd, Heller RS, Rompf J, Gee D. (1994) A case-management system for coronary risk factor modification after acute myocardial infarction. Ann Intern Med 120:721-9.

Delichatsios HK, Friedman RH, Glanz K, Tennstedt S, Smigelski C, Pinto BM, Kelley H, Gillman MW. (2001) Randomized trial of a "talking computer" to improve adults' eating habits. Am J Health Promot 15:215-24.

Eberhardt MD, Ingram DD, Makus DM. (2001) Urban and Rural Health Chartbook, Health, United States, 2001. Hyattsville, MD: National Center for Health Statistics.

Eisenberg DM, Davis RB, Ettner SL, Appel S, Wilkey S, Van Rompay M, Kessler RC. (1998) Trends in alternative medicine use in the United States, 1990-1997: results of a follow-up national survey. JAMA 280:1569-75.

Elder JP, Wildey M, de Moor C, Sallis JF Jr, Eckhardt L, Edwards C, Erickson A, Golbeck A, Hovell M, Johnston D.

(1993) The long-term prevention of tobacco use among junior high school students: classroom and telephone interventions. Am J Public Health 83:1239-44.

Eng TR, Butler WT, eds. (1997) The Hidden Epidemic: Confronting Sexually Transmitted Diseases, Executive summary. Washington, DC: National Academy Press.

Flegal KM, Carroll MD, Kuczmarski RJ, Johnson CL. (1998) Overweight and obesity in the United States: prevalence and trends, 1960-1994. Int J Obesity 22: 39-47.

Gartner Dataquest survey. (2001) http://www4.gartner.com/5_about/press_releases/2001/pr2001089b.html, accessed on 10/2/02.

Glasgow RE, Eakin EG, Fisher EB, Bacak SJ, Brownson RC. (2001) Physician advice and support for physical activity: results from a national survey. Am J Prev Med. 21:189-96.

Glasgow RE, Strycker LA.(2000) Preventive care practices for diabetes management in two primary care samples. Am J Prev Med. 19:9-14.

Goodman CC, Pynoos J. (1990) A model telephone information and support program for caregivers of Alzheimer's patients. Gerontologist 30:399-404.

Gorelick PB, Sacco RL, Smith DB, Alberts M, Mustone-Alexander L, Rader D, Ross JL, Raps E, Ozer MN, Brass LM, Malone ME, Goldberg S, Booss J, Hanley DF, Toole JF, Greengold NL, Rhew DC. (1999) Prevention of a first stroke: a review of guidelines and a multidisciplinary consensus statement from the National Stroke Association. JAMA 281(12):1112-20.

Grant JS, Elliott TR, Weaver M, Bartolucci AA, Giger JN. (2002) Telephone intervention with family caregivers of stroke survivors after rehabilitation.

Stroke 33:2060-5.

Greineder DK, Loane KC, Parks P. (1995) Reduction in resource utilization by an asthma outreach program. Arch Pediatr Adolesc Med 149:415-20.

Gustafson DH, Hawkins R, Boberg E, Pingree S, Serlin RE, Graziano F, Chan CL. (1999) Impact of a patient-centered, computer-based health information/support system. Am J Prev Med 16:1-9.

McDonald T. (2000) Americans turning to net for health info. E-Commerce Times http://www.ecommercetimes.com/perl/story/4000.html, accessed on 10/20/02.

Hellinger FJ, Fleishman JA. (2000) Estimating the national cost of treating people with HIV disease: Patient, payer, and provider data. J Acquired Immunodeficiency Syndromes 24:182-188.

Hersh WR, Helfand M, Wallace J, Kraemer D, Patterson P, Shapiro S, Greenlick M. (2001) Clinical outcomes resulting from telemedicine interventions: a systematic review. BMC Med Inform Decis Mak. 1:5. http://www.biomedcentral.com/1472-6947/1/5 accessed on 10/20/02.

Hoch DB, Norris D, Lester JE, Marcus AD. (1999) Information exchange in an epilepsy forum on the World Wide Web. Seizure 8:30-4.

Hughes RA, Carr ME, Huggett A, Thwaites CE. (2002) Review of the function of a telephone helpline in the treatment of outpatients with rheumatoid arthritis. Ann Rheum Dis 61:341-5.

Humphreys K, Klaw E. (2001) Can targeting nondependent problem drinkers and providing internet-based services expand access to assistance for alcohol problems? A study of the moderation management self-help/mutual aid organization. J Stud Alcohol 62:528-32.

Interstudy Competitive Edge Series. (1999) HMO Industry Report 9.1. Interstudy

Publications: St. Paul, MN.

Keating NL, Green DC, Kao AC, Gazmararian JA, Wu VY, Cleary PD. (2002) How are patients' specific ambulatory care experiences related to trust, satisfaction, and considering changing physicians? J Gen Intern Med. 17:29-39.

Klein SR, Manning WL. (1995) Telemedicine and the law. Healthc Inf Manage 9(3):35-40.

Knowler WC, Barrett-Connor E, Fowler SE, Hamman RF, Lachin JM, Walker EA, Nathan DM, Diabetes Prevention Program Research Group. (2002) Reduction in the incidence of type 2 diabetes with lifestyle intervention or metformin. N Engl J Med 346:393-403.

Lorig KR, Laurent DD, Deyo RA, Marnell ME, Minor MA, Ritter PL. (2002) Can a Back Pain E-mail Discussion Group improve health status and lower health care costs?: A randomized study. Arch Intern Med 162:792-6.

Louis Harris & Associates, Inc. (1999) The 1999 National Pain Survey. http://www.ultram.com/painsurvey/, accessed on 10/20/02.

MacLean CH, Louie R, Leake B, McCaffrey DF, Paulus HE, Brook RH, Shekelle PG. (2000) Quality of care for patients with rheumatoid arthritis. JAMA 284(8):984-92.

Mair F, Whitten P. (2000) Systematic Review of Studies of Patient Satisfaction with Telemedicine, BMJ 320: 1517-1520.

Mannino DM, Homa DM, Pertowski CA, Ashizawa A, Nixon LL, Johnson CA, Ball, LB, Jack E, Kang DS. (1998) Surveillance for Asthma—United States, 1960-1995. MMWR 47(SS-1): 1-28, http://www.cdc.gov/mmwr/preview/mmwrhtml/00052262.htm, accessed on 8/27/03.

Marks JS. (1999) Public Health and Chronic Disease in an Aging Society. Chronic Disease Notes and Reports 12(3): 2-6,

http://www.cdc.gov/nccdphp/cdfall99.pdf, accessed 8/27/03.

Miller LS, Zhang X, Novotny T, Rice DP, Max W. (1998) State estimates of Medicaid expenditures attributable to cigarette smoking, fiscal year 1993. Public Health 113:140-51.

Miller SM, Siejak KK, Schroeder CM, Lerman C, Hernandez E, Helm CW. (1997) Enhancing adherence following abnormal Pap smears among low-income minority women: a preventive telephone counseling strategy. J Natl Cancer Inst 89:703-8.

Moyer CA, Stern DT, Dobias KS, Cox DT, Katz SJ. (2002) Bridging the electronic divide: patient and provider perspectives on e-mail communication in primary care. Am J Manag Care 8:427-33.

National Stroke Association. (2002) http://www.stroke.org/brain_stat.cfm, accessed on 10/20/02.

National Osteoporosis Foundation (2002) Disease Statistics: Fast Facts, http://www.nof.org/osteoporosis/stats.htm , accessed on 10/20/02.

Noell J, Ary D, Duncan T. (1997) Development and evaluation of a sexual decision-making and social skills program: "the choice is yours--preventing HIV/STDs". Health Educ Behav 24:87-101.

Office of National Drug Control Policy (2001) The economic costs of drug abuse in the United States, 1992-1998. Washington, DC: Executive Office of the President. Publication No. NCJ-190636. NIH Publication number 98-4327, http://www.whitehousedrugpolicy.gov/publications/pdf/economic_costs98.pdf, accessed on 8/27/03.

Ohinmaa A, Hailey D, Roine D. (1999) The Assessment of Telemedicine: General Principles and a Systematic Review. Finnish Office for Health Care Technology Assessment: Helsinki,

Finland.

Ornish D, Scherwitz LW, Billings JH, Brown SE, Gould KL, Merritt TA, Sparler S, Armstrong WT, Ports TA, Kirkeeide RL, Hogeboom C, Brand RJ. (1998) Intensive lifestyle changes for reversal of coronary heart disease.JAMA 280:2001-7.

Partnership for Solutions. (2002) Medicare: Cost and prevalence of Chronic Conditions http://www.partnershipforsolutions.org/statistics/issue_briefs.cfm, accessed on 8/27/03.

Partnership for Solutions (2002) Statistics and Research Cost. http://www.partnershipforsolutions.org/statistics/out_of_pocket.cfm, accessed on 8/27/03.

Piette JD, Weinberger M, McPhee SJ, Mah CA, Kraemer FB, Crapo LM. (2000) Do automated calls with nurse follow-up improve self-care and glycemic control among vulnerable patients with diabetes? Am J Med 108:20-7.

Puschel K, Thompson B, Coronado GD, Lopez LC, Kimball AM. (2001) Factors related to cancer screening in Hispanics: a comparison of the perceptions of Hispanic community members, health care providers, and representatives of organizations that serve Hispanics. Health Educ Behav. 28:573-90.

Reekie D, Devlin H. (1998) Preventing failed appointments in general dental practice: a comparison of reminder methods. Br Dent J 185:472-4.

Rice DP, Miller L. (1998) Health economics and cost implications of anxiety and other mental disorders in the United States. Brit J Psychiatr supp 34: 4-9.

Rogers AE, Addington-Hall JM, Abery AJ, McCoy AS, Bulpitt C, Coats AJ, Gibbs JS. (2000) Knowledge and communication difficulties for patients with chronic heart failure: qualitative study. BMJ 321:605-7.

Rupp A, Gause EM, Reiger DA. (1998) Research policy implications of cost-of-illness studies for mental disorders. Brit J Psychiatr, supp 36: 19-25.

Saelens BE, Sallis JF, Wilfley DE, Patrick K, Cella JA, Buchta R. (2002) Behavioral weight control for overweight adolescents initiated in primary care. Obes Res 10:22-32.

Simon GE, Von Korff M, Ludman EJ, Katon WJ, Rutter C, Unutzer J, Lin EH, Bush T, Walker E. (2002) Cost-effectiveness of a program to prevent depression relapse in primary care. Med Care 40:941-50.

Stafford RS, Saglam D, Causino N, Starfield B, Culpepper L, Marder WD, Blumenthal D. (1999) Trends in adult visits to primary care physicians in the United States. Arch Fam Med 8:26-32.

Stanton BF, Li X, Galbraith J, Feigelman S, Kaljee L. (1996) Sexually transmitted diseases, human immunodeficiency virus, and pregnancy prevention. Combined contraceptive practices among urban African-American early adolescents. Arch Pediatr Adolesc Med 150:17-24.

Sturm R. (2002) The effects of obesity, smoking, and drinking on medical problems and costs. Obesity outranks both smoking and drinking in its deleterious effects on health and health costs. Health Aff (Millwood) 21:245-53.

Tsu RC, Burm ML, Gilhooly JA, Sells CW. (2002) Telephone vs. face-to-face notification of HIV results in high-risk youth. J Adolesc Health 30:154-60.

Turnin MC, Beddok RH, Clottes JP, Martini PF, Abadie RG, Buisson JC, Soule-Dupuy C, Bonneu M, Camare R, Anton JP. (1992) Telematic expert system Diabeto. New tool for diet self-monitoring for diabetic patients. Diabetes Care15:204-12.

Weinberger M, Tierney WM, Booher P, Katz BP. (1989) Can the provision of information to patients with osteoarthritis improve functional status? A randomized, controlled trial. Arthritis Rheum 32:1577-83.

Whitten P, Kingsley C, Grigsby J. (2000) Results of a Meta-Analysis of Cost-Benefit Research: Is this a Question Worth Asking? J Telemed Telecare 6: S4-S6.

Wolf AM, Colditz GA.(1998) Current estimates of the economic cost of obesity in the United States. Obesity Res 6: 97-106.

Wu S, Green A. (2000) Projection of Chronic Illness and Caregiving. RAND Health, Santa Monica, CA.

Young GP, Wagner MB, Kellermann AL, Ellis J, Bouley D. (1996) Ambulatory visits to hospital emergency departments. Patterns and reasons for use. 24 Hours in the ED Study Group. JAMA 276:460-5.

Zhu SH, Anderson CM, Tedeschi GJ, Rosbrook B, Johnson CE, Byrd M, Gutierrez-Terrell E. (2002) Evidence of real-world effectiveness of a telephone quitline for smokers. N Engl J Med 347:1087-93.

The letters *f* or *t* following a page number refer to a figure or table on that page.

The letters *f* or *t* following a page number refer to a figure or table on that page.

The letters *f* or *t* following a page number refer to a figure or table on that page.

The letters *f* or *t* following a page number refer to a figure or table on that page.

The letters *f* or *t* following a page number refer to a figure or table on that page.

The letters *f* or *t* following a page number refer to a figure or table on that page.

The letters *f* or *t* following a page number refer to a figure or table on that page.

The letters *f* or *t* following a page number refer to a figure or table on that page.

The letters *f* or *t* following a page number refer to a figure or table on that page.

The letters *f* or *t* following a page number refer to a figure or table on that page.

I

The letters *f* or *t* following a page number refer to a figure or table on that page.

The letters *f* or *t* following a page number refer to a figure or table on that page.

The letters *f* or *t* following a page number refer to a figure or table on that page.

The letters *f* or *t* following a page number refer to a figure or table on that page.

The letters *f* or *t* following a page number refer to a figure or table on that page.

Z

The letters *f* or *t* following a page number refer to a figure or table on that page.